The Loire

written and researched by

James McConnachie

with contributions from

Hugh Cleary

ROUGH
GUIDES

NEW YORK · LONDON · DELHI

www.roughguides.com

Contents

The château colour
section following p.160

The River Loire colour
section following p.256

3

Introduction to

The Loire

When the River Loire reaches its halfway point in the very centre of France and turns west towards the Atlantic, locals say that it ceases to be a mere *rivière*, it becomes a *fleuve* – which is something altogether grander. In this proudest stretch, from the hills of Sancerre to the floodplains of Anjou, the Loire flows past an extraordinary parade of castles, palaces and fine mansions. In fact, there are so many of these châteaux that when it came to choosing which should be awarded the title of World Heritage Site, UNESCO just bestowed the label on the entire valley.

But behind the myriad châteaux – not to mention the abbeys, churches and cathedrals – lies a modest region known for its *douceur*, or gentleness. This reputation is partly owed to the balanced climate, and partly to the landscape, which is kindly rather than dramatic. But the Loire's *douceur* also stems from something harder to define, an alluring air of nostalgia perhaps: from being the noblest waterway of France and the favourite home of the court, the river valley has literally become a backwater, as trade has taken to the roads and railways. This is a slow-moving, provincial corner of France, much further removed from Paris's energies and fashions than would seem likely, given how close it is to the capital. The main regional cities may be vigorous and dynamic, but contemporary life elsewhere seems subtly undermined by the relative grandeur of the past.

The Loire is, after all, the most palpably historic of French regions. It lay at the heart of the great but short-lived Plantagenet empire, and the endless battles of the Hundred Years War between England and France were largely fought here. Warfare left its mark in the shape of powerful fortresses and proudly turreted mansions, as well as abiding memories of resonant figures such as Eleanor of Aquitaine and Joan of Arc. Later generations grew more refined. It was in the Loire Valley that the great Renaissance monarchs re-created the vibrant

▲ Place Plumereau, Tours

civilization they had discovered in Italy. At the beginning of the sixteenth century, François I even brought Leonardo da Vinci, in person, to his miniature court at Amboise. When the court abandoned the Loire for Paris, in the mid-sixteenth century, the region slipped back into provincial obscurity.

If there's no single word for "the Loire region", it's because there's no such thing. Historically, the area is divided into separate regions, though these were replaced after the Revolution by administrative *départements* named after local rivers. Touraine became Indre-et-Loire, Anjou changed to Maine-et-Loire and the Orléanais was saddled with the name of a tiny backwater, the Loiret. Yet local people never accepted the new names, and in recent years tourist boards have revived the old ones. As for the region as a whole, the nearest you can get in French is "Val de Loire", meaning the classic royal stretch of the Loire Valley, or the made-up adjective *ligerien*, from Ligeris, the Latin name for the Loire.

Where to go

The Loire isn't all châteaux. The riverbanks make idyllic spots to picnic with supplies of local cheese, fruit and wine, and there are some superb restaurants in which it's easy to while away a surprising number of hours. More active visitors can rent **canoes** and kayaks, follow the well-marked **footpaths** that run throughout the region, and ride the dedicated **Loire à Vélo cycle network**, which mirrors the course of the river for almost its entire length; even where there's no official route,

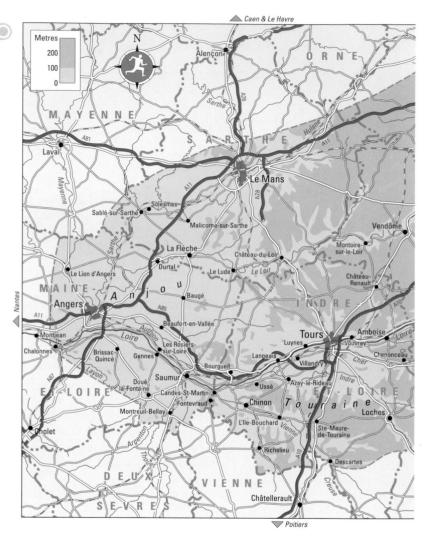

bikes make an excellent way to get around. That said, most visitors tour by **car**, as relying on public transport mostly restricts you to the towns.

The heartland region of **Touraine**, long known as "the garden of France", has the best wines, the most delicious goat's cheese, the most regal history and, it's argued, the purest French accent in the land. It also has two of the finest châteaux – **Chenonceau** and **Chambord** – and by far the most developed tourist industry. But Touraine also takes in three of the Loire's most pleasant tributaries: the **Cher**, **Indre** and **Vienne**, each of which can be explored at a slower, more intimate pace. The attractive towns of **Blois**

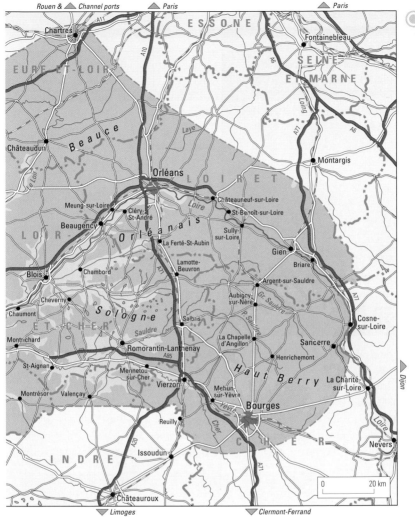

and **Amboise**, which have their own exceptional châteaux, make good bases for visiting the area upstream of Tours, including the wild and watery region of the **Sologne**. Downstream, around handsome **Saumur**, fascinating troglodyte dwellings have been carved out of the soft local rock. If you have just a week to spare for the region, these are the parts to spend it in.

Of the three main cities, energetic, historic **Tours** provides the best urban base, though **Angers**, the friendly, low-key capital of Anjou, and **Orléans**, the commercial-minded seat of the government of the Centre *région*, have their own urbane nineteenth-century charm. Each city has

7
■

The heartland region of Touraine, long known as "the garden of France", has the best wines, the most delicious goat's cheese, the most regal history and, it's argued, the purest French accent in the land

its distinctive cathedral, though none is as impressive as the three found in outlying regions: the hybrid Romanesque-Gothic cathedral of **Le Mans**, the perfectly harmonious structure of **Chartres** and the epic scale of **Bourges**.

Touring the Loire without visiting any **châteaux** would be rather eccentric, and yet the sheer number of them can make choosing bewildering. Trying to pack in the maximum can quickly blunt your sensibilities, and you'll get most out of your stay by alternating château tours with visits to vineyards and gardens, enjoying long picnics and restaurant meals, and exploring the towns and the countryside on foot. The most famous châteaux usually justify the crowds they draw, but it's often wise to time your visit for lunchtime, or first and last thing. The headline attractions at less well-known sites may not be as compelling, but it's well worth visiting at least one minor château, as you'll often have the place deliciously to yourself.

Among the A-list châteaux, **Azay-le-Rideau** and **Chenonceau** both belong exclusively to the Renaissance period, and their settings, in the middle of moat and river respectively, are very beautiful, rivalled only by the wonderful Renaissance gardens of **Villandry**. **Blois**, with its four wings

▼ Château de Chambord, near Blois

Cathédrale St-Etienne, Bourges

representing four distinct eras, and **Amboise**, rearing cliff-like above the Loire, are extremely impressive, as is the monstrously huge **Chambord**, the triumph of François I's Renaissance. More pristinely elegant are **Valençay**, with its Napoleonic interiors, and **Cheverny**, the prime example of seventeenth-century magnificence.

Many châteaux that started life as serious military defences were turned into luxurious residences by their regal or ducal owners: good examples are **Brissac**, **Chaumont** and **Ussé**, the most fairy-tale of them all. **Langeais**, **Le Plessis-Bourré** and **Sully** show how elegance and defence can be satisfyingly combined, while other feudal fortresses have preserved their medieval feel, among them ruined **Chinon**, noble **Saumur** and the entire citadel of **Loches**. Others are more compelling for their contents than their architecture: **Beauregard** is most famous for its portrait gallery, while at **Angers** the stark, largely ruined medieval castle houses the *Tapestry of the Apocalypse*, the greatest work of art in the entire Loire Valley.

When to go

The Loire's climate is dreamily perfect. The region's situation at the centre of France makes it distinctly warmer than neighbouring coastal regions, and warm Atlantic air follows the Loire Valley inland, creating a pleasantly temperate microclimate. Even at the height of summer the Loire rarely suffers the excessive heat of the south of

France. Rainfall is moderate and spread throughout the year, though wet days are more frequent in the autumn months.

Spring can be surprisingly cold earlier on, and sometimes wet too, though the sunnier days and the intense green of the countryside make this one of the loveliest times of all to visit, especially from around mid-April. Be wary of coming before **Easter**, as most of the sights are only open for relatively restricted hours. **Summers** are hot but

▼ Asperges Blanches, Montoir-sur-le-Loir

rarely sweltering. The chief drawback of visiting during **July** and especially **August** is that these months make up the high **tourist season**; in the more popular places, châteaux can get packed out by tour parties, and you'll need to book accommodation – especially if you're renting by the week – and restaurants well in advance. **June** and **September** are particularly lovely months, offering summery temperatures without the crowds. **Autumn** can be a fine time to visit, especially for lovers of game and mushrooms; it's also the season for wine fairs celebrating the harvest. Few travellers visit in **winter**. It's not especially cold, but many sights and hotels are closed.

Average Loire monthly temperatures and rainfall

	°C	°F	rainfall/mm	rainfall/inches
Jan	4	39	49	1.9
Feb	5	41	41	1.6
March	8	46	45	1.8
April	10	50	49	1.9
May	14	57	57	2.3
June	17	63	55	2.2
July	20	68	54	2.1
Aug	19	66	53	2.1
Sept	17	63	50	2.0
Oct	13	55	62	2.4
Nov	8	46	59	2.3
Dec	6	43	54	2.1

things not to miss

It's not possible to see everything that the Loire Valley has to offer in one trip – and we don't suggest you try. What follows, in no particular order, is a selective and subjective taste of the region's highlights: abbeys, cathedrals, gardens, canoe trips, wine and of course châteaux – both to visit and to stay in. They're arranged in five colour-coded categories to help you find the very best things to see, do and experience. All entries have a page reference to take you straight into the guide, where you can find out more.

01 **Château de Blois** Page **144** • The interior of the château at Blois is as colourful as its violent history.

02 Châteaudun Page 307 •
Looming over the river on its clifftop height, little-visited Châteaudun is an eerily Gothic château.

04 Villandry's gardens
Page 101 • These superb gardens exactly re-create the intricate designs of the Renaissance, right down to the geometrically planned vegetable plot.

03 Au Cabernet d'Anjou Page
291 • This former Loire mariners' bar enjoys a sun-flooded terrace overlooking one of the prettiest stretches of the river.

05 Montsoreau and Candes-St-Martin Page
253 • If the heart of the Loire region lies anywhere, it is in these twin villages straddling the border of Touraine and the Saumurois, with their ancient abbey (pictured) and château looking out across the water.

06 Canoe and kayak trips

Page **42** • The best way to get to know the River Loire is by boat, and you can rent canoes and kayaks all over the region.

08 Food markets

Page **34** • Every town has its lively, traditional weekly market where you can stock up on picnic provisions and local specialities.

07 Chartres cathedral

Page **303** • Almost all of Chartres' magnificent stained glass survives from the early thirteenth century, when the cathedral was originally built.

09 Loire à Vélo

Page **42** • A brand new network of cycle-paths and cycle routes on minor roads now makes cycling along the River Loire even more enjoyable – and safer – than it was before.

10 **Chenonceau** Page **89** • The most graceful of all the Loire châteaux arches its way right across the placid River Cher.

11 **Son-et-lumière** Page **38** • The biggest châteaux put on elaborate sound-and-light shows on summer evenings. The best, such as the ones at Azay-le-Rideau and Blois (pictured), give the building a magical new perspective.

13 **Loire wildlife** Page **44** • The Loire is rich in wildlife, particularly in summer, when swallows and swifts swarm in the evening air, coypus fish in the shallows and agile terns swoop over the rapids.

12 **Montgeoffroy** Page **296** • Built on the eve of the Revolution, and hardly altered since, Montgeoffroy is a shrine to the vanished elegance of the ancien régime.

14 **Sparkling wine** Page **352** • You can visit vineyards right across the region, tasting and buying the elegant local wines direct from the growers. In Saumur and Vouvray, call in at the vast sparkling wine *caves* quarried out of the tufa.

15 Staying in a château

Page **32** • You can find chambres d'hôtes in anything from full-scale princely palaces to relatively humble turreted farmhouses.

16 Chambord

Page **154** • At François I's gargantuan "hunting lodge", you can explore the whole building freely, taking in the strange double-helix staircase and the forest of chimneys above the roof terrace.

17 Tapestry of the Apocalypse

Page **278** • Angers' château guards one of the world's great medieval treasures: a hundred-metre-long tapestry depicting the Apocalypse in nightmarishly vivid colours.

18 **Plantagenet tombs** Page **257** • The favoured abbey of the Plantagenet family still houses their serene, polychrome tombs, including those of Eleanor of Aquitaine and her son Richard the Lionheart.

19 **Loches** Page **126** • This small, provincial town sits at the foot of a complete medieval citadel, incorporating an eleventh-century keep and fifteenth-century royal *logis*.

21 **Touring le Loir** Page **307** • The green valley of le Loir has all the castles, cave-houses, churches and vineyards that characterize its big sister, la Loire, but everything is smaller, sleepier and more hidden-away.

20 **Azay-le-Rideau** Page **106** • Set on an island in the sleepy River Indre, Azay-le-Rideau is a Renaissance gem.

22 **Cathédrale St-Julien** Page **318** • At the centre of Le Mans' giant, hybrid cathedral, the chapel vault is painted with glorious angel musicians.

Basics

Basics

Getting there

Direct flights connect London with Tours, in the heart of the Loire Valley. The main alternative is to fly to Paris and travel south overland: Tours is just one hour from the capital by rail, and two hours by road. British visitors can also use the cross-Channel or Normandy ferries, and the Channel Tunnel (by car or Eurostar train).

Airfares tend to be more expensive in summer and around Christmas. Cheap fares can often be found online, or by booking through a travel agent or flight consolidator, and there are discounted deals available to students and young people through specialist travel agents.

From the UK

Getting to the Loire from the UK is potentially bewildering, such is the wealth of options. Much depends on where you're travelling from in the UK, whether you want to avoid Paris or make a short stay in the capital part of your trip, and which part of the Loire you're making for. Ryanair's direct **flights** from London Stansted to Tours are fast and cheap. If you want to bring your own **car**, taking a cross-Channel ferry to Le Havre or Caen allows you an enjoyable approach from the north, through Normandy, but it's faster and often cheaper to cross by ferry or Eurotunnel to Calais and then follow the motorways down past Paris. If you plan to travel via Paris, the **Eurostar** train is an attractive – and green – option, especially if you're coming from the southeast; otherwise, it's worth looking into flights from regional airports to Paris and travelling overland from there. Contact details for the following methods of transport are given on pp.23–26.

By plane

Ryanair's daily direct flight from **London Stansted to Tours** is often the cheapest and quickest route to the Loire. Fares rise as the plane fills up, so to get the best deals you should book as far in advance as possible. Once taxes are factored in, you might end up paying anything between £50 and £150 for a return flight.

If you're flying **from UK regional airports**, or if the Tours flight is full or over priced, consider **flying to Paris** and making your way south from there (see box on p.24). The best fares to Paris are often on the budget airlines Bmibaby, easyJet and Ryanair; again, try to book well in advance and travel off-peak – £80–120 is a fairly typical fare. Routes change frequently, but **bmibaby** generally flies from Durham Tees Valley, Leeds Bradford, London Heathrow and Nottingham EMA to Paris Charles de Gaulle (Paris CDG); **easyJet** from Belfast, Bristol, Liverpool, London Luton and Newcastle to Paris CDG; and **Ryanair** from Glasgow Prestwick to Paris Beauvais airport, which is rather inconveniently situated 65km to the northwest of the city. For wider regional airport coverage, and for the occasional promotional fare, check out the routes and fares offered to Paris by the big scheduled flight carriers: Air France, BMI and British Airways.

If you're flying on a **budget airline**, it's simplest to book the ticket directly with the airline, by phone or on their website. Website addresses and contact details are given on p.23; specialist travel agents are listed on p.23. Young people under 26 may be able to find discounted fares at agents such as STA Travel and Usit NOW.

By Eurostar

Travelling to the Loire **by train** means getting on the **Eurostar** at London Waterloo (or Ashford International in Kent) and whizzing through the Channel Tunnel to Paris Gare du Nord – a journey of just over two and a half hours. Unfortunately, to get an onward train from Paris to the Loire you have to transfer between the Gare du Nord and the **Gare Montparnasse** (for Angers, Chartres, Le

Fly less – stay longer! Travel and climate change

Climate change is the single biggest issue facing our planet. It is caused by a build-up in the atmosphere of carbon dioxide and other greenhouse gases, which are emitted by many sources – including planes. Already, flights account for around 3–4% of human-induced global warming: that figure may sound small, but it is rising year on year and threatens to counteract the progress made by reducing greenhouse emissions in other areas.

Rough Guides regard travel, overall, as a global benefit, and feel strongly that the advantages to developing economies are important, as are the opportunities for greater contact and awareness among peoples. But we all have a responsibility to limit our personal "carbon footprint". That means giving thought to how often we fly and what we can do to redress the harm that our trips create.

Flying and climate change

Pretty much every form of motorized travel generates CO_2, but planes are particularly bad offenders, releasing large volumes of greenhouse gases at altitudes where their impact is far more harmful. Flying also allows us to travel much further than we would contemplate doing by road or rail, so the emissions attributable to each passenger are greater. For example, one person taking a return flight between Europe and California produces the equivalent impact of 2.5 tonnes of CO_2 – similar to the yearly output of the average UK car.

Less harmful planes may evolve but it will be decades before they replace the current fleet – which could be too late for avoiding climate chaos. In the meantime, there are limited options for concerned travellers: to reduce the amount we travel by air (take fewer trips, stay longer!), to avoid night flights (when plane contrails trap heat from Earth but can't reflect sunlight back to space), and to make the trips we do take "climate neutral" via a carbon offset scheme.

Carbon offset schemes

Offset schemes run by **climatecare.org, carbonneutral**.com and others allow you to "neutralize" the greenhouse gases that you are responsible for releasing. Their websites have simple calculators that let you work out the impact of any flight. Once that's done, you can pay to fund projects that will reduce future carbon emissions by an equivalent amount (such the distribution of low-energy lightbulbs and cooking stoves in developing countries). Please take the time to visit our website and make your trip climate neutral.

ⓦwww.roughguides.com/climatechange

Mans and Tours) or **Gare d'Austerlitz** (for Bourges and Orléans), which means taking a taxi or the métro across Paris. For tips on crossing Paris, and for details on travel from Paris to various destinations in the Loire region, see the box on p.24.

If you want to avoid the Paris interchange, there is an alternative, as long as you can be flexible about your departure time. A couple of Eurostar trains per day stop at **Lille Europe**, where you can take the high-speed TGV south to Tours. The whole journey takes just under six hours, which is roughly the same as travelling via Paris, and infinitely more leisurely.

Prices of **Eurostar tickets** depend on how far in advance you book, and how much flexibility you need. The lowest fares are almost always for early-morning trains, especially those departing mid-week. You'll usually pay more if you don't stay over a Saturday night. It's possible to find tickets for as little as £70, but you'll often pay double that. A number of discounted seats are set aside on each train for students under-26 and for the over-60s; the longer you book in advance the better your chances are of securing one of these. Eurostar tickets can be bought from travel agents or by phone or online directly from Eurostar, but for through-ticketing to train stations in the Loire it's better to book at mainline railway stations in Britain, through Rail Europe (℡08708/371 371, ⓦwww .raileurope.co.uk), or on the SNCF website (ⓦwww.voyages-sncf.co.uk).

By car

If you're bringing a car from the UK, the quickest route is via the Channel Tunnel, using the frequent **Eurotunnel** shuttle service between the Folkestone and Calais terminals. The **car ferries** from **Dover to Calais** or Boulogne are slower but less expensive than Eurotunnel. Taking a ferry direct to the **Normandy** coast is a relaxing alternative, with less driving time at the end of the crossing. However, unless you take a high-speed **catamaran**, it's likely to be slower than zooming down the motorway from Calais – unless you live in the southwest of England.

Fares vary according to season, with school and bank holidays being the most expensive, but expect to pay around £200 per car for the Eurotunnel, £50–150 on a ferry, depending on when you travel and, on certain routes, how many passengers there are. Lower fares are usually available if you can avoid travelling out on Fridays and Saturdays. On ferries, **bicycles** carry – at most – a nominal charge in peak season.

Eurotunnel

Eurotunnel's car-carrying trains leave every fifteen minutes or so from the terminal near Folkestone (one per hour midnight–6am); just take the heavily signposted exit off the M20 at Junction 11A, drive up to the ticket booths to buy a ticket, wait half an hour or so and then drive straight onto one of the double-decker railway carriages. However, to get the lowest fares and to avoid queues, especially during peak school holiday periods, it's worth **booking ahead** – in which case you have to arrive at least thirty mintes before departure. The cheapest fares are usually for late-evening crossings, after around 10pm. Once aboard, you can walk around in the comfortable, garage-like chamber during the 35-minute trip.

You surface just outside Calais, and well-signposted slip roads lead straight onto the **Paris-bound motorways**. Unless you're heading to the easternmost side of the Loire, it's simplest to take the A16 motorway via Boulogne and Amiens, which approaches Paris from the west, but the A26/A1 via St-Omer and Arras is often just as quick, if slightly longer. On either route, allow five hours from Calais to Tours.

Cross-channel ferries

Sea France and **P&O Ferries** both sail from Dover to Calais (at least hourly; 1hr 30min), so you can usually get away without booking ahead, though it's advisable in summer. The excellent new budget carrier, SpeedFerries, runs car-carrying catamarans between Dover and Boulogne (3–5 daily; 1hr). The lowest fares are usually to be found for travel midweek or on Sundays, departing very early or late in the day. As with Eurotunnel, you're left with a fairly long drive south at the end of all these crossings (see above), though going via Boulogne gives you a thirty-kilometre headstart on Calais.

Normandy ferries

The gentlemanly alternative is to take the long sea route to the Normandy coast. The crossing may be slow but this allows time for a meal, a stroll on deck and perhaps a film in the small cinema; the ferry companies make fairly good provision for children, too. Night crossings are even more leisurely, and you can book a cabin for around £20 per person. It's important to book in advance for the Normandy ferries.

Brittany Ferries sails from Portsmouth to Caen (1–3 daily; 6hr), with a single daily high-speed crossing (4hr); **LD Lines** sails overnight from Portsmouth to Le Havre (1 daily; 7hr 30min); and **Transmanche** ferries sail from Newhaven to Dieppe (2–3 daily; 4hr). There are generally fewer crossings to the Normandy coast in winter.

The advantage of all these routes is the approach to the Loire region: **the drive south** is mostly along ordinary roads rather than toll-paying, petrol-guzzling motorways. You won't save all that much driving time – Caen is a little over three hours away from Tours, and Le Havre and Dieppe are an hour or so further – but you could plan an attractive route through the rolling Norman countryside, which is particularly appealing in the so-called Suisse Normande immediately south of Caen, where villages such as Thury-Harcourt and Pont d'Ouilly make tempting overnight stops, and in the Pays d'Auge, south of Lisieux, the home of Camembert and Livarot. Alternatively, you could push through to the cathedral towns of Le Mans or Chartres, and the fringe territory to the north of the Loire, which is covered in a dedicated chapter of the Guide, "The Northern approaches", on pp.299–324.

There are ferry routes to Cherbourg, too, but Cherbourg to Tours takes up to five hours by car – no faster than coming from Calais, and the crossing is longer and more expensive. If you're heading to the westernmost part of the region, around Anjou, consider Brittany Ferries' overnight Portsmouth to **St-Malo** service (4–7 weekly; 10hr 45min), or Condor Ferries' Poole to St-Malo crossing, which runs from late May to the end of September via Jersey or Guernsey (1 daily; 4hr 35min).

From Ireland

The most obvious route to the Loire from Ireland is to **fly to Paris** with Aer Lingus, Air France or Ryanair, and continue south from there (see box on p.24), but you can also fly **Ryanair to London Stansted** and then pick up their flight to Tours – which can sometimes work out cheaper, but you're more at the mercy of missed connections.

A much slower alternative – but one that lets you bring your own car – is to take a **ferry** to the Normandy port of Cherbourg, which is around five hours' drive from the centre of the Loire region. Irish Ferries and Celtic Link Ferries make the crossing from Rosslare to Cherbourg (2–4 weekly; 19hr). You could also look at Brittany Ferries' summer-only route between Cork and Roscoff (1 weekly; 14hr); conveniently, it leaves on a Friday evening, but there's a lengthy drive through Brittany at the end of it.

From the US and Canada

Getting to the Loire from anywhere in North America means **flying to Paris** and making your way from there by road or rail – the distances are so small that it doesn't really make sense to connect with an internal flight. If you're arriving at Orly or Charles de Gaulle (CDG) airports, you don't even need to travel into central Paris to pick up a high-speed train straight to the centre of the Loire valley, though you may of course want to spend time in the capital. For details of onward travel to the Loire from Paris and Paris's airports, see the box on p.24.

The widest choice of flights to Paris is offered by **Air France**, with regular, non-stop, scheduled services to CDG from across the US. From New York, there are up to eight departures a day. American Airlines and Continental are usually a little cheaper, but you may have to stop off en route from smaller cities. Typical midweek **fares** range from around US$500 in low season to US$1000 in high season. Note that from New York or Washington DC you can expect to pay around US$50–200 less. Flying at weekends is more expensive.

Air France and Air Canada both fly non-stop to Paris from all the major cities in **Canada**. There's little to choose between them in terms of fares: count on CDN$1000/1600 (low/high season) from Montréal, Québec and Toronto, and CDN$1400/1900 from Vancouver.

From Australia and New Zealand

There are scheduled **flights to Paris** from Auckland, Brisbane, Cairns, Melbourne, Perth and Sydney, but you can find a wider range of options by flying to another European capital – usually London – and making a connection from there. The best

---

Travelling with pets from the UK

The Department for Environment, Food and Rural Affairs' (DEFRA) **Pet Travel Scheme** allows owners of cats and dogs to take them on holiday to France. Your pet will need to be appropriately microchipped, vaccinated, blood-tested and documented, and you'll need to begin the process at least seven months ahead of travel. For information on regulations and the necessary documentation, check out ⓦwww.defra.gov.uk or ring the PETS helpline on ☏0870/241 1710.

deals from Australia or New Zealand to Europe are routed via Asia, often with a transfer or overnight stop in the airline's home city. Flights via the US are usually slightly more expensive. From Paris, you'll have to make your way overland to the Loire – all of an hour from Paris to Tours by train, or two hours in a rental car (see box on p.24).

Fares are priced according to the French tourist seasons: the brief low season runs from early January to the end of February and through October and November; high season lasts from mid-May to the end of August and from December to early January. From Australia, you should be able to find scheduled fares to Paris for around AUS$2000 in low season, or AUS$2500 in high season. From Auckland, you might pay from NZ$2200 right up to NZ$3000 in peak season.

Online booking

ⓦ www.expedia.co.uk (in UK), ⓦ www.expedia.com (in US), ⓦ www.expedia.ca (in Canada)
ⓦ www.lastminute.com (in UK)
ⓦ www.opodo.co.uk (in UK)
ⓦ www.orbitz.com (in US)
ⓦ www.travelocity.co.uk (in UK), ⓦ www.travelocity.com (in US), ⓦ www.travelocity.ca (in Canada)
ⓦ www.zuji.com.au (in Australia), ⓦ www.zuji.co.nz (in New Zealand)

Airlines

Aer Lingus Ireland ☏ 0818/365 000, ⓦ www.aerlingus.com.
Air Canada US and Canada ☏ 1-888/247-2262, ⓦ www.aircanada.com.
Air France UK ☏ 0870/142 43443, Ireland ☏ 01/605 0383, US ☏ 1-800/237-2747, Canada ☏ 1-800/667-2747, Australia ☏ 1300/390 190, ⓦ www.airfrance.com.
Air India Australia ☏ 02/9283 4020, New Zealand ☏ 09/303 1301, ⓦ www.airindia.com.
American Airlines US ☏ 1-800/433-7300, ⓦ www.aa.com.
bmi UK UK ☏ 0870/607 0555, ⓦ www.flybmi.co.uk.
Bmibaby UK ☏ 0871/224 0224, ⓦ www.bmibaby.co.uk.
British Airways UK ☏ 0870/850 9850, Australia ☏ 1300/767 177, New Zealand ☏ 09/966 9777, ⓦ www.ba.com.
Cathay Pacific Australia ☏ 13 17 47, New Zealand ☏ 09/379 0861, ⓦ www.cathaypacific.com.

Continental US Airlines ☏ 1-800/523-3273, ⓦ www.continental.com.
Delta US ☏ 1-800/221-1212, ⓦ www.delta.com.
easyJet UK ☏ 0870/600 0000, ⓦ www.easyjet.co.uk.
Garuda Indonesia Australia ☏ 1300/365 330, New Zealand ☏ 09/366 1862, ⓦ www.garuda-indonesia.com.
JAL Japan Airlines Australia ☏ 02/9272 1111, New Zealand ☏ 09/379 9906, ⓦ www.jal.com.
KLM Australia ☏ 1300/303 747, New Zealand ☏ 09/921 6040, ⓦ www.klm.com.
Lufthansa Australia ☏ 1300/655 727, ⓦ www.lufthansa.com.
Malaysia Airlines Australia ☏ 13 26 27, New Zealand ☏ 0800/777 747, ⓦ www.malaysia-airlines.com.
Northwest Airlines US ☏ 1-800/225-2525, ⓦ www.nwa.com.
Qantas Australia ☏ 13 13 13, New Zealand ☏ 0800/808 767, ⓦ www.qantas.com.
Ryanair UK ☏ 0871/246 0000, Ireland ☏ 0818/303 030 ⓦ www.ryanair.com.
Thai Airways Australia ☏ 1300/651 960, New Zealand ☏ 09/377 3886, ⓦ www.thaiair.com.
United Airlines US ☏ 1-800/UNITED-1, Australia ☏ 13 17 77, ⓦ www.united.com.

Agents and operators

North South Travel ☏ 01245/608 291, ⓦ www.northsouthtravel.co.uk. Friendly, competitive travel agency. Profits are used to support projects in the developing world, especially the promotion of sustainable tourism.
STA Travel ☏ 0870/160 0599, ⓦ www.statravel.co.uk. Worldwide specialists in low-cost flights, overlands and holiday deals. Good discounts for students and under-26s.
Trailfinders ☏ 020/7938 3939, ⓦ www.trailfinders.com. Well-informed and efficient agents for independent travellers.
Travel Bag ☏ 0870/890 1456, ⓦ www.travelbag.co.uk. Discount deals worldwide.
Travel Care ☏ 0870/112 0085, ⓦ www.travelcare.co.uk. Flights, and holiday deals, run on ethical principles by the Co-operative group.
USIT Ireland ☏ 01/602 1904, ⓦ www.usit.ie. Specialists in student, youth and independent travel – flights, trains, TEFL and more.
World Travel Centre Ireland ☏ 01/416 7007, ⓦ www.worldtravel.ie. Dublin-based agent.

Specialist tour operators

Arblaster and Clarke Wine Tours UK ☏ 01730 893344, ⓦ www.arblasterandclarke.com.

Getting to the Loire from Paris

Trains to the Loire depart from the Gare Montparnasse, in the south of Paris, or the Gare d'Austerlitz, in the southeast; the station depends on your destination. You may want to pick up a **rental car** (see p.27) in Paris and head down to the Loire valley under your own steam. If so, there are three main motorway routes from Paris towards the Loire valle; for detailed **route descriptions**, check the online planner at ⓦwww.viamichelin.com.

By train from central Paris

The simplest and quickest rail route is the breathtaking TGV high-speed line from Paris's **Gare Montparnasse** to **Tours**, which usually takes just over an hour. At the time of writing, a single, adult, off-peak **ticket** cost €25.60. You usually arrive at the TGV station, Tours St-Pierre-des-Corps, where you sometimes have to disembark, walk across the platform and pick up the shuttle train on to Tours' central station – all of which adds on a few minutes. From Tours you can pick up public transport to destinations all over the region, notably **Blois**, **Chinon** and **Saumur**.

Hourly trains run from the **Gare Montparnasse** to **Chartres**, and there's also a good TGV service to **Le Mans** (1hr) and **Angers** (1hr 30min), though the high-speed part of the line currently only extends as far as Le Mans. From the **Gare d'Austerlitz** there are frequent TGV departures for **Orléans** (1hr; some include a shuttle train from the suburban station at Fleury-les-Aubray to Orléans' central station), a handful of direct trains to **Bourges** (2hr) and slow, mainline SNCF trains to **Tours** (2hr 20min). Trains for **Gien** (1hr 30min–2hr) leave every couple of hours from the **Gare de Lyon**. If you're travelling from London by train, note that a couple of Eurostar trains stop at **Lille Europe** station in good time to make a connection with the TGV to Tours; for more details, see p.19.

If you need to **travel between mainline stations in Paris**, allow at least an hour between arrival and departure times – a little more if you have to book your onward ticket. If you're taking the métro, it's useful to keep some euro coins handy for the ticket (€1.30 single). Note that the métro's credit-card ticket machines are temperamental about accepting foreign plastic. From the Gare du Nord, take métro line 4 (pink) signposted "Direction Porte d'Orléans" for the Gare de Montparnasse; or line 5 (orange) "Direction Place d'Italie" for the Gare d'Austerlitz.

Whichever train you catch, don't forget to **validate your ticket** (*compostez votre billet*) before you depart; just push it into the slot in the orange stamping-machines on every platform.

Wine-and-walking and just plain wine tours of the Loire, among many other regions.

Backroads US ☎1-800/GO-ACTIVE or 510/527-1555, ⓦwww.backroads.com. Biking and touring in the Loire valley, with the chance to kayak on the tranquil Cher.

Belle France UK ☎01892/559 595, ⓦwww.bellefrance.co.uk. Independent UK company offering cycling and walking holidays in the châteaux country around Amboise and Blois.

Château to Château FR☎+33-(0)6.19.75.30.23, ⓦwww.chateautochateau.com. Experienced French company specializing in the Loire, and offering cycling and wine itineraries – or both combined – of between four and eight days. They'll sort out all the details – you just have to peddle, and drink.

Classic Journeys US ☎1-800/200-3887 or 858/454-5004, ⓦwww.classicjourneys.com. Walking and cultural tours in Europe. Currently offers a seven-day tour combining walking in châteaux country with a barge trip on the canals of Burgundy.

Cosmos US ☎1-800/276-1241, ⓦwww.cosmosvacations.com. Planned-vacation packages with an independent focus. The tours of France all include a whole day in "châteaux country".

DuVine Adventures US ☎1-888/396 5383, ⓦwww.duvine.com. Offers an independent but guide-supported six-day cycling and wine-tasting tour of Touraine.

EC Tours US ☎1-800/388-0877, ⓦwww.ectours.com. California-based tour operator,

By car from central Paris

All three motorway routes to the Loire are fast and usually congestion-free. From Paris through to Tours, the distance is 240km, or two and a half hours, with **motorway tolls** to pay of just under €20.

The ordinary route follows the **Autoroute d'Aquitaine** (A10) south to Orléans, a distance of 127km. A second route, the **Autoroute de l'Océane** (A11) branches off the A10 some 30km out of Paris, from where it runs roughly west towards Chartres – 83km in all. From Chartres you can follow the little River Loir downstream (see p.22), or continue along the A11 as far as Le Mans and Angers. If you're making for Bourges or the eastern portion of the Loire, you could choose a third motorway route, which breaks away from the A6 just beyond Nemours, some 35km south of Paris, and becomes the **A77** to Gien.

If you want to avoid the *autoroutes*, there are three alternative routes, two of which lead past wonderful châteaux – though bear in mind that there are plenty more ahead. The N20 runs from Paris's Porte d'Orléans direct to **Orléans** (117km); the D910 heads east from the Ponte de Sèvres to Versailles, from where the D10/N10 continues to **Chartres**; and the N7 leads southeast from Paris's Porte d'Italie to Fontainebleau and on south towards **Gien** and Sancerre.

From Paris airports

If you're arriving in Paris by air, it's possible to reach Tours and Angers without the hassle of crossing central Paris – as long as your arrival time matches up reasonably well with a **train** departure. From **Charles de Gaulle (CDG)** airport there are four or five high-speed TGV trains every day direct to Tours (1hr 50min), and around two TGVs daily to Angers (2hr 15min). If the train times don't match your flight, you can take the RER B suburban line to Massy Palaiseau (roughly 1hr), and connect there with reasonably frequent TGV trains to Tours and Angers. The TGV and RER stations at Massy Palaiseau are just 200m apart. If you're arriving at **Orly airport**, Massy Palaiseau is only fifteen minutes away on the RER line C2.

If you're picking up a **rental car** at **CDG**, you'll have to make your way right round Paris to continue down to the Loire valley. The best bet, avoiding the route-finding nightmare of the *périphérique*, is to take the succession of *autoroutes* (A1/A3/A86/A10) that skirt the southeastern side of Paris.

---

offering inexpensive two- to ten-day French tours taking in any or all of Paris, Normandy, Brittany and the Loire Valley.
Euro-Bike & Walking Tours US ☎ 1-800/321-6060, ⊛ www.eurobike.com. Runs cycling and walking trips in Europe, with a seven-day dedicated cycling trip around "la Loire".
French Travel Connection Australia ☎ 03/9531 8787, ⊛ www.frenchtravel.com.au. Everything to do with travel to and around France, including accommodation, canal boats, train travel, car rental and more. Offers a wide choice of self-guided cycling and walking tours in the Loire, as well as wine tours taking in the Loire.
Headwater UK UK ☎ 01606/720 099, ⊛ www .headwater.com. Walking and cycling holidays in the

Loire and Berry. Sadly, no canoeing options at the time of writing, though it may be something they offer in the future.
Inntravel UK ☎ 01653/629 000, ⊛ www.inntravel .co.uk. This award-winning company offers four- and seven-day cycling and walking holidays near Chinon or along the Cher.
Loire Valley Travel FR☎ +33-(0)2.54.78.62.52, ⊛ loire-valley-travel.com. This well-established, Blois-based cycle-tourism specialist offers a long list of unguided cycle holidays in the Loire. They'll arrange bike rental, accommodation – ranging from tents to luxury châteaux – baggage transfer, routes and maps. Most packages last less than a week. A few walking tours are also available.

Martin Randall Travel UK ☎020/8742 3355, Australia ☎1300/559 595, New Zealand +61-7/3377-0141, ⓦwww.martinrandall.com. British company running small-group cultural tours in the Touraine and Berry, led by an expert lecturer.

National Registration Centre for Study Abroad US ☎(414)278-0631, ⓦwww.nrcsa.com. Language courses in Amboise and Angers, as well as home-study language programmes based in Tours.

Off the Beaten Path US ☎1-877/846-2831, ⓦwww.traveloffthebeatenpath.com. Small-group walking, wine and cultural tours, specializing in France. The seven-day Loire tour features cooking lessons, wine and food tastings, and, of course, châteaux visits.

Travel Notions Australia ☎02/9552 3355, ⓦwww.unitednotions.com.au/travelnotions. France specialists, and agents for leisurely "Cycling for Softies" tours, including one in western Touraine and another around the Sarthe and Mayenne valleys.

Rail contacts

European Rail UK ☎020/7387 0444, ⓦwww.europeanrail.com.

Eurostar UK ☎0870/5-186186, ⓦwww.eurostar.com.

Rail Europe UK ☎0870/837 1371, ⓦwww.raileurope.co.uk; US ☎1-877/257-2887, Canada ☎1-800/361-RAIL, ⓦwww.raileurope.com/us.

SNCF ☎08.36.35.35.35 (France only), ⓦwww.voyages-sncf.co.uk.

Ferry contacts

Brittany Ferries UK ☎0870/366 5333, Republic of Ireland ☎021/4277 801, ⓦwww.brittanyferries.co.uk.

Celtic Link Ferries Republic of Ireland ☎01/823 0126, ⓦwww.celticlinkferries.com.

Condor Ferries UK ☎0870/243 5140, ⓦwww.condorferries.co.uk.

Eurodrive UK ☎0871/423 5540, ⓦwww.eurodrive.co.uk.

Ferrysavers UK ☎0870/990 8492, ⓦwww.ferrysavers.com.

Irish Ferries Republic of Ireland ☎1890/313131, ⓦwww.irishferries.com.

LD Lines UK ☎0870/428 4335, ⓦwww.ldlines.co.uk.

P&O Ferries UK ☎0870/520 2020, ⓦwww.poferries.com.

Sea France UK ☎0870/571 1711, ⓦwww.seafrance.com.

Speed Ferries UK ☎0870/220 0570, ⓦwww.speedferries.com.

Transmanche Ferries UK ☎0870/917 1201, ⓦwww.transmancheferries.com.

Channel tunnel

Eurotunnel UK ☎0870/535 3535, ⓦwww.eurotunnel.com.

Getting around

To make the most of the Loire you'll need a car or a bike. Efficient, regular SNCF trains serve all the main towns in the Loire as well as many of the most popular châteaux, but this limits you to the beaten track. You can also book yourself onto a coach or minibus tour from the big cities, notably Tours (see p.67), but again these only visit the major destinations. Beyond the rail network, bus services are typically infrequent (though reliable), so to get to many of the less well-known sites and villages covered in the Guide you'll need your own wheels. Renting or bringing a car is the obvious choice, but bear in mind that the Loire is ideal cycling country. Unfortunately, the Loire itself isn't navigable by anything other than very small boats.

For advice on **cycling**, **walking** and **kayaking**, see "Outdoor activities", on p.41. **Hitching** is unusual in this region, and you'd be unwise to rely on it for getting around; you may want to consider safety issues, too, especially if travelling alone.

By car

The pros of travelling by car are evident. The main disadvantage is cost, but you also see a less attractive side of the Loire countryside from the main roads and motorways. There are numerous car-rental agencies in all the main Loire towns, notably Tours, Blois, Orléans and Angers. Tours airport has booths for both Hertz and Europcar; the former is Ryanair's partner, so there are usually long queues for the Hertz booth on arrival. **Car rental** costs something in the region of €300 a week, or at least €50 a day. It can be less expensive to book in advance from abroad. Under-25s pay an extra insurance premium of upwards of €20 a day; you must still be over 21 and have driven for at least one year. OTU Voyages (℡01.55.82.32.32, ⓦwww .otu.fr) can arrange car rental for drivers under 21. North Americans and Australians should note that it is very difficult to find rental cars with automatic transmission; if you can't drive a manual/stick-shift vehicle, try to book an automatic well in advance and be prepared to pay for it.

At the time of writing, **petrol/gas** (*essence*) costs around €1.30 a litre for unleaded (*super sans plomb*), with a small premium for leaded four-star (*super*), while diesel (*gasoil*)

costs around €1.15 a litre – figure on about $4 per gallon. Supermarkets tend to have the lowest prices for fuel.

Traffic **congestion** is only a problem on the busiest summer weekends – especially around July 14, August 15 and the beginning and end of August – but you may find yourself ambling along behind lorries or caravans on the arterial roads that run alongside the Loire at any time. Traffic or no, it's almost always worth planning a slower route along the lovelier minor roads. If you're in a tearing hurry, the **autoroute** network is fast, mostly free of traffic, and serves the main cities of the region – though at the time of writing there was still a fifty-kilometre hiatus along the Cher heading east of Tours towards Bourges. You have to pay tolls for the privilege of riding the *autoroute*, but any trips within the scope of this guidebook will come in under €20. For an excellent **route-planner**, check out the bilingual website, ⓦwww .viamichelin.com.

You're never far from a garage or a petrol station in France. If you have **mechanical difficulties**, look in the *Yellow Pages* (*Pages Jaunes*) of the phone book under "*Garages d'automobiles*", or "*dépannages*" for breakdowns. If you have an accident or a break-in, you may need to get a report from the local police in order to make an insurance claim – contact your insurer/rental company as soon as possible to check what you should do. It may help if you note down as many details as you can, especially contact details for other drivers involved, and in the event of a serious

Mileage and journey times

Angers to: Blois (2hr; 195km); Caen (2hr 45min; 255km); Calais (4hr 40min; 515km); Le Havre (3hr; 330km); Nantes, Brittany (1hr; 88km); Orléans (2hr 30min; 245km); Paris (3hr; 300km); Saumur (55min; 48km); Tours (1hr 30min; 125km).

Orléans to: Blois (45min; 63km); Bourges (1hr 25min; 120km); Caen (3hr 25min; 320km); Calais (4hr 10min; 420km); Chartres (1hr; 81km); Le Havre (3hr 10min; 280km); Paris (1hr 30min; 135km); Tours (1hr 10min; 115km).

Tours to: Blois (45min; 65km); Bordeaux (3hr 30min; 335km); Bourges (2hr; 155km); Caen (2hr 50min; 265km); Calais (4hr 50min; 525km); Chartres (2hr; 140km); Le Havre (3hr 10min; 340km); Le Mans (1hr 10min; 95km); Paris (2hr 30min; 240km); Saumur (1hr 10min; 71km); Poitiers (1hr 5min; 100km).

problem, you should get a report from the police. For motoring vocabulary, see p.368.

For minor driving offences, the police may turn a blind eye to foreign drivers, or they may impose an on-the-spot fine. Reckless speeding and other more serious violations will lead to you having your licence taken away, and drink driving is taken very seriously in France (see opposite).

Car rental agencies

Avis UK ☎ 0870/606 0100, Republic of Ireland ☎ 021/428 1111, US ☎ 1-800-230-4898, Canada ☎ 1-800-272-5871, Australia ☎ 13 63 33 or 02/9353 9000, New Zealand ☎ 09/526 2847 or 0800/655 111, ⊛ www.avis.com.
Budget UK ☎ 0870/156 5656, US ☎ 1-800-527-0700, Canada ☎ 1-800-268-8900, Australia ☎ 1300/362 848, New Zealand ☎ 0800/283 438, ⊛ www.budget.com.
Europcar UK ☎ 0870/607 5000, Republic of Ireland ☎ 01/614 2800, US & Canada ☎ 1-877-940 6900, Australia ☎ 393/306 160, ⊛ www.europcar.com.
Hertz UK ☎ 020/7026 0077, Republic of Ireland ☎ 01/870 5777, US & Canada ☎ 1-800-654-3131, New Zealand ☎ 0800/654 321, ⊛ www.hertz.com.
National UK ☎ 0870/400 4581, US ☎ 1-800-CAR-RENT, Australia ☎ 0870/600 6666, New Zealand ☎ 03/366 5574, ⊛ www.nationalcar.com.
Skycars UK ☎ 0870/789 7789, ⊛ www.skycars.com.
Thrifty UK ☎ 01494/751 540, Republic of Ireland ☎ 01/844 1950, US and Canada ☎ 1-800-847-4389, Australia ☎ 1300/367 227, New Zealand ☎ 09/256 1405, ⊛ www.thrifty.com.

Rules of the road

British, Irish, Australian, Canadian, New Zealand, US and all EU **driving licences** are valid in France. You're required to keep your licence on you if you're driving, along with insurance papers. Rented cars must also have their registration document (*carte grise*). The minimum driving age is 18, and provisional licences are not valid.

All EU-issued **motor insurance** is now valid in all EU countries, so there's no requirement to upgrade your policy, though UK drivers should note that they may only have third-party cover while driving in France. You can pay extra to buy a "**green card**" from your policy provider that upgrades you to comprehensive cover while abroad.

Drivers of British cars have to adjust the headlight dip to the right, or fit glare deflectors that do the same job – these are sold in ferry ports and the Eurostar terminal. You're also supposed to carry a red triangle, spare headlight bulbs and fit national identification plates – "GB", etc.

French law still stipulates that unless signs indicate otherwise you should give way to traffic coming from the right – the notorious **priorité à droite** rule. To add to the confusion, main roads are an exception, as they now almost always have priority, shown by a *passage protégé* sign of a yellow diamond on a white background. The same sign with a black slash indicates that vehicles coming from your right have priority. Cars already on roundabouts are another exception, as they have priority over cars joining the roundabout (from the right…). As a rule, take great care at junctions – occasionally, older motorists blithely expect to have priority when turning onto a main road. *Cédez le passage* means "Give way", and *déviation* (in yellow) means "diversion" – these diversions can sometimes take you some distance out of your way on wandering rural roads.

The **speed limit** in built-up areas is 50kph (31mph). Other limits change according to whether the conditions are wet or dry; drivers with less than two years' experience must follow the lower limit. *Autoroute* limits are 130kph (80mph), or 110kph (68mph) in the wet; urban *autoroutes* and dual carriageways with a central reservation are 110kph, or 100kph (62mph) in the wet; main roads are 90kph (55mph), or 80kph (50mph) in the wet. There are stiff fines for speeding, and they are being more rigorously enforced than in the past.

The **alcohol limit** is set low, at the EU standard of 50mg alcohol per 100ml of blood (0.05% BAC), which is just over half the UK level of 80mg, or the 80–100mg levels imposed in most US states. In most adults, the limit equates to roughly one glass of wine. Drink driving is severely punished, and there are frequent random checks. **Seat belts** are compulsory in the back and front; children under 10 must sit in the back unless you have a rear-facing car seat.

By train

Trains in the Loire are admirably clean, reliable and inexpensive. The operator is the nationally owned SNCF, divided locally into two regional networks: TER Centre in the east, TER Pays de Loire in the west. The main line runs from Angers to Orléans, passing through Saumur, Tours and Blois, and keeping close to the Loire for much of its length. There are a number of branch lines as well, notably those radiating from Tours; unfortunately, many more minor branches now suffer from infrequent services, and occasional or total replacement by **SNCF buses**. These buses are ticketed as for trains and arrive and depart from train stations. Over and above the normal train network, two high-speed **TGV** lines connect Tours and Le Mans with Paris. TGVs are timetabled separately from normal TER trains, but connecting tickets are sold as standard.

For national **train information** you can phone (☎08.36.35.35.35, within France only) or check online at ⓦwww.sncf.com, which has an English-language option, and

offers online booking. Individual **timetable** leaflets are available for each route; the display shelves at stations are usually well stocked, but you can always ask if they've run out. You can also pick up a free *SNCF Guide Voyageur* for each regional network, which includes maps as well as lots of general information (in French).

Tickets can be bought online and at all train stations – given the French name of **gare SNCF** throughout the Guide. Smaller stations may be only sporadically manned, but there's always an automatic ticket machine. Before boarding, make sure to validate your ticket at the orange machine on the platform marked **compostez votre billet**, though conductors are often lenient with forgetful foreigners.

Fares are inexpensive: around €15 single from Tours to Angers, for example. Children under-12 travel for half price and under-4s travel free. There are various discounted "**découverte**" fares on off-peak days, especially for under-26s and over-60s; you could look up the exact details of who's eligible in the official *SNCF Guide Voyageur*, but staff are invariably helpful in finding you the best tariff. **Bikes** travel free on most trains.

Various **rail passes** and discount cards can be bought, but you're unlikely to make enough train journeys within the Loire area to make any of these worthwhile.

By bus

On major routes, trains are faster and more frequent than buses (though marginally more expensive), but where no train service exists you may have to fall back on the buses. Two kinds of bus services operate in the Loire region: **SNCF buses**, which have replaced some or all trains on many branch lines; and **public buses**, mostly run by private companies, which can be useful for local and cross-country journeys. SNCF buses are ticketed just like trains, and arrive and depart from train stations.

Timetables on ordinary public buses are usually scheduled to suit working, market and school hours. Early and end-of-school services may also be supplemented by one or two extra buses during the day on certain routes. You'll have to plan carefully; note that services can be skeletal on Sundays and during school holidays. Tickets can be bought on board public buses.

Larger towns always have a **gare routière** (bus station), often next to the gare SNCF, but many buses also call at town-centre stops. In smaller towns you can usually rely on the bus stopping at the Mairie (town hall) or market square.

Boat trips and inland waterways

First-time visitors are often surprised to find that the Loire river is no longer navigable: the most you'll get from a river **boat** on the Loire is a short cruise. The **Sarthe** and **Mayenne** rivers above Angers, however, are plied by various cruise boats, detailed in the relevant sections of the Guide.

The great **canal** networks of central France lie mostly to the east of the Loire, outside the scope of this book, but there are stretches to be explored, notably the **Canal Latéral à la Loire**, which links Briare to Sancerre before continuing upstream into Burgundy. Vestiges of the long-closed **Canal du Berry** still exist alongside the upper reaches of the Cher, but they aren't much used commercially. For information on **canoeing** and **kayaking**, see p.42.

Accommodation

The chance to spend the night in a château is one of the great lures of the Loire region, and needn't cost the earth. If you can't afford this luxury, the region has scores of attractive, family-run hotels, and there are as many homely chambres d'hôtes – rooms in private homes rented out by the night. You can usually find a room just by turning up, but in high summer and in the period after Easter, or if you plan to stay somewhere special, it's well worth booking ahead. All hoteliers speak enough English to take a telephone booking.

Hotels

All French hotels are given official **star** ratings, but the system has more to do with size and fittings of bathrooms than with genuine quality. Most tourist hotels in the Loire are two-stars, though there is a solid foundation of no-star and one-star hotels at the budget end of the range, and a smattering of often rather chintzy three-stars at the top. The handful of four-star hotels are almost all converted châteaux deep in the countryside.

At the bottom end of the scale (❶, or less than €30) you're likely to be in an old-fashioned, family-run **budget hotel**, often used by local workers, and typically above a bar or simple restaurant. Such places may be charming – with rickety wooden floors, cast-iron radiators and peeling paint on the shutters

– or depressing. Rooms usually have a sink (*lavabo*) in one corner, sometimes with a toilet (*WC*) behind a screen as well; bathrooms and showers (*douches*) are almost invariably found on the landing – referred to as *douche et WC dans le palier*.

For a little more money (❷, or around €35), you'll either find yourself in one of the better rooms offered by a simple **one-star hotel**, often with refreshed paintwork and a simple bathroom (*salle de bain*) added in a corner, or in one of the budget rooms at a **two-star**, perhaps an old-fashioned attic room with a shared bathroom, or something modernized but spartan. The majority of good **tourist hotels** in the Loire fall within the next category up (❸, often at around €45). You can usually rely on hotels at this price to be professionally run, with reasonably new bathrooms and

Accommodation price codes

All hotels and chambres d'hôtes in this book have been given price codes according to the following scale. The symbol indicates the price of the **least expensive double room in high season**.

Although many hotels offer a range of rooms at different prices, a range of prices (such as ❷–❺) is only given when the spectrum is especially broad, or where there are relatively few rooms in the lowest category. Prices given for dorm beds in hostels are per person per night.

❶ Under €30	❹ €55–70	❼ €100–125
❷ €30–40	❺ €70–85	❽ €125–150
❸ €40–55	❻ €85–100	❾ Over €150

decent furnishings, but don't expect stylish interior design at this price level; at best, owners will have made a feature of ancient beams or fireplaces.

Prices in touristy areas, especially at swankier places with posh restaurants, can rise into the next price category (❹, or between €55 and €70), but you may not get much for the extra money – perhaps satellite TV and a mini bar. Above this level (❺ and up) you're definitely moving into the territory of **luxury hotels**. Some are absolutely delightful, set in historic townhouses or country châteaux and gracefully converted – real honeymoon territory – while others are aimed more at the business market. Note that relatively inexpensive rooms at the best hotels are occasionally disappointing – in a modern annexe, perhaps, or lacking the view – so be sure to ask when you book.

Many family-run hotels **close** for two or three weeks in winter. Only really out-of-the-way places are shut in summer these days. In smaller towns and villages, hotels may also close for one or two nights a week but if you ring in advance you may be able to arrange to pick up a key, or stay on if you arrived on a previous night. Details are given in the Guide, but note that dates vary from year to year, so phone ahead to be sure.

Single rooms are rare, and it's rarer still to be offered a discount on a double room; you may, however, be offered one of a hotel's relatively inexpensive rooms. Many hotels have a few rooms with **extra beds**, on the other hand, and even if they don't they'll willingly add a bed for only a small supplement to the normal price.

The old-fashioned habit of insisting on **half-board** (*démi-pension*) has almost universally been replaced by a polite enquiry as to whether or not you'll be eating dinner at the hotel. Don't dismiss the offer: hotel restaurants are often the best in town, and the set dinners at budget hotels can be astoundingly good value.

Breakfast is not normally included in the price of the room. Again, you'll probably be asked whether you'll be eating breakfast (*prendre le petit déjeuner*) when you check in. At roughly €5 or so, it costs scarcely more than a cup of coffee, an indifferent orange juice and a croissant in a café – which, in fact, is often exactly what you'll get.

Hotel chains and associations

You're not likely to need them in the Loire, and they won't crop up in the listings in the Guide, but it's worth knowing that you can find a very inexpensive, basically decent room at the French budget **chain hotels**. Formule 1 (☎08.92.68.56.85, ⓦwww.hotelformule1 .com), B&B (☎08.20.90.29.29, ⓦwww .hotel-bb.com) and Premiere Classe (☎01.64.62.46.46, ⓦwww.premiereclasse.fr) have inexpensive hotels in the industrial/commercial zones of all the Loire's major cities. At Formule 1, if you reserve in advance you can let yourself in at any time of the day or night using your credit card.

Slightly more upmarket chain hotels include Ibis, Sofitel, Kyriad, Première Classe and Campanile, most of them run by the Accor group (ⓦwww.accorhotels.com), which also manages the relatively swanky Mercure chain of good, if businesslike, hotels in Tours, Blois, Orléans, Bourges, Angers and Le Mans.

An organization to know about is **Logis de France** (☎01.45.84.83.84, ⊛www.logis-de-france.fr), more a French institution than an association. It markets and to some extent regulates its three-thousand-odd members, and its distinctive green and yellow sign showing a hearth and a map of France can be a welcome sight if you're arriving somewhere late or unexpectedly. Standards are far from uniform, and its members tend to be of the old-fashioned school of hotel-keeping – which can be either a very good or a bad thing – but you can rely on reasonable prices and cleanliness.

Chambres d'hôtes

Staying in **chambres d'hôtes** – "hosts' rooms", or **bed-and-breakfast** accommodation in a private home – is an excellent way to get off the beaten track and meet local people. You shouldn't expect hotel-like services such as daily changes of sheets and towels, but standards and availability have soared in recent years, and you can now find chambres d'hôtes in many towns as well as in more traditional countryside cottages or farmhouses.

The pick of the bunch are detailed in the Guide alongside hotel recommendations, but be sure to ring ahead: some proprietors may open and close from one year to the next, the best places get booked long in advance and, in any case, you'll often need to speak to your host to get accurate directions – many chambres d'hôtes are found deep in the countryside.

Tourist offices often stock folders full of pictures and details of chambres d'hôtes in their area; if you're booking from home, a phone call will often result in a choice local recommendation. Alternatively, buy one of the official booklets published by the national promotional agency, **Gîtes de France** (☎01.49.70.75.75, ⊛www.gites-de-france.fr): *Chambres et Tables d'Hôtes* or *Chambres d'hôtes de Charme*. You can find these at international tourist board offices (see p.55) and in French bookshops and tourist offices; both booklets cost €22. For the most comprehensive listings, ask for the dedicated guide for the

région (Centre or Pays-de-la-Loire) or even the individual *département* you plan to visit, or get online – the fully searchable database is translated into English.

Costs are around €45–60 a night – equivalent to the better class of two-star hotel. By and large, standards are high, with typically simple and pleasant décor. The best chambres d'hôtes, whether historic townhouses, ancient farmhouses or mini-châteaux, are far and away the loveliest places to stay in the region: real, lovingly cared-for homes with antique furniture and exquisite period details. At the very top end of the scale, you can find chambres d'hôtes in full-blooded châteaux (see below). Prices rise steeply above €100 at this level, and the boundary between such places and hotels may be blurred.

Some proprietors also offer evening meals or **tables d'hôtes**. If you want to take advantage of this you'll usually need to let your hosts know at least a day or two in advance.

Châteaux

Accommodation in a **château** can take the form of a swish hotel or a room in a private home let out by the blue-blooded proprietor in an attempt to keep the taxman from the door. Either way, what's on offer varies as much as any other kind of accommodation.

Details of many châteaux offering accommodation are given in the Guide alongside hotels and chambres d'hôtes, but if you decide to plan your holiday around staying somewhere really special, you might want to consider getting hold of a **specialist guide**. Many are listed in the standard chambres d'hôtes guide (see above), but the best guide by far is *Bienvenue au Château – Western France*, published in conjunction by the tourist boards of the Centre, Pays-de-la-Loire, Normandy, Brittany and Poitou-Charentes régions. Updated each year, and written in both English and French, the guide lists and describes some 150 châteaux and manor houses that offer rooms. Text and photos are also available online at ⊛www.bienvenue-au-chateau.com.

Alternatively, check out *Châteaux et Hotels de France* (reservations ☎01.72.72.92.02, ⊛www.chateauxhotels.com), a free guide for the whole of France, which covers posh hotels as well as châteaux; note that all of the places listed have paid for the privilege. The similar Relais et Châteaux association (France ☎08.25.32.32.32, UK ☎0800/2000 0002, US ☎1-800/735 2478, ⓦwww.relaischateaux.fr) promotes a handful of luxury châteaux-hotels in the region; you can find their catalogue in tourist offices and on their website.

Gîtes and other rented accommodation

Your first port of call is likely to be **Gîtes de France** (☎01.49.70.75.75, ⓦwww.gites-de -france.fr), the national association promoting self-catering accommodation as well as bed-and-breakfast and camping on farms. You can get the catalogue of self-catering cottages rented by the week – from tourist boards, local tourist offices and some bookshops, or search the organization's excellent website.

For **private rentals**, British travellers should look in the classified ads in the Sunday papers. Otherwise, there are hosts of online booking agencies acting as agents for private owners: ⓦwww.frenchconnections.co.uk, ⓦwww.bvdirect.co.uk and ⓦwww.cheznous .com are well established.

Youth hostels

Auberges de jeunesse (youth hostels) may be handy for lone travellers looking to save money, but people travelling in pairs or groups may as well opt for an inexpensive hotel. Prices are given per person throughout the guide, but if you're not already a member of Hostelling International

(HI) you'll have to factor in paying to join as well – which you can do on the spot in any HI hostel by paying an extra €2.90 a night. Once you've paid this for six nights, you're awarded a year's membership, worth €17.40. You'll only find HI hostels – known as FUAJ hostels in France – in the larger towns: Amboise, Angers, Beaugency, Blois, Bourges, Orléans, Saumur and Tours. Some are in awkward locations out in the suburbs (or, in the case of Amboise and Saumur, on an island in the Loire). The big cities will also have a **Foyer des Jeunes Travailleurs**, a residential hostel aimed at young workers, though travellers can stay there, too; there's no membership fee for these.

Camping

Almost every town or village in the Loire has its own municipal **camping** (campsite), usually located in a pleasant spot by the nearest riverbank. Multi-starred private campsites, many with swimming pools and other facilities, cater to the swankier class of camper and caravanner – many of them French people from outside the region or Dutch holidaymakers. Prices at campsites vary according to facilities and whether you have a tent, a car or a caravan: count on around €5–10 per person. Most campsites stay open from March or April to the end of September or mid-October.

You'll find few opportunities for camping rough (*le camping sauvage*) in the Loire, but you could try asking at farms. Some farms have their own little official campsites anyway, signposted as **camping à la ferme**.

Food and drink

The cuisine of the Loire is famously light and simple, with good-quality ingredients unmasked by complex sauces or over-fussy treatment. There's an obvious local fondness for river fish and fine mushrooms – the latter are grown all over the region – but you'll find plenty of other dishes based on the excellent local wines and local vegetables: Touraine is not called "the garden of France" for nothing. So while the Loire may not have achieved the international gastronomic profile of, say, Burgundy, you can expect to eat and drink extremely well.

The Language section of Contexts (see p.365) includes a French–English glossary that you can use as a **menu reader**. For detailed discussion of the Loire's light and incredibly varied **wines**, see p.352.

Eating out is excellent value, especially at lunchtime. In the evening, you can often find three courses for under €15, and even posh places typically have a come-hither menu priced at under €20. Mark-ups on bottles of wine are surprisingly high, but many restaurants offer inexpensive wine by the carafe. Unless you go for simple fare, picnic food is relatively expensive, but the quality of pâtés, cold meats and prepared salads is high. The sting in the tail may be café costs, which can really add up.

Breakfast

Hotel **breakfasts** are almost universally unimaginative. You'll be served a length of baguette (sometimes a croissant, too) with pre-wrapped butter and jam, a glass of indifferent orange juice and a cup of filter coffee. It often comes served on a paper napkin rather than a plate; you're allowed to leave crumbs on the table. It's easy to do it yourself for a couple of euros less: *boulangeries* (bakeries) can sell you a can of orange juice along with your croissant, *pain au chocolat* or *pain aux raisins*, and in the morning you can usually find croissants in a rack on the counter at cafés and bars.

Picnics and snacks

For **light meals** and **snacks**, cafés and bars often sell inexpensive baguette sandwiches, *tartines* (buttered half-slices of baguette) and *croques-monsieurs* (toasted sandwiches with cheese and ham). Thin, pancake-like crêpes are another option. You'll get a better and usually healthier meal shopping at a **charcuterie** (delicatessen), as found in every small village. These are ideal places to buy delicious **picnic food** such as pâtés, cold meats and prepared salads, though it can work out surprisingly expensive once you've added up *une tranche* (a slice) of this and *une barquette* (a carton) of that. A nearby **boulangerie-pâtisserie** will often have a selection of quiches, cakes and sweet pastries alongside the racks of narrow baguettes and the thicker, longer-lasting *pains*. For fruit and vegetables, you'll have to look for the rarer *épicerie* (grocery), or head for a supermarket.

Salons de thé (tea rooms) are mostly found in larger towns, where they are often chi-chi little places serving small savoury dishes, cakes and lots of different teas.

Service, tipping and the bill

The **service charge** is always included (*service compris*) in the prices listed on the menu, and you're not expected to **tip**. It's polite to round up the bill, however, and you might leave a euro or two if you've been particularly impressed.

To get the **bill**, attract the waiter or waitress's attention – for a man, it's always *monsieur* and never *garçon*, whatever you've learnt in school – and ask for **l'addition, s'il vous plaît**.

Restaurants

Every village has its **restaurant**, most of them serving old-fashioned French dishes perked up by local ingredients, sometimes with a dedicated menu of local specialities. **Opening hours** are short and usually inflexible, typically noon to 2pm and 7.30pm to 9pm or 9.30pm, sometimes a little later in touristy places or large towns – but don't expect to turn up outside a restaurant's stated hours and be served. Almost all restaurants are closed one day of the week, often a Monday, and often for one regular evening and one lunchtime session, too; details of when a restaurant is closed are given with every review.

If it's a weekend night or you're travelling in high season, it's wise to **reserve** – phoning or calling the same day is usually fine. Telephone numbers are given in the Guide whenever you might need them – at less touristy places this is really weekends only. Many restaurants double as hotels – don't ignore them for this reason, as the emphasis is typically on the cooking. Children are almost universally welcomed with an inexpensive and unpatronizing *menu enfant*.

For more glamorous, chef-concocted cuisine, you'll have to book at the more expensive and formal type of restaurant, commonly located in the middle of the countryside. Livelier, more modern, **bistrot**-type places are only really found in the big towns, along with **ethnic restaurants** – mostly Indian, North African and Chinese – and traditional brasseries, which serve straightforward French food at all hours.

In French, a **menu** means a fixed-price set meal, which is usually the best way to eat. All restaurants have a selection of these menus, often starting with a bargain-priced **menu touristique** with no more than a couple of choices for each of two or three courses, and a price tag of as little as €10–15. You'll find more interesting pickings in the mid-priced menus, especially if there's a **menu du terroir** of regional specialities. At the top of the range you may find a multi-course **menu gastronomique** or, at the showiest places, a *menu dégustation*, which may even have a different wine served with each course. The menu itself is called *la carte*, and eating **à la carte** means you can choose from all the dishes on offer, which works out a lot more expensive.

At **lunchtime**, most restaurants offer excellent-value two- or three-course menus for around €10–15, or a simple, inexpensive **plat du jour** (dish of the day).

In France, salads and often vegetables, too, come separately from main dishes, and cheeses come before dessert. First-timers from **North America** should note that *entrée* means an appetizer or starter – main courses are *les plats*, or *plats principals*. At the end of the meal, you'll always be offered *un café* – which means an espresso – and it's never included in the price of the menu.

Regional cuisine

There is no such thing as traditional **Loire cuisine** for the simple reason that the Loire is not a traditional French region. Some dishes, such as *sandre au beurre blanc* (pike-perch in a butter-based sauce) and *la friture de la Loire* (small fried fish), find their way onto menus across the region, but real specialities are highly localized – the prunes of Tours, for example, or the famous green lentils of the Berry.

Freshwater fish is a firm favourite, though sadly it rarely comes from the Loire itself – in fact, if it's salmon, you can be certain that it doesn't, as salmon fishing has been banned for many years. If you want to eat fish fresh from the local rivers, go for *la friture*, a plate heaped high with little smelt-like *goujons*

Vegetarians

Vegetarians have a hard time in French restaurants, and the Loire is no exception. If you don't eat fish you'll often have to make do with yet another omelette or tomato salad, and ordering off-menu, even for simple dishes such as these, is relatively expensive. Sympathetic restaurants may well fix you something special if you say *je suis végétarien(ne), est-ce qu'il y a quelques plats sans viande?* (I'm vegetarian, are there any non-meat dishes?), but you shouldn't rely on this. There is, however, a top-flight restaurant in Tours that offers a genuinely gastronomic, all-vegetable menu – the renowned *Jean Bardet* (see p.78).

(gudgeon), *gardons* (roach) and *éperlans* (smelt), all deep-fried in a light, milky batter. Other traditional favourites include the small, herring-like *alose* (shad) and the rare *lamproie* (river lamprey), both caught in spring in long nets stretched across the river. *Brochet* (pike) and the wonderful *anguilles* (eel) – best served *en matelote*, in a heady red-wine stew – are well worth trying.

Ubiquitous on regional menus is *sandre* (pike-perch or zander), a large, white-fleshed species introduced from Eastern Europe and usually served with **beurre blanc**, a favourite regional sauce made with butter, shallots and white wine or *vinaigre d'Orléans*, whisked into a light emulsion. Imported **salmon**, often poached in Vouvray wine or flavoured with sorrel, is still common, as is stuffed bream.

Meat is less of a speciality, though the *géline Tourangelle* (a black-feathered, corn-fed chicken from Touraine with a distinctive flavour) and *volailles de Loué* (chickens raised according to strict regulations in the Sarthe) are renowned in France. Touraine focuses on pork. The local rillons, great cubes of fatty pork, are tasty but rather off-putting to outsiders unless you find them sliced up and served on a green salad with goat's cheese, in which case they taste rather like particularly good *lardons* (bacon bits). You may find *rillettes* more tempting – this paste of pork mashed with lard and liver is perfect when spooned onto a bit of French bread, and both Tours and Le Mans make a fetish of it. *Andouilles* are cooked pork sausages usually served grilled (they are no relation to the Cajun smoked *andouille* or the ubiquitous French *andouillette*); those from Jargeau and Mennetou-sur-Salon are particularly renowned. In Touraine charcuteries, you'll also find *pâté au biquion*, made from pork, veal and goat.

The favoured meat of the forested eastern Loire is **game**. Pheasant, guinea fowl, pigeon, duck, quails, young rabbit, venison and even wild boar are all hunted in the Sologne. You're more likely to find farmed game on restaurant menus than the real thing, even within the autumn game season, but it's arguable that the farmed stuff tastes better anyway. Game is often served in a rich sauce made from autumnal forest fruits, or **wild mushrooms** such as *girolles* (chanterelles), *cèpes* (ceps, or edible boletus) and *trompettes de la mort* (horns of plenty) – all of which thrive in the region's many forests.

Cultivated **mushrooms** have been big in the Loire ever since it was first discovered back in the late nineteenth century that you could grow the ordinary *champignons de Paris* in the caves that honeycomb the riverside escarpments. In recent years, some producers have experimented with **exotic mushroom varieties** such as *pleurotes* (oyster mushrooms), shiitake mushrooms and *pieds bleu*, and chefs are responding with new sauces.

The Loire valley is also superb **vegetable**-growing country. Anjou and the Orléanais are famous for horticultural research, while the gardens of Touraine produce the wonderfully sweet *haricots verts* (French beans) and leeks – known as poor man's asparagus. The sandy soil of the Sologne is ideal for the real thing, cultivated in distinctive deep rows; locals rate the fleshy white or purple-tinged variety above the smaller green asparagus. It's usually eaten simply accompanied by a vinaigrette made with local walnut oil, or with a hollandaise or mousseline sauce. Turnips are a particular favourite: eaten raw they taste like radishes infused with the taste of violets; otherwise they may find their way into a potent *soupe Tourangelle* along with cabbage, leeks and bacon. Finally, from Berry, come *lentilles vertes* (green lentils), second only to those from Puy among connoisseurs; they traditionally accompany salmon, trout or oxtail.

Anjou's orchards produce greengages called *reine Claudes* after François I's queen, and the succulent Anjou pear. Tours has long been famous for its **prunes**, and you'll often find them on regional menus, steeped in sweet Vouvray wine, stuffed with apricots and apples and flambéed in rum, or even served with pork. A few villages in the Saumurois have revived the tradition of *poires* or **pommes tapées** – oven-dried apples and pears, delicious with duck or poached in wine. But of all local dishes, the most famous is **tarte Tatin**, an upside-down apple tart whose fame originates in the small town of Lamotte-Beuvron, in the Sologne.

The region makes a cult of its **goat's cheese**. A local *chèvre fermier* (farm-produced goat's cheese) can be a revelation, but four named cheeses are found on most restaurants' boards. Each can be recognized by its distinctive shape: soft Ste-Maure takes the form of a long cylinder with a piece of straw running through the middle; the richer Pouligny-St-Pierre and Valençay are pyramid-shaped; while creamier, nutty Selles-sur-Cher is flat and round, like a miniature Camembert. Sancerre has its own tiny, round, tangy *crottin de Chavignol*. *Chèvre* may be presented in any stage of readiness from a creamy, soft *frais*, often dusted with ash, to a dry, powerful *sec* that all but reeks of billy goat. **Cow's milk cheeses** are more unusual, though just south of Orléans they make the delicious *Olivet bleu* and *Olivet cendré*, while in the north of the Orléanais, around Pithiviers, they make the soft *bond-aroy au foin*. Touraine, meanwhile, has a good ewe's milk cheese: *Perrusson*.

The heritage industry makes a lot of noise about **fouaces** (or *fouées* in some regions), a kind of wheat bread fast-cooked in the oven, usually with goat's cheese or *rillons* as a stuffing – though Rabelais' original recipe specifies eggs, butter, spices and saffron. It's particularly popular in tourist-trap cave-restaurants in Touraine and Anjou, and can be very good in a hearty way.

Drink

You can drink **water** from the tap anywhere in the Loire region, but when eating out many locals eschew it in favour of bottled mineral waters (*eau minérale*), either sparkling (*gazeuse*) or still (*eau plate*).

The vineyards of the Loire, which stretch from Sancerre in the east down to the Atlantic estuary, produce an incredible variety of **wines**, ranging from acid Muscadet to honeyed Côteaux du Layon, and from sparkling Saumur to the fruity reds of Chinon and Bourgueil. Bought wholesale from the vineyard, or in supermarkets, wine is incredibly cheap, even if it's AOC (*Appellation d'Origine Contrôlée*) – an indication of quality. You can get a decent bottle for €5, and anything above €10 is moving into more serious territory. For a full discussion of **Loire wine**, see p.352.

As for **drinking** the stuff, you'll find regional wines dominate most restaurant menus. In bars, you'll be served the local plonk – just ask for *un rouge* (a glass of red) or *un blanc* (a glass of white), or even *un vin mousseux* (a sparkling wine). Not all restaurants sell wine by the glass, which is a pity, as it's an excellent way to taste. At moderately priced restaurants there's usually a **pichet** (*carafe*) of something local and decent on offer – you can order *un quart* (quarter litre) or *un demi* (half-litre). You'll often find a few bottles priced somewhere a little over the €10 mark. Be careful if you're drinking fine wines, however, as restaurant mark-ups can be stratospheric.

Beer (*bière*) is popular among younger people; the standard 25cl glass of lager from the tap is ordered as *une (deux, trois) pression(s), s'il vous plaît*. The usual beer on offer is Kronenbourg, but you may be lucky enough to come across one of François Loubriat's artisanal, bottled beers: Leonardo, Sologne, Réserve de Château and others. Despite their local billing – the headquarters is in Tour-en-Sologne – they're currently brewed in the north of France, though there are plans to start brewing in the Sologne itself.

Spirits have less of a following in the Loire than in other regions of France, partly because of the abundance of good wine, and partly because little hard liquor is produced locally, with the notable exception of the big Cointreau (triple sec) distillery just outside Angers. That said, *apéritifs* – *les apéros* in slang – are regularly drunk before a meal; *digestifs* such as Cognac and Armagnac, on the other hand, may be reserved for more special occasions.

Canned **soft drinks** are available everywhere, most commonly Coke (*Coca*), lemonade (*limonade*), Orangina (a pulpy orange-ade), Lipton's (lemon- or peach-flavoured ice tea) and Minute Maid (unsweetened orange or apple juice). Otherwise, you can try a gaudy-coloured *sirop*, a flavoured syrup to mix with water or lemonade: mint (*sirop de menthe*) and grenadine are popular.

In **cafés**, it's cheaper to drink at the counter (*au comptoir*) than inside, while the outdoor *terrasse* commands premium prices. Cafés serve beer, wine and hard drinks as well as **coffee**. Daytime coffee is always *un crème – un café au lait* is a big bowl of very milky coffee served in French homes for breakfast. After a meal you'll be offered a small, black café (*espresso*, or *un express*). You can ask for *un déca* (decaffeinated coffee). **Hot chocolate** (*chocolat chaud*) is popular in the morning, and **tea** in the afternoon. The latter comes as a glass of hot water with a bag of Lipton's-brand tea; if you want the English version, ask for milk on the side – *un peu de lait frais à part* – and add it yourself once the tea has finished brewing. **Herb teas** (*infusions* or *tisanes*) are popular, especially *camomille* (camomile), *menthe* (mint), *tilleul* (lime flowers) and *verveine* (verbena).

Festivals

It would be hard to holiday in the Loire without coming across at least one festival. Even the tiniest villages celebrate their saint's feast day, or put on a festival dedicated to sometimes surprisingly specific items of food. Among larger festivals, there are endless wine fairs, rock, folk and classical music seasons, medieval and night markets, and elaborate, after-dark son-et-lumière shows at some of the bigger châteaux. The most important festival of all, the Jour de Loire (late May or early June), celebrates the river itself, with events organized right the way along the valley.

Major festivals include the half-millennium-old celebrations for Joan of Arc's relief of the siege of Orléans (early May), Chambord's mammoth game fair (June), Saumur's horse-show spectacular (July), the rose festival of Doué-la-Fontaine (August) and Romorantin-Lanthenay's grand feast for the food of the Sologne (October) – not forgetting the classic **24 Heures du Mans'** motor race (June). Big **rock festivals** include Blois' Tous sur le Pont (late May to mid-June), the Printemps de Bourges (April) and the Aucard de Tours festival (May). Look out for the frequent programmes of **classical music** in abbeys and churches across the region, and the numerous **folk music** jamborees, such as those at Pierrefitte-sur-Sauldre (April) and Montoire-sur-le-Loir (August).

Most other festivals in the Loire region focus on food, wine, gardens or music. The **calendar of events** pp.39–41 is by no means comprehensive, and does not include certain "festivals" that run over a period of months and are really season attractions: **Chaumont's garden festival**, for example, which attracts over 100,000 people a year,

lasts from late May to late October and really counts as one of the château's attractions more than an "event". The same applies to the many horse shows and competitions organized throughout the year by the riding school in Saumur, the **Cadre Noir** (see p.245), the **son-et-lumière spectacles** (see below) put on by many châteaux during the summer months or the "festivals" of music and theatre set up in many big towns. All these events are covered in the relevant section of the Guide.

Son-et-lumière spectacles

A particular feature of the French heritage industry, and seen *par excellence* in the châteaux of the Loire is the son-et-lumière. The phrase literally means "sound and light" but there's no real translation. These shows are designed to turn a château into a kind of musical-historical extravaganza using elaborate sound and lighting effects, sometimes with a melodramatic voice-over or antique music, sometimes with professional actors and local townspeople in costume. The trend these days is to allow visitors to wander freely around the site admiring the various effects. At their worst, son-et-lumières are dreary affairs, a travesty of the history and architecture of an ancient building; at their best and most original they can transform the way you see a château. Children may find them equally hit and miss as well. **Starting times** usually vary according to season between about 9.30pm and 10.30pm. The list below covers all the major son-et-lumière performances.

Amboise À la Cour du Roy François ℡02.47.57.14.47, Ⓦwww.renaissance-amboise.com. Costumed spectacular on the high terrace in front of the château with seemingly hundreds of dancing locals and images projected onto the walls. Wed & Sat from late June to end Aug. Adults €13 (€17 in the grandstand), children aged 6–14 €7.

Azay-le-Rideau Songes et Lumières ℡02.47.45.42.04, Ⓦwww.monum.fr. Original and enthralling use of just light and Renaissance music, allowing you to wander freely round the château grounds. July to early Sept. €12 combined entry with château (€9 separately); young people aged 12–18 €5; under-12s free.

Blois Ainsi Blois Vous est Conté. ℡02.54.90.33.32. One of the best, in the atmospheric setting of the enclosed courtyard. Actors' voices tell the story of the château and its bloody history while ultra-high-tech lighting effects pick out details of the architecture. English-language version on Wednesdays. Mid-April to end Sept. €10 combined ticket with château (€6.50 separately); children aged 6–17 €5.50 (€3 separately).

Bourges Les Nuits Lumière de Bourges. Low-key but relatively sophisticated circuit of the old city, following a trail of blue streetlamps past historic buildings lit up by moving projections, while soft music plays. July & Aug daily; May, June & Sept Thurs–Sat. Free.

Chambord Les Métamorphoses de Chambord. ℡02.54.33.39.16, Ⓦwww.chambord.org. Free-ranging "promenade" round the château grounds, taking in clever lighting effects playing on the surface of the stone, and piped Renaissance music. Daily July & Aug; Fri & Sat in Sept. Free.

Chenonceau Nocturne à Chenonceau. Ⓦwww.chenonceau.com Little more than an evening stroll in the elaborately lit-up gardens – to the tune of Corelli. No need to book. July & Aug, plus weekends in June. €5, under-7s free.

Major festival dates

Festival dates are notoriously changeable from one year to the next, depending on factors such as Easter, when the weekend falls or the whims of the organizers. Many of the dates given below are deliberately vague, therefore, and you should always check with the local tourist office or online – websites are given where appropriate. Where festivals straddle more than one month, they are listed below under the month in which they begin.

January and February

Angers Premiers Plans (second half of Jan; Ⓦwww.premiersplans.org) Season of European directors' first films.

Montlouis-sur-Loire and around Les Rencontres Musicales de l'Est Tourangeau (late Jan and early Feb) Diverse and high-quality two-week programme of mostly classical concerts.

March

Chalonnes-sur-Loire (first Sat of March) Festival of Anjou wines, with parades and outdoor banqueting over one weekend.

Orléans (second week of March; Ⓦwww.oci-piano.com) Prestigious, week-long competition for young international players of twentieth-century piano music.

Bourgueil (early/mid-March) Annual wine fair.

Vouvray (late March) Annual wine fair.

Azay-le-Rideau (late March) Annual wine fair.

Prieuré de St-Cosme, Tours Le Printemps Musical de St-Cosme (late March) Two weekends of chamber music.

Around Easter (variable)

Amboise (Easter weekend) Wine fair.

Selles-sur-Cher (second weekend after Easter) Annual wine fair.

Montrésor (Pentecost, ie seventh weekend after Easter) Medieval festival every even-numbered year, with night-time market, processions and dancing.

April

Saumur (April) Books and wine fair, with celebrity French authors.

Le Mans 24 Heures Motos (mid-April; Ⓦwww.lemans.org) Le Mans' classic 24-hour motorcycle race.

Chinon (mid-April) Wine and food fair.

Bourges Le Printemps de Bourges (April; Ⓦwww.printemps-bourges.com) Huge, week-long rock festival featuring artists such as The Dresden Dolls and Arctic Monkeys (in 2006).

Pierrefitte-sur-Sauldre Les Musicalies de Sologne (last weekend in April; ⓦwww.ucps.fr.st) Eight thousand people come for this festival of Sologne folk music.

Orléans (29 April) Commemoration of Joan of Arc's entry into the city, followed on May 1 by celebrations of the taking of the Bastille St-Loup.

May

Orléans (May 7–8) Presentation of Joan of Arc's standard to the people of Orléans, in front of the cathedral in the evening of May 7, followed by Mass and a long procession on the morning of May 8.

Le Mans Festival de l'Epau (mid- to late May; ⓦwww.epau.org) High-quality classical concerts.

Tours Aucard de Tours (last week of May) Big rock festival with a one-off free concert.

Tours Florilège Vocal (late May/early June; ⓦwww.florilegevocal.com) Weekend festival of choral music.

Various locations Jour de Loire (late May/early June; ⓦwww.jourdeloire.com) Concerts, fireworks, nature walks and boat trips along the length of the Loire, from Anjou to the Orléanais.

Blois Tous sur le Pont (late May to mid-June) Festival of rock and world music attracting well-respected domestic names, with small free concerts in the day.

Sully-sur-Loire (late May to late June; ⓦwww.festival-sully.com) Month-long programme of classical concerts, attracting big names (Michel Béroff in 2003!).

June

Amboise (early June) Marching and competing brass bands in the streets of Amboise.

Prieuré de St-Cosme, Tours Les Journées de la Rose (early June) Renowned exhibition of hundreds of rose varieties.

Sancerre (early June) The big festival for Sancerre wines.

Le Mans 24 Heures du Mans (mid-June; ⓦwww.lemans.org) World-famous 24-hour car race.

Orléans (mid-June) Jazz festival, with concerts in the amazing setting of the Campo Santo.

La Châtonnière near Azay-le-Rideau (mid-June) Garden festival of roses and lilies.

Anjou Festival d'Anjou (mid-June to mid-July; ⓦwww.festivaldanjou.com) A month of plays in historic outdoor settings throughout Anjou.

Bourgueil, Langeais, Azay-le-Rideau (mid-June to Aug) Gourmet night market (Fri 6pm–midnight), visiting each of the three towns in turn.

Chambord (third weekend in June; ⓦwww.gamefair.fr) Europe's premier game fair. Set

in the château grounds, with dogs, horns, all sorts of manufacturers' stands and hordes of hunt enthusiasts.

Saumur (last Sunday of June) Festival of military music in odd-numbered years; mask festival in even-numbered years.

Tours Fêtes Musicales de Touraine (late June/early July) Ten days of top-quality classical music in historic locations.

Bourges Un Eté à Bourges (late June to late Sept) Programme of concerts and theatre.

July

Chartres (July & Aug; ⓦhttp://orgues.chartres.free.fr) Two-month-long organ festival and competition, with concerts every Sunday.

Angers Festival Angers L'Été (July & Aug) Lively two-month programme of world and French music concerts, in the lovely surroundings of the Cloître Toussaint.

Le-Puy-Notre-Dame (second weekend of July) Wine and mushroom fair.

Everywhere La Fête Nationale, or Bastille Day (14 July) Fireworks and community celebrations in every corner of France.

Doué-la-Fontaine (mid-July; ⓦwww.journeesdelarose.com) Thousands des3cend to see the rose harvest arranged inside local caves.

Tours (July 23) Garlic and basil fair on the feast day of Sainte Anne.

Saumur Carrousel de Saumur (mid-July) Three days of horse spectaculars.

Richelieu (late July) "Cape and sword" seventeenth-century weekend.

August

Northern Anjou (Aug; ⓦhttp://heuresmusicales.free.fr/) Month-long programme of classical music in churches and château across the region.

Genillé Festival Cosmopolite (second week in Aug; ⓦhttp://festivalgenille.free.fr) Two days of rock, reggae and metal, and one of world music.

Montoire-sur-le-Loir Folklores du Monde (second week in Aug) Large festival of world folk music.

Beaulieu-sur-Layon (second weekend of Aug) Wine and omelette fair.

Bourgueil Fête des Vins du Val de Loire (Aug 15) Festival and showcase for all Loire wines.

Vouvray and Amboise (Aug 15) Wine fairs.

Thouarcé (Aug 15) Bonnezeaux wine festival.

Cunault Les Heures Musicales (mid-July to mid-Aug) Week-long feast of organ and chamber music.

Chedigny (mid-Aug; ⓦwww.blues-in-chedigny.com) Three days of blues and gospel.

Sablé-sur-Sarthe (late Aug) Prestigious four-day festival of Baroque music.

September

Bourges Fête des Marais (first weekend in Sept) Garden and general town festival of Bourges' marshes.

Angers Les Accroche-Cœurs (early Sept) Four bizarre days of street art and theatre all over the city.

Montlouis Jazz en Touraine (early Sept) Major jazz week in and around Montlouis.

Château de la Bourdaisière, Montlouis-sur-Loire (second week in Sept) Gardeners' tomato festival, with tastings.

Château du Rivau (mid-Sept) Pumpkin, vine and children's fairy-tale festival.

Chartres and around (late Sept to early Oct; ⓦwww.journees-lyriques.com) High-quality, week-long festival of opera and classical music in historic buildings.

Various locations Journées du Patrimoine (third weekend in Sept; ⓦwww.journeesdupatrimoine .culture.fr) Hundreds of historic buildings normally closed to the public open their doors.

Orléans Festival de Loire (late Sept; ⓦwww .festivaldeloire.com) Scores of old-style boats descend on Orléans for a five-day river fiesta.

Western Anjou Marathon de la Loire (end Sept) Canoe race down the Loire from Gennes to Bouchemaine.

October

Montrichard Rendez-vous du Pain (first weekend of Oct) Three-day fair of bread and baking.

Le Lion d'Angers Mondial du Lion (mid-Oct; ⓦwww.mondialdulion.com) Major date in the eventing calendar, focusing on young horses. Held in a small town northwest of Angers.

Romorantin-Lanthenay (last weekend of Oct) Gastronomic festival of the Sologne, attracting twenty thousand people.

Azay-le Rideau (late Oct/early Nov) Weekend apple festival.

Outdoor activities

What it lacks in sheer adventure – there are no mountain rock-faces or white-water river-runs – the Loire makes up for in gentle walks, excursions in kayaks or old-fashioned Loire river-craft, and, of course, cycling expeditions. It's ideal terrain for families and older or less adrenaline-fixed travellers. If you're determined on a heart-in-mouth trip, you could always try floating over rivers and châteaux in a balloon.

Touraine's tourist board produces a particularly useful bilingual guide to activities, walks, canoe trips, riding routes and cycle rides called *Loisirs & Randonnées*, and many other *départements* publish equivalent leaflets or booklets – just ask at any tourist office. **Fishing** enthusiasts should contact tourist offices for details of local fishing clubs – the best way to get hold of the necessary licence.

Cycling

Cycling is one of the best ways to travel in the region, especially now a dedicated cycle route, **La Loire à Vélo**, follows the river for almost the entire area covered in this Guide.

Details of this route, and of cycling in the Loire in general, are given in the box on p.42. Even if you don't follow the organized routes, you couldn't hope for better cycling terrain, although you should steer clear of the arterial main or national roads – marked thick red on most maps. The flat *levées* (dykes) running along the Loire are a classic of French cycle-touring, and elsewhere you'll find gradients mostly gentle and roads largely traffic-free. It's surprising how much ground you can cover in one day if you pace yourself. With a modicum of fitness, and well-judged rest stops, most people can comfortably manage a leisurely 40km a day, often much more.

Full details of **bike rental**, including the excellent pick-up and drop-off schemes for bikes and luggage alike, are given in the box below. Standard rental rates are around €15 a day, or €10 for a half day. Theft is rare, but be aware that your rented bike is unlikely to be insured. Mountain bikes (*VTT* in French) are most commonly available, though a touring bike is actually more suitable for road use. Every town has its cycle repair shop, and municipal authorities are building cycle lanes in many Loire cities. As for maps, Michelin's 1:200,000 regional series (see p.53) is perfectly adequate, though it doesn't show contours – not that there are many along the Loire. For detail you're best off with IGN's 1:100,000 Carte de Promenade series – full details are given under "Walking" (see opposite).

Bikes go free on many **trains** and on certain TGVs – indicated by a cycle symbol at the top of the timetable. Newer SNCF carriages have dedicated bike racks. You can take your bike on all car ferries, usually for free if you ring in advance. On Eurostar you have to dismantle the wheels, pedals and handlebars, and parcel the whole thing up in a bag of some kind if you want to take it as hand luggage, otherwise you can send it on as freight 24 hours in advance. Both methods are free of charge.

Canoeing and kayaking

Taking a **canoe** or **kayak** out on the Loire is one of the best ways to experience the river, with its shifting sandbanks, busy bird life and, of course, its château-dominated vistas. On the stretch covered by this guidebook,

---

Loire à Vélo – cycling the Loire

Bicycles (*vélos*) have high status in France, and cyclists are habitually treated with respect by car-drivers, café-owners and train staff alike. Now, thanks to the **Loire à Vélo** scheme, the Loire region is one of the loveliest and safest places in France to have a cycling holiday or take a day out on a rented bike. A new and meticulously signposted cycle route runs all the way along the Loire from Orléans to beyond Angers – a distance of over 300km, of which a quarter is on cycle-only tracks, a quarter on no-through-roads used by local traffic only, and ten percent on cycle-lanes separated from the main road. The remaining two-fifths of the route follows quiet minor roads. At the time of writing, there was a single, fifty-kilometre gap upstream of Tours, which meant if you wanted to cycle the entire route you'd have to follow ordinary roads between Tours and Candé-sur-Beuvron, 14km short of Blois. Work is now underway to fill this gap, however, and to extend the network further up- and downstream. By 2009 the route will extend all the way from Sancerre to the Atlantic. Tourist offices can provide detailed **maps** and other information, and you can download most details, including maps, online at ⓦ www.loire-a-velo.fr.

The region around Blois, meanwhile, offers an additional, 300-kilometre network of routes, **Châteaux à vélo**, which threads inland among the forests and links the area's many châteaux. Full details are given in chapter 2 (see box on p.152), and you can find out more online at ⓦ www.chateauxavelo.com.

All larger towns and many smaller ones have at least one bike rental and repair agency, detailed in the Guide, and bikes can also be rented at a number of hotels, campsites, tourist offices, train stations and even restaurants along the way. A good hundred hotels and campsites have joined the **Accueil Vélo** or **Welcomebike** scheme, which means they offer not just bike rental, but good locking facilities and repair equipment, and can arrange to transport your luggage to your next destination (costs for this vary but aren't generally too expensive). A number of hotels and restaurants have also signed up to **Detours de Loire** (☎02.47.61.22.23, ⓦ www.locationdevelos.com), a fantastic service which picks up your bike in one place and drops it off in another; the organizers will also deliver a rental bike to any location of your choice. You pay a very reasonable fee of €6 per bike plus €2 per "zone" crossed; transporting two bikes from Blois to Tours (across two zones), for example, would cost €16.

there's no white water as such, but you should be very cautious at bridges. Particularly lovely trips can also be made on the Loire's smaller tributaries – especially the Cher, Indre, Loir and Vienne.

To go canoeing and kayaking on any of the region's rivers, including the Loire itself, contact one of the **clubs** listed in the Guide, or any of the members of FFCK, the French Canoë-Kayak association (☎02.38.49.88.80, ⓦwww.ffcanoe.asso.fr). This organization publishes lists of canoe/kayak clubs – available at tourist offices or online. Canoe clubs are often found at a "*Base Nautique*" near a large town.

Canoes and kayaks are usually rented out for around €8 an hour or €15 for a half-day, and you can often join a guided half-day or day-long *descente* of the river for a small surcharge.

If you're canoeing without a guide, a useful, free English-language booklet, *Canoe-kayak*, is produced by the Centre *région*, with tips on good routes and safety. It's available online at ⓦwww.canoe-regioncentre.org.

Boat trips

Sadly, the Loire is no longer used by river traffic, and indeed the only places you can take a proper river or canal cruise are up the **Mayenne** and **Sarthe** rivers, north of Angers; along the **Canal Latéral à la Loire**, north of Sancerre; or on stretches of the Cher. Shorter excursions in old-style Loire boats are easy to arrange, however. You can take a turn in an old-fashioned wooden *gabare* or *toue cabanée* from an ever-growing number of town quays, and many of the **Maisons de la Loire** (river and wildlife information offices) also run trips. Details of all river excursions are given in the relevant sections of the Guide.

Swimming

Swimming pools (*piscines*) are found in every town of any consequence, and privately run campsites often have elaborate pools with waterslides and other facilities. While you're not allowed to swim in the Loire – or the Cher downstream of Tours – because of the serious **dangers** of currents, whirlpools and collapsing sandbanks, many towns on the Loire's tributary rivers have a small artificial beach or grassy sward, often

next to the municipal campsite. It's usually safe enough to swim in any of the smaller rivers, though it's sometimes hard to find a decent spot. Avoid entering the water anywhere near sandbanks, especially ones that have little vegetation and are therefore likely to be newly formed and unstable. Obviously, don't swim during floods.

The safest option for swimming "in the wild" is a freshwater **lake** (*lac* or *plan d'eau*) with a dedicated, sandy beach area. Often referred to as **Bases de Loisirs**, there are many such facilities in the region, often with cafeterias, and with canoes, kayaks and windsurfers for rent.

Walking

Most people think of walking in the Loire only in terms of gentle **day rambles** and indeed almost every village seems to have its signposted *promenade* or *randonnée*, and tourist offices can enthusiastically hand out little maps of the locale. For **short walks** – anything from two to six hours – look out for the excellent hiking **guidebooks** produced by the FFRP (Fédération Française de la Randonnée Pédestre, ⓦwww.ffrandonnee.fr), including *Les Châteaux de la Loire à pied*, *La Touraine à pied*, *De L'Anjou au Pays nantais à pied*, *La Sarthe à pied*, and *La Sologne à pied*, among many others. Each details twenty or thirty walks that keep mostly to footpaths and provides good maps and route descriptions alongside. The guides are only available in French (prices vary from €8 to €13), but it's reasonably clear what's going on even if you don't speak any; a small dictionary might prevent confusion. You can buy the guides, or smaller packs of **route cards**, in French bookshops or tourist offices.

While the Loire is not typical hiking country – there's no wilderness as such – some superb **long-distance footpaths** do extend right across the region. The foremost of these *sentiers de grande randonnée*, or **GR trails**, is the GR3, which runs along the Loire itself from Angers though to Gien. Other major trails include the GR41 from Tours along the River Cher; the GR46 from Tours to Loches along the River Indre; the GR36 from Le Mans to Saumur and south to Montreuil-Bellay; and the GR48 from Chinon up the River Vienne. Good side-trails include the

GR3D through the Layon valley from Chalonnes-sur-Loire to Doué-la-Fontaine, and the GR3C from Gien through the Sologne towards Chambord. There are also a number of Country Trails or **GRP**s, including one circuit around Bourgueil, one route down the Loir from Châteaudun towards Tours, and lots of short routes through the Sologne.

The best **maps** for walking are from IGN's Carte de Promenade series, which shows contours and footpaths, and has a usable scale of 1:100,000. Three maps cover the entire area: *25 Angers–Chinon*, *26 Orléans–Tours* and *27 Orléans–La Charité-sur-Loire*. IGN also publish 1:25,000 super-scale maps, but you shouldn't need this level of detail.

Riding

If you want to go **riding**, the obvious place to make for is **Saumur**, home of the famous Ecole Nationale d'Equitation (Cadre Noir) and one of the foremost areas of France for all things horsey. For details of local stables contact the Saumur tourist office (see p.245). Another fine place to ride is in the ancient hunting forest of **Chambord**, where you can hire horses from the historic stables built by the Maréchal de Saxe (☎02.54.20.31.01). But you don't have to restrict yourself to these two centres. Tourist offices all over the region can supply full lists of **Centres de Tourisme Equestre**, which may be fully fledged stables or farms where you can find instruction or pony-trekking. Costs vary considerably depending on what exactly you're doing, but for pony-trekking expect to pay from €15 an hour. A half-day can cost anything from €30 to €60.

If you're interested in organized riding tours in small groups, ⓦwww.cheval-et-chateaux .com is a good place to start looking. Tours aren't cheap, but can include château accommodation.

Balloon and helicopter rides

At around €200 per person for an hour in the air, a **balloon ride** might seem expensive, but it can be an incredibly refreshing way to view a château. Trips are always just after dawn or a couple of hours before dusk, and there's usually champagne thrown in. Flights are highly weather-dependent, so you may be asked to reschedule at the last minute. A trip in a **helicopter** is less romantic, but you can cover a lot more ground.

Aérocom ☎02.54.33.55.00, ⓦwww.aerocom.fr. Balloon flights from the Blois area, at €200 per person, or €175 if in a group of four or more. Children under 13 pay €150.

Au Gré des Vents ☎02.54.46.42.40, ⓦwww .au-gre-des-vents.com. Balloon trips from near Blois: Cheverny, Beauvais, Villesavin, Valençay. €190 per person, or €165 if three or more people book; children aged 8–16 €145.

France Montgolfières ☎02.54.71.75.40 ⓦwww .franceballoons.com. Balloon flights from Chenonceau, Amboise or Loches, with experienced and professional Anglo-French guides. €225 per person, or €180 on a weekday; children aged 6–12 €150.

Heli Sphere ☎02.38.46.04.32, ⓔhelispheres @aol.com. Hardly green tourism, but certainly exhilarating. A thirty-minute helicopter ride from Orléans aerodrome takes you over the Loire as far as St-Benoît and Sully (€70), but it's worth paying the extra to go as far as Chambord (1hr; €130).

Bird- and wildlife spotting

In summer, you can't fail to notice swallows and house martins darting about the roofs of the towns, and swifts wheeling high above, but if you want to see more unusual **birds** you should head for the rivers. Two species of tern – a bird like a gull built for racing – nest in the sandbanks: the black-capped, red-beaked common tern and the smaller, rarer, yellow-beaked little tern; the latter has become a symbol for all Loire **wildlife**. You can often see herons and all-white egrets fishing in the shallows, little ringed plovers and sandpipers trotting about on the sand, and cormorants flying low over the water in winter. Kingfishers are rarer, but are sometimes seen on tributary waters. Otters are even harder to spot; the coypu, a North American water rat, is more commonly seen. Marshy areas such as the Sologne are rich in bird life: marsh harriers, reed, sedge and Sevi's warblers, bitterns, herons, and endless types of duck and grebe. The poplar plantations of the river meadows offer relatively poor pickings, but in the larger oak, birch and chestnut forests you can spot buzzards, goshawks, sparrowhawks and woodpeckers of all kinds, as well as red deer, roe deer and, if you're lucky, wild boar.

Travelling with children

The Loire is a justifiably popular destination for families travelling with children. Canoeing, swimming and visits to the region's many caves, zoos and theme parks are obvious choices, and while traipsing round on a guided tour of a château and its wonderful collection of Louis XV chairs might sound like purgatory to most kids, don't underestimate the power of many châteaux to enthral. As for practicalities, there are few dangers or annoyances in the Loire, and children are welcomed in almost all restaurants and hotels – children old enough to sit reasonably still and quietly, at any rate.

Hotels charge the same rates for a room no matter who is occupying it, but you can usually save money by asking for an additional bed in a double room, often for only a small or even nominal supplement. Family rooms aren't all that common, but where they are available they may cost only a little more than a double. Most **restaurants** list an inexpensive *menu enfant*, usually with foolproof choices such as steak and chips. Younger children may be happier with an extra plate and a choice of what they can see you eating.

The cost of **entry tickets** can add up, though in state-run monuments, children under 12 go free and young people under 18 pay half price. Age limits elsewhere may vary, but tickets are almost always free for children under 4, with a discounted tariff for children under 12. You may need to carry some proof of age for children on the borderline. On SNCF **trains and buses**, children under 4 years travel free, and children between 4 and 12 pay half fares.

If you're travelling with a **baby**, be aware that most French baby foods have added sugar and salt, and the milk powders may be richer than your baby is accustomed to – soy-based milk is only available at pharmacies, and is very expensive. Many hotels, especially the better two-stars, can provide a cot (*un lit à enfant*) in your room for a small or no charge. Disposable nappies/diapers (*couches à jeter*) are available everywhere.

Activities and sights

Tourist offices are well used to offering advice on local sights and activities that are suitable for children, and should probably be your first port of call. The tourist boards of Anjou and Touraine have co-ordinated various châteaux and other sights under the label "Sur la piste de l'enfant Roy" (@www.piste-enfant-roy .com), or "On the Trail of the Childe Kinge". All the sights taking part in the scheme have special activities and leaflets for children but as yet there is little translated into English.

For details of **outdoor activities** such as swimming, kayaking, cycling and riding, see pp.41–44.

Châteaux for children

Don't rule out **château visits**. Dragging a reluctant 12-year-old round an elegant – or "boring" – eighteenth-century home is probably not a great idea, but if you pick your châteaux judiciously and prepare the ground well it can be amazing how children who are otherwise completely unengaged with history or fine buildings can seize upon a certain feature of the building or a particular historical tale. One trick is to let your charges pick their own château, perhaps from a selection of postcards. the following châteaux may be particularly suitable for children, though it's impossible to guarantee success.

Any château with a **grand aspect**, such as those lording it over the river (Amboise, Chaumont, Chenonceau, Chinon, Montsoreau, Saumur), and those with fine **moats** (Azay-le-Rideau, Le Plessis-Bourré, Sully-sur-Loire) or medieval **towers** (Chinon, Langeais, Loches, Mehun-sur-Yèvre, Montrichard) are likely candidates. Otherwise, châteaux with **dungeons** or particularly **bloody histories** (Amboise, Blois, Chambord, Loches,

Meung-sur-Loire) may be a good bet. **Chambord** is particularly popular for its double-spiral staircase, which has amused children for centuries, and you can take rent **boats** at Chambord, Chenonceau and Cheverny. St-Brisson and Chinon have **catapult** demonstrations in summer.

Some châteaux make a virtue of being child-friendly. **La Ferté-St-Aubin** allows children to explore the interior with complete freedom and has an "enchanted island" and miniature farm in its grounds; **Ussé** sells its connections with *Sleeping Beauty* hard, with a high tower stocked with fairy-tale scenes acted out by shop-window dummies; **Brézé** has a rabbit-warren of underground passages to explore; **Valençay** has a small zoo and maze; the **Château du Rivau** has fairy-tale-themed gardens. Even in otherwise adult-oriented châteaux you can sometimes find special activities or worksheets for children (though not always with English-language versions), and many guides are expert at a well-aimed joke or story designed to make children feel included. The national monuments website (Ⓦwww.monum.fr) includes some child-oriented pages.

Older children and **teenagers** seem to particularly go for Le Clos-Lucé, in Amboise, with its models of Leonardo da Vinci's inventions, and the tapestries of the apocalypse and the Chant du Monde, in Angers.

Other sights

A good choice may be to visit some of the **caves** in the rocky escarpments lining the rivers. The area around Saumur is particularly rich. Doué-la-Fontaine (see p.260) has "cathedral caves", a zoo, a cave full of satirical carved figures, another used as a quarry for medieval stone coffins, and an entire cave village. The sparkling wine caves of Saumur, meanwhile are impressive, and older children will be able to taste the product. Just downstream of Saumur, fantastical **miniature châteaux** have been carved out of the soft rock (see p.266). "**Troglodyte**" cave-dwellings can be explored at Trôo (see p.312), on the Loir, and at the wonderful farm-village of les Goupillières (see p.111), near Azay-le-Rideau. You can descend into subterranean **mushroom farms** all over the region, while near Villandry, you can watch objects being slowly "petrified" by slow-dripping cave water (see p.103).

French families are particularly keen on **zoos**. As well as the wonderful semi-underground cave-zoo at Doué-la-Fontaine (see p.261), there's a large and impressive zoo at St-Aignan (see p.177). Welfare at both is generally good, but if you or your children aren't keen, you could try the **aquarium** just outside Amboise (see p.88).

You might also want to consider taking the children to Holly Park (see p.295), an outdoors-oriented activity park near Baugé, in Central Anjou; the witchcraft museum (see p.237) at Concressault, in the Haut Berry; or the Parc Mini-Châteaux (see p.88) near Amboise, the name of which says it all.

Travel essentials

Costs

The Loire is not an expensive region to visit, at least not in northern European terms. Accommodation and meals can be as cheap or pricey as you like, with hotel rooms available for less than €30, and good restaurant menus for half that. That said, it's easy to splash out on luxurious château accommodation and refined gastronomy, and entry tickets to châteaux and other attractions can add up.

Typical costs might work out at €100 a day per person, based on sharing the cost of a double room (typically around €45 in a standard two-star hotel), eating a simple breakfast (€5), a good picnic lunch (€10) and a proper restaurant meal in the evening (€20), visiting a couple of châteaux, museums or other attractions (€15), and adding a little for cafés and local travel. Hiring a car will add to the cost. On a tighter budget, you could get by on less than €60 by staying in youth hostels, campsites or no-star hotels, and eating in more modest places.

Admission charges to châteaux, museums and other sites can be off-putting. Lazing by the river or wandering the streets is fine, but you'll have to dig into your pocket to get the best out of the Loire's châteaux, troglodyte sites and museums. Students and under-26s, as well as those over 60, can usually take advantage of **discounted entry** – bring your passport as proof of age. Children under 18 go free at state-run monuments, and most commercial attractions offer discounted entry for children, or special family tickets. If you're planning on making a lot of visits, some towns and regions offer multi-entry tickets for a number of museums and monuments (detailed in the Guide). For €25 you can buy a single ticket, La Clef des Temps, to all the Monum (state-run) châteaux in the wider Loire valley region; it might not be worth it, however, unless you're travelling a lot, as the seven Monum châteaux within the ambit of this book – Angers, Chambord, Châteaudun, Chaumont, Fontevraud, Fougeres-sur-Bièvre and Talcy – are mostly fairly distant from each other.

Note that **service** is included in restaurant bills, so you don't need to leave more than small change as a tip (see box on p.34).

Crime and personal safety

The Loire is a sedate, largely **trouble-free** place to travel. Even the cities aren't all that big, and have few of the problems associated with, for example, Paris or Marseille. Violent crime against tourists is almost unheard of, and petty theft unusual. The usual advice applies: don't carry excessive amounts of cash; be wary of pickpockets at train stations; don't leave cameras and valuables lying around in rental cars or hotel rooms; and keep a separate note of credit card and cheque numbers – and the phone numbers for cancelling them.

The **Police Nationale** deal with crime and traffic in towns, where you'll find them at the Commissariat de Police. **Gendarmes** are a separate force in charge of rural areas (and run by the Ministry of Defence). In practice, you can be in trouble with either, and you can go to either for help. If you are **robbed** and want to claim on insurance, you'll need to **report the theft** officially at the nearest Commissariat de Police – addresses in the main cities are given in the "Listings" at the end of the relevant city account. There you can fill out a *constat de vol*, but you probably shouldn't expect much assistance beyond this.

Drug use is as risky, as severely punished and as common in France as anywhere else in Europe. That said, people in the Loire are traditionally minded in their drugs of choice: they are of the prescription or grape-based kinds, for the most part. If you are **arrested** on any charge, you have the right to contact your consulate. If you're discreet, you're probably not likely to get caught, but don't expect the authorities – or your consulate – to be sympathetic just because you're on holiday.

47

Culture and etiquette

As one of the more **conservative** parts of France, the Loire has generally "old-fashioned" manners. People greet each other when entering (or leaving) shops, for instance, and are generally courteous to the point of formality. Travellers with idiosyncratic manners (or, indeed, clothing) will often be received with pursed-lips and a lack of helpfulness. Similarly, excessive warmth or sudden intimacy are usually counter-productive. Straight-talking, however, is generally appreciated: the reputation French people have for rudeness stems largely from their fearlessness about speaking their mind – and opinions are rarely in short supply.

When **addressing people** a simple *"bonjour"* is not enough: you should always use *Monsieur* ("muh-syuh") for a man, *Madame* for a woman, *Mademoiselle* ("mam-zelle") for a young woman or girl. This has its uses when you've forgotten someone's name or want to attract someone's attention. *"Bonjour"* can be used well into the afternoon, and people may start saying *"bonsoir"* surprisingly early in the evening, often as a way of saying goodbye.

If you're actually introduced to someone, it's polite to shake hands – though more traditional women tend to leave this to the men. As a **greeting**, kissing is reserved for friends and family – who may receive anything up to four light touches of cheek to cheek. American-style embraces are almost universally avoided.

The Loire, like the rest of western France, doesn't live up to the unfortunate national reputation for **racism**, and harrassment is unlikely to be a problem. That said, black or Asian visitors may encounter various degrees of curiosity and/or suspicion. There are occasional reports of unpleasant incidents such as restaurants claiming to be fully booked, or shopkeepers with a suspicious eye, but it's no worse than anyone might find in other conservative, ethnically very uniform regions of the world. Travellers of North African or Arab appearance, on the other hand, may be unlucky enough to encounter outright hostility or excessive police interest, though once again, the Loire is relatively unproblematic. Full-on **sexual harassment** is extremely unusual, though women travellers from Anglophone countries may find ordinary male behaviour chauvinistic.

Once a defining national pasttime, **smoking** is slowly waning as a French habit, though restaurants are often distinctly smoky, especially come coffee time – few have the officially required non-smoking areas. Asking a neighbouring diner not to smoke, however, is likely to be considered gauche at best and, at worst, an assault on liberty itself. Smoking is forbidden (*fumer interdit*) in museums, châteaux and on public transport.

Tipping is optional in restaurants, where you don't need to leave more than small change (see box on p.34). Taxi drivers and hairdressers expect around ten percent. You should only tip at the most expensive hotels; in other cases, you're probably tipping the proprietor or their family. Tips for château guides are optional; you could leave a euro or two if you're particularly impressed.

For public **toilets**, ask for *les toilettes* or look for signs to the WC (pronounced "vay say"). If you're caught short, most bars will oblige. You'll occasionally find automated toilet booths in town centres, for which you need thirty or forty cents in change.

Disabled travellers

Travellers with disabilities won't encounter many difficulties peculiar to the Loire – few steep, stepped villages, for instance – but neither are there many specific concessions. Wheelchair users, in particular, will find dedicated access is unusual anywhere outside major public institutions. Few hotels, for example, have lifts or even ramps, though many trains are now wheelchair-friendly. Narrow entrances are commonplace in hotels and restaurants alike, and many

Emergency numbers

Police ☎17
Medical emergencies/ambulance ☎15
Fire brigade/paramedics ☎18
Rape crisis (*SOS* Viol) ☎08.00.05.95.95
All emergency numbers are toll-free.

French towns are awkward to negotiate in themselves: the combination of slender pavements, parked cars, medieval street-plans and dog poo is not exactly ideal for wheelchair use.

To **get to France**, Eurotunnel is the simplest option if you have limited mobility, as you don't have to leave your car, while Eurostar trains have dedicated wheelchair spaces in First Class, at ordinary prices. If you're flying, note that no-frills airlines may lack the experience or resources to guarantee a smooth journey, though on paper they are obliged to offer wheelchair access to anyone who needs it. At the time of writing, for instance, Ryanair crew carried wheelchair passengers down the steps to the tarmac at Tours airport in a narrow (strapless) aisle-sized chair – full marks for effort, none for equipment. All the ferry companies have lifts to get you on and off the car deck, though you may encounter problems moving freely between decks once aboard.

Public transport in France is slowly adapting to the needs of people using wheelchairs, with ramp access available at most stations for boarding and disembarking from **trains**. Timetables show a wheelchair symbol if a train has special on-board facilities, and the SNCF's free guide, the *Mémento du Voyageur à Mobilité Réduite*, is available at all stations. If your French is up to it, you can also call the free information line, ☎08.00.15.47.53 (within France only). If in any doubt, arrive early and make yourself known to the conductor or station-attendant. **Taxi**-drivers are legally obliged to help passengers into and out of their vehicle, and to carry passengers' guide dogs. Hertz and Europcar (see p.28 for listings) can provide **rental cars** with special hand controls, if notified well in advance.

Travellers using wheelchairs may find they have to pay a little more and prepare a little further in advance for **accommodation**, as inexpensive hotels, especially those in rural areas, rarely have lift access or even ground-floor rooms. The omnipresent Logis de France hotel federation (see p.32) has listings of hotels with special facilities, but otherwise you should always ring in advance to find out whether a hotel is able to match your needs. Chambres d'hôtes are typically on upper floors, but you can contact Gîtes de France (see p.32) for information on places with adapted facilities.

It's hardly surprising that visits to ancient **châteaux** can be fraught with access problems. Even before you get to the building, there is often a sea of gravel to negotiate – for which a chair with proper, large rear wheels rather than four small ones is essential. Once inside, wheelchair-users may have to resign themselves to being carried up lots of steps, or restrict themselves to ground-floor rooms. At the major châteaux run by the national agency **Monum**, however, there are sometimes facilities for disabled visitors, and it may be possible to arrange assistance where there are not. The website ⓦwww .monum.fr indicates if a site is "Access for All" or not.

Local contacts

APF (Association des Paralysés de France) 17 bd Auguste Blanqui, 75013 Paris ☎01.40.78.69.00, ⓦwww.apf.asso.fr. National organization that can answer general enquiries and put you in touch with local offices.
Tourisme-handicaps 280 bd St-Germain, 75007 Paris. ☎01.45.55.99.60, ⓦwww.tourisme -handicaps.org. Campaigns for better access in the tourism sector, with a nationwide sticker-scheme for hotels, restaurants and tourist sites. Aimed at tourism professionals rather than tourists themselves, but does maintain comprehensive lists of accessible sites.

Electricity

Electricity is at 220v. Plugs have two round pins. Transformers are best bought at home, but you can buy them in big department stores in France.

Entry requirements

Citizens of **European Union** (EU) countries can travel freely in France, while those from **Australia**, **Canada**, the **United States** and **New Zealand** do not need any sort of visa to enter the country, and can stay for up to ninety days. The situation is unlikely to change, but if you're in any doubt check with your nearest French embassy or consulate before departure. South Africans need to apply for a short-stay visa at the French consulates in Johannesburg or Cape Town – full details are given on the

South African French embassy website, Ⓦwww.ambafrance-rsa.org. A complete list of all **French government websites**, including embassies and consulates, can be found at Ⓦwww.diplomatie.gouv.fr /annuaire.

Anyone staying in France longer than three months is officially supposed to apply for a **Carte de Séjour** (see opposite). If you're an EU citizen, however, your passport is unlikely to be stamped on entry, so there is no evidence of how long you've been in the country. Even if your passport does get stamped, you can cross the border and re-enter for another ninety days legitimately.

Gay and lesbian travellers

France is relatively liberal as regards **homosexuality**, with legal consent starting at 16 and laws protecting gay couples' rights – including the right to form civil partnerships (se pacser). The big cities have upfront gay communities. In rural areas, gay and lesbian couples may encounter curiosity and sometimes outright shock, but full-on prejudice or hostility is much rarer. You'll find useful contacts and listings in the excellent glossy magazine Têtu (Ⓦwww.tetu.com). The French government tourist office publishes a useful booklet, FranceGuide for the Gay Traveler. At the time of writing, there were plans to make it available for downloading via the main site, Ⓦwww .franceguide.com.

Health

With its gentle climate, easy pace of life and world-beating healthcare system, France is one of the world's healthiest destinations. All **tap-water** is safe to drink (except from taps labelled "eau non potable") and there are no nasty local maladies. No visitor requires any vaccinations.

Pharmacies, marked out by flashing neon green crosses – not to mention semi-nude adverts advertising cellulite treatments – are expensive, but well stocked and extremely efficient. For most minor ailments, the pharmacist is well qualified to dispense advice as well as remedies. Opening hours are normally the same as shops (roughly 8/9am–noon & 2/3–6pm). Cities maintain a pharmacie de garde that stays open 24 hours according to a rota; addresses and hours are displayed in all pharmacy windows.

For more **serious complaints**, pharmacists, tourist offices or police stations can direct you to a **doctor**, or you can always find one yourself by looking under "Médecins généralistes" in the Yellow Pages (Pages Jaunes). Many speak reasonably good English. Consultation fees, which you have to pay upfront, are €20 for a government-registered doctor (un médecin conventionné) – though fees are sometimes waived on an informal basis, partly to avoid paperwork. Non-registered doctors (médécins non-conventionné), however, particularly specialists, may charge considerably more.

In serious **emergencies** you should take yourself off to the nearest Centre Hospitalier (hospital), or call an **ambulance** (SAMU) on ℡15. In an accident or injury situation, the **fire service** (les pompiers) is usually fastest, and firemen and women are trained in first aid: call ℡18. Hospital phone numbers are given in "Listings" at the end of the main city accounts in the Guide.

Healthcare charges and refunds

EU citizens are entitled to a refund (usually around seventy percent) of the standard fees of registered doctors and dentists. To apply for this refund, British citizens technically need a **European Health Insurance Card** (EHIC), available from post offices – note that this has replaced the old form E111. In practice, the card exists mainly to smooth the refund process rather than to guarantee it. If you don't have a card and need one, you can always apply for a "provisional replacement certificate". **Non-EU visitors**, including North Americans, should be sure to have adequate medical insurance cover – note that many ordinary policies already cover foreign travel.

French doctors are enthusiastic issuers of prescriptions (ordonnances), which can add to the final cost of treatment. You will be given a **Statement of Treatment** (feuille de soins) with little stickers (vignettes) for each medicine prescribed, and you can use this to claim against insurance. EU citizens, alternatively, can use it to claim back between 35 and 65 percent of the cost of prescription drugs and remedies. You have to take your *feuille de soins* to a local **Caisse Primaire d'Assurance-Maladie** (CPAM), or "Sickness Insurance Office" – ask the pharmacist for details – then wait around two months for the refund to be sent to you.

Similarly, if you're **treated at a hospital**, you'll have to pay upfront for out-patient treatment and then claim a refund at a CPAM branch. If you are hospitalized, inpatients who are EU citizens can proffer their European Health Insurance Card to get 75 percent refunds on bills. The other 25 percent, and a daily hospital charge (*forfait journalier*), however, are non-refundable.

Insurance

The Loire is one of the world's safer travel destinations, but you may want to take out **insurance** before travelling against theft, loss and flight cancellations. As for illness or injury, even though EU travellers can get most of their health needs free from the French healthcare system (see opposite for more), peripheral expenses in the event of a serious problem can add up. Before paying for a new policy, it's worth checking whether your existing home insurance or medical policies already give you cover. If you need to **make a claim**, you should keep receipts for medicines and medical treatment, and in the event you have anything **stolen**, you must obtain an official statement from the police (called a *constat de vol*).

Rough Guides has teamed up with Columbus Direct to offer you **travel insurance** that can be tailored to suit your needs. Products include a low-cost **backpacker** option for long stays; a **short break** option for city getaways; a typical **holiday package** option; and others. There are also annual **multi-trip** policies for those who travel regularly. Different sports and activities (trekking, skiing, etc) can be usually be covered if required.

Visit (⊛www.roughguidesinsurance.com) for eligibility and purchasing options. Alternatively, UK residents should call ☎0870/033 9988; Australians should call ☎1300/669 999 and New Zealanders should call ☎0800/55 9911. All other nationalities should call ☎+44 870/890 2843.

Internet

Signing up to a free Web-based **email** account such as Yahoo (⊛www.yahoo.com) or Hotmail (⊛www.hotmail.com) is the easiest way to keep in touch while you're away. The major cities in the Loire all have a number of cybercafés or other **Internet access** points – *point internet* in French; addresses are given in the "Listings" sections at the end of the relevant city accounts in the Guide. Cybercafés typically charge upwards of €4 an hour. Outside the big cities you may be able to get online at some post offices and even in the odd café or shop, but you shouldn't depend on it.

Laptop-users should note that French phone sockets take a non-standard plug, though you'll often find a standard RJ-11 female socket in the back of the male unit, enabling you to plug straight in. The website ⊛www.kropla.com offers useful advice on dial tones and other potential problems.

Laundry

Laveries automatiques (laundries/laundromats) are only found in the larger towns; listings are given at the end of the relevant city account. Dry-cleaning – *teinturerie* or *pressing* – is a possible fall-back. Most hotels dislike clients washing more than a few smalls.

Living in the Loire

It's hard to find **work** in France unless you have a marketable skill or good local contacts. Even casual work on the grape harvest or in bars and clubs is likely to go to locals, unless you can actually sell yourself on your foreign credentials – in an Irish pub, for example. Teaching English is a relatively reliable option as there is always demand from businesspeople and those who want to work in the tourist industry. If you plan to study French, consider the many language schools in Tours, which is full of international language students in summer.

EU citizens can freely live and work in France, though officially you're supposed to pick up a **Carte de Séjour** if you stay more than three months – and to do this within two months of your arrival. In practice, so few EU citizens actually apply for this card that it may be more hassle than it's worth to either you or the Préfecture (the headquarters of your *département*) or Commissariat de Police from which it's supposed to be issued. Non-EU citizens should be much more careful to follow the rules, and will need a work permit for anything other than the most casual jobs – for information, contact the French embassy in your home country or, if already in France, the Mairie.

Finding work

If you plan to find a job in the Loire, it might be worth getting hold of the **book** *Live and Work in France*, by Victoria Pybus, published by Vacation Work. Once **in France**, check the job offers in the regional newspaper, *La Nouvelle République*, which has a searchable online facility at ⓦwww.nr-emploi.com. Young people may be able to get help and advice in a CIDJ, or Centre d'Information et de Documentation Jeunesse (ⓦwww.cidj .com). The main regional office is in Orléans, 3–5 boulevard de Verdun (☏02.38.78.91.78, ⓦwww.informationjeunesse-centre.fr). The national **employment agency**, the Agence Nationale pour l'Emploi (ANPE; ⓦwww .anpe.fr), advertises vacancies but doesn't go out of its way to help non-French citizens, especially non-French-speakers.

There is much more work available **apple picking** (Sept) than in the late-September or early-October *vendange*, or **wine harvest**, which is increasingly mechanized or requires skilled workers. In late summer, however, the ANPE attempts to match vineyards and orchards to workers from abroad. You can find contact details on the website, and each major city has an office. The best bet, though you'll need to speak some French and be persistent, is to get a list of producers from a tourist office and phone round – or, better still, do the rounds in person.

You're more likely to find work **teaching English**, though if you specifically want to find a job in the Loire region you'll probably have to forgo the usual sources of TEFL jobs and ask at language schools locally: look under "Enseignement: Langues" in the local *Yellow Pages* (*Pages Jaunes*) directory. Offering private lessons is a competitive business. The best opportunities are probably in the big cities, especially commercial centres such as Orléans.

Language study

As the home of "the purest French in France", **Touraine** has a long history of teaching French as a foreign language. In summer, the international student social scene in Tours is pretty hectic; for a quieter stay, or more intensive immersion, consider Amboise or Blois. All the language schools listed below can help to arrange accommodation with local families. Course prices vary a lot (from around €200 a week), partly depending on the size of the group and the number of hours of teaching on offer – usually either 20 or 25 hours a week.

Centre Linguistique pour Etrangers (CLE) 7 place Châteauneuf, Tours ☏02.47.64.06.19, ⓦhttp://centrelinguistique.com. Small classes of around seven students; fairly upmarket.

Eurocentres Amboise 9 Mail St-Thomas, Amboise ☏02.47.23.10.60, ⓦwww.eurocentres .com. Large, relatively inexpensive chain of language schools, offering classes of around a dozen. Amboise is a more sedate place to learn French than Tours.

Institut de Touraine 1 rue de la Grandière, Tours ☏02.47.05.76.83, ⓦwww.institut-touraine.asso.fr. Long-established language school, running classes for fifteen or so, ranging from two weeks to three months.

Tours Langues 36 rue Briçonnet, Tours ☏02.47.66.01.00, ⓦwww.langues.com. Small school right in the centre of old Tours. Offers relatively inexpensive classes for eight to ten students, with morning-only options.

Mail

Most **post offices** (*la poste*) are open Monday to Friday from 8am to around 6pm or 7pm, and Saturday from 9am to noon, though smaller post offices may keep shorter hours and close for an hour or two at lunch, and city-centre offices keep slightly longer hours.

You can buy and send a pre-paid *aérogramme* at any post office, but the easiest place to buy **ordinary stamps** is at a *tabac* (tobacconist). Postboxes are bright yellow.

You can receive letters **poste restante** – addressed to you at Poste Restante, Poste Centrale, Town x, Postcode – but most people these days use email (see p.51) instead.

Maps

To back up the maps in the Guide, you may want to pick up free town plans or regional maps from tourist offices, but there's no substitute for a good **road map**, particularly if you're heading off down minor roads in search of *chambres d'hôtes*, vineyards or lesser-known châteaux.

There's no single map showing the entire area covered in this guide. Of the two main series, IGN's brown Carte Régionale 1:250,000 maps have the edge. IGN covers the area in two sheets: IGN R08 *Centre* and R07 *Pays de la Loire;* the former includes all of Touraine and extends north to cover Le Mans, Chartres and even Paris; the latter covers Saumur, Angers and the Western Loire. The alternative, **Michelin**'s Local series, covers most of the Loire region in two 1:150,000 maps: *317 Indre-et-Loire and 318 Loiret, Loir-et-Cher*. Neither of these show any of the area covered in chapter 7 of this Guide, however, so you'd have to rely on the chapter map shown on p.302 – or fork out for maps 310 (the Sarthe river, Le Lude and Le Mans) and 311 (Le Loir, Vendôme, Châteaudun and Chartres). For detail, clarity and town plans, there's little to choose between IGN and Michelin.

If you're looking for really large-scale maps – for **walking**, perhaps – go for IGN's Carte de Promenade 1:100,000 series (see p.44); for serious detail, check out their local maps at 1:25,000.

The Media

France's leading **national newspaper** is the left-leaning *Le Monde* (⊛www.lemonde .fr). The main **regional paper** for the Loire is *La Nouvelle République* (⊛www .lanouvellerepublique.fr). Copies of **UK and US newspapers** – usually the *Financial Times*, *Guardian*, *International Herald Tribune*, *Times* and *USA Today* – can be found in kiosks in most large towns, as well as in tobacconists' (*tabacs*) and stationers' shops (*papeteries*) that advertise themselves as selling *journaux* (newspapers). All newspapers have to be sold at the marked euro price, exactly.

Hotels with three or more stars, and one or two with fewer, usually have **satellite television**, typically showing BBC World and sometimes CNN, among other channels.

Money

Since January 2002, France's unit of **currency** has been the euro (€), divided into

100 cents. When speaking, locals may occasionally estimate prices in terms of francs, and cents are invariably referred to as centimes, but the changeover is otherwise complete. There are seven euro notes (5, 10, 20, 50, 100, 200 and 500) and eight different coins (from 1 cent to 2 euros).

For most of its short life, the euro has been worth roughly one US dollar. At the time of writing, however, the **exchange rate** was relatively poor for non-Euroland visitors, at €0.80 to the US dollar, €1.50 to the British pound. For up-to-date, exact exchange rates, consult newspapers or the Currency Converter website, ⊛www.oanda.com.

Banking hours are Monday to Friday 9am to noon and 2pm to 4.30pm, though larger branches may also open at lunchtime and on Saturday mornings. Smaller branches may close on Mondays, and all banks are closed on Sundays and public holidays. If you're **changing money**, banks are the best option, though rates and commissions do vary, so shop around. Where "no commission" is advertised, the exchange rate may be disadvantageous. Avoid **bureaux de change**, especially at tourist hotspots, where commissions tend to be high and exchange rates very poor; the only benefit of these places is their long opening hours.

By far the easiest way to access money in France is with your own **ATM card**. Most foreign bank cards will work in a French ATM/ cash machine (called a *distributeur* or *point argent*), especially if they carry the Cirrus, Plus or Link symbol; on-screen instructions are given in a choice of foreign languages. Banks charge reasonable exchange rates but add piratical rates of commission, depending on the bank – between 1 and 5 percent commission for foreign cash withdrawals. Note that there is often a minimum charge as well, so it may be worth getting out a sizeable sum each time you use the machine.

Credit cards are accepted in all but the most inexpensive shops, hotels and restaurants. **Visa** (called *Carte Bleue* in France) is the front-runner, with MasterCard and American Express coming a distant second. Be aware that French credit cards carry a small gold-coloured chip (*puce*) on the front, which allows card-users to enter a PIN code to authorize their purchases; if your card works using a magnetic strip (*bande magnétique*) on the back and a signature, you may need to explain. Most retailers and hoteliers in the Loire, however, are well accustomed to foreign cards.

Traveller's cheques are, of course more secure than cash. Any major brand will do. **US dollar** cheques are widely accepted in tourist areas, and cheques denominated in other major currencies are usually accepted as well. Be sure to keep the purchase agreement and a record of cheque serial numbers safe and separate from the cheques themselves. In the event that cheques are lost or stolen, the issuing company will expect you to report the loss immediately, using the emergency number given with the cheques. Most companies claim to replace lost or stolen cheques within 24 hours.

Opening hours and public holidays

Except in the height of summer, when tourist attractions and businesses forgo the customary two-hour lunch break, everything **shuts down** in the middle of the day. Restaurants usually remain closed at least one night a week (often two nights in winter), and usually on the following lunchtime as well. Don't get caught out by the official closing days at state-owned museums and smaller châteaux – usually Monday or Tuesday – and remember that in cathedrals, Sunday mornings are set aside for worshippers. Note, too, that all sights and attractions keep Sunday hours on public holidays.

Shop opening hours in France are usually Monday to Saturday 8am to noon, and 2pm to 6.30pm, though many shops, especially in rural areas, may open and close an hour later in the morning and afternoon, while shops and businesses in cities may stay open throughout the day. Sunday opening is rare, though food shops may stay open on Sunday morning and close on Monday instead. In summer, larger tourist offices and museums tend to stay open without interruption, and closing times are often extended by an hour or more into the evening.

Some **major châteaux** offer late-night opening once a week, or a night-time son-et-lumière show (see p.38). **Smaller**

museums and **private châteaux** may only offer two short morning and afternoon sessions: from around 10am to noon, and 2pm (3pm in summer) until 5pm (or 6pm). **Churches** and **cathedrals** are almost always open from early in the morning until dusk, or around 8pm in summer. Occasionally, you'll find a rural church locked shut, but there's sometimes a note telling you which door to knock on to get the key. Failing that, you could try to find the priest's house, or *presbytère*.

Public transport is mostly timetabled from Monday to Friday, with a slightly reduced Saturday service and very little if any action at all on *dimanches et jours fériés* (Sundays and public holidays).

France celebrates eleven **national holidays** (*jours fériés* or *j.f.*), not counting the two that fall on a Sunday anyway – Easter Sunday (*la Fête de Pâques*) and Whitsun (*Pentecôte*). Throughout the Guide, opening hours on public holidays are the same as for **Sundays**, unless detailed otherwise. With three and sometimes four holidays, **May** is a particularly festive month. If a public holiday falls on a Tuesday or a Thursday, many people *faire le pont* ("bridge it") by taking an unofficial day off on the adjacent Monday or Friday.

January 1 *Le Jour de l'an*
Easter Monday *Lundi de Pâques*
May 1 *La Fête du travail* (Labour Day)
May 8 *La Fête de la Victoire 1945* (VE Day)
40 days after Easter (May) *L'Ascension* (Ascension Day)
7th Monday after Easter (mid-May to early June) *Lundi de Pentecôte* (Whit Monday)
July 14 *La Fête nationale* (Bastille Day)
August 15 *L'Assomption* (Feast of the Assumption)
November 1 *La Toussaint* (All Saints' Day)
November 11 *L'Armistice 1918* (Armistice Day)
December 25 *Noël*

Phones

Phone boxes are plentiful, but you'll often need to buy a **phonecard** (*télécarte*) to use them. The easiest option – though by no means the cheapest – is to use a **mobile phone**. If you plan to make a lot of calls you might consider buying a French mobile (*portable*) using pre-paid charge-up cards (*mobicartes*); inexpensive deals are always on offer from one of the big companies. Note

Calling France from abroad

To make a call **to France from abroad**, use the IDD code for your country (00 or 011 in most cases) followed by the French country code (33), then the local number minus the initial "0".

From the UK, Ireland, New Zealand and the Netherlands ℡00 33 (0), from South Africa ℡09 33 (0). From the US, Canada and Australia ℡011 33 (0).

that France operates on the European GSM standard, so US cellphones won't work in France unless they're tri-band.

If you're **calling within France** you'll always need to dial the regional code first – ℡02 for all of the area covered by the Guide. Phone numbers prefixed ℡08 are special: ℡08.00 is free-to-dial; ℡08.10 is charged at local rates, no matter where you're calling from; all other ℡08 numbers cost €0.34 per minute and can't be accessed from outside France. Mobile numbers begin ℡06. International access numbers for phoning abroad are shown in the box above. International off-peak hours are the same as for domestic phone calls.

Shopping

Among the best purchases in the Loire are **wine** (see Contexts, p.352) and **food**. Both are generally far better and cheaper than their equivalents in Anglo countries. Touring the vineyards is certainly the most enjoyable way to buy wine, and with enough tasting you'll be able to identify a wine you really like, but be aware that wines from the bigger names are usually available from supermarkets at comparable prices. France in general is, of course, famous for fashion, but clothes are relatively expensive, and the Loire's cities are generally disappointing in terms of designer wear – the region's more stylish residents prefer to shop in Paris.

Visitors from outside the EU can claim **value added tax** (VAT) refunds on any non-business purchases in a single shop of over €175 – if the shop in question signs up to the scheme. Ask for the relevant forms when you buy.

Time

France is in the **Central European Time Zone** (GMT+1): one hour ahead of the UK, six hours ahead of Eastern Standard Time. Daylight Saving Time (+1hr) lasts from the last Sunday of March through to the last Sunday of October, so for one week in late March and/or early April North American clocks lag an extra hour behind.

Tourist information

A French government tourist office, or **Maison de la France** can be found in most major capital cities around the world. For a full list of addresses, see ⓦwww.franceguide.com. Their brochures, maps and lists of campsites, hotels, festivals and so on can be handy, but much of the best material covers only one of the many official *régions* or *départements* that divide up the area – it's difficult to find information on the Loire as a whole.

Once in France, you'll find a tourist office – **Office du Tourisme** (OTSI) – in even the smallest towns and villages. Addresses, opening hours and websites are given in the Guide for all but the most minor. All staff speak English and can provide free town plans and exhaustive lists of activities, sights and accommodation, including *chambres d'hôtes* – in fact, about the only thing they can't do is recommend a restaurant, though you may get personal advice with a nod and a wink. Many tourist offices also produce walking maps and offer town tours.

Some towns along the Loire also have a **Maison de la Loire**, which acts as a kind of river and wildlife information and resource centre. They vary in levels of activity, but you can usually sign up for river and bird-watching walks, arrange trips in old-style river boats, and pick up lots of information on the ecology of the area. Some house small local museums as well.

Tourist offices and government sites

This guidebook covers an area of France administered by two government *régions*, including all six *départements* of the Centre *région*, and two *départements* of the Pays-de-la-Loire *région* – namely the Maine-et-Loire and the Sarthe. Each has its own Départementale du Tourisme, or **tourist board**, listed below. The websites of the two Comités Régionales are ⓦ www.visaloire.com, for the Centre *region*, and ⓦ www.paysdelaloire.fr.

Cher 5 rue de Séraucourt, 18000 Bourges ☎ 02.48.48.00.10, ⓦ www.berrylecher.com.

Eure-et-Loir 10 rue du Docteur Maunoury, 28002 Chartres ☎ 02.37.84.01.00, ⓦ www.tourisme28.com.

Indre 1 rue St Martin, 36003 Châteauroux ☎ 02.54.07.36.36, ⓦ http://tourisme.cyberindre.org.

Indre-et-Loire (Touraine) 9 rue Buffon, 37000 Tours ☎ 02.47.31.42.52, ⓦ www.tourism -touraine.com.

Loiret (Orléanais) 8 rue d'Escures, 45000 Orléans ☎ 02.38.78.04.04, ⓦ www.tourismeloiret.com.

Loir-et-Cher 5 rue de la Voûte du Château, 41005 Blois ☎ 02.54.57.00.41, ⓦ www.chambordcountry.com.

Maine-et-Loire (Anjou) place Kennedy, 49021 Angers ☎ 02.41.23.51.51, ⓦ www.anjou -tourisme.com.

Sarthe 40 rue Joinville, 72000, Le Mans ☎ 02.43.40.22.50, ⓦ www.sarthe-tourisme.com.

Tourism and recreation sites

Camping France ⓦ www.campingfrance.com. Large database of French campsites, with an English-language option. Gives opening seasons and contact details, and icons indicate facilities.

Jardins de France ⓦ www.jardins-de-france.com. Association of private gardens in the Loire valley, with links and descriptions of all those open to the public.

Loire-France ⓦ www.loire-france.com. French-language site dedicated to the history and culture of the entire Loire region.

Maison de la France ⓦ www.franceguide.com. The English-language section of the French government tourist-office website offers news, details of events, links to local and regional tourist offices, historic monuments and the like.

Monum ⓦ www.monum.fr. The website of the state monuments agency, which manages many of the biggest and finest châteaux in the Loire region. Each historic building has its own English-language pages, with details of opening hours, access and events and dedicated pages for children.

Parc Naturel Régional Loire-Anjou-Touraine ⓦ www.parc-loire-anjou-touraine.fr. French-language website for the regional natural park at the heart of the Loire, with contacts and details of guided walks and excursions throughout the year.

Via France ⓦ www.viafrance.com. Bilingual events database (including concerts, theatre, festivals, markets and sports) organized by category and region.

Guide

Guide

1

Touraine

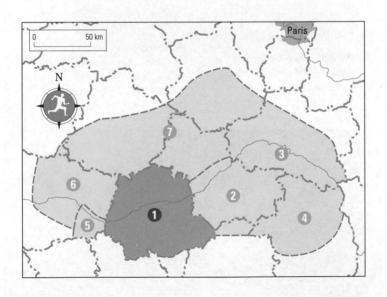

CHAPTER 1　# Highlights

* **St-Gatien** Tours' magnificent Gothic cathedral has two extravagantly sculpted towers and a fascinating interior. See p.69

* **Chenonceau** The graceful arched gallery of Chenonceau bridges the placid River Cher. See p.89

* **Villandry** If you thought a vegetable patch couldn't be fabulous, you haven't been to Villandry, where the château overlooks perfect gardens re-created in a sixteenth-century style. See p.101

* **Au Bout du Monde** Hidden away at "the end of the world", as its name translates, this restaurant near Villandry offers the best of Loire cuisine. See p.104

* **Les Goupillières** Local cave-dwelling traditions are brought to life at this subterranean medieval farm. See p.111

* **Chapelle Ste-Radegonde** Hewn out of the cliffs above Chinon, this ancient hermit's chapel shelters a Plantagenet wall-painting. See p.119

* **Loches** The brutal keep and refined château of the citadel of Loches are encircled by fortified walls. See p.126

* **Montrésor** This picturesque village has a superb Renaissance tomb in its church and fine art in its château. See p.133

△ Villandry gardens

Touraine

I f the Loure Valley conjures up an image of gentle rivers and exquisite châteaux, it is **Touraine**, the historic region around the cathedral city of Tours, that best matches the ideal. Touraine isn't any richer in history than neighbouring regions, or more densely populated with fine churches and châteaux, but it is somehow closer to the idea of *la France profonde* – the great French cultural myth of "deepest France". It certainly receives the most tourists of any Loire region.

The writer Rabelais called Touraine the "**garden of France**", and the name still aptly describes its air of well-tended prosperity: the shallow, well-watered valleys are soft and fertile, the orchards and vineyards fruitful, and every back road takes you past carefully maintained gardens and vegetable plots. It's the perfect backdrop for the scores of pale stone châteaux that dot the landscape. Between the soft rivers, the plateaux are surprisingly bleak, empty of anything but farms, modest villages, vineyards and the occasional patch of ancient forest.

Although no larger than other cities in the Loire region, **Tours** stands pre-eminent by virtue of its history and cultural status. It was a key centre of early Christianity in France, and the favoured city of the French monarchy in the Renaissance. The Valois kings have long since departed, but Tours remains a place of government as the administrative capital of the *département* of the Indre-et-Loire – the modern bureaucratic name for Touraine. If you don't have your own transport, the city is the obvious Loure Valley base, with both bus and train connections to many of the region's most notable châteaux.

From Tours, you can follow the course of the Loire east past the vineyards of **Vouvray** and **Montlouis–sur–Loire**, which together produce some of the region's finest white and sparkling wines, and on to **Amboise**, whose fine Renaissance château stands high on natural battlements overlooking the river. A short distance south, the graceful, much-visited **château de Chenonceau** bridges the lovely Cher river, creating one of the quintessential images of idyllic Loire life.

West of Tours, the north bank of the Loire sees relatively few visitors, though you can visit the grand châteaux of **Luynes** and **Champchevrier** and the dramatic, superbly furnished château at **Langeais** on the way to the wine-growing town of **Bourgueil**. To the south, the sleepy **River Indre** runs in a great arc through the heart of Touraine, lined with ruined abbeys, watermills and châteaux – none of them more beautiful than the Renaissance pearl of **Azay-le-Rideau**, mirrored in the streams that flow past its walls. Nearby lie the fairy-tale château of **Ussé** and Balzac's summer writing home at **Saché**. Just short of the nearby confluence of the Loire and Cher, Renaissance gardens have been spectacularly re-created at the château **Villandry**.

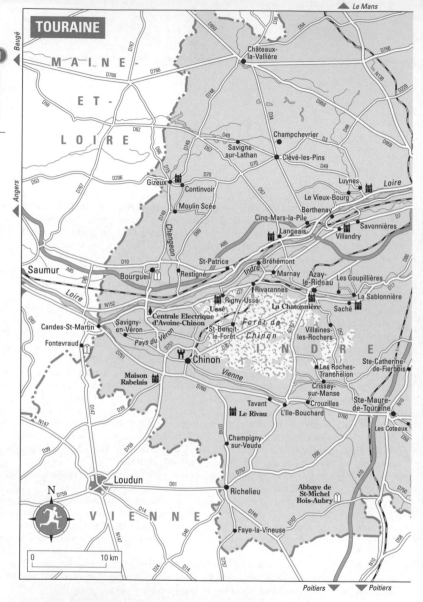

The southwestern corner of Touraine is watered by the broad river **Vienne**, whose confluence with the Loire marks the border with the Saumurois. The chief town is **Chinon**, whose ruined castle was built by Henry Plantagenet on a cave–riddled escarpment overlooking the river. You can follow the Vienne upstream past **Tavant**, with its bright Romanesque mural paintings, and **L'Ile Bouchard**'s ruined abbey, then up onto the plateau surrounding

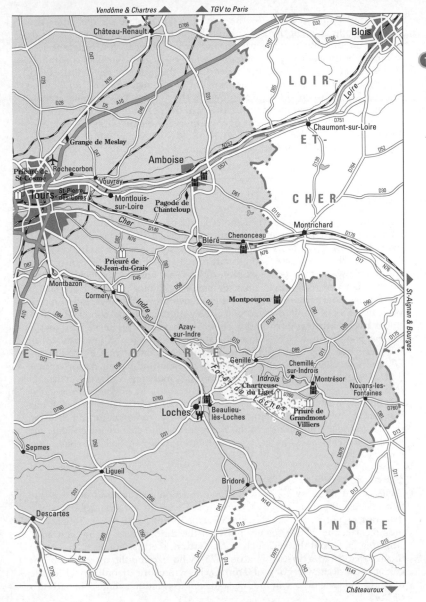

Ste-Maure-de-Touraine, which produces some of the region's most renowned goat's cheese. Alternatively, head south up the River Veude to the stunning chapel at **Champigny-sur-Veude** and the weird seventeenth-century planned town of **Richelieu**.

The main draw in southern Touraine is **Loches**, a quiet provincial town at the foot of a stunning medieval citadel. If you travel beyond Loches, you'll really leave other tourists behind. To the east you can explore up the little river **Indrois**, stopping off at the half-ruined abbeys hidden in the ancient Forêt de Loches on the way to the château and abbey church at **Montrésor** – a contender for the title of prettiest little town in the region. North of the Indrois, within striking distance of the river Cher, the isolated forest château of **Montpoupon** houses a fascinating museum of hunting. The wet and wooded countryside **north of the Loire**, known as the **Gâtine Tourangelle**, is more popular with wild boar than tourists.**Information** on Tours and the surrounding region can be found online at ⓦwww.tourism-touraine.com. For details of **bus** times, contact Filvert (☎02.47.47.17.18, ⓦwww.touraine-filvert.com), the operating company for the whole of Touraine.

Tours

Straddling a spit of land between the rivers Loire and Cher, the ancient cathedral city of **TOURS** has an air of quiet confidence. It may be the chief town of the Loire Valley, but Tours has long had a reputation as a staid, bourgeois place, the home of lawyers and administrators rather than, say, artists or factory workers. However, the city's proximity to Paris – it's now less than an hour away on the high-speed TGV line – has tempered its nature, ensuring that Tours is indefinably more switched on than other French provincial cities, and in recent years an influx of commuters has perceptibly modified Tours' conservative feel.

The **lively atmosphere** of the centre is thanks in no small part to the student population, which is domestic through the year and international in summer. There are scores of bustling bars and cafés, an active if limited nightlife, and some fine restaurants – among the best in the region. As for culture, Tours has an excellent art gallery, some unusual museums – of wine, crafts and stained glass – and a great many fine buildings, not least of which is the glorious St-Gatien cathedral. The city's prettified old quarter is perfect for idle wandering, its fourteenth- to sixteenth-century townhouses still bearing witness to the industriousness of the bourgeoisie, who rose to power while the nobility frittered away its energy on hunting, château-building and other country pastimes.

Some history

Tours' recorded history begins with the foundation of **Caesarodunum** in the first century BC, but the city's name harks back to earlier inhabitants, the **Turones**, one of many Gaulish tribes to settle in this fertile region. Tours was a prominent centre of Christianity between the third and the eighth centuries, attracting saints and thinkers such as **St Gatien**, the first bishop of Tours; the much-loved **St Martin** (see box on p.75), who became the focus of a major cult after his death; **Gregory of Tours**, who wrote an extraordinary chronicle of world and local history in the late sixth century; and the philosopher **Alcuin of York**.

Attacks by **Vikings**, who sailed right up the Loire in the mid-ninth century, heralded an era of conflict and insecurity. The main attraction was the wealth of the churches, and Tours was a major target. Martinopolis, the new centre that had grown up around the shrine of St Martin, was razed and then rebuilt with serious defences, leading it to be renamed Châteauneuf. The city became part of the fief of the counts of Blois and then, in 1044, fell to the Angevins. Under their aegis, a new centre, the Bourg des Arcis, grew up between Martinopolis

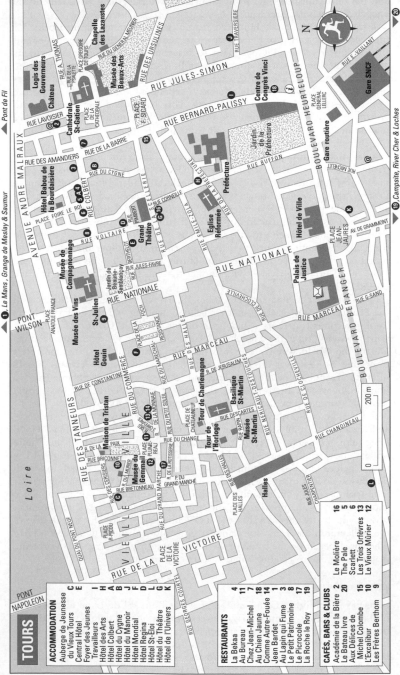

Orléans · St-Pierre-des-Corps (Gare TGV) & Airport

Le Mans, Grange de Meslay & Saumur
Pont de Fil

Campsite, River Cher & Loches

N

Gare SNCF

TOURS

ACCOMMODATION

Auberge de Jeunesse du Vieux Tours	C
Central Hôtel	E
Foyer des Jeunes Travailleurs	I
Hôtel des Arts	H
Hôtel Colbert	A
Hôtel du Cygne	B
Hôtel du Manoir	J
Hôtel Mondial	F
Hôtel Regina	D
Hôtel St-Éloi	L
Hôtel du Théâtre	G
Hôtel de l'Univers	K

RESTAURANTS

La Bekaa	4
Au Bureau	11
Chez Jean-Michel	7
Au Chien Jaune	18
Comme Autre-Fouée	14
Jean Bardet	1
Au Lapin qui Fume	3
Le Petit Patrimoine	8
Le Picrocole	17
La Roche le Roy	19

Le Molière	16
The Pale	5
Scarlett	6
Les Trois Orfèvres	13
Le Vieux Mûrier	12

CAFÉS, BARS & CLUBS

Académie de la Bière	2
Le Bateau Ivre	20
Aux Délices de Michel Colombe	15
L'Excalibur	10
Les Frères Berthom	9

PONT NAPOLEON

PONT WILSON

Loire

Prieuré de St-Cosme

and the old Roman centre. In the fourteenth century new city walls finally encircled the whole conurbation.

In the aftermath of the Hundred Years War, the paranoid king **Louis XI** made Tours the capital of his kingdom, attracting the artist Jean Fouquet and the composer Johannes Ockeghem to his court, and bringing silkworkers and worms from Lyon to found the **silk industry**. Mulberry trees, the favoured food of the worms, were planted all around the city and Tours boomed as a major commercial centre, dependent on the trade along the Loire. The **financiers** and merchants who bankrolled the military and courtly excesses of the monarchs from Louis XI onwards built ever finer mansions, aping the excesses of their royal and aristocratic masters by building châteaux in the countryside nearby.

Tours' **Protestant** population grew steadily from the sixteenth century, particularly among the merchant classes and workers in the 20,000-strong silk industry. When the 1685 Edict of Fontainebleau ended official toleration of Protestantism, however, thousands fled the city, trade declined, and Tours gradually became just another conservative, provincial town. Eighteenth-century works such as the construction of the axial **rue Royale** (now rue Nationale) failed to stimulate much growth, and it was only when the railway arrived in the mid-nineteenth century that the city started to prosper once more. The proud civic centrepiece of **place Jean-Jaurès** was built by the train lines and some 800m from the river – symbolically, the city had finally turned its back on the Loire.

There was brief excitement in October 1870 – when Léon Gambetta escaped the Prussian siege of Paris by hot air balloon, landing and forming the short-lived government in Tours – and again during the 1920 **Congress of Tours**, which famously split the French Left into socialist and Communist factions. During the **World War II**, Tours was again the national capital – for three days from June 10, 1940 – as the French army fled the advancing Germans. For 48 hours the Loire became the front line, and Tours suffered incredibly destructive bombardments and firestorms. Yet the face of the modern city was mostly seriously rearranged by the postwar reconstruction that followed.

In 1959 the conservative but vastly energetic **Jean Royer** became mayor – and remained so until 1995, acquiring the nickname of *le bon roi Jean* ("Good King John"). During his "reign", **place Plumereau** and much of the **Vielle Ville** were carefully restored, and France gained the so-called *loi Royer*, a law which helped protect traditional town-centre shops from competition with out-of-town retail giants. While Tours may have failed to keep pace with the industrial successes of its neighbour, Orléans, it has found new pride, confidence and prosperity in the postwar era, and in the late 1990s, the city's development was crowned with the arrival of the **TGV** line from Paris. The first decade of the millennium has seen city planners once more turning their attention to where it all began, on the banks of the Loire, but it may be some years yet before major works like re-creating the quays are carried out.

Arrival

Ryanair's daily **flights** from London arrive at Tours Val de Loire **airport**, 4lm northeast of the city centre. Arrival is very straightforward thanks to the aiport's tiny size. Booths for the major car-rental companies (see p.28) are found in the small waiting room on the far side of customs, next to the exit. A bus waits immediately outside to take you into the centre of town (€5), a journey of about twenty minutes. Taxis cost around €12.

The **gare routière** and **gare SNCF** are situated about 500m south of the centre, on the south side of place Général Leclerc. Most **TGV**s from Paris stop at **St-Pierre-des-Corps** station, in an industrial estate deep in the suburbs, but frequent shuttle trains (or sometimes buses) provide a link to the main central station; transferring is usually a matter of stepping off the TGV and across to an ordinary train waiting at the next platform, but if you're in any doubt just follow the crowd.

Information

On the opposite side of the square from the gare SNCF is the city's excellent **tourist office**, on the corner of rue Bernard Palissy and boulevard Heurteloup, next to the landmark Centre de Congrès Vinci (mid-April to mid-Oct Mon–Sat 8.30am–7pm, Sun 10am–12.30pm & 2.30–5pm; mid-Oct to mid-April Mon–Sat 9am–12.30pm & 1.30–6pm, Sun 10am–1pm; ☎02.47.70.37.37, ⓦwww .ligeris.com). It sells a **museum pass** (*carte multi-visites*; €7) that acts as a ticket for all five city museums, including the Musée des Beaux-Arts and the Musée du Gemmail, and can give information on **château tours** (see box below).

The centre of Tours is small enough to cover on foot. The best place for **bike rental** is Store Trek, 31 bd Heurteloup (☎02.47.61.22.35). It's right opposite the tourist office and charges around €15 a day or €50 a week. Its offshoot, Détours de Loire, 5 rue du Rempard (☎02.47.61.22.23, ⓦwww .locationdevelos.com) runs an incredibly useful service which allows you to pick up and drop off bikes at various locations along the Loire à Vélo route (see p.42), for a small extra charge.

Accommodation

Tours has a good range of inexpensive **accommodation**, with some excellent budget and two-star hotels in the area just west of the cathedral. There's less

---

Château and wine tours

It's possible to visit most of the popular châteaux by public transport, but if you're short of time it's worth considering a day or half-day minibus trip. A number of companies run **excursions** from Tours, and on most schedules you'll find the following: Amboise, Azay-le-Rideau, Blois, Chambord, Chenonceau, Cheverny, Clos Lucé (in Amboise), Fougères-sur-Bièvre, Langeais, Ussé and Villandry. **Ticket** prices are usually around €19 for a morning trip, taking in a couple of châteaux; €25–32 for an afternoon tour – often with a third château or a wine-tasting; and €40–50 for a full-day tour. Prices do not usually include entrance fees or lunch. Be aware that you may not have as much time as you'd like to explore each châteaux thoroughly.

Ask at tourist offices or contact the following Touraine-based **agencies** directly: Acco Dispo ☎06.82.00.64.51, ⓦwww.accodispo-tours.com; Saint-Eloi Excursions ☎06.70.82.78.75, ⓦwww.chateauxexcursions.com; Alienor Excursions ☎06.10.85.35.39, ⓦwww.alienortours.com; and Quart de Tours ☎06.30.65.52.01, ⓦwww.quartdetours .com. Most pick up from the tourist office in Tours or your hotel.

If you want to tour the vineyards and don't have your own transport – or do, and don't want to drive it – the wine tours offered by Détours de Loire, 5 rue du Rempard (☎02.47.61.22.23, ✉thewinetour@orange.fr) are an excellent option. Led by the best of experts – a former sommelier at the top Touraine restaurant, *Jean Bardet* – there's the opportunity to taste and buy freely. The afternoon "white tour" of Vouvray costs €29; the all-day "red tour" of Chinon and Bourgueil includes a picnic lunch, and costs €43. Tailored tours can also be arranged.

choice at the higher end of the market. It's worth booking in advance, particularly in the summer months.

Hotels

Central Hôtel 21 rue Berthelot ☎02.47.05.46.44, ⓦwww.tours-online.com/central-hotel. The best bet at the upper end of the market, though it's overpriced and part of a chain (Best Western). The atmosphere suffers from a largely business clientele, but rooms are large and high-ceilinged, and there's a small garden, plus garage parking for €9 a night. The more expensive rooms (€137) have baths rather than showers, and a bit more space. ❻

Hôtel des Arts 40 rue de la Préfecture ☎02.47.05.05.00, ⓔhoteldesartstours@orange.fr. This newly opened hotel has been done up in warm yellows and oranges, with some nice pieces of antique furniture here and there. Rooms are all comfortable and have en-suite showers. Garret-like attic rooms cost just €32; the larger rooms on lower floors are significantly dearer. ❸

Hôtel Colbert 78 rue Colbert ☎02.47.66.61.56, ⓦwww.hotelcolbert.net. Pleasant, well-furnished family-run hotel in a good location on the restaurant strip, near the cathedral. Rooms are modern in style, with TVs and new bathrooms. Those overlooking the small garden at the back have baths rather than showers and are a little more expensive (€53) than those on the street (€48), but double glazing means there's no problem with noise even at the front. ❸

🏃 **Hôtel du Cygne** 6 rue du Cygne ☎02.47.66.66.41, ⓦperso.orange.fr /hotelcygne.tours. Pleasantly old-fashioned and well-run hotel on a quiet street, its delightful eighteenth-century frontage spilling over with flowers and grey shutters. The rooms are relatively unmodernized, with unattractive carpeting, but they're comfortable and preserve some of the flavour of the house, with mantelpieces, side-lamps and oddments of old-fashioned furniture. There are some family rooms and smaller, inexpensive (€45) singles on the top floor. Offstreet parking is available for a small charge. ❹

Hôtel du Manoir 2 rue Traversière ☎02.47.05.37.37, ⓦsite.voila.fr/hotel.manoir .tours. This nineteenth-century townhouse has a very pleasant situation, on a peaceful backstreet with a small garden and parking area out front. Inside, the feel has been slightly spoilt by over-modernization, but the hotel is friendly, comfortable and in a good location between the cathedral and train station. ❸

Hôtel Mondial 3 place de la Résistance ☎02.47.05.62.68, ⓦwww.hotelmondialtours.com. Ideally situated, on a pleasant enough square halfway between the restaurant hotspots of place Plumereau and rue Colbert. The rooms are new and functional, with pine-wood flooring, pastel-shaded walls and sparkling bathroom fittings. Those looking onto the square have small balconies with pretty window boxes. ❸

Hôtel Regina 2 rue Pimbert ☎02.47.05.25.36, ⓕ02.47.66.08.72. Friendly and well-run budget place right in the town centre, with simple, clean rooms and some cheery and varied artwork on the walls. Popular with backpackers, and offers a range of prices: the more expensive rooms (€34) have en-suite showers. ❶

Hôtel St-Éloi 79 bd Béranger ☎02.47.37.67.34, ⓕ02.47.39.34.67. Excellent-value, especially for small groups who don't mind sharing – you can have a room with three beds for €39. All the rooms are in good condition, and have en-suite bathrooms and TV. It's also one of the few options on the western side of town, nearer to the nightlife round place Plumereau. ❷

Hôtel du Théâtre 57 rue de la Scellerie ☎02.47.05.31.29, ⓔhoteldutheatre.tours @orange.fr. Under the same friendly ownership as the *Mondial,* this charming hotel is set in a tastefully restored medieval townhouse in the cathedral quarter. Ancient, exposed beams and stone walls are matched with bright paintwork, brand-new bathrooms and double glazing throughout. The downside is the presence of a rather seedy "gentlemen's" club next door. ❸

Hôtel de l'Univers 5 bd Heurteloup ☎02.47.05.37.12, ⓦwww.hotel-univers.fr. The grandest and most historic hotel in town, right opposite the town hall. The foyer is stunning, illustrated by portraits of celebrities who have stayed here – from Winston Churchill to Edith Piaf – but, disappointingly, the rooms are fairly ordinary for the price (€193 for the "standard" rooms), though stuffed with all the mod cons imaginable. ❾

Hostels and campsite

There is no campsite in Tours itself, but there is a decent camping option within striking distance of the city. Campers could also try the sites at Vouvray (see p.81) and Luynes (see p.94).

Auberge de Jeunesse du Vieux Tours 5 rue Bretonneau ☎02.47.37.81.58, ✆tours@fuaj.org. This large, modern youth hostel has an excellent location right in the heart of the old centre. Most of the rooms are singles, but there are twenty-odd twin-bed rooms as well. Reception 8am–noon & 6–11pm. Beds cost €16.70 per night and HI membership is required, but you can join on the spot. Bicycles are rented at reasonable prices.

Foyer des Jeunes Travailleurs 16 rue Bernard-Palissy ☎02.47.60.51.51, ✆ajh.ufjt.tours@numericable.fr. A fairly smart, central workers' hostel and cafeteria for under-25s. Reception closed Sun. €18 per night in a single room or €13 if you're sharing. Price includes breakfast.

Camping Les Rives du Cher St-Avertin ☎02.47.27.27.60, ✆contact@camping-lesrivesducher.com. Four kilometres southeast of the city, but still the nearest campsite to the centre of town, and accessible by bus #5 from place Jean-Jaurès. Closed mid-Oct to March.

The city centre

The centre of Tours fills a three-kilometre-wide strip of flat land between the Loire and its tributary, the Cher, but the city has spread far across both banks, with industrial Tours eating up the area north of the Loire. Neither river is a particular feature of the town, though there are parks on islands in both, and an attractive new footbridge leads across the Loire from the site of the old château. The city's two distinct quarters lie on either side of the axial rue Nationale, a strip of commercial no-man's-land hastily built in the aftermath of the war. The quieter of the two quarters, where most of the hotels are found, lies around the **cathedral**, while the so-called **Vielle Ville**, some 600m to the west, is more developed and more touristy, centred on picturesque place Plumereau.

Cathédrale St-Gatien

The great west towers of the **Cathédrale St-Gatien**, known locally as *la Gatienne*, are visible all over the city, rising in tier upon tier like a vision of the heavenly city they were intended to represent. Their surfaces crawl with lace-like stonework in the Flamboyant Gothic style, and even the early Renaissance belfries that cap them share the same spirit of refined exuberance. Inside, the stonework becomes more tight-lipped as it moves back in time through the fourteenth-century nave and back towards the relatively sober mid-thirteenth-century choir.

The architecture of the **choir** may be relatively restrained, but its **stained-glass windows** are glorious. Inspired by St Louis' work at the Sainte Chapelle in Paris – and largely paid for by him – they form a giant band of jewelled colour under the vaults. The life of **St Martin** (see box on p.75) is shown in the second tall window right of the centre – on the final panel on the top right, you can clearly see the boat transporting his corpse along the Loire from Candes-St-Martin. Immediately right of this window, on the flat south wall of the choir, are two large windows depicting the bishops of Tours and canons of Loches; these are renowned for their unusual monochrome bands, or *grisailles*.

The choir was originally tacked onto the end of a much earlier Merovingian nave, which was in turn demolished and rebuilt a century later. You can see an awkward kink where the join was made, and in the line of the pillars on the east wall of the **north transept**. The structural problems this caused can be seen in the **rose window** of the Heavenly Jerusalem, whose perfection is spoiled by a great stone prop running through its middle. Just beyond the **south transept** stands the **tomb** of the sons of Charles VIII and Anne de Bretagne. The sarcophagus betrays the Italian origins of its sculptor, Girolamo da Fiesole, while the lifelike figures of the distressingly young princes were carved by a pupil of the great local sculptor, Michel Colombe. After the deaths of the little princes – at 3 years and at 25 days – and the accidental death of their father (see p.84), the Valois line proper came to an end, and Anne was obliged by law to marry Charles's cousin, Louis XII. Behind the tomb, a mural painting shows St Martin dividing his cloak.

A door in the north aisle leads through to the **Cloître de la Psalette** (April–Sept Mon–Sat 9.30am–12.30pm & 2–6pm, Sun 2–6pm; Oct–March Wed–Sun 9.30am–12.30pm & 2–5pm; €2.30), a cloister which has an unfinished air, thanks to the great foot of a flying buttress planted in the southeast corner – another attempt to solve the problem of the nave's misalignment – and the missing south arcade, which was lost when a road was driven through in 1802 by the same progressive, anticlerical prefect who destroyed the basilica of St-Martin (see p.74).

On the north and east sides, late Gothic is disrupted by Renaissance details, especially on the small but perfect spiral staircase, with its tightly twisting central pillar. You can climb up it to the gallery level, which leads through to the library on the cloister's west side, with its mullioned windows.

Musée des Beaux-Arts

Immediately south of the cathedral, the **Musée des Beaux-Arts**, 18 place François-Sicard (daily except Tues 9am–12.45pm & 2–6pm; €4), is housed in what used to be the archbishop's palace, overshadowed by an enormous, 200-year-old cedar of Lebanon in the peaceful courtyard garden. The handsome seventeenth- and eighteenth-century building was briefly used by the provisional national government as it fled from the advancing Prussians in 1870. Today, it proves an elegant setting for a fine collection of paintings. The star attraction is a pair of works in the basement by the Italian Renaissance master Andrea **Mantegna**: the *Resurrection* and the *Agony in the Garden* (1457–9). Napoleon stole both from San Zeno, in Verona, in 1797, along with a *Crucifixion* which now hangs in the Louvre. Together, the three paintings formed the predella below the altarpiece, though the main upper section was returned to San Zeno in 1815. Even outside their proper setting, the two paintings are superb, grippingly intense in mood, the action dominated by a magical Biblical-Italian landscape. The small collection of early Italian masterpieces alongside are somewhat overshadowed, though there's a fine *Coronation of the Virgin* by Lorenzo Veneziano and two saints by Antonio Vivarini.

The visit actually begins on the **first floor** of the museum, which consists of a stately, loosely chronological progression of palatial seventeenth- and eighteenth-century rooms, each furnished and decorated to match the era of the paintings it displays. There's a lot of indifferent eighteenth-century stuff, but a few celebrity works are scattered through the collection. The **Salon Louis XV** has a flowery mythological work by François Boucher – the favourite artist of the king's lover, Mme de Pompadour – that depicts Sylvia fleeing a wolf. The small **Cabinet Rembrandt** houses Rembrandt's moody study, the *Flight into Egypt*, opposite **Rubens'** hasty *Virgin and Child*. Engravings of *The Five Senses* by the locally born **Abraham Bosse** have been interpreted as full-size canvases in the handsome **Salle Louis XIII**, which is furnished with characteristically twisty-legged chairs and a gilded, polychrome fireplace, and offers a fine view of the cathedral.

Upstairs on the **second floor** are two rooms of works by local painters, and a suite that runs from eighteenth-century Neoclassicism through to contemporary works. Look out for the 1787 panorama of Tours and **Boulanger**'s portrait of a faintly corpulent Balzac. The **Salle Réaliste** has **Degas'** vibrant, hasty interpretation of the Mantegna *Crucifixion* in the Louvre, and an arresting autopsy scene by Feyer-Perrin, while the next room is named after **Monet**, who is represented by a bleak and drizzly riverbank scene dating from 1878.

On the left of the main gate as you leave, in one of the stable buildings, there's a surprising exhibit: the stuffed remains of an elephant that caused a sensation in Tours in the early part of the twentieth century. Occasional classical **concerts** are held inside the museum; ask for details or call ☎02.47.05.68.73.

The cathedral quarter

On the north side of the cathedral, between rue Albert-Thomas and the river, just two towers remain of the medieval **château** of Tours. In 1593, the northern tower was the scene of the dramatic escape of the prince de Joinville, imprisoned here after his father, the duc de Guise, was murdered at Blois (see box on p.147). The prince apparently out-sprinted his captors up the steps of the tower, locked the door behind him and shinned down the outer wall to freedom. You can get inside a section of the château when exhibitions are held, but there's nothing much to see otherwise. In the sixteenth-century **Logis des Gouverneurs** (Wed & Sat 2–6pm; sometimes closed during school holidays; free), just across the remnants of the city's Gallo-Roman wall, there's an exhibition on the history of Tours that gives an excellent impression of how the city has developed over the centuries, though it's depressing to see so many fine buildings that no longer exist. Opposite the château, a suspension footbridge aptly nicknamed the **Pont de Fil** ("wire bridge") leads across the river to the St-Symphorien quarter via the sports fields of the **Ile Aucard**.

The area behind the cathedral and museum, to the east, is good for a short stroll. There's a fine view from **place Grégoire de Tours** of the spidery buttresses supporting the cathedral's painfully thin-walled apse. Overlooking the square is the oldest wing of the archbishop's palace, whose end wall is a mongrel of Romanesque and eighteenth-century work, with an early sixteenth-century projecting balcony once used by clerics to address their flock.

Leading off the square, rue Général Meunier traces the line of the now-vanished Roman amphitheatre, ascending past affluent private mansions, high-walled religious institutions and the decrepit **Chapelle des Lazaristes**. From this chapel, you can continue down rue de la Porte Rouline, then left along rue des Ursulines, past the cinema Les Studios and the conservatoire, to a half-hidden muncipal garden overlooked by the tall remains of the city's **Roman walls**. Alternatively, head back down rue Manceau and through to **rue de la Psalette**, which offers a fine view of the cathedral's great north rose window, with its unfortunate buttress. On the corner of this street is the eighteenth-century house where **Balzac** set his novella *Le Curé de Tours*, a withering attack on the petit-bourgeois concerns of the provincial clergy. Half hidden by walls and foliage, the house looks just the part.

Rue Colbert and the river

From the cathedral quarter, **rue Colbert** runs west as straight as the Roman road it once was, with down-at-heel bars, ethnic restaurants and excellent little bistros competing for attention along most of its length. Heading off down to the river, **place Foire-le-Roi** recalls the fairs instituted by François I. There are some fine old half-timbered houses at the bottom end, and on the east side, at no. 8, is the handsome **Hôtel Babou de la Bourdaisière**, built for François I's finance minister in the 1520s. West of rue Voltaire, the foot of rue Colbert was widened and modernized after the destruction of the World War II. A few historic houses survived well enough to be rebuilt, notably the house at no. 39 – now a shoe shop – where **Joan of Arc** is said to have had her suit of armour made.

Behind the corner of rue Colbert and rue Nationale hides the **Jardin de Beaune-Semblançay**, whose pretty, sixteenth-century fountain stands in front of the sad remnants of the house of Jacques de Beaune-Semblançay, François I's finance minister (see p.334). The propped-up, three-quarters ruined facade, the result of wartime shelling, stands as an ironic testament to the financier's career, which was spent vainly trying to fund the king's lavish court expenditure and expensive foreign military excursions with ever-dwindling royal income – while creaming off the funds necessary to build this, his own fabulous Renaissance mansion. As a placard explains, the shabby garden was once a palatial complex of houses, but the only other remnant is a **chapel**, whose elegant arches are now glazed in to form an enclosed space behind – which serves as a lamp shop.

At the north end of rue Nationale lies the **River Loire**, its scruffy walkways overlooked by statues of Descartes and Rabelais. There are plans to develop the riverfront, but for now it's a sad place, bombed out and bereft of the roaring river trade that once filled the quays with merchandise. You can sometimes see terns wheeling and diving in the rapids formed by the arches of the **Pont Wilson**, a much-patched-up eighteenth-century bridge which locals refer to prosaically as the Pont de Pierre, or "stone bridge". In summer, you'll see one or more old-fashioned wooden boats tied up at the jetty just downstream from the Pont Wilson; you can make an hour-long guided **river trip** aboard one of these (usually July & Aug Fri– Sun 2.30–6.30pm, but it's best to check at the tourist office first or call Alain Lacroix on ☎06.83.57.89.20; €6).

St-Julien

On the northeast corner of rue Colbert and rue Nationale stands the **église St-Julien**, which once belonged to the Benedictine abbey founded by the great chronicler and sixth-century bishop, Gregory of Tours. The heavy Romanesque tower is one of the few remnants of an older church which collapsed in a storm in 1244; the rest is a high-shouldered and slightly awkward Gothic construction. The most interesting features inside are the eleventh-century mural depicting the story of Moses, just visible from the passage above the organ, and the modern stained glass which replaced the windows destroyed when the Pont Wilson was blown up by the retreating French army in June 1940.

The old monastic buildings are home to two museums. The dry-as-dust **Musée des Vins**, at 16 rue Nationale (daily except Tues 9am–noon & 2–6pm; €4.20), is only worth visiting for its location in the barn-like twelfth-century cellars of the abbey, although if your French is up to it, there's a comprehensive display on the history, mythology and production of wine. Behind the museum, a Gallo-Roman winepress from Cheillé sits in the former cloisters of the church. The **Musée de Compagnonnage**, at 8 rue Nationale (mid-June to mid-Sept daily 9am–noon & 2–6pm; rest of year closed Tues; €4), is housed in the eleventh-century guesthouse and sixteenth-century monks' dormitory. It honours the peculiarly French cult of the artisan, displaying a bizarre miscellany of the *chefs d'œuvre*, the "masterpieces", that craftsmen had to create in order to join their craft guild as a fully-fledged *compagnon* (master craftsman). The skills are unquestionable, but many of these showpieces, displaying arts as diverse as cake-making and carpentry, locksmithery and bricklaying, are breathtakingly vulgar. The guilds still exist, but membership is no longer a passport to work.

Around place Jean-Jaurès

The centre of Tours is divided by the wide, soulless modern avenue of **rue Nationale**. What you see today is the drab result of hasty reconstruction following the bombardments of 1944; the street began life as the more prestigious rue Royale, and as rue Napoléon it was the birthplace of Balzac, in May 1799. At its tail is the huge, traffic-ridden **place Jean-Jaurès**, site of the Doric

Palais de Justice, which dates from the 1840s. The grandiose **Hôtel de Ville** was designed at the beginning of the twentieth century by local boy Victor Laloux, with four large telamons (columns in the form of male figures) supporting its balcony, each representing a river god. Laloux's talent seems to have been better suited to train stations, however: the noble **gare SNCF**, 200m further east along busy boulevard Heurteloup, was also his design, as was Paris's world-famous Gare (now Musée) d'Orsay. The steel and glass curves of the **Centre de Congrès Vinci**, opposite the station, are the work of France's current celebrity architect, Jean Nouvel, the creator of Paris's Institut du Monde Arabe, among other buildings. Eye-catching though it is, the Vinci congress centre has proved to be something of a white elephant.

To the west of place Jean-Jaurès, a giant **flower market** takes over boulevard Béranger on Wednesdays and Saturdays, lasting from 8am into the early evening.

Around place Plumereau

One hundred metres west of rue Nationale, the **Hôtel Gouin**, at 25 rue du Commerce, has a Renaissance facade to stop you in your tracks, but the **museum** inside (Tues–Sun 10am–1pm & 2–6pm; €4.50) is a dull collection of archeological oddments and the remnants of a private scientific laboratory from Chenonceau – more rich man's toys than cutting-edge research tools.

A few steps further west, the pulse of the city quickens as you approach **place Plumereau** – or place Plum' as it's known locally. The square's tightly clustered ancient houses have been carefully restored as the city's showpiece, transforming what was once a slum into a vibrant and wealthy quarter. On sunny days, the

△ Place Plum'

square is packed almost end to end with café tables, and students and families drink and dine out until late in the evening. To some extent, the restoration project has been the victim of its own success; Irish pubs, pizza restaurants and international ice-cream chains are shouldering their way in and the noisy party atmosphere is driving out longer-term residents from the vicinity.

One of the less brash places on the square is the café *Le Vieux Mûrier*, so named for the large **mulberry tree** outside, a reminder of the days when Tours' silkworms used to feed on mulberries planted in their thousands in and around the city. Fine woodworking and slate cladding adorns the pair of medieval houses on the southeast corner of the square, while the central quartet on the southern side display elaborate brick patternwork. The handsome white stone house over on the northwest corner, with its wrought-iron balconies, is a nineteenth-century creation.

To escape the bustle, slip north down **rue Briçonnet** into a miniature maze of quiet, ancient streets. Opposite an oddly Venetian-looking fourteenth-century house, at 41 rue Briçonnet, a passageway leads past a palm tree and an ancient outdoor staircase to the quiet and insulated **Jardin de St-Pierre-le-Puellier**. In its centre lie the dug-out ruins of a conventual church, while twin brick-and-wood tower-staircases prop up the backs of the houses on place Plumereau. Further down rue Briçonnet, at no. 16, just before the heavily modernized riverfront, is the elaborate **Maison de Tristan**. Built for a chamberlain of Louis XI in the then-fashionable style, its ornate Gothic doorway and rose-motif carvings are well worth a look.

Musée du Gemmail

Off rue Briconnet, at 7 rue du Mûrier, the **Musée du Gemmail** (April to mid-Oct Tues–Sun 10am–noon & 2–6pm; mid-Oct to March Sat & Sun 10am–noon & 2–6pm; €5.40; ⓦwww.gemmail.com) is dedicated to an obscure, locally invented modern art form that uses fragments of backlit stained glass as a medium. Although some of the works are signed by such luminaries as **Raoul Dufy**, **Modigliani** and **Picasso**, the actual execution is by professional technicians working from a design. Picasso was enamoured of the technique, and his two works displayed here are among the finest examples of the style. The way colour is built up using layer after layer of coloured shards over a white background light, in some ways like a watercolour, is interesting, but a tackier side of the art form is seen in the reproductions of the Mona Lisa and various Gauguin paintings.

St-Martin quarter

Immediately south of place Plumereau lay the pilgrim city once known as Martinopolis after **St Martin**, a key figure in the spread of Christianity through France (see box opposite). There was a chapel here from the fifth century, but the site reached its apotheosis with a vast Romanesque basilica, which stretched along rue des Halles from rue des Trois-Pavées-Ronds almost to place de Châteauneuf. Sadly, very little remains. The Huguenot riots of 1562 severely damaged the interior, and the whole structure finally collapsed in 1797, seemingly in protest at its desecration by Revolutionary troops, who used it as a stables. Only the northern **Tour de Charlemagne** and the western clock tower now survive, but the outline of the structure is traced out in the street. The Charlemagne tower half-collapsed in 1928, but was glued back together with a modern image of a cloak-rending St Martin on its south face. At its foot stands a precious carved capital, one of 140 which once graced the basilica's forest of columns.

St Martin of Tours

As a patron saint of France, **St Martin of Tours** stands in the shadow of his higher profile peers Anne (mother of Mary), Joan of Arc and St Denis. Yet during the first millennium the cult of St Martin was the most important in France, and it was only when St Denis was promoted by the Paris-based Capetian dynasty that St Martin's fame was eclipsed. Locally, however, St Martin still cuts quite a figure – you'll see images from his life all over the Loire Valley, especially in Touraine.

The saint was born in Pannonia, in modern-day Hungary, in about 316. His father was a Roman tribune and as a young man Martin was duly sent off to do military service in Gaul. The most significant – and most often depicted – event of his life occurred at Amiens, when he met a ragged beggar at the city gates. Moved by compassion, he cut his **cloak** in two, reached down from his horse, and gave the beggar one half. He later asked to be baptized and left the Roman army. The cloak became the most treasured relic of the Merovingian and Carolingian kings, and eventually gave its name (*capella*, in Latin) to the oratory where it was preserved – hence the English word "chapel".

After various adventures in Italy, Martin returned to Gaul in 361 to set up a monastery at Ligugé, just outside Poitiers, where he lived as a hermit. In 371 he was tricked into visiting Tours and, on arrival, was acclaimed as bishop – legend has it that he tried to hide but was revealed by honking **geese**, which became his symbol. Martin and his entourage lived just outside Tours at **Marmoutier**, a monastery built in the chalky riverside cliffs on the road to Vouvray – its remains now lie in the grounds of a private school and, sadly, can't be visited. He remained as bishop for 26 years, living a life of model simplicity, performing miracles and acquiring a reputation as the scourge of idolaters. One story tells how a group of villagers would only cut down their sacred **pine tree** if he sat in its path. The saint agreed, but as the tree fell he made the sign of the cross, miraculously deflecting it.

In around 397 or 400, while staying at **Candes** (see p.254), on the western border of Touraine, Martin fell ill and died. Monks transported his body back up the Loire to Tours in a boat – another familiar scene from the saint's iconography – where he was buried at his own request in the cemetery of the poor.

On the other side of rue des Halles, the **Basilique de St-Martin** is a sorry neo-Byzantine replacement for the original. It was erected at the end of the nineteenth century by local architect Victor Laloux to honour the relics of St Martin, which were rediscovered in 1860 and are now housed in the crypt, which sits on the original site of the basilica's altar – hence the unusual north–south alignment of the modern church. St Martin still has a strong local following, evident from the hundreds of votive prayers carved into the walls and the vigorous celebrations of his feast day, on November 11.

Nearby, the **Musée St-Martin**, 3 rue Rapin (mid-March to mid-Nov Wed–Sun 9.30am–12.30pm & 2–5.30pm; €2), tells the story of the saint and displays various artefacts related to him and his shrine, including a fragment of his fifth-century tomb and a copy of the huge capital under the Tour Charlemagne. Sadly, the adjacent Cloître de St-Martin, all that survives of the basilica's beautiful Renaissance cloister, seems to be closed for the foreseeable future.

A short distance away, down rue des Halles, lies the huge, modern **Halles**, or covered market – an excellent place to browse for a picnic in the morning.

The suburbs

If you're leaving Tours on the way to the enticing countryside of Touraine, the suburbs look particularly uninspiring, a mix of bland, medium-rise apartment blocks, semi-wasteland riverbanks and endless slip roads. But a trio of unusually inspiring sites hidden away in the suburbs makes a refreshing change from the usual château itineraries. The old Le Manach **silk factory**, on the right bank of the Loire, is fascinating for its archaic working looms, Ronsard's **Prieuré de St-Cosme** is a place of pilgrimage for poetry lovers and rose enthusiasts alike, while the huge **Grange de Meslay**, out near the airport, is a useful reminder of the ultimate source of all Touraine's wealth: the land.

Le Manach silk factory

The silkworks of **Le Manach**, at 35 quai Paul Bert, on the north bank of the Loire, east of the Pont Wilson, can only be visited on occasional tours organized by the tourist office (℡02.47.70.37.37; €11), but if you understand French it's well worth enquiring, as the visit is fascinating, and unique in the region. The "factory" – which has been here since 1829 – still uses some eighty original **Jacquard looms**, some dating from the eighteenth century, on which exquisite made-to-order and stock silks, brocades and velours, many of which grace the walls of restored châteaux across France, are woven. You can see the whole weaving process in action, with local artisans energetically operating the looms by hand and foot, and watch the complex and archaic processes for reeling, bobbining, warping and the like. Small cushions and other samples are sold at the end of the visit.

Prieuré de St-Cosme

In May, when the roses are in full bloom, the **Prieuré de St-Cosme**, 3km west of the centre (mid-March to mid-Oct daily 10am–6pm (till 7pm May–Aug); mid-Oct to mid-March daily except Tues 10am–12.30pm & 2–5pm; €4.50), is one of the loveliest and most melancholy sites in Touraine, for all that it is hemmed in by suburbs and barred off from the nearby Loire by a trunk road. Once an island priory, now a semi-ruin, it was here that **Pierre de Ronsard** – arguably France's greatest poet – was prior from 1565 until his death, in 1585. The site was a dependency of the great monastery of Marmoutier (see box on p.75), and vestiges of many monastic buildings survive, including the refectory, the prior's house (where you can see Ronsard's study), and half an apse, which is all that remains of the priory church. But the most affecting sight is the lovingly tended **garden of roses**, flowers which Ronsard described as having "the perfume of gods" and obsessively used as symbols of beauty – and, inevitably, decay – in his poetry. The garden has some 2000 rose bushes, and 250 varieties – including the tightly rounded, pink rose called "Pierre de Ronsard".

Occasional classical **concerts** are held between May and November, and there's a jazz festival at the end of June. On the weekend of Pentecost, in late May or early June, there's a special festival and market of roses; call ℡02.47.37.32.70 for details. To get to the Prieuré de St-Cosme by **bus**, take #7 from immediately outside the Palais de Justice, on place Jean-Jaurès, towards La Riche-Petit Plessis, getting off at the La Pléiade stop.

Sadly, you can't get inside the **château de Plessis**, but it's only 1km to the southeast, and its history has a repellent fascination. It was here that the paranoid King Louis XI immured himself – as the chronicler Philippe de Commynes put it, behind "great bars of iron in the form of a thick grating" … "with ten bowmen in the ditches to shoot at any man who dared approach the castle" – and finally died, in 1483. The brick and stone building, a rump of the original structure, is typical of the style of the era.

Grange de Meslay

As a giant barn beside the airport, the **Grange de Meslay**, 6km northeast of the centre of Tours (Easter–Oct Sat & Sun 3–6pm; €4), may not immediately seem worth the trip. But then it is no ordinary barn, and unlike the more glamorous châteaux of the Loire you'll almost certainly have the place to yourself. The last remnant of a medieval priory, now destroyed, it was built in about 1220 to store the tithes due to the abbey of Marmoutier (see box on p.75). The facade echoes that of a Romanesque church, but it's plainer and more rustic. Similarly, the interior uses wood where you might expect to find stone, like an agricultural version of a cathedral. Occasional classical music **concerts** and other events take place here throughout the year; call ☎02.47.29.19.29 for details, or visit ⓦwww.meslay.com. To get there **by car**, follow signs towards Vendôme and the main, northbound N10; 1km after the interchange signposted to the A10 motorway (at junction 19), take the signposted turn-off to the Grange de Meslay.

Eating and drinking

The streets around **place Plumereau**, especially rue du Grand Marché, are lined with jostling and mostly overpriced cafés, bars and **bistros**. If you're looking for pizza, pasta or steak frites and don't mind paying a little extra for an outside table, this is the area to head for. Most of the bar-restaurants with tables on the square serve until around midnight. On the cathedral side of rue Nationale, **rue Colbert** is lined with much less touristy **bars** and ethnic eateries, as well as a few good family restaurants serving regional dishes such as *rillettes*, river fish in sauces based on local wines, and the famous prunes of Tours, soaked in sweet Vouvray wine. If you have your own transport, you could also consider heading outside Tours itself; some of the restaurants around Villandry (see p.104) are worth every one of the twenty-odd minutes it'll take to get to them.

Chocolate freaks should make a detour to the enticing *La Chocolatière*, 6 rue de la Scellerie. The main **market** halls are to the west of St-Martin at the end of rue des Halles.

Cafés

Aux Délices de Michel Colombe 1 place François-Sicard. This café-bakery offers an inspiring array of chocolates and pâtisseries – including their speciality, macaroons – and is open through the day. The handful of pavement tables makes for a very pleasant place to have breakfast or afternoon tea while gazing at the tips of the cathedral's towers.

Le Molière Cnr rue de la Scellerie & rue Corneille. Directly in front of the Grand Théâtre, this large Belle Époque café has faded frescoes and a relaxed atmosphere. Good for a daytime coffee or drink.

Scarlett 70 rue Colbert. Relaxed tearoom serving all the tea varieties you could desire, as well as delicious hot chocolates and cakes. Open till 7pm. Closed Sun.

Le Vieux Mûrier 11 place Plumereau. One of the oldest and best cafés on place Plum', with an old-fashioned decor of faded wallpaper and black and white photographs. Serves drinks only, from 11am to around 2am. Closed Mon.

Restaurants

La Bekaa 80 rue Colbert ☎02.47.61.27.01. This long-established and popular Lebanese restaurant offers various buffet-type options from €14 per person. Closed Sun lunch & Mon lunch.

Au Bureau place Plumereau. One of a number of places serving pizzas and simple dishes on the square, but worth recommending for its decent *plats du jour* – *moules frites* are around €7.50. The late-night service and happy atmosphere at the outside tables is the main draw, but don't expect anything special in terms of cuisine. Serves until midnight daily.

Chez Jean-Michel 123 rue Colbert ☎02.47.20.80.20. This intimate wine bar and restaurant is immaculately run by proprietor Jean-Michel and manages to be elegant and relaxed at the same time. It serves tasty regional dishes to go along with the excellent local wines, of which there's a large selection. Starters cost around €6.50 and main courses €15. Closed Sat & Sun.

Au Chien Jaune 75 rue Bernard Palissy. Carefully re-created brasserie interior, with a real *zinc* (bartop) and old posters and brass everywhere. The food is comforting if unexceptional regional cuisine and brasserie classics; the location is very handy for the gare SNCF and tourist office. Menus €17–28. Closed Sun.

Comme Autre-Fouée 11 rue de la Monnaie ☎02.47.05.94.78. Something of a gimmick, in that the food is a revival of the archaic *fouace* (or *fouée*) breads praised by Rabelais. They're served hot and heavily garnished with local titbits such as hot goat's cheese or *rillettes*. It's good, unsophisticated fun. The evening menu is €19.50 with wine, while the lighter lunch menu is €10. Closed Sun, Mon & Tues lunch.

Jean Bardet Château Belmont, 57 rue Groison ☎02.47.41.41.11, ⓦwww .jeanbardet.com. Tours' top restaurant, in an opulent Second Empire building on the north side of the Loire. It offers extremely sophisticated, healthy food with rare varieties of vegetables straight from the hotel's renowned garden. Menus are at €60, €125, €165, with an unmissable all-vegetable menu at €69. Worth a splurge. Closed Mon lunch Tues & Sat lunch; Nov–March also closed Sun eve and all day Mon.

Au Lapin qui Fume 90 rue Colbert ☎02.47.66.95.49. Relaxed but elegant miniature restaurant with a meaty menu that's half from the Loire and half from the south of France. There's lots of *lapin* (rabbit) – as a terrine, as a fricassée with rosemary, as a confit leg – but it's not obligatory; other dishes include fish stew with Chinon wine. Half-litres of wine at €8. Menu €19, or from €11 at lunch. Closed Sun & Mon.

Le Petit Patrimoine 58 rue Colbert ☎02.47.66.05.81. Romantic little place squeezed into an atmospheric, stone-lined street-front site, with one or two tables out on the pavement. Serves rich, lovingly prepared Loire dishes and wines, as well as fresh, well-dressed salads. Menus €13.50–26. Closed Sun & Mon.

Le Picrocole 28–30 rue du Grand Marché ☎02..47.20.68.13. One of the better choices among the host of commercial restaurants behind place Plumereau, with a few outside tables in the narrow, bustling street. Serves traditional grilled meat and fish dishes, and has a good selection of wines from the region. Menus at €11.60 and €18.10. Open daily.

La Roche le Roy 55 rte de St-Avertin ☎02.47.27.22.00, ⓦwww.rocheleroy.com. Truly gastronomic cuisine without bank-breaking prices. Chef Alain Couturier makes a speciality of regional ingredients, and you can try wonderful dishes such as eels in white Vouvray, or in red Chinon with prunes, and veal sweetbreads with creamed morel mushrooms. The setting sounds unpromising – just off the A10 motorway bypass south, exit 22 – but the building is in fact a lovely eighteenth-century mansion, with tables in the garden. Menus €55 and €70, or €34 at lunch.

Nightlife and entertainment

Packed with tables and chairs, picturesque place Plumereau is *the* place to start the evening, with an open-air apéritif, and to finish it, with a coffee. Giant Irish **pubs**, pizzerias and branded ice-cream parlours are slowly making inroads into the area, but it's easy to pick out somewhere less commercial in the busy streets around. Even in summer, when local students are away, the nearby **nightclubs** fill up with backpackers, locals and language students, though things don't usually get going until past midnight. The musical diet is more good-time than cutting-edge.

For **gigs**, try *Le Bateau Ivre*, 146 rue Édouard-Vaillant (☎02.47.44.77.22, ⓦwww.bateau-ivre.org), to the south of the gare SNCF, which attracts international reggae, world music and hip-hop acts, as well as occasionally hosting French *chanson* (entry €9–18). Touraine's tourist office has details of **classical music** concerts, in their free monthly events magazine, *Détours et des nuits*. The main venues are the Grand Théâtre, 34 rue de la Scellerie (☎02.47.60.20.20), which also stages plays, opera and ballet, and the Salle Jean de Ockeghem, 15 place Châteauneuf (☎02.47.20.71.95), which runs a varied programme of recitals and concerts by local and visiting groups. Many of the best concerts are held in abbeys and churches outside the city, but good smaller venues in Tours itself include the Cloître de la Psalette (see p.70), Musée des Beaux-Arts (see p.70) and Prieuré de St-Cosme (see p.76). For **cinema**, the best venue is the Studio, rue des Ursulines (☎08.36.68.20.15, ⓦwww.studiocine.com), which shows international classics in their original language, usually subtitled in French, as well as mostly arty French films.

Bars and clubs

Académie de la Bière 43 rue Lavoisier. A predominantly studenty bar, so it's a bit quiet in summer. It's a friendly place, though, and stays open until 5am, with a small dance-floor at the back which can be lively enough in term time. Closed Sun & Mon.

L'Excalibur 35 rue Briçonnet. Just off place Plum', this cellar club has a medieval theme, with stone walls and portcullis-type grates separating the two main rooms. It plays a mixture of pop and more serious dance music, in an attempt to find something for everybody. Open Tues–Sat 11pm–5am, entry is €8 with one drink.

Les Frères Berthom 5 rue du Commerce. The outside tables get packed in summer for the early evening happy hour (7–9pm except Sat). Inside you'll find a cosy pub with a forest of wooden beams and overhanging foliage, and a decent range of beers.

The Pale cnr of rue Colbert and place Foire-le-Roi. Popular Irish pub with pool table, dartboard and big screen showing sport. Jazz or Irish folk concerts usually take place on the first Thursday of the month.

Les Trois Orfèvres 6 rue des Orfèvres, ⓦwww.3orfevres.com. Probably the most popular club in the town centre, playing unashamedly mainstream pop and rock music. From September to June they also have a couple of live concerts a month and various themed nights. Open Wed–Sat 11pm–5am. Entry is technically free, but you're obliged to pay for the cloakroom and at least one drink – about €8 in all.

Festivals and markets

May is the biggest month for festivals in Tours. The rock festival **Aucard de Tours** stages concerts on the Ile Aucard, while around Pentecost (usually late May), a choral festival, **Florilège Vocal de Tours**, takes place in the Grand Théâtre on rue de la Scellerie, finishing with a free concert on place Plum'. The major Loire Valley **wine fair**, Vitiloire, takes place during the second week of May; it's aimed at professionals, but there's plenty for the casual drinker or buyer to see and taste. In the summer, a festive market devoted to garlic and onions is held on place du Grand Marché on 26 July. Since 2005, a new summer programme of concerts and open-air cinema, called **Tours sur Loire** (mid-June to mid-Sept), has taken place on the south bank of the Loire just west of pont Wilson. A bar and restaurant are open there until 11pm daily, but it's liveliest at the weekend.

Traditional fruit-and-veg **street markets** take place every morning of the week (except Mondays) – you'd be hard pressed not to come across one if you just walk through town. It's worth making a special trip, however, to one of the **speciality markets**: the flower market (Wed & Sat) and the marché artisanal, or craft market (Sat), are both on Place des Halles; the marché gourmand, or speciality foods market, convenes on Place de la Résistance on the first Friday of the month (4–10pm).

Listings

Books There is a good selection of English-language books at La Boîte à livres de l'étranger, 2 rue du Commerce ☎02.47.05.67.29.
Car rental Avis, gare de Tours ☎02.47.20.53.27; Budget, 194 av André Maginot 02.47.88.00.50;

Europcar, 76 rue Bernard-Palissy ☎02.47.64.47.76; Hertz, 57 rue Marcel Tribut ☎02.47.75.50.00. All offer pickup/drop at Tours airport, at St-Pierre-des-Corps TGV station or near the gare SNCF in Tours.

Emergencies Ambulance ☎15; different hospital departments are spread around the city – call ☎02.47.47.47.47 to check where to head, or ask at the tourist office; late-night pharmacy, phone police (see below) for address.
Internet The tourist office on boulevard Heurteloup (see p.67) offers inexpensive Internet access. Otherwise try Le Paradis Vert, 9 rue Michelet (€4–10/hr, depending on the time of day), which is near the

gare SNCF; or Cyberspace, 27 rue Lavoisier (€3/hr).
Police Commisariat Central 70–72 rue Marceau ☎02.47.70.88.88.
Taxis Groupement Taxis Radio Tours ☎02.47.20.30.40.
Wine Vinothèque de Tours 16 rue Michelet ☎02.47.64.75.27, ⊛www.vinotheque-tours.fr. Mon 4–7.30pm, Tues–Sat 9am–12.30pm & 4–7.30pm.

Vouvray's wine villages

The main reason to visit the cluster of villages that makes up the wine region of **VOUVRAY**, 10km east of Tours on the north bank, is to taste the **wines**, which range from honeyed demi-secs to brisk sparklers. The main road leading into the actual village of Vouvray is unappealing, a choked section of ribbon-strip agri-business that joins the village to neighbouring **ROCHECORBON** and **MONCONTOUR**, the whole thing squeezed between the heights of the north bank – into which the wine *caves* (cellars) are cut – and the river's edge.

If you climb the escarpment behind the villages, however, everything changes. The view of the vines combing across the chalky plateau above town is intoxicating. You can follow the **Route du Vouvray** by car, or explore the footpaths signposted **Vouvray les vins**; both thread their way among the vines towards the *domaine* of individual producers, many of whom offer wines for tasting. Tourist offices can give you a map, including one with two signposted walking routes. Alternatively, you can join the "white tour" organized by Détours de Loire (see p.67), which takes you to three Vouvray vineyards in the course of an afternoon, and costs €29.

A name to look out for is Domaine Huët, based in Le Haut-Lieu, 1.5km northeast of Vouvray itself, where organic techniques are used. You can combine wine-tasting with a visit to the impressive, Renaissance-style terraced gardens and early sixteenth-century troglodyte chapel at the **château de Valmer** (May–June Sat & Sun 2–7pm; July & Aug Tues–Sun 2–7pm; Sept Tues–Sun 10am–12.30pm & 2–6pm; ⊛www.chateau-de-valmer.com; €7.50), beyond Chançay, just off the D46; or visit the small museum of wine-making at the **château de Moncontour** (Easter to mid-Oct daily 10am–7pm; ⊛www.moncontour.com; free), a château so handsome that it was Balzac's favourite. For a broad spread of Vouvray wines, especially sparkling styles, make for the co-operative **Caves des Producteurs de Vouvray**, 3km west of Vouvray's centre at 18 rue de la Vallée Coquette (daily: mid-May to mid-Sept 9am–7pm; mid-Sept to mid-May 9.30am–12.30pm & 2–7pm), which sells the wines of around fifty small growers and offers guided tours of the large, rock-cut *caves*. For more on the wines of Vouvray, see p.353.

Two branches of a well-known Vouvray **charcuterie**, Hardouin, stand in the centre of Vouvray, on rue de la République, and on the main road; either is a good place to stock up on picnic supplies. The **tourist office**, 100m off the main road on rue Rabelais (May–Oct Mon–Sat 9.30am–1pm & 2–6.30pm, Sun 1–7pm; Nov–April Tues–Sat 9.30am–1pm & 2–5.30pm; ☎02.47.52.68.73), can provide details of exact dates, addresses of *vignerons*, and information on guided tours, but all the steep valleys leading up to the plateau are riddled with *caves*. Vouvray's lively Foire aux Vins takes place for four or five days around August 15, with smaller-scale festivities for the tasting of the new vintage in early

March, Pentecost weekend, and sometimes for the *vin nouveau* in early November.

The better places to **eat** tend to be in the hotel dining rooms, though in Rochecorbon there's *L'Oubliette*, at 34 rue des Clouets (℡02.47.52.50.49; closed Sunday eve, Mon & Wed), which serves good local specialities and wines in a tufa (soft limestone) *cave*, with a range of menus starting at around €20. In Vouvray itself, the *Domaine des Bidaudières*, rue du Peu Morier (℡02.47.52.66.85, ⓦwww.bandb-loire-valley.com; ❼), is a delightful place to **stay**, a luxury bed-and-breakfast halfway up the escarpment, with a swimming pool. Vouvray also has a pleasant hotel with a rather grand restaurant, the *Grand Vatel*, 8 ave L. Brulé (℡02.47.52.70.32, ⓕ02.47.52.74.52; ❷; hotel closed first week of March; restaurant closed Sun evening & Mon; menus €20–71), and a **campsite** between the Loire and the Cisse (℡02.47.52.68.81; closed Oct–April).

To get to Vouvray by public transport, take the regular **bus** #61 from place Jean-Jaurès in Toures, which travels via Rochecorbon. A single **cruise boat**, the *Saint-Martin-de-Tours*, makes fifty-minute afternoon excursions downriver to Tours most days of the week, departing from the quai de la Loire in Rochecorbon, 2km out of Tours. For timetables and reservations, contact Georges Marchand (℡02.47.52.68.88, ⓦwww.chateau-croisiere.com); tickets cost €9.

Montlouis-sur-Loire

If you're driving on the quieter, less touristy route to Amboise and Chenonceaux, along the south side of the river, **MONTLOUIS-SUR-LOIRE** makes a pleasant place to stop. The little village huddles on the hilltop to the north of its pretty church, and like Vouvray the tufa rock is honeycombed with cool *caves*.

Montlouis' **wines** are similar to Vouvray's, if less well-regarded by connoisseurs – though local legend has it that men traditionally prefer them to Vouvray's somehow more feminine vintages. At any rate, a Montlouis tends to be slightly less expensive than an equivalent Vouvray, and will mature faster. The best place to sample and buy is the friendly **Cave Touristique** (April–Nov daily 10am–noon & 2–7pm), an association of independent *viticulteurs* who almost always have an English-speaker on hand.

Down on the riverfront at 60 quai Albert Baillet, the **Maison de la Loire** (Tues–Sun 2–6pm; €3; ⓦmaisonloire.free.fr) has a small exhibition on the wildlife and ecology of the Loire. It's a good place to pick up information on walks and guided outings in the area. The festival **Jazz en Touraine** (℡02.47.50.72.70, ⓦwww.ville-montlouis-loire.fr), which takes place in and around Montlouis-sur-Loire in the second week of September, encompasses blues and world music.

If you want to stay, *Le Colombier*, 4 Grande Rue, Husseau, 4km east of the village (℡02.47.50.85.24, ⓦwww.lecolombier-loirevalley.com; ❹), has an unmissable **chambres d'hôtes** in a converted dovecote; two children can sleep below, or you can book one of two rooms in the main house. Set within its own private wood, you can visit or, preferably, stay at the *château de la* **Bourdaisière**, 1km south of Montlouis-sur-Loire (daily 10am–noon & 2–6pm; €6; ℡02.47.45.16.31, ⓦwww.chateaulabourdaisiere.com; ❽). The heart of the château was built in the early sixteenth century, but has been much added to and modified over the years. It has been beautifully restored by the owners, two brothers from the princely Broglie family, with terraced gardens, atmospheric nineteenth-century interiors and a pool. The estate produces its own wine, which you can taste and buy here, and its own garden tools – the expensive kind, as sold in the Jardin du Palais Royal in Paris. You can visit the walled garden, which hothouses around five hundred varieties of tomatoes, with tastings in June and July, and a dedicated **festival** in September attracting foodies and garden enthusiasts alike.

Amboise and around

Twenty kilometres upstream of Tours, **AMBOISE** is a twee riverside town trading on long-gone splendours, notably its impressive **château** and Leonardo da Vinci's peaceful residence of **Clos-Lucé**. The town draws a busy tourist trade that may detract from the quieter pleasures of strolling along the riverbank, but makes it a good destination for children – if they're unpersuaded by the bloodier elements of the château's history, they may go for the out-of-town aquarium and mini-châteaux park.

The approach from Tours along the main N152 on the north side of the river is busy but dramatic: the bridge carries the road across the midstream Ile d'Or towards the château's magnificent facade, propped up by mammoth towers. The D751 along the left bank, on the other hand, is quieter and has the advantage of passing through a glorious parade of plane trees at the town limits.

Arrival and information

The **gare SNCF** is on the north bank of the river, at the end of rue Jules Ferry, about 1km from the château. There are good connections to Tours and Blois. Information on Amboise and its environs, including the vineyards of the Touraine-Amboise *appellation*, is available at the **tourist office** on quai du

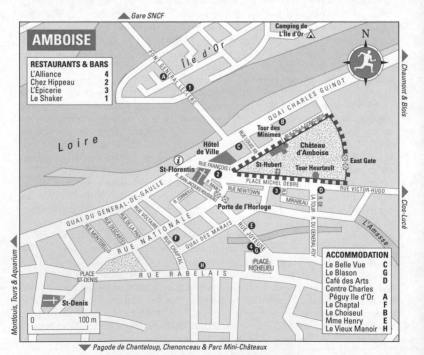

AMBOISE

RESTAURANTS & BARS

L'Alliance	4
Chez Hippeau	2
L'Épicerie	3
Le Shaker	1

ACCOMMODATION

Le Belle Vue	C
Le Blason	G
Café des Arts	D
Centre Charles Péguy Ile d'Or	A
Le Chaptal	F
Le Choiseul	B
Mme Henry	E
Le Vieux Manoir	H

Pagode de Chanteloup, Chenonceau & Parc Mini-Châteaux

Général-de-Gaulle, on the riverfront (June & Sept Mon–Sat 9.30am–1pm & 2–6.30pm, Sun 10am–1pm & 3–6pm; July & Aug Mon–Sat 9am–8pm, Sun 10am–6pm; Oct–May Mon–Sat 10am–1pm & 2–6pm; ℡02.47.57.09.28, ⓦwww.amboise-valdeloire.com).

Bikes can be rented from Cycles Richard, 2bis rue Nazelles, near the station (℡02.47.57.01.79), or Locacycle, on rue Jean-Jacques Rousseau (April–Oct; ℡02.47.57.00.28). **Canoes** are available from the Club de Canoë-Kayak, at the Base de l'Ile d'Or (℡02.47.23.26.52, ⓦwww.loire-aventure.com), which also runs guided trips. These are an excellent way to get to know the ecology of the Loire, and are reasonably priced – the twenty-kilometre trip down from Chaumont (see p.165), for example, costs around €20.

Accommodation

The town's **hotels** are relatively pricey and get booked up in summer some time in advance, but there are some excellent choices around town, including some lovely chambres d'hôtes. A good **campsite** can be found on the island across from the castle, the *Camping de l'Ile d'Or* (℡02.47.57.23.37; closed Oct–March), alongside the hostel.

Le Belle Vue 12 quai Charles Guinot ℡02.47.57.02.26, ⓔbellevuehotel.amboise @orange.fr. Long-established Logis de France three-star situated just below the château, with comfortable, old-fashioned bedrooms. Some rooms at the front give onto a small balcony overlooking the Loire, but road noise makes this less agreeable than it might sound. Closed mid-Nov to mid-March. ❹

Le Blason 11 place Richelieu ℡02.47.23.22.41, ⓦwww.leblason.fr. Very smartly kept, homely hotel in a quiet corner of Amboise. The furnishings are modern, but unobtrusively so, and all rooms have pretty exposed beams and white walls. Triples and quads are also available, and parking and Internet access are free. ❸

Café des Arts place Michel Debré ℡02.47.57.25.04. A simple but friendly backpacker-oriented place set up behind and above a simple, inexpensive café. Rooms are clean, bright and simple – think pine bunk beds and hard-wearing carpets. €25 for two bunks, €36 for a private room. ❶

Centre Charles Péguy Ile d'Or ℡02.47.30.60.90, ⓔcis.amboise@orange.fr. Ordinary but well done-up hostel in a pleasant location on the midstream island, halfway across the town bridge, with a small summer swimming pool. Reception is open Mon–Fri 3–8pm, but it's best to reserve in advance. Prices vary, but beds cost no more than €11.50 a night.

Le Chaptal 13 rue Chaptal ℡02.47.57.14.46. One of the few relatively low-budget options. The rooms are plain and rather spartan, and the welcome is not exactly effusive, but it's perfectly decent. All rooms are equipped with bathrooms and TVs. ❷

Château de Pintray Lussault ℡02.47.23.22.84, ⓦwww.chateau -de-pintray.com. This delightful, blue-shuttered grand country home among the vines is outside Amboise itself, but easy enough to find if you follow signs from Lussault, 6km downstream, towards the Aquarium de Touraine. It offers gorgeous chambres d'hôtes, all nineteenth-century loveliness with canopied beds and little occasional tables. ❼

Le Choiseul 36 quai Charles-Guinot ℡02.47.30.45.45, ⓦwww.le-choiseul.com. Serious elegance, set in an eighteenth-century riverside mansion almost below the château. The luxuriously furnished rooms have heavy curtains, thick carpets and fresh flowers – the best have views over the river. There is an open-air swimming pool in summer. Room prices range from €180 to €290. ❾

Mme Henry 3 rue Joyeuse ℡02.47.57.52.91. Charming chambres d'hôtes in an old house hidden away behind a high wall, with welcoming owners and views of the modest Renaissance townhouse opposite. There are two spacious double rooms available, and a pair of good-value singles (€32). ❸

Le Vieux Manoir 13 rue Rabelais ℡02.47.30.41.27, ⓦwww.le-vieux-manoir .com. This is the best place in town for a thoroughly romantic stay. It's an eighteenth-century mini-manor house converted for use as a luxury bed-and-breakfast, its antique furniture coupled with air-conditioning and brand new fittings. As well as the six double rooms (€140–175), there's an attractive annexe for four people, with its own kitchen and dining room (€280). Closed mid-Nov to mid-Feb. ❽

The Town

The town centre has two main axes vying for lack of appeal: the busy main road that runs alongside the river, quai du Général de Gaulle/quai Charles-Guinot, and the long pedestrianized street that runs parallel to it one block in, **rue Nationale**, which is lined with cheap souvenir shops and crêperies. Things look up as soon as you approach the **château**, with the fifteenth-century **Porte de l'Horloge** guarding the entrance to **place Michel Debré**, which occupies a dramatic position under the soaring walls of the **château**. The heavy defensive lines of the buttresses smoothly transform themselves into ornately sculpted window bays as they fly upwards towards the exquisite chapelle de St-Hubert, perched incongruously above.

The château

Rising above the river like a sculpted and decorated cliff, the **château d'Amboise** (daily: Feb to mid-March 9am–noon & 1.30–5.30pm; mid-March to end March & Sept to mid-Nov 9am–6pm; April–June 9am–6.30pm; July & Aug 9am–7pm; mid-Nov to Jan 9am–noon & 2–4.45pm; €8, Ⓦwww.chateau-amboise.com) dominates the town at its feet. The entrance is via the Tour Heurtault, at the upper end of place Michel Debré.

In July and August, the château hosts a **son-et-lumière** spectacular at around 10pm (Wed & Sat; adults from €12, children 6–14 from €6; Ⓦwww.renaissance-amboise.com), with Leonardo images projected on the walls and costumed actors prancing about to loud Renaissance-style music.

Some history

Following his marriage to Anne de Bretagne at Langeais in 1491 (see box on p.97), Charles VIII decided to turn the heavily fortified old castle of his child-hood days into an extravagant and luxurious palace, adding the chapelle de St-Hubert and the Flamboyant Gothic wing that still looks down graciously on the Loire. In 1494, however, Charles left Amboise to conquer the **kingdom of Naples**, and while there he fell in love with the delights of the Italian Renaissance, writing to his brother that "you would not believe how beautiful are the gardens I have in this city, for upon my faith, it seems that they lack only Adam and Eve to make them an earthly paradise". Resolving to re-create this Eden at home, he brought back artisans from Naples – along with France's first syphilis epidemic. The work of these artists and craftsmen was an early taste of the Renaissance, provoking an appetite for Italian design which was to dominate the next century.

Charles lost Naples within a couple of years, and his ambitions for life at Amboise fared little better. In April 1498, on leaving the queen's bedchamber to watch a game of tennis, he walked through the now-destroyed **Hacquelebac gallery** where, the chronicler Philippe de Commynes observed, "everyone used to piss", and managed to hit his head on a door lintel. Nine hours later, he collapsed and died. As de Commynes pointed out, this was an ignoble end for a king who had tried to bring together at Amboise "all the beauties that he had seen . . . in France, Italy or Flanders". Sadly, much of Charles's Italianate work has been demolished, as has the wretched gallery.

Charles left the kingdom – and his wife (see box on p.97) – to his cousin, **Louis XII**, who spent most of his time at Blois but built a new wing at Amboise to house his nearest male relative, the young François d'Angoulême, thereby keeping him within easy reach. When he acceded to the throne as François I, he didn't forget his childhood home. He embellished the newer wing and invited Leonardo da Vinci to work in Amboise under his protection (see box on p.87). François eventually died in the château's collegiate église St-Florentin, which has long since been destroyed.

The château today is a mere remnant of what once stood on this airy site, four-fifths of the original structure having been demolished in the Napoleonic era to save money on upkeep. It is extremely handsome nonetheless, encapsulating all the styles of the early Renaissance. The older Charles VIII wing is parallel with the river, the wing built by Louis XII, with its extra storey added by François I, standing at right angles to it. The dormer windows of the two wings seem very similar on first glance, but a closer look reveals how the later windows have been subtly transformed under the influence of Classical ideas.

Inside the château, there's a fairly atmospheric progression of large rooms on the **ground floor**, hung with Aubusson tapestries and furnished in sixteenth- or seventeenth-century style, with suits of armour to offset the bare walls and floors. The **Salle des Etats** is particularly fine, its four white marble columns marching down the centre of the room, carved alternately with the symbols of France (the fleur de lys) and Brittany (the ermine's tail). The effect, offset against red brick, is impressive, though much is fanciful restoration work. The **Salle Henri II** has been attractively furnished in an attempt to re-create the feel of a royal Renaissance bedroom. The **first floor** switches abruptly in style to the stuffy, 1830s post-First Empire period, as the apartments were converted for holiday use by the last French king, Louis-Philippe. There's an anxious-looking portrait of him in the **Salle de Musique**. His descendant, Henri d'Orleans – who adopted the title **comte de Paris** and managed to spend literally a king's inheritance before he died in 1999 – set up the foundation which now owns the château.

The most exciting part of the visit comes at the end, as you climb up to the top of the **Tour des Minimes**, from where there's a fabulous panorama of the Loire. You can also see across the château's facade and notorious iron balcony, which played a grisly role in one of the first skirmishes in the Wars of Religion, known as the **Tumult of Amboise**. Persecuted by the Guise brothers, the powerful advisers of the sickly young king, François II, Huguenot conspirators set out for Amboise in 1560 to "rescue" their king and establish a more tolerant monarchy under their Protestant tutelage. They were ambushed by royal troops and local zealots in woods outside the town. Some were drowned in the Loire below the château, some beheaded in the grounds, and others hanged from the balcony. Descending the Tour des Minimes by its massive internal ramp, it's easy to see that it was designed for the maximum number of fully armoured men on horseback to get in and out as quickly as possible.

Chapelle de St-Hubert and the grounds

In the grounds of the château, the perfectly miniature **chapelle de St-Hubert**, on the south side of the terrace, is well worth lingering over. The most interesting of the carvings above its doorway depicts St Hubert confronting the mystical vision of a deer with a cross between its horns, which converted him from a life of idle hunting to one of religious contemplation. This model of behaviour seems to have had little influence over the French monarchs, who were attracted to Amboise as much by its hunting as by anything else. Inside, the modern stained-glass windows are by the prolific twentieth-century glazier, Max Ingrand. A plaque marks the resting place of the probable remains of Leonardo da Vinci, which were discovered in the château **grounds** in the nineteenth century, on the site of the collegiate church, and transferred here.

It's worth exploring the **grounds** a little further. Head past the château towards the **east gate**, a medieval structure which was once the château's principal entrance. On the left, running along a terrace overlooking the Loire, is the site of the famous **garden** created by the Neapolitan Pacello da Mercogliano on the orders of Charles VIII. The garden you see today is not designed to be a copy of the original, but has been planned in the style of a Renaissance garden, with neat rows of spherical box bushes, bordered by exotic-looking cypresses. The best view of the château is from the slight hill in the eastern corner of the garden, where you'll also find a rather surprising cemetery, which serves as a reminder of one of the château's more unlikely guests. **Abd El-Kader**, the leader of the Algerian forces who fought against the French colonialist army in the 1830s, spent four years in captivity in Amboise after his defeat, and the twenty-six tombstones commemorate various members of his family and entourage who died during his stay. The large monument in the centre of the cemetery was paid for in 1853 by the citizens of Amboise, who had overcome their initial bewilderment at the strange appearance and behaviour of the Algerian contingent, and apparently felt a deep fondness for its leader by the time he left.

Clos-Lucé

Following his campaigns in Lombardy, François I decided that the best way to bring back the ideas of the Italian Renaissance was to import one of the finest exponents of the new arts. In 1516, **Leonardo da Vinci** ventured across the Alps in response to the royal invitation, and for three years before his death in 1519, he made his home at the **Clos-Lucé**, at the end of rue Victor-Hugo, five minutes' walk from the centre (daily: Jan 10am–5pm; Feb, March, Nov & Dec 9am–6pm; April–June, Sept & Oct 9am–7pm; July & Aug 9am–8pm; April–Oct €12; Nov–March €9). Leonardo seems to have enjoyed a semi-retirement at Amboise (see box opposite), devoting himself to inventions of varying brilliance and impracticability, and enjoying conversation with his royal patron. The house – an attractive brick mansion with Italianate details added by Charles VIII's Neapolitan craftsmen – is now an overpriced museum to Leonardo. If you can ignore the persistent piped Renaissance music, the reconstructed interior, with its suspiciously new beams and giant stone fireplaces, is pleasant enough. The **oratoire d'Anne de Bretagne**, built by Charles VIII for his new wife, is the loveliest room, a tiny chapel with a vaulted ceiling probably frescoed by Leonardo's last pupil, Francesco de Melzi. If the frescoes are by de Melzi, however, they only show how ill-equipped he was to take up his master's brushes.

Down in the basement are forty fascinating models of Leonardo's **mechanical inventions**; from the suspension bridge to the paddle-wheel boat and turbine, all are meticulously constructed according to the inventor's plans and sketches and are a particular hit with kids and teenagers.

The rest of town

In summer, it's worth pausing at the **Musée de l'Hôtel de Ville**, on rue François I (July–Sept Mon–Fri & Sun 10am–12.30pm & 2–6pm; free), just down from place Michel Debré towards the river. The handful of little rooms hold little of note, just some busts of Leonardo and second-rate tapestries and oil paintings, but look out for the sublime fourteenth-century sculpture of a smiling Virgin, which used to stand under the belfry of the Porte de l'Horloge.

At the other end of rue Nationale, some 500m to the west of the château, the Romanesque **église St-Denis** (daily 9am–6pm) is well worth visiting,

Leonardo's retirement

When **Leonardo da Vinci** arrived in Amboise in 1516, it was his first visit to France, but not the first time he had worked for the French, or heard the name of Amboise. When Louis XII conquered Milan in 1500, he captured Leonardo's first patron, Duke Ludovico Sforza, and imprisoned him in France – most notoriously, in a dungeon at Loches (see p.131). During the French army's ongoing Italian campaigns, Leonardo was put to work by Charles II d'Amboise, Louis XII's governor of Milan, on military engineering schemes, and he was soon engaged in various sculptural and architectural projects as well. This work came to an end with Louis XII's renunciation of Milan in 1513, but when **François I** came to the throne, he wasted little time in tempting Leonardo away from Italy with an offer of safety and comfort at Amboise, and a fat pension of 700 gold écus a year.

Leonardo brought some of his greatest canvases with him across the Alps, probably including the **Mona Lisa** – at least, when Cardinal Louis of Aragon visited the ageing painter in October 1517, the cardinal's secretary, Antonio de Beatis, wrote that they were shown "one of a certain Florentine lady, done from life, at the request of the late Magnificent, Giuliano de' Medici". Sadly, Leonardo seems to have done little or no painting in Amboise. The sculptor and goldsmith Benvenuto Cellini, another Italian working in France, blames François I for rarely leaving him alone: "for this reason he did not have the opportunity of putting into actual use the splendid studies which he had carried on with such devotion." An aside by de Beatis gives the slightly more plausible explanation that "on account of a certain paralysis having seized him in the right hand one cannot expect more fine things from him" – though Leonardo was actually left-handed. Perhaps he was simply settling into a dignified retirement, freely pursuing the unorthodox **inventions** that characterized this last period of his life. Celebrity culture makes much of these as proof of his "**universal genius**", but in fact Leonardo's achievements were outstripped by many contemporaries, and few of his inventions were either practical or original. Their fame really rests on the fact that some seem to foretell future technologies – though Leonardo rarely worked out the actual details, as with his absurd sketch for a man-powered helicopter.

Leonardo also worked on a design for a château at Romorantin, some of the features of which may have influenced the construction of **Chambord** (see p.154), and re-created his famous mechanical lion, which took part in an elaborate masquerade at Blois. The beast apparently walked several menacing steps towards the king before its head split open to reveal the royal lilies set against a blue background.

For all this uneven output, the old man grew close to his employer, François I. Cellini heard the king say "that he believed no man had been born into the world who knew as much as Leonardo, and this not only in matters concerning sculpture, painting and architecture, but because he was a very great philosopher". A poignant anecdote relates that in the harsh winter of 1518–19, which was so cold that ice broke down an arch of Amboise's bridge, Leonardo rescued a swallow that was too frail to continue its southward migration. He kept it in his rooms at the Clos-Lucé as a companion to his decline, and died on May 2, 1519 – legend has it, in the arms of the king.

with a great view back across town to the château's battlements. The first two pairs of capitals at the westernmost end are richly carved, but the finest stonework is to be seen in two sixteenth-century works: a wonderful, polychrome Entombment group, in the corner halfway down the south aisle of the church, and the troubling figure of a drowned woman's semi-naked corpse, nearby. Local legend has it that François I himself modelled for the Christ of the Entombment, surrounded by likenesses of the Babou family of La Bourdaisière (see p.81).

Just upstream from the Pont Général Leclerc are six extraordinary brick and tufa silos, **Les Greniers de César**, their entrance at 36 quai Charles-Guinot. Strange, almost spaceship-like constructions, they were built in the sixteenth century to store grain. The easiest way to visit the silos is to join one of the tourist office's regular costumed guided tours of the city (€5), which take place all year in French or English. Otherwise, it may be possible to arrange special openings for groups; call ☎02.47.30.45.45.

Children, in particular, may enjoy investigating a rather unusual sculptural concession to twentieth-century art. On the riverfront 50m downstream from the tourist office, in front of the spot where the **market** takes place every Friday and Sunday morning, stands a fountain by German Surrealist **Max Ernst** showing lots of weird froggy and tortoise-like creatures spitting jets of water.

Eating

Most of the eateries in town specialize in crêpes and overpriced snacks, and there are only a handful of decent possibilities outside the hotel **restaurants**. For a real blow-out meal, make for Pascal Bouvier's Michelin-starred dining room at the hotel *Le Choiseul* (☎02.47.30.45.45; menus at €59 & €90). There are two enticing choices for ordinary mortals, both of which need to be booked in advance in summer. ☀ *L'Épicerie*, 46 place Michel Debré (☎02.47.57.08.94; menus €11–37; closed Mon & Tues except July & Aug), has a lovely situation overlooked by the chapelle St-Hubert, and serves good and fairly refined country cuisine. The highly regarded *L'Alliance*, 14 rue Joyeuse (☎02.47.30.52.13; menus €18–43; closed Wed & Jan), meanwhile, serves mainly fish, though the

---

Family attractions near Amboise

Just south of town on the D751 to Chenonceaux, near the Pagode de Chanteloup, lies the **Parc Mini-Châteaux** (daily: April–June, Sept & Oct 10am–6pm, July & Aug 10am–7pm; €12, children 4–15 years €8, ⊛www.mini-chateaux.com; various family tickets are available that also include entry to the aquarium, below). It houses more than forty surprisingly good large-scale models of the chief Loire châteaux, made convincing by careful weathering and thousands of bonsai trees. Some are particularly large and impressive, including Loches, where they've modelled the whole citadel and all its houses. There's even a model TGV rattling by. Suitable attire for knights or princesses can be loaned to children.

At Lussault, 6km west of Amboise towards Tours, is the mammoth **Aquarium de Touraine** (daily: Sept–June 10am–6pm, July & Aug 10am–7pm; closed last two weeks of Nov & last two weeks of Jan; adults €12, children 4–15 years €8; ⊛www .aquariumduvaldeloire.com). It boasts 10,000 fish, and a special sequence of tanks features all the Loire species, from native bream and carp to introduced giants such as sturgeon, pike-perch and the frankly terrifying *silure*. There's also a small tropical section with turtles and alligators, and a tunnel that leads you through a large shark tank. Children can touch fish in a special tank, and watch regular piranha feeding frenzies.

For more energetic distractions, book in advance for the **Fantasy Forest** activity park, in Mosnes, 11km from Amboise on the road to Chaumont-sur-Loire (April–June Wed–Sat 10am–6pm; July & Aug daily 10am–7pm; Sept & Oct Sat & Sun 10am–6pm; ☎02.47.30.50.90, ⊛www.fantasyforest.fr). There's a go-kart luge-type affair (€9 for five descents), paintball sessions (€18.50), canoeing on the Loire (€14 per person), mountain bike rental (€6.50 for a half-day), inflatable castles and an adventure playground for younger children (€9.50). The signature activity, the "Parcours Acrobatique" (€10–22.50, depending on height) involves clambering through the trees on all kinds of rope bridges, while securely attached to wires.

house foie gras often features as a starter. For something more lively, *Chez Hippeau*, 1 rue François I (☎02.47.57.26.30; menus €11–30), is a bustling brasserie next to the Hôtel de Ville, with good lunchtime menus and pleasant outdoor seating out back, under the walls of St-Florentin church. Most places stop serving at around 10pm, but if you fancy another drink, head over to the Ile d'Or, where you'll find the friendly and popular cocktail bar *Le Shaker* (6pm–2am; closed Mon), whose outside terrace has great views across to the illuminated castle.

Around Amboise: Pagode de Chanteloup

If you take the main road south out of Amboise towards Bléré and Chenon-ceaux and turn right just before the junction with the D31, less than 1km from the centre, you'll arrive at a long, tree-lined avenue leading to an unlikely-looking eighteenth-century **pagoda** (April Mon–Fri 10am–noon & 2–6pm, Sat & Sun 10am–6pm; May & Sept daily 10am–6.30pm; June daily 10am–7pm; July & Aug daily 9.30am–7.30pm; Oct to mid-Nov Sat & Sun 10am–5pm; €6.90). It once belonged to the now-demolished château of **Chanteloup**, which was one of the largest, finest and most fashionable country houses of its eighteenth-century heyday. The pagoda's weird structure owes something to the fashion for Orientalism and something to the serene Classicism of the day, and you can climb to the top up a skilfully constructed staircase, though you'll have to negotiate 142 narrow steps.

You can also play some addictive medieval skittle-like **games and puzzles** in the grounds, hire a **boat** on the lake and explore the surrounding park. Plans are also afoot to make more of the structure's oriental connections, through displays and artwork on an Asian theme.

Chenonceaux and around

The gentle River Cher flows so slowly and passively between the exquisite arches of the **château de Chenonceau**, 35km east of Tours, that you are almost always assured of a perfect reflection. As nineteenth-century novelist Gustave Flaubert put it: "All is peaceful and gentle, elegant yet robust. It has calm without boredom, and melancholy without bitterness." The château is not visible from the road and you will have to pay to get even a peek. The little village of **CHENONCEAUX** (spelt with an x) is not much more than a cluster of pleasant hotels and restaurants built to serve the hordes of visitors that arrive here – the château vies with Chambord for the title of most-visited sight in the region, and it's a prime stop on the coach-party circuit. During summer the place teems with people, and it can become uncomfortably crowded mid-morning and mid-afternoon.

The relatively untouristed upper reaches of the Cher, including the pretty town of **Montrichard**, just 9km upriver, are covered in Chapter 2, "Blois and the Sologne" (see p.173).

Château de Chenonceau

Women always controlled the building of the **château de Chenonceau** (daily: March 16 to Sept 15 9am–7pm; Sept 16 to end Sept 9am–6.30pm; Oct 1 to Oct 15 & March 1 to March 15 9am–6pm; Oct 16 to end Oct & Feb 16 to end Feb 9am–5.30pm; Nov 1 to Nov 15 & Feb 1 to Feb 15 9am–5pm; Nov 16 to Jan

9am–4.30pm; €9, or €10.50 with Musée de Cires; **ⓦ**www.chenonceau.com). Catherine Briçonnet – whose husband Thomas Bohier bought the site on the proceeds of embezzling from his master, François I – hired the first architects in 1515 and had them begin building on the foundations of an old mill that stood on the granite bed of the Cher. At the same time, they destroyed the old castle belonging to the Marques, a venerable noble family which the ambitious new owners had helped along the road to financial ruin. Its moat-surrounded foundations now form a kind of island courtyard and prelude to the château. Anxious to guarantee – and advertise – their newly bought seigneurial status, the Bohiers left the corner **keep** alone, adding a few fancy windows to make it look less starkly Gothic, and engraving their initials at the base of the door. Their new château rose from the water alongside, combining in its architecture the fresh, rational ideas and Classical details of the Renaissance with the dizzy turrets and chimneys of late Gothic's courtly spirit. The Bohiers didn't have long to enjoy their ennoblement; the disgrace of financier Jacques de Beaune-Semblançay (see p.334) brought down their son Antoine as part of a general inspection of royal accounts, and the château was given up to the Crown.

The château's most characteristic feature, the set of arches spanning the River Cher, was added later in the century by **Diane de Poitiers**, who had been given the château by her lover, Henri II. Only five years later, following the accidental death of Henri II in 1559, Diane in turn was forced to hand over the château to the indomitable **Catherine de Médicis**, Henri II's widow, in return for Chaumont (see p.165). Catherine added lots of fashionable Mannerist details, including a set of giant caryatids (columns in the form of female figures) on the entrance facade; these now stand in the park. But her most important contribution was to build on top of the bridge. Laid out as three smoothly horizontal storeys, this section of the building has shaken off the febrile, more vertically orientated Gothic air that still clings to the main body of the château.

△ Château de Chenonceau

The more you look, the more different the two parts seem, although they are only separated by fifty-odd years and both could be called Renaissance.

After a long period of disuse, one **Mme Dupin** brought the fashionable life of the eighteenth century to this gorgeous residence, along with her guests Voltaire, Montesquieu and Rousseau, whom she had hired as tutor to her son and who became, according to his own account, "fat as a monk" during his stay. Saved by her local charitable works, Mme Dupin continued to live here until after the Revolution, château and owner slipping into old age together. Restoration back to the sixteenth-century designs – which involved removing many of Catherine de Médicis' additions – was completed by another woman, **Mme Pelouze**, in the late nineteenth century. The château is now a profitable business, owned and run by the Menier family firm, of chocolate fame.

The interior

Inside, the château is surprising small, with four main rooms set either side of a central corridor on all three floors, but there's a huge array of arresting tapestries, chimneys, ceilings, floors and furniture on show. The surprisingly good collection of **paintings** includes works by or attributed to Veronese, Tintoretto, Coreggio, Murillo and Rubens, as well as a number of portraits of the château's female owners, which helps to flesh out the history. Many of the tiled floors are original.

As soon as you step inside the château, it's obvious that this is no rambling medieval building. The layout is symmetrical and logical, with two main rooms on either side of a central hall with a beautiful Renaissance ceiling, its stone vaults strangely offset in a zigzag pattern. On the ground floor, the tapestry-hung **Guards' Room**, on the left, leads through to the modest chapel and on to Catherine de Médicis' green-velvet-lined **study** and **Diane de Poitiers' bedroom**, its fine chimney created by great Mannerist sculptor Jean Goujon. On the other side of the hall, the impressive **François I room** features Zurbarán's superb *Archimedes*, alongside two contrasting images of the goddess Diana; one is in fact a portrait of Diane de Poitiers, attributed to Primaticcio, while the other represents a relatively aristocratic-looking Gabrielle d'Estrées, the mistress of Henri IV. Mme Dupin's winsome portrait hangs in the **Louis XIV room**, next door, giving an impression only slightly more composed than when the philosopher Jean-Jacques Rousseau first met her: "her arms were uncovered, her hair was loose, her peignoir in disarray. . . it quite turned my poor head". Rigaud's portrait of Louis XIV was apparently given by the king as a souvenir of his own visit. Down the steps, the vaulted **kitchens**, conveniently positioned just above the water level, are well worth a look.

The section of the château that spans the Cher is relatively empty. The seemingly incongruous checkerboard flooring of the elegant **long gallery** is in fact true to the Renaissance design, though potted plants have replaced the Classical statues Louis XIV carried off to Versailles. Catherine de Médicis used to hold wild parties here, all naked nymphs and Italian fireworks. She intended the door on the far side to continue into another building on the south bank, but the project was never begun, and these days the gallery gives onto quiet, wooded gardens. In 1940, the Cher briefly formed the boundary between occupied and "free" France. The current proprietors, who rode out Nazi occupation, like to make out that the château's gallery was much used as an escape route. Given that their adjacent farm quartered a German garrison, it would have been a risky one. Today, the door is open only in July and August (you are given a token for re-entry), when you can cross through to the woods on the far bank of the Cher. Something of the quiet spirit of Mme Dupin's twilight years can be felt on this bank, especially if you stroll over to her dilapi-dated **tomb**, which is inscribed with a dedication to the Virtues, Genius and the Graces.

Being both straight, and inside the main building, the carved stone **staircase** is another piece typical of Renaissance design. The first and second floors are usually much quieter than the lower floors so there's more space to admire unique decorative details such as the seventeenth-century window-frame in the **César de Vendôme room**, supported by two carved caryatids, and the moving ceiling in the **bedroom of Louise de Lorraine**, which mourns Louise's murdered husband Henri III in black paint picked out with painted tears and the couple's intertwined initials. She lived out her widowhood at Chenonceau, always dressed in the white of royal mourning.

The grounds

The **gardens** on the near bank were the scene of wild celebrations for the marriage of the Dauphin François II and Mary Stuart, Queen of Scots, in 1558. Court ladies dressed in rustic style stood at the foot of every tree waving ribbons, and as the newlyweds crossed the bridge, fireworks went off – a first for France – and thirty cannon fired from the quay, causing so much smoke and flame that, according to a captain of the guard, "the very water seemed to burn". At Catherine's last party, in June 1577, Henri III and his favourites arrived dressed as women, while Catherine's infamous ladies in waiting, known as the "Flying Squadron", are said to have appeared half naked, with their hair flowing. The story certainly fits the popular image of Catherine's court as a den of vice, a legend much put about by Huguenot detractors.

Various outbuildings allow you to escape the crowds. The immaculately restored **farm courtyard** can be visited freely, along with its huge flower and vegetable garden. The adjacent stables now house the **Musée de Cires** (€10.50 including château entry), a collection of waxworks acting out various historical scenes associated with the château. Adults may find the figures interesting for their meticulously recreated clothes, which show off some of the precious textiles worn by sixteenth-century aristocrats, but it's too worthy for most children. A better bet is the *labyrinthe*, or **maze**, or renting a boat on the River Cher (July & Aug only; €2 for 30min). You might also want to try the own-label **wine** – the shop is signposted off the main path. It's not top-notch stuff, but certainly has curiosity value.

In July and August (and weekends in June), as part of the **Nocturne à Chenonceau**, the gardens and château are lit up between 9.30pm and 11pm, with atmosphere provided by Baroque chamber music played through speakers. The exterior-only evening ticket costs €5.

Practicalities

The tiny village of Chenonceaux has been almost entirely taken over by a handful of comfortable **hotels**, any of which would make a good base for exploring further up the Cher, though there's nothing much to see between forays. All of them are on rue du Docteur-Bretonneau, within easy reach of the château and the **gare SNCF** – which has decent train connections to Tours and up the Cher towards Bourges. The *Hôtel du Roy* at no. 9 (☎02.47.23.90.17, ⓕ02.47.23.89.81; ❸; closed mid-Nov to Jan) is relatively inexpensive, while *La Roseraie*, at no. 7 (☎02.47.23.90.09, Ⓦwww.charmingroseraie.com; ❹–❼; closed mid-Nov to March), is very welcoming, with air-conditioned rooms, good food, extensive grounds and a swimming pool. At no. 6, the four-star

Auberge du Bon Laboureur (☎02.47.23.90.02, ⑭www.bonlaboureur.com; ❼) has 25 rooms spread around five former village houses, now ivy-clad and luxuriously appointed; there's also an award-winning **restaurant** and a pool. For **camping**, there's a modest site (☎02.47.23.90.13; closed Oct–Easter) between the railway line and the river.

At Chisseaux, 2km upstream of the château, you can book yourself on an hour-long **boat tour** (tours depart: April & Oct 4.15pm; May, June & Sept 11am, 3.15pm & 4.15pm; July & Aug 11am, 2.15pm, 3.15pm, 4.15pm & 5.30pm; €8.50–9.25). There are two boats: the old-fashioned wooden riverboat, or *gabare*, is more fun than the modern mini-cruiser, but less well-protected from the elements. You can pay extra for snacks, or book yourself on a two-hour dinner cruise (7pm, €43.50).

Around Chenonceaux: Prieuré de St-Jean-du-Grais

The road from Tours to Chenonceaux on the left bank of the Cher, the N76, passes through a number of small riverside towns. Three kilometres south of one of the prettier of them, **Azay-sur-Cher**, is the crumbling old priory complex of **ST-JEAN-DU-GRAIS** (Easter–June Sun 2.30–6.30pm; July & Aug daily 2.30–6.30pm; €5). Despite the proximity of Tours, just 18km to the west, it's possible to sense how isolated the priory must have been in the mid-twelfth century, when it was built as a Cistercian monastery. The surrounding farmland is still broken up by remnants of the ancient forêt de Bréchenay, which once stretched north and south as far as the Cher and Indre rivers. The priory itself has been half-ruined since the Revolution, but the visit is fascinating, thanks in large part to guide and resident owner Martin Darrasse, who can show you the restoration work carried out by his own father between the wars and the very bed in which he himself was born – in the fifteenth-century *hôtellerie*, or prior's house.

M. Darrasse isn't able to guide all visitors personally, but even on your own it's well worth having a good poke around. The **priory** isn't large, forming just three sides of a square with a well at the centre. Its strangest feature is the lone bell tower in the southeastern corner, which is all that remains of the now-demolished priory church. The priory was founded in the wake of the crusades and it's thought that the weird, bullet-like shape of its stone spire may have beeen influenced by Arab architecture. On the west side of the square, opposite, the chapterhouse preserves its Plantagenet vaulting, which supports the long monk's dormitory above. The refectory completes the north side of the square. It still has its stunning, original roof beams, and the pulpit from which lessons were read while the monks ate in silence. A faded, thirteenth-century fresco looms high on the west wall. Throughout the prior, the **windows** have been replaced with modern stained glass, by the artist Sarkis. The dormitory windows are blue, symbolizing night, yellow windows light the refectory, representing day, while the chapterhouse and refectory pulpit have red windows, for the word of god.

The north bank west of Tours

The north bank of the Loire, to the west of Tours, is often neglected. The honeypot châteaux lie mostly on the south side of the river, and once you're on the main road west it's easy to speed past towards Saumur and Anjou. But the elegant private château at **Luynes** and the strange Gallo-Roman tower of **Cinq-Mars-la-Pile** have their own low-key appeal, and even if the main focus of your visit lies to the south it is well worth making a foray across the river to the splendidly furnished and quintessentially late-medieval château at **Langeais**. North of Cinq-Mars, the privately owned château of **Champchevrier** is set in the typical flat, wooded *landes* country of northern Touraine. At the western limits of Touraine, the attractive market town of **Bourgueil**, with its ancient abbey and opportunities to buy the excellent local wine, makes for a pleasant stop. Deep in the verdant country north of Bourgueil, **Gizeux** is worth visiting for its château's wall-paintings and its church's Renaissance tombs.

If you don't have your own transport, you can visit Cinq-Mars-la-Pile and Langeais by **train**, while Luynes is on Tours' excellent suburban **bus** network. The distances mean that it's possible to visit some of the châteaux by **bicycle**, perhaps returning to Tours via Villandry (see p.101). You'd have to be fairly committed to make it round via the bridge at Langeais in a day – a round trip of just under 50km – but you could easily take the train one way. The main N152 road along the riverbank *levée* can be easily avoided for almost all of its length.

Luynes and around

Roughly 1km back from the river and 11km west of Tours, the small town of **LUYNES** nestles under the cliff-like walls of its lofty **château** (April–Sept daily 10am–12.30pm & 2–6pm; €8.50), which is buttressed by an imposing row of four round towers. In 1619, the château became the ducal home of Charles d'Albret, a favourite of the young Louis XIII, and it has remained in the family ever since. As it stands today, the building is an unsettling jumble of styles, its courtyard enclosed by a grim thirteenth-century curtain wall that faces the refined residential wing, itself split into a romantic, brick-built section dating from the 1460s and an elegant, late-seventeenth century wing. The longevity of the Luynes' ownership is palpable if you take the guided tour of the interior, which is richly furnished with the aristocratic apparatus of the last four centuries: family portraits and photographs, weapons, hunting trophies and fine furnishings. Down on the main square, the fifteenth-century wooden-beamed **market hall** dominates place des Halles.

Frequent **buses** (line #55) make the journey out from Tours. On the edge of town, there's a three-star **campsite**, *Les Granges* (☎02.47.55.60.85). For local accommodation, head a couple of kilometres north of town along the D49, following the signposts to the **chambres d'hôtes** at *Le Moulin Hodoux* (☎02.47.55.76.27, ⓦmoulinhodoux.free.fr; ❹), set in a converted watermill on the peaceful little Bresme river, with a small swimming pool and a pretty garden.

If you're in the mood for further exploration, two minor sights lie close at hand. A short detour 3km west along the road signposted to St-Etienne-de-Chigny will take you to **LE VIEUX-BOURG**, where the **church** is a perfectly preserved mid-sixteenth-century construction. The tie-beams of the timber roof are spewed from the mouths of carved monsters, while the east window features a gorgeous stained-glass Crucifixion. Two kilometres northeast of Luynes, off the road towards Fondettes, you can follow a fragment of the course of a **Gallo-Roman aqueduct** along a signposted lane. A handful of tall stone piers, some with brick-lined arches intact, are all that is left of a structure that once carried water from a nearby spring all the way to the Roman town of Caesarodunum, now Tours.

Cinq-Mars-la-Pile

The main road west follows the Loire embankment as far as **CINQ-MARS-LA-PILE**, 18km from Tours, where the Tours–Angers railway line crosses to the northern bank. If you're coming into town by road from Tours, you pass close by the strange *pile* (pillar) from which the town gets its name just before you enter the city limits. Rising roughly thirty perfectly square metres from base to top, or exactly one hundred Roman feet, the brick tower is probably a Gallo-Roman memorial from the second century, though it lacks any inscriptions or the statue niche found in similar structures in southern France. The monumental banality of its construction, adorned only by a few crumbling geometric patterns on the upper part – the turrets are later additions – only adds to the enigma of why it was built. The other part of the town's name, Cinq-Mars, is probably a corruption of St-Médard, the name of the largely Romanesque **church**, which is capped by an octagonal stone spire.

In summer, you can walk around the overgrown ruins of the **château** (April-June & mid-Sept to end Oct Sat & Sun 11am–6pm; July & Aug daily except Tues 11am–8pm; €4), which consists of two crumbling twelfth-century towers incorporating a couple of original vaulted ceilings. The present state of decay dates from the treason of Henri Ruzé d'Effiat, the marquis of Cinq-Mars and another of Louis XIII's favourites, who supported Gaston d'Orléans' bid to overthrow Cardinal Richelieu in 1642. As the Loches-born writer Alfred de Vigny describes in his novel, *Cinq-Mars*, d'Effiat was beheaded and his château rendered uninhabitable. You can **stay** in two chambres d'hôtes in a low outbuilding (T02.47.96.40.49, E chateau-cinq-mars@orange.fr; ❹); they're not especially romantic, but the artist-owner is welcoming.

Château de Champchevrier

At Cinq-Mars-la-Pile, the D34 breaks away from the Loure Valley and shoots northward, straight as an arrow, across the flats of northern Touraine. This is the little-explored *landes* country, an area of hard-working villages and farms hidden in the great swathe of woodland that stretches all the way north to the river *le* Loir (see p.205) – which follows a parallel course to its big sister *la* Loire some 40km to the north, just over the Touraine border.

Civilization in the Loire region has always followed the major river valleys, and as a result there's little to tempt the visitor into northern Touraine – an area known as the **Gâtine Tourangelle**, where lakelets and little streams punctuate the near-endless forest. One landmark exception to this monotony stands 13km north of Cinq-Mars, just beyond the village of Cléré-les-Pins. The **château de Champchevrier** (mid-June to mid-Sept Mon–Sat 10am–6pm, Sun 2–6pm; €7.50; W www.champchevrier.com) is truly a creature of its environment, the product of centuries of aristocratic traditions that even the French Revolution could not uproot. Its name means "the field of the roebuck" and deer-filled woods stretch for miles all around, happy hunting grounds for the pack of seventy-odd dogs still kennelled here. Its attractions were no doubt lost on the British ambassador and his team, who briefly took up residence here in 1940, as they and the French government retreated before the German advance.

The château itself is is Renaissance at core, albeit "modernized" and expanded after 1728, when the estate was bought by Jean-Baptiste de la Rûe du Can, the first Baron de Champchevrier. Nine generations later, the baron's descendants still live here year-round. The happy result of such long, unbroken occupation is a treasury of precious furnishings, whose stories are explained on the (obligatory) **guided tour**. There are paintings by French Classical greats such as Pierre

Mignard and Hyacinthe Rigaud, but the most fabulous items are the tapestries, especially those in the **cabinet du roi**, or king's bedchamber. These were manufactured in the 1630s and 40s from cartoons by Simon Vouet depicting the loves of classical gods, and have been protected from the sun with rare diligence ever since, thus preserving colours of unrivalled depth.

Langeais

LANGEAIS, 23km west of Tours, is utterly dominated by its forbidding château, which rises up, sheer, at the end of the town's main street. Otherwise, the small town is peaceful but fairly insipid, though a few fifteenth-century houses are dotted about the centre, notably one immediately opposite the château's drawbridge. Even if you're not stopping in Langeais, it's worth taking a good look at the bridge over the Loire, a 1930s construction whose bizarre concrete towers are intended to mimic the château.

North of Langeais lies the beautifully wooded *landes* country of **Castel-valérie**; the tourist office (see opposite) can provide recommendations of signposted walks and horse-riding centres.

The château

Any hints of luxury and welcome provided by the elegant windows of the **château** (daily: Feb–June & Sept to mid-Nov 9.30am–6.30pm; July & Aug 9am–7pm; mid-Nov to Jan 10am–5pm; €7.20) are obliterated by the combined effect of drawbridge, stone walls and massive towers. The most extraordinary feature of the exterior is the *chemin-de-ronde*, or guard-walk, which smoothly wraps its way round the topmost level of the walls, resting on perfect stone machicolations. On closer inspection, the warlike impression is moderated by subtle details: between each machicolation is a carved trefoil, and the sheer regularity of the structure puts it in a different league from the average medieval fortress built higgledy-piggledy for war.

The château is sometimes described as one of the first stirrings of a new architectural age. It was the work of one **Jean Bourré**, who, as a bourgeois lawyer in the service of Louis XI, was himself a sign of the new era. He built numerous châteaux, including Le Plessis-Bourré, in Anjou (see p.292), but Langeais was particularly important: its construction was at the king's command, and it had the power to stop incursions up the Loire by the Bretons. This threat ended with Charles VIII and Anne de Bretagne's marriage in December 1491, which was celebrated at Langeais (see box opposite).

If you're tired of the bare rooms or misplaced eighteenth-century furnishings of so many châteaux, Langeais is a relief: for once, the furnishings are mostly fifteenth century, to match the building, even if the other decorations are mostly reconstructions. The château is owned by the Institut de France, the wealthy and powerful state foundation which encompasses the Académie Française, among other august bodies. When it was bequeathed the château by the nineteenth-century collector Jacques Siegfried, it also took over his unrivalled and exceptionally valuable **collection of furniture**. This creates a lived-in impression that's rare even in châteaux a century or two younger. There are fascinating tapestries, some rare paintings and polychrome Madonnas, cots and beds, and a number of imposing *chaires*, or seigneurial thrones.

The **chambre de parement** contains a true four-poster bed and one of the most precious objects in the collection, a tapestry of the Crucifixion from the workshop of Rogier van der Weyden. The best is saved for the huge **marriage chamber**, whose centrepiece is Anne's gilded and bejewelled **wedding coffer**.

The marriage of Anne de Bretagne

On December 6, 1491, a deal was made at the château de Langeais which secured the future of the French kingdom and finally ended Brittany's independence: **Charles VIII** married **Anne, duchess of Brittany**. The ceremony was conducted under tight security, and the couple travelled separately to Langeais under cover of night.

Secrecy was necessary because of the marriage's enormous significance and its shady political circumstances. Anne was technically already married to **Maximilian**, the Habsburg emperor, who ruled over Austria, the Netherlands, Franche-Comté, Alsace and parts of Burgundy. If he were to inherit Anne's Breton lands, the French kingdom would be all but surrounded by an implacable enemy. Mindful of the threat, France invaded Brittany in December 1488, and by June 1491 Anne was besieged at Rennes. When the city finally fell in October, Anne was forced to give up either her duchy or her marriage to Maximilian. She chose the latter, and Pope Innocent VIII granted a dispensation annulling her unconsummated marriage to Maximilian (she was only 15). For his part, Charles was already engaged to Maximilian's daughter, Margaret of Austria. Unusually, the couple seem to have been deeply in love – Margaret is known to have wept on hearing of Charles's marriage, and kept his portrait with her until she died – but political necessity prevailed.

The marriage stipulated that Charles would not become duke of Brittany, but it was the end of the duchy's independence anyway, as if Charles were to die before Anne, she would be obliged to marry his successor. Having apparently secured his future, Charles decided to create a fabulous new home for Anne in Amboise (see p.84).

Figures of the apostles, as well as the wise and foolish virgins, are depicted on the lid, while the main body is carved with a miniature Annunciation – an ironic choice, with hindsight, as none of Charles and Anne's four children survived them, thus bringing the Valois dynasty to an end. A diptych of the couple portrays them looking less than joyous at their union, while on the walls is a set of tapestries showing seven of the "Nine Prow Knights", models of chivalric virtue drawn from the Bible, antiquity and early Christianity. The upper-floor **chapel room** – which isn't in fact a chapel, though it has a marvellous, church-like wooden ceiling – has a waxwork recreation of the royal wedding, along with piped music and a histrionic French commentary. From here you can access the **guard-walk**, which you can follow all the way round the château – as long as you're not put off by the dizzy views over the rooftops and out to the river. In summer, swarms of swallows and house martins take up residence, swooping and darting around the machicolations.

The **gardens** are overlooked by the grim remnants of a **keep**, one of the first strategic constructions of the warlike count, Foulque Nerra. Built in around 1000 – which makes it one of the earliest keeps in France – the tower marks Foulque's determination not to relinquish the territories he had wrested from the counts of Blois, who held the rest of Touraine. His grip may not have been as strong as he thought: a contemporary recounts him trying to win back the castle in 1038.

Practicalities

The **gare SNCF**, which has good connections to Tours, Saumur and Angers, is practically in the middle of town. The **tourist office** is next door on place du 14 Juillet (July & Aug Mon–Sat 9.30am–7pm, Sun 10am–12.30pm & 3.30–6pm; rest of year Mon–Sat 9.30am–12.30pm & 2.30–6pm, Sun 10am–12.30pm; ☏02.47.96.58.22, ⓦwww.tourisme-langeais.com).

Langeais is a peaceful place to overnight, and it has a pleasant, thoroughly old-fashioned three-star **hotel**, the *Errard-Hosten*, 2 rue Gambetta (☏02.47.96.82.12,

ⓦwww.errard.com; ❺), which offers plain but spacious rooms as an adjunct to its excellent **restaurant** (menus €27–49). There's also a decent, two-star Logis de France hotel, *La Duchesse Anne* (℡02.47.96.82.03; ❸), which has a relatively inexpensive but good restaurant. Best of all, there's the 🍴 *Anne de Bretagne*, 27 rue Anne de Bretagne (℡02.47.96.08.52; ❸), which offers some genuinely exceptional **chambres d'hôtes** in a beautifully restored early-nineteenth-century home almost under the walls of the château. If you're not up for the *Errard-Hosten*, you can enjoy simple bruschettas and Italian dishes in the garden of *Au Coin des Halles*, 20m short of the château at 9 rue Gambetta (closed Tues eve & Wed).

For a really refined place to stay, head 16km north along the D57 to the *Vieux Château d'Hommes*, just outside the village of Hommes (℡02.47.24.95.13, ⓦwww.le-vieux-chateau-de-hommes.com; ❼), where the well-furnished rooms are in a fifteenth-century outhouse of the main château; one room even occupies a pepper-pot tower, and there's a good-sized pool. Six kilometres west of Langeais along the main road to Bourgeuil, at St-Patrice, the sumptuous *Château de Rochecotte*, 43 rue Dorothée de Dino (℡02.47.96.16.16, ⓦwww .chateau-de-rochecotte.fr; ❽) offers a taste of eighteenth-century luxury in modern, four-star guise: the rooms are beautifully furnished (well, they cost from €139 to over €200), the restaurant is serious, and there's a terrace overlooking the Loire, a large swimming pool and extensive grounds. The attractive municipal **campsite** is 1km from town, off the main road to Tours (℡02.47.96.85.80; closed mid-Sept to May).

Bourgueil

Until the Revolution, the wine town of **BOURGUEIL**, 45km west of Tours on the north bank of the Loire, lay just outside the boundaries of Touraine. It now falls within the *département* of the Indre-et-Loire, Touraine's modern replacement, and for mosts visitors it is inextricably linked with Chinon, 18km to the south, as the two are great rivals for the title of the producer of the greatest red **wine** in the Loire region. You can taste and buy the wines at the **Maison des Vins**, 18 place de l'Eglise (mid-May to mid-Sept Tues–Sat 10am–12.30pm & 3–7pm; mid-Sept to mid-May Fri 2–6pm, Sat 10am–noon & 2–6pm; free), which is owned and run by local winegrowers; they can also recommend individual *caves* to visit.

The town itself is surprisingly sleepy, though it comes to life on Tuesday mornings, as the network of narrow streets and little squares off the central rue du Commerce fill up with **market** stalls selling local produce – lots of garlic – inexpensive clothing, hunting gear and the like. The chief sights in the handsome old town centre are the large **covered market** on place des Halles and the adjacent church on place de l'Eglise, **St-Germain**, which was over-restored in the nineteenth century but has an unusual Angevin-style choir running the entire width of the nave and aisles. But the showpiece is the ancient **Abbaye de Bourgueil**, which lies at the foot of rue de Tours, on the eastern edge of the town. Unfortunately, the more impressive thirteenth- to seventeenth-century section is occupied by nuns, and can't be visited, but the eighteenth-century wing, with its fine staircase, has been converted into a modest municipal **museum** of folk traditions (April–June, Sept & Oct Sat & Sun 2–6pm; July & Aug Mon & Thurs–Sun 2–6pm; €5), and the town cinema. Just outside town, in the northeastern suburb of Sablons, off the road to Restigné, the **Musée Van Oeveren** (July & Aug Tues–Sun 2–6pm; €6.50; ⓦwww.musee-escrime.com) shows off the owner's collection of fencing and duelling weapons and ephemera.

△ Garlic market

Bourgueil's main **festival** is the Fête du Vin du Val de Loire, which attracts some fifty winegrowers on August 15; on the third Tuesday in July the town celebrates garlic; and on the third Tuesday in October chestnuts are honoured. An evening "gourmet market", with stalls selling wines and hot and cold local specialities, arrives in Bourgueil on the third Friday of July and August.

Practicalities

The **tourist office**, 16 place de l'Eglise (Mon 3–5.30pm, Tues–Sat 9am–1pm & 2–6pm, Sun 10am–12.30pm; ☎02.47.97.91.39, ⓦwww.ot-bourgueil.fr), can give advice on visiting the surrounding region, including the handful of **Boule de Fort** clubs, where you can watch or join in the Angevin version of bowls, which is played on a curved, wooden floor.

The best two **hotels** lie cheek by jowl on the narrow rue de Tours, just a few steps from the covered market. The ageing but comfortably bourgeois *Ecu de France*, 9 rue de Tours (☎02.47.97.70.18, ⓔecu-de-france@orange.fr; ❷), occupies a handsome old posthouse, and has attractive, old-fashioned rooms with boxed-off shower units in the corner. Next door, *Le Faisan Doré*, 5 rue de Tours (℡02.47.97.72.44, ℻02.47.97.95.64; ❶), is more working-class in tone, with a bar and an admirably inexpensive evening menu; there are cheap, rather mean rooms in an annexe out back (❶), and better rooms in the main building (❸). Both hotels have good restaurants, and serve lunch or dinner at street-side tables.

If you don't want to eat at one of Bourgueil's hotel **restaurants**, try the *Moulin Bleu*, 7 rte du Moulin Bleu, 2km out of town on the road to St-Nicolas-de-Bourgueil (℡02.47.97.73.13; menus from €16–36; closed Tues & Sun evening, and Wed), which serves lots of good, winey regional specialities, and has a lovely rural situation.

Gizeux

North of Bourgueil, you can follow the little river Changeon upstream through heavily wooded, sparsely populated backcountry to the tranquil village of **GIZEUX**, 13km away. At the end of a long avenue of giant plane trees, the **château** (May–Sept Mon–Sat 10am–6pm, Sun 2–6pm; €6.50; ⓦwww .chateaudegizeux.com) extends like a game of dominoes around its grassy grounds, each wing dating from a different epoch. A resident theatre company arrives every summer – offering children's workshops and classics of French theatre presented as a walkabout on Friday and Saturday evenings – but the main reason for English-speakers to visit is to see two remarkable sets of **wall-paintings**.

The core of the château was built in the sixteenth century by the **du Bellay** family – from the Plessis-Macé branch (see p.292), rather than that of the poet Joachim. In the 1590s, Marie de Yvetôt, the wife of René du Bellay, commissioned an unknown artist to decorate the wooden panelling of the central **salon**, and the result still graces the walls in its original, unrestored state. Colourful floral designs compete with monochrome biblical and mythological *grisailles*, set against an ancient terracotta floor scattered with threadbare chairs from the eras of Louis XIII, Louis XIV and Louis XV. Roughly one hundred years later, one Anne de la Frézollière bought the château from the daughters of the du Bellay family, which had no male heirs, and ordered a rival decoration for the **long gallery**. She offered the blank walls to pupils from the painting school at Fontainebleau, who set about practising views of great French châteaux. Initially, the result is hilariously cack-handed, with châteaux such as Chambord rendered with amazingly bad proportions (and suspiciously identical dogs), but as you progress down the gallery the work becomes more assured.

A signposted circuit offers a four-kilometre **walk** around the village, passing the château and the adjacent **église Notre-Dame**, where you can see the white marble **tomb** effigies of René du Bellay and his severe-looking wife Marie, kneeling in the south transept in prayer. It's one of the finest works of the Tourangeau sculptor Nicolas Guillain, and strangely affecting if you've just admired the Du Bellays' home improvements at the château. Across in the north transept, the superficially similar tomb of Martin du Bellay and his wife Louise de Savennières was sculpted less than twenty years later, but the style of the stonework and the costumes is already quite different.

If you're approaching from Bourgueil in the afternoon, you can visit a working seventeenth-century watermill on the way. Turn off after 8km at a signpost for the **Moulin Scée** (May–Aug Tues–Sun at 4pm; €4.50), then drive 1km along a rural backroad. The charming – but monolingual – miller will happily show you round, and demonstrate the process by which he makes flour for discerning local *boulangeries*.

The northern half of the circular GRP **footpath**, the Côteaux de Bourgueil, encompasses the whole Changeon valley; walking the complete northern route from Bourgeuil to Gizeux and back would be an ambitious full-day expedition, taking you through undulating woodland and past the occasional hamlet. The FFRP's walking guide, *La Touraine à pied* (see Basics, p.43) outlines a shorter, three-hour circuit around Continvoir, 2km east of Gizeux, taking you through beautiful, lightly wooded countryside.

Villandry and around

Even if gardens aren't your thing, those at the **château de Villandry** are definitely worth a visit – and the château itself is a beautifully restored Renaissance gem. Even getting there can be a pleasure, as Villandry is a superb cycle ride from Tours, 13km east along the Cher, following dedicated cyclepaths for most of its route.

The château

The **château de Villandry** (daily: Jan, Nov & Dec 9am–5pm; Feb 9am–5.30pm; March 9am–6pm; April–June & Sept 9am–7pm; July & Aug 9am–7.30pm; Oct 9am–6.30pm; château closes 30–60min earlier, and is closed mid-Nov to mid-Dec; €8 château and gardens, €5.50 gardens only; Ⓦwww.chateauvillandry .com) is one of the highlights of the region, so if you want to explore in peace, arrive early, late or at lunchtime.

The château was erected in the 1530s by one of François I's royal financiers, **Jean le Breton**. Like so many of the court's banker-accountants, Le Breton was eager to legitimize his new status – and launder his fortune – so he purchased and then knocked down the twelfth-century château des Colombiers (see box p.102), preserving only the feudal keep as a symbol of his arrival as an aristocrat. Le Breton's Renaissance structure still abuts this keep, arranged around three sides of a *cour d'honneur*, the fourth wing having been demolished in the eighteenth century, at the same time as the apparently Renaissance details around the windows and dormers were recarved. The square towers closing off the courtyard, which look more like eighteenth-century work, are actually an extremely novel part of Le Breton's original scheme – by the time that Le Breton began building here, the court had quit the Loure Valley for Fontainebleau, and the sober architecture of Paris and its Ile-de-France region was in the ascendant.

Little is known about the original design of the gardens, as they were totally remodelled in the nineteenth century in the then-fashionable style of an English country park. In 1906, however, the château was bought by an American heiress, Ann Coleman, whose husband, **Joachim Carvallo**, a Spanish doctor, decided to re-create a French garden in the grandest and most historically accurate style.

The gardens

Carvallo's research led him to believe that gardens were as much symbolical as ornamental or practical, so at the topmost level, very much in the elevated Classical spirit, is the **water garden**, a large pond surrounded by neat lawns and meticulously pruned lime trees. Water flows down from it through a small canal that runs underneath the walls of the old keep and fills the château's moat. Next down, at the level of the château itself, the **ornamental garden** "serves as an extension of the salon", according to Carvallo. It reflects the middle state of the human condition, poised between divine rationality and base animal desires. Four geometrical arrangements of immaculately trimmed box hedges symbolize different kinds of love: tender, passionate, fickle and tragic – the dark green of the box enflamed by red flowers in summer. At the top end of this section are three crosses – Maltese, Languedoc and Basque – while another box garden on the opposite side of the canal acts as a less successful allegory of music.

The highlight, spread out across 12,500 square metres of perfectly flat ground, is the **potager**, or Renaissance kitchen garden. Symbolically and physically, it may be the lowest and most vulgar part of the gardens, but it is the most fascinating. Carrots, cabbages and aubergines are arranged into intricate patterns, while rose bowers and miniature box hedges form a kind of frame. Even in winter, there is almost always something to see, as the entire area is replanted twice a year. Sadly, the vegetables are not sold for consumption, but when the beds are thinned out in the summer months you can often find tomatoes, aubergines, peppers and the like in a box in the far southeast corner of the garden – just leave a coin for the gardeners' annual dinner. Other vegetables are simply mulched. Up close, keen amateurs can admire rare and beautifully presented varieties, while city-bred kids may get a kick out of trying simply to work out which vegetable is which – placards provide a key. At the far end of the garden, overlooked by the squat tower of the village church, beautiful vine-shaded paths give onto the medieval **herb garden** and the **maze**. Just beyond, there's a children's playground.

There are various **festivals** throughout the year, notably the *potager* weekend, at the end of September, with lots of workshops and demonstrations, and the Nuits des Mille Feux, on the first weekend of July, when the gardens are lit by hundreds of candles at night.

The interior

It's worth paying the extra to visit the **château**, if only for the unmissable turret-top view over the gardens and out to the confluence of the Loire and Cher. Inside, the château is the epitome of eighteenth-century elegance,

---

The last days of Henry Plantagenet

By the summer of 1189, **Henry II**, king of England and ruler of the great Angevin empire, was old, fat and suffering from a severe anal abscess, but he hadn't lost his appetite for fighting. His son, Richard the Lionheart, had joined forces with his arch-enemy, the French king Philippe-Auguste, and their combined armies had captured Le Mans, Henry's beloved birthplace. Henry watched as the city burned, cursing God "thou hast vilely taken away the city I loved best on earth ... I will pay thee back as best I can." The French armies pursued Henry as he fled south towards his castle of Chinon (see p.112). They captured Tours on the way, leaving Henry nowhere to hide. Philippe-Auguste summoned Henry to a conference at Colombiers, modern **Villandry**, and demanded that he do homage to the French king for all his territories on the Continent. Further, Richard was to be confirmed as heir, and would be allowed to marry his betrothed, Alais – who had become Henry's mistress. Henry could hardly remain upright on his horse but refused to dismount. As he agreed to submit to the terms, and bent forward to give his son the kiss of peace, he whispered, "God grant that I may not die till I have had a fitting revenge on you." He was then carried back to **Chinon**, where he plotted vengeance even as he lay dying. But when he learned that his youngest son, John, had also joined the rebellion, Henry turned his face to the wall saying, "I care no more for myself nor for aught in this world." Hours later, he died in delirious agony, shouting over and over, "Shame, shame on a vanquished king."

Carvallo having decided that restoring Renaissance standards of comfort wouldn't make for an ideal home. The **dining room** suggests the transition from inside to outdoors, with its Provençal marble fountain and bizarre terracotta stove, and windows looking onto the ornamental garden. The nearby staircase is an eighteenth-century addition, replacing the unfashionably medieval spiral staircase which used to stand in the *cour d'honneur*. The exquisite bedrooms on the first floor offer improved views over the gardens. The **long gallery** is lined with the Carvallos' collection of Spanish paintings, many of them distressingly religiose, and leads to a stunning **Mudejar ceiling**, which was brought to Villandry from a fifteenth-century palace in Toledo and painstakingly reassembled. On first sight, the intricate arabesques and geometric patterns in gilded and coloured wood are pure Moorish work, but Spanish Christian motifs recur, notably the scallops – the symbol of St James of Compostela – that frame each corner. Upstairs, the **library** and various bedrooms have been lovingly restored.

Savonnières

The small village of **SAVONNIÈRES**, 2km east of the château de Villandry on the main road to Tours, has a pretty situation overlooking the Cher – its high bridge is the last before the river flows into the Loire 3km downstream. On the far side of the bridge, the hidden-away spit of land between the Cher and Loire rivers is known locally as *le bout du monde*, or "the end of the world". A circuit of the very tip of the peninsula, west of Savonnières' bridge is a lovely twelve-kilometre cycle ride. On the south side, facing Villandry across the Cher is an area of sand that's sometimes used by locals for sunbathing; swimming, as ever, is strongly discouraged because of the danger of collapsing sandbanks, though you may see the odd bold – and knowledgable – local risking it.

Savonnière's main sight lies just outside the village, heading towards Villandry. The **Grottes Pétrifiantes de Savonnières** (Feb, March & Oct to mid-Nov daily 9am–noon & 2–5.30pm; April–Sept daily 9am–6.30pm; mid-Nov to mid-Dec daily except Thurs 9am–noon & 2–5.30pm; €5.60; ⓦwww.grottes -savonnieres.com) are not in fact caves but abandoned medieval quarries. The slow trickle of water through calcite has formed plenty of natural stalactites and stalagmites, however, some of them moderately impressive. The owners have turned the process to commercial use, producing an amazingly kitsch array of petrified objects by leaving dolls, pots and little statuettes exposed to the flow, all of which are for sale in the shop. It gets chilly during the forty-plus-minute tour through underground tunnels, so bring a jumper.

Practicalities

The best way to **get to Villandry** is to cycle along the charming "Loire à Vélo" path (see p.42), which avoids even the modest traffic on the D7 for most of its route – the only drawback is making your way through the suburbs of Tours. In summer you can take a **minibus** directly from Tours (ⓣ02.47.70.37.37); the service leaves from the tourist office at 10am and 2.30pm and costs €16 return. There is no useful public transport.

For **accommodation**, the most appealing options are two chambres d'hôtes near the confluence of the Loire and Cher rivers: head north across the bridge at Savonnières and follow the signs for 2km to the village of Berthenay, then continue 1km west, following the Loire along a minor road running along the embankment; turn left when you see the signs. At *La Grange aux Moines* (ⓣ02.47.50.06.91, ⓦgrangeauxmoines.free.fr; ❸), the rooms are in a handsome old farmhouse. *La Fouacière* (☎02.47.43.50.82, ⓦlafouaciere.site.voila.fr; ❸), some 100m beyond, is slightly more modest but very welcoming. Both have swimming pools. For more luxurious accommodation, make for the *Château du Vau*, 6km east of Villandry, between Savonnières and Ballan-Miré (☎02.47.67.84.04, ☎www.chez.com/chateauduvau; ❼); as private châteaux come, this one is rather hulking, but it has four deeply old-fashioned, antique-furnished guest rooms, extensive grounds and a swimming pool. The best **campsite** hereabouts, *Camping de la Confluence* (☎02.47.50.00.25; closed Oct–May), is right beside the Cher in the village of Savonnières.

There are some top-class options for **eating out** in and around Villandry. Good snack meals are served on the terrace next to the château gates, but it's well worth venturing into Villandry's tiny village, where you'll find a wonderful establishment combining the roles of delicatessen, tearoom, wine-bar and **restaurant**, ⚒ *L'Epicerie Gourmande* (☎02.47.43.37.49). Tucked away behind the *Hôtel Le Colombier*, it offers delicious gourmet specialities from the Loire and further afield, and can match your dish with carefully chosen and unusual wines: you could have a glass of a sparkling wine from Poitiers with an *assiette* of smoked fish or fine cheeses (€12), and a smoked duck salad (€8), or go for a hot dish of Basque tripe (€15) with a powerful southern red. Food is served all day, and in the evenings at weekends; weekday evenings are often possible as well if you call ahead – it's well worth doing so.

Just outside Savonnières, along the road to Villandry, the warm and classy *Maison Tourangelle*, 9 rue des Grottes Pétrifiantes (☎02.47.50.30.05; closed Wed, Sat lunch & Sun eve; menus €25–50) offers excellent, refined Loire cuisine, along with a gorgeous terrace with a view onto the Cher. For something heartier, head out from Villandry and 1km down the D121 towards Druye, where there's an upmarket farmhouse restaurant, the *Etape Gourmande* at the Domaine de la Giraudière (☎02.47.50.08.60; menus €15–30; closed mid-Nov to mid-March). It throngs with families enjoying meals in the courtyard on summer evenings, and the food is honest home-cooked fare, with the farm's own goat's cheese featuring prominently.

But the best place to eat around Villandry is ⚒ *Au Bout du Monde*, beside the Loire in Berthenay (☎02.47.43.51.50; evening menus €28–52) closed Sun eve, Mon eve & Tues). It has a children's playground and a lovely garden setting, but the fresh, light, imaginative local food is the thing: for starters, think perfect fish *rillettes* or grated turnip with snails and thyme; for mains, eel stew with frog's legs and artichoke, or pikeperch with morille mushrooms and polenta.

Azay-le-Rideau

Even without its château, the quiet village of **AZAY-LE-RIDEAU**, 27km southwest of Tours, would bask in its serene setting, complete with an old mill by the bridge and an ancient church. On its little island in the Indre, the château is one of the loveliest in the entire Loire region: perfect turreted early Renaissance, pure in style down to the blood-red paint of its window frames. The village's apparently odd name needs some explanation: *rideau* doesn't actually mean "curtain", but derives from the Ridel family, who occupied a minor fortress at Azay in the thirteenth century. In fact, the village was known for centuries as Azay-le-Brûlé ("the burnt"), after the Dauphin Charles smoked out a Burgundian garrison here in 1418.

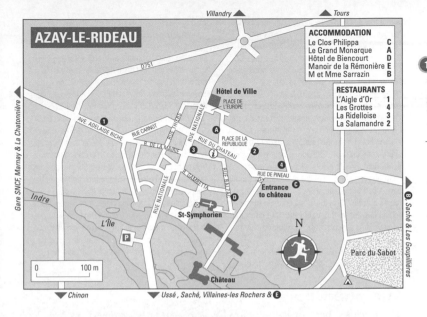

Arrival and information

Trains from Tours call at Azay-le-Rideau on their way to Chinon roughly every two hours (some services are replaced by SNCF buses). Cyclists should pick up the SNCF's useful leaflet, *Autour du Train* (W autourdutrain.free.fr), which gives timetable information and recommends a thirty-kilometre one-way route, stopping off at Villandry on the way between Tours and Azay-le-Rideau. The **gare SNCF** is awkwardly situated a fifteen-minute walk west of the centre, along ave Riché.

Azay's **tourist office** (May, June & Sept Mon–Sat 9am–1pm & 2–6pm, Sun 10am–1pm & 2–5pm; July & Aug Mon–Sat 9am–7pm, Sun 10am–6pm; Oct–April Mon–Sat 9am–1pm & 2–6pm; T 02.47.45.44.40, W www .ot-paysazaylerideau.fr) sits just off the village's main square, place de la République. The **bus stop** is just behind, next to the Hôtel de Ville.

You can rent **bikes** from Cycles Leprovost, 13 rue Carnot (T 02.47.45.40.94; closed Mon & Sun). **Canoes** can be rented from *La Plage*, on L'Ile – just before town when approaching from the south (daily 11am–7pm; T 06.61.21.80.29).

Accommodation

Azay-le-Rideau has a trio of pleasant **hotels**, budget, mid-range and fairly expensive, clustered round its main square, as well as two excellent chambres d'hôtes and a fantastic château offering accommodation. The nearest **campsite**, *Camping du Sabot* (T 02.47.45.42.72; closed Nov–March), lies upstream from the château, signposted off the D84 to Saché.

Le Clos Philippa 10 rue de Pineau
T 02.47.45.26.49. Delightful chambres
d'hôtes in an old, L-shaped house a few steps
away from the château. Rooms are large and well
appointed with tiled floors or floorboards, water

decanters by the beds and swags of good French
fabrics giving an antique feel. ❹
Le Grand Monarque 3 place de la République
T 02.47.45.40.08, W www.legrandmonarque.com.
The poshest hotel in the village, a solid three-star

with a traditional, slightly formal atmosphere and handsome, attractively furnished rooms with "historic" touches such as beams and exposed stone walls. The more expensive rooms (❻–❾) overlook a pleasant walled garden – a good place for breakfast. Closed mid-Dec to Jan. ❹

Hôtel de Biencourt 7 rue Balzac ☎02.47.45.20.75, ⓦwww.hotelbiencourt.com. This attractive and unpretentious two-star hotel has a great location on a quiet side-street leading down from the market square to the church and château. The actual building is eighteenth-century – in lovely white stone, with charming red shutters – but the interiors are all-new, albeit in a rustic style. Perhaps the nicest rooms are the "Directoire" styled ones in the old school building at the end of the little garden. Big family rooms are available. Closed mid-Nov to Feb. ❸

🚶 **Manoir de la Rémonière** 1km from Azay on the opposite side of the Indre, on the road to Saché ☎02.47.45.24.88, ⓦwww .manoirdelaremoniere.com. The best option, if you can afford it – prices range from €120 to €180. Once the château's fifteenth-century hunting lodge, it now does bed and breakfast, with some atmospheric and slightly ramshackle rooms in the main building, and less interesting ones in the outbuildings. Has a small, unheated outdoor pool. ❼

🚶 **M et Mme Sarrazin** 9 chemin des Caves Mecquelines ☎02.47.45.31.25, ⓦwww .troglododo.com. The friendly young owners offer a rare chance to actually sleep in a troglodyte room, in a quiet location just out of the village on the D84 heading east. There are two rooms, both adorable: one is small and cosy, with a hollowed-out bedchamber off the living room, a miniature kitchenette and a wonderful hacked-out bathroom deep in the rock; the other is large, with a big central fireplace, a proper kitchen, a mezzanine level for the main bed and spare beds for an extra two people. ❹

The château

The romantic hero of Balzac's novel *Le Lys dans la Vallée* described Azay-le-Rideau's **château** (daily: April–June & Sept 9.30am–6pm; July & Aug 9.30am–7pm; Oct–March 10am–12.30pm & 2–5.30pm; €7.50; ⓦwww.monum.fr) as "a diamond cut with facets, set in the Indre, and mounted on piles hidden by flowers". The flowers may have been tidied away in the last century and a half but "diamond" remains exactly the right word: Azay really is the most precious and captivating of all the Loire's châteaux – and the one requiring the most minute examination if you want to discover its true value. The setting in the waters of the Indre remains as exquisite as when Balzac saw it, the famous reflection now fringed by the mature trees of landscaped gardens. You'll have to pay the entrance fee if you want to have a good look at the outside, as the château is hidden away behind high walls and a leafy driveway.

Begun in 1518, Azay was one of the very first truly Renaissance châteaux to be built in France, an expression of the new wealth, power and cultural ambition of the merchants and bankers of Tours who surrounded Louis XII and François I. Azay's builder, **Gilles Berthelot**, was one of four powerful French treasurers. He was also a close relation of Jacques de Beaune-Semblançay, the great banker behind François I's overspending, and a cousin of Catherine Briçonnet, the *grande dame* of the château de Chenonceau, which predates Azay by just five years. In an atmosphere of fierce rivalry for cultivated extravagance, Berthelot threw up his château as fast as he could, famously getting his team of mason Etienne Rousseau, sculptor Pierre Maupoint and carpenter Jacques Thoreau – all Frenchmen, despite the Italian influences in their designs – to work literally day and night. Even so, Azay wasn't finished before Berthelot and his cronies fell from favour in the huge corruption scandal of 1527 (see p.334), and what stands today is probably only half a château. It's likely that the original plan would have been for four identical wings enclosing a courtyard, and you can still see a rough edge where work stopped in 1527, when Berthelot fled for Metz.

The **courtyard** is dominated by the great open **staircase**, a structure as important as the feudal towers of earlier châteaux in defining the status of the *seigneur*. It even looks like a tower in reverse, a space carved out of the main body of the château, with flat, lace-like encrustations of stone carving defining the space behind. The balustrades on the first- and third-floor levels of the staircase bear the emblems of François I and his wife, the salamander and the ermine, while delicately carved Classical motifs crawl over the creamy stone. The loggia-like pairs of the staircase's window arches are particularly Italian in inspiration. There is one anomaly: the large tower on the right as you approach the courtyard was added in the mid-nineteenth century, replacing an incongruous-looking medieval tower that Berthelot never got round to demolishing.

You don't need to know anything about architecture to love the **southern facade** of the château: it's breathtakingly pretty, rising out of a broad, pool-like meander of the slow-moving Indre. The perfect symmetry is striking, each corner finished off by an *échauguette* tower daintily suspended just above the water level, each row of windows defined by a neat horizontal stringcourse and delicate pilasters pointing up to the dormers in the roof, the whole facade drawn together by the noble windows of the central axis. A guard-walk runs all the way round the topmost level, but it's hardly a fortification – the machicolations look suspiciously like a Classical cornice.

The **interior**, dolled up with the usual miscellany of period and reproduction furnishings and tapestries of all eras, doesn't add much to the experience, but the grand staircase is worth seeing close up. The medallions of the kings and queens of France on the first flight are nineteenth-century additions, while those in the loggia above date from the sixteenth century, depicting kings, philosophers and possibly Gilles Berthelot and his Blésoise wife Philippe Lesbahy. The ground floor was refitted by the **Marquis de Biencourt**, the château's owner in the nineteenth century, with the obligatory library and billiard room. The **gardens** are another of Biencourt's additions, fashionably styled as an English landscaped park.

Azay's **nocturnal spectacle**, "Songes et Lumières" (July & August daily; early Sept Fri & Sat only; €9, or €12 with daytime château entry), is one of the region's better efforts. Beginning at nightfall (times vary from 9pm to 9.45pm), elaborate lighting and sound effects transform the château into the centrepiece of a fantasy world, with fantastic creatures projected onto the facade. You can wander freely round the grounds admiring the spectacle from all angles, while being serenaded by loudspeakers hidden behind bushes.

St-Symphorien

Relatively few visitors make the effort to visit the **église St-Symphorien** (daily 9am–7pm), though it's right next to the château and its western front is adorned with one of the strangest and most compelling bits of stonework in the region, a rare survival of the **Carolingian renaissance** of the ninth century. High above the main door, two rows of strange, doll-like statues stand impassively below triangular patches of lozenge-shaped stones that seem to mimic roofs. The whole thing looks like a facade within a facade, but sadly the lower row of figures was rudely cut through by a window in the thirteenth century, when the current church was built. The crossed halo of the central figure in the upper row indicates Christ, but the identities of the other statues are disputed. Curiously, the saints on Christ's left have halos, while the figures on the right – perhaps disciples of St-Symphorien – have none. The nave aisle on the left of the main facade, with its beautiful wide door, was added in 1578.

Eating and drinking

For something simple, *La Salamandre*, a **restaurant** and pizzeria with a terrace overlooking the main square, will serve, but you'll do much better at *La Ridelloise*, 24 rue Nationale (☎02.47.45.46.53; menus €11–33), which has a pleasant stone-and-beams setting matched with a family atmosphere and excellent-value cooking. For a really special meal out, make for ✱ *L'Aigle d'Or*, 10 ave Adélaïde Riché (☎02.47.45.24.58; menus €24–60; closed Wed & Sun evening), which serves elegant and sometimes inspired cuisine in its delightful garden, shaded by a catalpa tree; lots of dishes come in sauces of local wine, and bottles are reasonably priced. At *Les Grottes*, 23ter rue de Pineau (☎02.47.45.21.04; menus €24–44; closed Thurs lunch & Wed), you can eat good regional specialities in a troglodyte cave carved out of the rock, but it's touristy and slightly overpriced.

Other options dot the countryside around Azay-le-Rideau: of especial note are *L'Auberge du XII Siècle*, in Saché (see p.112) and the restaurants in Bréhémont (see opposite).

Around Azay-le-Rideau

I found infinite love written in the long ribbon of water streaming in the sun between two green banks, in the rows of poplars adorning this vale of love with their flickering lacework, in the oak trees rising between the vineyards on the ever-changing slopes that the river rounds off, and in the shadowy horizons shifting athwart each other.

Honoré de Balzac, *Le Lys dans la Vallée*

Around Azay-le-Rideau, the shy **River Indre** lies mostly concealed by thickets of willows and poplars, or hidden in the middle of wide water meadows that soak up the regular floods. You'll only actually see the river when you cross it, which you can do at Azay-le-Rideau, or downstream at marshy **Marnay** where there's a giant museum of motor vehicles. The gardens at nearby **La Chatonnière** make the most of the well-watered, sunny climate. Southwest of Marnay, the Indre makes a dogleg and begins to parallel the line of the Loire, less than a kilometre away. The broad, shared floodplain is overlooked to the south by the wooded heights of the Forêt de Chinon (see p.120), at the edge of which stands the fairy-tale **château d'Ussé** and the village of **Rivarennes**, where a rustic technique for drying pears is still practised. Elsewhere in the Indre valley, it is apples that dominate. The swathes of **orchards** – growing Golden Delicious, for the most part – are at their best in late spring, when the trees blossom. Upstream of Azay-le-Rideau, you can visit the cave-village of **Les Goupillières** on the way to another Indre bridge at **Saché**, where Balzac had his summer writing retreat. Nearby, a tiny, willow-rich tributary valley conceals the village of **Villaines-les-Rochers**, a miniature centre for basket-weaving.

The tourist office in Azay-le-Rideau offers a free leaflet showing three well-signposted **cycle routes** covering this area. The circuits range from 34–55km – fairly manageable on a bike, even if you're not much used to it.

Downstream of Azay-le-Rideau

Four kilometres from Azay-le-Rideau, just off the D57, which runs west along the right bank of the Indre, lie the exceptional **gardens** at **LA CHATONNIÈRE** (mid-March to mid-Nov 10am–7pm; €6; ⓦ www.lachatonniere.com).

The setting alone – in a fold of the valley, under the shadow of a private Renaissance château – is gorgeous, while the gardens themselves are a showpiece for French-style design. Master gardener Ahmed Azéronal has developed nine gardens (so far) since 1995, all following carefully considered themes. Among the most enticing are the Jardin de l'Elégance, set around lawns with statues and ponds; the Jardin des Sens, with hundreds of tea roses – at their best in May and early July; the Jardin de l'Abondance, a *potager* of endless varieties of vegetables beautifully presented in a leaf-shaped area; and the Jardin des Sciences, made up of medicinal herbs. Behind it all are six hectares of wildflowers appropriately named the Jardin de l'Exuberance.

If you follow the Indre downstream from Azay-le-Rideau, along the D57 then D120, after 6km of lovely backroad motoring you'll reach **MARNAY** and the **Musée Maurice Defresne** (daily: Feb, March, Oct & Nov 10am–6pm; April–Sept 9.15am–7pm; €10; ⓦ www.musee-dufresne.com). This giant collection of motorized vehicles, especially tractors, was brought together by M. Dufresne himself, a successful local manufacturer of tractor trailers and dealer in agricultural implements. There are endless tractors, of course, but also scooters, cars, planes and motorized ploughs, plus a British double-decker bus, Blériot's 1909 plane, a working turbine watermill and even a Revolution-era guillotine. It's magical or interminable, according to your point of view: there always seem to be local grandads showing their grandchildren round, but you probably need to be something of a petrol-head to really enjoy it, or get a shiver of nostalgia when you see a 1930s Massey-Ferguson.

West of Marnay, a spit of watery land separates the Indre and Loire rivers. Less than a kilometre west of Marnay the D7 crosses over to the south bank of the Indre, but you can follow a sideroad (the D119) north for two kilometres, re-crossing the Indre on the way to the handsome village of **BREHEMONT**, which basks on the south bank of the Loire, its broad quays testifying to its long-vanished status as a significant river port. This beautiful stretch of the Loire can be explored on pedalo-type tandem canoes, the Aquacycles de Bréhémont (Easter–Oct ⓣ06.71.64.67.22, ⓦ www.loirevelonature.com; €25–30, under-12s €15). The main draw is not so much the boats themselves, though they are charming – designed for exploring mangrove swamps, apparently – or even the delicious picnic of *rillettes*, goat's cheese and Loire wine, but the bilingual commentary on the Loire wildlife supplied by the naturalist guides. Excursions leave three times a day, at 9am, 2pm and 6pm, and last three hours. The evening trip is probably the most satisfying, when sunset lights up the river, birds settle on the sandbanks and it's often possible to see beavers.

Bréhémont has a modest but good little **hotel-restaurant**, La Clé d'Or (ⓣ02.47.96.70.26; ❷). The rooms are plain but clean, but the main draw is the restaurant's riverfront situation – outdoor tables allow you to enjoy simple local cuisine overlooking the Loire itself (menus €18–24).

If you ignore the Bréhémont turn-off and continue on the D7 from Marnay towards Rigny-Ussé, after 3km you'll come to the pretty village of **RIVAR-ENNES**, where the inhabitants have revived a bizarre local speciality: "hammered pears". An old barn houses the tiny, co-operatively run **Musée des Poires Tapées** (April & May daily except Mon 2–6.30pm; June–Sept daily except Mon 10am–12.30pm & 2–6.30pm; July & Aug daily 10am–12.30pm & 2–6.30pm; €2.50), where you can find out how the pears are traditionally dried in ovens and "tapped" to check their moisture content. A video describes how the technique died out in the 1930s but was successfully revived in the late 1980s, and you can taste and buy the actual product – it's amazing cooked with duck, or steeped in wine and sugar.

Rigny-Ussé

With its shimmering white towers and terraced gardens, the **château d'Ussé** (daily: mid-Feb to March & Sept to mid-Nov 10am–6pm; April–June 10am–7pm; July & Aug 9.30–7pm; €11; Ⓦ www.chateaudusse.com) is the quintessence of a fairy-tale castle – so much so that it's supposed to have inspired Charles Perrault's classic retelling of the **Sleeping Beauty** myth, *La Belle au bois dormant*. The château lies on the edge of the village of **RIGNY-USSÉ**, 14km west of Azay-le-Rideau, as the Indre approaches its confluence with the Loire.

The exterior is beautiful, a late-fifteenth-century vision of white turrets and machicolations largely built by Antoine de Bueil, comte de Sancerre, who married the illegitmate daughter of Charles VII and Agnès Sorel (see p.129). The inner courtyard was once closed by a fourth wing, demolished in the seventeenth century to improve the picturesque view. Unfortunately, the **interior** isn't as compelling as you might expect, and hardly worth the swingeing entrance fee. The signposted visit begins with the Oriental collections of a nineteenth-century duc de Blacas – the ancestor of the present proprietors, then proceeds to the old chapel, now fitted out as an aristocratic drawing room full of tapestries and furnishings from across the centuries, including a rare Mazarin-style desk inlaid with lemon wood. Next come the vaulted kitchens and a long, tapestry-lined eighteenth-century gallery, then a rather fine iron-balustraded staircase designed by François Mansard. On the first floor, the so-called King's Bedchamber has some choice eighteenth-century wall-hangings of Tours silk.

The outbuildings are more interesting. You can ascend the stairs of the tall **round tower**, where the attic rooms are populated by dressed-up dummies illustrating the story of Sleeping Beauty – a hit with younger and perhaps more

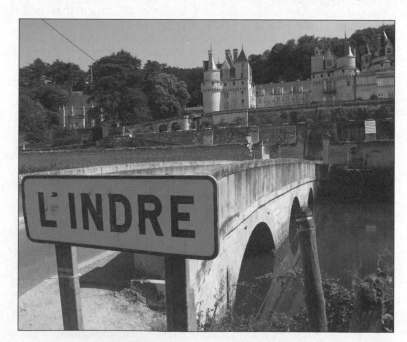

△ L'Indre at Ussé

sentimental children. The perfect little Renaissance **chapel**, shaded by ancient cedars, is definitely not to be missed. Its pale tufa stone is graced by Classical-style decorative stonework, while inside you can admire a classic Lucca della Robbia enammelled terracotta Virgin, and fine choir stalls carved by the greatest French Renaissance sculptor, Jean Goujon.

Practicalities

The **village** is little more than a few houses stretching along the road, but there's a very welcoming family-run hotel, *Le Clos d'Ussé* (℡ & ℻ 02.47.95.55.47; ❸), which offers eight simple, old-fashioned rooms; the hotel restaurant is inexpensive and homely. Set in a tranquil, wooded fold of the valley behind the château, the ⚑ *Domaine de la Juranvillerie*, 15 rue des Fougères (℡ 02.47.95.57.85, ⓦ www.lajuranvillerie.com; ❸), is a charming little group of cottages, one housing a simple, attractive **chambre d'hôtes** with a bedroom upstairs and a dining room below (the medieval-themed table d'hôte costs €28) – which can also be rented out weekly as a gîte. The friendly owners are enthusiastic naturalists and can advise on walks in the Forêt de Chinon. To get there, take the D7 east of Ussé and turn right after about 2km at the signpost; it lies just beyond the ruined abbey of **Turpenay**.

La Vallée Troglodytique des Goupillières

As the D84 backroad passes out of Azay-le-Rideau, heading east, it's overshadowed on the left by low, creamy cliffs riddled with **caves** used as storehouses, wine *caves* and even homes – one of which offers chambres d'hôtes (see p.105). These chambers are the modern-day remnants of the region's fascinating *troglodyte* (cave-dwelling) traditions, which can be explored at the fascinating complex of **LES GOUPILLIÈRES**, 3km from Azay-le-Rideau (April–Nov Mon–Fri 10am–7pm, Sat & Sun 2–7pm; €4; ⓦ www.troglodytedesgoupillieres .fr). The "**troglodyte valley**" is actually a paddock-like area depressed five or six metres below the level of the surrounding farmland, its outer edges burrowed away to create cave farmhouses, barns, grain silos and even a cave rabbit-hutch.

The whole "village" was hacked out of the soft tufa rock by hand over hundreds of years, new rooms and dwellings being added – or rather subtracted – as need arose. It was gradually abandoned around a hundred years ago, but has been rediscovered and re-excavated by a knowledgeable local family, who now run the guided tours with infectious enthusiasm. They also keep goats, hens, ducks, geese and even pot-bellied pigs, making the site feel more like a well-tended, working farm than a sterile archeological dig. In one of the more ancient caves you can see the niches used for silkworm production – the silk is sold at Tours. Another was used in medieval times as a refuge from marauding bands of mercenaries and soldiers; as you're shown the false tunnel leading to a **murder-hole**, the real tunnel plunging deeper underground to a chamber big enough for all the village and its animals, the insecurity of peasant life is shockingly brought home.

Saché

Continuing east from Les Goupillières on the D84, you pass the hamlet of **LA SABLONNIÈRE**. Just to the north, on top of a hill surrounded by vines, with beautiful views of the Indre valley, was the last *atelier* of **Alexander Calder**, sculptor of mobiles and "stabiles". Calder also worked at **La Chevrière**, just down the slope to the east.

One of the artist's toy-like mobiles decorates the main square of **SACHÉ**, 8km from Azay-le-Rideau. However, it is **Honoré de Balzac** rather than Calder who draws the pilgrims to Saché, as the writer often stayed at the small château, describing it as "a melancholy abode full of harmonies". He sought peace and inspiration here, though complaining that "there's no peace living in a château. People come to visit and you have to dress at a particular time. Provincial people find it very odd that anyone should want to miss dinner in order to pursue an idea." He nevertheless managed to write several of his 91 novels at Saché, notably *Le Père Goriot* and *Le Lys dans la Vallée*. The sixteenth- and seventeenth-century manor house has been turned into the **Musée Balzac** (daily: April–June & Sept 10am–6pm; July & Aug 10am–7pm; Oct–March 10am–12.30pm & 2–5pm; €4.50, grounds only €2), with lots of imprints, caricatures and bits of manuscripts. The most compelling rooms are those decorated in full, florid nineteenth-century style, preserved or restored exactly as they were when Balzac stayed here. The vestibule is heavy with the sound of a grandfather clock, the dining room thickly carpeted and painted with lurid, mint-green walls, and the walls of the *salon* decorated imperial-style with swags of painted cloth apparently hanging from lion's-face medallions. Upstairs, in Balzac's writing room and bedroom, a crucifix hangs over his cot-like bed; adjacent, his writing desk stands next to the window and the view across the valley.

Saché has a top-class gastronomic **restaurant**, ☕ *L'Auberge du XII Siècle* (☎02.47.26.88.77; closed Sun eve, Tues lunch & Mon). The setting in an old, heavily beamed tavern is wonderful and the menus, which range from €30 to €65 are inventive and good value; book in advance.

Villaines-les-Rochers

Six kilometres south of Azay-le-Rideau is the troglodyte village of **VILLAINES-LES-ROCHERS**, famous for its wickerwork co-operative, set up in 1849 by the local curate to keep the village economically sustainable. It's a weird place, tucked into an enclosed valley bristling with pollarded willows, and there are now seventy-odd *vanneries* (wicker workshops) in and around the village – wickerwork signs seem to hang from every house. You can visit the **Musée de la Vannerie** (May, June & Sept daily except Mon 2.30–6.30pm; July & Aug Tues, Sat & Sun 2.30–6.30pm, Wed–Fri 11am–1pm & 2.30–6.30pm; €3), which has surprisingly interesting exhibitions on the theme of wickerwork and willow, and buy baskets, chairs and so forth from the **Coopérative de Vannerie**, 1 rue de la Cheneillère (daily: April–June, Sept & Oct 9am–noon & 2–7pm; July & Aug 9am–7pm; mid-Oct to March 10am–noon & 2–7pm; Ⓦwww.vannerie.com), or at one of the many *vanneries* dotted around the village. Many are dug into the rock, providing the perfect humid conditions for keeping the willow supple.

Chinon

You could be forgiven for thinking that **CHINON**, 52km southwest of Tours, was still a Plantagenet fief. More than 100,000 tourists visit each year, ten times the local population, and an unusual proportion of them are English. The physical attractions are obvious – the huge ruined castle, the medieval streets, the noble situation on the banks of the smooth Vienne, the excellent local vineyards – but many Chinonais believe that something deeper is at work, an abiding sense that Chinon, for all its quintessential provincial Frenchness, is in some way part of the English patrimony. Increasingly, it actually is: scores of the fine old manor houses in the countryside round Chinon now belong to English people, both holiday-makers and permanent residents.

Arrival and information

The train line from Tours and Azay-le-Rideau passes through the beautiful, thickly wooded Forêt de Chinon before terminating at Chinon's **gare SNCF**, which lies to the east of the town. From here, ave Pierre Labussière and rue du 11-Novembre lead to the **gare routière** on the large place Jeanne-d'Arc, ten minutes' walk away, at the eastern edge of the old town. Keep heading west, either along the riverbank or across place Mirabeau into rue Rabelais, and you'll soon reach the old quarter. The **tourist office** is on place d'Hofheim, off the central rue Jean-Jacques Rousseau (May–Sept daily 10am–7pm; Oct–April Mon–Sat 10am–noon & 2–6pm; ℡02.47.93.17.85, ⓦwww.chinon.com), and can provide addresses of local vineyards where you can taste Chinon's famous red wine.

If you plan to visit a number of sights in the region, consider buying the Pass' Découverte Ouest Touraine, a leaflet that gives **reductions** of a euro or two off the entry tickets to many châteaux and other sites in western Touraine, especially in the Chinon region. You can pick it up free at any participating attraction, though you pay the first entry fee at the full rate.

An antiques and flea market takes place on the third Sunday of every month, while regular **market day** is Thursday. On the south bank of the Vienne, just beside the campsite, Chinon Loisirs Activités Nature (℡06.23.82.96.33) rents out **canoes** and kayaks from April to September, and runs half-day and full-day guided trips. **Bathing** in the Vienne near Chinon is discouraged, as it's potentially dangerous due to collapsing sandbanks and freak currents.

Accommodation

Chinon has an excellent selection of **hotels**, and there are some enticing **châteaux** offering accommodation in the countryside around. For a full list of chambres d'hôtes, including châteaux, contact the tourist office. The **campsite**, *Camping de l'Ile Auger* (℡02.47.93.08.35; closed mid-Oct to mid-March), overlooks the old town and château from the south bank of the Vienne.

Chambres d'hôte Cheviré 11 rue basse, Savigny-en-Véron, 10km from Chinon ℡02.47.58.42.49, ⓦperso.orange.fr/chevire. This delightful bed-and-breakfast sits in the heart of the peaceful Véron countryside west of Chinon. The charming owners have tastefully converted the grange adjoining their stone house, leaving exposed stone walls and wooden beams in the two main rooms. Antique furnishings and fresh flowers make the finishing touches, and guests can use the kitchen. A third, inexpensive room with a bathroom across the corridor isn't quite as nice. ❸

Château de Coulaine Beaumont-en-Véron, 6km from Chinon ℡02.47.93.01.27. Superb late-medieval château with an oversized tower and three simple chambres d'hôtes. The owners make excellent wines and there's a large park to stroll in. Closed mid-Nov to mid-March. ❹

Château de Danzay Near Avoine, 5km north of Chinon ℡02.47.98.44.51, ⓦwww.chateaudedanzay.com. This miniature medieval castle could almost be a large farmhouse poshed up with a turret and Renaissance windows. As a hotel, it's a real hideaway gem. There are only seven rooms, with rich, medieval-stye colour schemes, stone walls, huge fireplaces, four-poster beds tucked under the roof beams and lots of luxurious little touches. Outside, there's a heated swimming pool and expensively manicured gardens. Prices begin at €180. Closed Oct–April. ❾

Hôtel Agnès Sorel 4 quai Pasteur ℡02.47.93.04.37, ⓦwww.agnes-sorel.com. The hotel's situation by the main road along the riverbank, at the western edge of the old town, lacks atmosphere and is awkward for the train station, but it's very clean and welcoming inside. The two

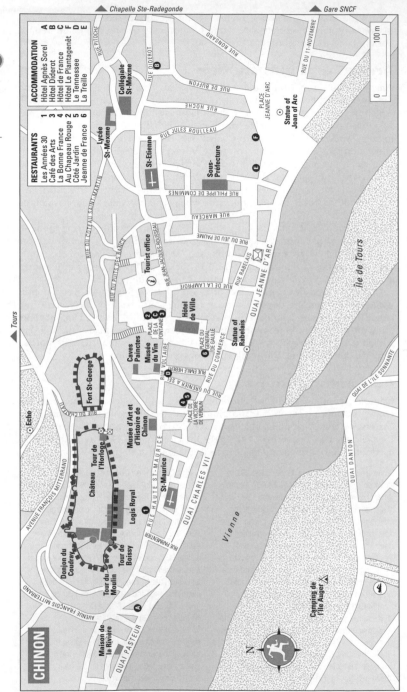

CHINON

▲ Chapelle Ste-Radegonde   ▲ Gare SNCF

RESTAURANTS
Les Années 30   1
Café des Arts   3
La Bonne France   4
Au Chapeau Rouge   2
Côté Jardin   5
Jeanne de France   6

ACCOMMODATION
Hôtel Agnès Sorel   A
Hôtel Diderot   B
Hôtel de France   C
Hôtel Le Plantagenêt   F
Le Tennessee   D
La Treille   E

0   100 m

▲ Tours

Collégiale St-Mexme
Lycée St-Mexme
St-Etienne
Sous-Préfecture
Statue of Joan of Arc
Place Jeanne d'Arc
Tourist office
Caves Painctes
Musée du Vin
Hôtel de Ville
Statue of Rabelais
Fort St-George
Musée d'Art et d'Histoire de Chinon
Château   Tour de l'Horloge
Logis Royal
St-Maurice
Donjon du Coudray
Tour de Boissy
Tour du Moulin
Echo
Maison de la Rivière
Camping de l'Ile Auger

RUE PITOCHE
RUE DIDEROT
RUE DU 11-NOVEMBRE
RUE RONSARD
RUE DE BUFFON
RUE HOCHE
RUE JULES ROULLEAU
RUE PHILIPPE DE COMMINES
RUE MARCEAU
RUE DU JEU DE PAUME
RUE JEAN JACQUES-ROUSSEAU
RUE DE LA LAMPROIE
RUE RABELAIS
QUAI JEANNE D'ARC
RUE DU PUITS DES BANCS
RUE DU COTEAU SAINT-MARTIN
RUE VOLTAIRE
RUE EMILE HERBIER
RUE DU GRENIER A SEL
RUE DU COMMERCE
PLACE DE LA FONTAINE
PLACE DU GENERAL DE GAULLE
PLACE DE LA VICTOIRE DE VERDUN
RUE HAUTE ST-MAURICE
RUE PARMENTIER
QUAI CHARLES VII
AVENUE FRANÇOIS MITTERRAND
QUAI PASTEUR
RUE DU CHATEAU
Vienne
Île de Tours
QUAI DE L'ILE SONNANTE
QUAI DANTON

Île de Tours

Vienne

N

more expensive rooms in the annexe (**6**) have nice balconies overlooking a little courtyard, while other rooms are modern but reasonably tasteful. Bikes are rented to all-comers. **3**

🏃 **Hôtel Diderot** 7 rue Diderot
☏02.47.93.18.87, ⓦ www.hoteldiderot.com. Solidly bourgeois hotel hidden away in a venerable townhouse in the quiet, historic streets just east of St-Mexme church. It has some grand old rooms with antique furnishings in the main building (**4**), and some brighter modern ones in the annexe, which fronts pretty floral terraces. Offers an old-fashioned welcome and an excellent breakfast. **3**

Hôtel de France 47–49 place du Général de Gaulle ☏02.47.93.33.91, ⓦ www.bestwestern.com/fr/hoteldefrancechinon. The historic town-centre hotel, with wrought-iron balconies overlooking the top part of the leafy main square, known locally as place de la Fontaine. Best Western welcomes you on the doormat, but five hundred years of hotel history still manage to cut through the corporate sheen, and the standards are high. Rooms are attractive and cosy, with big comfy beds, beams and exposed stone walls, and only the occasional bit of cheap repro wood to spoil the effect. Some rooms have a partial view of the château, but prices depend on size and whether you go for a bath (**5**) or shower. **4**

Hôtel Le Plantagenet 12 place Jeanne d'Arc ☏02.47.93.36.92, ⓦ www.hotel-plantagenet.com. Decent two-star hotel on the large market square on the eastern edge of town. Rooms in the main, nineteenth-century house are pleasantly decorated, some with wooden beams and floorboards – the three on the top floor have views of the château. Those in the annexe at the end of the garden are rather characterless, but have the bonus of air-con. Family rooms available. **3**

Manoir de la Giraudière Beaumont en Véron, 5km from Chinon ☏02.47.58.40.36, ⓦ www.hotels-france.com/giraudiere. This rural hotel spreads around various old buildings set in peaceful, spacious grounds. Many of the two dozen rooms preserve old chimneys and roof beams, and they're all well furnished and comfortable. At the centre of the whole operation is a refined and fairly formal restaurant. **4**

Manoir de la Tesserie Le Vieux Bourg, Cravant-les-Côteaux, 9km from Chinon ☏02.47.93.39.96, ⓦ www.tesserie.fr.st. Two top-class chambres d'hôtes in a lovely fifteenth-century manor house at the edge of the village, with private grounds and a small swimming pool. **5**

Le Tennessee 11 rue Voltaire ☏02.47.93.02.85. Three basic but acceptable rooms tucked away on the second floor above a Tex-Mex bar and restaurant. It's a good budget choice, as it's right in the centre of the old town. **2**

🏃 **La Treille** 4 place Jeanne d'Arc ☏02.47.93.07.71. Tiny, spartan and full of character. A handful of clean and very simply decorated rooms – wood-effect lino, white walls, old shutters – are shoehorned onto the first floor of this ancient building. Below is a friendly local bar and restaurant run by a husband-and-wife team; *monsieur* looks after the cooking (see review on p.119). Book well in advance, as there are just four rooms. **2**

The Town

The spectacular line of **towers and ramparts** rearing up on the high ridge behind town look as if they must enclose one of the best of this region's châteaux, but for centuries now, almost all has been ruined within, the result of neglect – and local borrowing of ready-dressed masonry. At the time of writing, however, the most important section of the château, the Logis Royal was being partially rebuilt. During the works, which are expected to continue until 2008 at least, the château's skyline won't be as romantic as it once was, but you will be able to access the site and watch traditional craftsmen at work. It should be fascinating, but if a building site isn't high on your wishlist there'll still be the château's **dramatic history** to ponder, and the fine view of the grey walls and roofs of the medieval town below, crammed in between the heights of the cliffs and the broad River Vienne.

The château

A fortress of one kind or another has existed at Chinon since the Stone Age, but it was under the overlordship of **Henri Plantagenet**, who became king of England as Henry II, that the heart of the medieval **château** was built. Henry also added the **Fort St-Georges** to the east, isolating it from the main body of the château by a dry moat, and the round **Tour du Moulin**, at the far west end of the escarpment. Chinon became the setting for the most tragic events of Henry's life. It was from here that his son Henry, the "Young King", fled to the court of the French king Louis VII, an act which kickstarted the rebellion of Henry's wife **Eleanor of Aquitaine** (see box on p.256) and their younger son Richard the Lionheart. When Henry crushed the rebels in 1174, he is thought to have imprisoned Eleanor at Chinon. Fifteen years later, the wheel had turned: defeated by the unholy alliance of Louis VII's son Philippe-Auguste and his own son Richard, Henry died at Chinon in 1189 (see box on p.102). It didn't take long for Richard to fall out with his French ally, and local legend claims that he breathed his last in Chinon after being wounded in a battle in 1199, though he was probably dead on arrival.

The Plantagenet lands passed to Henry's youngest son, John, who presided over the final humiliation: after a year's siege in 1204–05, Philippe Auguste finally took the castle and put an end to Plantagenet rule over Touraine and Anjou. To assert his mastery, he bolstered the exterior walls with towers and erected the central **Donjon du Coudray**. He also dug a deep, dry moat between the main body of the château and the fortifications on the west side, which thus became the separate **Fort du Coudray**. Chinon now seemed truly impregnable: a castle sandwiched between two satellite fortresses. Apparently, the defences still weren't enough: in the middle of the fourteenth century, the exceptionally tall, narrow **Tour de l'Horloge** was added to guard the east gate.

When Charles VII met **Joan of Arc** in the grande salle of the Plantagenet-era **Logis Royal**, in 1429, (see box below), Chinon's defensive security must have been welcome: Charles was a king on the run. By the time he and Joan had finished with the English (see box on p.191), however, the château's role could change. In the second half of the fifteenth century the Logis Royal was enlarged and improved with a second storey and high, Gothic windows. Sadly, few

---

The miracle at Chinon

During the Lenten fast of 1429, the Dauphin Charles was sequestered at Chinon, one of the few strongholds left to him by the English in the disastrous aftermath of Agincourt. It was a bleak time for the French cause, but everything changed at a stroke with the arrival of a peasant girl from Lorraine, **Joan of Arc**, who somehow talked her way into meeting Charles. The usual story, repeated everywhere, is that Charles's courtiers set up a test by concealing him anonymously among the assembled nobles, but Joan miraculously picked him out straight away. It sounds more like a conjuring trick than an epoch-changing miracle and turns out to be based only on an eyewitness report that "when the king learned that she was approaching, he withdrew behind the others, but Joan recognized him perfectly, bowed to him and spoke to him for some minutes". Another tale claims that Joan revealed herself as Charles's illegitimate half-sister, and revealed details of a dream he'd had about his own legitimacy – but this is just royalist fantasy.

Joan herself told a different and far more powerful story. Interrogated in prison, she claimed that the king received a sign that made him believe in her. Under pressure from her inquisitors, she revealed that the sign was "beautiful, honourable and good", and later confessed that an angel appeared – a real one that "stepped on the ground" and "entered the room by the door" – and gave a golden crown to the archbishop of Reims, who in turn gave it to Charles. Perhaps she was talking about herself. In any case, the symbolism could hardly have been clearer, and it wasn't lost on Charles, who finally set about recovering his kingdom. For more on Joan, see the box on p.191.

monarchs thereafter chose to enjoy it, and Chinon fell into disuse, becoming little more than a military arsenal. Successive rulers tried to have it demolished, including Henri III, who feared it would be occupied by Huguenot rebels, and **Cardinal Richelieu**, who became the owner of the château in 1632. Contrary to the local legend that he promptly stole the stone for his own château (see p.125), Richelieu seems to have done little more than dismantle the grande salle – which remains ruined – and lop the tops off the defensive towers.

Ever since locals started carting off the stone in the early nineteenth century, the **château** (during works opening times may vary, but the standard hours are daily: April–Sept 9am–7pm; Oct–March 9.30–11.30am & 2–5.30pm; €3) has been little more than a ring of tumbledown walls and broken towers – albeit one of the most impressive such rings in France, if not Europe. The finest and most intact building, the **Logis Royal**, is being partially rebuilt under a new roof, with works expected to continue at least until the end of 2008. The **grands** and **petits comblés** will recover their fifteenth-century appearance, complete with brand-new roofs built in local, seasoned oak and tiled in Angevin slate. The famous grande salle will remain a ruin, however, its generous first-floor fireplace continuing to project futilely over empty space. The **Fort St-George**, to the east, is being rebuilt as a modern visitor centre.

Access will be permitted throughout the restoration works, so you will be able to watch stonemasons shaping shining new tufa, and roofers and other traditional artisans at work alongside the cranes and diggers. An exhibition will explain the techniques involved. All in all, it's likely to be more interesting than the peaceful but rather heartless shell that existed before, though the success of the plans for the interiors remains to be judged: the current project imagines an interactive medieval experience complete with sound-effects and wafting odours of spices.

The interior walls of Philippe-Auguste's **Donjon du Coudray**, over to the west, are covered with intricate thirteenth-century graffiti carved by imprisoned Knights Templar, who awaited burning here after their dangerously wealthy and powerful quasi-monastic order was smashed by Philippe IV "le Bel", in 1307. Works are in progress to reconstruct the original first-floor entrance, and allow access to the topmost, defensive level – which should offer excellent views. The grim lower-ground level, with its stone-vaulted roof, will be accessed once more by a staircase in the thickness of the wall. To the east, over the main gate, the **Tour de l'Horloge** looks set to continue to house an eccentric little museum of Joan-related odds and ends.

Rue Voltaire to the river

The heart of town is **place du Général de Gaulle**, overlooked by the town hall and set out with café tables under the false acacias. At its foot is the river and the town's statue of local hero **Rabelais** (see p.121), slumped louchely atop his marble pillar. At the top end of the square is **place de la Fontaine** – named after a cast-iron statue of the three Graces – which gives onto steep stone stairs leading up to the château.

Leading east, **rue Voltaire** is lined with half-timbered and sculpted townhouses – look out for nos. 10 and 12, which date from the fifteenth century, and the old salt-storage house at no. 20. It's best to skip the tacky wine- and barrel-making museum, the Musée du Vin, with its second-rate animated coopers, but the tour of the so-called **Caves Painctes**, just off rue Voltaire (July to mid-Sept Tues–Sun 11am, 3pm, 4.30pm & 6pm; €3) is moderately diverting, though the paintings suggested by the name are long vanished, if they ever existed – no one's sure. There's little inside now except a dark tunnel, a fountain lined with

The echo

If you take the road leading up between the château and Fort St-George, then turn down the small, seemingly private lane that doubles back alongside the Clos de l'Echo vineyard, you'll come to a small, overgrown vantage point after about 200m, signalled by what must be the oddest road sign in France – "**ICI L'écho**" – pointing through a hedge roughly in the direction of the high walls of the château. Try it: your voice comes back bright and hard off the château's walls.

Local tradition uses the timing of the echo to deliver a misogynistic rhyme: "Les femmes de Chinon sont-elles fidèles?", you ask – "ELLES?", the echo replies. "Oui, les femmes de Chinon", you confirm – and back comes the riposte, "NON!" ("Are the women of Chinon faithful?"; "THEM?"; "Yes, the women of Chinon"; "NO!")

two thousand-odd empty bottles and a huge, hollowed-out space used for local weddings and the functions of the local wine guild, but you get a glass of wine at the end of the tour.

At the end of rue Voltaire, beyond a series of beautiful fourteenth- and fifteenth-century houses, is the lovingly kept **Musée d'Art et d'Histoire de Chinon**, 44 rue Haute St-Maurice (June–Sept daily 10.30am–12.30pm & 2–6pm; Oct–May Mon–Fri 2.15–6pm; €3), where the Etats Généraux met in 1428 to raise the funds for Joan of Arc's mission of reconquest. The highlights of the museum's small collection are the **Chape de St-Mexme**, a chasuble-like Sassanid (Persian, roughly sixth-century) garment with a design of multiple leopards that was probably spoil from the Crusades, and a powerful bas-relief of the Crucifixion from the eleventh-century, with Christ's head framed by images of the sun and moon. Stairs lead up to a vaulted upper room where Delacroix's portrait of a fruity-looking Rabelais looks down on a collection of nineteenth-century crockery – *faïence*, to be exact – from Langeais.

Ancient **rue Haute St-Maurice** – though this section of the road is still known locally as rue Voltaire – passes below the walls of the château's *logis* as it gradually slopes its way down towards the river. Just set back from the riverbank, at the western limits of town, the summer-only **Maison de la Rivière**, 2 quai Minster (July & Aug Tues–Fri 10am–12.30pm & 2–5.30pm, Sat & Sun 3–5.30pm; €3; ☎02.47.93.21.34, Ⓦwww.cpie-val-de-loire.org) celebrates the once-thriving Loire shipping industry with lots of detailed models of the many kinds of strange, narrow sailboats and steamships, and a full-size cutaway *fûtreau* – a traditional kind of sailboat built by a local craftsman. On weekend afternoons in summer, you can even take a 45-minute trip (€6) on a traditional *fûtreau* or *toue* (large punt), and staff lead regular guided nature walks.

St-Mexme and the Chapelle Ste-Radegonde

The eastern side of town is much quieter and less touristy. **Rue Jean-Jacques-Rousseau**, with more half-timbered houses, leads past the tourist office and the **église St-Etienne**, a fifteenth-century affair with a beautiful Flamboyant Gothic portal, on its way to the **collégiale St-Mexme**. Only the west tower and a half-shell of the nave remain of what was once an important Romanesque church, and it's only just possible to make out heavily weathered geometric and floral patterns, and what may be a figure of Christ. Rue Hoche runs down to the river at place Jeanne d'Arc, an expanse of tarmac designed in the nineteenth century to accommodate the **weekly market**, which still takes place here on Thursdays, with delicious fresh food stalls open till midday and lots of less enticing stands selling cheap clothing, accordion music, hunting hats and the like right through the day. The square is dominated by an extraordinary equestrian **sculpture of Joan of Arc** in mid-charge, all flying hooves, sword and standard, which was given to the town by its sculptor, Jules Roulleau, in 1893.

Evidence of Chinon's renowned sunny micro-climate can be seen on the north side of the square, where one of the town's many palm trees flourishes behind the high walls of the odd-looking Lycée St-Mexme. A lane, rue Pitoche, leads east past this school, climbing slowly and then contouring along the cliffs past numerous **troglodyte dwellings**, some of which are still inhabited. After a kilometre or so the path peters out at the **chapelle Ste-Radegonde**, a rock-cut church which is part of a complex of cave dwellings once occupied by hermits. Sainte Radegonde was a sixth-century German princess who renounced the world and her husband – probably not a great sacrifice, since he eventually murdered her brother – in order to devote her life to God. The chapel's guardian has lived in the troglodyte house next door for nearly thirty years and often takes visitors into the chapel and caves behind – check with the tourist office in advance, or ask politely. High on one wall of the chapel, a captivating **painting** depicts a horseback cortege of regal figures, probably the Plantagenet royal family. It's uncertain whether it celebrates the marriage of King John in 1200 or marks the end of **Eleanor of Aquitaine**'s captivity in Chinon (see box on p.256). The leading figure is probably Henry II, followed by his wife Eleanor (crowned, centre) and their daughter Jeanne, followed in turn by their sons Richard the Lionheart (receiving a falcon, which may symbolize his succession to the duchy of Aquitaine) and John Lackland. Dated to the end of the twelfth century, it may be the only contemporary portrait of Eleanor in the world – not counting the effigy on her tomb in Fontevraud.

Eating and drinking

There aren't as many **restaurants** in Chinon as you might expect. Some have gone for the touristy medieval theme in a big way, but if you choose carefully you can find an excellent and not overpriced meal.

Les Années 30 78 rue Haute St-Maurice, aka rue Voltaire ☎02.47.93.37.18. Tiny, cosy restaurant with a bar in the corner in the old-fashioned way. Serves reliable *cuisine bourgeoise*, with one or two more adventurous dishes. Menus at €23 and €36. Closed Wed.

Café des Arts place du Général de Gaulle. The food isn't anything special – salads and brasserie fare, mostly – but it's a pleasant place to have a drink or a simple meal out on the square.

La Bonne France 4 place de la Victoire de Verdun ☎02.47.98.01.34. Something of a local secret, tucked away on a tiny old square just behind the bridge. Offers good-value menus at €14.50, and has a nice terrace out on the square. There's also an excellent value weekday lunch menu at €9 and an evening menu at €22. Closed Thurs evening & Wed.

Au Chapeau Rouge 49 place du Général de Gaulle, ☎02.47.98.08.08. One of the best restaurants in Chinon, with an inviting situation on the "place Fontaine" part of the main square and lots of outside tables. Indoors is a bit more formal, with white tablecloths. Specializes in local ingredients, including fresh, wild Loire fish, *poires tapées* from Rivarennes and of course Chinon wines. Menus at €26, €37 and €55. Closed Sun evening & Mon.

Côté Jardin place de la Victoire de Verdun, ☎02.47.93.10.97. Menus €13–25. The food isn't terribly special – big, hearty salads and classic French meat dishes, mostly – but the courtyard garden setting makes it very popular with foreign visitors.

Jeanne de France 12 place du Général de Gaulle. Sometimes you don't want eel stewed in Chinon wine, you want pizza – and this pizzeria-crêperie at the lower end of the main square (with outside tables) does good ones. Prices range from €8 to €11.

La Treille 4 place Jeanne d'Arc ☎02.47.93.07.71. Utterly old-fashioned hotel restaurant with wooden tables and a sparse but homely decor. The speciality is wild plants, and you may find your salad laced with flower petals and herb-like leaves. Otherwise the cooking is careful and homely. Expect to pay around €30, plus wine. Closed Wed, and Thurs evening.

The Chinonais

The countryside around Chinon, the **Chinonais**, was made famous by Rabelais as the setting for the Picrocholine wars of his satirical epic, *Gargantua*. It's the epitome of a Loire landscape: northeast of Chinon lies the ancient **Forêt de Chinon** while to the west is the soft **Pays du Véron**, a slice of rural land squeezed between the Loire and Vienne. Over on the southern bank of the Vienne lies the rich countryside made mythical by **Rabelais**, whose birthplace you can visit at **La Devinière**. But the main sights of the Chinonais lie to the east, up the Vienne, whose northern bank rises to low tufa cliffs riddled with caves, some of them still used as wine cellars, storage rooms or even houses. The ruined churches at **Tavant**, with its Romanesque wall-paintings, and **L'Île Bouchard** may draw you upstream, and you could continue up the peaceful **Manse** valley towards the relatively bleak plateau of **Ste-Maure-de-Touraine**, which divides the western and eastern parts of southern Touraine. Just north of Ste-Maure, the impressive church at **Ste-Catherine-de-Fierbois** is a little-known stop on the Joan of Arc circuit.

Forêt de Chinon and Pays du Véron

Northeast of Chinon, the elevated terrain of the *landes* is covered by the ancient **Forêt de Chinon**, crisscrossed by roads and forest alleys that make for delightful cycling or walking – the GR3 long-distance footpath runs right through from Chinon to Azay-le-Rideau (see p.104). Even the rail route from Azay is superb. If you want to **stay** in the area, there's a good **chambres d'hôtes** near Rigny-Ussé (see p.110). Just outside St-Benoît-la-Forêt, the village in the heart of the forest, is a woodland adventure park, **Saint-Benoît Aventure** (Easter school holidays daily 1.30–7pm; May & June Sat & Sun 10am–7pm; July & Aug daily 10am–8pm; Sept & Oct Sat & Sun 1.30–7pm; children under 8 years €8, under 13 years €13, under 16 years €16; adults €20; ☎06.89.07.18.96, ⓦwww .stbenoitaventure.new.fr). It offers a chance to let kids off the leash – or rather attach them to it, in the form of an alarming aerial ropeway assault course that threads its way through the trees. There's also a mountain bike circuit and a nature walk.

The west is far more tranquil. The **Pays du Véron**, between the Loire and Vienne rivers, feels like the softly beating heart of the Loire landscape. It's an especially lovely corner of the region, characterized in the east, between Huismes and Chinon, by fields and vineyards interspersed with *puys*, or low, rounded chalk hills. The relatively dry soil of these *puys* – they're raised above the flood plain – allows them to be topped with stands of oak and pine, with orchids, anemones and Mediterranean-type herbs like rosemary and sage growing among the grasses. In the west, towards Savigny-en-Véron and the confluence of the Loire and Vienne, the narrow meadows of the floodplain are fringed by hedgerows of ash and pedunculate oak – a classic Loire landscape known as *bocage*. Unfortunately, this rich ecological idyll is somewhat overshadowed by the nuclear power station near **Avoine**, a nightmarish vision of futuristic 1960s design. As if to compensate, Avoine does have one of the better outdoor **swimming pools** in the region, complete with water-slide.

In the furthest corner of the Pays du Véron, the sleepy village of **SAVIGNY-EN-VERON**, 7km west of Chinon, hosts the **Ecomusée du Véron** (April–Sept daily except Tues 10am–12.30pm & 2–6pm; Oct–March 9am–12.30pm & 2–5pm, Sat & Sun 2–7pm; €3.50; ⓦwww.cc-veron.fr/ecomusee), a museum with exhibitions on local wine-making in history, traditional lace caps and the ecology of the Loire's flood zone. It also runs excellent guided nature walks in summer, and gives out leaflets showing the routes of the many signposted walking circuits in the area.

The Maison Rabelais at La Devinière

The sixteenth-century monk, doctor, humanist, *bon viveur* and writer **François Rabelais** was probably born at his family's manor farm of **La Devinière**, 6km southwest of Chinon. Local tradition holds that he was born on the road from Chinon, however, and Rabelais' most famous work, the very loosely autobiographical *Gargantua*, suggests he was actually born in a nearby willow grove – but then, it also famously claims that Gargantua entered the world clamouring for wine, "climbing through the diaphragm to a point above the shoulders where this vein divides in two, he took the left fork and came out by the left ear. As soon as he was born he cried out, not like other children: 'Mies! Mies!' but 'Drink! Drink! Drink!'" (see p.343).

The manor house itself is modest, fitting Rabelais' father's station as a lawyer in Chinon, and the main attraction is inside, where there's an excellent but dry **museum** (April–June & Sept Mon & Wed–Sun 10am–12.30pm & 2–6pm; July & Aug daily 10am–7pm; Oct–March Mon & Wed–Sun 10am–12.30pm & 2–5pm; €4,50; ⓦwww.musee-rabelais.fr) dedicated to the writer's life and works. You'll need to speak French or be familiar with *Gargantua* and *Pantagruel* to get the most out of the exhibits, as the museum is dominated by old texts, plus a few portraits and engravings and a couple of roughly reconstructed rooms. The countryside around is beautiful, the gentle slopes lined with vines, and true Rabelais enthusiasts will want to imagine it as Grandgousier's monstrously inflated kingdom. The château of Le Coudray-Montpensier, on the other side of the valley beyond Seuilly, is private and cannot be visited.

Tavant

The more attractive road east of Chinon runs along the rocky right bank of the Vienne, but the southern route, along the flat D760, has the advantage of passing through **TAVANT**, 16m from Chinon. Roughly 100m back from the main road, a little jewel-box of a church, **St-Nicolas** (March–Nov Wed–Sun 10am–12.30pm & 1.30–6pm, closed first Sun of every month; €3), shelters an extraordinary collection of **Romanesque wall-paintings** in a **crypt** that ranks among the finest in Europe. It's an extraordinary claustrophobic space, thick with four pairs of columns, its vault almost entirely covered with 27 early twelfth-century images. Many scenes show a subtle mastery of captured movement. Two of the most enigmatic figures frame the entrance, both holding lilies; they're clearly important, as the finely sculpted capitals below indicate, but their identities remain obscure. In fact, it's hard to know why this crypt should have been so richly painted at all, as it hasn't been identified with any major relic cult or tomb – though the chapel was associated with a priory, whose remnants survive on the other side of the main road.

It's thought that the entire structure, inside and out, would once have been painted in bright colours, but today only fragments of mid-twelfth-century paintings survive in the upper church, as well as a giant figure of Christ in Majesty on the half-dome of the apse. Fine stone carving remains on the west portal, however, and on the capitals of the crossing, where griffons are matched with sirens, two-bodied monsters and a tree with a serpent. If the chapel isn't open when you arrive, ask for the guardian at the nearby Mairie.

L'Ile-Bouchard

The island referred to in **L'ILE BOUCHARD**, 18km east of Chinon, turns out to be a bland car park of a square encircled by two branches of the river Vienne. The more interesting features of this little town lie on either bank. Roughly 500m south of the island centre lies the melancholy ruin of the **Prieuré St-Léonard**. The apse is all that's left of an eleventh-century priory church, standing in a grassy enclosure under a practical little modern roof and looking like a broken-down theatrical backdrop. The astonishing stonework is remarkably well preserved, however, especially the lovingly sculpted scenes from the life of Christ, clearly visible on both sides of the capitals. The gate is always open to visitors and you may well be joined by the site's guardian, who lives in an adjacent house and gives out explanatory leaflets.

On the north side of the river, in the village-like centre of town, the little **église St-Gilles** was the scene of a meticulously documented miracle that took place over six days in December 1947, when the Virgin and the Angel Gabriel repeatedly appeared to four local schoolgirls, one of whom, now a retired teacher, still lives in the village. The Virgin apparently commanded the girls to pray for France – to be rescued from Communism, according to local interpretation – and to build a special golden grotto of an Annunciation scene, a triumph of kitsch that now stands in the north aisle of the church, the focus of veneration by scores of pilgrims every day.

Practicalities

A couple of places on the fringes of town offer pleasant **chambres d'hôtes**. On the road in from Ste-Maure-de-Touraine, the *Moulin de Saussaye* (☎02.47.58.50.44; ❸) has simple, inexpensive rooms dotted around the old farm and watermill buildings, but the main draw is the simple but excellent farm **restaurant** (open weekends and most evenings in summer – ring to check; menus for under €20), serving fresh duck and chicken dishes straight from the farm in a very welcoming, homely atmosphere. Halfway up the wooded bluff to the south of town – follow the signs off the road to Champigny-sur-Veude for about 1km – the ⚜ *Château de la Commanderie* (☎02.47.58.63.13, ⓦwww .lacommanderie.com; ❸) is set in a grand old house with an appealingly rustic atmosphere created by exposed stone walls and floorboards; the friendly owners also do a table d'hôte (€25 with wine) on reservation.

The island at the centre of L'Ile Bouchard has a good **restaurant**, *L'Auberge de l'Ile* (☎02.47.58.51.07; menus from €25; closed Tues & Wed), though the dining room is unprepossessing, despite the river view. The *Auberge du Val de Vienne*, 6km west of the village on the road to Chinon, at Sazilly, (☎02.47.95.26.49; menus from €25; closed Sun eve & Mon), has a similarly sophisticated menu, but a more invitingly rustic atmosphere.

The lower Manse valley

The willow- and mill-lined **Manse valley**, which slopes away from the Vienne at L'Ile Bouchard towards the plateau of Ste-Maure, is one of the more bucolic corners of Touraine, its gentle rises populated by sleepy villages, woods and tiny vineyards. The attractive village of **CRISSAY-SUR-MANSE**, 8km from L'Ile Bouchard, is dotted with medieval and Renaissance mansions built in more energetic days and now occupied by wealthy refugees from the cities. Behind high walls you can just see the remains of the château which once belonged to the wealthy Turpin-de-Crissé family, while the church at the bottom end of the village has some beautiful Flamboyant Gothic windows.

On the western side of the village, at the junction with the C2 to Crouzilles, a signposted road threads 2km north across the undulating countryside to **ROCHES-TRANCHELLION**, where you can explore the ruins of an early sixteenth-century **collegiate church** – look for the steps leading up beside a farmhouse with hundreds of exotic caged birds in the courtyard. The west front preserves some fine Renaissance chisel-work.

Ste-Maure-de-Touraine

For most visitors, **STE-MAURE-DE-TOURAINE**, 18km east of L'Ile Bouchard, means little more than a roadside stop on the thundering N10 highway, though Ste-Maure-de-Touraine is also the quality-controlled name of one of the region's best-known **goat's cheeses**, distinguished by its flattened cylindrical shape and the straw running down the middle. There is a small, reasonably attractive old centre on the hill above the road, with an old covered market sporting seventeenth-century carved doors, a small château housing a museum of local history and a heavily restored church. If you want to look round the modest local **museum** (€3.85) – there's a tasting of local wine and goat's cheese at the end – you have to ask for an accompanied visit at the **tourist office**, next door to the château (Feb, April–June, Sept & Oct Tues–Sat 10am–noon & 2–6pm; March & Nov–Jan Mon–Fri 2–5pm; July & Aug Mon–Sat 9am–noon & 2–6pm ☎02.47.65.66.20). Staff can also give advice on visiting local **goat farms** and can sometimes be persuaded to lead tours of the church's Romanesque **crypt**.

An infrequent **bus** service (line #H) makes the trip from Tours via Ste-Catherine-de-Fierbois. There's little reason to stop at any of the string of **hotels** lining the main road, but some 4km west of Ste-Maure-de-Touraine, near Noyant-de-Touraine, the fifteenth-century 🏕 *Château de Brou* (☎02.47.65.80.80, 🌐www.chateau-de-brou.fr; ❽) is worth going out of your way for. It has been converted into a romantic and very luxurious three-star hotel, set at the end of a long drive among 100 hectares of wooded grounds. Each of the dozen rooms is beautifully and very carefully decorated with bright, chintzy fabrics and furnishings that range from the old and handsome to the plain eccentric.

The **Manse valley** (see opposite) continues southeast past Ste-Maure-de-Touraine; if you're heading east towards Loches, consider travelling via the troglodyte village of **Les Côteaux**. A delightful back road, the C3, passes neat vegetable plots, grazing goats, tumbledown cave cottages and endless poplar trees on its way to the village of **Sepmes**, 7km southeast of Ste-Maure-de-Touraine.

Ste-Catherine-de-Fierbois

Seven kilometres north of Ste-Maure-de-Touraine, the fifteenth-century church at **STE-CATHERINE-DE-FIERBOIS** is bizarrely impressive for such an inconsequential little village. The first chapel here is supposed to have been established by Charles Martel after his historic defeat of a Moorish army in 732, a battle that turned the tide of the Moors' northward thrust from Spain. Seven hundred years later, **Joan of Arc** (see box on p.191) slept at the chapel and heard three Masses the following morning – St Catherine was especially precious to her as one of her "voices" – before continuing to Chinon. Two months later Joan ordered her aides to return to collect a sword "marked with five crosses" that she assured them would be hidden behind the altar – probably left there as a votive offering by a soldier. It became one of her most powerful symbols, but was shattered and lost – the legend goes – when Joan beat a prostitute with it after the defeated attack on Paris.

The size and importance of the existing **church** is entirely due to an archbishop of Tours who acted for Joan at her rehabilitation trial and erected this church in her memory. The wide vault is eye-catching, and fine scraps of Flamboyant Gothic carving decorate the doors on either side of the altar, but the *pièce de résistance* is the recently restored west front.

Once you've looked at the **statue of Joan** in the square and the facade of the adjacent **Maison du Dauphin**, built in around 1415, there's nothing else to do except have a meal or a drink at the homely *Auberge Jeanne d'Arc* (☎02.47.65.68.61; menus €16–24; mid-May to mid-Sept closed Mon; mid-Sept to mid-May closed all weekday evenings, and Sat). If you're moving on towards Chinon, take the back roads via St-Epain (the D101) and down the Manse valley (the D21).

Richelieu and around

RICHELIEU, 24km south of Chinon, is an extraordinary place. If it wasn't for the ambitions of Cardinal Richelieu, it would look more like what it really is, a small, provincial town of no particular pretensions. In the 1630s, though, the Cardinal decided to celebrate his new status as a top-rank nobleman by creating what the brown-nosing poet La Fontaine was to call "the most beautiful village in the universe", with a château to match. He rushed the initial work through in less than a dozen years and then ran out of steam.

The nexus of town is the perfectly symmetrical **Grande Rue**, lined with 28 noble townhouses. Although they are almost identical inside and out, the houses were actually put up by individual speculators attracted by – or arm-twisted into supporting – the Cardinal's scheme, and willing to follow the exact building specifications of his architect, Jacques Lemercier. Several have plaques outside with brief biographies of their original owners. No. 15, named after one Louis Barbier, houses the little **Musée du Chat** (May to mid-Sept Mon & Wed–Sun 2.30–6pm; mid-Sept to April Mon & Wed–Sun 2–3pm; €4). Even if you're not interested in modern cartoon-caricatures of Richelieu's fourteen cats (which apparently went everywhere with him), or cat-related stamps, books and objects, or even the four real moggies that roam the house, it's well worth visiting for the chance to look round the almost untouched interior, which preserves the stipulated layout. A sixteen-metre-long central passage, which has its obligatory "large room with a fireplace" on one side and "kitchen with a cellar and pantry" on the other, leads through to a 56-metre-long garden.

The townhouse at number 28 has been converted into a small **exhibition** space (July & Aug daily except Tues 2–6pm; first two weeks of Sept Sat & Sun 2–6pm; €2), with a permanent display on the vanished château (see opposite). In the absence of the real thing, one has to award points for effort: there are even 3D images to help get across a sense of what was lost.

The Grande Rue terminates at each end in a perfectly quadrangular square closed by a grand gate. The more impressive of the two is the southern square, **place du Grand Marché**, framed on either side by a huge **covered market**, whose high roof is supported by a fantastically timbered chestnut-and-oak frame, and the **church**, built in a frigid but nevertheless awe-inspiring version of the Baroque style. The roads that run east and west off the square, rue de Loudun and rue des Halles, apparently end in two more gates, but one of them is actually a blind, backing onto the little river Mable. The northern square, **place des Religieuses**, is more modest, its pollarded plane trees and parking spaces frowned over by former conventual buildings.

The layout of the old town still fits within a perfect grid, surrounded by high walls and a moat, but sadly only the two squares and the Grande Rue are really grand, the rest of the town's houses only having been built in succeeding, and less ambitious, centuries. The greatest tragedy to befall Richelieu's modest tourist industry, however, is the loss of its **château**, whose absence is as palpable as a missing limb as you pass through the impressive **Porte de Châtellerault**, at the southern end of the Grande Rue, across the circular place du Cardinal and into a huge and empty park. Built at the same time as the town, the château was absolutely vast, only rivalled in scale and ambition by Louis XIV's Versailles, which was begun some thirty years later. Its disappearance is the result of Richelieu's heirs selling it off in the aftermath of the Revolution to a contractor who quarried it for ready-cut stone. You can see reproductions of engravings of the château in the tourist office, or get a dim sense of what it must have been like if you enter the 480-hectare **park** (daily: April–Oct 10am–7pm; Nov–March 10am–6pm; free), where a single pavillion, the **"Dôme"**, and part of the Orangerie survive. The rest of the park is given up to avenues of trees and meadows, with a deer-hunting forest behind. Bizarrely, the whole thing belongs to the University of Paris. In summer, you can rent **boats** (daily: mid-June to Sept €2.50/hr) and splash about on the remnants of the canal; **bikes** are also rented out here.

Practicalities

The skeletal school bus service runs during term time only, so you'll need your own **transport** to get around the surrounding area of the Richelais. The **tourist office**, 7 place Louis XIII (April–Oct Mon–Sat 9am–12.30pm & 2–5.30/6pm; Nov–March Mon, Tues, Thurs–Sat 9am–12.30pm & 2–5.30pm; ☎02.47.58.13.62, ⊛www.cc-pays-de-richelieu.fr), can provide lots of information on Richelieu and the country around, and produces an excellent free booklet in English, *Round and About the City of the Cardinal*.

Richelieu has a lovely **chambres d'hôtes**, *La Maison*, 6 rue Henri Proust (☎02.47.58.29.40, ⊛www.lamaisondemichele.com; ❻), a beautifully decorated early nineteenth-century house with four spacious, high-ceilinged rooms with polished wood floors set around a grand old staircase and hall, and a large garden behind. The long-standing town **hotel**, *Le Puits Doré*, 24 place du Marché (☎02.47.58.16.02; ❹), occupies a prominent corner of the main square; the rooms are newly renovated, with some pretty ones under the roof beams; the **restaurant** serves traditional bourgeois fare. A reliable alternative for an evening meal is the *Auberge Le Cardinal*, 3 rue des Ecluses (☎02.47.58.18.57; menus from €12), facing the park gates.

Champigny-sur-Veude

Like Richelieu, 7km south, **CHAMPIGNY-SUR-VEUDE** is missing its château, which was destroyed on the orders of the Cardinal himself – as popular legend would have it, he wanted to ensure nothing competed with his own palace. Running alongside the main road, the old château walls still guard substantial sixteenth-century *communs* and the oversized white stone buttresses and steeply pitched roof of the **chapelle St-Louis** (May Sat & Sun 2.30–5.30pm; June Wed–Sun 2.30–5.30pm; July & Aug Mon–Fri 2.30–6pm, Sat & Sun 10am–12.30pm & 2.30–6pm; Sept Mon–Thurs, Sat & Sun 2.30–5.30pm; €4), which possesses some of the finest Renaissance **stained-glass windows** in France. The chapel's architecture is an odd mix of Gothic and Renaissance, but the windows follow a purer later style, having been were fitted by local master glaziers in the latter half of the sixteenth century. The uppermost tier depicts scenes from the Passion and Resurrection, the middle row follows the life of St Louis and the lower level acts as a portrait gallery for the Bourbon-Montpensier family, who owned the château. The highlight is the apse, filled with a staggering Crucifixion scene of three powerfully muscular figures set against a deep blue sky.

Château du Rivau

Their shape is perfectly medieval, but the white-stone towers and conical turrets of the **château du Rivau** (May & Oct Wed–Sun 2–7pm; June & Sept Mon & Wed–Sun 10am–12.30pm & 2–7pm; July & Aug daily 10am–7pm; €8; Ⓦwww.chateaudurivau.com), 11km north of Richelieu, have had such a good clean-up that they look almost new. All this effort aims to provide a suitable backdrop for the **gardens**, which have been developed as a whimsical attraction in recent years.

The ambitions of the project are obvious as soon as you walk past the lavender knot garden, through the gates and into the ancient *basse cour*, which is lorded over by a high gatehouse keep and filled by the **potager de Gargantua**, in which giant vegetables are brought on through late summer and autumn. Beyond lies the austerely medieval château, which is plain and empty inside. The main attraction is the **garden**, which features an arbour of climbing roses, an orchard and a fantastical forested area littered with modern sculptures such as giant wooden legs apparently running through the forest, little gardeners entirely made of terracotta pots and lovers' benches watched over by poetic quotations. One corner is devoted to children, with gnomes, toadstools and fairy-tale creatures hiding among the shrubs.

South and east of Richelieu

The hilltop village of **FAYE-LA-VINEUSE**, 7km south of Richelieu, once had a population of over 10,000 and stood behind high walls like a medieval Tuscan town. The walls are gone, but the village still has a handsome setting, with a number of fine old houses in the narrow streets of the village centre. The chief relic of grander days is the twelfth-century **collégiale St-Georges**, which has some fascinating carved capitals in its large crypt.

Deep in the countryside some 20km east of Richelieu, the twelfth- to fifteenth-century **Abbaye de St-Michel** at **BOIS–AUBRY**, 3km southeast of Luzé, is largely a romantic ruin, though a dramatic fifty-metre-high belfry and a serenely vaulted Romanesque chapterhouse still stand, along with various Gothic fragments. Monks returned in 1978 to set up a small community, and they now offer ten simple **chambres d'hôtes** (℡02.47.58.34.48; ❷), equipped with bunk beds, which attract occasional overnight visitors and Christians on retreat.

Loches

LOCHES, 36km southeast of Tours, is the obvious place to head for in the southeastern part of Touraine. Its walled **citadel** is by far the most impressive of the Loire Valley fortresses, its unbreached ramparts and the Renaissance houses below still partly enclosed by the outer wall of the medieval town. Tours is only an hour away by bus or train, but Loches makes for a quiet, relatively untouristy base for exploring the Cher valley, or the much lesser-known country along the Indre and Indrois rivers.

Arrival and information

From Tours, trains and buses alike arrive at the **gare SNCF** on the east side of the Indre, just up from place de la Marne, where the **tourist office** is housed in a little wooden chalet (April–June & Sept Mon–Sat 9.30am–12.30pm & 1.30–6.30pm, Sun 10am–12.30pm & 1.30–6pm; July & Aug Mon–Sat 9am–7pm, Sun 10am–12.30pm & 1.30–6pm; Oct–March Mon–Sat 10am–12.30pm & 2.30–6pm; ☎02.47.91.82.82, ⓦwww.loches-tourainecotesud.com).

Accommodation

Most visitors to Loches come on day-trips, so the **accommodation** options are fairly limited. Loches' three-star **campsite**, *Camping La Citadelle*

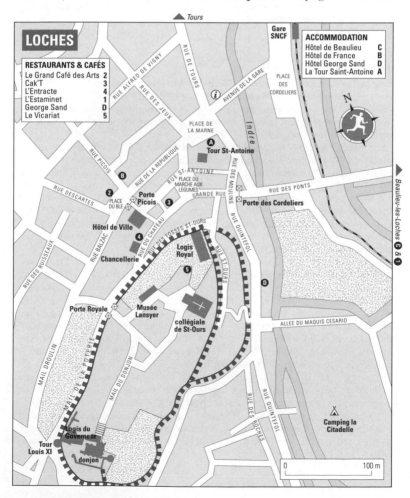

(☎02.47.59.05.91, ⓦwww.lacitadelle.com; closed mid-Oct to mid-March), is situated between two branches of the Indre, by the swimming pool and stadium, looking up at the east side of the citadel.

Hôtel de Beaulieu 3 rue Foulques Nerra, Beaulieu-lès-Loches ☎02.47.91.60.80. Charming, tumbledown sixteenth-century house right next to the abbey, with just nine plain old rooms. It's an independent-spirited place, and often closed in the afternoons, so be sure to ring in advance. **➋**

Hôtel de France 6 rue Picois, near the Porte Picois ☎02.47.59.00.32, ⓦwww .hoteldefranceloches.com. Friendly, pleasantly old-fashioned posthouse hotel with parking in the small courtyard out back. The bedrooms are welcoming and full of character, mixing fine original features like chimneys and wooden windows with good quality repro furniture. Closed Sun evening & Mon, except in July and Aug. **➌**

Hôtel George Sand 37 rue Quintefol ☎02.47.59.39.74, ⓦwww.hotelrestaurant -georgesand.com. This much-rebuilt fifteenth-century coaching inn sits between the eastern ramparts of the citadel and the Indre. The facilities are good – it has three stars – and the best rooms are at the back, looking onto the river. **➎**

La Tour Saint-Antoine 2 rue des Moulins ☎02.47.59.01.06, ⓦwww.latoursaintantoine.com. Looks like a large, tourist-oriented hotel from the outside, with lots of flags fluttering over the large, roadside restaurant, but the welcome is warm when you arrive and the simple rooms are good value. **➋–➌**

The lower town

The isolated, sixteenth-century **Tour St-Antoine** stands sentinel over the wide, central **place de la Marne**, at the foot of the old town. Everything looks dull and modern down here, but things quickly get better, Loches' onion-skin-like layout meaning that as you penetrate each layer of town walls the buildings get more and more impressive.

From the place de la Marne, rue de la République slopes up to the miniature **place du Blé**, where the town's two main cafés face each other across the square. Just to one side, a secretive, tunnel-like gateway leads under one of the town's two surviving fifteenth-century towers, the **Porte Picois**, and into the old town proper. This is a tiny area, but very attractive, with narrow cobbled streets falling away from the main axis of rue du Château and the Grande Rue. On market days (Wednesday and Saturday mornings), these streets thrum with locals shopping for fruit, vegetables and lots of local produce, notably goat's cheeses, pâtés and the like.

A number of the old town's Renaissance mansions are worth a closer look. The tall **Hôtel de Ville**, abutting the inner side of the Porte Picois, was built under François I and still has his distinctive salamander symbol carved over its windows. Over on rue du Château, check out the curious scene of an archer confronting a centaur carved high on the end wall of the so-called **House of the Centaur**, and the beautiful Italiante details on the facade of the adjacent **Chancellerie**. The latter houses a good exhibition on the history of Loches (daily: March, April, Sept & Oct 10.30am–12.30pm & 2.30–5pm; June–Aug 10am–12.30pm & 1.30–6pm; free), with lots of engravings and old town plans, with explanations in English. A special exhibition (€5) of some dodgy seventeenth-century copies of works by Caravaggio – "discovered" in a local church and claimed as "possibly" original – looks set to run and run. Rue du Château continues up to the mighty twelfth-century gatehouse known as the **Porte Royale**, the main entrance to the citadel, while the Grande Rue slopes down to the **Porte des Cordeliers**, down by the River Indre.

The citadel

The **citadel of Loches** is a remarkable relic: a miniature town, complete with elegant private houses, all entirely enclosed behind high fortifications. The modern world is largely banished to the outside of these walls, and as you walk along the cobbled streets it's easy to conjure Loches' medieval heyday. At the near end of the citadel, overlooking the modern town, is the graceful Logis Royal. From here a long avenue, the Mail du Donjon, stretches back past the grey Collégiale de St-Ours to the ruined – but still lofty – *donjon*, or keep, at the far, southern end.

Turn left just after the Porte Royale for the **Musée Lansyer** (April–Oct daily except Tues 10.30am–12.30pm & 2.30–5pm; €3), which occupies the house of local nineteenth-century landscape painter Emmanuel Lansyer. Despite briefly studying under Gustave Courbet – too briefly, perhaps – his paintings are nothing to write home about, but there are some pleasant local landscapes and the museum's rooms are attractively decorated in period style.

Collégiale de St-Ours

A few steps beyond the Musée Lansyer lies the **collégiale de St-Ours** (same hours as château, though sometimes closes earlier in the evening; free). Its distinctively eccentric roof-line looks like the spiny back of a prehistoric animal, its two octagonal stone pyramids, called *dubes*, lined up between a pair of relatively conventional spires. In essence it's a Romanesque structure, built in the eleventh and twelfth centuries as a kind of private chapel for the counts of Anjou, but it has one or two extremely early Gothic features, notably the Plantagenet vault of the porch. Inside the porch, the west portal is elaborately carved with all manner of humans, animals and monstrous figures, and preserves traces of its original bright paint. Look out for the allegories of the seven Liberal Arts on the outer arch, under the figures of the Virgin Mary and the Magi. In the nave, the hollow octagonal vaults grab most of the attention, with their strange, fish-scale-like decoration on the triangular pendentives. But the church's highlight is the shining white **tomb of Agnès Sorel**, the mistress of the Dauphin Charles VII. She had the good fortune to own a manor at Beauté-sur-Marne as well as one at Loches, thus giving her the title of "La dame de Beauté" (the Lady of Beauty). If her effigy, a beautiful recumbent figure tenderly watched over by angels, does her justice, the title was well deserved. The alabaster is rather more pristine than it should be, as it had to be restored after anticlerical Revolutionary soldiers mistook her for a saint – an easy error to make. Elsewhere in the church, there are a handful of ornately sculpted capitals to examine, as well as the stoup, or basin for holy water, which was once a Gallo-Roman altar.

For three weeks in August you can follow a night-time **son-et-lumière** circuit around the citadel, watching fancy light projections and performers acting out historical scenes (Fri & Sat and occasional other days from 10pm; €11, children 6–12 years €6).

The Logis Royal

The northern end of the citadel is occupied by the **Logis Royal**, or royal lodgings, of Charles VII and his three successors (daily: Jan–March & Oct–Dec 9.30am–5pm; April–Sept 9am–7pm; €5, €7 including the *donjon*). It has two distinct halves, similar at first glance, but separated by a century in which the medieval need for defence began to give way to a more courtly, luxurious lifestyle. The first section, the **Vieux Logis**, was built in the late fourteenth century as a kind of pleasure palace for the Dauphin Charles and Agnès Sorel. A copy of Charles's portrait by Fouquet can be seen in the antechamber to the **Grande Salle**, where in June 1429 the Dauphin met the second woman of importance in his life: Joan of Arc, who came here victorious from Orléans to give the defeatist Dauphin another pep talk about coronations. The chamber today has been dressed in late medieval style, with a bare terracotta floor under the roof beams, and various weapons, chests and tapestries against the pale stone walls.

A doorway leads through from here to the second part of the *logis*, the **late-fifteenth-century wing**. In the first room hang two copies of portraits of Agnès Sorel by which you can judge her famous beauty. One depicts her as a regal Madonna, surrounded by strange red cherubs, while the other shows her more intimately, in drabber garb; bizarrely, her bared breast – in both pictures – was no artist's fantasy, but a courtly trend set by Agnès herself. The **triptych** that dominates the next room is an original work of 1485 painted for the Chartreuse du Liget (see p.132) by an unknown artist working within the School of Tours. It's a brilliantly coloured and splendidly composed Crucifixion scene with a strong Flemish influence. Beyond lie the two rooms of Anne de Bretagne's **oratory**, whose every surface is carved with Franciscan knotted tassels and the stylized ermines' tails of Brittany, the homeland of Charles VIII's wife (see box on p.97). Originally, they would have been painted silver against a black background. Works to restore the oratory – and limit access so that you can only peer in from outside – are due to take place in 2008.

The donjon

From the Logis Royal, cobbled streets overlooked by handsome townhouses wind through to the far end of the elevated citadel, where the **donjon** (same hours as Logis Royal; €5, €7 including Logis Royal), begun by Foulque Nerra, the eleventh-century count of Anjou, stands in grim ruin. Vertiginous gantry

△ Loches *donjon*

stairways climb up through the empty shell of the massive **keep** to its very top, but the main interest lies in the dungeons and lesser towers.

After the Logis du Gouverneur, which now houses the ticket office, you come to the **Tour Louis XI**, or Tour Ronde, built under Louis XI to provide a platform for artillery. It also served as a prison for Louis XI's adviser, Cardinal Balue, though the most dungeon-like room, underneath, was probably used for storing grain. Instead, Balue was kept locked up in a wooden cage (a reproduction hangs over the courtyard outside) in one of the upper rooms, perhaps the extraordinary **graffiti chamber** on the second floor, which is decorated with an enigmatic series of deeply carved, soldier-like figures apparently wearing top hats, which are linked together almost all the way round the walls like a paper chain. There's also a small but elaborate altar-cum-shrine. It's not known when either was carved – perhaps the thirteenth century, or even earlier.

From the courtyard, steps lead down into the bowels of the **Martelet**, which became the home of a more famous prisoner: Ludovico "Il Moro" Sforza, Duke of Milan, patron of Leonardo da Vinci and captive of Louis XII. In the four years he was imprisoned here, he found time to decorate his cave-like cell with ruddy wall-paintings that are still faintly visible, though nothing like as impressive as they once were, to judge by the reconstructed drawing on the plaque. The dungeons peter out into quarried-out galleries which produced the stone for the keep.

Beaulieu-lès-Loches

The ancient suburb-village of **Beaulieu-lès-Loches** is a little-visited place, despite being only 1km from the centre of Loches, on the other side of the Indre. Its parish church is built into the ruins of the **Abbaye de la Trinité**, a Benedictine abbey church built to house the bones of Foulque Nerra, the dreaded count of Anjou who also established the keep at Loches. A twelfth-century belfry still towers over the ruins of the Romanesque nave, which was damaged by fire in the fourteenth and fifteenth centuries. The monks simply rebuilt, using stones from the original, creating the stark Gothic church that now seems to prop up the ruins. You can take a stroll round the back of the whole structure, catching glimpses of some Romanesque chapels and the wonderful stone carving on the gable of the ruined north transept, which seems to depict a hunting scene.

Eating and drinking

For a drink or a simple **meal**, either of the simple café-brasseries on the central place du Blé makes a reasonable choice: *Le Grand Café des Arts* is slightly more elaborate, but still has an appealingly local character. In the old town, *Cak'T*, 6 Grande Rue, offers all kinds of teas, coffees and cakes in a bright, homely setting. For something more substantial, *L'Entracte*, 4 Grande Rue (☎02.47.94.05.70, closed Sun; menus from €10) does hearty, generous bistro food, with excellent, substantial salads, and has a lovely courtyard out back. Over in Beaulieu-lès-Loches, there's an inexpensive but excellent little bistro right next door to the abbey, *L'Estaminet* (menus €8–12; closed Mon). The restaurant at the *Hôtel de France*, 6 rue Picois (menus €18–50) is fairly formal but serves good, sometimes imaginative regional specialities. The hotel-restaurant at the *George Sand*, 37 rue Quintefol (menus €17–44), can be patchy but has a lovely, sunny dining terrace overlooking a weir on an arm of the River Indre. If you aren't put off by the waiters in medieval costume, *Le Vicariat*, next to the château on place Charles VII (☎02.47.59.08.79; closed Mon & Sun eve; menus €19–43), can be fun; it offers some fascinating – sometimes delicious – re-creations of medieval recipes, and has a great outside terrace.

The excellent **market** takes place in the winding streets just above the château gate on Wednesday and Saturday mornings.

The Lochois

For once, the most interesting sights in the **Lochois**, the region around Loches, don't lie along the river. In a modest way, the **River Indre** is certainly pretty, dotted with watermills and old villages, but you're better off making forays into the remnants of the ancient **Forêt de Loches**, which covers the modest uplands between the Indre and Indrois, immediately east of town. Here you'll find a quartet of monastic buildings. On the far side of the forest, astride the little River Indrois, **Montrésor** is famously one of the prettiest villages in the Loire region, with its still-inhabited château and Renaissance church. North and east lies sparsely populated land that has only partially been reclaimed from the forest. Bizarrely, the one-horse hamlet of **Nouans-les-Fontaines** is the guardian of a rare fifteenth-century masterpiece, which hangs in its church, while the **château de Montpoupon**, isolated in a woodland clearing to the north, possesses a less surprising attraction – a museum dedicated to hunting.

The Forêt de Loches

Only a remnant survives of the **Forêt Domaniale de Loches**, but it's still a large and forbidding swathe of ancient woodland, and seems to close in on the D760 as it motors east from Beaulieu-lès-Loches. The presence of a quartet of half-ruined religious buildings only adds to the forest's brooding feel. The first you come to as you head east from Loches is the oddly circular chapel of **St-Jean-du-Liget**, standing in a wheat field surrounded by forest, roughly 300m off the main road. The beautiful series of wall-paintings inside depicts scenes from the life of Christ, along with a Tree of Jesse and various saints. They date from around 1180, though the chapel itself may be even older.

To get inside to see them, you may need to call in first at the **Chartreuse du Liget**, 1km further along the road, its incongruous eighteenth-century gateway topped by a bas-relief of the dynamic, cross-wielding figure of St Bruno, the founder of the strict Carthusian order. The *chartreuse*, or charterhouse, was founded by Henry II Plantagenet in order to atone for the murder of Thomas Becket, but nothing remains of the original abbey church besides a pile of ruins surrounded by eighteenth-century outbuildings, now in private hands. If you want to have a proper look round, or visit St-Jean-du-Liget, you need to ask the owner and purchase a small explanatory leaflet (€0.50): knock at the door on the left of the main building, indicated by a small plaque (official hours are daily 8am–6pm, but there's not always anybody there, so it's best to ring in advance on ☏02.47.92.60.02).

Another kilometre up the road, another clearing in the woods shelters **La Corroirie** (April to mid-Nov 10.45am–7.45pm; €3), a collection of fifteenth-century buildings that once housed the lay brothers attached to the charterhouse. The distance between the two foundations emphasized the strict sequestration of the hard-core Carthusians proper. The remnants of the twelfth-century church are intriguing, and panels help explain the history of the site. Look out for the fresco of the Crucifixion, and the remains of a watermill.

The last of the quartet, the **Prieuré de Grandmont-Villiers**, sits at the end of a long farm track that leaves the main road opposite the turning to Chemillé-sur-Indrois, roughly 2km beyond the Chartreuse du Liget. The priory was another of the institutions set up by Henry II in his sudden outpouring of religious remorse and, for once, is still in use as a religious foundation. Its new occupiers follow the strict and little-known Grandmont rule, an austere Augustinian monastic order established in the eleventh century, suppressed under Louis XV, and, somewhat bizarrely, revived in 1979. They follow hermit-like principles of living, which seem admirably suited to this backwoods area: the three brothers live a humble, withdrawn life, scratching out an existence by raising chickens and livestock and growing vegetables. One of them is always on public duty, however, and will happily, if quietly, show you round the roughly rebuilt church and the cloister buildings, which incorporate lots of ancient fragments of stonework, notably a fine Renaissance window in the priory itself.

If you want to **walk** or **cycle** in the forest, contact the tourist office at Loches (see p.127), which can supply details of signposted routes.

Montrésor and around

The name of this utterly picturesque village, 19km east of Loches, says it all. In modern French, **MONTRÉSOR** means "my treasure", and once you've passed through the forbidding Forêt de Loches, turned down into the hidden valley of the Indrois and discovered the picture-postcard château rising above the river meadows, you'll feel as if you've discovered something really precious. What's more, Montrésor harbours a collection of artworks quite disproportionate to its size and significance. Disappointingly, the real etymology of the name probably stems from the Latinate "Mont Thesauri".

Montrésor is unlucky enough to have been officially classified as one of "The Most Beautiful Villages in France", but it doesn't seem to have affected it in the slightest, nor brought hordes of tourists. There's just one café, one *tabac* and the inevitable hairdresser's salon, though admittedly the antiques shop and jeweller's are probably concessions to out-of-town visitors. One of the nicest things to do is take the short, signposted **circular walk** that runs along the Grande Rue, across the footbridge at the west end of the village, then through the meadows beside the River Indrois – from where there's a fabulous view of the village panorama – then across the pretty, nineteenth-century iron footbridge and back up into the village below the church. On the way round the Grande Rue, make a short detour to the **Halle des Cardeux**, a seventeenth-century covered market with a handsome timber roof.

Like so many others in the region, the **château** (April–Nov daily 10am–6pm; Dec–March 2–5pm; €7) dates back to Foulque Nerra, the belligerent eleventh-century count of Anjou, but its earliest visible parts are the curtain wall and stumps of towers built by Henry II Plantagenet in the late twelfth century in a vain attempt to save his French dependencies from the French king, Philippe-Auguste (see box on p.102). The château's main wing, however, was put up at the end of the fifteenth century by the magnificently named Ymbert de Bastarnay, who, as an adviser to Louis XI, Charles VIII, Louis XII and François I, must have been some political operator. He built the château in the middle part of his career, before the First Renaissance had really got going, so it preserves a basically late medieval look. **Inside**, however, it's perfect nineteenth century, the work of a Polish émigré called Xavier Branicki, who bought the estate in 1849 and made all the latest improvements. His descendants still own the château, and they'll either give you an excellent guided tour or allow you to wander around freely, taking in the just-as-he-left-it feel, with its grand-scale, dusty furnishings, heavy wallpapers and lots of Polish artworks and hunting trophies. Sadly, if the painting of *Christ and the Woman Taken in Adultery* is indeed by Veronese, it's not his best.

The **collégiale** (daily: 9am–7pm) now acts as the parish church, but it was originally built for one purpose: to sanctify the remains of the family of Ymbert de Bastarnay. His **tomb** still stands at the western end of the nave, a pale alabaster figure lying in prayer on a sombre black slab, accompanied by his wife and son. The tomb was broken up in the Revolution and only reassembled in 1875, but the amazing realism of details such as the pillows and the painfully aged face of Ymbert make it easy to agree with the tentative attribution to Jean Goujon, the premier sculptor of the French Renaissance. The church itself took just over twenty years to build, beginning in 1519, a period which saw the flowering of the First Renaissance. The basic concept, therefore, is Flamboyant Gothic, but Renaissance details such as the frieze above the west portal intrude insistently. The original **stained-glass window** at the east end shows three scenes from the Passion. Don't miss the amusingly carved misericords of the choir stalls, or the mawkish Annunciation by the great seventeenth-century painter **Philippe de Champaigne** in the north chapel.

Practicalities

The **tourist office**, on the central Grande Rue (Jan–March & Nov Mon–Fri 10am–noon & 2–6pm; April & Oct Mon–Fri 10am–noon & 2–6pm, Sat & Sun 2.30–6pm; May, June & Sept daily 10am–12.30pm & 2.30–6.30pm; July & Aug daily 10am–12.30pm & 2.30–7pm; Dec Tues–Fri 2.30–6pm, Sat & Sun 10am–noon & 2–6pm; ☎02.47.92.70.71, ⊛www.tourisme-valdindrois-montresor .com), can provide lots of information on chambres d'hôtes and other attractions in the area. There's no hotel in Montrésor, and just one **restaurant**, the relaxed, inexpensive *Café de la Ville*, 29 Grande Rue (☎02.47.92.75.31). At Genillé, 12km to the northwest, the *Relais Agnès Sorel*, 6 place Agnès Sorel (☎02.47.59.50.17; lunch menus at €17, evening menus from €38; Sept–June closed Sun evening, Tues lunch & Mon; July & Aug closed Tues), has three simple **rooms** (❸) above its excellent, inventive **restaurant**.

Three kilometres northwest of Montrésor, there's **camping** at **CHEMILLE-SUR-INDROIS**, where an artificial lake has been developed with a small beach for swimming, and pedalos and kayaks are rented out. There's a posh campsite *Camping du Lac* (☎02.47.92.77.83, ⊛www.lescoteauxdulac.com; closed Oct–March), and on the opposite side of the lake, the *Moulin de Chaudé* **restaurant** (☎02.47.92.71.31; menus €15–32; closed Mon), which has a wood-fired grill and a pleasant outdoor terrace.

Nouans-les-Fontaines

The hamlet of **NOUANS-LES-FONTAINES**, 10km east of Montrésor, is scarcely more than an isolated crossroads in the middle of undulating fields, a junction for the main D760 to Loches and the D675 that cuts razor-straight across the countryside between the Cher and the wetlands of the Brenne. As such, its parish **church** (daily 10am–6pm) is an unlikely repository for one of France's greatest fifteenth-century paintings, but it makes the experience of viewing it all the richer. Jean Fouquet's wonderful **altarpiece** is usually referred to as a Pietà, and the central focus is indeed on the heart-rending figure of Mary kneeling beside her son's body, but it's also closely related to the Entombment scenes so popular in France, with the familiar bearded and be-hatted figures of Nicodemus and Joseph of Arimathea seen lowering Jesus's slim, muscular body onto a winding sheet. The painting was probably cut down at some stage in its life, only adding to the incredible, almost claustrophobic intimacy of the scene. The frame is further crowded by two kneeling donors. The white-surpliced man is usually identified as one Jean Bernard, a bishop of Tours, though another theory claims that it may be the great Jacques Cœur of Bourges (see p.228), based on the presence of the watching figure of St James (St Jacques). Be sure to bring a two-euro coin to illuminate the panel behind its over sized, bullet-proof glass case.

The rest of the church is fairly dull, and there's nothing to see or do in the village, unless you decide to have a meal at the family-run **restaurant** – only in France would a village this small have a good restaurant – *Le Lion d'Or* (℡02.47.92.62.19), which offers regional-focused menus at €20 and €28.

Montpoupon

The woodland setting of the **château de Montpoupon** (Feb, March & Oct–Dec Sat & Sun 10am–noon & 2–4pm; April–June & Sept daily 10am–noon & 2–6pm; July & Aug daily 10am–6pm; closed Jan; €7, Ⓦ www.montpoupon .com), which lords it over a sudden forest clearing some 24km northeast of Loches, betrays its entire *raison d'être*. Hunting has always been the passion of its owners, and it's now the theme of an intriguing museum that's well worth a visit even if you're no supporter.

The site is an ancient one, well defended on a rise set in a small valley, but the current structure dates mostly from the thirteenth to fifteenth centuries. Tall, crenellated circular towers prop up the noble *logis*, whose mullioned windows were opened up in around 1460, and the whole site is encircled by the remains of a curtain wall, guarded by an impressive sixteenth-century gatehouse. The historic owners, the de Prie family, sold the estate in 1763 to the marquis de Tristan, whose heirs split the 1200-hectare forested estate from the château. The latter was bought by one Jean Baptiste de la Motte Saint Pierre, whose descendant, the elderly Mlle de le Motte St-Pierre, still lives here. It's her nephew, a Parisian art dealer, who has created the **museum of hunting** in the stables and outbuildings.

You'll need quite an interest in hunting to get round it all. You begin with a collection of carts and carriages, then the *pigeonnier* (see p.161), with its original turning mechanism for inspecting the pigeonholes, then the **Logis de Veneur**, the huntsman's lodge, which houses a reconstruction of a real saddlery that ceased to be used in 1997 and was transported here lock, stock and barrel, as well as the nineteenth-century living quarters of a chief huntsman. On the opposite side of the courtyard are scores of watercolours, photographs, hunting costumes, hunting instruments and hunt-inspired Hermès scarves – Hermès was originally a saddler. Finally, there's a taxidermist's studio, a reconstruction of a gamekeeper's home and full-size models of horses in their stables.

Hunting continues to be a theme **inside the château**, which you can see on hourly guided visits. There's a stag theme in the tiled flooring of the entrance hall, a light made out of an old hunting shop sign and a fine series of seven-teenth-century Beauvais tapestries. But the furnishings are mostly elegant antiques, which the guide describes in some detail. The tour ends in the kitch-ens, which were supplied with electricity as early as 1870 – almost a hundred years before the nearby village of Céré-la-Ronde.

The friendly *Auberge du Château*, just 200m away (℡02.47.94.25.53; menus from €17.50; closed Mon), provides a very huntsman-like setting for a meal; simple dishes like steaks, omelettes and salads are also available.

Travel details

Trains

Tours to: Amboise (18 daily; 20min); Azay-le-Rideau (7 daily; 30min); Blois (18 daily; 40min); Bourges (usually requires change at Vierzon; 6–8 daily; 1hr 30min–2hr 15min); Chartres (usually requires change; 3–5 daily; 2hr 30min–3hr); Chenonceaux (5 daily; 25–45min); Chinon (7 daily; 45min); Cinq-Mars-la-Pile (4 daily; 20min); Langeais (8 daily; 25min); Le Mans (7 daily; 1hr); Loches (1–2 daily; 1hr); Montlouis (6 daily; 15min); Montrichard (10 daily; 30min); Orléans (12–18 daily; 1hr–1hr 30min); Saumur (12 daily; 45min); Vendôme (9 daily; 30min–1hr).

Buses

Chinon to: Azay-le-Rideau (2 daily; 1hr); Langeais (2 daily; 1hr); Port-Boulet (for Saumur; 2–3 daily; 15min); Richelieu (2–3 daily; 40min).

Tours to: Amboise (7 daily; 50min); Azay-le-Rideau (2 daily; 50min); Chartres (2 daily; 1hr 40min); Chinon (2 daily; 1hr 10min); Loches (12 daily; 40min); Luynes (18 daily; 30min); Richelieu (1–4 daily; 1hr 50min); Ste-Maure-de-Touraine (4–6 daily; 50min); Vouvray (16 daily; 20min).

2

Blois and the Sologne

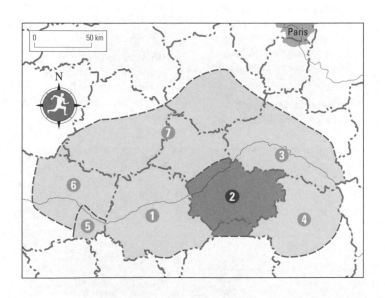

CHAPTER 2 # Highlights

* **Château de Blois** The breathtaking architecture of this royal château spans centuries, while its history is stained with a notorious royal murder. See p.144

* **Au Rendez-Vous des Pêcheurs, Blois** Serious about its cooking but unpretentious, this is one of the region's best restaurants. See p.151

* **Cycling between châteaux** A network of cycle routes connects Blois with the many fine châteaux that stud the wooded country to the south. See p.152

* **Château de Chambord** A behemoth of a Renaissance palace topped by a soaring stone crown, Chambord is the most kingly château of them all. See p.154

* **Château de Cheverny** Gleaming white in its carefully manicured park, Cheverny is the ultimate expression of the French nobility's elegance. See p.162

* **The Sologne** Walking or cycling are the best ways to explore the pine woods and wetlands of the Sologne. See p.167

* **Château de Chémery** You can taste the life of a château-owner at this homely, yet wonderfully medieval bed and breakfast. See p.178

△ Château St-Aignan

Blois and the Sologne

The low-lying country between the rivers **Loire** and **Cher**, south of the ancient city of Blois, still feels wedded to its feudal past. The area is dominated by swathes of ancient forest, much of it set aside for hunting, while scores of pristine châteaux stand in strong contrast to the relatively unimpressive villages and hamlets that dot the backroads. After the Revolution, the region's historic name, the Blésois, was replaced with the more businesslike Loir-et-Cher, but when you're standing in a aristocrat-owned château surrounded by miles of private woodland, you could be forgiven for thinking these changes are rather cosmetic.

Unlike its neighbours on the Loire, Tours and Orléans, **Blois** has never really made the leap from provincial capital to fully fledged modern city. It does, however, contain one of the most fascinating châteaux in France, standing on a rocky pedestal in the heart of the city, and the presence of significant numbers of tourists means there are plenty of good restaurants and bars. Blois' modest size, meanwhile, means it's easy to escape into the countryside. The southern hinterland of the city has long been famous for its game, making this prime territory for aristocrats looking to build a country residence. As a consequence, the area is studded with fine châteaux, and two in particular are ranked among the finest palaces in Europe: mammoth **Chambord** and refined **Cheverny**, two white-stone gems set in the green of their extensive private parks.

A little further south and east of Blois lies the forested, watery and wildlife-rich area known as the **Sologne**. Châteaux are thicker on the ground here than anywhere else in the region, but they're almost all closed to the hoi polloi. The best way to visit the area is on foot or by bicycle, or by spending a night in a country hotel sampling the renowned cuisine, with its rich, seasonal flavours of local forest mushrooms, game, stewed hare, freshwater fish and asparagus.

Even compared with other gentle tributaries of the Loire, the slow-flowing **River Cher**, which forms the southern boundary of the region, is unusually placid. In tourist terms, the valley's tranquillity is partly enforced by the château de Chenonceau, in Touraine (see p.89), whose arched bridge seems to act as a kind of weir for tourists – the coach parties just don't get upstream. The towns along this middle stretch of the Cher are relatively unassuming, though **Montrichard** and **St-Aignan** make attractive bases for a few days' stay. Most visitors come for St-Aignan's **zoo**, or to see the great château of **Valençay**, a short distance south of the Cher, which combines Renaissance ambition with cool Classical elegance.

Train lines run along the Loire and the Cher, with a third branch connecting Valençay with the provincial towns of Romorantin-Lanthenay and Salbris, in the Sologne. **Public transport** elsewhere in the region is sparse, with just a

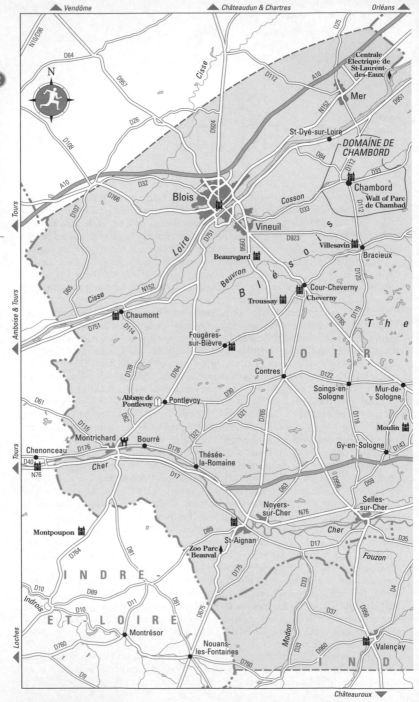

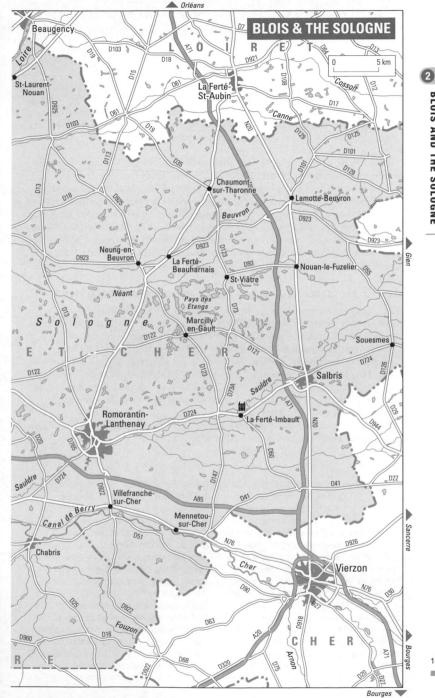

BLOIS & THE SOLOGNE

Orléans

Beaugency

St-Laurent-Nouan

La Ferté-St-Aubin

Chaumont-sur-Tharonne

Lamotte-Beuvron

Beuvron

Neung-en-Beuvron

La Ferté-Beauharnais

St-Viâtre

Nouan-le-Fuzelier

Néant

Pays des Etangs

Souesmes

S o l o g n e

Marcilly-en-Gault

E T C H E R

Salbris

Romorantin-Lanthenay

La Ferté-Imbault

Sauldre

Villefranche-sur-Cher

Canal de Berry

Mennetou-sur-Cher

Chabris

Cher

Vierzon

Fouzon

C H E R

R E

Bourges

Gien

Sancerre

Bourges

Arnon

handful of infrequent buses run by Transports du Loir et Cher (☎02.54.58.55.55, ⓦwww.tlcinfo.net).

Blois

The small but historic city of **BLOIS**, on the Loire 53km east of Tours, is entirely dominated by its château. A favoured residence of the sixteenth-century Valois kings, it is one of the most fascinating châteaux in France, with its airy esplanade, dramatic courtyard and gaudily painted rooms steeped in bloody events.

The city, pleasant though it is, comes a distant second. While it flourished briefly under Louis XII, who had his court here, Blois has long lagged behind its neighbours, Tours and Orléans, both in terms of size and economic importance. That said, it is still large enough to feel much less devoted to tourism than château-towns such as Amboise or Saumur. There are few sights of particular interest other than the château and the excellent Musée de l'Objet, but it's fun to explore: narrow roads wind up the steep inclines, hidden squares shelter cafés, restaurants and fine old townhouses, and flights of steps cut down to the river, which is spanned by one of the Loire's most handsome bridges.

Arrival, information and accommodation

Blois is compact and easy to get around on foot: avenue Jean-Laigret is the main street leading east from the **gare SNCF** to place Victor-Hugo and the château, and past it to the town centre. The **gare routière** is directly in front of the gare SNCF, with buses leaving three times a day (at most) for Cheverny and Chambord. The **tourist office**, at 23 place du Château (May–Sept Tues–Sat 9am–7pm, Sun & Mon 10am–7pm; Oct–April Mon–Sat 9am–12.30pm & 2–6pm, Sun 9.30am–12.30pm; ☎02.54.90.41.41, ⓦwww.loiredeschateaux .com), organizes hotel rooms for a small fee and can provide information on day coach tours of Chambord and Cheverny.

There's a good range of inexpensive and decent **hotels** in Blois, but the choice at the upper end of the market is rather limited.

Hotels

Côté Loire 2 place de la Grève ☎02.54.78.07.86, ⓦwww.coteloire.com. Tucked away in a quiet corner of town by the river, this is Blois' most charming hotel. The seven rooms all have antique furnishings, a cheery decor and brand new bathrooms. Front-facing rooms have views of the river, while on the other side is a leafy inner courtyard where you can eat breakfast. Downstairs is a tiny dining room with a grandfather clock, where you can enjoy a three-course regional menu for €24. ❹

Hôtel du Bellay 12 rue des Minimes ☎02.54.78.23.62, ⓦhoteldubellay.free.fr. Friendly budget option, with rooms which are well worn but clean, and much cheered up with pictures of local sights and the odd wooden beam. The standard doubles (€37) are quiet and comfortable,

while at the top of the steep wooden staircase are excellent-value rooms aimed at backpackers, containing up to three single beds for €25. ❷

Hôtel de France et de Guise 3 rue Gallois ☎02.54.78.00.53, ⓦannedebretagne.free.fr. An attractive and comfortable hotel on a busy road just below the château. It was once the Guise townhouse and, while little evidence of the old building remains, some rooms still have balconies with views of the château loggia. ❸

Mercure Blois Centre 28 quai St-Jean ☎02.54.56.66.66, ⓦwww.mercure.com. No character whatsoever, but this chain hotel certainly offers *tout confort* – all mod cons, including a pool. Overlooks the river to the east of the town centre. ❼

Le Monarque 61 rue Porte Chartraine ☎02.54.78.02.35, ⓦannedebretagne.free.fr.

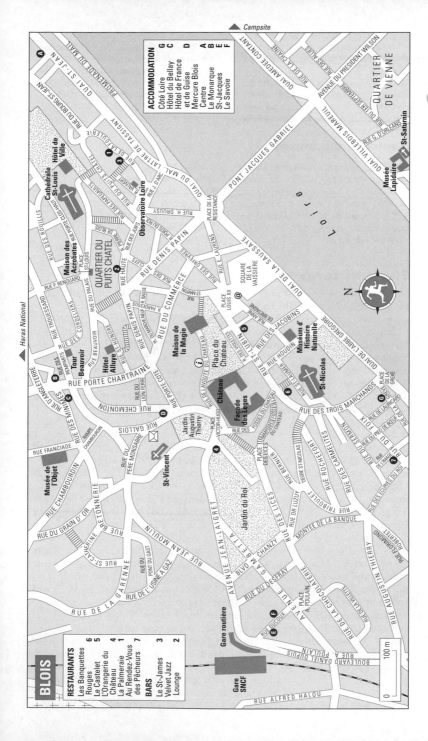

▲ Campsite

ACCOMMODATION
Côté Loire   G
Hôtel du Bellay   C
Hôtel de France
et de Guise   D
Mercure Blois   A
Centre   B
Le Monarque   E
St-Jacques   F
Le Savoie

BLOIS

RESTAURANTS
Les Banquettes
Rouges   6
Le Castelet   5
L'Orangerie du
Château   4
La Palmeraie   1
Au Rendez-Vous
des Pêcheurs   7

BARS
Le St-James   3
Velvet Jazz
Lounge   2

0   100 m

Professional and energetically managed hotel with a cheerful yellow and blue colour scheme and some bright artwork. Usefully located at the top end of town. ❸

St-Jacques 7 rue Ducoux ☎02.54.78.04.15, ⓦwww.hotelsaintjacquesblois.com. Plain and institutional, but rooms are fully equipped and in good nick, and it's opposite the train station. ❸

Le Savoie 6 rue Ducoux ☎02.54.74.32.21, ⓔhotel.le.savoie@orange.fr. The more attractive and friendly of the pair of two-stars opposite the station, with modern fittings and spacious rooms. There are family rooms for up to four people (€66) and downstairs is a bar exclusively for clients of the hotel. ❸

Hostel and campsite

Auberge de Jeunesse Les Grouets 18 rue de l'Hôtel-Pasquier ☎02.54.78.27.21, ⓔblois@fuaj.org. Awkwardly but peacefully located five kilometres downstream from Blois, between the Forêt de Blois and the river. Bus #4 runs at least once an hour but stops at around 7pm. Closed mid-Nov to Feb. €9.70.

Camping Rives de Loire Vineuil ☎02.54.78.82.05, ⓦwww.camping-blois.com. Pleasant, wooded campsite on the south bank of the Loire, 4km from the town centre. Has a good-sized outdoor pool. Bus #3C (stop "Mairie Vineuil") runs only four times daily. Closed Oct–May.

The château

You can glimpse different angles of the **château de Blois** (daily: April–Sept 9am–6.30pm; Nov–March 9am–12.30pm & 2–5.30pm; €6.50) from all over town, but the best view is from inside the extraordinary inner courtyard – for which you have to pay the entrance fee. You can also get into the courtyard as part of the evening **son-et-lumière** show (see box, opposite), which evocatively conjures up the château's history, but it would be a shame to miss the garishly decorated interior of the château. The two-hour, guided **visite privilégiée** (July & Aug daily at 3pm; English-language tour sometimes available on request, call ☎02.54.90.33.33; €7.50) explores parts of the château not normally seen, such as the roof and cellars, and the foundations of the medieval towers.

Some history

Blois' château began life as the powerful fortress base of the warring **counts of Blois**, the great rivals of the counts of Anjou, but by 1391 it had passed into the hands of Louis d'Orléans, brother of the mad king Charles VI. The Orléans family didn't have much luck with their acquisition. In 1407, Louis d'Orléans was assassinated in Paris by henchmen of the Burgundian duke Jean Sans Peur. His widow retired to Blois, where she died of grief a year later, while their son, the poet-duke **Charles d'Orléans**, was imprisoned in England following the French defeat at Agincourt in 1415 – where he wrote poetry as the self-styled "Scholar of Melancholy" – and was only ransomed 25 years later. When Charles returned to Blois, he established a fine library and organized poetry competitions that drew the brilliant and notorious **François Villon**, another poet-jailbird (see p.341), who was awarded a pension. At the age of 68, Charles finally had a son, Louis. He did a turn in prison too, at Bourges, but then unexpectedly came to the throne in 1498 as **Louis XII**, following the sudden death of his cousin Charles VIII at Amboise. The luck of the Orléans family seemed to have turned.

Louis XII made Blois his main residence, knocking down the outmoded feudal towers inherited from his father and building a fine new lodging with trendy Italianate details for Anne de Bretagne, the wife he inherited from his cousin along with the kingdom. The chronicler Jean d'Auton wrote in 1506 that "there they passed the time in great joy and pleasure, for the king was very healthy and in good spirits, and all his country was happy and at peace, with

Blois' son-et-lumière

The **son-et-lumière** at the château of Blois is one of the best in the region, making the most of the enclosed courtyard setting. Crowds gather outside as dusk falls, before being let into the main courtyard. The beginning of the show is the best bit, clever lighting effects really bringing the chiselwork and the disparate architectural styles of the château to life, while a booming actor's voice recounts the story of its construction. The elaborate historical music-and-lighting show that follows is by turns kitsch, exciting and downright tacky, but the finale, following the duc de Guise step by step towards his murder, is dramatic – it was here, after all, that he was killed.

The show takes place just after dark on summer evenings (mid-April to late Sept), which means 10pm from mid-April to May, 10.30pm in June and July, 10pm in August and 9.30pm in September. **Tickets** (€6.50, or €10 including château entrance) can be booked in advance at the tourist office or by calling ☏02.54.90.33.33, although you can usually just turn up at the gate. The show is presented in English on Wednesdays.

wealth abounding". But Louis failed to produce a male heir, and when he died in 1515 he bequeathed throne and château to his second cousin, **François I**, who had married his daughter Claude. François lost no time in rebuilding the château's north wing in an up-to-date style that was even more indebted to the Italian Renaissance. François eventually received the Habsburg emperor Charles V here – a triumph of diplomacy, as the last time Charles had visited Blois was to be betrothed to Claude de France, now François' wife.

Unlike most Loire châteaux, Blois continued to remain an important royal residence throughout the sixteenth century, partly due to **Catherine de Médicis'** fondness for it. Catherine's son François II and his wife Mary Stuart ruled largely from Blois, and her younger sons Charles IX and Henri III continued to use it for hunting and festivals. But Blois' most significant moment in French history came when it was twice the venue for the French parliament (unlike its English equivalent, it convened wherever the court was to be found). The session of 1588, called to halt the Wars of Religion, culminated in the notorious assassinations of the **Guise brothers** (see box on p.147), on the orders of Henri III.

The religious conflicts ended with the accession of Henri IV. After his death, his widow, **Marie de Médicis,** was briefly consigned to house arrest at the château by her son, Louis XIII, but she escaped down the outer wall on the night of February 21, 1619. Louis later assigned the château, along with the titles of duc d'Orléans and comte de Blois, to his brother Gaston, who set about construction of an entirely new palace following the designs of the great architect François Mansart. Luckily for the old château, Gaston only succeeded in rebuilding the west wing before the birth of a son and heir to his brother made him reconsider the state of his fortunes – he had been spending heavily on his hobbies of clock-collecting, boating on the Loire and growing tobacco and tomatoes. Gaston died in the apartments of the François I wing in 1660, and thereafter the château lapsed into obscurity, barely surviving its use as an army barracks in the early nineteenth century. In the 1840s, following the politically fashionable "rediscovery" of the romance of French royal history, architect **Félix Duban** set about the radical restoration works still visible today.

Visiting the château

From the plateau-like esplanade in front of the château, you step through the little door to the right of the glamorous equestrian statue of Louis XII – a nineteenth-century copy – under the crowned porcupine that was Louis' emblem, through the ticket office and into the main **courtyard**, where you are confronted with an extraordinary clash of four architectural styles, only slightly muted by time. Tucked away in one corner is the plain stone of the Gothic **Salle des Etats**, the thirteenth-century manorial assembly hall, while the Flamboyant Gothic **Louis XII wing** is easily identified by the use of brick, the windows and doors dressed with stone and a few borrowed Italianate details. The graceful lines and inspired Renaissance stonework of the northern **François I wing** are interrupted by a giant spiral staircase, one of the last flowerings of the French medieval tradition before the fashion for straight, internal stairs took hold. As Balzac put it, the stone is "cut like a piece of Chinese ivory". Architecturally speaking, one of the most radical features of this wing is the giant sculpted cornice that almost conceals the dormer windows in the roof. The Classical designs tentatively introduced by Louis and François reach their apotheosis on the western side, in the **Gaston d'Orléans wing**, designed by François Mansart in the 1630s.

Salle des Etats

The visit begins in the oldest and most dramatic part of the building. The vast Grande Salle was built in the early thirteenth century by Thibaud VI, comte de Blois, just before the château passed out of the hands of his family. The room is usually called **Salle des Etats**, from the time the French parliament, the Etats-Généraux, was summoned here by Henri III in 1576 and again in 1588, to debate the religious crisis enveloping the kingdom. In 1588, when the king gave his opening speech to some five hundred representatives of the three "estates" of clergy, nobility and gentry, the walls would have been decked with rich tapestries; these days, the vaults, pillars and fireplaces are a riot of golds, reds and blues dating from architect **Félix Duban**'s mid-nineteenth-century efforts to turn the empty château into a showcase for sixteenth-century decorative motifs. The paint wasn't long dry when revolutionaries were tried here for conspiring to assassinate Napoleon III, a year before the Paris Commune of 1870.

François I wing

A door leads through to the **François I wing**, where an **archeological museum** on the ground floor displays original stonework from the staircase and dormer windows, as well as carved details rescued from other châteaux. The collection shows how badly tufa stone weathers over time, and how much of the stonework you see today must therefore be completely "restored". The upper floors, while mostly empty, are enlivened by the rich colours of Duban's bold reinvention of the interiors – to call it a restoration would be pushing it, though his work is at least loosely faithful to the original decorative spirit. François I's salamander emblem recurs ostentatiously, along with the ermine and ermines' tails of his wife Claude de France, duchess of Brittany. The interior is surprisingly narrow, with just two flanking rows of rooms separated by an astonishingly thick wall – this was the original outer wall of the château before François I tacked the **Façade des Loges** to the outside.

The **first-floor** suite belonged to Henri III's notorious mother, Catherine de Médicis. The rooms are decorated in extraordinarily vivid golds, reds and blues, but the most striking chamber is the *cabinet*, or **study** – the only room in the château to have preserved its original decor. According to Alexandre Dumas' novel, *La Reine Margot*, Catherine kept poison in the hidden cupboards that lurk behind four of the study's 237 carved wooden panels, but these are actually fairly standard accoutrements in the Italian-inspired *studiolo* – *cabinet* in French

The murder of the duc de Guise

In 1588, the French parliament convened in Blois' medieval Grande Salle. **Henri III** opened proceedings by attacking "the unbounded ambitions of certain subjects". No one had any doubt who he meant. The powerful **Henri, duc de Guise**, and his brother, the Cardinal of Lorraine, were the populist leaders of the ultra-Catholic **Holy League**, which claimed to defend the faith against Protestantism and the king's weak, compromising policies. Back in 1560, it was Guise who was the target of the Huguenot rebels at Amboise (see p.85), and Guise who was most diligent in the executions that followed. In the quarter-century since the Tumult, France had fallen into open civil war, with Protestants and Leaguers alike raising armies to fight each other and, on occasion, the king.

The conflict became known as the **War of the Three Henrys**, with Henri, duc de Guise, Henri III and the Protestant Henri de Navarre as leaders of the main factions. The king decided that the only solution was to get rid of Guise, who was rumoured to be setting himself up as heir to the throne on the basis of his family's claimed descent from Charlemagne. Guise was secretly receiving money from Philip II of Spain.

At dinner on December 22, the duke found a note on a napkin warning him of the threat to his life. Contemptuously, he scribbled on it, "they wouldn't dare", and retired to spend the night with the beautiful Catherine de Beaune-Semblançay. Early the following morning, while waiting for a meeting to begin in the **Salle du Conseil**, Guise received a message from the king asking him to attend him in the nearby Vieux Cabinet (now destroyed). To get there, Guise had to pass through the **royal bedroom**, which lay just the other side of the thick partition wall of the château; there he was set upon by the king's loyal bodyguard, the **Forty-Five**. He received a stab wound in the neck but fought on, fending off his attackers "like a wounded bull" – the noise of their feet could be clearly heard on the floor below. When he finally succumbed, he cried out "God have mercy!" and fell to the ground. Legend has it that the king came through to deliver a contemptuous kick to his rival's body, commenting, "My God, he looks even bigger dead than alive". Guise's brother, the cardinal, was murdered soon after, and both bodies were burned in secret.

The royal family didn't have long to enjoy their newly asserted mastery of the kingdom. Henri's mother, Catherine de Médicis, died at Blois just ten days after the murders, and the Guises were avenged a year later when a monk assassinated the king – stabbing him as he rode through the streets of Paris in his coach.

– a private room for contemplation, study and safe storage of fine art. You can see the concealed foot pedals in the skirting that spring open the cubby-holes, which are usually left open to display Renaissance objets d'art.

Stairs lead up through the thickness of the internal wall to the **second floor**, the province of Catherine's son, Henri III, with more fabulously colourful neo-Renaissance decoration. It was in the **royal bedroom**, now graced by a reconstructed four-poster bed, that the duc de Guise was hacked to death by the king's assassins (see box, above). As Flaubert noticed, the king's oratory lies just two doors away, "a coincidence not unusual in itself but which strikes one forcibly here, in a man whose sensuality was stimulated by religion and whose cruelty was whetted by fear". A large adjoining room displays nineteenth-century paintings of the Guise murder, including two full-length portraits of a suitably effete Henri III and a duc de Guise who looks as if he could have fought off Henri's gang of murderous *mignons* with one hand tied behind his back.

Gaston d'Orléans wing

Few visitors bother to penetrate inside the severe **Gaston d'Orléans wing**, but it's well worth having a look at Mansart's breathtaking internal staircase, with its framed trompe-l'oeil cupola. A seventeenth-century painting in the adjacent, fifteenth-century **chapelle St-Calais** shows Gaston, along with his brother Louis XIII, adoring the holy sacrament. The chapel is sadly over-restored, though there's a fine Gothic vault given the full technicolour Duban treatment and some interesting 1950s stained-glass windows by the prolific Max Ingrand. A gap alongside the chapel allows you to walk through to a terrace known as the **Perche aux Bretons**, after the lodgings of Anne de Bretagne's bodyguard of a hundred Breton gentlemen, which once stood on this spot. At the edge of the ramparts, the **Tour du Foix** is one of the few visible vestiges of the thirteenth-century château of the counts of Blois. From the terrace there are excellent views over the city.

Louis XII wing

Back in the main courtyard, the **Louis XII wing** is relatively disappointing on the inside, for all that it bears witness to Blois' heyday. The ground floor houses an undistinguished **Musée des Beaux-Arts**, whose finest room features seventeenth- and eighteenth-century French and Flemish work, with a strong focus on portraits and scenes connected with the French royal family. Alongside are a few sixteenth-century paintings, a lot of nineteenth-century sculptures and a collection of tapestries, one of which, from the Parisian Gobelins workshop, shows the château as it appeared in the early eighteenth century.

The rest of the city

The twists and turns, hills and stairs of the city centre make it an enjoyably confusing place to walk around, though the area is in fact very small. The higher ground forms a horseshoe shape around the **place de la Résistance**, which lies at the north end of the main town bridge, the **Pont Jacques Gabriel**. On the west side of the horseshoe, the **château** perches above the abbey church of **St-Nicolas** and the river, while the **cathédrale St-Louis** stands on the eastern slopes above the winding streets of the old **Quartier du Puits Châtel**, where Blois' limited nightlife is to be found.

Around the château

For all its attractive airiness, there's little to do on **Place du Château** except wander around with an ice cream, unless you plan on taking a half-hour cart-horse-and-carriage tour (April–June & Sept 2–6pm; July & Aug 11am–7pm; €6) or visiting the tourist office. In July and August, however, a local produce market takes place every Thursday afternoon.

The tall building at the far end from the château is the less-than-magical **Maison de la Magie** (April–Sept daily 10am–12.30pm & 2–6pm; €7.50 or €12 with château entry; ⓦwww.maisondelamagie.fr). Children are unlikely to be convinced by the rather shoddy optical illusions inside, or the stuffy room dedicated to local impresario Robert-Houdin, but the afternoon magic shows are in mime, so at least there's no need to understand French. Younger children may want to catch the mechanical dragons stretching their golden necks through the front windows, on the hour. Steps lead down from here to the pleasant place Louis XII, centred round the rump of a fifteenth-century fountain that survived the artillery storm of June 1940.

From the square, you can continue down to the river, or take rue Anne de Bretagne west to the **Muséum d'Histoire Naturelle** (Tues–Sun 2–6pm; €2.70). Instructive dioramas explain various regional environments and the birds and animals that live in them, but children aren't likely to find it very exciting, still less the dusty **Musée d'Art Réligieux** (Tues–Sat 2–6pm; free) – all shabby mitres and gilt reliquaries – that occupies the same building. Rue St-Lubin, home of Blois' better bistro-restaurants, heads west of place Louis XII towards the **église St-Nicolas** (daily 9am–6.30pm), which once belonged to the Benedictine abbey of St-Laumer. It's very bare inside, but the choir is a handsome example of the Romanesque style, and there's a fine cupola over the crossing. The abbey buildings alongside were rebuilt in the seventeenth century, following the destruction of the old monastery by rampaging Huguenots.

Turning back north, rue des Fossés du Château climbs round under the Gaston d'Orléans wing of the château before ending up at place Victor Hugo, where there's a small public garden ringed by traffic and overlooked by the Baroque **église St-Vincent**. The modest greenery is a pleasant reminder of the fabulous Renaissance gardens designed by Pacello Mercogliano that once stood here, but the main reason to come is to look up at the extraordinary **Façade des Loges**, the masterpiece of François I's château, modelled on a loggia of the Vatican designed by Bramante and Raphael – François had met Pope Leo X while campaigning in Italy. Rising smoothly from the natural rock that led the counts of Blois to build their fortress here in the first place, it stretches like a great Italianate cliff from the old Salle des Etats on the left to one of the surviving medieval towers on the right, before coming up short against the relatively brutal Gaston d'Orléans wing. A covered bridge once led across from here to the raised garden terraces. Rue de la Voûte du Château leads back up to the esplanade.

The cathedral quarter

The cafés on **place de la Résistance** are popular on summer evenings, though the real action goes on in the atmospheric streets immediately north, around the **Quartier du Puits Châtel**. A number of medieval houses survive here, particularly on rue des Juifs, where the old ghetto lay, on rue Vauvert and rue Pierre de Blois. On the south side of the handsome **place St-Louis**, the **Maison des Acrobates** is a particular fine half-timbered construction decorated with sculpted tumbling figures.

The **cathédrale St-Louis** (daily 7.30am–6pm), at the west end of the square, rests on Carolingian foundations and leans against a weighty bell tower. The lowest storey of the tower is twelfth century, while the top was only completed in the mid-sixteenth century. Surprisingly, the Gothic body of the cathedral actually postdates the tower. The interior is fairly bare; indeed some of the stone blocks above the nave arcade are still blind, waiting for the sculptor's chisel. The crypt contains the bones of St-Solenne, a bishop of Chartres who died at Blois, but the most interesting feature is the modern **stained-glass windows**, completed in 2003 by the Dutch artist Jan Dibbets working in collaboration with a French glassmaker. They follow a careful programme of colour symbolism, adorned with biblical tags in Latin.

Leading off place St-Louis, rue du Palais runs along the high ground above the town centre, passing the long stairs which swoop down to rue Denis Papin. A few paces west is the elaborate **Hôtel Alluye**, at 8 rue St-Honoré, the private house of the royal treasurer Florimond Robertet and is a rare survivor of Blois' golden years under Louis XII. At the top of the hill, the twelfth-century **Tour Beauvoir**, on rue des Cordeliers was the town prison until the end of World War II. It is now pretty derelict, but the grim, barred windows bear witness to its former purpose.

Pont Jacques Gabriel and St-Saturnin

The highly distinctive angular humpback of the **Pont Jacques Gabriel** dates from 1724, though as the monument at the bridge's apex explains, it has been partially destroyed many times – unusually, because of warfare rather than flooding. The last demolition job protected the retreat of the German army in 1944. The suburb on the far side of the city, the **Quartier de Vienne**, is home to the **église St-Saturnin**, whose Flamboyant Gothic west portal dates from the time of Anne de Bretagne, who commissioned it. The cloister-like structure alongside is in fact an unusual walled cemetery from the era of François I, now used to show off the **Musée Lapidaire**, a collection of sculptural fragments gathered from the rubble after the bombardments of 1940, which is usually only visitable on occasional tours organized by the tourist office (see p.142).

Musée de l'Objet

It's well worth slogging uphill to the unusual **Musée de l'Objet**, set back from the town centre at 6 rue Franciade (March–June & Sept–Nov Sat & Sun 1.30–6.30pm; July & Aug Wed–Sun 1.30–6.30pm; €4). The museum celebrates conceptual sculpture, and most of the works here have been made using found objects rather than traditional materials. The entrance sets the tone: hanging from the ceiling of the staircase, a forest of hammers gradually morphs into handbags – a work entitled *Passage André Breton* (1996), by Jean-Jacques Lebel. The two long, spacious galleries are filled with similarly witty or alarming artworks and installations, including some by major figures in modern art: **Christo** is represented by a disturbing wrapped mannequin, while the conceptual artist **Joseph Kosuth** has a piece called *Leaning Glass* (1965), which is exactly that. Other, more fun pieces include *Le Couple de Damas* (1986), a life-size couple dancing on a kitsch bit of carpet cut out in the shape of a tiger skin, by the French group Présence Panchounette, and the plunks and twangs of Joe Jones's *Guitare* (1973), which emanate from a guitar randomly strummed by a dangling, jerking plectrum.

Haras National

A solid bet for horse lovers, and no doubt many children too, is the **Haras National**, 62 ave Maunory (mid-March to May & Oct Mon–Fri 2.30pm, Sat 2.30pm & 4pm; June & Sept Mon–Sat 2.30pm & 4pm; July & Aug Mon–Sat 10.30am, 2.30pm, 3.30pm & 4.30pm, Sun 10.30am & 3pm; Nov to mid-March Mon–Sat 2.30pm; €6), one of 23 studs distributed around the country. It's odd to find a stud so close to the centre of town, especially as there's no field for the forty-odd stallions to gallop around in. The reason is quite simple: the horses are all here for breeding only – as becomes clear when you are shown the extraordinary leather horse used to goad the stallions into doing their bit for artificial insemination.

Elsewhere there's a horse shower and solarium – for drying, not tanning up – a working saddlery, a vet's room, an old stables full of carriages and a smithy where you can sometimes see the blacksmiths at work. As for the stallions, they're an impressively virile lot, best seen exercising on the little sandy circuit on the front lawn. In the second set of stables you are shown the stud's much-loved carthorses, including four massive **Percherons**, a breed which gets its name from La Perche, the region just north of Le Mans. Astonishingly, these horses can weigh up to 1000kg. The ninety-minute visits are always guided, and usually in French – though you're given an excellent English leaflet.

Eating, drinking and entertainment

Most of Blois' traditional **restaurants** can be found on or around rue St-Lubin, between the château and the river, and you'll find reasonably priced brasseries nearby on place Louis XII. On the east side of town, there's a cluster of bars and eateries in the Quartier du Puits Châtel; the delightful little square at the end of rue Vauvert, in particular, has a number of crêperies and pizzerias with tables set out under an Indian bean tree, and from here alleyways cut through to rue de la Foulerie, the best place for ethnic food – Portuguese, Moroccan and Indian – and late-night **bars**. The cocktail bar *Le St-James*, at 50 rue de la Foulerie, with its little square behind, is a good bet late on weekend nights. Nearby at 15bis rue Haute, the *Velvet Jazz Lounge*, with its stone-vaulted ceiling, is usually popular, if a little posy, and hosts a couple of concerts a month out of season.

Since 2003, a new **music festival**, Tous sur le Pont has taken place annually in early July with an impressive line-up of domestic, international and local acts, ranging from Rita Mitsouko to Juliette Greco and Manu Dibango. Gigs are held in locations all over the city, including the château and the Jardins de l'Evêche; for tickets, contact the organizers (☎02.54.58.84.56, ⊛www .toussurlepont.com) or the tourist office.

Restaurants

Les Banquettes Rouges 16 rue des Trois Marchands ☎02.54.78.74.92. Serves unusually adventurous food in a pretty lemon-yellow dining room with the red bench-seats from which it takes its name. You'll find some amazing dishes like pike-perch with frogs legs, and creative salads – featuring crab or veal, perhaps. You can have a startlingly good lunch for as little as €13.50, while evening menus start at €21. The service is very proper, but the modern bistro atmosphere is more relaxed than your typical restaurant. Closed Mon & Sun.

Le Castelet 40 rue St-Lubin ☎02.54.74.66.09. Specializes in homely Loire cuisine, using regional produce such as Sologne honey and *andouilles* from Vouvray, matched with local wines. You can have a platter of regional specialities for €15, and there's a reasonably imaginative vegetarian menu. A few tables sit out on the adjacent side-street. Sept–June closed Wed & Sun; July & Aug closed Wed lunch & Sun lunch.

L'Orangerie du Château 1 ave Jean-Laigret ☎02.54.78.05.36. The well-heeled flock to this posh restaurant, which offers seriously refined regional cuisine, though the atmosphere can suffer from the group banqueting factor, with over-fussy service. Dining rooms are spread across various wings and levels, the best situated in the echoey vaulted chamber to one side. There is a menu for €30, though you'll do better picking one in the €40–68 range. Closed Mon lunch, Sun evening & Wed.

La Palmeraie 44 rue de la Foulerie ☎02.54.56.02.02. A good alternative to the usual trad French, with decent couscous and tagines from around €14. The decor is souk-like, plus an attractive terrace hidden away at the back. Closed Mon.

Au Rendez-Vous des Pêcheurs 27 rue du Foix ☎02.54.74.67.48. Unquestionably the best gastronomic restaurant in town, with an impeccable, fresh, uncluttered dining room. Top chef Christophe Cosme offers some wonderfully elaborate fish dishes on the eight-course €74 menu *découverte*, such as pike stuffed with chestnuts on a bed of Puy lentils, or caramelized veal head with an eel Mousseline sauce. There is a come-hither €28 menu (not served Sat eve), but it's worth splashing out – at least on the €49 seasonal menu. Closed Mon lunch & Sun, and three weeks in Aug.

Listings

Bike rental Cycles Leblond, 44 levée des Tuileries (☎02.54.74.30.13; ⊛cycles.leblond.free.fr); Bike in Blois, 8 rue Henri Drussy (☎02.54.56.07.73; ⊛www.locationdevelos.com).

Boat trips The Observatoire Loire, 4 rue Vauvert ☎02.54.56.09.24; ⊛www.observatoire.loire.asso .fr. Two-hour excursions on an old-style *fûtreau* sailboat with a guided commentary (in French) on river wildlife. Tickets cost €8.50 and can be booked through the tourist office. It helps if you speak French, but some guides can get by in English. For groups of six or above, it will work out cheaper to hire the boat with a helmsman.

Canoes and kayaks Canoe Découverte, in La Chaussée Saint Victor, 2km upstream on the north bank (☎02.54.78.67.48; ⓦwww.canoe -decouverte.fr), rents out canoes and kayaks for trips downstream towards Chaumont and Amboise. Kayaks cost €8.50 an hour, while a two-man canoe costs €26 for half a day.

Email and Internet Au Nouveau Monde, place Louis XII. Mon, Tues & Thurs–Sat 9am–9pm; Sun 3.30–9pm.

Emergencies Ambulance ☎15; Centre Hospitalier de Blois, Mail Pierre Charlot ☎02.54.55.66.33; late-night pharmacy, phone police (see below) for address.

Police 42 quai St-Jean ☎02.54.55.17.78.

Taxis ☎02.54.78.07.55.

Blésois châteaux

Some of the finest **châteaux** in the whole Loire region are clustered on the left bank of the Loire, in the historic **Blésois region** – now known prosaically as

Blésois by bike

The beautiful wooded region south of Blois, stretching from the Loire Valley to the Sologne, is threaded through by some 300km of cycle routes, making up the Pays des Châteaux à Vélo network. The routes mostly follow tranquil backroads or arrow-straight forest alleys, though some sections are on dedicated cycle paths. There are eleven signposted circuits – though the signposts don't always tell you which circuit you're on, which can be awkward where they cross over. They're almost all between 20 and 30km, or an easy half-day's cycle ride, though you can cut short at least half of them by 10km or so by taking an alternative route. All the circuits can be seen at ⓦwww .chateauxavelo.com, and tourist offices have lists of places to rent bikes – including Blois (see p.151) and many of the smaller towns in this chapter. Tourists offices and bike outlets can give you free (and fairly basic) maps. For recommendations of more detailed road maps, see p.53. Full details, including costs, can also be found at ⓦwww .chateauxavelo.com. Charges are usually around €13 a day, or €8–9 for a half day.

Circuits 1 (25km) and 2 (16–24km) head south from Blois into the old manorial woodland of the Forêt Domaniale de Russy, and then on towards Chaumont to the west – though to make it all the way to the château, you'll have to follow a (yellow) D-road for a few kilometres. Circuits 2 and 3 (16km) pass the château at Fougères-sur-Bièvre. Circuits 4 (16–27km), 5 (9–23km) and 6 (23km) all centre on the château de Cheverny, though circuit 5 continues east as far as Bracieux, on the edge of the grand Chambord forest. Circuits 6 and 7 (29km) take you into true Sologne territory; the former makes a wonderful sweep south into the relatively open woodland of the Forêt de Cheverny, while the varied circuit 7 encompasses the mixed forest and little lakes around Fontaines-en-Sologne, as well as an impressively broad and straight forest avenue north of Bracieux. This "avenue" runs through the superb woodland of the Forêt de Boulogne and Parc de Chambord, an area also covered by circuits 8 (taking in the southwestern part; 28km) and 10 (covering the north and east; 29km). Circuit 10 also takes you right past the château de Chambord. Circuit 9 (11–33km) runs north from Chambord to St-Dyé (see p.160), on the banks of the Loire, following the Loire à Vélo route from there towards Blois, while circuit 11 (23km) takes you north and east towards the Loire at St-Laurent-Nouan.

There are only two gaps in the network where you'll have to share the road with a fair amount of traffic. The D112 runs south from Chambord for eight perfectly straight kilometres to Bracieux, but this forest avenue is so wide that it's not a problem. The traffic-ridden roads heading out of Blois, especially the D765 highway heading south-east towards Cheverny, are less pleasant and should be avoided if possible.

the *département* of the Loir-et-Cher. The location – within easy reach of Blois, on the edge of the semi-wilderness of the Sologne – explains the attraction for château-builders: this is prime hunting territory. Even the greatest château of them all, **Chambord**, started life as a hunting lodge, and it still sits within its own dedicated game reserve, the **Domaine de Chambord**, while the elegant, aristocratic **château de Cheverny** still maintains a pack of hounds.

These days, the châteaux themselves are the bait. Chambord alone attracts around 750,000 visitors each year, and while few sights in Europe compete in that league, both Cheverny and lofty **Chaumont**, perched on its terrace above the Loire, rank among the loveliest and busiest châteaux in the entire Loire region. But with its woods and quiet backroads, the area doesn't feel crowded, and you could even find yourself alone in smaller châteaux such as **Villesavin**, **Troussay** and **Fougères-sur-Bièvre**. Even the **château de Beauregard**, with its extraordinary portrait gallery, sees surprisingly few visitors.

Public transport in the area is very poor, with even the main routes served by only a couple of commuter buses a day, which means timings are less than helpful for sightseeing. Note, however, that the local bus company TLC (℡02.54.58.55.55, ⓦwww.tlcinfo.net) runs "Circuit Châteaux" **coach trips** to Chambord and Cheverny, with two morning and one lunchtime departure from Blois' **gare SNCF** (mid-May to Aug; €10.75, but offers discounted château entry tickets). Check exact times when you buy your ticket from the tourist office. Staff may also be able to find places on a chartered taxi or minibus tour. The best option is **cycling** (see box, opposite). If you want to **walk**, you're best off following one of the area's excellent GR footpaths (see box on p.168).

Château de Beauregard

The little-visited **château de Beauregard** (Feb 8 to end March, Oct, Nov & Dec 20 to end Dec daily except Wed 9.30–noon & 2–5pm; April–June & Sept daily 9.30am–noon & 2–7.30pm; July & Aug daily 9.30am–6.30pm; €6.50; ⓦwww.beauregard-loire.com) lies in the Forêt de Russy, an easy seven-kilometre cycle ride south of Blois, on the D956 to Contres. It's a satisfying château to visit, as the handful of rooms open to the public are especially magnificent.

Beauregard's existence is due to the efforts of a family of butchers from Blois, the Doulcets, to outgrow their humble origins. The first owner of the fief, Jean Doulcet, was ennobled by Louis d'Orléans in 1455, but it was left to his son to erect the first château, and the building as it stands today was largely rebuilt by Jean du Thier, a humanist and friend of Ronsard, in the 1550s. In the seventeenth century, the new owner, Paul Ardier, modified it again, adding the facade facing the garden and the long gallery. The result is sober and serene, very much at ease in its manicured park.

The highlight of the château is a richly decorated **portrait gallery**, its walls entirely panelled with 327 paintings of kings, queens and great nobles. They're hardly the finest paintings in the region, but the original object would have been to edify and amaze rather than display fine art, and the overall impression is staggering. Few of the portraits can have been done from life, but many are probably good likenesses nonetheless, as they would have been copied from well-known images where possible. If you've spent any time in the region, it can be rewarding to put faces to names – there's Jean de Berry, Maximilien de Béthune (the duc de Sully) and all of France's kings from Philippe VI (1328–50), who precipitated the Hundred Years War, to Louis XIII (1610–43), who occupied the throne when the gallery was created. In among the French notables are various European celebrities, including Habsburg Emperor

Charles V, Francis Drake and Anne Boleyn. Emperors, kings, nobles and executed wives alike are all given equal billing – except for Louis XIII, whose portrait takes up the space of nine others. The floor of blue-and-white Delft tiling – unfortunately partly covered by protective carpeting – depicts Louis' army on the march.

On the other side of the partition wall, the **southern gallery** is lined with fine old furnishings, including some impressive sixteenth- and seventeenth-century pieces. At the gallery's far end, the **Chamber of Bells** was installed by Jean du Thier. It's a little wood-scented oaken cube of a study, every surface painted, gilt or carved in the finest humanist tradition of the *studiolo*. No effort has been spared to create the right atmosphere of high-flown artistic brilliance, held to be most conducive to study and reflection. The painted panels show the proper activities for the Renaissance man, from music and sculpture to warfare, and from hunting and farming to, apparently, tennis.

The grounds slope down towards the River Beuvron, and it's well worth taking a stroll at least as far as the sunken **Jardin de Vivaces**, a Renaissance-influenced creation by contemporary landscaper Gilles Clément, who was responsible for Paris's futuristic Parc André Citroën. It could be better tended, but the garden's formal arrangement of hardy perennials – by colour of flower and foliage – is fascinating. Elsewhere in the grounds you'll find an alley of cyclamens, and cedars on the picnic lawns beside a pretty, reed-fringed lake. A garden festival is held here every year in early April.

Château de Chambord

The gargantuan **château de Chambord** (daily: April to mid-July & mid-Aug to end Sept 9am–6.15pm; mid-July to mid-Aug 9am–7.30pm; Oct–March 9am–5.15pm; July & Aug €9.50, Sept–June €8.50; under-26s €6, under-18s free; ⓦwww.chambord.org) has always inspired extravagant comparisons. The writer Châteaubriand thought it "like a woman whose hair had been blown about by the wind", while Touraine-born novelist Alfred de Vigny felt "as if an Oriental djinn, compelled by the power of some wonderful lamp, had snatched it away … from some country of the sun to conceal it in mistier lands". Henry James, more cynically, believed that "the whole thing was monstrous … the exaggeration of an exaggeration".

François I's "hunting lodge" is certainly one of the most bizarre and magnificent commissions of its age. Its patron's principal object – to outshine the Holy Roman Emperor Charles V – would, he claimed, leave him renowned as "one of the greatest builders in the universe". And yet for most of its life the château has stood empty and forgotten, a wilderness of stone surrounded by thick forest contained behind a giant wall. The cold, draughty size of the château made it unpopular as an actual residence – François I himself stayed there for some forty days during his 32-year reign – and Chambord's role in history is slight.

Before you even get close, the sheer scale of the palace is awe-inspiring. There are over 440 rooms and 85 staircases, and a petrified forest of 365 chimneys runs wild on the roof. In architectural terms, the mixture of styles is as outrageous as the size. François I wanted to establish prestigious **Italian Renaissance** art forms in France, and he certainly used Italian architects, but the labour would have been supplied by French masons. So the massive round towers with their conical tops and the explosion of chimneys, pinnacles and turrets on the roof bring to mind Flamboyant Gothic, but Italianate Classical details also proliferate, notably the niches decorated with shell-like domes, and the distinctive, diamond-shaped panels of Anjou slate done up to look like marble. An eighteenth-century

Leonardo's posthumous masterpiece?

The authorities in charge of looking after **Chambord** are desperate to attribute its plan to international superstar and marketing dream **Leonardo da Vinci**, even though he died four months before building began, in 1519. Their arguments come down to "it's so good it must be by him", backed up by cherry-picking in his notebooks for similar bits of design – a spiral staircase under a cupola here, a square-shaped palace with corner towers there and a single sketch of a curious staircase with four separate ramps climbing round a square well.

It is true that Leonardo had a close relationship with François I at Amboise (see p.87), and he certainly made sketches of an ideal city to be built near Romorantin, in the south of the Sologne, though little came of these plans. It's likely, however, that Chambord's design was by an obscure Italian architect called **Domenico da Cortona**, and that it was perfected by the French master masons supervising construction – not to mention the 1800 workmen who laboured and all too often died at the marshy site, plagued by mosquitoes and fever. Leonardo may have had at least some input. He made a note that he had met da Cortona, so they probably discussed their king's projects – perhaps Leonardo even suggested refinements.

The most brilliant architectural idea at Chambord, the **double-spiral staircase**, may in fact have come from the great Italian architect Giuliano da Sangallo. He is thought to have taught da Cortona in Italy, and is known to have created a double-spiral staircase at the Pozzo di San Patrizio in Orvieto – used by donkeys to bring up water from the well. Another Chambord curiosity, the belfry-like **lanterns** that top the conical roofs, may be François I's own idea. After his disastrous defeat at the **Battle of Pavia** in 1525, the king was taken prisoner and held at the Carthusian monastery near the city, where he wrote to his mother, "All is lost save my honour and my life". It would seem odd to commemorate such humiliation, even if François did think his honour intact, but there's no doubt that Chambord's roofscape, completed in the 1530s, bears a striking resemblance to the Charterhouse of Pavia.

survey counted eight hundred different capitals atop the many columns and pilasters, each a unique variation on one of the Classical orders.

Whoever the genius behind Chambord may be (see box, above), the design is pure Renaissance: rational, symmetrical and designed to express a single idea – the kingly power of its owner. Four hallways run crossways through the central keep, at the heart of which a great staircase rises up in two unconnected spirals before opening out into the great lantern tower, which draws the confusion of the roofscape together like a glorious crown.

The summer **events** and festivals calendar is a busy one, with costumed tours for children, classical concerts, night-time lighting displays and guided walks and wildlife-stalking in the forest, among other attractions. Check the main website at Ⓦ www.chambord.org for details.

The donjon, staircase and roof terrace

Chambord's design may be ingenious but, thanks to its confusing four-way symmetry and double-spiral staircase, it's not very practical. Marguerite de Navarre used to complain to her brother François I that she was always getting lost when he wasn't there to help her. These days, a free leaflet helps explain the basics. It's worth bearing in mind that when you get on the great staircase you come off it on the same side of the château as you got on – just one level up or down.

On each floor, the **donjon**, or keep, is divided up into four separate apartments grouped round the four corner towers. At the heart of the building is a

△ Château de Chambord

cavernous cross-shaped stone atrium. Two giant earthenware stoves can be seen here, decorated with the coat of arms of the notorious Maréchal de Saxe, victor of Fontenoy, who ordered them in a vain attempt to heat what served briefly as his home. At the centre of the atrium is the famous **staircase**. Children love to play on it, entranced by the fact that you can catch glimpses of other people on the second, interwinding flight, but never actually catch them up. It's not a modern fascination – Anne d'Orléans, known as "La Grande Mademoiselle", recalled that she used to play on the stairs with her father, Gaston d'Orléans: "he came down as I went up, and laughed aloud to see me run, thinking as I did to catch him." A good place to admire the structure is from the bottom of the narrow central well, accessible at the ground-floor level.

The great staircase ends at the roof level, sheltered by the stunning glazed space of the **lantern tower**, which then continues on skyward through a series of fantastical tiers, culminating in a gilded fleur-de-lis topped by a slender cross. The stairs give onto the **roof terrace**, Chambord's crazed highlight, where you can wander in a forest of chimneys, balconies, turrets, balustrades, finials, dormer windows and steeply pitched slate roofs. You can also eyeball the endlessly inventive Renaissance stonework and look across at the single-spiral staircase towers that serve the château's side wings. Beyond the château walls, moated lawns give way to the trim woodland of the surrounding park and the forested scrub of the Sologne.

The apartments

A number of rooms on the ground and first floors were fitted out by **Louis XIV**, one of the few French monarchs grand enough not to be dwarfed by the château – in fact, one of the few to spend any time here at all. Louis commissioned his architect Jules Hardouin-Mansart to complete the chapel and west wing, and made a number of autumn hunting trips here with his court. In 1670, the assembled nobles were famously entertained by the premiere of Molière's *Le Bourgeois Gentilhomme*.

As reconstructed today, the most interesting Louis XIV-era rooms are in the grand position at the front of the château's first floor, in the wing running between the north and west towers. The **Salle de Compagnie**, in the very centre of the facade, has one of the only pieces of original pre-Revolutionary furniture left in the château, a giant console table with a limestone top that is said to have been used for the embalming of the Maréchal de Saxe. The adjacent **Salle du Roi** has been sumptuously styled as Louis XIV's bedchamber. The

The château staircase

The entrance stair was perhaps the most significant part of any medieval château. It lay at the heart of the social life of the house, as front door, great hall and feudal symbol rolled into one. Staircases began, in the medieval era, as turret-enclosed spirals, usually partly separated from the main structure of the keep for the sake of defence. Cleverly, most castle spirals ascend in a clockwise direction, a design trick apparently intended to encumber the sword arm of a right-handed attacker and leave the defender free to swing and slash.

As defensive design gave way in the face of a more peaceable, luxurious era, the staircase slowly evolved. Its importance meant that it was often given the Renaissance treatment before any other feature, and in the early sixteenth century, Classical motifs began to be carved around staircase doorways. At first, the spiral form was preserved even if the decoration changed, as at Blois and the east wing of Chambord. This type of stair reached its apotheosis, however, in the main wing of Chambord. Here, François I and his architects took the radical step of bringing the staircase inside the body of the château, forming a strange kind of internal, central tower. This particular stair, of course, is all the stranger for following a bewildering double-spiral form.

Gradually, as Classical design took root more deeply in France, straight flights of stairs divided by landings became popular. These kinds of staircases could more easily be incorporated into the body of the building, but still, the earliest examples, as at Châteaudun and Azay-le-Rideau, still preserve the look of towers, and their windows were unglazed. It was only a small step from here, however, to a fully enclosed stairway. By the seventeenth century the only clue to the presence of a château's great staircase was a predilection for the central pavilion of a château to stand slightly proud of the facade or to have, perhaps, a higher or more pointed roof.

king's valet's room is preserved in the tower room alongside, the simple camp bed visible through an original wood-and-glass partition uncomfortably reminiscent of a shop-front.

The rest of the first floor is largely taken up by the **eighteenth-century apartments** installed by the marquis de Polignac, the château's governor in the last years before the Revolution. The marquis made the château habitable by lowering ceilings, constructing wooden floors, building small fireplaces within the larger ones, and cladding the walls in panelling and ornate wall-coverings – the latter at their (reproduced) best in the **Laurel** and **Indian chambers**. In the southeastern corner, the east tower apartments on this floor are occupied by the **Musée du Chambord**, dedicated to Henri, the count of that name and the last serious pretender to the French throne (see box, opposite). The large collection of miniature copper artillery pieces gathered in the last room was used for the count's military training, though as Henry James noted sniffily, "I wondered, if he should take it into his head to fire off his little canon, how much harm the comte de Chambord would do." You can spot the occasional French monarchist fanatic on pilgrimage, but to anyone else the museum is exceedingly dull, a sad collection of portraits, busts, sentimental knick-knacks and oppressive furnishings, though the gilded wooden regalia used for the count's funeral mass in the château's chapel have curiosity value.

Most people miss out the **second floor** altogether, but it's worth stepping off the staircase for the nobly coffered ceilings that vault over the vestibules. The half-empty apartment rooms house a rambling **Musée de la Chasse**. Even if you're not a hunting enthusiast, you can find some beautiful paintings and engravings of animals among the guns and glorificatory paintings, and you get a good sense of the emptiness and chilly silence that has so long been Chambord's lot. The finest exhibits are two superb seventeenth-century tapestry cycles, kept in the north tower suite. One set depicts Diana, goddess of the hunt; another, based on cartoons by Lebrun, tells the story of Meleager, the heroic huntsman from Ovid's *Metamorphoses*.

The side wings

François I's apartments were installed in the **east wing** in the early 1540s, served by their own separate tower staircase. The intimate sequence of inter-locking rooms may be largely bare and empty, but it gives a surprisingly good sense of a lived-in space. The highlights are the bedchamber, fitted out with Renaissance-style furnishings, and the light-filled *studiolo*, or private study, with its delicate coffered and vaulted roof inscribed with the royal fleur-de-lis and François' own flaming salamander emblem. You can also see panels from two wonderful series of tapestries known as *Les Chasses du roi François* ("King François' hunt"), most woven in the seventeenth century.

The **west wing** of the keep, accessed by another tower staircase, is almost entirely filled by the airy **chapel**. Each rib of the broad vault rests on twin columns, according to the fashion of the 1540s.

The stables and grounds

The **stables** just south of the château were turned into barracks by the **Maréchal de Saxe**, who was given Chambord to live in by Louis XV, in thanks for the great victory at Fontenoy during the War of the Austrian Succession. They housed the marshal's riotous-living private army, which stayed with Saxe during his 1748–50 sojourn, before he tired of the château's unhealthily marshy atmosphere. The buildings are now ruined, but an open-air

The last Bourbon

At his birth in September 1820, Henri, duc de Bordeaux, was acclaimed as the **enfant du miracle**, the "miracle child", as France thought it had seen the last of the Bourbons following the death of his father early the same year. There were enough loyalists left in the country to buy the child the **Château de Chambord**, the money having been raised by public subscription. Even more surprising than Henri's birth is the fact that he claimed the throne at all. The Bourbons had already been kicked out of France twice: in the Revolution and again when Henri's grandfather Charles X was chased from the throne in the Three Glorious Days of July 1830, to be replaced with his cousin, Louis-Philippe.

Henri's mother, Marie-Caroline de Bourbon-Sicile, was a vociferous "legitimist" – that is she supported the Bourbon claim rather than the "Orléanist" claim of Louis-Philippe's supporters – and she brought up her child in the old, pig-headed Bourbon way. Despite his unassuming new title of **comte de Chambord**, it was expected that Henri would reclaim his rightful throne – the child's collection of miniature artillery, now exhibited at the château, was intended as more than a plaything. After the fall of Napoleon III, in 1871, a conservative, royalist government took control of the National Assembly, and overtures were made to the count to return to Paris as Henri V. Everyone assumed he would take up the throne.

But with characteristic Bourbon arrogance, Henri released what has become known as the **White Flag Manifesto** of 5 July 1871, probably written while he spent his only three nights at Chambord. He claimed that he couldn't relinquish the Bourbon's white flag – "the standard of Henri IV, of François I and of Joan of Arc ... which floated over my cradle and will shade my tomb" – in favour of the Republican *tricolore*. What he meant was that he wouldn't submit to the Crown being awarded him by the National Assembly, rather than being due to him by God. As his final refusal letter of October 1873 admitted, with a certain integrity, "I do not want to be the legitimate king of the Revolution."

equestrian show (May, June & Sept Mon–Fri 11.45am, Sat & Sun 11.45am & 4.30pm; July & Aug daily 11.45am & 4.30pm; €8.50; ℡02.54.20.31.01, ⓦwww.chambord-horse-show.fr) uses the site for displays of trick riding, with costumed riders.

You can rent **bikes** and **boats** from the jetty where the Cosson passes alongside the main facade of the château (closed Oct–March). Rowboats cost around €10–20 per hour, depending on the number of people.

Practicalities

The line 2 **bus** from Blois picks up and drops off right in front of the château, but there's usually only one useful service, leaving from the gare SNCF in Blois at 12.20pm (Sun at 1.45pm), so check the exact departure time. Alternatively, you can take the inexpensive tourist bus (see p.153).

Accommodation in the village of **Chambord** itself can be found opposite the château (and beside the cafeterias and postcard stalls) at the *Hôtel du Grand St-Michel* (℡02.54.20.31.31; ⓦwww.saintmichel-chambord.com; ❸). The newly furnished rooms aren't particularly special, but taking in the sight of Chambord after the crowds have left is very satisfying, and the more expensive rooms (❻) have direct views of the château. Ten kilometres east, at Crouy-sur-Cosson, there are attractively floral chambres d'hôtes at the *Moulin de Crouy*, 3 rte de Cordellerie (℡02.54.87.56.19, ⓦlemoulindecrouy.com; ❹), an ivy-clad watermill set in large gardens, with a swimming pool.

The Domaine de Chambord and around

In 1528, the Venetian ambassador and traveller Andrea Navagero wrote that in the forests near Blois was a deer so marvellous that no one would hunt it, indeed "every respect is paid to it, such as one would show to a wonder of the world". Much of the forest has disappeared since then, but a well-protected game reserve, the **Domaine de Chambord**, survives behind 32km of wall. Wild boar roam freely, and badgers, foxes, hares, rabbits and even wild sheep live in the forest, though red deer are still the beasts you're most likely to spot, along with circling buzzards. Regional information is available online at Ⓦwww .chambordcountry.com.

Only two areas of the reserve are open for free exploration: the strip alongside the Cosson as it flows towards Blois, and the area west of the D112 road to Muides-sur-Loire, where there are four short circular routes along signposted paths. At various points along these you'll find hides for viewing animals. You can get around easily enough on foot, or rent a **bike** from the boat jetty next to the château de Chambord (see p.159). To get deeper into the forest you'll have to sign up at the château ticket office in advance for a **guided excursion**, such as the half-day horseback, bike or walking tours of the forest (€35, lunch included; summer only) – which often focus on seasonal events, such as the deer rut in autumn. You can also explore the reserve in a 4WD, but it's not the best way to see wildlife. A free leaflet available at the château gives details (French-language only, but all staff speak English and can help), or you can call ☎02.54.50.50.00 or visit Ⓦwww.chambord.org.

St-Dyé-sur-Loire

The materials used for building Chambord almost all arrived at the tiny riverside port of **ST-DYÉ-SUR-LOIRE**, 3km from Chambord (with a dedicated cycle path connecting the two). These days the riverside quays are mere embankments, but they make for a delightful place to stroll, especially at sunset when the sandbanks teem with birds. The friendly **Maison de la Loire**, 73 rue Nationale (Tues–Sun 10am–noon & 2–6pm; ☎02.54.81.65.45), has a small exhibition on the port and the building of Chambord, as well as lots of information on the natural history of the river (€2.50). Staff can organize inexpensive bird-watching trips and half-day nature trips canoeing down from St-Laurent.

A rather swanky **hotel**, the *Manoir Bel Air* (☎02.54.81.60.10; Ⓦwww .manoirdebelair.com; ❹), stands at the eastern end of the village; the more expensive rooms at the back (❺) have great river views, and there's a good riverside restaurant, but it can feel unfriendly and oversized. You're better off at M and Mme Bonnefoy's extremely friendly **chambres d'hôtes**, 102 rue Nationale, at the western end of the village (☎02.54.81.60.01; ❹). The interiors are furnished with antiques and the back gate gives onto a path that runs down a field and right onto the riverbank.

Bracieux

There's not a lot to **BRACIEUX**, a pleasant little town just beyond the southern wall of the Domaine de Chambord, but it makes a good base for exploring the surrounding châteaux, especially by bike. You can visit the **chocolaterie Vauché** (mid-June to Aug daily 10am–12.30pm & 2–7pm; Sept to mid-June Tues–Sat 10am–12.30pm & 2–7pm, Sun 3–7pm; free), though it's really just a glorified shop with a window overlooking the modest factory floor. On Thursday mornings (and Sunday mornings in summer), a **market** gathers under the ancient covered *halle*, which is the town's main sight.

The château

The word "château" can mean anything from a ruined castle keep to an exquisite eighteenth-century mansion, but the first châteaux in the Loire Valley were powerful, foursquare *donjons*. These tower-keeps were more than just defensive devices, more even than feudal symbols: they legally confirmed the nobility of their owner. Old keeps were rarely demolished in later years, even where the rest of a château was repeatedly rebuilt.

The most ancient *donjons*, as at **Langeais** and **Loches**, date back to Foulque Nerra, the belligerent eleventh-century count of Anjou. From the early thirteenth century onwards, thanks to Crusader techniques, giant curtain walls were constructed at strategic sites such as **Chinon** and **Angers**. Walls also began to enclose the *basse-cour*, an open space for trading and farm work at the château gates, flanked by *communs*, or outbuildings. These were originally labourers' dwellings but later became almost as elaborate as the châteaux themselves.

The medieval château was occupied by the seigneur, along with his feudal entourage, servants and garrison. Life focused on the first-floor *grande salle*, a large room used for anything from law-giving to feasting and guest accommodation. Servants congregated in a separate *salle basse*, below. Furniture was sparse, partly because most households moved regularly between a number of different châteaux. Chests and trunks doubled up as beds, and the cold walls were covered with tapestries. Meals could be taken anywhere, with trestle tables being brought in wherever required, including in the *chambres*, or bedrooms – which were usually shared.

Gothic castles

In the fourteenth and fifteenth centuries, the old keeps were transformed. Fine stone-carving was applied to doors and windows, and roofscapes came alive with balustrades, gables and exquisite leadwork. With the end of the Hundred Years War, châteaux began to be less defensively planned. Among the many built in the 1460s and 1470s, **Le Plessis-Bourré** has stout walls, a wide moat and a drawbridge, while **Langeais** is buttressed by towers. Both, however, have large, elaborately carved windows – of little use for defence.

Life inside the château began to change. Courts and households were still itinerant, capping the amount of attention spent on internal decoration or design, but for the first time châteaux incorporated private rooms. In the new *logis*, or "lodging", there would be two or more *chambres*: the outer room, was used for public audiences, while the inner *chambre de gîte* was used for sleeping and private conversations. Off it lay a latrine, and sometimes a private oratory or study. The basic layout is found all over the region, but is best preserved in the Vieux Logis at Loches.

▲ Langeais, Touraine

airy eighteenth-century work, though the current owners are slowly returning some of the windows to their original Renaissance shape.

For a lunch stop, the *Bistro d'Arian* (☎02.54.46.42.85; closed Thurs), in the village of Pont d'Arian, 1km south, is a traditional **restaurant** serving excellent *cuisine du terroir* – well-cooked food using lots of local produce, so lots of game in season – with menus from €14.

Château de Cheverny

Fourteen kilometres southeast of Blois, the **château de Cheverny** (daily: April–June & Sept 9.15am–6.15pm; July & Aug 9.15am–6.45pm; Oct–March 9.45am–5pm; ⓦwww.chateau-cheverny.fr; €6.50) is the perfect seventeenth-century château. Built largely in the 1620s and early 1630s and never altered, it presents an immaculate picture of symmetry, harmony and the aristocratic good life – descendants of the first owners still own, live in and go hunting from Cheverny today. The stone from which it is built – from Bourré on the River Cher (see p.174) – lightens with age, and the château gleams like a great white brick in its acres of rolling parkland.

The **Hurault** family have been the *seigneurs* of a château here since 1510, but the story of the present building begins a hundred years later, when one Henri Hurault was visiting the court of Henri IV. The legend goes that as he left the king's chamber, he caught a glimpse in a mirror of the king making the sign of a cuckold's horns behind his head. He galloped home in a jealous rage to Cheverny, where he surprised his wife in bed with her lover. After murdering the lover in the garden, he forced his wife to choose death by poison or pistol shot. She chose the bottle rather than the bullet – either way, Henri was free to marry again. His second wife, Marguerite, masterminded the building of the new château while her husband was an officer of Louis XIII's court.

For once, the old building was entirely expunged, and Marguerite took advantage of the clean sheet by building an entirely new kind of structure: purist, Classical and restrained. Cheverny's **architecture** seems unrelated to the feudal fortress, a new departure for a Loire château, but there are telltale throwbacks. In particular, the little room and steep roof that top off the central staircase block make it look rather like a tower, and the side pavilions could almost be corner turrets.

Since the château was first built, the Huraults have proved a tenacious lot. In 1764 they were forced to sell the château to a fellow aristocrat, Jean-Nicolas Dufort-de-Saint-Leu – who wanted to retire to a modest country retreat in order to put a cap on his outrageous spending at Versailles – but a descendant of the family, the marquis de Vibraye, managed to buy it back under the restored Bourbon king, Charles X. The current owner, Charles-Antoine de Vibraye, lives on the second floor with his wife and three children, whose photos litter pianos and occasional tables throughout the château.

Renaissance palaces

France's architectural Renaissance was kickstarted at the end of the fifteenth century by two dozen Italian craftsmen in the entourage of Charles VIII. At **Chaumont** and **Amboise** they worked on decorative, Classically inspired motifs, importing a whole new style into France. The Renaissance proper is usually held to begin with François I, whose new wing at Blois established the key design features of early Renaissance architecture. There was a new attention to symmetry and aesthetic balance: stone windows were framed by pilasters topped by carved capitals; decorative panels of marble

▲ Villandry, Touraine

(or locally available slate) were set into the stone for contrast; shallow-carved shells, scrolls and flowers proliferated; and regularly spaced window openings were alternated with plain stone walls divided by horizontal bands of stone. The flamboyance of the treatment, however, owed as much to local skills and the soft local stone, called tufa, as it did to imported ideas.

Nobles soon began to copy the new fashions, most elegantly at **Azay-le-Rideau** and **Chenonceau**. Delight in symmetry and decorative flair spilled over into garden design, and many châteaux were surrounded by elaborately planted terraces – as superbly re-created at **Villandry** – divided into the *parterre*, or raised flower-beds, and the *potager*, the vegetable garden.

Classical mansions

In the 1530s François I quit the Loire for Paris and Fontainebleau. Thereafter, Classical principles were applied with a new sobriety and elegance, as in Beauregard and the bridge section of Chenonceau. In the seventeenth century the basic arrangement of the medieval *logis* persisted. Floors were divided into *appartements*, with a succession of rooms of various degrees of privacy. The public salon became the lynchpin of social life, the home of polite "conversation" – another French invention of the era. Leading off the *salon* was the *antechambre*, then the *chambre*, which usually had an alcove for the bed, and finally the private *cabinet*.

New architectural fashions included *œil-de-bœuf* (bull's eye) and "French" windows. The former brought light into the topmost floors, which started to be occupied by servants, while the latter allowed the salon to flow into the gardens. In the Loire, serene, horizontally organized facades were built in the local white tufa , although an element of quintessentially French, tower-like verticality remained, however, with most châteaux divided up into discernible pavilions, as at **Cheverny** and the Gaston d'Orléans wing at Blois. The *basse-cour* began to be replaced by a symmetrically arranged *avant-cour* (forecourt), with formal gardens flanked by miniature moats and elegant pavilions or stable blocks. **La Ferté-St-Aubin**, south of Orléans, is a beautiful example.

▼ Cheverny, near Blois

▲ Cooking at La Ferté-St-Aubin, Orléanais

In the eighteenth century picturesque landscapes became the thing. Gardens were turned over to grass and trees in the "English" style, and at Chaumont, Villandry and **Ussé**, whole wings were torn down in order to open up the internal courtyard to the view. There was little new building out in what had become the sticks, though the exquisite Montgeoffroy is a notable exception.

The modern château

Nineteenth-century châteaux tended to ape the designs of the past, often on a vast scale. A distinctly English influence crept in, with a fad for great halls on the model of the stately home.

New bourgeois wealth meant that scores of châteaux were built all over the Sologne and Anjou; almost all remain in private hands.

In the twentieth century many châteaux were bought or bequeathed to the local or national governments, and new building was almost unheard of. Instead, **restoration** has been the keynote. France has traditionally followed a policy of returning monuments to their "original" condition, rather than merely arresting decay. Today, châteaux interiors are "brought back to life" with the help of restorers' brushes and "period" furniture snapped up from auction rooms around the world.

Nineteenth-century restorers, meanwhile, brutalized more stone-carving than the heritage industry cares to admit, and even today you can see whole areas of facade gleaming with new-cut white **tufa**. In fact, tufa is such a soft stone that almost *any* surface which has been exposed to the weather must have been recut at some point in its life, making the whole idea of "authenticity" seem rather redundant.

◄ Restoration at Talcy, Orléanais

There are two **hotels**: the decent *Hôtel du Cygne* (☎02.54.46.41.07, ⓦwww .hotelducygne.com; ❹), which has a pool; and the attractive *Hôtel de la Bonnheure*, 9 rue René Masson (☎02.54.46.41.57, ⓦwww.hoteldelabonnheur .com; ❹), which has a good range of rooms and apartments set around floral gardens. Both rent bikes to guests for a moderate price. Bracieux also has a large, three-star **campsite** (☎02.54.46.41.84; closed mid-Nov to mid-March) with a summer-only pool and the option to rent mobile homes (around €40 for up to six people). At the edge of the village, where the Chambord and Blois roads split, there's a top-flight **restaurant**, ⍟ *Le Relais de Bracieux* (☎02.54.46.41.22; menus €38–140; closed Tues & Wed), with a strong emphasis on local, seasonal produce – you might find a *croustillante* of Loire eels in Orléans vinegar, wild boar with spiced vegetables or hare fillet with juniper berries.

Château de Villesavin

Despite its prime location midway between Chambord and Cheverny, many visitors hurry past the graceful **château de Villesavin**, set back from the road 3km west of Bracieux (mid-Feb to May daily 10am–noon & 2–7pm; June–Sept daily 10am–7pm; Oct to mid-Nov daily 10am–noon & 2–6pm; mid-Nov to end Dec Sat & Sun 2–5pm; guided tour €7.50, grounds only €6; ⓦwww .chateauvillesavin.com). You'll need your own transport to get there and the entry ticket is expensive for what's on offer – a modest, low-slung set of white-stone buildings arranged around three sides of a courtyard – but as an antidote to the bombast of its neighbours, Villesavin is perfect.

The present structure is the work of **Jean le Breton**, who shared François I's defeat and imprisonment at the Battle of Pavia in 1525. On his return from Italy, Le Breton was rewarded with the task of managing the payments for the construction of Chambord, and he found time to build his own château nearby, starting construction in 1527 and finishing it only ten years later – having begun work at Villandry (see p.101) in the meantime. Legend has it that Villesavin was built with materials or funds earmarked for Chambord, but all that's really known is that many of the Italianate architectural ideas, and probably some of the craftsmen, were borrowed from the giant building site down the road.

Despite Le Breton's links with Chambord, in many ways Villesavin is closer in spirit to a Classical villa than a French château – and indeed a Roman "Villa Savinus" may once have stood at this spot. Over and above the obviously Classical details, the arrangement of the low-level buildings round a courtyard gives off a distinct whiff of Rome, suggesting refined but practical country living. There's even a statue of the goddess Diana in the centre of the facade, while the **chapel** is relegated to a side wing; inside, the walls and vaults are entirely painted in still-bright colours, with a fine sixteenth-century wall-painting of the Flagellation.

The outbuildings on the far side of the chapel house a bizarre museum dedicated to nineteenth-century marital garb, but persevere as far as the giant **dovecote** (see box, p.162), its 1500 pigeonholes still accessible by a ladder turning around a central spindle. From here you can walk round to the plainer southern facade of the château.

The guided tour of the **interior** is only moderately interesting, and usually in French only. This is, after all, a real home rather than a museum, lived in today by the comte and comtesse de Sparre. The only room in the château that preserves its sixteenth-century form is the kitchen, with its blackened beams and roasting spit in the huge fireplace. The rest of the rooms are graceful and

The interior

The château's **interior** decoration has only been added to, never destroyed, and the extravagant display of paintings, furniture, tapestries and armour against the gilded, sculpted and carved walls and ceilings is almost overwhelming. The most precious objects are hard to pick out from the sumptuous whole, but the highlight is the work of the painter Jean Monier, whose charming, cack-handed painted wall panels in the **dining room** tell stories from *Don Quixote*. From here, the signposts lead you upstairs to the congenial **Private Apartments**. They were in use until 1985, and give a rare glimpse of an elegant, contemporary château decor. On the far side of the central staircase, the beams and panels of the **Arms Room** are awash with mottos and flowers by Jean Monier, and the golden chimneypiece shows his version of the *Death of Adonis*. On the opposite side of the room, a seventeenth-century tapestry from the Parisian Gobelins workshop is extraordinary for its vibrant and unfaded colours. In the **King's Bedroom**, just beyond, the colours are yet more astonishing, with paintings by Monier of Perseus and Andromeda adorning almost every surface, four fabulously intricate tapestries on the walls and an original gilded and silk-hung sixteenth-century bed.

By way of contrast, the next room on the circuit, the **Great Drawing Room**, down on the ground floor, has a typically cluttered nineteenth-century feel, overstocked with Louis XIV chairs and other scraps of precious furniture. It is, however, hung with some very fine portraits, including an excellent Mignard effort over the fireplace showing Henri Hurault's grandson's wife, and a set depicting Louis XIII along with his wife, his brother Gaston d'Orléans and his niece Anne, Mlle de Montpensier. Between the windows on the north side of the room hangs a gorgeous portrait of Henri Hurtault's daughter Elisabeth, whom Mlle de Montpensier described as having "admirable hands and the loveliest elbow I have ever seen". On either side of the mirror opposite the chimneypiece are two remarkable pictures: one shows Cosimo de' Medici, future grand duke of Florence, and is attributed to **Titian**; the other is from the school of Raphael. But the most treasured paintings are in the **gallery** beyond, where the three small, sixteenth-century Hurault family portraits above the door are by François I's court painter, **François Clouet**.

The outbuildings and grounds

The rear facade of the château is very different from the front, its projecting towers and dressed stone windows and edges biting into the plainly rendered walls in what became the classic Louis XIII style. The low building at the far end of the lawns is the **Orangery**, built by the Duforts, no doubt as part of their penny-pinching regime.

Tintin in the Loire

Some visitors to Cheverny find the château oddly familiar. If they do, it's probably because Hergé used it as the model for Marlinspike Hall (Moulinsart in French), the ancestral home of Tintin's nautical friend, **Captain Haddock**. The only change Hergé made was to remove the large outer pavilions from his drawings.

The connection is celebrated in the slick exhibition, **Les Secrets de Moulinsart**, housed in the outbuilding next to the main gate (daily 9.30am–6.45pm; adults €11.50 with château ticket, children aged 7–14 €6.40 with château ticket), which retells various Tintin stories in rooms dressed up in the style of the cartoon, enlivened by audio-visual effects and well-made animation clips – the latter in French only.

Given its situation on the edge of the Sologne, the château has always been a centre for hunting with dogs. Near the main entrance, the **trophy room** holds around two thousand sets of antlers. The **kennels** alongside house a hundred lithe and odorous hunting hounds – a cross between foxhound and Poitevin – that mill and loll about while they wait for the next stag. If you can stomach it, feeding time (April to mid-Sept at 5pm) is something to be seen, the dogs obediently waiting for permission before tearing into their meat. Cheverny's hunt culls around thirty animals a year, a figure set by the National Forestry Office.

You can explore the elegant **grounds** on foot, or take a sedate, hour-long tour by golf-buggy and boat (April to mid-Nov; €11.20 including château entry).

Practicalities

Cheverny's small but very helpful **tourist office**, 12 rue de Chêne des Dames (daily: March–June & Sept 10–noon & 2–7pm; July & Aug Mon–Fri 10am–7pm, Sat & Sun closed 1-2pm; Oct–Feb 10am–noon & 2–6pm; Nov–Feb 2–6pm; ☎02.54.79.95.63), is on the main road 50m along from the château gates. **Bikes** can be rented from the four-star **campsite** *Les Saules* (☎02.54.79.90.01; closed mid-Oct to March), just beyond the village on the D102 south to Contres. A **bus** service connects Cheverny to Blois and Romorantin, running three times daily in each direction.

The village of **COUR CHEVERNY**, Cheverny's larger neighbour, 1km away, has a more basic, municipal campsite and a two-star hotel, the *Hôtel des Trois Marchands* (☎02.54.79.96.44, Ⓦwww.hoteldes3marchands.com; ❸; closed mid-Feb to mid-March). The hotel is full of provincial old-world character, though the decor in the rooms is rather tired. The restaurant, however, is elegant and rather smart (menus €23–33); there's also an inexpensive bar and grill next door. Set back from the road to Fougères-sur-Bièvre in its own park, a couple of kilometres out of town, the three-star ⚜ *Château de Breuil* (☎02.54.44.20.20, Ⓦwww.chateau-du-breuil.fr; ❸; closed Jan–March) is distinctly classy, with elegant, period-furnished bedrooms and a pool. Right opposite the château entrance, the **restaurant** *Le Pichet* (☎02.54.79.97.23; closed Sun evening & Mon) does decent regional fare, with menus from €17.

The surrounding countryside is packed with good **chambres d'hôtes**. The following are among the nicest, but Cheverny's tourist office can supply a more complete list. Six kilometres from Cheverny, near Chitenay, ⚜ *Le Clos Bigot* (☎02.54.44.21.28, Ⓦwww.gites-cheverny.com; ❸) is a picturesque collection of old buildings built round a courtyard. The rooms are all charmingly furnished, with plentiful roof beams and the like, but the suite in the dovecote (❻), with its huge fireplace and two levels, is the most desirable of all. Nearby, just off the road between Cormeray and Cellettes, is the modest but attractive *Château de la Coque* (☎02.54.70.33.92; ❻). At Contres, 10km south of Cheverny, *La Rabouillère*, chemin de Marçon (☎02.54.79.05.14, Ⓦwww.larabouillere.com; ❹), is a half-timbered farmhouse with two cosy and freshly decorated rooms, and two further rooms in a lovely detached cottage.

Château de Troussay

Three kilometres from Cheverny, on the road to Cormeray, the **château de Troussay** (April–June & Sept daily 10.30am–12.30pm & 2–6pm; July & Aug daily 10am–6.30pm, Tues 10am–10pm; Oct Sat & Sun 10.30am–12.30pm & 2–5.30pm; €5) is a little gem. It was originally built in the fifteenth century as a *gentilhommière*, or country manor, the noble details round chimneys and windows added only in the sixteenth century. In fact, some oddments of sculpture only found their way onto the facade after 1828, when the historian Louis de Saussaye rescued various bits of decoration from dilapidated châteaux in the region.

More purloined fragments can be seen on the French-language guided tour of the interior, notably the stained-glass windows from the Guises' *hôtel* in Blois and the delicately carved but heavy **oratory door**, a rare survival from the demolished château de Bury, arguably the first Renaissance château of them all. In all, the interior is handsome rather than spectacular, as fits the setting.

As is normal in a minor château, the *communs*, or outbuildings, run right up to the main front of the house, forming a large sandy yard – and Troussay was a working farm for much of its life. The links are acknowledged in a small exhibition on Sologne life in part of the old stables, which displays lots of old photos and agricultural implements, with meticulous homespun explanations (in French). A little room is entirely devoted to doing the laundry, but most curious is the section on light carts drawn by dogs, as used in the Sologne by everyone from schoolchildren to the postman.

Château de Fougères-sur-Bièvre

The proudly defensive **château de Fougères-sur-Bièvre** (mid-May to mid-Sept daily 9.30am–12.30pm & 2–6.30pm; mid-Sept to mid-May daily except Tues 10am–12.30pm & 2–5pm; €4.60) lies in the village of the same name, 10km southwest of Cheverny. The château was built in 1470 by Louis XI's chancellor, the aptly named Pierre de Refuge, who was clearly sceptical about long-term peace: unlike its more luxurious contemporaries this is a veritable fortress, turned tightly in on itself.

The inner **courtyard** is the most attractive feature. Spindly towers buttress the walls, little slate roofs crowded between and on top of them, and a long arcaded gallery runs the length of one side as far as the **chapel**, which housed a millwheel for most of the nineteenth century. Two decorated door lintels survive from Pierre de Refuge's day, but the rest of the stonework is plain. Inside, you can scurry freely about the many corridors, rooms and spiral staircases, even clambering under the oak-framed roof and strolling along the **guard walk**, and there are rarely other visitors to interfere with the medieval fantasy. Unfortunately, the château's more recent history as a mill and later a hostel means almost nothing survives apart from the bare walls, ceilings and fireplaces. Various exhibits along the way explain medieval building techniques, but you'll need fairly good French to appreciate the explanations.

Château de Chaumont

When Catherine de Médicis forced her rival, Diane de Poitiers, to hand over Chenonceau (see p.89) in return for the **château de Chaumont** (daily: April & late Sept 10.30am–5.30pm; May to mid-Sept 9.30am–6.30pm; Oct–March 10am–12.30pm & 1.30pm–5pm; €6.10; grounds open daily 9.30am–dusk; free), Diane is thought to have had the worst of the deal, although you can't help feeling that she didn't have much to complain about. Sitting on a low hilltop overlooking the Loire, 20km downstream from Blois, the château occupies one of the finest bits of real estate in the region. To get to the château you can take one of the frequent **trains** from Blois or Tours, get off at Onzain and stroll across the Loire – no more than a thirty-minute walk.

The original fortress on the site was destroyed by Louis XI in revenge for the part its owner, Pierre d'Amboise, played in the "League of Public Weal", an alliance of powerful nobles against the ever-increasing power of the monarch. But Pierre found his way back into the king's favour, and with his son Charles I, he was able to build much of the quintessentially medieval castle – complete with machicolated round towers, moat and drawbridge – that stands today. Under Louis XII, Pierre's grandson **Charles II d'Amboise** was sent to Milan as governor of the newly won French territories, where he became the patron of Leonardo da Vinci. With his uncle, the powerful Cardinal Georges d'Amboise, he was one of the first to import the fashionable ideas of the Italian Renaissance into France. His interlaced initials, as Charles de Chaumont, are repeated along the odd frieze that runs in a band across the exterior walls, alternating with what looks like a thorny, steaming dung heap but is supposed to signify *chaud mont* ("hot hill") – though the château's name actually comes from *chauve*, meaning bald, a reference to the woods cleared from the hilltop in order to build the original castle. More letter Cs appear on the elaborately allegorical plaque that overlooks the drawbridge, above the heads of two naked savages holding the family coat of arms. The building works were completed by **Diane de Poitiers**, who arrived in 1559, just nine years after Catherine de Médicis bought the château from the Amboise family.

The interior
Proto-Renaissance design is more obvious in the courtyard, which today forms three sides of a square, the fourth side having been demolished in 1739 to improve the views over the river, which are spectacular. Inside the château, the heavy nineteenth-century decor of the ground-floor rooms dates from the ownership of **Marie Say**, daughter of the millionaire sugar baron Constant Say, and her husband **Amédée de Broglie**, who together lived here in grand style until the bottom fell out of the sugar market and the château was sold to the French state in 1938.

A few rooms on the **first floor** have been remodelled in Renaissance style. The large council chamber is floored with seventeenth-century majolica tiles, its walls adorned with wonderfully busy sixteenth-century tapestries showing the gods of each of the seven planets known to exist at the time. Sadly, the stunning series of tapestries commissioned by Charles II to depict Petrarch's Triumphs – Time, Youth, Love, Eternity – are now kept in the Cleveland Museum of Art.

The grounds
The Broglie family also transformed the 21-hectare landscaped **park** into the fashionable English style – all rolling lawns and tall trees, with no fussy French flower-beds – and built the remarkable Belle Époque **stables**. These have porcelain troughs and elegant electric lamps for the benefit of the horses, at a time before the château itself was wired, let alone the rest of the country. A corner of the château grounds now plays host to an annual **Festival des Jardins** (May to mid-Oct daily 9.30am to dusk; €8.50, or €11 with château entry), a huge affair which shows off the extravagant efforts of scores of contemporary garden designers.

On weekends in summer, you can secure the best view of the château from the deck of a traditional Loire boat. Book in advance with the Association Millière Raboton (☎06.88.76.57.14, ⓦwww.milliere-raboton.net), whose **boat trips** (€12–15) leave from the quay immediately below the château, and last roughly an hour and a half. It's possible to organize an excursion pretty much any time from dawn to well after dusk – early and late are best for wildlife. You can even camp out overnight on an island sand bank, with a freshly caught fish supper and the services of an on-hand naturalist.

The Sologne

Viewed from the air, the **Sologne** is a bewildering wasteland of sparse woodland, bog, heath and field, studded with hundreds of gleaming *étangs* – or man-made lakes and ponds. Indeed, so ubiquitous is the *étang* that its characteristic, T-shaped sluice-gate has been adopted as the Sologne's symbol. On a dark, damp day the region really earns its soubriquet of *triste* ("sad") Sologne. But when the sun is shining on the water lilies and the broom is in golden, summer bloom, when the birches, oaks and beech trees are in their autumn colours, or when you catch a glimpse of a night heron, hear a bittern's boom, or stumble upon a butterfly orchid, the Sologne can be a revelation.

As revelations go, however, the Sologne's are somewhat hard to track down. The region remains the refuge of the French aristocracy, along with the descendants of rich industrialists who bought land and built châteaux here in the latter part of the nineteenth century. **Hunting** is the thing, not tourism, and much of the Sologne is out of bounds or simply physically impenetrable. This conservative culture means that it's a frustrating region to visit, with most châteaux cached in forests at the end of long, barred drives – Sologne estates are unusually large by French standards.

Even the Sologne's abundant **wildlife** requires patience and persistence to see. Find the right picnic spot or the right walk, however, and you may spot the wild boar or red and roe deer so eagerly sought by the hunters. You'll certainly see lots of birds. Alongside the plentiful gamebirds – ducks of all kinds, wood pigeons, pheasants and grey and red-legged partridge – the Sologne shelters rarer species such as the black-winged stilt, short-toed eagle, marsh harrier, black-necked grebe, and purple and night heron. Butterflies, damselflies and dragonflies are legion – as are more iniquitous biting beasties, from gnats to mosquitoes. You're not even safe underwater, as some *étangs* harbour leeches. These won't do you much harm if you decide to go for a rustic swim, but are highly unpleasant.

The Sologne's mosquitoes meant that it was long famous for **malaria**, and the disease was only finally stamped out in the nineteenth century by the efficient draining of the marshes – hence the endless artificial *étangs*. For centuries, these were used for **fish farming**. Carp were raised on a mammoth scale in the medieval era and transported live all over Europe, especially to the east. This trade had the added benefit that fish were the main predators of mosquito larvae. In the seventeenth and eighteenth centuries, however, the *étangs* fell into disuse. Today, line-fishermen are slowly introducing fish – mainly pike, zander and carp – back into the Sologne. The depredations of (legally protected) cormorants, however, mean that would-be pisciculturists can't begin to compete with the low-cost fish farms of – ironically enough – Eastern Europe. The region's sandy, acidic soil, meanwhile, remains too poor to support all but the most minimal farming. Industrialization of the Sologne's other traditional crop, hemp, which thrives on the region's sandy soil and has long been grown here for its fibre, is hampered by the need for crop licences.

The **Sologne** isn't an official French region, but spreads across three administrative *départements*: the Loir-et-Cher, the region's heartland, to the west; the Cher, to the east; and the Loiret, to the north. Only the western area that falls within the Loir-et-Cher *département* is covered in this section. The eastern and northern fringes of the region are discussed elsewhere in the guide, where you'll find accounts of **Aubigny-sur-Nère** (see p.236) and the area around **La Ferté-St-Aubin** (see p.197), with its rambling château and nearby nature reserve.

Walking in the Sologne

There are over 1000km of signposted **footpaths** in the Sologne, many accessible by bicycle, and tourist offices in most towns and villages can provide maps, along with details of horse-riding and bike rental. Two *grandes randonnées*, or national walking routes, lead through the Sologne, both variants of the main GR3 along the Loire – which turns a little inland south of Blois, passing close to the château de Beauregard before forking at rue de Meneuil, 5km northwest of the château de Villesavin. The northern **GR3C** runs through Chambord and east, mostly along forest roads, to Thoury and La Ferté-St-Cyr, where it rejoins the southern branch, the **GR31**, which takes a more attractive route through Bracieux and along footpaths through the southern part of the Forêt de Chambord. From La Ferté-St-Cyr you can continue on the wooded GR3C east towards Ménéstreau-en-Villette (see p.198), head southeast on the GR31 towards La Ferté-Beauharnais and Lamotte-Beuvron, where it turns south, or take the **GRP** (*grande randonnée de pays*) **Vallée des Rois** north towards Cléry-St-André, in the Orléanais (see p.201). A number of other GRP side-routes allow you to make circular walks.

The best **map** for all these routes is IGN 3615, *Sologne*. If you can follow French, the walkers' guidebook *La Sologne à Pied* (€7.50) details some twenty walks lasting from two to six hours – even if you don't speak French you can just follow the route maps. If you're exploring the Sologne during the **hunting season** (Oct 1–March 1), don't stray from the marked paths; there are endless stories of people being accidentally shot.

One of the few private châteaux to open its doors to visitors is the romantic **château de Moulin**, built in the handsome red brick typical of the region. Nearby, the large but exceedingly dull town of **Romorantin-Lanthenay** acts as something of an unofficial regional capital, but to get the best of the Sologne you'll have to head into the countryside, either to a country hotel like the one at **La Ferté–Imbault**, or out to a wilderness area such as the **Pays des Etangs**, around the little village of **St-Viâtre**.

Romorantin-Lanthenay

Forty kilometres southeast of Blois, **ROMORANTIN-LANTHENAY** is a French byword for stick-in-the-mud provincial dullness. Even the old Renault/ Matra factory which sustained the town for so long is finally closing its doors, leaving almost ten percent of Romorantin's inhabitants out of work. But it remains the biggest town in the Sologne, and has a great hotel-restaurant. The best time to visit is in the last weekend in October, during the **Journées Gastronomiques** food festival, when hundreds of street stalls tempt you with a mixture of traditional and novel dishes centred on game, wild mushrooms, apples and pumpkins.

The Town

Romorantin made a bid for stardom in the early sixteenth century, when Leonardo da Vinci drew up plans for a utopian city called Romolontino, or "little Rome", but his sketches were never realized, although some claim that they took shape further north, at the château of Chambord (see box on p.155). Today, Romorantin has just two sights of local interest. The **Musée de Sologne**, housed in the old mills astride the River Sauldre, just below the town centre (Mon & Wed–Sat 10am–noon & 2–6pm, Sun 2–6pm; €4.50; ⓦwww .museedesologne.com), is large and surprisingly glossy, with elaborately presented exhibits on the history, ecology and traditions of the area. But unless you read French, or you're particularly interested in brickworks, gamekeeping and local biscuit products, it's unlikely to enthrall. The **Musée Matra**, at 17 rue des Capucins, on the north side of the main road bridging the Sauldre (Mon & Wed–Fri 9am–noon & 2–6pm, Sat & Sun 10am–noon & 2–6pm; €4.57, or €7.62 with Musée de Sologne), shows off the Matra and Renault cars that were built at the factory on the site. There's a smattering of flashy racing cars, and a proud but less exciting display of the Renault Espace people-carrier, the most recent – and last – product of the factory.

Practicalities

For information on walking routes in the Sologne, contact the **tourist office** on the main square, place de la Paix (Mon 10am–12.15pm & 2–6.30pm, Tues–Sat 8.45am–12.15pm & 1.30–6.30pm; July & Aug also Sun 10am–noon; ☎02.54.76.43.89, ⓦwww.tourisme-romorantin.com). The tourist office can also put you in touch with the Romorantin-based organization Sologne Nature Environnement (☎02.54.76.27.18, ⓦwww.sologne-nature.org), which runs **guided walks** and nature-spotting expeditions throughout the Sologne right through the year. The town **campsite**, Camping Tournefeuille, rue de Long Eaton (☎02.54.76.16.60; closed Oct–April) rents out **bikes**, as well as **canoes** for trips on the River Sauldre.

If you fancy a splurge, head for the ⚘ *Grand Hôtel du Lion d'Or*, 69 rue G.-Clemenceau (☎02.54.94.15.15, ⓦwww.hotel-liondor.fr; ❾), an old manor house with a fabulous courtyard garden, sixteen well-appointed **rooms** and a stellar **restaurant** (meals over €100) where the chef is known for his use of organic ingredients and, sometimes, medieval spices; if you've never had frogs' legs in a seventeenth-century variety of wild garlic, this is the place to try it.

La Ferté-Imbault

One of the most impressive but definitely closed châteaux in the Sologne lies at the eastern edge of the village of **LA FERTÉ-IMBAULT**, 18km east of Romorantin. Surrounded by stables and well-tended lawns which stretch down to the main road, the noble, red-brick pile of the **château de la Ferté-Imbault** looks extremely moneyed. It should be – the château's estates once stretched across some 10,000 hectares, roughly twenty times the French average for a château. You can't get any closer to the château than the public road, but the village is pleasant to stroll around, with the remains of a Romanesque **chapel** standing among the pretty brick houses and floral displays of the little island of St-Taurin, and picnic tables on the banks of the River Sauldre.

There's a good traditional **hotel** on the main square, the *Auberge à la Tête de Lard*, 13 place des Tilleuls (☎02.54.96.22.32, ⓦwww.aubergealatetedelard.com; ❸), which has pleasant, quiet rooms and a good restaurant (menus €17–49; closed Mon, Tues lunch & Sun eve). It offers the whole Sologne experience, renting out mountain bikes to guests, leading canoe and hunting excursions, and maintaining a kilometre of riverbank for fishing.

Château du Moulin and around

Built almost entirely of brick, surrounded by water, and standing in romantic isolation at the end of a long avenue of oak trees, the **château du Moulin** (April–Sept daily except Wed 10am–11.30pm & 2–5.30pm; €7.50) is the quintessential Sologne château. It lies just outside the village of Lassay-sur-Croisne, 10km west of Romorantin-Lanthenay, and is still occupied year-round by its elderly owner, Mme de Marchéville, whose family bought it off the du Moulins in 1901.

The original builder, local *seigneur* Philippe du Moulin, earned the right to set himself up as a nobleman with a fortified château after saving Charles VIII's life at the 1495 Battle of Fornovo, the coda to the king's Italian campaigns at which he lost all his war booty. Only the main keep and the wide, low corner tower date from the original fifteenth-century fortifications, the rest of the defences having been cleared to leave a kind of open, moated courtyard, though the gatehouse block of tall, narrow towers was subsequently rebuilt. The château's brickwork is striking, curving smoothly around the various towers, the pink tint offset by an inlaid lozenge pattern in dark grey and window frames of white tufa stone. It's the same style made popular by Louis XII at Blois and elsewhere, but seems more natural here in the Sologne, where even the humblest houses are built of local brick.

Guided visits of the **interior** take place roughly every hour, and last around 45 minutes; if it's not too busy staff should be able to lay on an English-language tour. You're shown a series of half a dozen rooms in the main keep section, all beautifully furnished by the father-in-law of the current proprietor, one Louis de Marchéville. He also installed a clever central-heating system, the radiators disguised as traditional iron chimney-backs. The main **salle d'apparat** is one of the highlights, with its chestnut ceiling painted in the seventeenth century and the small polychrome statue of St Catherine, from the school of the great Tourangeau sculptor Michel Colombe. Upstairs, Mme de Marchéville's own bedroom is entirely furnished with seventeenth-century pieces. On the second floor, the **chambre de Philippe du Moulin** contains two extremely rare bits of fabric: the bedcover is actually made from material removed from the walls of the Sainte Chapelle in Paris, while the strange tapestry on the wall dates from the fourteenth century, in the semi-abstract patchwork style of Bergamo.

The restored stables now house the **Musée de la Fraise**, an exhibition celebrating the strawberry through history. Dozens of rare and delicious varieties are grown in the nearby *potager*, or kitchen garden, and visitors can taste them in season – usually from around late May to late June.

Locature de la Straize

To see how the other half lived, make for the nearby **Locature de la Straize** (April–Oct: Sat & Sun 10–11.30am & 3–6pm; Mon, Wed & Thurs call ☎02.54.83.82.89 to make an appointment; €4). The owner, who lives in an adjacent house, has reconstructed this sixteenth-century *locature* (farm-workers' cottage, in Sologne dialect) to its original sixteenth-century form, showing how it would have looked until the early part of the twentieth century: the barn on one side of the partition wall, and the simple one-room accommodation on the other. Sitting as it does on the edge of marshy fields and woodland, it's a rather moving contrast to the usual round of châteaux. Monsieur Picard has also collected an array of Solognot items in the barn next to his own house, creating a private **museum** of old clothing, tools and items in use in daily life, many of them from his own family. The hamlet of La Straize lies just a couple of kilometres west of the château du Moulin, but to get there you'll have to drive for some 6km until you get onto the road between Gy-en-Sologne and Soings-en-Sologne, which it lies halfway between.

St-Viâtre

In medieval times, the village of **ST-VIÂTRE**, which lies in the deepest Sologne, 30km northeast of Romorantin-Lanthenay, was part of the *seigneurie* or manor of Tremblevy or Tremblevif. The name says it all: this was an area long renowned for malaria, and the trembling fever fits it brought on. The last French death from malaria occurred here in 1840.

Today St-Viâtre is a tiny but robust rural community – there are two flower shops and no less than three hotel-restaurants – centred on its **church** and market square. The former is largely fifteenth-century, and has a wonderful barrel-vaulted roof, but its most remarkable features are the two Renaissance chapels. These were probably donated by Wolfgang Eberhard, count of Lupfen, a mercenary captain who had distinguished himself in François I's Italian campaign of 1515 and had been given the lordship of Tremblevy as a reward. The north chapel houses an original sixteenth-century **polyptych** of eight richly coloured and superbly realized panels, painted in the Flemish style. One side depicts the Passion of Christ, the other shows scenes from the life of St Viâtre. The saint's fifteenth-century **shrine** used to be housed in the crypt, but has now been rebuilt under a brick shelter at the north end of the village.

A panel in the centre of the village details circular walks in the locality, but the best place for information is the **Maison des Étangs**, 2 rue de la Poste (April–Oct 10am–noon & 2–6pm; rest of year call ☎02.54.88.23.00; ⓦwww .maison-des-etangs.com). It occupies a half-timbered house in the centre of St-Viâtre and contains a reconstruction of a nineteenth-century Solognot home, and an excellent exhibition on local social and natural history (€4.50), covering everything from the traditional construction of barrels, baskets and boats to wild plants and cultivated hemp. Most of the material is in French, but a guided visit in English can usually be arranged.

Practicalities

Bikes can be rented from the flower shop on the main square, La Malle aux Raboliots (☎02.54.88.43.75). If you're looking for somewhere to **stay** in the area, the *Auberge le Creusard*, 6 place de l'Eglise (☎02.54.88.91.33, Ⓕ02.54.96.18.06; ❸), is right in the middle of St-Viâtre, next to the church, and has a few unexceptional but pleasantly decorated rooms – avoid the unrefurbished ones; its **restaurant** (closed Tues evening & Wed) is good in a splendidly old-fashioned way. The restaurant at the *Lion d'Or*, next door, caters mostly for workers with its basic, but excellent, *plats du jour*.

Gastro-tourists should make the pilgrimage 15km northeast to the modest town of **LAMOTTE-BEUVRON**, where the large, well-to-do *Hôtel Tatin*, 5 ave de Vierzon (☎02.54.88.00.03, Ⓦwww.hotel-tatin.com; ❹; closed first week in Aug), is the original home of tarte Tatin – supposedly created by accident by the Tatin sisters, who once ran the hotel – and serves it all day long. It's some way to go for an upside-down apple tart, and the rooms are fairly ordinary, but the restaurant is good across the board, with refined menus from €21–51 – think sole *meunière* or duck with foie gras.

The Pays des Étangs

If you had to pinpoint the Sologne's marshy heart, it would lie in the area immediately southeast of St-Viâtre. Known as the **Pays des Étangs**, or "land of little lakes", this is the Sologne at its dampest. Bird watchers can spot great crested and black-necked grebes, marsh harriers, and endless types of ducks, with the chance to see ospreys in September and cranes in October and November. You may even hear bitterns in spring, and see black and whiskered terns nesting on the water lilies.

One of the best ways to see the area is by **bicycle** along the **route des Étangs**, which forms a 21km triangle between St-Viâtre, the village of Marcilly-en-Gault, some 7km southwest, and the Étang de Marcilly, a small lake 2km south of the little town of **LA FERTÉ-BEAUHARNAIS**. You pass endless lakes and ponds along the route, with lots of offshoot paths to explore for picnicking or bird-watching. Bikes can be rented at the *Camping de la Varenne,* 34 rue de Veillas (☎02.54.83.68.52; closed Oct–Easter), at **NEUNG-SUR-BEUVRON**, a tiny Sologne town 4km west of La Ferté-Beauharnais.

A pleasant **walking route** circles the muddy little Néant, a wooded stream just north of St-Viâtre. From the village, take the D123 towards Chaumont-sur-Tharonne and stop after 3km at Ste-Marie farm. From here a rough tarmac farm road heads east, passing the farm of St-Loup, where the odd brick structure used to house the relics of St-Loup, a local saint with reputed healing powers. The road follows the north bank of the Néant for some 4km, ending at the junction with the D49. Turn right at this main road, crossing the Néant, and then turn right again a short distance beyond the bridge at the signpost for the GR31 footpath. You then follow this footpath back along the south side of the Néant to the D123, ending up a few hundred metres south of where you started. The whole circuit from Ste-Marie is about 8km long.

△ Sologne Étang

The middle reaches of the Cher

The most attractive stretch of the Cher falls within what can be described as the river's middle reaches – defined here as the section of river bordering the Sologne, falling within the government *département* of the Loir-et-Cher. While this area lacks the historical and architectural glamour of the Touraine, to the west, or Blésois, to the north, the little towns and villages along the way have a pleasantly relaxed, backwater feel. The two main centres are **Montrichard** and **St-Aignan**, both with handsome châteaux lording it over the town – though Montrichard's is ruined and St-Aignan's closed to visitors. Near Montrichard you can make forays to low-key sights such as the restored abbey complex of **Pontlevoy**, the Gallo-Roman ruins at **Thésée-la-Romaine** and the mushroom and silkworm caves at **Bourré**, while just outside St-Aignan there's a large and professionally run **zoo**.

The exquisitely refined château of **Valençay** technically lies in the *déparement* of the Indre, but it's only a short excursion south of the Cher, close to the goat's-cheese-producing town of **Selles-sur-Cher**. If you're continuing upstream all the way to Bourges, you might want to stop off at the medieval town of **Mennetou-sur-Cher**. Beyond Mennetou, the river enters the Cher *département* at the industrial town of Vierzon, which is of no interest to visitors.

Public transport is relatively good, with **trains** serving all the towns along the Cher, from Tours and Chenonceaux, through to Montrichard, St-Aignan and on to Vierzon and Bourges.

Montrichard

A laid-back market town on the banks of the Cher, 34km south of Blois, **MONTRICHARD** also happens to have a full complement of medieval and Renaissance buildings, plus a hilltop **castle**, of which just the keep remains after Henri IV broke down the rest of the defences in the aftermath of the Wars of Religion. Between mid-July and mid-August, a medieval-costumed son-et-lumière spectacle (daily at 4.30pm and around 9pm; €15) make the most of the fortress's situation, but it's well worth walking up towards the castle at any time of year for the view over the Cher – though the keep itself is out of bounds. Various buildings on the way up to the keep contain the lovingly tended but rather dull town **museum** (daily: April & Sept 10am–noon & 2–5pm; May–Aug 10am–5pm; €5), which is divided into worthy sections on local archeology and history, paleontology, milling and, bizarrely, the archeology of the Sahara.

Montrichard's Romanesque **church** was where the disabled 12-year-old princess Jeanne de Valois, who would never be able to have children, married her cousin Louis, duc d'Orléans, in 1476. After the unlikely death of Charles VIII at Amboise, Louis became king, and politics dictated that he marry Charles VIII's widow, Anne de Bretagne. Poor Jeanne was divorced and sent off to govern Bourges, where she turned to religion, founding a new religious order. She eventually took the veil herself – though she wore her nun's habit under her clothes.

In summer, canoes, pedalos and **kayaks** can be rented (☎02.54.71.49.48; closed Sept to June) at the pleasant artificial **beach** on the opposite bank of the Cher – it's possible to paddle as far as Chenonceau, 7km downstream. Some locals swim from here, but you should be sure to seek advice before entering the water – and bear in mind that it's officially forbidden. For those feeling less energetic, the *Léonard de Vinci*, a miniature **cruise-boat**, usually makes ninety-minute trips upstream to Bourré (see p.174) and back, leaving from the main jetty (May, June, Sept & Oct Sat & Sun 3pm & 5pm; July & Aug daily 3pm &

5pm; ☎02.54.75.41.53; €9.50); at the time of writing, however, the service was uncertain, so check in advance.

On the edge of town on the D764 road north to Blois, the **Musée du Poids Lourd** (April–June & Sept Sat & Sun 1–6pm; July & Aug Tues–Sun 10am–5pm; €4) shows off a large collection of vintage lorries. You can also visit the **caves Monmousseau** (daily: April to mid-Nov 10am–6pm; mid-Nov to March 10am–noon & 2–5pm; €2.75), a ten-minute walk east of town along the road towards Bourré, where racks of bottles of sparkling wine line the quarried-out cellars. There's the usual tasting at the end of the tour, although it's not the highest-quality sparkler in the Loire.

Practicalities

Montrichard's **tourist office** is in the Maison Ave Maria, 1 rue du Pont (April–Sept Mon–Sat 9am–noon & 2–6pm, Sun 10am–noon; ☎02.54.32.05.10, ⓦ www.officetourisme-montrichard.com), an ancient house with saints and beasties sculpted down its beams. *La Tête Noir*, 24 rue de Tours (☎02.54.32.05.55, Ⓔg.galimard@orange.fr; ❹), is the more enticing of the two town hotels, with its plain but well-kept rooms and terrace on the river. You'd be better off, though, at the atmospheric ☝*Manoir de la Salle du Roc*, 69 rte de Vierzon (☎02.54.32.73.54, ⓦmanoirdelasalleduroc.monsite.orange.fr; ❺), which offers grand **chambres d'hôtes** set in an ancient manor house above the main road leading east from Montrichard towards Bourré. More upmarket still, if not quite as romantic, is the sixteenth-century, three-star *Château de la Ménaudière*, 3km from Montrichard on the D115 towards Amboise (☎02.54.71.23.45, ⓦwww.chateaumenaudiere.com; ❼), a tall, elegant building set in its own grounds, with a heated outdoor swimming pool and a classy restaurant. Montrichard also has a municipal **campsite**, *L'Étourneau* (☎02.54.32.10.16; closed mid-Sept to May), on the banks of the Cher. Decent **meals** can be had at *Les Tuffeaux*, an inexpensive brasserie on Montrichard's main square, place Barthélémy Gilbert.

Bourré

Three kilometres east of Montrichard, the escarpment that rises up above the Cher at **BOURRÉ** is riddled with seven layers of tunnelled quarries, extending over scores of kilometres. Bourré was the source of the finest château-building stone of all, as it has the unique quality of whitening as it weathers. As the local inhabitants quarried out their cliff, they turned the outer tunnels into houses. Even today, some 350 of the 700-odd inhabitants of the village are troglodytes, or **cave-dwellers** – that is to say, their houses, or at least parts of them, are carved out of the rock. These are not primitive dwellings: they are protected from the heat of summer and the cold of winter, and have chimneys – originally hollowed out as far as the clifftop above by children – central heating and full plumbing.

You can visit a fascinating troglodyte house at **La Magnanerie**, 4 chemin de la Croix-Bardin (guided tours only, in English and French: Easter to Aug Mon & Wed–Sun at 11am, 3pm, 4pm & 5pm; Sept Mon & Thurs–Sun at 3pm, 4pm & 5pm; Oct Fri–Sun at 4pm; €6). Park your car or bike at the foot of the slope and walk up a steep lane (indicated by a sign), enjoying the luxuriant foliage stimulated by the microclimate of the sheltered, sun-drenched cliff. The **tours** are led by the owner of the house, whose family have lived here for generations. He demonstrates how the soft stone was traditionally cut using a huge saw, and how all the necessities of daily life, from a lamp-stand to an abacus, could be fashioned from the stone walls of the cave itself. But the most interesting part of the tour is the seventeenth-century **silkworm chamber**. Silk production was one of the

Loire region's major sources of employment from the days of Louis XI through to the 1680s, when the flight of persecuted Huguenots from Touraine decimated the industry. The room is riddled with pigeonhole-like niches, stocked – from May to September – with living worms feeding on mulberry leaves, or spinning some 35cm of silk a minute as they construct their cocoons.

Some of the largest caves in Bourré are now used to cultivate mushrooms – big business in the Loire – a peculiar process that you can witness at the **Caves Champignonnières**, 40 rte des Roches (French-language guided tours daily: Easter to mid-Nov 10am, 11am, 2pm, 3pm, 4pm & 5pm; €6; Ⓦwww .le-champignon.com). You won't see any bulk growing here, but rather the boutique, showpiece production of *pleurotes* (oyster mushrooms), *pieds bleus* (blue-foot or Wood Blewit) and shiitakes, as well as a few white or cultivated mushrooms, known in France as *champignons de Paris*. A second tour (€6 or €10 for both tours) takes you to a "subterranean city" sculpted in recent years as a tourist attraction, and impressive enough in its way. An excellent shop sells mushrooms, including rare varieties, and mushroom products.

Bourré has a superb **chambre d'hôtes**, *Le Clos du Verêt*, 9 route des Vallées (Ⓣ02.54.32.75.51, Ⓦwww.lestabourelles-leveret.com; ❹), in an old convent house. The charming owners are winemakers, and their three immaculate guest rooms are full of character, with antique furnishings and old roof beams. The largest room can sleep up to four, and there's a kitchen and a large living room.

Thésée-la-Romaine and Pontlevoy

Ten kilometres upstream of Montrichard, the village of **THÉSÉE-LA-ROMAINE** gets its name from the Roman ruins that now stand alongside the D176 highway, 1km short of the village. As you approach along the riverbank road, you'll see a large sward of grass broken up by trenches, gravel paths and stony lines of walling, the remains of the second-century Gallo-Roman potters' community of Tasciaca, known locally as **Les Mazelles** (Easter–June Sat & Sun 2–6pm; July to mid-Sept daily except Tues 10am–12.30pm & 2–6.30pm; €3). There's little to see at the site itself, though one section of fortified wall still stands impressively high and smooth, the grey stone offset by narrow bands of brick. Most of the finds – figurines, coins and lots of pots and jars – are displayed in the **Musée Archéologique**, in the Mairie at Thésée (Easter–June Sat & Sun 2–6pm; July & Aug daily except Tues 2–6.30pm; €3), which is set among extensive gardens. Hidden in the forest a few kilometres north – follow the signs from Monthou-sur-Cher – the Centre Equestre du Gué-Péan (Ⓣ02.54.71.10.71) offers **pony trekking** for €12–16 an hour.

Eight kilometres northeast of Montrichard, on the road to Blois, the **Abbaye de Pontlevoy** (grounds open daily 9am–7pm; free) is no longer an abbey, but a private, American overseas campus. The main building in the complex dates from the abbey's sixteenth-century stint as a royal military academy – it has been a long time since the monks left. A vast and overweening sweep of austere classicism, it looks exactly like a wing of Paris's Les Invalides complex bizarrely transplanted to this sleepy corner of the Loire. If you call in advance and ask politely (Ⓣ02.54.32.99.39, Ⓦwww.eurabbey.com) you may be allowed to visit the equally anomalous **abbey church**, which rockets upwards as if part of a much larger building. It turns out to have been built as the choir of a huge, Gothic cathedral that was never completed. The interior, however, is pure, serene seventeenth century.

An excellent **chambre d'hôtes**, *La Cure*, 30 rue du Colonel Filloux (Ⓣ02.54.32.01.29, Ⓦwww.la-cure.com; ❼), stands almost opposite the abbey gates, catering to a largely American clientele. The rooms are luxuriously decorated in various period styles.

St-Aignan and around

ST-AIGNAN, 15km upstream of Montrichard, presents an extremely pictur-esque face to the world – as long as you're approaching from the right direc-tion. Seen from the opposite bank of the Cher, the town appears to nestle snugly at the foot of its outsized Romanesque church and château, which lines the top of a minor escarpment like a great wall of mismatched windows, chimneys and decorated brick and stonework. Meanwhile, the modern town leads a workaday life on the high ground behind, centred around **place du Président Wilson**, a large car park which is transformed into a **market** every Saturday morning.

Planted in the very centre of town, just up from the river off the axis of rue Constant Ragot, the solid stone buttresses of the **collégiale de St–Aignan** (Mon–Sat 9am–7pm, Sun 1–7pm) rise sturdily from the steep ground. The approaches are charming: up the slope from the river, or down the steps that lead from the château straight up to the west portal. Inside, the lofty nave is closed off by an airy, three-storey apse adorned with carved capitals – unfortu-nately most of them nineteenth-century re-creations. A leaflet points you towards the half-dozen twelfth-century originals – note the many-headed monster on the north side of the ambulatory, and the fighting rams over on the south side. The unusually tall eleventh-century **crypt** is renowned for its remarkably preserved, brightly coloured **wall-paintings**. The most striking of these is found on the half-dome vault of the central chapel, a late twelfth-century *Christ in Majesty*. On either side are two very different works dating from the fifteenth century, with captions flowing from the mouths of the protagonists like a comic strip. The large *Last Judgement* on the facing wall is later still, from the sixteenth century, while the oldest wall-paintings, hidden in the deeper recesses of the crypt, show scenes from the legend of Saint Gilles.

The **château** belongs to the wealthy duc de la Roche-Aymon, one of France's biggest landowners, and the country's major owner of forestry. His home, predictably, is closed to the hoi polloi. It's well worth wandering round the outside, however. A curving flight of 144 steps that's just crying out for a ballgo-wned princess climbs up from the collégiale to the gates, behind which is a grand gravelled terrace enclosed on one side by the L-shape of the Renaissance *logis*, and on the other by the remnants of the eleventh-century fortress. The delightful, harmonious sixteenth-century facade of the *logis* makes a powerful contrast with the mongrel appearance of the château as seen from below, its dressed white stone, decorated dormer windows and stone-crossed window frames recalling the finest creations of the First Renaissance. The octagonal **staircase tower**, however, is a confused nineteenth-century addition, marring the François I effect with anachronistic *œil-de-bœuf* ("bull's eye") windows and a Chambord-like pepper-grinder lantern perched on the top.

If the gate is open, you can cross to the far corner of the terrace, which leads through to a great **view** of the river. You can continue from here down the steep steps of the Degrés des Trois Gloirieuses to place du 8 Mai 1945, opposite the bridge. Alternatively, take the chestnut-lined Fossés du Château round towards the Hôtel de Ville, at the top end of rue Constant Ragot. For informa-tion on local Côteaux du Cher wines, the **Maison du Vin** (July & Aug daily 10am–noon & 3–6pm; Sept–June Tues & Thurs 8am–noon), on place Wilson, is open for tastings and sales.

The midstream **Ile des Trois Evêques** is used as a picnic area and informal beach, though swimming in the Cher is officially banned. However, there are indoor and outdoor **swimming pools** over on the downstream side of island (outdoor pool open July & Aug daily 11am–7.30pm; €2.70). You can rent **boats** – including beautiful wooden canoes – from Bâteaux Roussineau, 45 rue du Four à Chaux (☎02.54.75.00.57, ⓦwww.bateaux-roussineau.com). Alternatively, head 5km downstream to the Club Canoë Kayak de la Vallée du Cher (☎02.54.75.38.21), on the south bank at Mareuil-sur-Cher; they also offer guided descents of the Cher on Saturday afternoons. A more sedate vessel, the *Tasciaca* barge (July & Aug daily at 3pm, 4pm & 5pm; April–June, Sept & Oct Sat & Sun at 3pm, 4pm & 5pm; €7.50) **cruises** the Cher for an hour on summer afternoons, with a running commentary; tickets can be bought on board.

Practicalities

The **tourist office**, 60 rue Constant Ragot (May, June & Sept Mon–Sat 9.30am–12.30pm & 2–6pm, Sun 10am–noon; July & Aug Mon–Sat 9.30am–12.30pm & 2–6.30pm, Sun 10am–noon & 3–6pm; Oct–April Mon–Sat 10am–12.30pm & 2–6pm; ☎02.54.75.22.85, ⓦwww.tourisme-valdecher-staignan .com), is just off place Wilson, in the upper part of town. It can organize **narrowboat trips** (☎02.54.71.77.23) on the **Canal de Berry**, which ends its three-hundred-kilometre journey shown from the Auvergne at Noyers-sur-Cher, on the opposite bank from St-Aignan.

The only two **hotels** are both down beside the river, on either side of the bridge: the *Hôtel du Moulin*, 7 rue Novilliers (☎02.54.75.15.54; ❷; closed Sun), is a rambling and fairly basic but friendly place above a bar. *Le Grand Hôtel St-Aignan*, 7–9 quai J.-J.–Delorme (☎02.54.75.18.04, ⒺBgrand.hotel.st.aignan@ orange.fr; ❸), is a hushed, well-furnished affair, with a good restaurant (menus €13–36; Nov–March closed Sun evening, Mon & Tues lunch). Alternatively, **chambres d'hôtes** can be found at *Le Sousmont*, 66 rue Maurice-Berteaux (☎02.54.75.24.35; ❸); the situation on the main one-way road into town from the north is a bit noisy, but the inside is immaculately kept, with lots of charming nineteenth-century features, and the welcome is warm, with breakfast served in the flower-filled garden on fine days. St-Aignan has a nicely situated **campsite** on the bank of the river near Seigy, the *Camping des Cochards* (☎02.54.75.15.59, ⓦwww.lescochards.com; closed mid-Oct to March); it has a small pool and there are plans to rent out canoes and **pedalos**.

For an alternative to the *Grand Hotel's* **restaurant**, *Le Mange-Grenouille*, 10 rue Paul Boncour, below the collégiale (☎02.54.71.74.91; closed Tues eve & Wed) has delightful sixteenth-century decor and outside seating in its courtyard; it offers a delicous lunchtime menu at €14, and more elaborate regional specialities on the €23 and €28 evening menus. Two more informal restaurants make good use of the lime-shaded place de la Paix, just across from the collégiale, on the far side of rue Ragot: the welcoming *L'Amarena* (☎02.54.75.47.98, closed Mon lunch) serves inexpensive Italian food and pizzas and has outside tables; while *Chez Constant* (☎02.54.75.10.75; menus €12–17; closed Mon) serves up generous portions of regional specialities in an atmospheric old bar with a restaurant section at the back. For a **drink**, try *Au Cèpages*, 2 rue du Four, a café and wine bar just off the place de la Paix which also serves good plates of charcuterie and the like.

Zoo Parc Beauval

Unless you've just arrived in the region, you can hardly have escaped the advertising for the **Zoo Parc Beauval** (daily: 9am–dusk; €17; ⓦwww.zoobeauval .com), 4km to the south of St-Aignan on the D675. Despite the superficial commercialism, the zoo is spacious and attractive, with sumptuous flower-beds giving way to little streams and islanded lakes. The space given to the animals is adequate – most live in artificial mini-habitats rather than cages – and the zoo is part of various European programmes for breeding threatened species in captivity, so there are always babies to admire. Alongside the open-air enclosures for deer, giraffes, zebras, big cats, camels, bears and the like, there's a big monkey house, a vivarium and an Australian-themed hothouse with kangaroos and kookaburras in the adjacent enclosure. Seats at the two **spectacles** (frequent shows daily from April to mid-Nov) – performing seals and a raptor display – are included in the ticket price, and the **petting zoo** in the far corner goes down very well with smaller children.

Selles-sur-Cher

Since the château at **SELLES-SUR-CHER**, 15km upstream of St-Aignan, became a private residence once more, the main reason to visit has disappeared, unless you're bent on buying the famous local **goat's cheese**. There are no less than two excellent *fromageries* in town – Fromagerie Huchet, at 13 rue Jules Ferry, just off the main square, and Fromagerie Jacquin on rue du Docteur Massacré – and you can follow signs in the countryside around to local producers, most of whom will sell you some cheese *en directe*, and perhaps take you to meet the goats. There's a thriving Thursday morning **market**, and a dedicated **wine-and-cheese festival** on the last weekend in April, beginning on the Saturday afternoon.

Despite its modest attractions, Selles-sur-Cher remains a pleasant market town, centred on a wide square set some 50m back from the river, with the former abbey **church of St-Eusice** at its centre. The church's apse is Romanesque – don't miss the carved frieze on the outside – but over-restored, while the nave dates from the fourteenth century, though its vault was demolished by Huguenots in 1562 and has been replaced by a wooden structure that's visibly too light for the columns supporting it. The rough stone coffin of the saint lies on an altar in the crypt, surrounded by votive marble plaques and their modern equivalent – votive postcards.

Around the back of the church, the Hôtel de Ville incorporates the small **Musée du Val de Cher** (June to mid-Sept Tues–Sun 10am–noon & 2.30–5/6pm; €3.15), which uses small scenes acted out by dummies to explain various local phenomena, including the old laundry boats that were once moored on the river and the techniques used to make goat's cheese. The museum also allows access to the seventeenth-century cloister. A grassy embankment runs along the pleasant **riverfront** from the bridge towards the **château**, a grand combination of medieval fortifications and seventeenth-century luxury, the latter built in brick by Pierre-Philippe de Béthune, the brother of the duc de Sully (see p.213). Unfortunately, it is half-abandoned while the owners leaden-footedly pursue plans to convert it into a luxury hotel, and it remains closed to visitors.

Eight kilometres north of Selles-sur-Cher is a splendidly romantic **place to stay**, the tumbledown ⚘ *Château de Chémery*, (☎02.54.71.82.77, ⊜chateau dechemery@orange.fr; ➍). A handful of gorgeously ramshackle, antique-furnished rooms give onto the moat or the inner court of the castle, and a night or two here would be the perfect way to practise having your own château; reserve the table d'hôte (€21) in advance.

Château de Valençay

Fifteen kilometres south of Selles-sur-Cher, the **château de Valençay** (daily: April, May & Sept 10.30am–6pm; June 9.30am–6pm; July & Aug 9.30am–7.30pm; Oct

10.30am–5.30pm; €9; ⓦwww.chateau-valencay.com) is an isolated tourist destination in the otherwise almost completely unvisited *département* of the Indre. Architecturally, it's an overgrown mongrel of a château, but none the less beautiful for the mix of styles. The little Renaissance turrets of the keep clash with the enormous, bell-like tower pavilions, which jar in turn with the serene Neoclassical inner court, but the ensemble – all built of the palest tufa stone and capped by roofs of deep grey slate – is refined and impressive, set among handsome classical gardens. The mid-sixteenth-century wings were originally built to show off the enormous wealth of the d'Etampes family, but the lasting impression of a visit to the château today is the imperial legacy of a later owner, the great diplomat **Talleyrand** – famously described by his master Napoleon as "shit in a silk stocking".

An extraordinary political operator and survivor, Talleyrand owes his greatest fame to his post as Napoleon's foreign minister. A bishop before the Revolution, with a reputation for having the most desirable mistresses, he proposed the nationalization of church property, renounced his bishopric, escaped to America during the Terror, backed Napoleon, negotiated the imperial capitulation and then represented the restored Bourbons at the Congress of Vienna. One of his tasks for the emperor was keeping **Ferdinand VII of Spain** entertained at Valençay after the king had been forced to abdicate in favour of Napoleon's brother Joseph. Napoleon advised Talleyrand that "if you had a theatre at Valençay, and could arrange for actors to play there, it wouldn't be a bad idea". Talleyrand quickly had a stage built, which still exists here today, along with seventeen original stage sets. Six years after Ferdinand's arrival, the Treaty of Valençay, signed in the château in 1813, put an end to his enforced holiday and gave him back his Spanish throne. Talleyrand eventually fell from grace under the Bourbons, and retired to his château with his lover, the duchesse de Dino, who happened to be his nephew's wife. Together, they would entertain and politically seduce their guests with the help of elaborately structured dinners prepared by Marie-Antoine de Carême, the originator of French *grande cuisine*.

The **interior** dates from Talleyrand's glory days, and is consequently largely First Empire: elaborately embroidered chairs, Chinese vases, ornate inlays to all the tables, faux-Egyptian details, finicky clocks and chandeliers. A single discordant note is struck by the leg-brace and shoe displayed in a glass cabinet along with Talleyrand's uniforms – the statesman's deformed foot was concealed in every painting of the man, including the one displayed in the portrait gallery that runs the length of the graceful Neoclassical wing.

On occasional nights from late June to the end of August, you can visit after dusk, when the exterior is breathtakingly illuminated by thousands of candles. This **candlelit tour** (€13.50, or €15 with château entry) usually takes place once a week on a Thursday or Friday, but check in advance. The château **park** (same hours as above; €1.50) keeps a small collection of unhappy-looking camels, zebras, llamas and goats, and there's a small, imaginative **maze** – you'll need to understand some French in order to work out the riddling passwords that open the various doors, or ask for the answers at the ticket office. Theatricals take place in the courtyard or kitchens of the château roughly every hour (April–June, Sept & Oct Sat & Sun only; mid-July to Aug daily), with costumed actors replaying fanciful scenes from Talleyrand's time.

About 200m from the château gates, on the long straight road leading north of town, a **car museum** (daily: April–June, Sept & Oct 10am–12.30pm & 1.30–6pm; July & Aug 10am–12.30pm & 1.30–7.30pm; €5) houses an excellent collection of sixty-odd mostly prewar cars, though there are a few more recent vehicles, such as a covetable 1970s Renault Alpine, built for rallying. The **memorial** on top of the hill, at the edge of the forest, commemorates the wartime dead of F-section, known in the UK as the Special Operations Executive, whose mission was to aid and equip the French Resistance. It was here that the first spy's parachute drop took place, on the night of May 5, 1941.

Once you've seen the château, the car museum and the war memorial you've about exhausted the possibilities of Valençay. For something to **eat**, the best bet is *La Renaissance*, an informal restaurant which does pizza and reasonable-value *assiettes* of cold meats and salad for around €10.

To get to Valençay by public transport, you can take the **train** from Orléans (change at Salbris), passing through Romorantin-Lanthenay. It's also possible to join the branch line that runs along the Cher at Gièvres, but there's often a longish wait for a connection. An infrequent **bus** service connects with Blois.

Mennetou-sur-Cher

There's little of interest on the river upstream of Selles-sur-Cher, but if you're making your way to Bourges you might want to stop off at the miniature medieval town of **MENNETOU-SUR-CHER**, 15km west of Vierzon. The steep, pedestrianized, cobbled streets running between the fortified gates are perfect for a relaxed stroll, but the pride with which the town markets its local speciality, *andouillette à la ficelle* – a sausage of pig's intestine with a string running through the middle, celebrated with a festival on the first weekend of May – gives a clue as to the shortage of actual things to see and do. Once you've visited the Flamboyant Gothic **église St-Urbain**, near the thirteenth-century Porte d'en Bas, and wandered the length of the **Grande Rue** between the half-ruined Porte du Nord and the Porte Bonne Nouvelle, admiring the half-dozen fifteenth- and sixteenth-century houses, there's little left to do except cross the busy N76 road and the Canal du Berry that runs alongside it, then walk 100m down to a grassy sward shaded by weeping willows. You can **picnic** and **swim** in the Cher here, and there's a playground for children. The municipal **campsite** (℡02.54.98.11.02; closed mid-Sept to April) is just downstream, with a swimming pool.

Travel details

Trains

Blois to: Amboise (17 daily; 20min); Beaugency (20 daily; 25min); Meung-sur-Loire (20 daily; 35min); Onzain (for Chaumont; 17 daily; 10min); Orléans (22–26 daily; 40min); Tours (18 daily; 40min).
Valençay to: Montrichard (change at Gièvres; 3 daily; 1hr 30min); Romorantin-Lanthenay (6 daily; 35min); Tours (change at Gièvres; 3 daily; 2hr–2hr 30min).

Buses

Blois to: Bracieux (2–3 daily; 45min); Chambord (1–3 daily; 45min); Cour-Cheverny (3 daily; 35min); Romorantin-Lanthenay (3 daily; 1hr); St-Aignan (2–3 daily; 1hr 10min); Valençay (3 daily; 1hr 30min); Vendôme (2–3 daily; 1hr); Vierzon (3 daily; 2hr).
Romorantin-Lanthenay to: Mennetou-sur-Cher (5 daily; 20min); Vierzon (5 daily; 40min).

3

The Orléanais

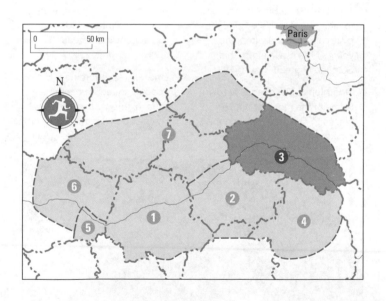

CHAPTER 3

Highlights

✳ **Rue de Bourgogne, Orléans**
Lively bars and relaxed restaurants line Orléans' old Roman road, the rue de Bourgogne.
See p.194

✳ **Fonderie Bollée** Time your visit for a Friday, and you can see church bells being cast using ancient techniques at this bell foundry just outside Orléans. See p.197

✳ **La Ferté-St-Aubin** You're free to sit in the armchairs, play the piano and generally imagine yourself the châtelain at this Sologne château. See p.197

✳ **Beaugency** This medieval town is one of the most attractive places to stay anywhere on the banks of the Loire. See p.201

✳ **Talcy** A foray north onto the plain of the Beauce brings you to the château where Cassandre, the muse of the poet Ronsard, lived. See p.205

✳ **St-Benoît-sur-Loire** The mortal remains of St Benedict brought pilgrims in their thousands to this handsome stone abbey. See p.210

✳ **Château des Pêcheurs** The aristocratic obsession with angling is all too evident at this eccentric château. See p.216

✳ **Briare** An extraordinary Belle-Époque aqueduct carries a canal high over the Loire itself. You can cross it on foot or on a canal-boat cruise. See p.217

△ Bell foundry, St-Jean-de-Braye

The Orléanais

T he **Orléanais** was the heartland or "navel" of druidic power in the
centuries before the Roman conquest, and the region was again thrust
into national prominence as the home fief of the Capetian dynasty,
which ruled France from the tenth to the fourteenth centuries. In the
great years of the French monarchy, however, the Orléanais had the misfortune
to fall between two poles of royal power: Touraine and the Ile-de-France, and
in the last few centuries the Orléanais has gently lapsed into provincial irrele-
vance. Even the region's modern title, the *département* of the Loiret, refers to a
tiny stream, in contrast to neighbours glowing under the relatively noble
names of the Cher and the Seine-et-Marne. This has always been – and
remains – a wealthy region, but the sense of departed grandeur is even stronger
here than in the rest of the Loire Valley: the châteaux seem quieter and more
abandoned, and the churches, forests and abbeys more ancient. On the left
bank, south of the Loire, lies the low-lying marshy woodland of the **Sologne**
(covered, for the most part, in Chapter 2, see p.167). On the right bank, the
dull, flat arable fields of the **Beauce** stretch away to the northwest, towards
Chartres, while the great, dark swathe of the **Forêt d'Orléans** looms to the
northeast. As a tourist destination, the Orléanais is an acquired taste – and
relatively few tourists make the effort.

Orléans itself has a very different feel to the rest of the region. Enterprising
and upbeat, the city seems more oriented towards Paris and the future than to
the river and the history that flows through it. But the city's past does bind it
firmly to the Orléanais, especially in the person of Joan of Arc, the "Maid of
Orléans", who is celebrated in the magnificent cathedral. Some excellent town
museums and a relaxed restaurant and nightlife scene make the city all the more
appealing. Directly south of Orléans and included in this chapter as an obvious
day-trip from the city, is the charming brick-built château at **La Ferté–St–
Aubin**, on the northern fringe of the Sologne.

Downriver of Orléans, the small, pretty towns of **Meung–sur–Loire** and
Beaugency huddle on the bank of the Loire within a few kilometres of each
other, each with its historic château in the very centre of town. Meung's château
is the more interesting of the two to visit, but Beaugency, with its cobbled
medieval squares and excellent hotels, is a more attractive place to stay. Interesting side-trips can be made to the **château de Talcy**, with its poetic links, and
the royal abbey church at **Cléry–St–André**.

Upriver from Orléans, the north bank is shadowed by the giant **Forêt
d'Orléans**, a good place to explore on a bike, or pass through on the way to
the **château de Chamerolles'** perfume museum. One fifteen-kilometre
stretch of the Loire is particularly fascinating: you can visit a jewel box of a

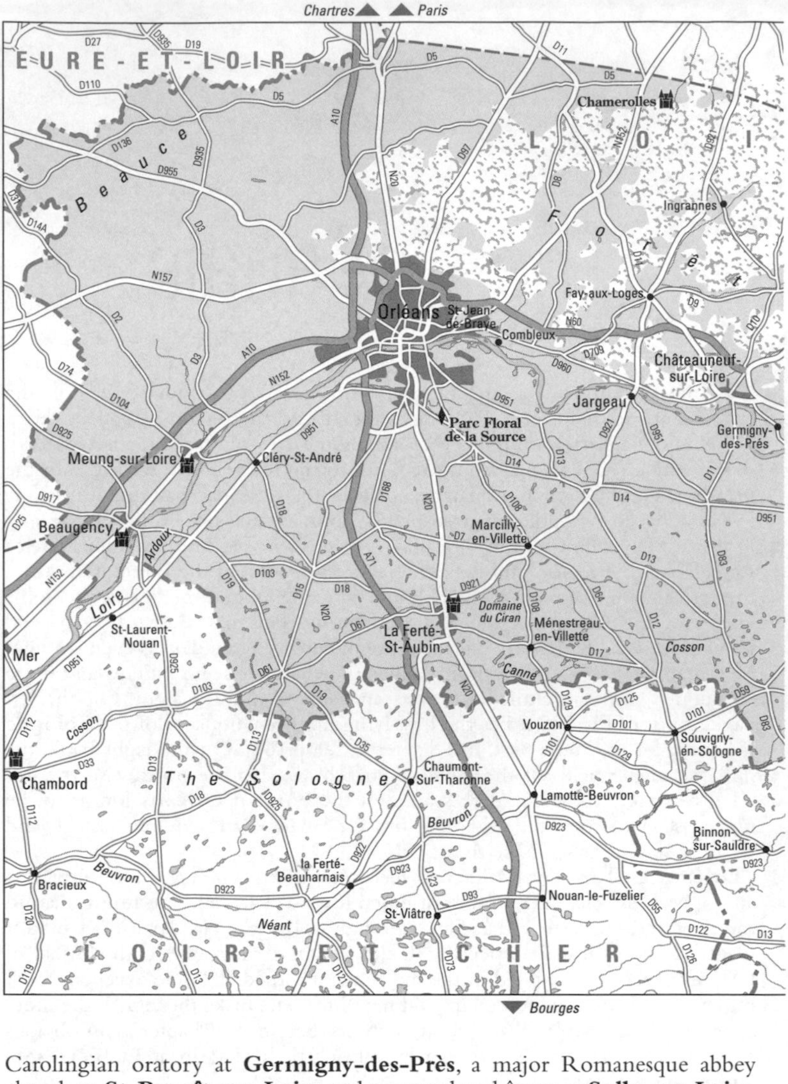
Chartres
Paris
EURE-ET-LOIR
Chamerolles
Beauce
Forêt
LOIRET
Ingrannes
Fay-aux-Loges
Orléans
St-Jean-de-Braye
Combleux
Châteauneuf-sur-Loire
Jargeau
Germigny-des-Prés
Parc Floral de la Source
Meung-sur-Loire
Cléry-St-André
Talcy
Beaugency
Ardoux
Marcilly-en-Villette
Loire
Blois & Tours
St-Laurent-Nouan
Mer
Domaine du Ciran
Ménestreau-en-Villette
La Ferté-St-Aubin
Cosson
Canne
Vouzon
Souvigny-en-Sologne
Chambord
The Sologne
Chaumont-Sur-Tharonne
Lamotte-Beuvron
Beuvron
Binnon-sur-Sauldre
Bracieux
la Ferté-Beauharnais
St-Viâtre
Nouan-le-Fuzelier
Néant
LOIR-ET-CHER
Bourges

Carolingian oratory at **Germigny-des-Près**, a major Romanesque abbey church at **St-Benoît-sur-Loire** and a muscular château at **Sully-sur-Loire**. A little further up the river, the brick-built château and town of **Gien** are often held to mark the end of the Loire Valley proper, but it's worth persevering as far as **Briare**, where the Canal Latéral crosses the river on an exquisite nineteenth-century aqueduct. Near Gien, the château at **St-Brisson-sur-Loire** and the Château des Pêcheurs at **La Bussière** – one devoted to medieval artillery, the other to fishing – are quirky and little-visited destinations.

Online **information** on the *département* of the Loiret and the Orléanais can be found at Ⓦwww.tourismloiret.com. Rapides du Val-de-Loire (Ⓣ02.38.61.90.00, Ⓦwww.rvl-info.com) operate almost all the area's **buses**, though services are only frequent enough to be useful downstream of Orléans

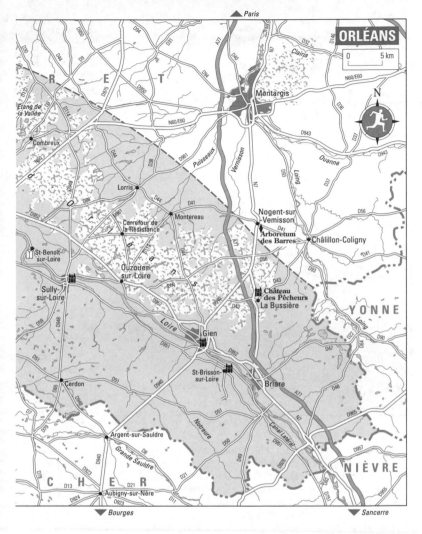

– an area which is better served by the train anyway. If you do want to use the bus, timetables can be viewed at Ⓦwww.ulys-loiret.com.

Orléans

ORLÉANS is the northernmost city on the Loire, sitting at the apex of a huge arc in the river as it switches direction and starts to flow southwest. Its proximity to Paris, just over 100km away, has always shaped this ancient city. Goods and passengers sailing up the Loire would disembark at Orléans for the journey to the capital and, despite the city being hundreds of kilometres inland, it developed as an important port – in 1663 the poet La Fontaine was surprised to see a

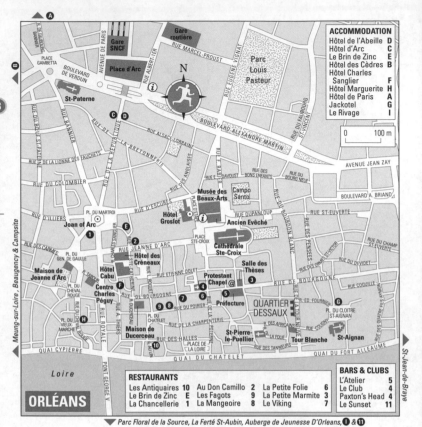

ORLÉANS

ACCOMMODATION

Hôtel de l'Abeille	D
Hôtel d'Arc	C
Le Brin de Zinc	E
Hôtel des Cèdres	B
Hôtel Charles Sanglier	F
Hôtel Marguerite	H
Hôtel de Paris	A
Jackotel	G
Le Rivage	I

0   100 m

RESTAURANTS

Les Antiquaires	10	Au Don Camillo	2	La Petite Folie	6
Le Brin de Zinc	E	Les Fagots	9	La Petite Marmite	3
La Chancellerie	1	La Mangeoire	8	Le Viking	7

BARS & CLUBS

L'Atelier	5
Le Club	4
Paxton's Head	4
Le Sunset	11

Parc Floral de la Source, La Ferté St-Aubin, Auberge de Jeunesse D'Orleans, ❶ & ⓫

"miniature Constantinople". The city's glory faded with the fortunes of the river, but in recent years high-speed motorway and rail links to Paris have underpinned an economic renaissance. Orléans is now one of the fastest growing cities in France, with a population of around a quarter of a million and an unemployment rate of around six percent – unusually low by French standards.

All this energy translates into a vibrant, exciting city to visit, its new-found municipal pride vigorously expressed in a lively restaurant and nightlife scene, redevelopment of the riverside quays and new, ultra-modern trams – a perfect foil to the handsome eighteenth- and nineteenth-century streets. For once, there's no château and historic sights are relatively thin on the ground – even the **cathedral** somehow lacks soul, and the giant **église St-Aignan** is semi-ruined – but the streets of the old city are fascinating to explore, and there are two excellent museums: the **Musée des Beaux-Arts**, which has an unusually good collection of paintings, and the **Hôtel Cabu**, with a strange display of third-century animal sculptures. One of the best times to visit is May 8 (**Joan of Arc Day**), when the city is filled with parades, fireworks and a medieval fair.

Some history

Orléans had a turbulent early history. It was a centre of revolt against Julius Caesar in 52 BC – a crime for which it was burnt to the ground, and was besieged by Attila the Hun in the mid-fifth century. In 498, Orléans was elevated to the position of temporary capital of the Frankish kingdom, while in the eleventh century it became a hotbed of Manicheanism – a heresy for which the cathedral's canons were burnt. Yet one event alone has defined Orléans. In 1429, the city was under siege by an English army eager to capture what was then the key to the Loire Valley and the last remaining territories of the Dauphin. On April 29, **Joan of Arc** (see box on p.191) relieved the siege by fighting her way through to the now-vanished Porte de Bourgogne, an event considered to be the turning point in the Hundred Years War.

A brief period of resurgence, during which a number of fine Renaissance mansions were built, was followed by the devastation of the sixteenth-century Wars of Religion, which affected Orléans – a centre of Protestant learning – particularly severely. After the peace of the Edict of Nantes, which granted rights to Protestants, however, the city prospered on the back of wheat from the Beauce to the north, wool from the Sologne to the south and timber from the Forêt d'Orléans to the east, while the **river trade** swelled with domestic and imported goods, especially muscovado sugar from the Caribbean. This wealth and activity came to an abrupt end with the arrival of the railways, which rendered river transport redundant. Six months of occupation by Prussian troops in 1870–71 began a period of relative decline, and the German bombardments of June 1940 only completed the humiliation, destroying a large part of the city centre. Since World War II, however, Orléans has vigorously reasserted itself, developing major engineering and "cosmo-ceuticals" industries in the hinterland, and making great strides in rebuilding what is once more a proud and thriving city.

Arrival, information and accommodation

The **gare SNCF** leads straight into the modern shopping centre on place d'Arc, which fronts onto a huge swathe of busy roads; the old city centre lies on the far side of the traffic, accessed by the pedestrian bridge that leads to rue de la République. On foot, count on ten to fifteen minutes to the cathedral, down rue de la Bretonnerie. If you don't want to walk, you could take **tram A** south from the terminus under place d'Arc to place du Général de Gaulle (€1.30), and then take bus 3 east from here to the cathedral (€1.30). The **gare routière**, on rue Marcel-Proust, is some 200m behind the train station, on the corner of rue Marçel-Proust.

The **tourist office** is opposite the cathedral at 2 place de l'Etape (April & May Mon–Sat 9.30am–1pm & 2–6.30pm; June & Sept Mon–Sat 9am–1pm & 2–7pm; July & Aug Mon–Sat 9am–7pm, Sun 10am–1pm; Oct–March Mon–Sat 10am–1pm & 2–6pm; ☏02.38.24.05.05, Ⓦwww.tourisme-orleans.com). If you're looking for information on events, Ⓦwww.orleanscity.com is a good resource, while the main city portal is Ⓦwww.ville-orleans.fr; you'll need some French to make sense of either.

Accommodation in Orléans is mostly uninspiring, but a few central two-stars stand out from the rest.

Hotels

Le Brin de Zinc 62 rue Ste-Catherine ☏02.38.53.88.77, Ⓦwww.brindezinc.fr. The bar of the busy brasserie below acts as reception, where you are given a key and sent round to the back door on a seedy back alley. Things get rather better

inside, where the well-priced and -located rooms are clean and comfortable. ❷

Hôtel de l'Abeille 64 rue Alsace Lorraine ☏02.38.53.54.87, Ⓦwww.hoteldelabeille .com. This thirty-room hotel has been in the same family for a century. The handsome Belle Epoque exterior and the reception area are very promising, while inside the rooms have been freshly painted, and are embellished by the odd handsome vase or old clock. Stands on the corner of the pedestrian-ized shopping street of rue de la République, which is convenient for the station. Prices vary depending the size of the room, and you pay more (④) for one with a bath. ③

Hôtel d'Arc 37 rue de la République ☎02.38.53.10.94, ⓦwww.hotelarc.fr. This long-established hotel boasts a striking sculpted Art Nouveau facade, and the rooms are fairly grand too, with a decor ranging from pastel artwork to period posters. The large, attractive "prestige deluxe" rooms (⑦) have small balconies looking down onto the tramlines and pedestrian street below. ⑥

Hôtel des Cèdres 17 rue Marèchal Foch ☎02.38.62.22.92, ⓦwww.hoteldescedres.com. Welcoming three-star with a garden, set in a peaceful street just outside the ring road encircling the old town. It's a good option for families, as the rooms are fairly spacious and a number of them have cots and communicating doors, and there's garaged parking for an extra €7. The rooms have been newly done-up with bright colour schemes and decent furnishings. ⑤

Hôtel Charles Sanglier 8 rue Charles-Sanglier ☎02.38.53.38.50, ⓔhotelsanglier@orange.fr. This friendly, well-run hotel is in a very central location, close to the best restaurants. On the down side, the unprepossessing modern building is a little shabby inside and out. The rooms are fairly small and most

have plastic shower units tucked away in the corner behind a screen. ③

Hôtel Marguerite 14 place du Vieux-Marché ☎02.38.53.74.32, ⓔhotel.marguerite@orange.fr. Central, friendly and very well run. Most of the large, immaculate rooms have been recently repainted in cheery colours, with comfortable, if slightly sterile, modern furnishings (④). The handful of non-renovated rooms retain a bit more charm, although the bathrooms aren't so pristine. ③

Hôtel de Paris 29 rue Faubourg-Bannier ☎02.38.53.39.58. Old-fashioned but clean rooms above a very ordinary bar, just behind the train station. The wooden stairs and floors are noisy and the fittings very basic, but the management is extremely helpful and prices are low. ①

Jackotel 18 place du Cloître-St-Aignan ☎02.38.54.48.48, ⓦwww.jackotel.com. Has a peaceful location overlooking the church of St-Aignan across a shaded square, in a quiet corner of the old town southeast of the cathedral. The sixty rooms are comfortable enough, with tidy modern furnishings, but have little character. ③

Le Rivage 635 rue de la Reine Blanche, Olivet ☎02.38.66.02.93, ⓔhotel-le-rivage.jpb @orange.fr. This professionally-run three star has a peaceful location in the suburb of Olivet, 3km due south of the city centre. The hotel backs onto the River Loiret, and has a lovely summer terrace where you can enjoy a sophisticated and elegant meal. Rooms have all the usual facilities, including a/c, but aren't especially appealing – the best ones are on the first floor, with balconies overlooking the river. ⑤

Hostel and campsite

Camping Gaston Marchand Chemin de la Roche, St-Jean-de-la-Ruelle ☎02.38.88.39.39. The municipal campsite, and the closest to Orléans, 5km away out on the Blois road, beside the Loire; bus #26, stop "Petite Espère". Closed Sept to June. **Auberge de Jeunesse d'Orléans La Source** Stade Omnisports, 7 av Beaumarchais ☎02.38.53.60.06, ⓔauberge.crjs@orange.fr. This

is a good hostel, with friendly management and very modern rooms and facilities. The major downside is the suburban location, underneath a stand of Orléans' stadium: get tram A from the train station, stop "Université l'Indien" (30min), then it's a ten-minute walk. Reception Mon–Fri 8am–7pm; €9 per night with HI membership – you can join on the spot.

The City

Joan turns up all over town, most notably on horseback in the centre of the **place du Martroi**, the pedestrianized square at the heart of the commercial end of town. The square lies at the foot of **rue de la République**, which runs due north to the gare SNCF, standing just set back from the main axis of **rue Jeanne d'Arc**, which runs east to the cathedral. Just to the north of the cathedral lie the modern **Musée des Beaux-Arts** and the Renaissance **Hôtel de Ville**, while the **old city** lies to the south, sloping down from the long, narrow **rue de**

Bourgogne – where Orléans' main restaurant and nightlife is to be found – to the **river**, whose quays are sadly mostly given over to high-speed traffic.

The cathedral

The grand nineteenth-century avenue of rue Jeanne d'Arc marches straight up to the giant doors of the **cathédrale Ste-Croix** (daily 9.15am–noon & 2–6.45pm), where Joan celebrated her victory over the English. The uniformly Gothic structure actually dates from well after her death: Huguenot iconoclasts destroyed the transepts in 1568, and in 1601 Henri IV inaugurated a rebuilding programme that lasted until the nineteenth century. The lofty towers of the west front, which culminate in a delicate stone palisade like a crown of thorns, were barely complete in time for the Revolution, while the skeletal spire wasn't finished until 1858.

△ Statue of Joan of Arc, Hôtel Groslot, Orléans

Inside, slender stone columns extend in a single vertical sweep from the cathedral floor to the vault: impressive but somehow too neat to be moving. Joan's canonization in 1920 is marked by a garish monumental altar next to the north transept, supported by two jagged, golden leopards that represent the English. The highlight is the late nineteenth-century **stained-glass window** sequence in the nave, which tells the usual romanticized version of Joan's life story (see box, opposite) in a series of cartoon-like images. Starting from the north transept and working back to the west doors, you see: Joan the shepherdess hearing voices; Joan finding the king in the crowd at Chinon; the miracle of the angel at Chinon; and Joan carrying her standard triumphantly into Orléans. Moving across the nave to the south aisle: the thanksgiving at Ste-Croix; Charles VII's coronation at Reims; Joan "rendered by treachery into the hands of the English"; Joan in prison; and Joan burnt at the stake. *L'Anglois perfide* ("perfidious Albion"), gets a rough ride, while the role of the Burgundians in her capture and the French clergy in her trial is rather skated over.

Before you move on from the cathedral, two inconspicuous statues at either end of the cathedral square are worth a look. On the north side, *La Beauce* depicts the flat, agricultural region north of Orléans in the form of a buxom woman holding golden ears of wheat; on the south side *La Loire* is shown as an idealized young woman with a bounteous skirtful of fruits.

Musée des Beaux-Arts

You are largely spared the Maid in the cavernous **Musée des Beaux-Arts**, next to the tourist office (Tues–Sat 10am–12.15pm & 1.30–5.45pm, Sun 2–6.30pm; €3; same ticket as Hôtel Cabu), which spreads across five floors. There's plenty of second-rate stuff, but lurking among it are a number of works that make this one of the best regional art museums in France – well worth a rainy or even a sunny afternoon. The museum regularly stages good temporary exhibitions too – the tourist office has details.

The main **French collection** occupies the first floor, arranged either side of the central staircase. The more interesting seventeenth-century works are on the right of the stairs, beyond a huge room lorded over by the *Four Church Fathers*, depicted in alarmingly Mannerist style by Martin Fréminet (1567–1619). Both these and Claude Deruet's *Four Elements*, displayed in the hexagonal room just beyond, once hung in the château de Richelieu. While apparently devoted to the four elements as seasons, Deruet's quartet actually glorifies the family of Louis XIII: the king, his wife Anne of Austria, his brother Gaston d'Orléans and the cardinal himself can be spotted presiding over lavish festivities. Next door, in room 3, the highlight is the Le Nain brothers' dream-like and compelling *Bacchus Discovering Ariane on Naxos* (c.1635), where the young god discovers Ariadne after she has cried herself to sleep following the departure of Theseus.

Eighteenth-century works occupy the rooms on the left of the staircase, notably the exquisite collection of **pastel portraits** in room 8. Jean-Baptiste Perronneau, a leading exponent of the art, who often visited Orléans, is represented by a number of subtle and refined pieces, but the gems are Maurice Quentin de la Tour's *Portrait of a Young Negro* (1751), and Chardin's irresistible *Self-portrait with Spectacles*, from 1773.

The two mezzanine levels immediately below offer an alluring taste of **French nineteenth-century art**. The doglegged corridor of the upper level runs past a large collection of works by the Romantic painter Léon Cogniet (1794–1880): look out for the horror expressed in his studies for *The Massacre of the Innocents*, and in Delacroix's *Head of an Old Woman*, but otherwise speed your way down to the large chamber on the lower mezzanine level. Here,

The Maid of Orléans

In 1429, during the **Hundred Years War** between England and France, a 17-year-old peasant girl in men's clothing somehow talked her way into meeting the heir to the French throne. She persuaded him to reconquer his kingdom, roused his army to the crucial victory at Orléans and guided him to his coronation. Less than three years later she was captured in battle, tried as a heretic and burnt at the stake. It took another 491 years for **Joan of Arc** – now nationalist heroine, feminist icon and Witness of the Faith – to be made a saint.

Everything Joan accomplished seems to have been through her own formidable charisma, with the help of mysterious, angelic "voices", which accompanied her until her death. She first heard them in around 1425 – three years after both the **Dauphin** (the heir to the French throne) Charles and Henry VI of England had declared themselves king of France – describing their sound as "sweet and low and beautiful". Joan understood that these voices brought a message directly from God, instructing her to go to the Dauphin and help him win back his kingdom. Her belief was ardent enough to convince almost everyone she met too, a process that finally ushered her into the presence of Charles at **Chinon**, in 1429.

No one knows what exactly happened at Chinon (see box on p.116), but it was enough to convince Charles that he was the legitimate heir to the French throne. Charles's supposed weakness, and the allegations of his bastardy, were not, as is often alleged, the obstacle. Instead, it was the 1420 **Treaty of Troyes**, a document of questionable legality in which Charles VI had disinherited his son in favour of Henry V of England. Joan's arrival, and the sign she brought, made the Dauphin believe that God was on his side and, whatever the legal arguments, in late medieval eyes that made him the rightful king.

And yet his kingdom hung by a thread. The strategic city of **Orléans**, just upstream from Chinon, was besieged by the English, and barely held by Charles's most heroic captain, **Jean Dunois**, the "Bastard of Orléans" (see p.308). Joan's role in the week-long battle that lifted the siege, in early May 1429, was probably slighter than is usually claimed, but her standard and sheer conviction certainly inspired the troops to victory. **Meung-sur-Loire** and **Beaugency** fell to the French in June and July, and on July 17 Charles was crowned at Reims, with Joan at his side.

For Joan, the turning point came in September, when her attack on English-held Paris failed. Charles, now looking for diplomatic solutions, disbanded the main army, leaving Joan to fight with a few hundred ill-supplied troops. On May 23 of the following year, after a disastrous winter campaign, Joan was captured by Burgundian troops at Compiègne. She was ransomed by the English, who turned her over to a hostile inquisitorial court in Rouen, a town they controlled.

The record of Joan's five-month **trial** survives, complete with her own defence. She comes across as spirited, precise and full of integrity, even as her interrogators tried to trap her into proving herself a heretic by claiming she had spoken to God through his angels. "I saw them with my bodily eyes as well as I see you," she protested, "and when they left me I wept, and I would have had them take me with them too." Along with her adoption of male clothing – an offence in the eyes of God and an outrage in those of men which she never explained, only saying that it was "at the command of God and his angels" – this claim was enough to condemn her.

Joan's sentence was enacted on **May 30, 1431**, in the marketplace at Rouen, the fire being built some distance from her so that death would be slow. Joan asked for a crucifix to be brought to her and, as she burned, called out the same word over and again: "Jesus!" "Everyone present could hear it," her executioner reported, "almost all wept with pity."

Realism takes over, set against walls painted blood-red and stacked with canvases in proper nineteenth-century style. Two works by Orléans-born artists dominate the room: the melodramatic *The Fire* (1850), by Alexandre Antigna, and *The Apotheosis of the Rabble* (1885), by Maurice Boutet de Monvel – an artist better known for his 1896 comic-book version of the life of Joan of Arc.

Twentieth-century art lurks in the basement. The big names are Gauguin, with a still life called *Fête Gloanec* (1888), Picasso, with *Woman's Head with a Collar* (1926), and Tamara de Lempicka, with an iconic painting of a fashionable skier entitled *Saint-Moritz* (1929), but the works with local connections are just as rewarding. A small inner chamber has a number of African-influenced sculptures by Henri Gaudier-Brzeska (1891–1915), who was born just outside Orléans at St-Jean-de-Braye (see p.197), and a number of works devoted to the poet and literary figure Max Jacob, who lived in nearby St-Benoît (see p.210) for many years.

Foreign art, mainly Flemish and Italian sixteenth- and seventeenth-century works, is banished to the second floor, where the highlights are Coreggio's renowned *Holy Family* (1522), a work of incredible tenderness, and Velázquez's overwrought *St Thomas* (1620), an early painting influenced by Caravaggio that shows the apostle hearing the news of Christ's resurrection.

Hôtel Groslot and Campo Santo

Opposite the cathedral and museum, on the other side of place d'Étape, the fancy, red-brick **Hôtel Groslot** (July–Sept Mon–Fri & Sun 9am–7pm, Sat 5–9pm; Oct–June Mon–Fri & Sun 10am–noon & 2–6pm, Sat 5–6pm; free) is thought to be the work of the sixteenth-century architect Jacques Androuet du Cerceau. It's now part of the Hôtel de Ville, and is used for civic ceremonies including marriages, which explains why it's closed to visits for most of Saturday. Joan appears in the courtyard, this time in pensive mood, with her skirt dented by twentieth-century bullets – the statue is actually by the daughter of Louis-Philippe, the last king of France. Inside, you can wander through the plush, neo-medieval reception rooms, where the mayors are listed back to 1569.

On the other, rather desolate side of the Musée des Beaux-Arts, the **Campo Santo**, off rue Fernand Rabier (daily 8am–dusk; free), was the town's main cemetery until just before the Revolution. It's a weird, hidden-away space, a blank square of green surrounded on three sides by pearly-white arcades that date from the fifteenth century. It comes to life during the town's jazz festival at the end of June, when it's used for concerts. The nearby **Ancien Évêché**, 100m down rue Dupanloup, was built for the bishops of Orléans in the 1640s; there's a fine view of the cathedral's apse from the stately garden at the back.

Rue Jeanne d'Arc and around

Handsome rue Jeanne d'Arc was largely built on the back of voluntary donations from the people of Orléans, who in 1825 managed to raise 400,000 gold francs within mere days to pay for it. The area to the north was heavily damaged by German bombing in 1940, though the centrepiece **place du Martroi** has been handsomely rebuilt round the equestrian statue of Joan by the sculptor Denis Foyatier, who was born at La Bussière (see p.216) in 1793. Joan's armoured appearance is in line with the nineteenth-century fashion for a warlike Maid; copper-green friezes round the base depict scenes from her life. North of the square, rue de la République is the main commercial and shopping drag, continuing across the busy ring road to the station via a pedestrian bridge.

The narrow streets to the south of rue Jeanne d'Arc are more enticing, with a number of Renaissance mansions to admire. The facade of the **Hôtel des Créneaux**, 32 rue Ste-Catherine, is particularly fine, while the **Maison de Ducerceau** at 6 rue Ducerceau, the continuation of rue Ste-Catherine, is a considered Classical structure. Like the Hôtel Groslot, it is thought to be by the architect Jacques Androuet du Cerceau, famous for his meticulous eagle's-eye drawings of Loire châteaux. The design of the ornate **Hôtel Cabu**, square Abbé-Desnoyers, off rue Ste-Catherine (May, June & Sept Tues–Sat 1.30–5.45pm, Sun 2–6.30pm; July & Aug Tues–Sat 9.30am–12.15pm & 1.30–5.45pm, Sun 2–6.30pm; Oct–April Wed 1.30–5.45pm, Sun 2–6.30pm; €3 – same ticket as Musée des Beaux-Arts), is also attributed to Du Cerceau. Inside, the **historical and archeological museum** houses the extraordinary **Treasure of Neuvy-en-Sullias**, a collection of bronze animals and figurines found near Orléans in 1861. The cache was probably buried in the second half of the third century AD to protect it from marauding Germanic invaders, or to save it from being melted down for coinage at a time of rampant inflation. The words inscribed on the base of the glorious, naturalistic horse sculpture states that it is an offering to Rudiobo – thought to be a god of war. The bronzes of wild boars are more stylized and may be treasured symbols of war or the priesthood – contrary to what Asterix readers may imagine, the Gauls had a deep respect for wild boars on account of their tenacity and belligerence. Discovered in the locality of the Forest of the Carnutes, where Celtic druids gathered for their annual shindig, it's possible that the collection represents the last flourishing of Celtic religion at the end of the Gallo-Roman period. The floors above house various medieval oddments and Joan-related pieces, as well as exhibits on the history of Orléans.

At the end of rue Jeanne d'Arc, beside the funky tram stops on place Général de Gaulle, stands the semi-timbered **Maison de Jeanne d'Arc** (Tues–Sun: May–Oct 10am–12.30pm & 1.30–6pm; Nov–April 1.30–6pm; €2). It's a disappointing place to visit: the house turns out to be a 1960s reconstruction, and the main exhibit is a fairly dull set of diorama models of the siege of Orléans, with recorded commentaries in French or English. Otherwise there are just a few Joan-related plates, books and engravings. A short distance from Joan's house, the **Centre Charles Péguy**, 11 rue Tabour (daily 1.30–6pm; free), houses a rather dry celebration of the life and work of Charles Péguy (1873–1914), a Christian Socialist writer from Orléans. The building itself is more interesting, an early sixteenth-century mansion that only reveals its richly sculpted heart once you've penetrated to the inner courtyard.

The old city

The scattered vestiges of the **old city** lie between **rue de Bourgogne**, which follows the line of the Gallo-Roman thoroughfare, and the river. The modern **Préfecture** at 9 rue de Bourgogne was built on the site of the Roman forum. In the basement, a spartan civic reception room provides odd surroundings for an excavated first-century dwelling and the walls of a ninth-century church. It's not a site as such, but you could ask the receptionist if you want to have a look. Across the street is the **Salles des Thèses**, all that remains of the medieval university of Orléans where the hardline Reformation theologian Calvin studied Roman law. A short distance further west on rue de Bourgogne, the circular **Protestant chapel** owes its style to the early nineteenth-century architectural fad known as Greek Revival.

In the area west of rue de la Tour Neuve are the various sites of the former **Dessaux vinegar works**. Orléans' vinegar-making traditions go back some six hundred years – to the times when wine would go off during the journey up the Loire. Since the Dessaux factory closed down in 1983, only one traditional vinegar-maker remains in the city, the Maison Martin-Pouret: the factory is in the suburb of Fleury-les-Aubrais, but you can buy bottles of their vinegar and mustard all over town. Until recently, the **Quartier Dessaux** was semi-derelict, but it has now been entirely renovated as part of the grand municipal scheme to bring the entire riverside quarter back to life, with blocks of flats and a large student residence on rue de la Folie. The former factory building known as the **Salle Eiffel**, at 15 rue de la Tour Neuve, was designed by the Eiffel architectural studios and is now a lecture theatre and concert hall. On the corner of rue des Africains and rue de la Folie, a plaque marks the house of Joan's brother and companion-in-arms, Pierre du Lys.

Part of the **Gallo-Roman city wall**, which marked the eastern limits of the ancient city, can be seen on rue de la Tour Neuve near rue Edouard Fournier and again in the base of the **Tour Blanche**, just south, which is occasionally used for exhibitions by the city council's archeological department. To the east of rue de la Tour Neuve lies the fifteenth-century **église St-Aignan**, begun by Charles VII and hugely extended by Louis XI; astonishingly, what you see is only the choir and transepts, the nave having been destroyed by Huguenots in 1567. Peaceful place du Cloître St-Aignan, on the north side of the church, was once the site of the monastic cloisters. It's worth checking at the tourist office to see if your stay coincides with one of their occasional tours of the remarkable **crypt** (otherwise closed to the public). It was built in the early eleventh century to house the relics of St Aignan, an early bishop of Orléans who, according to legend, saved the city from the warriors of Attila the Hun in 451. In the 1950s, beautiful polychrome capitals were discovered inset into the fifteenth-century walls, but the tomb itself is even more impressive, a great stone chamber with four holes through which pilgrims could catch a glimpse of the precious relics contained within.

West of the Quartier Dessaux, the transformation of the riverside area is at its most complete at the all-new **place de la Loire**, which slopes down to the river and its pedestrianized quays from a nine-screen cinema complex, its flagstones inset with a pattern that's supposed to suggest waves.

Eating, drinking and nightlife

There are one or two good places to eat on and around the place du Martroi – rue Ste-Catherine is especially lively – but rue de Bourgogne is where it's at for both **restaurants** and **nightlife**. You can choose from among French, Spanish, North African, Middle Eastern and Indian cuisines, all at reasonable prices. For buying your own provisions there are the covered **market halls** on place du Châtelet, near the river.

Restaurants

Les Antiquaires 2 & 4 rue au Lin☎02.38.53.63.48, ⓦwww.restaurantlesantiquaires.com. This is Orléans' best restaurant and must be booked in advance. Lobster consommé, wild turbot with girolle mushrooms and a pike-perch steak are some of its delights, served in a formal, beamed dining room. The excellent €38 menu (not available Sat evening or Sun) includes wine, otherwise there are menus at €46 and €66. Closed Sun evening, Mon & first three weeks of Aug.

Le Brin de Zinc 62 rue Ste-Catherine. This bustling bistro is just off Place du Martroi, in the hotel of the same name. The outside tables are usually packed with a noisy crowd tucking into huge seafood platters (€14–28) and *plats du jour* (€7.40).

La Chancellerie 27 place Martroi ☎02.38.53.57.54. Customers in the upmarket restaurant section get starched white tablecloths – even outside – and a distinctly classy €36 menu, but the café-brasserie is a good place for a drink on the square, with a fair lunch menu for €16.50.

Au Don Camillo 54 rue Ste-Catherine ℡02.38.53.38.97. Packed out at lunch and dinner, this restaurant has a smart interior, with limited outside seating in summer. It's known for giant pizzas (€7–10), but also does standard meat and fish dishes, and a lunchtime menu for €11.50.

Les Fagots 32 rue du Poirier ℡02.38.62.22.79. Wonderfully convivial place that looks like it has been crammed into someone's grandmother's kitchen, albeit a grandmother with a mania for collecting coffeepots. Excellent grilled meats are cooked on the griddle in one corner of the room. There are two menus, at €11 and €15, both including an apéritif. Closed Sun & Mon.

La Mangeoire 28 rue du Poirier ℡02.38.68.15.38. This is a real local secret: a homely, brightly lit bistro packed full of locals enjoying straightforward pasta, salads and French standards, with starters at €5 and mains from €10–15. Closed Sun.

La Petite Folie 223 rue de Bourgogne ℡02.38.53.39.87, ⦿www.lapetitefolie.fr. From the new wave of designer bar-restaurants, this is full of trendy twenty- and thirty-somethings

having a drink with friends or a light meal. The food is actually very good: fresh and healthy with lots of zingy, unconventional combinations. You might find asparagus flan, chicken with sauce Canadienne, then strawberry soup with wine – all for around €20. Closed Sun; Oct–April closed lunchtimes.

La Petite Marmite 178 rue de Bourgogne ℡02.38.54.23.83. The most highly regarded restaurant on this busy street mixes the hip with the homely: the owner presides over the warm, bustling, rustic interior with Almódovar-esque cool. The excellent €20 menu du terroir features local produce such as rabbit and guinea-fowl from the Sologne, and there are more expensive menus as well. Booking is essential. Closed Tues & Wed.

Le Viking 233 rue de Bourgogne ℡02.38.53.12.21. Camp, oddball mix of fancily upmarket and relaxed, with candelabras on the tables and a half-hearted attempt at maintaining the Viking theme. The food is similarly surprising, the flagship dishes being luxurious cheese- or fish-based galettes (€12–18). There's also one with snails. Closed Sun & Mon.

Bars and clubs

L'Atelier 203 rue de Bourgogne. Of all Orléans' nightlife venues, this cosy bar really stands out. It's an arty, studenty place, with regular concerts, painting exhibitions and even occasional play readings. The atmosphere is friendly rather than pretentious, and drinks are reasonably priced and include some inventive cocktails – be sure to try their petit vélo. Rarely closes much before 2am.

Le Club 266 rue de Bourgogne. Cellar club-bar with a tiny dance floor overlooked by a little mezzanine seating level, and a vaguely 1980s theme. The friendlier choice if you're out late at the weekend and want to push on past 2am or have a dance – otherwise don't bother. Entry €10 with a drink.

Paxton's Head 264–266 rue de Bourgogne. A pretty authentic rendition of an English pub, and a good spot for a relaxed drink in the afternoon. After midnight or so, the livelier punters descend to the club downstairs (see above). Daily 3pm–3am.

Le Sunset 108 ave du Loiret, beside the Pont du Loiret on the main road to Olivet. Orléans' best club, and worth making the journey out of town for – though only on Friday and Saturday after 1am, as otherwise it tends to be pretty quiet, unless a particular soirée has been advertised. Plays R&B, funk or club classics – depending on the night – to a relatively sophisticated crowd. Taxi essential. €9 with one drink.

Festivals

The **Fête de Jeanne d'Arc** is a series of period-costume parades held on April 29, May 1 and May 7–8, with the big set-pieces occurring in front of the cathedral on the night of May 7 and morning of the May 8. The **Festival de Jazz d'Orléans** (⦿www.orleans.fr/orleansjazz) is held in the second half of June, culminating in concerts held in the Campo Santo. For around ten days in August, the **Ciné-Jardins** festival displays open-air cinema at various places in town. Showings usually start at 10pm, and entry is free. Every other year in September (2007, 2009…), the **Festival de Loire** (⦿www.festivaldeloire.com) presents five days of concerts and shows, many held on old boats moored by the Châtelet quay; cafés and restaurants are set up on a terrace built out over the river.

Listings

Bike rental The only central option is CAD, 95 rue Faubourg Bannier ☎02.38.81.23.00. Otherwise, try Kit Loisirs, 1720 rue Marcel Belot (☎02.38.63.44.34, ⓦwww.kitloisirs.com), out in the suburb of Olivet.

Car rental Avis, Gare SNCF ☎02.38.62.27.04; Rent-a-Car, 3 rue Sansonnières ☎02.38.62.22.44; Europcar, 17 Av de Paris ☎02.38.73.00.40.

Cinemas Le Select, 45 rue Jeanne-d'Arc, often shows good art house movies in the original language; Cinema Multiplex Pathé, 45 rue des Halles, place de la Loire, sometimes shows

Hollywood blockbusters in English. Programme info for both is available on ☎08.92.68.69.25, ⓦwww.cinemaspathe.com.

Emergencies Ambulance ☎15; police ☎17; Centre Hospitalier, 1 rue Porte-Madeleine ☎02.38.51.44.44.

Internet Leader Best Phone, 196 rue de Bourgogne (July & Aug 11am–11.30pm; Sept–June 9.30am–11.30pm; €3 per hour).

Police 63 rue du Faubourg-St-Jean ☎02.38.24.30.00.

Taxis Taxi Radio d'Orléans ☎02.38.53.11.11.

Around Orléans

If you're spending more than a couple of days in **Orléans**, two sights in the outer suburbs may well draw you out of the city. Even if you're just passing through, the **Parc Floral** at Orléans-la-Source makes a good stop-off on the way south into the Sologne, and you could call in at the Fonderie Bollée (bell foundry) at **St-Jean-de-Braye** on your way upstream towards Gien.

The overgrown village of **La Ferté-St-Aubin** is only 21km south of Orléans, but the distinctive red brick of its low buildings is distinctively *Solognote* – from the backwoods region of the Sologne (most of which is covered in Chapter 2; see p.167). Most visitors come on day-trips from Orléans, to visit the entertaining château, lunch in one of the restaurants in and around town and maybe have a walk in the nearby Domaine du Ciran. Any one of the three makes for an enjoyable outing, especially for children, and all are accessible on **public transport**.

Parc Floral de la Source

Orléans expanded rapidly after World War II, and in 1959 the suburb of **Orléans-la-Source** was created to take some of the pressure off the city. The grounds of the château de la Source (which now belong to Orléans' campus university and doesn't have anything much to offer the visitor) have been transformed into the enormous **Parc Floral de la Source** (daily: April–Oct 10am–7pm; Nov–March 2–5pm; €4 ⓦwww.parc-floral-la-source.com), where you can wander among endless gardens of roses, irises and rhododendrons, visit the wonderful tropical butterfly-house (€2.70), and gaze on the principal source of the Loiret – which turns out to be a rather unimpressive stream, for all that it inspired the name of the château (*source* means "spring") and indeed the entire *département* of the Loiret.

To get to the park **by car**, take the Pont du Maréchal Joffre, heading south along the N20 towards Bourges, and then follow the signs for the Parc Floral. It's much more fun, and just as quick, however, to take the spanking-new **tram A** from place de Gaulle towards Hôpital de la Source, getting off at Université-Parc Floral; the journey takes twenty minutes.

St-Jean-de-Braye

The village of **ST-JEAN-DE-BRAYE**, where sculptor Henri Gaudier-Brzeska was born in 1891, is now a suburb of the city. Most visitors are businesspeople on their way to the giant cosmetics factory, which employs around 1800 people and manufactures almost all **Christian Dior**'s perfumes and make-up. There are no guided visits, however, and the few tourists that come to St-Jean are those who have heard about the **Fonderie Bollée** (Feb–Dec Fri–Sun 2–6pm; €3), which is one of only three working bell foundries in France. Generations of the same family of bellwrights have used traditional techniques here since the 1840s – and before then the Bollées were itinerant bell-makers. Even if you don't speak French, it's worth seeing the workshops and the modest museum, though bear in mind that the actual foundry – the most fascinating part of the visit – shuts down at weekends and for most of August. On Fridays during the rest of the year, however, you can see bells being dramatically liberated from their moulds or being finished off by hand – even seeing them cooling in their giant pit is impressive.

To make an excursion of it, take the path that runs along the Canal d'Orléans to the pretty village of **COMBLEUX** – count on around one hour one-way. In the centre of St-Jean-de-Braye, on place de la Commune, you can see a carillon of 35 small bells, which rings out the "Carillon de Vendôme" every day at noon (see box on p.203), and the "Ode to Joy" at 6pm.

There's a good and rather fashionable **restaurant** on the towpath at St-Jean-de-Braye, *Les Toqués*, 71 chemin du Halage (☎02.38.86.50.20; closed Mon & Sun). It serves classic dishes with a modern twist, but the outside seating is the main draw; expect to pay around €25–40. To get to the Fonderie, take **bus** #4 from the gare SNCF stop or bus #27 from the riverside quai du Châtelet, getting off at St-Loup. **By car**, it's easiest to follow the river west and turn off at the signs.

La Ferté-St-Aubin and around

The privately owned **château de la Ferté-St-Aubin** (April to mid-Nov daily 10am–7pm; €8, children aged 4–15 €5; ⓦwww.chateau-ferte-st-aubin.com) lies at the north end of the village from which it takes its name, set back from the busy N20 road behind its own moat and meadow. From the outside, it's one of the warmest and most enticing of all Loire châteaux, the combination of salmon-coloured brick, creamy limestone and dark roof slates almost irresistible, especially as the place is well worn at the edges.

The approach is exquisite: you cross a meadow and a moat, passing through a stone gate flanked by two doll-sized turrets, with *œil-de-bœuf* windows peering out of their hat-like roofs. The **stable** buildings stand symmetrically on either side, marked by seventeenth-century terracotta horses' heads, which rear under the central pediments – the block on the right is now used for exhibitions, but the left-hand row still stables the proprietor's horses.

The main château building in front is far less well ordered, falling down in three step-like wings of very unequal sizes: the smallest section, known as the **petit château**, dates from the late sixteenth century, while the **grand logis** to the right was completed in the 1630s. The interior is a surprise: this is a nineteenth-century-style home, and you are invited to treat it as such. You can wander freely into almost every room, playing billiards or the piano, picking up the old telephone, sitting on the worn armchairs or washing your hands in a porcelain sink; only the rather fancier **grand salon**, with its *boiseries* painted with views of the château and its antique furnishings, is cordoned off. The none-too-tidy **attic** floor is chaotically full of bits and pieces, as a good attic should be: there are roomfuls of antique children's toys and artisans' tools and dummies apparently ironing the laundry, and a section where an old *épicerie* (grocer's shop) has been transferred here in its entirety and set up just as it was when it closed.

Roughly every hour there are demonstrations down in the **kitchens** of how to make madeleine cakes – the sweet spongy biscuit that so inspired Proust. The charismatic cook is part of the husband-and-wife team that looks after the château, and she gives a fascinating tour of the old kitchens as she works. The show ends with a tasting.

At the rear of the château, also enclosed by the moat, is the so-called **Enchanted Island**. This really is a magical place for younger children, a patch of wooded ground cleverly set up with lots of games that encourage imaginative play: there's a fort (with sponge balls supplied for storming it), a Wendy house on stilts, little cabins with models acting out fairy-tales, a play farm with tools for digging, a kitchen hut, a play *épicerie*, rabbits in hutches, chickens in runs and goats running wild everywhere. Older children and adults can explore the reconstructed 1930s **station** building adjacent. You're free to clamber aboard the original *Compagnie des Wagons Lits* (Orient Express) carriages pulled up outside, still complete with their old-fashioned buffet and sleeper cars.

Practicalities

The **gare SNCF** is roughly 200m southwest of the main square, with around nine trains arriving daily from Orléans and continuing south to Vierzon and Bourges. Buses are geared to commuters, heading into Orléans in the mornings and returning in the afternoons only – useless for day-trips. The **tourist office**, rue des Jardins (April–Sept Tues–Sat 9.30am–12.30pm & 2.30–6.30pm, Sun 10am–noon; Oct–March Tues–Sat 9.30am–noon & 3–5pm; ☎02.38.64.67.93), can advise on travelling deeper into the Sologne.

There's no **hotel** in La Ferté-St-Aubin, but there is something much better: **chambres d'hôtes** in the château itself (☎02.38.76.52.72, ⓦwww .chateau-ferte-st-aubin.com; ❸–❾). The enormous suite in the main château building (€200) is the most stunning option, with its eighteenth-century furnishings, and there are other, less grand but no-less lovely options in the pavilion facing the château and in various historic outbuildings. Another special option is *La Ferme des Foucault* (☎02.38.76.94.41, ⓦwww.ferme-des-foucault .com; ❺), isolated at the end of a long, wooded farm road some 9km from La Ferté. It has luxuriously appointed rooms under the roof beams, books in English scattered everywhere and a heated swimming pool; to get there turn off at the signpost on the D64, halfway between Marcilly-en-Villette and Sennely. The handsome, brick-built eighteenth century *Château les Muids*, 5km south of La Ferté on the main N20 (☎02.38.64.65.14, ⓦwww.chateau-les-muids.com; ❻), has beautifully furnished rooms, though the ones at the front suffer a little from road noise. La Ferté's municipal **campsite** (☎02.38.76.55.90; closed Oct–March) is tucked away on the banks of the Cosson, on the opposite side of the N20 road from the château.

The proximity of the Sologne (see p.167), with all its game and fish, makes this a fantastic area for **eating**. At the *Auberge Solognote*, at 50 rue des Poulies (closed Tues evening & Wed), behind the covered market on La Ferté's main square, you can join local workmen in an inexpensive and excellent lunchtime *formule*.

Le Relais de Sologne, on the main square at Ménestreau-en-Villette, 7km east of La Ferté (☎02.38.76.97.40; closed Tues eve, Wed & Sun eve) has a rustic feel, with its fireplace and boar's head, but the carefully prepared seasonal dishes are distinctly upper-class – menus begin around €30. Heading deeper into the Sologne, *La Grenouillère*, on the edge of the village of Chaumont-sur-Tharonne, 12km south of La Ferté-St-Aubin along the D922 (℡02.54.88.50.71; closed Mon & Tues), features excellent, innovative cooking on the €38 and €45 evening menus, and has outside seating in summer. Further away still, in Souvigny-en-Sologne, 21km from La Ferté, *Le Souvignot* (℡02.54.88.44.20; closed Tues & Wed) is a wonderfully homely restaurant to make for, serving rich regional dishes – lots of game – by a huge fireplace, or at outside tables in summer; the evening menus are exceptionally good value at around €20.

Domaine du Ciran

Six kilometres east of La Ferté-St-Aubin, just off the D108 and halfway between Ménestreau-en-Villette and Marcilly-en-Villette, the **Domaine du Ciran** (daily except Tues: April–June & Sept 10am–noon & 2–6pm; July & Aug 10am–noon & 2–7pm; Oct–March 10am–noon & 2–5pm; €5; ⓦwww .domaineduciran.com) is a small nature reserve covering a number of classic Sologne environments: sandy pine forest, heathland, meadows and the inevitable marshy *étangs* (artificial lakes). There's a five-kilometre signposted circular walk, for which you should count on at least two hours to allow for diversions to various bird-hides, though two shortcuts allow you to reduce the length of the walk to 3 or 4km. No hunting has been allowed here since 1977, when the miniature château and its attached estate were bought by a private association, so the butterfly- and bird-life – especially herons and ducks – is wonderfully rich, and you may well catch a glimpse of wild deer. The best time to visit is before dusk, when you've also got the best chance of coming across wild boar – they're not especially threatening unless they're with their young, but definitely shouldn't be approached. **Camping** (May– Sept) is allowed in a small field near the gîtes used by visiting groups of schoolchildren.

Downriver from Orléans

Heading downriver from Orléans towards Blois, the D951, set just back from the main floodplain on the left bank, is much the more attractive road. The northern routes on the opposite bank are pretty depressing; whether you take the A10 motorway or the busy N152 highway, the success of the region's light industry is all too visible. If you're visiting either of the main towns described in this section, **Meung-sur-Loire** and **Beaugency**, it makes sense to approach from the south, via the D951 – crossing Beaugency's 23-arch bridge is a particular treat, and you can call in at the giant basilica at **Cléry St-André** on the way. West of Beaugency, the **château de Talcy** actually lies in the Loir-et-Cher *département*, centred on Blois, but is included here as an excursion.

Between four and six **buses** daily make the trip from Orléans to Beaugency on route #9, passing Meung-sur-Loire, but the **train** service is much more regular, as both towns lie on the main line to Blois and Tours. For Cléry-St-André and Talcy you'll need your own transport.

Meung-sur-Loire

Fourteen kilometres southwest of Orléans, **MEUNG-SUR-LOIRE** is an agreeable place to spend a couple of hours, visiting the rambling château and wandering around the small walled town. A gateway off the central place du Martroi leads up to the **château de Meung** (March–Nov daily 10am–7pm; Dec–Feb Sat & Sun 2–6pm; €7; ⓦ www.chateaudemeung.com), which is well hidden behind the church and a screen of trees. The château remained in the hands of the bishops of Orléans from its construction in the twelfth century to the Revolution, but since then has passed through the hands of seven or eight owners, many of whom struggled to maintain the château properly. There are 131 rooms, after all. The current owners are making huge efforts to restore the interiors, however, and most of the family live and work in the château. If you don't meet them at the ticket counter, you may see them stripping wallpaper, or re-arranging buckets to catch drips under the roof.

Inside and out, Meung is two very different châteaux in one. On the side facing the church, with its **thirteenth-century pepperpot towers**, the château looks grimly defensive, while the far side, facing the park, presents a much warmer face to the world, its eighteenth-century windows framed by salmon-pink stucco. The interiors of the medieval section were heavily remodelled in the nineteenth century, and the eighteenth-century wing, where the bishops entertained their guests in relative comfort, is much more impressive. The furnishings largely date from the epoch: fine stucco ceilings face parquet flooring heavy with old polish, and the rooms are filled with upright chairs, graceful sideboards and old mirrors. Perhaps most fascinating are the seventeenth- and eighteenth-century bathrooms, complete with antique smalls apparently hanging up to dry.

Children in particular may enjoy climbing up under the roof, where the owners have laid out a few ghostly surprises, and descending into the deep, chilly **cellars**, where criminals condemned by the episcopal courts were imprisoned. The most famous detainee was the poet François Villon (see p.341), whose writings indicate that he was imprisoned in the bottom of a well, outside the main body of the château, between May and October 1461. This seems a relatively short time until you actually look down into the dank hole touted as his prison – which, rather reassuringly, may in fact be an ice-house.

The rest of the town is perfect for an afternoon stroll, but there's little to detain you. Just next to the château gates, the thirteenth-century **église St-Lyphard** is renowned among architectural historians for the unusual trefoil-shaped floorplan of its choir. You can wander down from the square to the plane-tree-lined riverfront, where the bridge makes its way across the Loire, overlooked by a statue of Jean de Meun (see box, below). For a longer walk, a signposted route traces the little streams known as **les mauves** as they flow

---

Literary Meung

Meung has accumulated a number of literary associations over the years. Over seven hundred years ago one Jean Chopinel – named **Jean de Meun**, after his birthplace, in the old spelling – added 18,000 lines to the already 4000-line-long *Roman de la Rose* (see p.340), written half a century earlier in 1225 by Guillaume de Lorris, from the town of the same name in the nearby Forêt d'Orléans. Inspired by the philosophical spirit of the times, De Meun transformed De Lorris's exquisite, allegorical poem into a finely argued disquisition on the nature of love, and the resulting *roman* inspired generations of European writers, Chaucer among them. Poet **François Villon** was imprisoned in the château in 1461 (see above), while somewhat more recently the town featured in the works of **Georges Simenon** – his fictional hero, **Maigret**, takes his holidays here.

through town, taking you along stony backstreets and past the medieval town gate, the Porte d'Amont.

Practicalities

The **gare SNCF** has good connections by train to Blois and Orléans. Beaugency (see below) has more **accommodation** options, but *La Mouche de l'Abeille*, right on the riverbank on the east side of town (☎02.38.44.34.36, ⓦwww.chambres-hotes-loire.com; ❺), offers three **chambres d'hôtes** – two with wonderful river views – in an attractive old house. For something to **eat**, there's a good crêperie, *Les Hortensyas*, at 42bis rue Jehan-de-Meung (closed Mon evening & Thurs evening).

Cléry St-André

Cléry St-André, 6km east of Meung, is distinguished only by its enormous **basilica** (daily 8am to around one hour before dusk), which dwarfs the square at the centre of the tiny town. The church owes its surprising size and significance first to Notre Dame de Cléry – whose pint-sized, thirteenth-century statue in oak is still worshipped here, standing on the main altar – and secondly to **Louis XI**, who rebuilt a church destroyed by the English in the Hundred Years War. This act of piety was brought on by Louis' defeat of the English at Dieppe in 1443, one of the battles that helped bring the war to a close, and a victory the king attributed to the assistance of the Virgin. Between 1465 and 1483, Louis came here regularly to pray, as depicted by the moving effigy on his **tomb**, which stands by the north door. He is one of only three French kings not to be buried at St-Denis, just outside Paris. The present stone tomb actually dates from the reign of Louis XIII, the original having been destroyed by Huguenots in the Wars of Religion.

The fifteenth-century church building has suffered over the centuries, but still stands as a wonderful example of late Gothic architecture. You can visit a Neogothic chapel housing the tombs of the Dunois Longueville family (see p.308), the chapterhouse and the impressive chapelle de St-Jacques, built in the sixteenth century to welcome pilgrims on the road to Compostela. One of the finest details is the crawling sculpture over the portal into the **sacristy**. If you can find a caretaker to unlock the door, you can admire the fifteenth-century wooden panelling inside, and take a spiral staircase up to **Louis XI's private oratory**, which has a little window for watching the Mass. The bells in the tower occasionally ring out the carillon de Vendôme (see box on p.203).

Beaugency

Six kilometres down the Loire from Meung, the small town of **BEAUGENCY** survives almost intact behind its medieval walls, the atmosphere of genteel charm only ruffled by the lively Saturday market. The château is closed for restoration works until the end of 2008 – they may continue into 2009 – but the tightly packed streets, all built in local Beauce limestone, and the riverside quays make this one of the prettiest of all Loire towns, and the excellent choice of hotels makes it an appealing base for a night or two.

Arrival, information and accommodation

The **gare SNCF**, on place de la Gare, is five minutes' walk from the central place du Docteur Hyvernaud, where you'll find the small **tourist office** (Mon–Sat 9.30am–12.30pm & 2.30–6pm; June–Sept also Sun 10am–noon; ☎02.38.44.54.42, ⓦwww.beaugency.fr) beside the Hôtel de Ville.

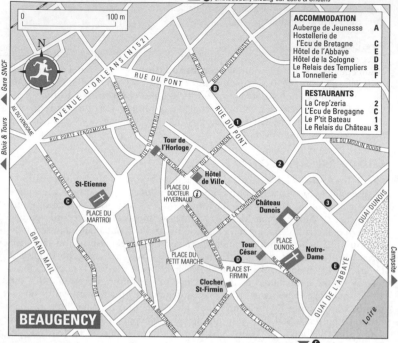

A, Châteaudun, Meung-sur-Loire & Orléans

0   100 m

N

Gare SNCF

Blois & Tours

AVENUE D'ORLÉANS (N152)

RUE DU PONT

RUE DU PUITS ROUSSY

RUE DU PONT

RUE DU VENDÔME

RUE PORTE VENDÔMOISE

RUE DES 3 MARCHANDS

RUE DE LA MAILLE D'OR

RUE DU MARTROI

RUE DU CHANGE

Tour de
l'Horloge

RUE DU CHAUMONT

Hôtel
de Ville

RUE DU MOULIN ROUGE

St-Etienne

PLACE DU
DOCTEUR
HYVERNAUD

PLACE DU
MARTROI

RUE DE LA CORDONNERIE

Château
Dunois

QUAI DUNOIS

GRAND MAIL

RUE DU CHAT QUI DORT

RUE DE L'OURS

RUE DU TRAINEAU

Tour
César

PLACE
DUNOIS

Notre-
Dame

Campsite

PLACE DU
PETIT MARCHE

PLACE ST-
FIRMIN

RUE DE L'ABBAYE

QUAI DE L'ABBAYE

Clocher
St-Firmin

RUE DE LA BRETONNERIE

RUE PORTE DE TAVERS

RUE DE L'EVÊCHE

Loire

BEAUGENCY

ACCOMMODATION

Auberge de Jeunesse	A
Hostellerie de	
l'Ecu de Bretagne	C
Hôtel de l'Abbaye	E
Hôtel de la Sologne	D
Le Relais des Templiers	B
La Tonnellerie	F

RESTAURANTS

La Crep'zeria	2
L'Ecu de Bregagne	C
Le P'tit Bateau	1
Le Relais du Château	3

Hotels

Hôtel de l'Abbaye 2 quai de l'Abbaye ☎02.38.44.67.35, ⓦwww.hotel -abbaye-beaugency.com. Its setting in a seventeenth-century abbey makes this one of the most interesting hotels in the region, and the stunning staircase, huge corridors and ancient wooden doorframes preserve the feel of historic grandeur. The actual bedrooms are a miscellaneous bunch: all are fairly luxurious, but the best have high ceilings, original features and views of the river. Try asking for room no. 7. ❼

Domaine de Montizeau Monçay, 9km from Beaugency ☎02.38.45.34.74, ⓦwww .domaine-montizeau.com. Four cosy chambres d'hôtes comprise one wing of a charming old farmhouse, set in its own green and well-tended grounds on the edge of the Sologne. Head southeast of Beaugency on the D19 and follow signs to Monçay; the house is 500m outside the village, off the road leading southwest. ❺

Hostellerie de l'Ecu de Bretagne 5 rue de la Maille d'Or ☎02.38.44.67.60, ⓦwww .ecudebretagne.fr. A classic old coaching inn beside the pleasant place du Martroi. Run in the best old

French manner, marrying the graciously formal with the warm and welcoming. The rooms are very well furnished and scrupulously maintained – some are found in the less attractive annexe, just down the street. Closed Sun evening mid-Nov to March. ❺

Le Relais des Templiers 68 rue du Pont ☎02.38.44.53.78, ⓦwww.hotel relaistempliers.com. Intimate, welcoming and enthusiastically run family hotel in a fine old building at the bottom end of town, close to the little stream that runs along the rue du Rû. The rooms are modern but tastefully furnished, and have solar-powered hot water. The best rooms are tucked away on the top floor under exposed rafters. ❸

Hôtel de la Sologne 6 place St-Firmin ☎02.38.44.50.27, ⓦwww.hotel delasologne.com. This delightful little stony-fronted, cream-shuttered hotel is set on the nicest of Beaugency's squares. There are sixteen rooms in all, four with views of the Tour de César, others set round a little internal courtyard with a glazed-over breakfast area. The bright, modern rooms are extremely comfortable, with elegant wallpaper and

furnishings that would not disgrace a much more expensive hotel. Prices for the largest rooms are around €65, otherwise ❸.
La Tonnellerie 12 rue des Eaux Bleues, Tavers ⓦ www.tonelri.com. Three kilometres southwest along the main N152, in the little village of Tavers,

this luxury hotel is set in a vine-covered building round a peaceful garden courtyard. The rooms are very swish, and the hotel has all the facilities you could think of, including a classy restaurant and a pool, but the prices are rather high – over €200 for a suite. ❽

Hostel and campsite

Auberge de Jeunesse de Beaugency 152 rte de Châteaudun, Vernon ☎ 02.38.44.61.31, ⓔ beaugency@fuaj.org. A genuinely attractive HI hostel set in a former schoolhouse located 2km north of town, on the main D925 to Châteaudun. HI membership is required, but you can join on the spot. Beds cost €11.50 a night. Closed Jan.

Camping Municipal du Val de Flux ☎ 02.38.44.50.39. One of the more pleasant campsites in the Orléanais: reasonably small, tree-shaded and making the most of its perfect riverside location on the opposite bank from town. Closed Oct–March.

The Town

The old town squeezes inside what remains of the medieval walls, clustered around a handful of central squares. At the top end of town, which slopes down from the the main N152 road to the river, **place du Martroi** is broad and handsome, but relatively uninteresting, its Romanesque priory church of **St-Etienne** sadly over-restored and used for exhibitions. Rue du Martroi leads off slightly downhill towards the **Tour de l'Horloge**, the old town gate, topped by its clock. The road leading through the tower gateway takes you to the tree-shaded **place du Docteur Hyvernaud**, presided over by the exquisite Renaissance **Hôtel de Ville**, a bizarrely proportioned structure with a curious carved frieze between the ground and first-floor levels. Inside, the main council chamber is graced by eight superb **tapestries** from the era of Louis XIII, but you'll have to ask at the tourist office, on the same square (see p.201), to be allowed inside to have a look – which somehow makes it more fun (Mon–Fri only; €1.70). The four tapestries on the left as you enter depict pagan traditions of sacrifice, while the slightly larger set on the opposite wall illustrates the four continents as perceived in the seventeenth century: a turbaned woman for the Americas; a bare-breasted (white) woman for Africa; Queen Anne of Austria, covered in a mantle of fleurs de lys, for Europe; and a mystical-looking woman for Asia.

The Dauphin's bells

Before Joan of Arc steeled him to fight for his kingdom and his coronation, the lands controlled by the Dauphin Charles were meagre indeed. A contemporary rhyme tells the litany of his possessions:

Mes amis que reste-t-il	O my friends, what land is there
A ce dauphin si gentil?	Left to this young prince and heir?
Orléans, Beaugency,	Orléans, Beaugency,
Notre-Dame de Cléry,	Our Lady of Cléry,
Vendôme, Vendôme.	Vendôme, Vendôme.

The poem was set to music, and the tune – known as the **carillon de Vendôme** – is now rung out three times daily by the bells at Beaugency and hourly at Vendôme. It's fun scrabbling to work out how the words fit the tune in time – it helps if you know that the first "Vendôme" runs straight on from "Cléry" and the second "Vendôme" gets four syllables.

The more interesting part of town lies down towards the river. Narrow rue du Traîneau runs below the market square to the lovely **place St-Firmin**, where a statue of Joan of Arc is overshadowed by the **Clocher St-Firmin**, a belfry tower whose carillon rings out a well-known tune (see box on p.203) at a few minutes past 8am, noon and 7pm. The square slopes down towards the massive shell of the eleventh-century **Tour César**, the brutal keep of the old château, which is only pierced by a few empty, anachronistic windows. On the downhill side of the tower lies **place Dunois**, bordered on one side by the rather grim fifteenth-century **château Dunois**, which Joan of Arc's companion in arms Dunois, the so-called Bastard of Orléans (see p.308), acquired by marriage. On the outside, look for the sign that has read "Quartier des Détenus" since the château was used as a debtor's prison. These days, it's even more firmly locked up, as restoration works will continue, perhaps into 2009.

Place Dunois is completed by the rather severe Romanesque abbey church of **Notre-Dame**, the venue for the Council of Beaugency in 1152 (see box, below). Inside, the superb wooden vault was installed in the mid-seventeenth century by the monks themselves – canons from the fraternity of Ste-Geneviève – but the most striking feature of the interior is the modern stained glass, which uses bold colours for symbolic effect, best seen in the choir, where Our Lady herself reigns pre-eminent in blue.

At the foot of place Dunois, a short, sloping alley runs down under an archway to **rue du Pont**; a left turn takes you some 300m to the pretty little **rue du Rû**, a narrow, flower-lined street with a little rivulet of a town stream flowing down the middle. A right turn takes you straight to the **river**. During the Hundred Years War, the **bridge** here was the only crossing between Orléans and Blois, making Beaugency a constant battleground – Joan of Arc liberated the town on her way to Orléans in 1429, in company with Dunois. Remarkably, the 26-arch medieval structure still stands, and from the parapet there's an excellent view of the keep and church towers rising above the leafy ranks of plane trees lining the quays. The large seventeenth-century building immediately upstream is what remains of the **abbey**, now a luxury hotel.

Eating and drinking

Even if you're not staying at the hotel, do consider the excellent **restaurant** at ✴ *L'Ecu de Bretagne* (see p.202), which has a deserved local reputation for using lots of fresh and home-made produce (menus €21–35). The other good restaurants in town are all found on rue du Pont, with very appealing outdoor seating alongside the little stream that runs down the middle of the street. The pick of

---

The Council of Beaugency

In 1152, the **Council of Beaugency** met in the abbey church of Notre-Dame to settle what turned out to be one of the most crucial questions in French history: could Eleanor of Aquitaine legally be divorced from Louis VII of France? The argument was based on the technical principle of consanguinity (kinship), and the council's decision that the couple were indeed too closely related freed Eleanor to marry the up-and-coming Henry Plantagenet – even though they were in fact even more closely related. Henry already controlled Normandy, Maine, Anjou and Touraine, and when he went on to become Henry II of England, Eleanor's huge land-holdings in southwest France fell under the sway of the English Crown. The ensuing struggles between the French and English kings over their claims to these territories – and to the French throne itself – continued for campaign after interminable campaign, acquiring the name of the Hundred Years War.

the bunch is *Le P'tit Bateau*, at no. 54 (☎02.38.44.56.38; menus €21–36; closed Mon), which offers carefully prepared traditional French dishes in an upmarket but unpretentious atmosphere, with big beams running between exposed stone walls and a floral terrace. One step down in terms of gastronomic pretensions is *Le Relais du Château*, just short of the bridge at no. 8 (☎02.38.44.55.10; menus €14–32; closed Thurs lunch & Wed), which has a simpler feel and specializes in fish. *La Crep'zeria*, at no. 32 (closed Mon, Sat & Sun lunch), does decent pizzas, salads and crêpes.

Château de Talcy

Fifteen kilometres west of Beaugency, the **château de Talcy** (April & Sept daily 10am–noon & 2–5pm; May & June daily 9.30am–noon & 2–6pm; July & Aug Mon–Fri 9.30am–noon & 2–6pm, Sat & Sun 9.30am–6pm; Oct–March daily except Tues 10am–noon & 2–5pm; €3.10; see map on p.202) is one of the few features in the otherwise featureless plain of the Petite Beauce, which runs north from this stretch of *la* Loire as far as its tributary, *le* Loir. The landscape seems particularly bleak along the D917 from Beaugency to Josnes, where ribbons of road are laid across scarcely undulating wheat fields, passing endless rows of pylons running north from the nuclear power station at St-Laurent-des-Eaux. Just before the village of Talcy, an old but working windmill is testament to the strength of the winds that scour the plain.

Talcy began life as a kind of fortified farmhouse, a role hinted at by the forbidding entry gate with its machicolations under the roof. Once you've entered the cobbled courtyard, however, the château's nobler incarnation is revealed in the shape of the arcaded Renaissance wing added by the Florentine financier Bernardo Salviati, who bought the château in 1517, bringing along his daughter Cassandra – who inspired Ronsard's groundbreaking sonnet sequence, *Les Amours de Cassandre*.

The numerous **eighteenth-century windows** hint at an even greater elegance within. In 1704, Talcy was bought by the Burgeats, a family of court officials who remodelled and refurnished the interiors in exquisite *ancien régime* style. Subsequent owners didn't meddle, and when the French state acquired the château lock, stock and barrel in 1932, all its fine furnishings and interiors were preserved intact. Since the completion of a major restoration programme in 2006, Talcy is now one of the Loire's most perfect châteaux. There are gorgeous furnishings to admire, but the loveliest feature is the original *boiserie*, or wood-panelling, that runs almost throughout. The attractive plainness of the panels, which are painted in pale French greys, greens and blues, is the result of Talcy being the Burgeat's supposedly modest second home in the country.

Horticulturalists will love the three-hectare **walled garden**, which presents endless varieties of apple, pear and cherry trees, many of them rare varieties little seen since the eighteenth century, and many shaped in arcane variations on the art of pruning. The huge fifteenth-century **dovecote** (see box on p.161), complete with 1500 pigeonholes and the wooden mechanism to access them, is also well worth seeing. In one of the outbuildings, a **film** on spirit hauntings is spookily projected onto wispy, blowing curtains.

The Forêt d'Orléans

East of Orléans, the ancient **Forêt d'Orléans** arcs its way along the right bank of the Loire, wrapping itself over the watershed that divides the Loire from the

Seine basin. This great swathe of woodland – one of the largest in France – is one of the ancient places of France. It is a last remnant of the great wood which once covered much of northwest Europe, and the druids are thought to have held their conventions here, at what Caesar called the "navel" of France. The forest is crisscrossed with arrow-straight roads and woodland tracks, but unless you're travelling with **bikes** strapped to the top of a car or you're a determined hiker, it can be difficult to get the best out of this area. No **buses** or **trains** serve the Forêt d'Orléans. There are few destinations as such, and the majority of visitors seem to be local retired people who drive out in the afternoons, find a spot on one of the many benches that supervise the forest crossroads and watch the world drive by.

The villages of **Ingrannes** and **Lorris** are useful bases for a more extended visit; both have fine **arboretums** within striking distance. The **château de Chamerolles**, with its gardens and perfume museum, makes a good destination on the forest's northern edge. Beyond the forest, the grain-growing plains of the Beauce stretch to the northwest, and the green fields of the Gâtinais to the northeast.

Ingrannes and around

One of the most peaceful ways to appreciate the forest flora is to arrive for one of the Sunday opening days of the **Arboretum des Grandes Bruyères** (April–Oct Sun 10am–6pm; also open on national holidays; closed Easter Sun, last Sun in July & first Sun in Aug; €10; ☏02.38.57.12.61, Ⓦwww.parcsdefrance.org), 1km outside the attractively soporific little village of **INGRANNES**, in the central part of the forest 9km north of Fay-aux-Loges, along a signposted side-road. The arboretum is really a huge woodland garden on the fringes of the forest, presided over by Scots pines and carpeted with heathers, with the occasional frog-rich pond or exotic tree, and wonderful clumps of magnolias and old roses scattered throughout. The charming owner-gardener, the comtesse de la Roche-foucauld, will happily swap tips (in exquisite English) and cuttings. Near Ingrannes, you can bathe, **camp** (☏02.38.59.35.77; closed Nov–March) and rent canoes and pedalos at the **Étang de la Vallée**, a lake just off the road to the extremely pretty village of **COMBREUX**, which lies on the Canal d'Orléans.

The obvious way to have lunch is to find a quiet forest clearing off the main road and make a **picnic**, but there's an excellent alternative at *Le Chêne Vert*, place de l'Eglise (☏02.38.57.11.97; closed Mon, Thurs evening & Sun evening; menus from €16), a splendidly rustic **restaurant** on the village green at Ingrannes. At Combreux there's an idyllic, twenty-room country **hotel**, the *Auberge de Combreux*, 34 rte de Gatinais (☏02.38.46.89.89, Ⓦwww.auberge -de-combreux.fr; ❹), with ivy on the walls, a swimming pool in the garden and a good but fairly expensive restaurant (menus at €18 in the week, otherwise around €30); guests can rent **bikes**.

Lorris

The small town of **LORRIS**, 18km northeast of Sully-sur-Loire, sells itself as the "Capital of the Forest of Orléans", though poetry enthusiasts may know it better as the birthplace of Guillaume de Lorris, the original author of the thirteenth-century *Roman de la Rose* (see box on p.200). With its ancient covered market and cluster of old-fashioned squares, the town is fairly appealing, and it's certainly a useful base for getting into the forest.

In town, you can visit the surprisingly imposing church of **Notre-Dame de Lorris**, a transitional Gothic structure with a really wonderful early sixteenth-century organ; the quirky little **Ecomusée Georges Lemoine** (accessed from the tourist office, see below for hours; free), which traces the life and work of a jeweller working in Lorris in the 1940s; and the excellent **Musée de la Résistance** (Mon & Wed–Sat 10am–noon & 2–6pm, Sun 2–6pm; €4), which is admirably well-presented, with models of Resistance fighters sending coded radio signals, and lots of old cartoons, photos and propaganda posters, though you'll need to read French to get the best out of the local history.

Giant stands of oak and even sequoias can be seen in the vicinity of the **Carrefour de la Résistance**, a woodland crossroads 10km south of town, in the heart of the forest. It was named after a group of *maquisards* encircled and shot here; ask at the **tourist office**, 2 rue des Halles (June–Aug Mon–Sat 9am–noon & 2–6pm, Sun 10am–noon & 3–5pm; Sept–May Mon–Sat 9am–noon & 2–6pm; ☏02.38.94.81.42, ✉otsi.lorris@tiscali.fr), for more precise directions and a map. From the crossroads, a signposted botanical walk leads off through the forest for 3km towards the **Étang du Ravoir**, a long forest lake that has become home to one of the few pairs of ospreys breeding in France. A special bird-hide has been built to tell the story of the so-called "fishing eagle", and if you're lucky there's even a chance to see ospreys nesting, or better still, dive-bombing the lake – though only in summer months; call the forestry office, the ONF, for details of how to get to the hide on ☏02.38.65.47.00. The ONF and the association Naturalistes Orléanais (☏02.38.56.69.84) also organize **guided walks** in the forest on Sunday afternoons in summer. At the **Étang des Bois**, 5km west of town along the D88, there's a pleasant artificial **beach** shaded by pines, with a sandy roped-off swimming area, and pedalos, canoes and windsurfers for rent. You can **camp** on one side of the lake (☏02.38.92.32.00; closed Nov–March).

There are no **buses** to or from Lorris, or any accommodation once you're there, so you'll need your own transport to get there. For getting around the area, **bikes** can be rented at Garage Delaveau, rte de Gien (☏02.38.92.40.02), 2km away from Lorris's town centre, in the light-industry zone.

Arboretum des Barres

If the native woodland of the Orléanais seems too prosaic, make for the **Arboretum des Barres**, 20km east of Lorris, just beyond the village of **Nogent-sur-Vernisson** (April–June, Sept & Oct Tues–Sun 10am–dusk; July & Aug daily 10am–dusk; €5). A national institution, the arboretum is one of the world's largest and most important collections of exotic trees, spreading across a huge and lovely area of parkland. If this was a zoo, it would be besieged by visitors.

You can follow three hour-long **walking circuits**. The Ornamental section focuses on America and the Mediterranean, taking you past some magnificent cedars and an superb "eighty-trunk" thuya. The Fructicetum section contains an extraordinary collection of fruit trees – wonderful when the blossom is out. Yet the largest and perhaps most impressive area is the Géographique collection, centred around the nineteenth-century château and presenting strange and stately trees from all over the world, notably the Far East. In summer you can also sign up for a two-hour **tree-climbing** session (July & Aug only; €31.50 per person); this isn't childish scrambling, but a serious sport, complete with ropes and harnesses.

In the village of Les Bézards, 5km south of Nogent on the main N7, there's an exceptionally swish country **hotel-restaurant**, *Les Templiers* (☏02.38.31.80.01; ❼). The main building is a handsome beamed coach-house dating back to the seventeenth century; inside the rooms are large and well-appointed to the extent of being fussy. The restaurant has a similar style, though the summer terrace is a little more relaxed. The food features high-end Sologne game and river fish given the full French gastronomic treatment; there are menus at €75 and €195, or €55 at lunch.

❸ Château de Chamerolles

On the northern side of the Forêt d'Orléans, the **château de Chamerolles** (Feb, March & Oct–Dec daily except Tues 10am–noon & 2–5pm; April–June & Sept daily except Tues 10am–6pm; July & Aug daily 10am–6pm; €5) stands outside the village of Chilleurs-aux-Bois, some 30km northeast of Orléans. It's a sedate, Sunday-afternoon-outing kind of place. The château's moat, drawbridge and pepper-pot towers, its Renaissance windows and arcade, and the perfect lozenge patterns set into its brickwork are delightful. The main attractions of the visit, however, are the **Promenade des Parfums**, a museum of perfume, and the **gardens**, beautifully restored by the current owners – the *département* of the Loiret.

The château was the work of one Lancelot 1er du Lac (named after the legendary Arthurian knight, but sadly no relation), who rose to the position of governor of Orléans under Louis XII in the early years of the sixteenth century. In the south wing, a suite of rooms presents various French interiors from the sixteenth century to the present day, with an emphasis on objects related to the *toilette* – bathing, personal grooming and the use of scent. Each room has a "press-and-sniff" button with a re-creation of a typical perfume of the era. Up on the first floor, under the rafters, there's a huge collection of 300-odd nineteenth- and twentieth-century perfumes and perfume bottles. It isn't as extensive as the racks of contemporary scents on sale in the **shop**, which are cleverly arranged by type rather than by brand. A little drawbridge leads out of the back of the château to the formal **gardens**, a large terrace of geometrically arranged herbs, flowers and fruit and veg, while the château's flank sets off a contrasting, "English-style" landscaped garden set around a reed- and iris-fringed lake.

There is an infrequent **bus** service from Orléans to Chilleurs-aux-Bois, but you'd have to walk the last 3km, so the trip only really makes sense by car – though cyclists can work out some great routes along the quieter forest roads.

Upriver from Orléans

Following the **Loire** upstream from Orléans, the greatest of the châteaux are left behind, along with the majority of the region's summer visitors, but there are some fascinating places to visit, notably the Romanesque abbey at **St-Benoît-sur-Loire** and the nearby Carolingian oratory at **Germigny-des-Près**, which bear witness to the region's venerable Christian roots. Further upstream, **Sully-sur-Loire** is a superb example of a moated castle, while the town of **Gien** has a fine setting, its brick-built château and church gazing down on an ancient, many-arched town bridge. Even more spectacular is the bridge at **Briare**, where an extravagant aqueduct crosses high above the Loire itself.

Bus route #3 passes through all the riverside towns covered in this section on its way between Orléans and Gien, but it is aimed squarely at commuter traffic, with only three or four services a day (one or two on Sundays), one of which leaves Orléans very early in the morning, while the others depart in the late afternoon. For **information** on this region, and the Forêt d'Orléans to boot, see Ⓦ www.loire-valdor-sologne.com.

Jargeau and Châteauneuf-sur-Loire

There's little to detain you immediately upstream of Orléans. Taking the left bank, you pass the pleasant town of **JARGEAU**, locally renowned for its largely twelfth-century church and its *andouilles* and *andouillettes* – delicious perfumed sausages made with pork and tripe. The more satisfying, right-bank route brings you to **CHÂTEAUNEUF-SUR-LOIRE**, 25km east of Orléans. The chief draw hides behind a monumental gate in the centre of town, where a splendid, thirty-five hectare **park** landscaped in the English style, with a huge collection of exotic trees and shrubs, extends down towards the Loire. There were some 350 species of ornamentals at the last count, including gingkoes, cedars and the unmistakable giant and coast redwoods. The wonderful **rhododendron garden** usually blooms in late May.

The seventeenth-century château to which the park belonged was mostly demolished after the Revolution, but the gleaming stable buildings survived. They now house the excellent **Musée de la Marine de Loire** (daily except Tues: April–Oct 10am–6pm; Nov–March 2–6pm; €3.50), which tells the story of the old Loire mariners and their boats – and of the vanished château. Pick up an English booklet from the reception desk if you want to make sense of the various exhibitions on boats, trade routes and the riverfaring way of life.

The town centre is dominated by the church of **St-Martial**. Poke a nose inside to gawp at the **tomb of Louis Phélypeaux**, marquis de la Vrillière and builder of the now-vanished "new" château from which the town takes its name. A Baroque work by the prolific Italian sculptor Domenico Guidi, it commemorates the death of the good marquis in the most extravagantly macabre fashion. If you've visited the museum, you may be inspired to head down to the abandoned **riverbank quays** for a meditative stroll.

Germigny-des-Près

Heading upstream along the right bank, the little D60 is a much more pleasant road than the main D952 to Gien, parading along the top of a grand lévee which protects against the Loire's wild winter floods. Five kilometres out of Châteauneuf, the village of **GERMIGNY-DES-PRÈS** is home to an outwardly unassuming **church** (daily: April–Oct 8.30am–7.30pm; Nov–March 8.30am–6pm; €2 coin needed for lighting) that incorporates one of the oldest buildings in France at its east end. The tiny, perfectly formed **oratory** is one of the few structures surviving anywhere from the Carolingian Renaissance. It was built in 806 for Theodulf, who was one of Charlemagne's counsellors as well as bishop of Orléans and abbot of St-Benoît (see p.210). The apparently Arabic horseshoe arches actually reflect Theodulf's Spanish-Visigotic origins, while the chapel itself is a typically Carolingian design, rationally planned in the shape of a Greek cross. The original structure lacks only its western apse, which was replaced by a long nave in the fifteenth century, although it was also damaged in the nineteenth century by too-perfect restoration work. Still, the unique gold and silver mosaic on the dome of the eastern chapel preserves all its rare beauty. Long covered by distemper, it was only discovered by accident in the middle of the nineteenth century, when children were found playing with coloured glass cubes in the church. Unusually, the mosaic represents the Ark of the Covenant, the biblical Jewish repository for the tablets of the Ten Commandments. The decision not to depict Christ in Majesty or the Virgin Mary, as was more common, may reflect Charlemagne's opposition to the cult of images.

St-Benoît-sur-Loire and around

Thirty-five kilometres upstream of Orléans, **ST-BENOÎT-SUR-LOIRE** derives its name and its considerable fame from a daring grave-robbery. In around 672, a group of monks from the **abbaye de Fleury** returned home from a raid on Monte Cassino in Lombard-occupied Italy with the remains of St Benedict (Saint Benoît), the sixth-century founder of the reforming Benedictine order. The presence of the relics secured a prestigious future for the abbey, and over the course of the next 1100 years, its abbots included many familiar names from French and Loire history, including Cardinal Louis II of Guise, who was murdered in the château at Blois (see box on p.147) and the great Cardinal Richelieu, who received the title of abbot as a political reward in 1621. For all its importance, the abbey stagnated as often as it flourished, and its population had dwindled to ten monks at the time of the Revolution, after which it was abandoned and dismantled. The church itself survived, and Benedictine monks returned in 1944. The community now numbers forty brothers, who observe the original Rule and can be heard singing Gregorian chant at the daily midday Mass (11am on Sunday). They earn their keep by producing some nine tonnes of sweets a year, as well as selling enamel paintings.

Built in warm, cream-coloured stone between 1020 and 1218, the present **church** (daily: April–Oct 7am–9pm; Nov–March 9am–7pm; free; ⓦwww .abbaye-fleury.com) dates from the abbey's greatest epoch. The oldest and most imposing part, the **porch tower**, illustrates St John's vision of the New Jerusalem in Revelation – foursquare, with twelve foundations and three open gates on each side. The fantastically sculpted capitals of the heavy pillars are alive with acanthus leaves, birds and exotic animals. Three of them depict scenes from the Apocalypse, with the horsemen clearly visible, while another shows Mary's flight into Egypt on a donkey.

The **interior** exemplifies the serene simplicity of the Romanesque style, though the vaults of the nave – the last section to be built – are just starting to point upwards in the half-way-to-Gothic style known as Transitional. A fascinating capital in the north aisle just before the choir shows St Benedict rolling in thorns to mortify his flesh and distract himself from the temptations of a prostitute. Look out for the strange moustachioed figure set into the west wall of the north transept, thought to represent a Visigoth. The light-filled **choir** is split into two levels divided by a wall pierced with tiny windows for viewing the relics: above, a marble mosaic of possible Roman origin covers the chancel floor; below, in the ancient **crypt**, the relics of St Benedict lie buried at the very root of the church's forest of columns and arches, in a modern reliquary designed by a monk from Solesmes (see p.323). Since the 2005 election of another Benedict as Pope, the relics have acquired a new importance within the Catholic community.

You can leave by the **north door**, where an unfinished Romanesque frieze, discovered only in 1996, shows the progress of sculpture from blind block of stone to finished work. On the outside of the north portal, a frieze under the figure of Christ Teaching depicts the translation of the relics of St Benedict – here shown as bones being carried off willy-nilly in a wicker basket.

Practicalities

The tiny **town** has little to offer other than a stroll around the old houses beside the quays, but visiting the abbey late in the evening might be appealing enough to make you want to stay a night. The **tourist office**, 44 rue Orléanaise (April–Sept Mon–Sat 9am–12.30pm & 2–6.30pm, Sun 10am–1pm; Oct–March Mon–Sat 9am–12.30pm & 2.30–6pm; ☎02.38.35.79.00, ⓦwww.saint-benoit -sur-loire.fr), occupies the house that once belonged to **Max Jacob**, the fashionable Montmartre-based poet who converted to Judaism and retired to St-Benoît. Jacob was interned in 1944 in the camp at Drancy, where he died, and there's a small (free) memorial exhibition to him above the tourist office. **Bikes** can be rented from Racing Cart, rte du Vieux Chemin (daily except Tues 10am–noon & 2–8pm; ☎02.38.35.76.46).

If you decide to **stay**, the *Hôtel du Labrador*, 7 place St-André (☎02.38.35.74.38, ⓦwww.hoteldulabrador.fr; ❹), has a great location right next to the abbey, but the rooms are an unappealing mix of the oppressively old-fashioned and the drably modernized – the latter in a new garden annexe. The attached **restaurant** (closed Mon, Sat lunch & Sun evening; menus from €23–45), however, is fairly good, if somewhat formal. You might be better off with **chambres d'hôtes**. Mme Bouin, 6 chemin de la Borde (☎02.38.35.70.53, ⓦwww.france -bonjour.com/la-borde; ❸), has six comfortable rooms in a modern farmhouse situated 2km from town, just off the D148 towards Ste-Scholastique; bikes can be rented and there's a table d'hôte on request. Mme Xavier, 8 rue de la Pigeonnière (☎02.38.35.72.93; ❹), has two rooms in an attractively renovated farmhouse, and offers an excellent table d'hôte – as well as half-day lessons in chocolate-making. The low-key **campsite**, *Camping du Port* (☎02.38.35.77.19; closed Oct–April), is particularly attractive, set beside a quiet stretch of river immediately below the village. You can rent **canoes** here in summer.

Sully-sur-Loire

SULLY-SUR-LOIRE, 8km southeast of St-Benoît, is a rare exception to the rule that seemingly states that all major towns must be founded on the right bank of the Loire. Approaching from the north, you pass over a bridge that was twice destroyed by savage wartime bombing (see p.213). The same bombs largely destroyed the tiny town, which has been innocuously rebuilt in red Sologne brick. The **château** that stands between town and river is a picture-book castle, complete with pointy-capped towers, machicolations and drawbridge. **Restoration works** are expected to be completed by the time this book goes to press, so you'll need to check with the tourist office (see p.213) for details of hours and ticket prices.

The original Sully family achieved brief fame under Maurice de Sully, the builder of Notre-Dame de Paris, but the male Sully line came to an abrupt end in the Hundred Years War. The domain passed by marriage to Georges de la Trémoïlle, an extravagantly tall, wealthy and fat man who, in 1400, had the château rebuilt by Raymond du Temple, the cutting-edge architect of the medieval Louvre palace. As one of Charles VII's favourites – he bankrolled the Dauphin's campaign – de la Trémoïlle infuriated **Joan of Arc** by encouraging the Dauphin to pursue a pacifying, diplomatic solution to the wars. After Joan's failure to liberate Paris in 1430, de la Trémoïlle attempted to ground her by virtually imprisoning her in the castle. She escaped, but was captured less than two months later at the disastrous battle of Compiègne. Three years later, an assassination attempt on de la Trémoïlle failed only because the sword failed to pierce his corpulent flesh.

The castle changed hands in 1602, this time being snapped up by Henri IV's hyperactive minister, Maximilien de Béthune, duc de Sully, who added the moat and park, and pushed out the riverbank to protect his glorious creation from

△ Château Sully-sur-Loire

the vagaries of the Loire. After Henri's death, the arrogant minister – known as
Le Grand Sully – was forced into retirement, which he spent writing his
memoirs at Sully. In the eighteenth century young Voltaire, exiled from Paris for
libellous political verse, spent time at the château, sharpening his wit in the
company of the society figures with whom the duc de Sully of the time
surrounded himself.

The last two centuries have been hard on the château. At the time of the
Revolution, the penultimate duke backed the new regime and saved his
château by partially dismantling the towers of the keep – potent symbols of
feudalism. When the last duke died without heir in 1807, the estate passed to
the Béthune-Desplanques family, who entirely remodelled the **Petit Château**
– the smaller, fifteenth-century wing on the southeast side – according to
nineteenth-century tastes. The towers of the keep were rebuilt in the 1900s,
but fire caused severe damage to the Petit Château in 1918 and at the height
of World War II all the furnishings were sold off. The current owner, the *département* of the Loiret, has been trying to buy them back ever since – if the
original pieces can't always be found, then antiques that once belonged to the
Sully family or, failing that, furnishings from the era of the fifth duke, are being
snapped up.

The greatest acquisition is the unusually beautiful series of **tapestries** depicting the story of Psyche, whose beauty made Eros himself fall in love with her
– much to the displeasure of his mother, Aphrodite. They were woven in the
reign of Henri IV for Maximilien de Béthune's birthplace of Rosny-sur-Seine,
and bought in 1994 for over €150,000. These are displayed in the **chambre de
psyche**, which has been restored – along with two adjoining rooms – in the
early eighteenth-century style of the fifth duc de Sully. The **cabinet** is decorated
with lovely *chinoiseries* in the then-fashionable Oriental style, while the
antichambre contains a tapestry of the *Dance of the Satyres*. When works are

The bridges of Sully-sur-Loire

Sully hasn't had much luck with its **bridges**. The earliest – washed away by a great flood in 1363 – was thought to have been an exceptionally long-lived Roman structure, but recent archeological digs have shown that it was actually built in around 1000. Even so, it was by far the longest-surviving bridge at this site. After its destruction, boats and ferries were the only means of crossing at Sully until a toll bridge was built – almost five hundred years later – in 1836. Optimistically constructed in oak, it didn't survive the flood of 1856, but was rebuilt and continued to be used until the local authorities completed a magnificent suspension bridge in 1933. Partially blown up by the retreating French army in June 1940, it was mended in 1943 and used until definitively destroyed by American aerial bombing in 1944. Yet another bridge was built immediately after the war, but succumbed to the pressure of ice in the big Loire freeze of January 1985. Today's ugly structure was built to last, in heavily reinforced concrete, and yet it's soon to be superseded by another bridge serving a brand new bypass that will cross the Loire a couple of kilometres downstream. Construction of this, Sully's latest river-crossing, is supposed to begin in 2010, though at the time of writing the decision as to exactly where the bridge will stand was yet to be made.

complete, you should be able to follow a spiral staircase and guard-walk to the **Great Garret**, a vast chamber lined with fifteen-metre-high, 600-year-old oak rafters. The absence of any trusses or tie beams is astonishing, and makes the rows of arching beams look like the ribs of some giant's sternum.

Practicalities

The **train station**, on the Bourges–Etampes line, is ten minutes' walk from the centre of the village, where the **tourist office** can be found on place de Gaulle (May–Sept Mon–Sat 9.45am–12.15pm & 2.30–6.30pm, Sun 10.30am–1pm; Oct–April Mon 10am–noon, Tues, Wed, Fri & Sat 10am–noon & 2–6pm, Thurs 2–6pm; ℡02.38.36.23.70, ℮ot.sully.sur.loire@orange.fr). **Bikes** are a good way to explore – especially if you're headed north into the Forêt d'Orléans (see p.205) – and can be rented from Passion Deux Roues, 10 rue des Epinettes (℡02.38.35.13.13).

Two reasonable **hotels** can be found near the central marketplace, which hums with life on a Monday, the local market day. The *Hostellerie du Grand Sully*, 10 boulevard du Champ-de-Foire (℡02.38.36.27.56, ℻02.38.36.44.54; ❸), is a very respectable place with comfortable rooms and an excellent restaurant (menus from €27; closed Sun evening & Mon). The *Hôtel de la Tour* (℡02.38.36.21.72; ❸) is above a very local bar, but has recently done up its rooms in an unfussy, modern way – the ones in the tower are good fun. The nearest **campsite**, *Camping Hortus* (℡02.38.36.35.94, ⓦwww.camping-hortus.com; closed Nov–April) is very swish and has a pretty riverbank location – though it's on the far, northern bank from town, which is awkward if you're on foot.

For **eating** out, *Côtes et Jardin*, at 8 rue du Grand Sully (℡02.38.36.35.89; €13 lunchtime menu, otherwise €20–30; closed Sun evening, Tues evening, Wed & last two weeks in Sept), serves classy and excellent-value French cuisine; it's easy to find – look for the town's sole-surviving Renaissance mansion, on the road to the château.

Sully's **International Music Festival** (ⓦwww.festival-sully.com) is usually held in the the first two weeks of June, featuring classical concerts held in a huge marquee in the grounds of the château.

Gien

On the right bank of the river, 23km upstream of Sully-sur-Loire, **GIEN** had the life bombed and burned out of it between 15 and 17 July 1940, when the rapidly advancing Germans caught up with the French army – which, for once, was not retreating fast enough. The damage was extensive, but a freak rainstorm saved most of the fifteenth-century **château**, and a postwar reconstruction in the local glazed brick has re-created some sense of the town's fifteenth-century quaintness. Unfortunately, Gien's hotels reflect the existence of its thriving manufacturing industry – which includes a major **toilet roll** manufacturer and a Japanese perfume factory – rather than tourism, so the choice is mostly uninspiring.

The sixteenth-century stone **bridge** spanning the river still offers excellent views of Gien's medieval-style mass, the château towering above town next to the modern church. Looking downstream, the four great cooling towers of the nuclear power station at Dampierre-en-Burly (see p.339), can also be seen, emitting tell-tale clouds of water vapour. An alarm siren is tested on the first Wednesday of every month, though it's not clear what the *Giennois* could do if it went off – local wits advise making for the wine cellars with a corkscrew.

The château and church

The architecture of the **château**, built in red brick inset with grey bricks in elaborate checkerboard and lozenge patterns, owes much to the local styles and materials of the Sologne (see p.167), a region to the west rich in clay but poor in stone. It's no farmhouse, however, and its elegant, proto-Renaissance style is a fine example of the architecture elaborated under Louis XI. The royal influence

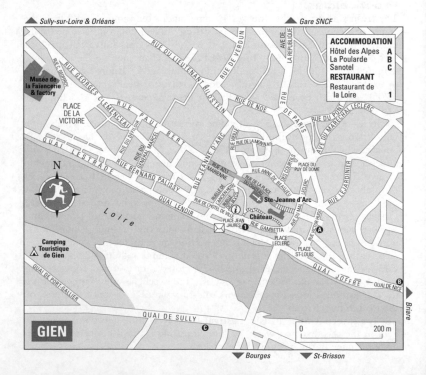

is hardly surprising, as the château was built by Louis' daughter, Anne de Beaujeu. As the elder sister of the young Charles VIII, Anne became the regent of France during her brother's strife-ridden minority. Building the château was practically a retirement hobby, as by 1494, when she began it, Charles had married and assumed full control of the kingdom. Some two hundred years later, in 1652, another great female regent arrived in the form of Anne of Austria, who sheltered in Gien with her young son and charge Louis XIV during the revolts against taxation known as the *Frondes*.

Little survives of the château's original interior, and the entire building has now been turned over to the **Musée International de la Chasse et de la Nature** (Feb–March & Oct–Dec daily except Tues 10am–noon & 2–5pm; April–June & Sept daily except Tues 10am–6pm; July & Aug daily 10am–6pm; €5), an appropriate theme for Gien, caught as it is between the rich hunting grounds of the Sologne and the Forêt d'Orléans. In fact, the countless exhibits venerating *la chasse* – hunting horns, tapestries, exquisite watercolours of horseback hunts, beautifully crafted guns, falconers' gear and noble oil portraits of dogs – rather outweigh *la nature*. If you're put off by the thought of a hunting museum, you might remind yourself of the deep significance of hunting in the French psyche: one of the great material gains of the Revolution was the right of ordinary people to hunt – a right zealously exercised today, particularly in the Sologne.

That said, the two topmost rooms are just grisly, the first adorned with five hundred-odd pairs of antlers, all shot by the trigger-happy Hettier de Boislambert – most impressive is the extraordinary wall of antelope and gazelle horns from Africa, twisted and curved and pointed in every conceivable shape – and the second displaying the hairier trophy collection of François de Grossouvre, featuring three entire leopards, two large buffalo heads and one gnu. The museum also hosts special exhibitions – some, focusing on animal sculpture and the like, will be of more interest to nature and animal lovers than hunters.

Next door to the château, the **église Ste-Jeanne d'Arc** was entirely rebuilt in the 1950s, only the massive stone bell tower having survived the war. Inside, Max Ingrand's fiery stained-glass windows recall the destruction of the old church, while Gien *faïencerie* makes up much of the religious artwork.

Musée de la Faïencerie

Like Nevers, further south on the Loire, Gien is well known in France for its faïence, or majolica, a technique of enamelling earthenware to produce fine china which came to Gien from Faenza via the rather roundabout route of England – one Thomas Hall introduced the technique in 1812. Gien lacks its own unique style, copying instead the blue patterns of Nevers and Italian-type multicoloured designs. A good half of the wares are now produced using a "chromographic" method similar to printing, rather than hand-painted in the traditional manner. A large factory still operates in Gien, employing over two hundred people, and you can buy the ordinary tableware in the **factory shop** on place de la Victoire, 1km west of the château and bridge (Mon–Sat 9am–noon & 2–6pm), and the hand-worked, arty stuff either in the shops found all over town, or direct from the **Musée de la Faïencerie** (Jan & Feb Mon–Fri 2–6pm, Sat 9am–noon & 2–6pm; March–Dec Mon–Sat 9am–noon & 2–6pm, Sun 10am–noon & 2–6pm; €3.50), which is next door to the factory shop. The museum is housed in the cellars of the old workshops, and displays the more extravagant plates, vases and gee-gaws produced over the last 180-odd years, ranging from exquisitely worked vases to some oversized and monstrously pretentious objets d'art. A video shows current fabrication techniques, which you may be able to see for real in the **factory** (closed July, Aug & Dec; ☎02.38.67.44.91), though tours are supposed to be reserved for groups only.

Practicalities

The **tourist office** is on the central place Jean Jaurès (June & Sept Mon–Sat 9am–12.30pm & 2–6.30pm; July & Aug Mon–Sat 9.30am–6.30pm, Sun 10am–noon; Oct–May Mon–Sat 9.30am–noon & 2–6pm; ☎02.38.67.25.28, ⓦwww.gien.fr), while the **gare SNCF** is a good 2km north of the old centre, at the end of ave de la République – not that you're likely to use it, as the only line runs south to Briare, Cosne and Nevers and north to Montargis. Bus #3, which runs between Briare and Orléans, stops at place Leclerc, at the north end of the bridge.

The best of Gien's **hotels** is *La Poularde*, 13 quai de Nice (☎02.38.67.36.05, ⒺLapoularde2@orange.fr; ❹), on the way out of town on the road to Briare, which has rooms looking out onto the river and an excellent restaurant (menus €29–50; closed Sun evening & Mon lunch). If it's full, you could try the air-conditioned rooms of the rather ugly, modern *Sanotel*, 21 quai de Sully, on the south bank of the river facing town (☎02.38.67.61.46, ⓦww.sanotel.fr; ❷), which is just about redeemed by the views from the river-facing rooms. The *Hôtel des Alpes*, 20 rue Victor Hugo (☎02.38.67.21.67; ❶), is a decent enough one-star in the town centre. The town **campsite**, *Camping Touristique de Gien* (☎02.38.67.12.50, ⓦwww.camping-gien.com; closed mid-Nov to Feb), has a swimming pool, and stands just back from the so-called Gien beach, a wide sandy strip bordering the river on the south bank of town; it lays on outdoor activities, including bike rental and canoe trips.

For an alternative to the **restaurant** at *La Poularde* (see above), make for the small strip of decent places on quai Lenoir, by the bridge; the pick of the bunch is the *Restaurant de la Loire*, at no. 18 (☎02.38.67.00.75; closed Mon) which is a refined place, serving lots of fish on menus from €18.50.

Château des Pêcheurs

Twelve kilometres northeast of Gien is a château dedicated to another of the Sologne's favourite activities – fishing. The so-called **château des Pêcheurs** at **La Bussière** (April–June & Sept to mid-Nov Mon & Wed–Sun 10am–noon & 2–6pm; July & Aug daily 10am–6pm; €7) is moored on the edge of its enormous, six-hectare fishpond, connected by a bridge to its large **gardens**, which were originally designed by Le Nôtre, the landscaper of Versailles. Initially a fortress, the château was turned into a luxurious residence at the beginning of the seventeenth century, but only the gateway and one pepperpot tower are recognizably medieval. Like Gien, the brick construction is typical of the Sologne. The impressive scale of the outbuildings is explained by the château's strategic location on the old trading route from Paris to the south, and to the vast taxes on grain imposed on its feudal lands.

Guided tours are available, but you're free to wander around, soaking up the exquisitely genteel atmosphere evoked by the handsome, largely nineteenth-century furnishings and the eccentrically huge collection of **freshwater fishing** memorabilia bequeathed by comte Henri de Chasseval, whose widow lives in an apartment in one of the outbuildings. Paintings, models, stuffed fish, engravings, flies and rods are scattered throughout the house, while a huge coelacanth, a giant prehistoric relic of a fish discovered in the Indian Ocean, lurks in a formaldehyde tank in the basement, next to the well-preserved kitchens and laundry. Keen gardeners can explore the elaborate **potager**, or formal vegetable garden, packed with flowers, herbs, vegetables and fruit trees.

Château de St-Brisson

On the south side of the Loire, halfway between Gien and Briare, medieval weaponry is the theme at the **château de St-Brisson** (April to mid-Nov daily except Wed 10am–noon & 2–6pm; €3.50), which is energetically run by the local village. In summer, costumed demonstrations (late June to mid-July & mid-Aug to mid-Sept Sun at 3.30pm & 4.30pm; mid-July to mid-Aug daily except Wed at 3.30pm; €2.60) of three different kinds of catapults and one small cannon are given in the moat. The château also hosts contemporary art exhibitions and occasional jazz and classical **concerts** (call ☎02.38.36.71.29 for information and reservations), both of which help to make up for the rather unattractive mix of styles (twelfth- to seventeenth-century) of the building itself. You can take guided tours of the interior, which is fairly ordinary for the most part, though the salon is rather fine, with its huge beams painted with the coats of arms of some of St-Brisson's owners.

If you're looking for somewhere quiet to **stay**, the *Auberge Chez Huguette*, 7 rue du Bizoir (☎02.38.36.70.10, ℗02.38.36.79.84; ❷), is welcoming and relaxed, with a good, inexpensive restaurant serving local produce.

Briare

The small town of **BRIARE**, 10km from Gien on the Orléans–Nevers road and the Paris–Nevers rail line, centres on its Belle Époque iron aqueduct, the **Pont Canal**, linking the Canal de Briare to the north with the Canal Lateral à la Loire, which runs south to the Saône. The design of the Pont Canal came from the workshops of Gustav Eiffel (of Tower fame), but parts of the canal scheme date back to the early seventeenth century, when internal waterways linking the Mediterranean, Atlantic and Channel coasts were devised. Poised high above the Loire, you can walk along the aqueduct's extraordinary 625-metre span, with its wrought-iron crested lamps and railings, hopefully without a cruise boat spoiling the effect.

At the far end of town, on the road out towards Gien, the tiny **Maison des Deux Marines** (daily: March–May & Oct 2–6pm; June–Sept 10am–12.30pm & 2–6.30pm; €5 or €8 with Musée de la Mosaïque) is dedicated to the rival boatmen who plied the Loire and the Canal Lateral. Its basement houses a modest aquarium of Loire species, including a pair of eels. Just across the street, the **Musée de la Mosaïque et des Emaux** (daily: Feb–May & Oct–Dec 2–6pm; June–Sept 10am–6.30pm; €4) has a small collection of reproduction and contemporary mosaics made using locally manufactured tiles – Briare's wares adorn sites as prestigious and varied as the mosque at Medina and Paris's RER stations.

The **tourist office** is at 1 place Charles-de-Gaulle (April–Sept Mon–Sat 10am–noon & 2–6pm, Sun 10am–noon; Oct–March Mon 2–5pm, Tues–Sat 10am–noon & 2–5pm; ☎02.38.31.24.51, ⓦwww.briare-le-canal.com) and can provide details of canoe rental as well as maps of footpaths, towpaths and locks. If you want to cross the Pont Canal in a **boat**, the simplest option is to reserve a place on the ninety-minute cruise run by Bateaux Touristiques (July & Aug daily at 3pm; April–June & Sept Sun at 3pm; €6.80, children under 15 €4.60; ☎02.38.37.12.75, ⓦwww.bateaux-touristiques.com). The same company also offers various canal trips and lunch/dinner excursions. Renting your own **canal**

boat is an expensive business, at upwards of €400 just for a weekend in the summer months, but you don't need a licence; contact Charmes et Nautiques, Port de Plaisance, Briare (☎02.38.31.28.73, ⓦwww.charmes-nautiques.com).

For **accommodation**, the modern *Auberge du Pont Canal*, 19 rue du Pont-Canal (☎02.38.31.24.24, nicolas.rou@orange.fr; ❷), is appealingly situated right next to the Pont Canal.

Travel details

Trains

Orléans to: Beaugency (15 daily; 20min); Blois (22–26 daily; 40min); Bourges (9 daily; 1hr–1hr 40min); La Ferté-St-Aubin (13 daily; 15–25min); Meung-sur-Loire (15 daily; 15min); Paris (at least hourly; 1hr); Romorantin-Lanthenay (change at Salbris; 7 daily; 1hr 30min); Tours (12–18 daily; 1hr–1hr 30min).

Buses

Orléans to: Beaugency (4–6 daily; 45min); Briare (1 daily; 2hr 20min); Chartres (9 daily; 1hr 10min–1hr 45min); Germigny-des-Près (3 daily; 1hr); Gien (3 daily; 1hr 50min); Meung-sur-Loire (8 daily; 35min); St-Benoît-sur-Loire (3 daily; 1hr); Sully-sur-Loire (2–3 daily; 45min–1hr 20min).

4

The Haut Berry

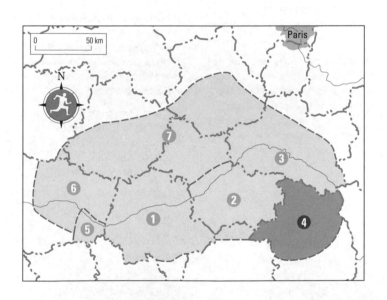

CHAPTER 4

Highlights

✱ **Cathédrale St-Etienne, Bourges** The early Gothic cathedral at Bourges is one of the most dramatic buildings in France, its immense interior illuminated by intensely coloured stained glass. **See p.225**

✱ **Les Bonnets Rouges, Bourges** You can stay in the heart of Bourges' atmospheric medieval quarter at this ancient, picturesque chambres d'hôtes. **See p.225**

✱ **Palais de Jacques-Cœur, Bourges** The refined mansion of the late-medieval financier Jacques Cœur has endless quirks, from the statues apparently looking out of an outside window to the unique internal steamroom. **See p.228**

✱ **Mehun-sur-Yèvre** Melancholy, broken towers are all that remain of the duc de Berry's beloved château. **See p.232**

✱ **La Borne** Scores of potters have settled in the backwater village of La Borne, and many have open studios where you can view and buy their wares. **See p.234**

✱ **Sancerre rouge** The dry white wine of Sancerre is one of France's best-loved wines, while the excellent, distinctive red is rarely seen outside the region. **See p.237**

✱ **Canoe trip from St-Satur** A canoe trip is the best way to get to know the river, and the stretch near Sancerre is particularly lovely. **See p.238**

△ Canoeing on the Loire near Sancerre

4

The Haut Berry

mong French people, the historic region of the **Berry** is a byword for
backwater obscurity. The roots of this area are resolutely peasant, encom-
passing a strong local tradition of sorcery and a deliciously humble
cuisine based on green lentils, potatoes, goat's cheese and nuts. In
geographical terms, the Berry is something of a no-man's land. It lies at the very
heart of France, cut off from the Loire by the semi-wilderness of the Sologne
and the rolling hills of the Sancerrois. The region has been divided in two since
the twelfth century, when the Lower, or Bas Berry, was part of the Plantagenet
empire (see p.329), while the Upper, or **Haut Berry**, remained one of the key
possessions of the French Crown. During the Revolution, the historic division
was institutionalized with new *département* names: the *département* of the Cher
corresponds with the Haut Berry, as covered in this chapter, while the Bas Berry
became the *département* of the Indre – a relatively dull region to the southwest
which lies outside the scope of this book. The Berry's principal attraction is the
ancient cathedral city of **Bourges**, the de facto capital of France under the
Dauphin Charles in the fifteenth century. It boasts two of the finest medieval
buildings in France: the fascinating **Palais de Jacques-Cœur** and the awesome
cathédrale St-Etienne. Nearby, the old town of **Mehun-sur-Yèvre** preserves
a moving ruin, one of the last vestiges of the late medieval palaces of the powerful duc de Berry. The little-known vineyards of **Reuilly** and **Quincy** lie close
at hand, as well as the amazing Romanesque wall-paintings at **Brinay**. After
Bourges, the Haut Berry's principal sight is the hilltop town of **Sancerre**,
which presides over a sweeping bend of the Loire and endless vine-combed
hillsides. For all its beauty, however, there's not a lot to see and do in the area,
and the main draw for most visitors is Sancerre's excellent **wine**.

West of Sancerre and north of Bourges, in the deeply rural country known as
the **Pays Fort**, things are quieter still. The region is hemmed in by slopes of the
Sancerrois to the south and the damp forests of the **Sologne Berrichonne** to
the west – the inspiration for Alain Fournier's classic Solognot novel *Le Grand
Meaulnes*. Fournier himself was born in **La Chapelle-d'Angillon**, one of three
small towns that punctuate the old road from Bourges to Paris, along with
Aubigny-sur-Nère and **Argent-sur Sauldre**. All three have modest château
museums to visit, but the more interesting sights lie deeper in the Pays Fort: the
potters' village of **La Borne** and the **château de Maupas**, with its huge
collection of fine china plates, testify to the region's history of ceramic production, while the children's museum of sorcery just outside **Concressault** draws
on murkier local traditions.

There is a good **train** service between Bourges and Mehun-sur-Yèvre, but the
only practical way to get around the rest of the Haut Berry is by **car**. The few

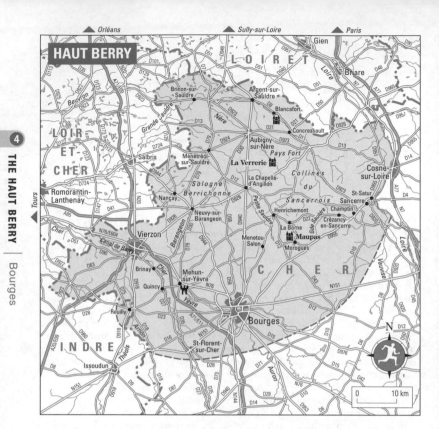

bus routes in the Pays Fort and Sancerrois are closely tied to the time tables of commuters or school students.

Bourges

The attractive medieval city of **BOURGES** feels oddly remote, a deeply provincial city isolated on the flat plain of the Berry, stranded at the geographic centre of France. It lies some distance from the Loire Valley proper – both Blois and Orléans are around 120km away – but the city's historical links with surrounding regions are strong, and the presence of one of the finest and largest Gothic cathedrals in France, rising gloriously out of the handsome medieval quarter, provides reason enough for making a detour. Bourges also offers an impressive late medieval mansion, the Palais de Jacques-Cœur, a remarkably successful outdoor sound-and-light show on summer evenings and an excellent programme of festivals and events. Sadly, the citizens of Bourges aren't called "Bourgeois" but "Berruyer".

Some history

You might not think it from its modest size today, but Bourges was intimately connected with the French monarchy through much of the Middle Ages. On

Christmas Day in 1137, the coronation of Louis VII was solemnized in the cathedral, along with that of his new queen, **Eleanor of Aquitaine** (see box on p.256), who only ten days before had inherited the vast duchy of Aquitaine from her father. When Eleanor remarried, fifteen years later, her husband Henry II gained control over her extensive lands, and Bourges became an isolated outpost – the only royal territory south of the Loire – of what was now a rump French kingdom. Henry's Plantagenet empire collapsed with his own death, however, and under Philippe-Auguste Bourges once more became the chief city of an important duchy. From the 1190s, new walls were built, and the city commissioned an avant-garde **cathedral** in the radical new Gothic style.

By the mid-fourteenth century, Bourges had become a wealthy mercantile centre, despite the endless warfare provoked by marauding English armies. In 1360, the city and the duchy of the Berry were granted to **Jean de France**, a highly cultivated grandson of the French king, Jean le Bon. As the **duc de Berry** (see box on p.226), he was reluctantly drawn into politics in the 1390s when his nephew Charles VI began to suffer bouts of insanity – famously, Charles was convinced that he was made of glass and would break unless iron rods were inserted in his clothing. The king's three uncles, the dukes of Anjou, Berry and Burgundy, were forced to act as co-regents. Inevitably, they fell out, and when Louis d'Anjou was assassinated in 1407, Jean found himself at the head of the anti-Burgundian cause. Within five years, the Burgundians had Bourges under siege; soon after, in 1415, Henry V of England spectacularly won the battle of **Agincourt**. Jean de Berry is supposed to have died from despair in the aftermath of the French defeat.

Jean de France's successor as duc de Berry was the disinherited Dauphin Charles, later **Charles VII**, who took refuge in the city. All of northern France had fallen under the English heel, while most of the south of France lay in the hands of the Duke of Burgundy. Charles's rump kingdom consisted of little more than Berry and the Loire Valley, causing the English to dub him "the little king of Bourges". It looked as if it would take a miracle to win back the kingdom, and one duly arrived in the shape of Joan of Arc. A lesser-known figure behind Charles's dramatic comeback was **Jacques Cœur**, a pioneering merchant, arms-dealer, taxman and financier who controlled and supplemented the royal finances from his palace at Bourges.

Charles turned his back on Bourges after his coronation, and in 1487, a **fire** destroyed as much as half the city. Subsequent French monarchs were more interested in the fine hunting grounds of the Loire Valley and the metropolitan attractions of Paris, and apart from a brief flourish of rebuilding in the early Renaissance, Bourges has languished as an ordinary, albeit wealthy provincial city for most of the last half-millennium – though Napoleon III established France's central **armaments industry** here in 1861, a trade which thrives to this day.

Arrival, information and accommodation

The **gare SNCF** lies 1km to the north of the old city centre, at the end of avenue Jean Jaurès and its continuation, avenue Henri Laudier, while the **gare routière** stands just west of the city, beyond boulevard Juranville, on rue du Prado. The **tourist office**, at 21 rue Victor Hugo (April–Sept Mon–Sat 9am–7pm, Sun 10am–7pm; Oct–March Mon–Sat 9am–6pm, Sun 2–5pm; ⊤02.48.23.02.65, ⓦwww.bourgestourisme.com), is just round the corner from the south facade of the cathedral; there is also a regional tourist office a short

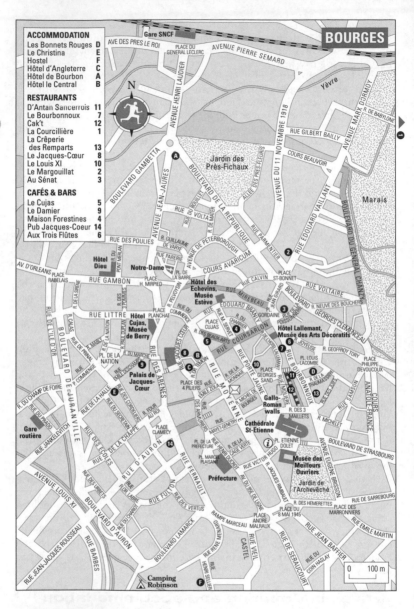

BOURGES

ACCOMMODATION
Les Bonnets Rouges	D
Le Christina	E
Hostel	F
Hôtel d'Angleterre	C
Hôtel de Bourbon	A
Hôtel le Central	B

RESTAURANTS
D'Antan Sancerrois	11
Le Bourbonnoux	7
Cak't	12
La Courcillière	1
La Crêperie des Remparts	13
Le Jacques-Cœur	8
Le Louis XI	10
Le Margouillat	2
Au Sénat	3

CAFÉS & BARS
Le Cujas	5
Le Damier	9
Maison Forestines	4
Pub Jacques-Coeur	14
Aux Trois Flûtes	6

distance south at 5 rue de Séraucourt (Mon–Fri 9am–noon & 1.30–5pm; ☎02.48.48.00.10, ⓦwww.berrylecher.com). To rent a **bike**, you'll have to make your way to the cycle shop Narcy, 39 ave Max Dormoy (☎02.48.70.15.84; closed Sun & Mon), ten minutes' walk north of the city centre. **Internet** access is available over on the other side of town at Tie-Break, 78 rue Jean-Baffier – a fifteen-minute walk south of the cathedral, or take bus #1 or #2 from place de la Nation to stop "Foch".

Most **accommodation** in Bourges fails to make the best of the old city. The only really attractive, central option is the *Bonnets Rouges* chambres d'hôtes, but there are a number of decent hotels.

Hotels and chambres d'hôtes

Les Bonnets Rouges 3 rue de la Thaumassière ☎02.48.65.79.92, ⓦbonnets-rouges .bourges.net. Five characterful chambres d'hôtes, furnished with nineteenth-century antiques and decorated in a handsome, old-fashioned style, are set in a beautiful seventeenth-century house built around a tiny, hidden courtyard. The attic rooms have splendid views of the cathedral. ❻

Le Christina 5 rue de la Halle ☎02.48.70.56.50, ⓦwww.le-christina.com. The modern, plain, six-storey exterior is uninspiring, but inside you'll find a friendly, professionally run hotel with seventy rooms, that's likely to have space if others are full. The rooms are cheerfully and freshly decorated, though the inexpensive ones (with showers rather than baths) are quite small, and those at the back are a little dark. The larger rooms (❹) also come with a/c. In all, good value and close to the old centre, although it could have more character. ❸

Hôtel d'Angleterre 1 place des Quatre-Piliers ☎02.48.24.68.51, ⓦwww.bestwestern.fr /hoteldangleterre. This is the old, traditional town-centre hotel, with an excellent location right next to the Palais de Jacques-Cœur. A recent refurbishment has made it conform to the three star standards of the Best Western chain, but it retains a degree of old-fashioned charm. The rooms are fully equipped, but the less expensive ones are very small for the price. ❻

Hôtel de Bourbon bd de la République ☎02.48.70.70.00, ⓦwww.hoteldebourbon.fr. This, the poshest hotel in Bourges, has been partially built in the ruins of a seventeenth-century abbey, with an extraordinary-looking but rather expensive restaurant created out of the chapel. The rooms don't make much of the ancient building, however: they're standard luxury hotel-chain fare, all plush carpets, minibars and over-dressed modern furniture. The location isn't great, either, on a busy road between the old centre and the train station. ❼

Hôtel le Central 6 rue du Docteur Témoin ☎02.48.24.10.25. This delightfully simple hotel, above a friendly bar just off the central rue Moyenne, offers inexpensive, old-fashioned rooms (including singles, at €25) with creaky, soft beds. Showers and toilets are on the landing. ❷

Hostel and campsite

Auberge de Jeunesse Jacques-Cœur 22 rue Henri-Sellier ☎02.48.24.58.09, ⓔbourges@fuaj. org. Pleasant, modern and recently refurbished hostel located a short way southwest of the centre, on a pleasant site overlooking the River Auron. Bus #1 to "Val d'Auron", stop "Condé"; or a 10min walk from the cathedral or gare routière. Daily 8am–noon & 5–10pm; closed mid-Dec to mid-Jan. HI membership required, but you can join on the spot.

Camping Robinson 26 bd de l'Industrie ☎02.48.20.16.85. Decently sized three-star site located south of the HI hostel. Bus #1, stop "Joffre", or it's a 10min walk from the gare routière. Closed mid-Nov to mid-March.

The City

The centre of Bourges sits on a low hill rising from the marshes of the River Yèvre. The city's main axis is **rue Moyenne**, which runs south–north between the cathedral, at the top end, and the Palais de Jacques-Cœur, at the bottom, with the narrow streets of the small medieval quarter falling away on either side.

The cathedral

Despite its huge size, the **cathédrale St-Etienne** (daily: April–June & Sept 8.30am–7.15pm; July & Aug 8.30am–7.45pm; Oct–March 9am–5.45pm; free) looks almost delicate from the outside, the smooth lines of its paper-thin nave walls supported by a regular, skeleton-like structure of flying buttresses. The cathedral owes its size to the importance of the archbishops of Bourges, who as primates of Aquitaine oversaw a vast territory stretching across central and southern France. Its design owes much to Paris's Notre-Dame, though it incorporates innovations such as the astonishing height of the inner aisles. Like Chartres cathedral, St-Etienne is one of the great achievements of the High Gothic style, which dominated the first quarter of the thirteenth century.

The facade of the west front, unlike the rest of the cathedral, is something of a hotch-potch of styles. The exquisitely narrow nave is dramatically pierced by the **Grand Housteau**, a rose window created under Jean de Berry. The taller tower on the left, the **Tour de Beurre**, had to be rebuilt after the original collapsed on New Year's Eve 1506. At the lowest level, five great **portals** yawn open, reflecting the five-aisle design inside. The sculpture of the tympanum above the central door could engross you for hours with its tableau of the Last Judgement; thirteenth-century imagination has been given full rein in the depiction of the devils, complete with snakes' tails, winged bottoms and faces appearing from below the waist, representing the soul in the service of sinful appetites. One of the damned souls in a cauldron appears to be wearing a bishop's mitre. It's fascinating to compare the style of the carving on the west portals with the older stonework of the inner **north** and **south portals**, which were incorporated from the earlier Romanesque cathedral, and date mostly from the 1160s.

The duc de Berry

At the age of 20, **Jean de Berry** (1340–1416), the third son of Jean II le Bon, was granted the duchies of Berry and Auvergne. He made **Bourges** his capital, creating a miniature court that could vie in magnificence with those of his three brothers – Charles, who would become Charles V, Philippe le Hardi of Burgundy and Louis d'Anjou. All three brothers were renowned as much for their artistic patronage as for their wealth and power. Jean de Berry must have been especially lavish in his spending, as when he died – as legend has it, of a broken heart after the defeat at Agincourt – there was too little ready money left to pay for his funeral.

During his lifetime, the duke built new châteaux all over France and amassed a vast collection of objets d'art, including twenty rubies, one of which is said to have weighed 240 carats. In Bourges, he commissioned his master architect, Guy de Dammartin, to remodel the cathedral's facade, build a fine new palace and construct a Sainte Chapelle in homage to the original in Paris. He built another new château at **Mehun-sur-Yèvre** (see p.232), where he kept a zoo of exotic animals that included ostriches, camels and a pet bear called Martin – the bear was the duke's personal emblem. Palace, château, zoo and Sainte Chapelle have all been largely destroyed, and all that remains intact – though dispersed – is Jean de Berry's fabulous **library**.

Chief among the hundreds of precious manuscripts it contained were the gorgeously illuminated "books of hours", or prayer-book calendars, and most exquisite among these was the celebrated **Très Riches Heures du Duc de Berry**. Painted by the Flemish Limbourg brothers in the International Gothic style, it is one of the finest illuminated manuscripts ever created – the swansong of the era before the invention of printing – and contains detailed, contemporary depictions of medieval châteaux. Jean de Berry himself is seen feasting in the illustration for the month of January, while the month of September is represented by **Saumur** (see p.244) at its chivalric best, its sheer walls and tall towers culminating in a glorious encrustation of machicolations and finials. The illustration for the first Sunday of Lent depicts the sweeping, delicately sculpted towers of Mehun-sur-Yèvre. Today, the manuscript is kept in the Musée Condé at Chantilly, outside Paris, and is far too precious and fragile to be viewed by anyone other than serious scholars. Art books full of reproductions are easy to find, however (see p.350), and you can view the complete work online at Ⓦwww.christusrex.org/www2/berry/.

The interior's best feature is its magnificent **stained glass**. There are geometric designs in the main body of the cathedral, but the most glorious windows, with astonishing deep colours, are on the lower level behind the **choir**. They were all created between 1215 and 1225, in the first phase of building. Working upwards from the bottom left pane, you can follow the stories of the Prodigal Son, the Rich Man and Lazarus, Joseph (you can spot him by his coat of many colours), the Virgin, the Good Samaritan, Christ's Crucifixion, the Last Judgement and the Apocalypse. On either side of the central absidal chapel, polychrome figures kneel in prayer; these are **Jean de Berry** and his wife, their fleur-de-lys cloaks advertising their royal connections. The bodies were carved by Jean de Cambrai, a Flemish sculptor working for Jean de Berry in the 1400s, but the heads are nineteenth-century recreations following a drawing by Holbein.

On the north side of the nave aisle, just before the ambulatory, the **chapelle Jacques-Cœur** has a wonderful mid-fifteenth century stained-glass window. At the western end of the nave, the painted decoration of the fascinating **astronomical clock** celebrates the wedding of Charles VII, who married Marie d'Anjou here on April 22, 1422. Above looms the giant, oak-built seventeenth-century **organ**, which thunders out for Mass (Sundays at 11am) and at occasional concerts.

The Tour de Beurre and crypt

On the far side of the nave aisle is the door to the **Tour de Beurre** (daily except Sun morning: April & Sept 9.45–11.45am & 2–5.30pm; May & June 9.30–11.30am & 2–6pm; July & Aug 9.30am–6.15pm; Oct–March 9.30–11.30am & 2–4.45pm; €5, or €9 with the crypt and Palais de Jacques-Cœur), which you can climb unsupervised for fantastic views over the old city, the marshes and the countryside beyond. The same ticket allows you to join a guided tour of the **crypt** (same hours and ticket; tours roughly every hour), where you can see the puggish but impressive alabaster statue of Jean de Berry. It is one of the few remaining parts of his original, elaborate tomb, alongside a few pieces at the Louvre and the Musée du Berry (see p.228). A small bear, symbol of strength, lies asleep at the duke's feet. Alongside are rare fragments of the cathedral's original rood screen, which survived the Protestant siege of 1562 but not the modernizers of the mid-eighteenth century. At the centre of the crypt you'll find a wonderful polychrome *Entombment*, dating from the 1530s; behind it lie the dark vestiges of the old Romanesque crypt, where the relics of St Etienne were kept, until the Revolution.

Around the cathedral

Next to the cathedral, on place Étienne-Dolet, the **Musée des Meilleurs Ouvriers de France** (Tues–Sat 10am–noon & 2–5/6pm, Sun 2–5/6pm; free) displays flamboyant demonstration pieces by contemporary French artisans in what was once the archbishop's palace. The theme changes each year; recent exhibitions have featured glass-blowing, woodwork, pastry-making, while in 2007 lamps will get their spell in the limelight. Behind lies the **Jardin de l'Archevêché**, a formal garden that's perfect for a stroll, offering good views of the fifteenth-century chapels whose weird octagonal spires rise up from the cathedral's apse.

Admirers of Jean de Berry can walk down rue Victor-Hugo and across rue Ducrot to the **Préfecture**, which incorporates fragments of the **ducal palace**, including a couple of windows on the facade. If you ask politely at reception (Mon 8.45am–4pm, Tues–Thurs 8.45–11.15am & 12.45–4pm, Fri 8.45am–2.30pm), you may be allowed inside to see the two main remnants: the **salle d'apparat**, or audience chamber, on the ground floor, and the council chamber up on the second floor, where there's a famous but over-zealously restored chimneypiece known as the **cheminée aux Ours** after the delightful, miniature carved bears – Jean de Berry's mascot – that cavort across it.

Palais de Jacques-Cœur

The **Palais de Jacques-Cœur** (daily: May & June 9.45–11am & 2–5.15pm; July & Aug 9.45–11.30am & 2–5.45pm; Sept–April 9.45–11am & 2–4.15pm; guided tours every 30min–1hr, depending on the season; €6.10) was the most luxurious and futuristic house built in the region during the fifteenth century, even incorporating a steamroom. It was the head office, stock exchange, dealing rooms and home of Jacques Cœur, a medieval magnate with a remarkable life story. Born in Bourges in around 1400, he started out working for his father, supplying luxury goods to the court, and quickly built up a lucrative portfolio of royal offices. After a successful expedition to the Near East in 1432, he imported spices, furs, exotic textiles, jewels, wine, salt and weapons from all over the Mediterranean. By the late 1440s, he was rich enough to finance Charles VII's military campaigns, but was denounced as a traitor at the height of his power, and arrested. After successfully escaping to the Vatican, he died leading a naval expedition against the Turks in 1456.

The building itself reflects the flamboyance and energy of its owner, starting with the fake windows on the facade of the entrance pavilion, from which two whimsical sculpted figures look down into the street. The inner **courtyard** is dominated by a staircase tower elegantly sculpted with bas-reliefs of everyday characters, including two thought to depict Jacques Cœur and his wife. The arcaded galleries on either side were designed to facilitate socializing and business deals.

Inside, there are hardly any furnishings, but much of the decoration of the house's stonework recalls the man who had it built. There are numerous hearts (for *cœur*) and scallop shells (for *coquilles St-Jacques*), along with inscriptions of Jacques Cœur's mottos: "dire, faire, taire de ma joie" ("speak, act, be silent of my joy") and "à vaillant riens impossible" ("nothing is impossible for the brave"). Above the door of a first-floor bedchamber there's a wonderful sculpture of a *galéasse* in full sail, with a reconstruction of the **tomb of Jean de Berry** nearby. But the finest piece of original decoration lies on the second floor, where angels fill the starry spaces between the ribs of the vaults of the **chapel**.

Musée du Berry

A flight of stone steps leads down beside the Palais de Jacques-Cœur to rue des Arènes and the sixteenth-century **Hôtel Cujas**, a classic Loire structure with pale, carved stone window frames and little *échauguette* half-towers. Inside, the **Musée du Berry** (Mon & Wed–Sat 10am–noon & 2–5/6pm, Sun 2–5/6pm; free) would be just another moderately interesting local history museum if it wasn't for its precious collection of **pleurants**. These cloaked, cowled, weeping figures are only a little over a foot high, but they're among the most precious pieces of French medieval sculpture. They were commissioned by Charles VII in around 1450, from the sculptors Etienne Bobillet and Paul de Mosselman, to complete the tomb of Jean de Berry for Bourges' Sainte-Chapelle, which was demolished in 1757. Almost half of the forty-odd figures have been lost. Among the survivors, apart from the ten examples here, one graces the New York Met, there's a pair in the Louvre, another in the château de la Verrerie (see p.237) and another in Paris's Musée Rodin – the sculptor paid 6000 francs for a single figure shortly before his death.

△ *Cul-de-lampe* at Hôtel Lallement, Bourges

Other sections of the museum display collections of Etruscan bronzes and Roman funerary monuments, bearing witness to Bourges' ancient roots, while a thorough exhibition on the theme of old-fashioned rural life occupies the first floor, testimony to the region's strong peasant traditions.

Hôtel Lallemant

At the foot of rue Bourbonnoux stands the impressive **Hôtel Lallemant**, an Italianate private mansion begun by a cloth merchant called Jean Lallemant in 1494, and finished by his two sons – both also called Jean – in 1520. After a stint in the nineteenth century as a primary school for poor girls, it now houses the **Musée des Arts Décoratifs** (Mon & Wed–Sat 10am–noon & 2–5/6pm, Sun 2–5/6pm; free), an exquisite museum of paintings, tapestries, furniture and objets d'art, including works by the Berrichon artist Jean Boucher (1575–1633) in the **Salon Bleu**. Each room is decorated and furnished in the style of a different era, covering the heyday of French elegance, from the sixteenth through to the nineteenth centuries. At the top of the stairs, the tiny **oratory** is a miniature masterpiece, its coffered ceiling carved with obscure alchemical symbols that include flaming spheres, an eagle on a skull and cavorting dolphins.

Even if you don't visit the museum, you can take the tunnel-like staircase through to the **inner courtyard**, a delightful stony enclosure replete with little towers, sculpted windows and stone medallions. Take a close look at the *cul-de-lampe* at the base of the small corner tower, which is carved with the grotesque, scaly figure of a merman. On the opposite, higher-level side of the courtyard, the loggia is decorated with seventeenth-century frescoes whose ruinous state says something about the difference between the Italian climate and that of Bourges.

The rest of the old city

The catastrophic fire of 1487 provoked a minor building boom, and the old city contains several handsome survivors from this era. Sloping down from the apse of the cathedral, **rue Bourbonnoux** is lined with ancient, timber-framed buildings, its cobblestones and restaurants making it one of the city's most attractive streets. A short distance down from the cathedral, a narrow passage cuts in to a picturesque back alley, the **Promenade des Remparts**, which gets its name from the high, crumbling remains of the **Gallo-Roman ramparts** that hem it in.

At the north end of rue Bourbonnoux, just beyond the Hôtel Lallemant (see above) lies **place Gordaine**, the old market square, ringed by half-timbered townhouses and informal café-restaurants. The pedestrianized shopping street of rue Coursalon runs west from here towards the leafy open space of **place Cujas**. You can peek at the much-restored arcades of a former convent on rue Mirebeau, immediately north, but the more impressive building is the adjacent **Hôtel des Échevins**, off rue Edouard Branly. The main body of the *hôtel* was built in 1489, its facade half-obscured by an extraordinary octagonal staircase tower whose four storeys are picked out in restrained bas-reliefs that mimic Flamboyant Gothic arches. An elegantly arcaded Classical wing runs at right angles. Inside, the **Musée Estève** (Mon & Wed–Sat 10am–noon & 2–5/6pm, Sun 2–5/6pm; free) is dedicated to highly coloured, mostly abstract paintings and tapestries created by locally-born artist Maurice Estève, who died in 2001.

A few steps west, along rue Mirebeau, lie half-timbered houses, a convent where Calvin studied and, at the end, the pleasant **place Notre-Dame**, with its sixteenth-century church. Just beyond that, on rue Gambon, stands the **Hôtel-Dieu**, a late medieval hospice building with a restored chapel.

The Marais

Just 200m from the cathedral, a great boggy swathe of allotments, canals, fishponds and meadows stretches away to the northeast. Known as **Les Marais** ("the marshes"), this is where Bourges's bourgeois residents get in touch with their peasant roots, raising vegetables for the dinner table, fishing and exercising their hunting dogs. A sign on a toolshed sums up the spirit of the place: "*liberté, santé, tranquillité*" ("liberty, health, tranquillity"). The Marais may be half-tamed by sluice gates and little dykes but it still floods regularly, attracting plentiful wildlife of a modest kind – ducks, moorhens, dragonflies and various pond-dwelling creatures. A good circuit of about an hour's duration leads north from the gate just east of place Philippe Devoucoux, winding through the heart of the Marais and exiting via rue de Babylone, from where it's a twenty-minute walk back to the centre. It's hard to get very lost, as the towers of the cathedral offer a constant reference point.

Eating and drinking

Bourges's main centre for **eating** is along rue Bourbonnoux, which runs between place Gordaine and the cathedral. Place Gordaine itself is attractively medieval but mostly good for pizzas. For tea and pâtisseries, there's a small tearoom by the counter of the excellent pâtisserie *Aux Trois Flûtes*, on the corner of rues Joyeuse and Bourbonnoux (closed Mon). For chocolates and the local sweet speciality of *fourrées au praliné* try the imposing *Maison Forestines*, on place Cujas (closed Mon morning & Sun).

On warm nights, lively place Cujas is also the best spot for **drinking** – the bar *Le Cujas* has plenty of outside seating. After that, you're down to the inevitable "pubs": the *Pub Jacques-Coeur*, on rue d'Auron, is popular with a young crowd. There's a tiny dance-floor at the cocktail bar *Le Damier*, 5 rue Emile Deschamps, which gets going at about midnight at weekends.

Restaurants

D'Antan Sancerrois 50 rue Bourbonnoux ☎02.48.65.96.26. Good and occasionally imaginative local cuisine with interesting specials on the blackboard. The dining room is rather odd – high-ceilinged and in a faintly 1980s style – but that needn't put you off. À la carte mains from €17–19. Closed Mon lunch & Sun.

Le Bourbonnoux 44 rue Bourbonnoux ☎02.48.24.14.76. This friendly basement restaurant has a good selection of inexpensive menus (€13–30), with dishes ranging from well-cooked classics to more ambitious regional specialities. Closed Sat lunch & Fri, also closed Sun evening Sept–June.

Cak't promenade des Remparts, rue Bourbonnoux ☎02.48.24.94.60. A refined tearoom in a handsome vaulted chamber with lace tablecloths and classical music. Tea and cakes are on offer every afternoon (3–7pm), while from Tuesday to Saturday it opens at 11am, offering delicious, home-made quiches and tarts on an excellent-value, mainly vegetarian menu (€10).

La Courcillière rue de Babylone ☎02.48.24.41.91. Given its situation deep among the allotments and tiny canals of the *marais* – a good 1.5km from the old centre – this feels almost like a country restaurant, with its outdoor terrace shaded by pollarded willows. The food is meaty and unpretentious, with lots of fish dishes, steaks and a rôtisserie. Menus at €17, €23 & €28. Closed Tues evening, Sun evening & Wed.

La Crêperie des Remparts 59 rue Bourbonnoux ☎02.48.24.55.44. Cosy, rustic-looking crêperie with a better-than-usual range of crêpes, galettes and salads – and a magnificent, two-person fishy fondue Bretagne (€46; order in advance). It's very family-friendly too, with a children's menu which shouldn't break the piggy-bank (€5) and a good stash of picture books. Closed Sun & Mon.

Le Jacques-Cœur 3 place Jacques-Cœur ☎02.48.26.53.01. This restaurant has a solid local reputation as one of Bourges' best for top-class regional specialities like mackerel in white wine or *paté Bérichon* – made from potatoes. It's in a cracking location too – book early for the tables looking straight out onto the palace. Menus €20–60. Closed Sun evening & Mon.

Le Louis XI 11 rue Porte Jaune ☎02.48.70.92.14. Serves impeccable steaks and char-grilled meats in a small, informal dining room crammed with tables and chairs. *Plat du jour* at €10, menus €17–26. Closed Sun.

Le Margouillat 53 rue Edouard Vaillant ☎02.48.24.08.13. For a complete change from provincial French cooking, this friendly, fun bistro offers delicious food from Réunion such as samosas and giant prawns flavoured with lots of ginger, spices and the odd dash of rum, with delicious tropical desserts to follow. Menus €17–23. Closed Mon lunch, Sat lunch & Sun.

Au Sénat 8 rue de la Poissonnerie ☎02.48.24.02.56. A Bourges institution, this smart restaurant just off place Gordaine has been open since 1866. In winter, the old dining room is still used, with an open fire in the hearth, while in summer you can sit out in the pedestrianized street. The traditional menu has a particularly good range of fish dishes. Menus €17–33. Closed Wed & Thurs.

Festivals and Les Nuits Lumière

Bourges's **music festival** programme is impressive. **Les Printemps de Bourges** (ⓦ www.printemps-bourges.com) features hundreds of contemporary music acts, from new rock groups to big-name rappers, and lasts for a week during the French Easter holidays. Concerts take place in pubs and bars all over the city. The **Festival Synthèse**, an electronic and acoustic music bash, takes place during the first week of June, while **Un Été à Bourges** (late June to late Sept) is a long line-up of mainly free outdoor performances of anything from local organ music to Chinese jazz, running throughout the summer.

In the summer months, you can follow a circuit through the streets of the old city between imaginatively lit-up landmark buildings, called **Les Nuits Lumière de Bourges**. Historically themed moving slide shows are projected onto the walls of various Renaissance and medieval mansions, while atmospheric lute and choral music plays. Even if it doesn't sound like your kind of thing, the circuit is remarkably well done, and the strange blue streetlights that indicate the route are decidedly eerie. The show is free and begins at sundown every day in July and August, and on Thursdays, Fridays and Saturdays in May, June and September.

West of Bourges

Two waterways lead west of Bourges, the placid river **Yèvre** and the **Canal de Berry**. Both leave the Berry region just downstream of the largely featureless industrial town of Vierzon, which straddles the Cher some 30km west of Bourges. Vierzon really doesn't repay a visit – indeed there's nothing much to detain you until Mennetou-sur-Cher, another 15km west (see p.164) – but close to Bourges there's a trio of rather recherché attractions: the ruined château of the duc de Berry at **Mehun-sur-Yèvre**, the Romanesque wall-paintings at **Brinay** and the isolated vineyards of **Reuilly** and **Quincy**.

Mehun-sur-Yèvre

The château at **MEHUN-SUR-YÈVRE**, a quiet market town 17km west of Bourges, was once to Bourges what Versailles is to Paris – the favourite country seat of the court. It was the extravagant home of the duc de Berry, and was frequently used by Charles VII, who died here of starvation in 1461 – some say he was unable to feed himself because of lockjaw, others that it was through a perfectly justifiable fear of being poisoned by the agents of his rebellious son, Louis XI.

A lightning strike in 1555 largely ruined the **château**, but it's still an evocative, if melancholy, stopping place on the trail of the duc de Berry. Two towers stand among the ruinous foundations, one relatively intact – though the famous picture in the *Très Riches Heures du Duc de Berry* (see box on p.226) shows that it was once half as tall again, capped by an elaborate superstructure. Fragments of original stonework, including some apostles' heads that may be the work of Jean de Berry's Flemish sculptor Jean de Cambrai and a few bits of the six-metre-tall tower-top statue, can be seen in the small **museum** inside (March, April & Oct Sat & Sun 2–6pm; May, June & Sept Tues–Sun 2–6pm; July & Aug 10am–noon & 2–6pm; €4.60 combined ticket with Pôle de la Porcelaine – see below). You can climb to the top of the **tower**, which stands 40m above the town and the meadows to the south where the duke had his world-beating library and zoo of exotic beasts.

Below the château, the flashily presented **Pôle de la Porcelaine** (same hours and ticket as château) displays excellent and exhaustive collections of local fine china, and can book you on a guided tour of the Pillivuyt porcelain factory, which lies on the far side of the Canal de Berry. Between museum and factory lie the **Jardins du Duc de Berry**, a kind of municipal park made up of interconnected islands in the muddy river Yèvre. The town itself is fairly pretty but quickly exhausted, its main features being a pair of gate-towers, the **Porte de l'Horloge**, and the **collégiale Notre-Dame**, a barn-like church with an unusual horseshoe-shaped choir, some dramatic modern stained glass and a set of nineteenth-century frescoes of Joan of Arc, who rested at Mehun with Charles VII in the extraordinary year of 1429 (see box on p.191).

Brinay

Halfway between Mehun-sur-Yèvre and Vierzon, on the south bank of the Cher, the modest Romanesque church at tiny **BRINAY** conceals one of the most complete sequences of twelfth-century **wall-paintings** found anywhere in France. Scenes from the life of Christ run right round the walls of the sanctuary, though, interestingly, there's no Crucifixion scene, as this topic didn't become popular until the thirteenth century. Around the inside of the almost-horseshoe arch that divides the nave from the sanctuary, you can just make out the labours of the months – look out for February, warming his hands at a fire, and the grape-crushers of September.

If you want to overnight in the area, look no further than the two prettily furnished **chambres d'hôtes** at the *Château de Brinay* (☏02.48.51.38.31, ⓦwww.chateaudebrinay.fr.st; ④), a substantial old pile set in quiet grounds between the church and the main road, with a swimming pool.

Reuilly and Quincy

Twenty-five kilometres west of Bourges, the village of **REUILLY** would be as sleepy as any in the Bas Berry – it just falls within the *département* of the Indre, on the edge of the flat plains of the Champagne Berrichonne – if it wasn't for a recent fashion for the minuscule local wine *appellation*. Buoyed by this unexpected fame, the **tourist office** (Tues–Sun 10am–noon & 2–6pm; ☏02.54.49.24.94, ⓦwww.ot-reuilly.fr) now runs a tiny wine museum and local art gallery. Staff can point you in the direction of local wine-producers, as well as various private châteaux in the vicinity, some of which open their doors to the hoi polloi in July and August. The most interesting local sight is the village **church**, which has a characteristic *passage Berrichon*

– a passageway leading behind the pillars of the nave to the transepts – and a claustrophobic ancient crypt that dates back to the Carolingian era. Fifteen kilometres northeast of Reuilly, the wines of **QUINCY** are a serious rival. There's nothing much to see in the village, but it's easy to hunt down producers' *caves* if you follow the signs. Most are open Monday to Friday, some on Saturday too.

On the road leading out of Reuilly towards the little **gare SNCF** – with good connections to Orléans – the friendly *Hôtel des Trois Cepages* (☎02.54.49.26.90; ③) has plain, bright, modern **rooms** and a homely restaurant.

The Pays Fort and Sancerrois

The main D940 trunk road flies arrow-straight due north of Bourges towards the bridge over the Loire at Gien (see p.214), the ancient gateway to Paris. As it goes, it effectively divides the gently undulating pastures of the **Pays Fort**, to the east, from the low-lying forests and reedy *étangs* of the **Sologne Berrichonne**, to the west. Both are deeply rural areas, relatively unused to outsiders and correspondingly welcoming. Sights are low key or even eccentric – one route recommended by local tourist offices takes you round granaries with pyramid-shaped roofs – but there's a satisfying sense of having stepped well off the beaten track.

The most interesting attractions are the potteries of **La Borne**, near **Henrichemont**, and the châteaux of **Maupas**, **La Chapelle d'Anguillon** and **La Verrerie**, while the old town of **Aubigny-sur-Nère** is handsome, if uneventful. To the southeast, the slopes become steeper, and cows and sheep are replaced by the more valuable vines of the **Sancerrois** – the region around the picturesque hilltop town of **Sancerre**.

Henrichemont and around

You don't have to travel far from Bourges towards Sancerre before the land begins to undulate, with trees foresting the ridgetops and vines stetching down the slopes. **Menetou-Salon**, 20km north of Bourges, is the hub of its own well-regarded *Appellation d'Origine Contrôlée* wine region, while down in the valley, 9km north, squats **HENRICHEMONT**, the area's principal town. The most interesting feature is the perfectly symmetrical layout conceived by Henri IV's loyal administrator, the duc de Sully (see p.211), as the centrepiece for the once-independent principality of Boisbelle, a Monaco-like anomaly which he bought in 1605. Sadly, the model Renaissance town he envisaged never came to fruition, and only a couple of fairly indifferent mansion houses were ever built round the broad market square. The town is otherwise resolutely ordinary – and no longer independent – but if you want to explore the surrounding area ask at the **tourist office** on place de l'Hôtel de Ville (Tues–Sun 10am–12.30pm & 2–5.30pm; ☎02.48.26.74.13, ⓦwww .henrichemont.info).

The most rewarding local excursion is to the potters' village of **LA BORNE**, strung out along a wooded ridge 4km southeast of Henrichemont. La Borne has been known for its rough stoneware since the seventeenth century, but in the post war period it has become a centre for artistic and experimental pottery, attracting scores of artisans from all over France and beyond, almost all of whom keep open house for visitors and potential customers – more than one in ten residents are artisans of one sort or another so just follow the signs and knock on doors. There are three more formal exhibition spaces: the excellent **Musée Vassil Ivanoff** (May–Sept Mon & Fri–Sun 2–7pm; €2.30) showcases the sensual creations of the Bulgarian master potter who invigorated La Borne's contemporary pottery scene when he arrived here in 1946; the **Musée de la Poterie** archives La Borne's traditional pottery (Easter to mid-Nov Sat & Sun 3–7pm; also open Mon–Fri 3–7pm during school holidays; €3; Ⓦwww .la-borne.com/museepot); and the **Centre de Création Céramique** (mid-March to mid-Jan daily except Tues 2–7pm; also open Tues during school holidays; free; Ⓦwww.ceramiclaborne.org), which exhibits and sells the works of some of the fifty-odd potters who live and work in and around the village. The range of wholesome and exotic foods at *L'Epicerie*, the central village grocery and deli, says a lot about the village's "alternative" traditions; you can get drinks and snacks at the tearoom here, as well as a reasonably priced "*menu surprise*" – it's usually excellent.

From La Borne, the D46 winds down for 8km through beautiful woodland to **MOROGUES**, the main wine-growers' village in the Menetou-Salon *appellation* (see Contexts, p.359). There are plenty of opportunities to taste and buy wine, while 1km beyond the village is the **château de Maupas** (Easter–Sept Mon–Sat 2–7pm, Sun 10am–noon & 2–7pm; €6.50; Ⓦwww.chateaudemaupas .fr), an attractive mishmash of local brickwork from La Borne and older stone turrets. In the nineteenth century the château was heavily restored, inside and out, by an ancestor of the current marquis who was close to the so-called comte de Chambord (see box on p.159). The guided tour takes in lots of fussily decorated rooms filled with fine furnishings and valuable objets d'art, but the highlight of the visit is the extraordinary two-storey display of almost 900 eighteenth- and nineteenth-century china plates which lines the grand staircase.

Lovers of the magical early twentieth-century novel, *Le Grand Meaulnes* (see p.346), may want to make the pilgrimage to **LA CHAPELLE-D'ANGILLON**, 11km north of Henrichemont on the main road to Gien, as it was here that author Alain-Fournier was born – as plain Henri Fournier – in 1886. Sadly, there's nothing much to see, although there is an Alain-Fournier museum in the **château** (July & Aug Mon–Sat 9.30am–7pm, Sun 2–6pm; Sept–June Mon–Sat 9.30am–noon & 2–6pm; Sun 2–6pm; €8; Ⓦwww.chateau-angillon.com). It's a modest affair, and would hardly seem worth the rather steep entrance fee, but Comte Jean d'Ogny takes many tours himself, and is a fascinating and ebullient guide. You also get to see a beautiful Renaissance gallery once used for the *jeu de paume* – an early kind of royal tennis – and the eccentric but rather lovely collection of regalia deposited here in 1983 by Léka I, the current claimant to the throne of Albania.

Aubigny-sur-Nère

AUBIGNY-SUR-NERE, 14km north of La Chapelle-d'Angillon, makes much of its connections with the **Stuarts**, hosting a grand Franco-Scottish festival in mid-July. These aren't the royal Stuarts, however, but the descendants of one John Stuart, who helped Charles VII reclaim his throne in the fifteenth century and was granted the territory as reward. Curiously, a distant relative, Louise de Keroualle, was one of the many mistresses of Charles II, last Stuart king of England, and was granted the château at Aubigny by Louis XIV in return for her services as a spy.

The town is fairly picturesque, dotted with half-timbered and stone houses, especially along **rue du Prieuré**, the broad and bustling main street. At the top end of the street stands the **église St-Martin** (Easter–Nov Mon–Fri 2.30–6.30pm, Sat & Sun 10.30am–12.30pm & 2.30–6pm), a rather fine early sixteenth-century Gothic church with a beautiful stained-glass window of the life of St Martin; sadly, the **château** at the bottom end has barely survived transformation into the local Mairie. Inside the château, you can visit two small **museums** (April–June & mid-Sept to Oct Sat & Sun 2.30–6pm; July to mid-Sept daily 3–7pm; Nov–March Sun 2.30–6pm; €3), dedicated to the Franco-Scottish "Auld Alliance" and to the works of a minor local writer, Marguerite Audoux, but both are rather dull.

Practicalities

The **tourist office** at Aubigny-sur-Nère is in a half-timbered old house next to the church, at 1 rue de l'Eglise (May–Sept Mon 10am–1pm & 2–6.30pm, Tues–Fri 9.30am–1pm & 2–6.30pm, Sat 9am–12.30pm & 2.30–7pm, Sun 10am–12.30pm & 2.30–5.30pm; Oct–April closes 1hr earlier; ☎02.48.58.40.20). The town has a pair of **hotels**, both on the fringe of the old centre. The *Auberge de la Fontaine*, 2 ave du Général-Leclerc, on the road to Bourges (☎02.48.58.02.59, ℉02.48.58.36.80; ❸), is friendly and comfortable, with large, well-appointed rooms, some featuring exposed brick and stonework. *La Chaumière*, 2 rue Paul Lasnier (☎02.48.58.04.01, ⓦwww.hotel-restaurant-la-chaumiere.com; ❹), has modern-styled rooms set in an old, smartly renovated house beside the busy road to Sancerre. Both hotels have good, moderately priced **restaurants**, but you might want to try the relatively funky *Bien Aller* at 3 rue des Dames (☎02.48.58.03.92; closed Tues & Wed evening), a good-value bistro with some interesting variations on the usual trad fare marked up on its specials board – think confit of Sologne pigeon, or foie gras tart in a cream-of-lentils sauce; menus start at €14.

Around Aubigny-sur-Nère

The rather plain village of **ARGENT-SUR-SAULDRE**, 9km north of Aubigny, has lost its château, but the grand old outbuildings have been turned into the **Musée des Métiers et Traditions de France** (April–Oct Mon–Fri 2–6.30pm, Sat & Sun 10am–noon & 2–6.30pm; Nov–March Thurs & Fri 2.30–6pm, Sat & Sun 10.30am–noon & 2.30–6pm; €4.30). The museum uses old looms, bizarre machines for making brooms and clogs and a display about the production of weathercocks to create a nostalgic meander through local crafts and trades. A comfortable **hotel** directly opposite the château, the *Relais de la Poste* (☎02.48.81.53.90, ℉02.48.73.30.62; ❸), makes for a good place to stop over, and has a decent **restaurant** (closed Sun). If you want to dip a toe into the Sologne, try *La Solognote*, Grande Rue, Brinon-sur-Sauldre (☎02.48.58.50.29, ℉02.48.58.56.00; ❹; closes occasionally for holidays, so call in advance), a quiet country hotel in a deeply rustic village 16km west of Argent-sur-Sauldre. The rooms aren't particularly special but the restaurant (menus €22–68) is excellent, featuring lots of Sologne produce – as one might expect. The hotel rents bikes and can recommend walks and book pony trekking excursions in the surrounding countryside.

Eleven kilometres east of Aubigny, along the D21, is the **Musée de la Sorcellerie** (April, May & Oct daily 10am–6pm; June–Sept daily 10am–7pm; €5.80; Ⓦwww.musee-sorcellerie.fr), a witchcraft museum just outside **CONCRESSAULT**. It's a bit over the top, with animated reconstructions of witchcraft trials, but kids will have fun, and some of the prints and paintings of legendary witches are interesting.

Louise de Kerouaille, the owner of the château d'Aubigny, was also proprietor of the much lovelier **château de la Verrerie**, on the river Nère 11km upstream of Aubigny (Easter–June, Sept & Oct Sun 11am–6pm; July & Aug daily 11am–6pm; €10), though her descendants sold it in 1841 to the de Vogüe family, who now run it as a tourist attraction and luxury **chambres d'hôtes**. The setting is beautiful, with two wings half enclosing a courtyard and a slope of sward that descends to the banks of the lake. The southern wing has a fine Renaissance arcade, but the chief draw is the elaborately frescoed chapel. The stories behind both are told on the interesting – but obligatory and rather pricey – guided tour, but you can just walk in the park for free. The gorgeously furnished 🛏 **chambres d'hôtes** (☏02.48.81.51.60, 🖷02.48.58.21.25; ❾) are in the grand style, with exquisitely old-fashioned but luxurious bathrooms. Prices start at around €155, climbing to over €360 for the top suite, with its study in the ancient tower. The restaurant in the gatehouse is attractively chintzy, and offers reliable evening meals for around €35, with wine.

Sancerre and St-Satur

At the easternmost edge of the low-lying Loire region – and its highest point at a dizzy 342m – is **SANCERRE**, a name better known in wine circles than on tourist circuits. Apart from eating and drinking – the preoccupation of most visitors – there are few particular sights or attractions in the town itself, but the countryside around is certainly picturesque: seen from the south, the vision of Sancerre huddling at the top of its steep, round hill, with vineyards furrowing the hillsides all around, could almost be Tuscany.

The first port of call for wine enthusiasts should be the **Maison de Sancerre**, 3 rue du Méridien (daily: June–Sept 10am–7pm; April, May, Oct & Nov 10am–6pm; €5; Ⓦwww.maison-des-sancerre.com), which has an elaborate permanent exhibition on winemaking in Sancerre, and a garden of aromatic plants representing the sixty key flavours found in Sancerre wines. The building itself is a fine fourteenth-century townhouse whose tower-top offers a great view over the rolling, vine-clad hills around. It's an enticing prospect, and endless *caves* offer tastings of the local **wine** (see box on p.238). The dry whites, made from the Sauvignon Blanc grape, are by far the best known, but don't ignore the unusual and extremely appealing reds, which are light in colour but rich in earthy, spicy flavours. The local **crottin de Chavignol**, an *appellation contrôlée* goat's cheese named after a neighbouring village, is well suited to the wines.

The counts of Sancerre long presided over the town. The most distinguished was Jean de Bueil, known as the "Scourge of the English" for his military successes under Charles VII in the early fifteenth century – exploits he later fictionalized in his classic account of the war, *Le Jouvencel*. During the Wars of Religion, the increasingly powerful merchants and townspeople sided with the Protestant cause,

Sancerre wine tours

Unusually, Sancerre wines aren't allowed to carry the name of an individual vineyard, as most are owned by a number of different producers, each in possession of a small, precious "parcel" of land. Instead, most wines are sold under the producer's name or, in exceptional cases, are given an individual *cuvée* name that just may give away the identity of the vineyard it came from, but only to those in the know. If you want to seek out good local vineyards, you're best off with a guide, and the friendly, informative agency **Aronde Sancerroise**, at 4 rue de la Tour, just off the central Nouvelle Place (Easter–May Mon–Fri 10.30am–12.30pm & 2.30–6.30pm, June–Sept daily 10.30am–12.30pm & 2.30–6.30pm; Oct–Dec & Feb–Easter Mon–Wed & Fri 10.30am–12.30pm & 2.30–6.30pm; closed during wine tours; ☏02.48.78.05.72), offers excellent half-day minibus **tours** (up to eight people; €218). If you just want to buy, there are also free, informative tastings on the spot – but no swallowing is allowed.

If you want to do it yourself, the Maison de Sancerre or tourist office can supply a list of over three hundred **vignerons** in the immediate area – or check out ⓦwww .vins-centre-loire.com. Wine outlets in Sancerre itself belong to the most famous names – Mellot, Vacheron – and have mark-ups to match, but most *vignerons* outside town are small-scale, traditional winemakers and welcome visitors every day – although some are closed on Sundays. There are particularly rich pickings in the cluster of villages between Sancerre and Crézancy-en-Sancerre, 11km southwest; try the **Dauny** *cave*, in Champtin (daily 8am–8pm; ☏02.48.79.05.75) – this family has been making excellent organic wines for three generations, including the rarer, pale red Sancerre. For a lesser-known buy, it's well worth exploring the neighbouring areas of Menetou-Salon, around 30km to the southwest, and Pouilly-Fumé, some 10km upriver.

and it took a six-month siege in 1573 to bring them to heel. Later defections to Protestantism led to the old château being almost completely destroyed, and today only the **Tour des Fiefs** remains, ruinous at the apex of the hill. You can climb it for spectacular views most afternoons; if it's shut, the view from the **rampart walks** which ring the old town are almost as satisfying. The simple **church of Notre-Dame**, on place du Beffroi, is notable for its mighty **belfry tower**, which was built by the city's merchants in the late fifteenth century as an expression of their civic pride; sadly, it lacks its original spire.

St-Satur

The two chief sights of **ST-SATUR**, the village at the foot of the hill below Sancerre, are the Gothic **abbey church**, which once belonged to the monks who first planted vines at Sancerre, and the 430-metre-long curving **viaduct**, which has been open to walkers since the railway shut down in 1968. There are a couple of good hotels in town (see opposite), but the main reason to visit is to take a guided **kayak trip** with Loire Nature Découverte (April–Oct 7.30am–9pm; ☏02.48.78.00.34, ⓦwww.loirenaturedecouverte.com), quai de Loire, down beside the campsite. The owner, Yvan Thibaudat, is something of a naturalist, and his guided half- or full-day expeditions (€15/21 per person) are fascinating. You are usually driven upstream and then float back down through the **Réserve Naturelle du Val de Loire**, a nature reserve created along a twenty-kilometre corridor of little islands and sandbanks that is particularly rich and diverse in wildlife. Yvan's partner, Karine Boucher, leads guided **pony treks** in the Pays Fort – a ninety-minute excursion costs just €17, and longer trips are possible. To get to the shop, turn left just before the Pont de St-Thibault, which bridges the Loire, following signs to the campsite. Just beyond the campsite there's a huge, heated open-air **swimming pool**, Les Godilles (July & Aug 11am–7pm).

Practicalities

Sancerre's **tourist office** is in the modern building at the centre of the Nouvelle Place (March, Oct & Nov Mon–Fri 2.30–5pm, Sat & Sun 10am–12.30pm & 2.30–5pm; April–Sept daily 10am–12.30pm & 2–5.30pm; ☏02.48.54.08.21, ⓦwww.sancerre.fr). To visit the vineyards you'll need your own **transport**, though SNCF runs a bus service four times daily from Sancerre through St-Satur and across the river to Cosne-sur-Loire, in time to meet the train to Gien.

The choice of **hotels** in Sancerre itself is rather disappointing. *Le Saint-Martin*, 10 rue St-Martin (☏02.48.54.21.11, ⓔhotel.saint-martin@orange.fr; ❸), is central and pleasant enough, but needs a refit inside. *Le Panoramic*, Rempart des Augustins (☏02.48.54.22.44, ⓦwww.panoramicotel.com; ❹), is smart and has a fine view and a wonderful outdoor swimming pool, but it's a disagreeably modern building, and you have to pay extra for the rooms with a view (❺). Luckily, there are two charming **chambres d'hôtes**. ⚑ *Le Logis du Grillon*, 3 rue du Chantre (☏02.48.78.09.45, ⓦwww.sancerre.biz; ❹), has four pretty, spotless little rooms, with pleasant antique furnishings; there's also a large, well-equipped kitchen and a comfortingly rustic living room, complete with exposed roof beams. The friendly *La Belle Epoque* on rue St-André (☏02.48.78.00.04; ❸) offers a single large, beamed room stuffed with antiques. If you want a really good hotel you'll have to descend to St-Thibault, the riverside quarter of St-Satur, which sits at the bottom of the hill below Sancerre. The large rooms at the ⚑ *Hôtel de la Loire*, 2 quai de la Loire (☏02.48.78.22.22, ⓦwww.hotel-de-la-loire.com; ❹–❺), are scrupulously maintained and beautifully furnished in an array of antique styles, while the five simple, clean bedrooms above the welcoming *Auberge de St-Thibault*, 37 rue J. Combes (☏02.48.78.04.10; ❶), a block away from the river, are exceptional value. The large, well-equipped three-star **campsite** *René Foltzer* (☏02.48.54.04.67; closed Oct–April) is 200m north of the bridge, on the St-Satur side of the river.

Book ahead if you want to dine at either of Sancerre's two best traditional **restaurants**. ⚑ *La Pomme d'Or*, 1 rue de la Panneterie (☏02.48.54.13.30; closed Tues evening & Wed) is the local favourite, serving local freshwater fish dishes in delicate sauces and good Charolais steaks; menus are excellent value at €18 and €26. The elegant ⚑ *La Tour*, 31 Nouvelle Place (☏02.48.54.00.81; menus €19–51), is more formal, with a heavy-beamed and carpeted dining room. Both have excellent wine lists. The food at the *Auberge Joseph Mellot*, Nouvelle Place (☏02.48.54.20.53; closed Sun evening, Tues evening & Wed), is designed to complement its own top-notch wines; the atmosphere is quintessentially French *café-bistrot*, and you'll pay from €12 for a simple *plat du jour*, pudding and glass of wine.

La Collina, 10 place du Connétable (☏02.48.54.11.16; closed Mon, Sept & Dec), is a surprisingly good Italian trattoria, though the pizzas are starter-sized. If you don't mind driving, consider making the three-kilometre trip out to Chavignol, where ⚑ *La Côte des Monts Damnés* (☏02.48.54.01.72; closed Sun evening, Tues evening & Wed) is aiming at a Michelin star, but remains friendly and excellent value, with menus in the €20–40 range and a superb wine list. The menus change constantly, but you might order tagliatelle with local *chèvre* and nutmeg butter followed by sea bream on a bed of spinach with an emulsion of sea-urchin's roe.

4

THE HAUT BERRY | The Pays Fort and Sancerrois

Travel details

Trains

Bourges to: Mehun-sur-Yèvre (14 daily; 10min); Orléans (9 daily; 1hr–1hr 40min); Tours (12 daily; 1hr 40min).

Buses

Sancerre to: Bourges (1–3 daily; 1hr 15min); Cosne-sur-Loire (for Gien; 3–4 daily; 15min).

5

The Saumurois

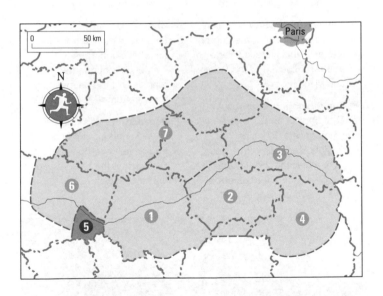

Highlights

Carrousel de Saumur Saumur's cavalry traditions take over the town during this festival of old-fashioned military muscle, held in late July. See p.245

Saumur Brut Matured inside vast cave-cellars, the sparkling wines of Saumur are a serious rival to Champagne's. See p.250

Candes-St-Martin An ancient and beautiful collegiate church stands in this historic village at the confluence of the Loire and Vienne. See p.254

The Plantagenet tombs The graceful tombs of the Plantagenets, kings of England and dukes of Anjou, lie in melancholy splendour in the giant Romanesque abbey of Fontevraud. See p.257

Zoo de Doué The zoo at Doué-la-Fontaine has a bizarre but humane setting in an old quarry filled with semi-tropical plants. See p.261

Montreuil-Bellay Its picture-book castle rising above the poplar-lined River Thouet, Montreuil-Bellay is one of the prettiest small towns in the Loire Valley. See p.262

Château de Brézé This château is most remarkable for what's underneath it – a network of quarried-out tunnels and the deepest dry moat in Europe. See pÈ.264

Bed-and-breakfast in a cave Spend a night in a troglodyte cave-house at *Les Bateliers*, in the pretty village of Cunault. See p.266

△ Riverbank and château, Saumur

The Saumurois

T he stretch of the Loire valley between Chinon and Angers is known as the **Saumurois** after its chief town, Saumur. The gentle slopes of the south bank are clothed in patches of woodland and sunny vineyards. Across the water, on the north bank, rich meadows watered by the River Authion are given over to grazing and market gardens. The main east–west route, the D952, lies on the north side, sweeping along the raised embankment of the *grande levée*, a flood wall first raised by Henry II Plantagenet in the twelfth century. It's a grand road, but all the sights covered in this chapter lie on the prettier, quieter south bank. Here you'll find one of the sweetest of all Loire regions; less grand than Touraine, maybe, but equally fascinating.

Historically and administratively, the Saumurois is no more than an enclave of greater Anjou – even the chief local town, **Saumur**, is a deeply provincial place compared to the regional capital, Angers, though its haughty château, proud cavalry traditions and classy sparkling wines give it status well beyond its size.

To the **east of Saumur**, on the border with Touraine, lie the twin villages of **Montsoreau** and **Candes-St-Martin**. The pair present very different faces to the world, the former with its noble château, the latter with its ancient church dedicated to the local patron, St Martin. A few kilometres south is the great Romanesque abbey of **Fontevraud**, where the medieval tombs of the Plantagenet royal family are one of the highlights of the whole Loire region. Heading **west of Saumur** towards Angers, still on the south bank, you can visit the sleepy villages of **Trèves** and **Cunault**, the latter with another remarkable Romanesque church.

But the most fascinating local sights are **troglodyte dwellings** – homes gouged out of the soft tufa rock. There are more in this region than anywhere else in France, and it's reckoned that in the twelfth century half the local population lived underground. Today, some of the rock dwellings have surprising uses – nearly two-thirds of France's mushroom cultivation originates in Saumurois caves, while others have been turned into "*troglo*" bars and restaurants. The region around **Doué-la-Fontaine** is particularly rich in bizarre troglodyte attractions, ranging from cathedral-like quarries and underground farmhouses to a cavern sculpted with satirical human figures in the sixteenth century. Close by, the picturesque château-town of **Montreuil-Bellay** stands astride the River Thouet at the southern bounds of the region. From here you can make forays to see the Girdle of the Virgin at **Le Puy-Notre-Dame**, or the rock-cut passages underneath the **château de Brézé**.

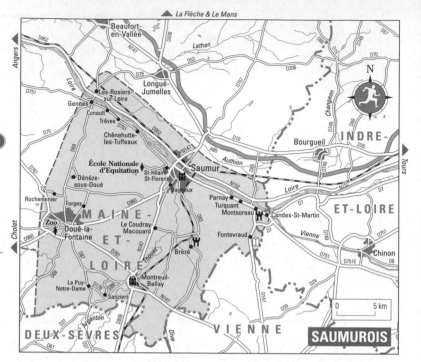

Saumur

Of all the comfortably bourgeois towns along the Loire, **SAUMUR** is the most genteel, with its graceful château, elegant sparkling wines and 250-year association with the military. The town is still the home of the aristocratic French Cavalry Academy and its successor, the Armoured Corps Academy, and you can sometimes see uniformed officers strolling about, though the tanks are mostly kept out at the military camp near Fontevraud. Once you've seen the château and the sparkling wine *caves*, and strolled along the river quays, there isn't a tremendous amount to do, but Saumur makes a pleasant base for exploring the delightful countryside to the west, or foraging east towards Touraine.

Saumur reached its chivalric apogee under **King René** (see box on p.277), and later achieved notoriety as a Protestant stronghold in the late sixteenth and early seventeenth century – a horrified Louise de Bourbon, abbess of Fontevraud, called the town a "second Geneva", a potential rival to Calvin's Swiss power-base. Henri IV's governor of Saumur, the "Protestant Pope" **Philippe Duplessis-Mornay**, helped draft the Edict of Nantes, which granted religious tolerance, and founded Saumur's **Académie Protestante**, whose students, scholars and publishers underpinned a miniature economic and cultural boom – the academy's riding school attracted co-religionists from as far away as England and Holland.

When the Edict of Nantes was revoked in 1685, causing the departure of the Protestant population, the town was only saved from ruin by the river trade.

In 1767, the government minister Choiseul brought the national riding school to Saumur, ensuring the survival of the town's proud equestrian traditions. The school was extended in 1824 and renamed the École Royale de Cavalerie; today, it's a military college with the full title of the École d'Application de l'Armé Blindée et de Cavalerie, or Armoured Corps Academy. Saumur's present-day elite riding school, the **École d'Équitation**, is a non-military institution out in the suburbs, though its instructors have taken on the illustrious name of the old cavalry officers, dubbed the **Cadre Noir** after their all-black uniforms.

Throughout the nineteenth century, the merchant classes grew wealthy on the back of the town's textile industry. Balzac's vicious satire on Saumur's mid-nineteenth-century bourgeois-provincial society, *Eugénie Grandet*, dented the town's reputation, but the heroic defence of the Loire in 1940 (see box on p.250) helped salvage civic pride. Today, the thriving wine, equine and tourist industries provide solid foundations for Saumur's evident prosperity.

Moving on from Saumur to Angers, you can either take the train, bus #5 along the south bank, bus #11 along the north bank or buses #10/15 via Beaufort-en-Vallée (see p.296). Heading east, the train runs along the north bank to Tours. Connecting buses to Chinon usually meet some of these trains at Le Port Boulet, on the Loire 13km north of Chinon, but check locally as timetables may change.

Arrival and information

Arriving at the **gare SNCF**, you'll find yourself on the north bank of the Loire: turn right onto ave David d'Angers and either take bus #30 to the centre or cross the bridge to the Île d'Offard on foot. From the island the old **Pont Cessart** leads across to the main part of the town on the south bank, where you'll find the **gare routière**, a couple of blocks west of the bridge on place St-Nicolas, and the **tourist office**, next to the bridge on place de la Bilange (mid-May to mid-Oct Mon–Sat 9.15am–7pm, Sun 10.30am–5.30pm; mid-Oct to mid-May Mon–Sat 9.15am–12.30pm & 2–6pm, Sun 10am–noon; ☎02.41.40.20.60, ⓦwww.saumur-tourisme.com).

The old quarter lies in the **lower town**, between the château and the Hôtel de Ville – an unmistakeable landmark on the riverbank a few steps east of the Pont Cessart. **Internet** access is available at Welcome Services Copy, 20 rue du Portail Louis and Config Système, 9 rue de la Petite Bilange. You can **rent bikes** at Détours de Loire, 2 ave David d'Angers (☎02.41.53.01.01), near the gare SNCF.

Festivals and river trips

The famous **Carrousel de Saumur** takes place over two weekends in mid- to late July on the huge place du Chardonnet, a swathe of open ground overlooked by the old École de Cavalerie, which has been used for knights' tournaments since the eleventh century. The Carrousel usually features some kind of horse-dance spectacle and a drive-by from the tank museum, as well as the main presentation by the elite Cadre Noir riding school; tickets are best purchased well in advance through the tourist office (see above). In late May, the École Nationale d'Équitation (see p.249) invites foreign riding schools to perform, while the second weekend of October sees **Les Musicales du Cadre Noir**, a horse show set to classical music. A **military band festival** takes place in late June (odd-numbered years only), with contingents from all over the world invited to blow and stamp and wheel about.

SAUMUR

| 0 | 300 m |

RESTAURANTS
Les Ardilliers	6
Auberge Reine de Sicile	1
Les Forges de St-Pierre	3
Le Grand Bleu	2
Les Ménéstrels	4
L'Orangeraie	5

ACCOMMODATION
Anne d'Anjou	F
La Bouère-Salée	A
Centre International de Séjour	C
Cristal Hôtel	B
Hôtel de Londres	D
Hôtel St-Pierre	E
Le Volney	G

Angers · Gare SNCF · Tours

Bagneux & Doué-la-Fontaine · Musée des Blindés · Montsoreau & Fontevraud

In summer, you can take **river trips** aboard the *Saumur-Loire* (mid-June to mid-Sept daily; 2.30pm, 3.30pm & 4.30pm; €7), departing from quai Lucien Gautier, in front of the tourist office. The town tours in a horse-drawn *calèche* are less worthwhile. **Canoes and kayaks** can be rentd from the Base de Loisirs de Millocheau, on the riverfront in St-Hilaire-St-Florent, the suburb immediately west of the centre (July & Aug daily; May, June & Sept Sat & Sun; ☎02.41.50.62.72).

Accommodation

Accommodation in Saumur is mostly upmarket and attractive, if pricey. The **campsite** is crowded in summer, but has a good location on the Île d'Offard, next to the youth hostel.

Hotels and chambres d'hôtes

Anne d'Anjou 32 quai Mayaud ☎02.41.67.30.30, ⓦwww.hotel -anneanjou.com. This rather grand hotel is set in a listed eighteenth-century building with a magnificent, sweeping staircase. The location, on the main road along the riverfront, is usefully central, and the hotel offers a wide range of attractively decorated and good-sized rooms, some with views up to the château. The garden restaurant, *Les Ménestrels* (see p.252), is one of the poshest in Saumur. **⑤**

La Bouère-Salée rue Grange-Couronne ☎02.41.67.38.85, 🌐www.ifrance.com/labouere. This appealing and good-value bed-and-breakfast occupies a handsome nineteenth-century townhouse. The only drawback is the inconvenient location, 300m north of the train station off rue des Maraîchers. ❸

Cristal Hôtel 10–12 place de la République ☎02.41.51.09.54, 🌐www.cristal-hotel.fr. One of the nicer hotels in town, with friendly proprietors. The situation on the riverfront is great, and there are river or château views from most rooms – the ones on the side street, though, can be noisy. Family rooms, and some inexpensive attic rooms (❷), are also available. ❸

Hôtel de Londres 48 rue d'Orléans ☎02.41.51.23.98, 🌐www.lelondres.com. This big, old town-centre hotel is comfortable and well-run. It has been spotlessly renovated in recent years, but preserves some older features such as a lovely, iron-balustraded staircase. Some rooms have a low-key cartoon theme – you might even find yourself staying in a fond (and subtle) re-creation of Tintin's bedroom, for instance. Offers secure private parking and a wide range of rooms, including family suites. ❸

Hôtel St-Pierre 3 rue Haute-St-Pierre ☎02.41.50.33.00, 🌐www.saintpierresaumur.com. This boutique hotel aims at a hushed, prestigious atmosphere with its plush decor, ancient beams and stone spiral staircase, but the rooms are a little overpriced and over-fussy for some tastes. Nevertheless, a very comfortable, reliable address. ❼

Le Volney 1 rue Volney ☎02.41.51.25.41, 🌐www.le-volney.com. This budget hotel lies just south of the centre. It's a bit tired around the edges, but perfectly decent, and the management are friendly. There are a couple of larger family rooms, and a few inexpensive but cosy little rooms with shared bathrooms tucked away under the roof. ❷

Hostel and campsite

Centre International de Séjour rue de Verden, Île d'Offard ☎02.41.40.30.00, 🌐www.hebergement-international-saumur.com. Large hostel at the east end of the island with laundry facilities, views of the château and use of the swimming pool at the campsite next door. Reception 9am–noon & 2–7pm. Boat and bike rental available. Closed Nov–Feb.

Camping de l'Ile d'Offard rue de Verden, Île d'Offard ☎02.41.40.30.00, 🌐www.cvtloisirs.com. This big, well-run site is next door to the hostel. There's a heated pool, and well-informed locals sometimes swim in the Bras des Sept Voies – the minor, northern channel of the Loire. It's potentially dangerous, however, so seek advice before taking a dip.

The Town

The main attraction of central Saumur is the climb up to its **château**, though the interior is closed for restoration works until 2008. You can spend a pleasant hour or two exploring the tiny old quarter, as described by Balzac in *Eugénie Grandet* (see p.345), and strolling along the **river esplanade**. Sadly, the historic cavalry school, now called the École d'Application de l'Armé Blindée et de Cavalerie, is closed to visits, but a trio of **churches**, each from a different epoch, is worth visiting. Most visitors head out to the suburbs (see p.249) where, unusually, some of the town's most interesting sights are found.

The château

Set high above town, Saumur's airy white fantasy of a **château** (exterior only: daily except Tues 10am–1pm & 2–5.30pm; €2), may seem oddly familiar, but then its famous depiction in *Les Très Riches Heures du Duc de Berry* (see box on p.226), the most celebrated of all the medieval books of hours, is reproduced all over the region. It was largely built in the latter half of the fourteenth century by Louis I, duc d'Anjou, who wanted to compete with his brothers Jean, duc de Berry, and Charles V. The threat of marauding bands of English soldiers made the masons work flat out – they weren't even allowed to stop for feast days. After the death of René d'Anjou (see p.277) in 1480, ownership of the château passed over to the French Crown, after which it fell into gradual decline, being used variously as an arsenal, a prison and a munitions store.

The château's serenely impregnable image took a knock in April 2001, when a huge chunk of the star-shaped outer fortifications added by Philippe Duplessis-Mornay collapsed down the hill towards the river. The château itself is built on more solid ground, but in the aftermath of the disaster, the alarmed authorities decided to embark on a major renovation programme, which looks likely to continue until 2008.

Until works are complete, large parts of the interior will remain closed to visitors, including the formerly excellent **Musée des Arts Décoratifs**. If it reopens according to plan, it will once again show off an impressive collection of European china, as well as some superb fifteenth-century tapestries. One pair of tapestries, from Tournai, shows knights fighting savages in the first scene, and then happily socializing with their hairy brethren in the second. Another, longer tapestry series tells the story of St-Florent, a local Roman soldier who worked miracles in the fourth century. It's to be hoped the other château museum, the **Musée du Cheval**, will also open once restoration is complete. The breadth of its collection allows you to get an overview of the evolution of bridles and stirrups over the centuries, culminating with a diverse collection of elaborate, lovingly worked saddles from Tibet, Morocco, Mexico and all over the world.

The lower town

The oldest, most atmospheric quarter of Saumur is centred on **place St-Pierre**, the ancient crossroads at the heart of town. A pair of half-timbered houses survives from the sixteenth century, one of which has a facade carved with lifelike figures. **Rue Fourrier** and the streets leading south of **rue Dacier** are dotted with houses dating from the sixteenth century and earlier. On rue des Païens, the **Tour Grénetière** (July & Aug daily except Tues 10am–1pm & 2–5.30pm; €2) survives from the early fifteenth-century town walls, though it was later used as a prison for smugglers avoiding the salt tax; you can climb to the top for a view across town. The **église St-Pierre**, off rue Haute St-Pierre (daily 9am–noon & 2–5pm), hides behind a Counter-Reformation facade built as part of the church's efforts to overawe Saumur's persistently Protestant population. Its unusual half-Gothic, half-Romanesque interior is more subdued, though the choir stalls are exuberantly carved and the sixteenth-century tapestry sequence depicting the life of St Peter is richly coloured.

The **riverside quays** once stood outside the town walls, and hummed with river trade; these days, cars are the only traffic, though you can stroll along the slipway below the embankments when the river isn't in flood. The partly sixteenth-century **Hôtel de Ville**, on quai Lucien Gautier, dominates the river frontage. Next door, you can try Saumur's sparkling wines at the **Maison du Vin** (April–Sept Mon 2–7pm, Tues–Sat 9am–1pm & 2–7pm, Sun 9am–1pm; Oct–March Tues–Sat 10.30am–12.30pm & 3–6pm; Ⓦwww.interloire.com). Staff can also provide addresses of wine-growers and *caves* to visit, and help you find your way to the sparkling wine cellars of St-Hilaire-St-Florent (see p.250).

Two of Saumur's most interesting sights, both churches, lie on the fringes of the old town. Down by the public gardens south of the château, Saumur's oldest church, **Notre-Dame de Nantilly** (daily 9am–6pm), houses a fine tapestry collection dating mostly from the sixteenth and seventeenth centuries. The church itself is beautiful in a severe, Romanesque way, its daringly wide tunnel vault supported by four-metre-thick walls. Don't miss the statue of Our Lady herself, carved in wood in the twelfth century and now tucked away in the right transept.

Notre-Dame des Ardilliers, down by the river on the eastern edge of town (daily 8am–noon & 2–6.30pm) was founded at the site of a spring – now dry – where a statue of the Pietà was miraculously discovered in the fifteen. century. The church was dedicated by Louis XIV, and is a typically grandios، Baroque affair dominated by the tremendous dome of its rotunda, which had to be rebuilt after the bombings of June 1940. The adjacent Oratory buildings once belonged to a theological college created to fight the battle of dogma with the Protestant academy in the town proper; they now shelter a home for retired clergymen, a Catholic school for girls and a small community of nuns, the Communauté Jeanne Delanoue.

The suburbs

Some of Saumur's biggest attractions lie out in the suburbs, particularly in and around the satellite villages of **St–Hilaire–St–Florent**, 2km west of the centre and separated from Saumur proper by the little river Thouet. The great **sparkling wine caves** are here, along with the distinguished **École Nationale d'Équitation**, the national riding school. Closer to hand, but also on the western side of the Thouet, the undistinguished suburb of **Bagneux** is the surprise home of one of France's most impressive dolmens, while the semi-industrial southeastern quarter of town houses the **Musée des Blindés**, a gargantuan tank museum.

Musée des Blindés

Even if you're not a military buff, there's something awesome about the giant collection of old tanks at the **Musée des Blindés**, at 1043 route de Fontevraud, 3km south of the town centre (daily: May–Sept 9.30am–6.30pm; Oct–April 10am–5pm; €6; Ⓦ www.musee-des-blindes.asso.fr). Walking through the huge, hangar-like space, it's possible to grasp the evolution of the beast from the glorified armoured cars produced by Panhard and Renault in World War I to the highly technical behemoth of a killing machine that is the modern French army's Leclerc tank. In between you'll stumble over swarms of tanks, howitzers and other bits of armour, their strong and weak points explained by bilingual placards. The World War II section could make up a division on its own, and there's a moment of real frisson when you spot the lethal Panzer, which so harried the French army in 1940.

The museum is well signposted for motorists; alternatively, **bus** #32 towards "Chemin Vert" and bus #30 to Hôpital Vigneau pass close by; both leave from rue Franklin Roosevelt at the junction with rue Dacier and rue Beaurepaire in Saumur; get off at the stop "Borêt".

École Nationale d'Équitation

The region's horsey roots extend back to the Arab thoroughbreds introduced by Richard the Lionheart, but the **École Nationale d'Équitation**, 4km from the town centre, just outside St-Hilaire-St-Florent, was only created in 1972. This distinctly aristocratic institution exists to train up the cream of French horsemen and women and has to some extent taken on the mantle of the old École Royale de Cavalerie, though most of the forty-odd Écuyers du Cadre Noir – the black-clad riding instructors – are now civilians. Even the evocatively named Colonel de la Porte du Treil, the current chief of the school, turns out to be a colonel in the *gendarmerie* only.

The school (April–Sept Mon 2–6pm; Tues–Fri 9am–6pm, Sat 9am–12.30pm; mornings €7, afternoons €5) offers excellent guided **tours** of the whole massive complex – only the longer morning tours allow you to watch a training session as well. You can see the state-of-the-art tack room, saddlery and

5

t of June 18, 1940, towns and cities all along the Loire were declar-
es "open" to the invading German armies. As the local populations
their troglodyte caves and cellars, much as they would have done in
dieval times, refugees streamed south across the river. On the radio, Pétain was
calling for an armistice, and de Gaulle was making his first rebellious broadcasts
from London. In Saumur, Colonel Daniel Michon, the commandant of the École de
Cavalerie, received the order to withdraw south, but he decided to apply it to the
horses only, addressing his students with the stirring words: "Gentlemen, for the
school it is a mission of sacrifice. France is depending on you." Guns were set up
on the town bandstand and at the river crossings, and for three days, Saumur's two
thousand cadets and instructors held a forty-kilometre stretch of the Loire against
the Germans, repulsing wave after wave of boat attacks. De Gaulle called it the first
act of the Resistance, but it could also be called the last chivalric battle fought on
French soil – by strange chance, the 18,000 attacking troops belonged to the deeply
aristocratic 1st Cavalry Division, from the elite Hanoverian Panzer school.

The fighting was fierce but hopelessly unequal, and by late evening on June 21 the
Germans had occupied the heights around the château. Saumur was outflanked and
no longer defensible. News came through that Pétain had signed the armistice, and
the surviving cadets either retreated on bicycles towards Fontevraud or surrendered
to the occupying troops. Most of the captives – who almost alone in the French army
had won the respect of their opponents – were quickly released and force-marched
into the Unoccupied Zone, saluted by German troops and cheered by French crowds
as they went.

veterinary hospital, and endless rows of stables whose hot and cold showers and
equine sun beds service some four hundred blue-blooded horses. The Cadre
Noir's displays of dressage, anachronistic battle manoeuvres and the secret-
recipe trick jumps – *courbette*, *croupade* and *cabriole* – are regular events at the
school's stadium-sized show ring. The tourist office in Saumur has programme
details, or you can check online at ⓦ www.cadrenoir.fr.

To **get there** by public transport take bus #31 from the south end of rue
Franklin Roosevelt to the "Alouette" stop, then continue down the route de
Marson, turning right at the signpost; it's about ten to fifteen minutes' walk. If
your enthusiasm for horses won't wait, take yourself off to the **Petit Souper**
riding school, 500m short of the École Nationale d'Équitation, where an hour's
instruction at any level costs around €20 – or €10 for a half-hour on a Shetland
pony for tots. Book at least one day in advance on ☎02.41.50.29.90, ⓦ www
.saumuréquitation.fr.

Sparkling wine cellars

The main D561 leading west from Saumur towards Gennes passes through the
suburban *commune* of **St-Hilaire-St-Florent**. The central stretch of the road,
along rue Ackerman and rue Leopold Palustre, is lined with the impressive
entrances to the cellars of Saumur's most prestigious makers of sparkling wine.
Choosing between Ackerman-Laurance, Bouvet-Ladubay, Langlois-Château,
Gratien & Meyer and Veuve Amiot is a matter of personal taste, and possibly a
question of opening hours, though most are open all day every day throughout
the warmer months (generally 10am–6pm), though most close for a couple
of hours at lunchtime out of season. All offer the chance to see spectacular
cellars carved out of the soft rock, lined with millions of bottles undergoing the
obligatory second fermentation. You might be persuaded by Veuve Amiot's free

tour (currently all the others charge €2.50), or Ackerman-Laurance's eighteen-metre-high underground chamber, but these two producers are not generally regarded as the best. Indeed, the bottles in Ackerman's caves are full of bleach and water – the actual fermentation is done on an industrial scale elsewhere. The smaller producer, Bouvet-Ladubay (Ⓦwww.bouvet-ladubay.fr), makes for a more worthwhile visit: the wines are top-notch, and the *caves* have sculpted columns and an impressive "underground cathedral". If you're tasting, don't miss Bouvet's bizarre sparkling red, and the Brut Zéro, an ultra-dry sparkler which has no added sugar in the final stage.

To get to St-Hilaire-St-Florent by public transport, take **bus** #31 or #05 from rue Franklin Roosevelt to the "Senatorerie" stop. If you don't fancy getting on the bus, you can make for the **Caves Louis de Grenelle**, 20 rue Marceau (Jan–April, Oct & Nov Mon–Fri 9.30am–noon & 1.30–6pm; May–Sept daily 9.30am–6.30pm; Dec Mon–Sat 10am–noon & 1.30–6pm; Ⓦwww.caves-de-Grenelle.fr), which are about fifteen minutes' walk beyond Notre-Dame de Nantilly, on the southwest side of town. Another easy-access option is the **Caves Coopératives** at St-Cyr-en-Bourg (May–Sept daily 9.30am–12.30pm & 2–6.30pm; Oct–April closed Sun; €2.50; Ⓣ02.41.53.06.08), a short train hop south of Saumur and near the station. Neither *cave* is as prestigious as, say Bouvet-Ladubay, but there are the same kilometres of tufa-cut cellars, and a glass of bubbly at the end of them. For more on sparkling wines, see Contexts, p.361.

The Dolmen de Bagneux

Take the main road south of town towards Montreuil-Bellay, the N147, and after just over 2km you'll come to the dispiriting suburb of **BAGNEUX**. Persevere a little, however – take the rue du Dolmen which leads left past the Mairie – and you'll be well rewarded. The **Dolmen de Bagneux** (mid-June to mid-Sept daily 9am–7pm; mid-Sept to mid-June daily except Wed 9am–7pm; €3.50; Ⓦwww.saumur-dolmen.com), squatting incongruously in the garden of the friendly but ordinary bar at no. 56, is the chief among the cluster of megalithic tombs found in the region downstream of Saumur. It is proably some 5000 years old. The owner jokingly calls it his "garden shed"; in fact, it's one of the largest and best-preserved such monuments in Europe, a 23-metre, 500-tonne rectangle of gravestone-like slabs capped by an enormous roof of three flat stones. Sadly, the smattering of archeological finds have been carried off to various museums. At the time of writing, the dolmen, and attached bar, were for sale – price on application. If and when the sale goes through, the dolmen should remain open to the public, though the hours may change.

Eating and drinking

Saumur's choice of good **restaurants** isn't quite as extensive as you'd hope, but there are several reasonably inexpensive places around place St-Pierre, many of which offer a chance to enjoy a glass of sparkling Saumur brut at an outside table. Almost everything closes up fairly early, and there's nothing much to do after hours except seek out a café or "pub" that's still serving. The area around place St-Pierre is the best bet; alternatively, try the bar of the *Hôtel Cristal*, down on the riverfront.

Les Ardilliers 35 rue Rabelais Ⓣ02.41.67.12.86. This relaxed bistro-restaurant on the way out towards Notre-Dame des Ardilliers has a contemporary edge to it. There's a sleek bar area with cosy armchairs, a purple colour-scheme and some modern twists on the classic dishes – three fish and three meat, every day – that make up the backbone of the menu. There's a pleasant summer terrace and a great wine list. Menus €15–30. Closed Tues lunch, Sun evening & Mon.

Auberge Reine de Sicile 71 rue Waldeck-Rousseau, Île d'Offard. ☎02.41.67.30.48. Over the bridge, on the Île d'Offard, this handsome restaurant stands next to the medieval home of King René's mother, the queen of Sicily. The dining room is atmospherically ancient and the food is delicious, with fish dishes grilled in front of you in the old chimneyplace. Try the *matelote d'anguilles* – eel stew. Menus at €19 and €33. Closed Mon & Sun evening, and for the last week in Aug and first week in Sept.

Les Forges de St-Pierre 1 place St-Pierre ☎02.41.38.21.79. Specializing in grilled meats, this is another of the busy, slightly touristy but ultimately enjoyable restaurants on the atmospheric old place St-Pierre. Steaks around €10–15. Closed Tues evening & Sun.

Le Grand Bleu 6 rue du Marché ☎02.41.67.41.83. Specializes in fish, not so much from the Loire as from the sea. Brittany is, after all, not so far away. Has a pleasant situation on a miniature square, with outside seating in summer. Menus from €14–26. Closed Wed.

🏃 **Les Ménestrels** At the *Hôtel Anne d'Anjou*, 32 quai Mayaud ☎02.41.67.71.10. Saumur's best place for serious, formal gastronomy, though the stone walls and exposed beams add a note of rustic relaxation. It's usually not too touristy, unless the hotel has a tour party staying. The set lunch menu is a bargain at €19, but expect to pay at least twice that for an evening meal.

L'Orangeraie Château esplanade ☎02.41.67.12.88. This brasserie does enjoyable cusine bourgeoise, but the main draw is the lofty location, up on the high ground right next to the château. Menus from €18. Closed Mon, Tues evening & Sun evening.

East of Saumur

East of Saumur, the sunny microclimate and rocky soil provides the ideal conditions for making red wine, which is produced locally under the renowned *appellation* of Saumur-Champigny (see Contexts, p.359). You can find winegrowers' caves in the pretty villages of **Parnay** and **Turquant**, both of which are utterly typical of the Saumurois. Set well back from the Loire's floodplain in the shelter of the tufa escarpment, the sandy stone walls of their ancient houses are hardly distinguishable from the surrounding natural rock. On the cliff-tops behind, traditional *moulins caviers* – windmills built on cone-shaped stone platforms – stand out against the sky, though few still turn. Behind them, the mild vine-covered slopes stretch away to the south, with apple orchards around **Le Val-Hulin**.

A little further upstream, handsome **Montsoreau** is more substantial, its slate-roofed houses spreading out in the shadow of the tall, tufa-built château. Montsoreau's immediate neighbour, the picturesque village of **Candes-St-Martin**, overlooks the confluence of the Loire and Vienne. Its ancient church, and the giant abbey at **Fontevraud**, just inland, are two of the most palpably historic places in the whole Loire region.

Two **buses** serve all the towns along the riverbank as far as Montsoreau, where they turn inland to Fontevraud: the #1 leaves from Saumur's gare routière, but it's not a frequent service (2–4 daily) and the timetable varies throughout the year, so check with the tourist office in advance. You'll be much more independent with a car or bicycle.

Parnay to Turquant

At **PARNAY**, 7km upstream from Saumur, a tiny valley cuts into the escarpment at right angles to the river. Lined with gardens and orchards – some tenderly cultivated, others romantically abandoned – it's a lovely place to stroll, and the river sandbank below the village is a good spot for bird-watching. A couple of kilometres further on, in **LE VAL-HULIN**, you can find the last producers of the once-common Saumurois dried apple – known as the *pomme* *tapée*, as each apple, after drying, is given a little expert tap to check its readiness. You can tour one of the workshops at **Le Troglo des Pommes Tapées** (Easter–June & Sept to mid-Nov Sat & Sun 10am–noon & 2.30–6pm; July & Aug Tues–Sun 2.30–6pm; €5), where you are taken through the apple-drying and -tapping process before finishing with a tasting.

TURQUANT, a few hundred metres beyond Le Val-Hulin, is the starting point for a **sentier d'interprétation**, a fascinating two-hour circular walk around the village following signposts set up by the Parc Naturel Régional Loire-Anjou-Touraine (see box, below). Turquant also has two very appealing **accommodation** options. The rooms at the beautiful, fifteenth-century 𝕬 *Demeure de la Vignole*, 3 impasse Marguerite d'Anjou, Turquant (☎02.41.53.67.00, ⓦdemeure-vignole.com; ❺), have roof beams, warm stone walls and black-and-white tiled floors; there's even a troglodyte suite (❼) set into the adjoining tufa cliffs. In the centre of the village, the relatively basic but still charming chambres d'hôtes at *Le Balcon Bleu*, 2 rue des Martyrs, Turquant (☎02.41.38.10.31, ⓦlebalconbleuturquant.free.fr; ❷) are set around a small courtyard garden; two of the rooms (❸) have kitchen facilities.

Montsoreau

Montsoreau (March Sat & Sun 2–6pm; April & Oct to mid-Nov daily 2–6pm; May–Sept daily 10am–7pm; €8.10; ⓦwww.chateau-montsoreau.com) is one of the most photogenic châteaux of them all, its north side rising cliff-like almost straight out of the river while its south walls present a more elaborately decorated face to the sun. It was built in the 1450s by Jean de Chambes, one of Charles VII's cronies, and added to piecemeal in succeeding centuries. The most obvious later feature is the Renaissance staircase tower, with its exquisitely sculpted bas-relief panels showing the heraldic devices of the Chambes family – "je le ferai" (I will do it) – and various allegorical scenes of Italian inspiration.

The château has been recently turned into an elaborately presented and child-friendly **museum**. There are over a dozen rooms of strategically lit models, video projections and slide shows backed by ambient music and

---

Parc Naturel Régional Loire-Anjou-Touraine

The boundaries of the **Parc Naturel Régional Loire-Anjou-Touraine** are wide, extending down both sides of the Loire from Villandry west to St-Georges-des-Sept-Voies, as well as north towards Beaufort-en-Vallée and south to Montreuil-Bellay – which roughly matches the area covered in this chapter, plus a good chunk of western Touraine. Given the dense local population, this is no fenced-off nature reserve or wilderness park, more a locally designated area of particular natural beauty. The **Maison du Parc**, in the centre of Montsoreau, behind the château (☎02.41.53.66.00, ⓦwww.parc-loire-anjou-touraine.fr) can provide information on the park's most interesting activities for visitors, including fascinating nature walks led by experts and the ten circuits known as "Sentiers d'Interpretation" – signposted walks of a couple of hours' duration that take you past bilingual information points describing local flora, fauna and traditions. There are two delightful four-kilometre walks in the Saumurois: one starts outside the collégiale at **Le Puy-Notre-Dame** and takes you round the vineyards, while the other begins in the centre of **Turquant** and takes you through the vines and past troglodyte caves, orchards and woods. If you plan to explore the park in detail, it's worth going to a good bookshop and getting hold of IGN's dedicated **map**, *Parc Naturel Régional Loire-Anjou-Touraine*, which has a detailed 1:80,000 scale.

French-language commentaries (a translation is available). On the ground floor is an exhibition on the history of the Loire and its role as a trading route, using some beautiful models of old river-boats. The first-floor rooms tell the story of the château itself, including its most famous incarnation as the setting for Alexandre Dumas' novel *La Dame de Montsoreau*. The upper rooms house a miscellany of excellent exhibitions on local windmills, weather-vane designs, troglodyte caves and so on, but the real treat is the panoramic view from the open-air battlements, right at the top.

A major local attraction is the **Champignonnière de Saut aux Loups** (daily: March–June & Sept to mid-Nov 10am–noon & 2–6pm; July & Aug 10am–6.30pm; €5.20; Ⓦwww.troglo-sautauxloups.com), where the traditional troglodyte housefronts conceal vast, underground mushroom-growing caves. You'll be offered a tour (in English if they're not too busy) followed by the chance to eat rather expensive menus (from €20) featuring *galipettes* – giant, oven-cooked mushrooms garnished with goat's cheese, *rillettes* and other tasty morsels.

Practicalities

The welcoming and well-run ⚘ *Hôtel le Bussy*, 4 rue Jehanne d'Arc (☎02.41.38.11.11, Ⓔhotel.lebussy@orange.fr; ❹), has just twelve rooms and an enviable situation right behind the château; the rooms with river views cost a little more (❺). The best **restaurant** in town is the *Diane de Meridor*, 12 quai Philippe-de-Commines (☎02.41.51.71.76), which serves classic regional specialities with a good-value lunch menu at €13.50. The *Aigue-Marine*, a boat moored to the riverbank at the east end of town, is a fun place to eat, though the food is pretty basic.

Candes-St-Martin

Where Montsoreau proudly faces out across the Loire, its ancient little neighbour, **CANDES–ST-MARTIN**, seems to hide away from it behind high walls. The village gets the second half of its name from the great Tourangeau saint, St Martin (see box on p.75), who died here in around 400 while trying to settle a dispute between squabbling monks. This is a beautiful corner of the region, the village set under a rocky bluff overlooking the confluence of the Loire and Vienne. Discreet plaques point out the village's many handsome old buildings – though it's often hard to actually catch a glimpse of them – notably the well-walled fifteenth-century Château Vieux and seventeenth-century Château Neuf, once the summer residences of the archbishops of Tours. You won't need help finding the **collégiale**, however, which stands squarely at the centre of the village. Its **porch** is one of the architectural delights of the Saumurois; its ranks of statues – headless, for the most part – stand sheltered by a tent-like vault which springs dramatically from a slender central pillar. Unusually, the porch is oriented to the north in order to welcome the many pilgrims who would have arrived by water.

Inside the church proper, the **nave** feels incredibly spacious, a sensation created by the cool, pale stone walls and lofty, dome-like Plantagenet vault. The nave is taller than was originally planned for, a fact given away by the oddly placed statuettes of saints, which were originally carved to mark the point at which the ribs of the vault would spring away from their supporting columns, but now hover awkwardly some distance below. The oldest part of the church, though heavily restored, is the **chapelle St-Martin**, on the left of the choir, where you can trace the life of the saint in nineteenth-century stained-glass windows.

Don't miss the view of the confluence from the hilltop just sor village – the road is helpfully signposted "**Panorama**". Down explore the remnants of the old **quays**. A number of the o' houses have been occupied by local **artisans**, and there's usual, photography exhibition on somewhere in the village.

The risk of collapsing sandbanks makes **bathing** in the Loire ɧ dangerous, but you may see locals swimming quite happily from a well-lished sandy island, accessible from the bridge some 500m upstream. A perilous way to enjoy the river is to take a **cruise**. There are two options, both based in the village: the **Comptoir du Confluent** environmental visitor centre, on rue du Confluent (mid-April to June & Sept Sat & Sun 2–6pm; July & Aug Tues–Sun 10am–12.30pm & 2–7pm; ☎02.47.95.86.40, ⓦwww .cpie-val-de-loire.org) runs summer nature-watching cruises in their traditional *toue cabanée*, or sailing-barge. In May, June and September you'll need to book a weekend afternoon cruise in advance; in July and August there are regular departures (usually Wed–Sun 2.30pm, 3.30pm & 4.30pm; €7).

Alternatively, you can take a trip on the showier *L'Amarante* (☎02.47.95.80.85 or ☎06.33.34.57.16), a handsome wooden river-boat with a glazed cabin – you'll find it moored down by the quays. It sails every day at 3pm on a ninety-minute trip (€12, children aged under 12 €7), but you can book longer cruises: on the enticing overnight trip (€290 for two people), you are served a sunset barbecue of stuffed mushrooms and sparkling Saumur then left to bed down for the night while moored beside a midstream islet.

Practicalities

Right beside the church, in a building apparently falling apart with age, the ⅍ *Auberge de la Route d'Or*, place de l'Eglise (☎02.47.95.81.10; closed Wed, Sept–June also closed Tues), is an excellent **restaurant** for local specialities like *alose* (shad) and *anguilles* (eels), with a lunch menu at €15 and evening menus from €26; service is relaxed and the atmosphere unstuffy, and in summer tables are laid outside on the gorgeous church square. If you're looking for somewhere to **stay**, *La Fontaine*, 14 rte de Compostelle, on the main road just before Montsoreau (☎02.47.95.83.66; ❸), offers simple but pleasant chambres d'hôtes, some with views straight onto the river. On the high ground behind Candes-St-Martin, *Les Sarments*, 15 rue Trochet (☎02.47.95.93.40, ⓦlessarments.free .fr; ❸), has three pretty rooms under the eaves, and there's a good view from the terrace.

Fontevraud

At the heart of the stunning Romanesque complex of the **abbaye de Fontevraud**, 13km southeast of Saumur and 5km inland from Montsoreau, are the tombs of the Plantagenet royal family, eerily lifelike works of funereal art that powerfully evoke the historical bonds between England and France. The tiny village of **FONTEVRAUD-L'ABBAYE** seems to hover at the abbey gates, servicing the hordes of visitors that arrive here with a single hotel and a handful of café-restaurants and gift shops.

Some history

Fontevraud was first established in around 1100 by an ascetic hermit-preacher, **Robert d'Arbrissel**, who had previously lived in a kind of woodland commune with both male and female followers. Gradually, the beds of leaves were replaced by huts and stone buildings, but unusually the institution

nained both nunnery and monastery. When d'Arbrissel died he declared that
s successor should always be a woman – a deeply unconventional move that
on the one hand rejected the commonplace medieval notion that women were
innately sinful, and on the other allowed the monks to profit spiritually from
the humiliation of serving under an abbess. During the course of the twelfth

Eleanor of Aquitaine

Eleanor of Aquitaine, the woman described in Shakespeare's *King John* as a "cankered grandam" and a "monstrous injurer of heaven and earth", was born in Poitiers in 1122, the granddaughter of troubadour-duke Guillaume IX. Her crime was to have behaved with the same vigour and fierce independence as the great male rulers of her age. At the age of 15, Alienor, as she is called in French, inherited the duchy of Aquitaine, which then covered most of southwestern France. Soon after, she married Louis VII, king of France. It was not a successful union – the cultivated, beautiful southern heiress being ill-matched with her monkish husband from the relatively boorish north. In 1147, Eleanor scandalized contemporaries by accompanying Louis on the disastrous Second Crusade, during which it is thought she embarked on a brief affair with her urbane uncle, Raymond of Toulouse.

Back in Paris, a disillusioned Eleanor met and fell in love with the fiery, volatile **Henry Plantagenet**, the son of Geoffroi le Bel, count of Anjou, and Matilda, titular queen of England. By 1152, she had persuaded the Council of Beaugency (see box on p.204) to annul her marriage, and eight weeks later, Henry Plantagenet arrived in Poitiers for his wedding. The marriage caused alarm throughout Europe as it united Aquitaine with the Plantagenet lands of Normandy, Anjou, Maine and Touraine, creating a huge new power bloc across western France. The following year Henry inherited the English throne from his mother, and became Henry II.

Eleanor spent much of the next twenty years alternately travelling through and governing the Plantagenet domains, both as regent for Henry – while he was away on one of his frequent wars against Louis and his allies – and as ruler of Aquitaine in her own right. She gave birth to eight children, and all three elder boys inherited their mother's independence of spirit; the youngest, John, turned out a little different, perhaps because he was sent away to Fontevraud to be educated by the nuns. By the late 1160s, Henry was tiring of his now middle-aged wife and began publicly flaunting a new lover, causing Eleanor to return in fury to Aquitaine. Meanwhile, trouble was brewing between Henry and his sons, who were demanding autonomy in ruling their apportioned lands, much to Henry's displeasure. The crisis came in the aftermath of Henry's murder of Thomas Becket, when the whole family assembled at Chinon at Christmas 1172. In March, the eldest – Henry, the "Young King" – suddenly fled to Louis VII in Paris, seeking a more generous overlord. Geoffrey and Richard also sided with the French king, and it seems that even Eleanor plotted with her first husband against her second. Henry fought back with characteristic speed and fury, however, fighting and burning his way through Touraine, seizing Eleanor at Poitiers and dragging her north to captivity, first in Chinon and then in Salisbury.

By the time Henry died in 1189 (see box on p.102), Eleanor had been a prisoner for sixteen years. Despite being almost 70 years old, she travelled to Navarre to find a bride – Bérengère of Navarre (see p.320) – for her son Richard the Lionheart, presented her at Messina, in Sicily, where the troops were gathering for the Third Crusade, and then travelled back by way of Rome. By 1194, however, Eleanor's energy had finally abated, and she retired to Fontevraud as a royal guest of the nuns. Here she buried her son Richard – killed by an arrow in 1199 – and watched the Plantagenet empire crumble under the assaults of Philippe-Auguste, the formidable new French king. She died in 1204, at the then extraordinary age of 82, honoured and hated in equal measure, but incontrovertibly one of the greatest women of her age.

The River Loire

From its source in the mountains of the Ardèche to its mouth on the Atlantic coast of Brittany, the Loire flows for a full 1000km, making it the longest river in France. The Loire is most renowned not for its length, however, but its wildness. In summer, it's hard to imagine that this tranquil river of golden sandbanks and slow meanders could be transformed into a savage torrent. But in winter and spring, dramatic floods can swell in a matter of hours. Many communities still commemorate the three catastrophic inundations of the mid-nineteenth century, when the river raged up to seven metres above the low-water mark. At Orléans, the flow at the flood's peak was 300 times the recorded minimum. It's reckoned that a repeat performance today would threaten the homes of 300,000 people and cause €6 billion damage.

The last wild river in Europe

The Loire may be brutal and unpredictable, but it is called "the last wild river in Europe" for another, more appealing reason. Uniquely among the continent's major waterways, the Loire has not been turned into a glorified canal. Its waters flow among half-overgrown islands and shifting sandbanks, making it barely navigable. These *ilots* and *grèves*, however, are an ideal habitat for wildlife. Egrets and herons use them as fishing platforms, black-headed or "laughing" gulls gather on them, stone curlews wail from them at night and pied wagtails and little ringed plovers skip about on their sand all day long. In May, the loveliest of all the Loire's birds, the little and common terns, actually nest in the sandbanks.

Aquatic mammals are plentiful in and around the river. You'll be lucky to see a native otter or beaver (the latter were reintroduced in the 1970s), but two American rodent imports, the sleek muskrat and the bulky coypu, are fairly easy to spot. The willow- and poplar-forested banks shelter roe deer and wild boar, along with plentiful birdlife: blue tits, woodpigeons, common and lesser spotted woodpeckers, and the occasional hobby or glorious golden oriole. The walls of old sandbanks provide homes for sand martins and kingfishers.

There is one last reason for the Loire's "wild" reputation: it can kill. In fact it's actually illegal to swim in the Loire or the lower Cher. Strong currents are one problem, but the main danger is from those tempting sandbanks, which have a habit of becoming waterlogged and undermined, meaning that sand that looks reassuringly solid can suddenly dissolve under your feet. Well-established vegetation is a good clue to where it's safe to wander, but *always* seek local advice before exploring.

▲ Kingfisher

▼ Swimming Prohibited

Boats, bridges and dykes

The Loire may be wild but it is not, of course, free from human intervention. The valley has been settled for at least 100,000 years and, today, a good million people live alongside the river in the central "Loire Valley" or *Loire moyenne* – the area covered in this book. The major cities of Orléans, Tours and Angers alone have populations of a quarter-million apiece. Humans have always attempted to shape and control the Loire, and each city contributes its own bridges, embankments and, inevitably, **pollutants** to the river.

Outside the cities, dykes have been built along the Loire's banks since the twelfth century, when the Plantagenets constructed their Angevin *turcies* to reclaim agricultural land. Many more were built in later centuries to aid river navigation, and the Loire is now embanked almost all the way from above Sancerre to Angers – a distance of some 800km. The greatest dykes, like Anjou's seventeenth-century Grande Levée, which swoops along the right bank, are sights in themselves.

For much of its life, the Loire was a major transportation artery, and the earringed *marigniers* – river-boatmen who sailed up and drifted down the river in flat-bottomed, square-sailed *gabares* – were served by scores of river ports whose quays rivalled anything found on the coast. The cities were once entirely oriented to the river that was the source of their wealth. In 1663, a visitor to Orléans was so amazed by the river-traffic that he imagined himself in the port of Constantinople.

By the early nineteenth century over half a million tonnes of **charcoal** alone were being transported through Orléans by river. Yet, by the 1860s, the total had dropped to zero. The river's untameable currents, shallow water and changeable channels meant that as soon as an alternative arrived, in the form of the railway, commercial river traffic died. Nowadays, the old quays remain largely forgotten, although a tourism-fuelled resurgence in boat building means that you can often see – and take trips on – *gabares*, *fûtreaux* and other traditional craft.

▼ The Loire at Montsoreau

Dams, nukes and disappearing salmon

The twentieth century has seen three major threats to the life of the Loire. First, there was industrial-scale **sand and gravel extraction**, which caused worrying drops in the Loire's water level until it was banned in the 1990s. Next came nuclear power

▲ Nuclear Power Station at St-Laurent-des-Eaux

stations: France gets eighty percent of its electricity from nuclear power, and the country's first **nuclear station** was opened at Avoine, near Chinon, in 1963. Three more followed: at Belleville and Dampierre-en-Burly, both near Gien, and St-Laurent-des-Eaux, near Beaugency.

The question of potential (or suppressed) leaks aside, the power stations' major effect on the Loire was to require regulation of the water level. **Hydroelectric power** and reservoirs were added incentives to build dams, and in the 1970s and 80s almost two dozen were built on the tributaries of the Upper Loire. There are so many on the River Allier, the Loire's major upstream tributary, that they're lined up like dominoes.

The unforseen consequence was the devastation of the Loire's salmon population. At the end of the nineteenth century, 50,000–100,000 salmon swam upriver on the great annual migration from Greenland to the spawning grounds in the Upper Loire. The **Atlantic salmon** was the symbol of the river, the star of local cuisine and the backbone of a major local industry – 200 tonnes a year were once fished out of the river every year. As more and more dams were built, however, the migration was thwarted, and by the early 1990s numbers had fallen to a mere 100.

The government reacted with rare resolution. Salmon fishing was banned outright and key dams were actually demolished. The Maisons-Rouges dam, which blocked the Vienne and Creuse rivers, was destroyed in 1998, while the sole dam in the Loire Valley proper, a movable barrage upstream of Blois, was removed in 2005. Salmon numbers are now up to around 1000. Sadly, it's too late for the native sturgeon, the last of which was seen in the Loire in 1940. The eel, meanwhile, once another staple of Loire cuisine, is also seriously threatened, with a population teetering around the 500 mark. In the Loire, as everywhere, fish remain in crisis.

◀ Ducks and terns on the Loire, Saumurois

century, the patronage of the counts of Anjou enabled the creation ~
Romanesque complex that can be seen today.

Typically, the abbesses were members of the Angevin aristocracy. Matu
second of the line, was the aunt of **Henry II Plantagenet**, count of Ai.
who visited Fontevraud in 1154 shortly before sailing to England for his cor
nation. His son John, later king of England, even lived here for five years as a
child, and when Henry died at Chinon in 1189, Fontevraud was the obvious
choice for his burial – though it seems to have been against his wishes. Henry's
widow, **Eleanor of Aquitaine** (see box, opposite), lived out the last decade of
her life at Fontevraud, and was on hand to organize the creation of a second
tomb for her son **Richard the Lionheart**, who died in 1199. When the
tombs of the two kings were joined by Eleanor's own, probably shortly after
her death in 1204, a royal necropolis seemed to be under construction. Ironically, even as the Plantagenet line was being celebrated in funereal art, King
John was losing all his continental lands to his Capetian suzerain, Philippe-
Auguste – who was extending and redesigning his own royal burial complex
at St-Denis, near Paris.

The abbey declined in the wake of the Plantagenets' fall from power, but was
periodically revived by unusually committed and industrious abbesses, most
notably by the aristocratic **Bourbon abbesses**, beginning with Renée de
Bourbon in the early sixteenth century and culminating in the rule of Louise
de Bourbon Lavedan and her successor, Jeanne-Baptiste de Bourbon, who died
in 1670. In the latest period the rules were applied with renewed strictness, and
the (men's) monastery surrounded by a deep moat, with two hawthorn hedges
for good measure. This barrier apparently wasn't sufficient to prevent incursions,
however, as stone walls had to be added two years later. The nuns were finally sent
away by the revolutionaries in 1792, after which Fontevraud was used as a prison
until 1963. Since 1975 the site has been occupied by the **Centre Culturel de
l'Ouest** (CCO), an important centre for medieval archeology that has been a
thorough if sometimes over zealous restorer of Fontevraud – the entire complex
now gleams with newly cut tufa stone and well-tended gardens.

The abbey complex

The buildings of the **abbaye de Fontevraud** (daily: April, May & Oct
10am–6pm; June–Sept 9am–6.30pm; Nov–March 10am–5.30pm; €7.90) cover
a large area, as they were originally built to house and segregate not only nuns
and monks but also the sick, lepers and repentant prostitutes, and were repeatedly extended at high points in the abbey's long history. The English-language
guided tours (mid-June to mid-Sept; roughly four times daily) are excellent, but
you're free to explore on your own.

The **Plantagenet tombs** lie in the serene and spacious abbey church:
Henry II flanks his wife Eleanor of Aquitaine – her notorious youthful beauty
preserved in painted stone, her hands clasping an open book – while at their
feet are Richard the Lionheart and Isabelle of Angoulême, the widow of King
John, whose tomb (the only one in wood, rather than stone) joined the other
three in 1254. The tombs may originally have lain in the last bay of the nave,
next to the northwest pillar, but were moved in 1504 and again in 1638 to
allow the whole community to worship in the nave – at which time two effigies of Joan, Henry's daughter, and her son, Raymond VII of Toulouse, were
replaced by more conveniently shaped kneeling figures. Ten days after Louis
XVI was guillotined in 1793, the tombs were broken open and damaged, but
they at least survived decapitation. A worse fate almost befell the Plantagenets
in the nineteenth century, when Queen Victoria successfully lobbied Empress

·ch itself is an enormous building ninety metres long, its unobscured by fanciful decoration. Powerful pillars support ntury choir, while the nave, completed some fifty years later, c, with its sequence of strangely dome-like Angevin vaults. y of the **Grand-Moûtier**, the glorious cloister adjoining ın on Gothic precepts, but masons with experience of the ..vere gradually brought in, and by the time the other three wings were built, beginning in 1540, Classical principles had fully taken root.

An exquisitely carved doorway leads through to the vaulted **chapterhouse**, decorated with intense sixteenth-century wall-paintings by the Angevin artist Thomas Pot, to which most of the Bourbon abbesses later had their portraits added. Nearby, you can visit the community room, where the nuns worked on handicrafts, the vaulted cells of the noviciate and the **refectory**, on the opposite side of the cloisters to the church. The last is an impressively vast space, with distended Gothic vaulting surmounting Romanesque walls. A beautiful Renaissance staircase leads up to the **dormitory**, a seventy-metre-long space arched over by vast roof beams.

All the cooking for the religious community, which would have numbered several hundred, was done in the bizarre-looking twelfth-century **kitchen**, an octagonal structure bristling with 21 spiky chimneys and a foiled, fish-scale-like roof. The design is virtually a unique survival, though it does recall the cone-shaped bays of St-Ours, in Loches (see p.129). Elsewhere in the complex, you can explore the infirmaries, the leper-house **prieuré de St-Lazare**, the **St-Benoît hospital** – where there's a beautiful fragment of a sculpted early thirteenth-century Last Judgement – and lots of restored rooms sometimes used for art exhibitions or concerts. An exhibition gives useful background on the extensive and meticulously re-created **gardens**, which include flower, medicinal and vegetable areas.

Practicalities

Unless you have a car or bicycle, **getting to Fontevraud** is a matter of catching bus #1 from Saumur (2–4 daily; 30min); services aren't frequent, so get an up-to-date timetable from the tourist office or gare routière. Fontevraud has its own little **tourist office**, on allée Ste-Catherine (May Tues–Sat 9.30am–12.30pm & 2–6pm, Sun 10.30am–12.30pm & 2.30–5.30pm; June–Aug Tues–Sat 9.30am–12.30pm & 1.30–7pm, Sun 10.30am–12.30pm & 2.30–5.30pm; Sept Tues–Sat 9.30am–12.30pm & 1.30–7pm; ☎02.41.51.79.45), where staff can advise on visiting Fontevraud's other churches and chapels, and suggest some good routes for walks. For details of the frequent concerts, lectures, art exhibitions and theatre programmes at the abbey, contact the Centre Culturel de l'Ouest directly (☎02.41.51.73.52, ⓦwww.abbaye-fontevraud.com), or ask at the tourist office.

The most appealing **place to stay** is the ⅔ *Prieuré St-Lazare* (☎02.41.51.73.16, ⓦwww.hotelfp-fontevraud.com; ❹). It's actually within the abbey complex, though sadly the rooms are more like a modern hotel's than a monastic cell; there's also a posh restaurant, an inexpensive brasserie and a tearoom. In the village, ⅔ *La Croix Blanche* (☎02.41.51.71.11, ⓦwww.fontevraud.net; ❺) is a large and well-run hotel. All the rooms have been freshly renovated, but if you can afford it, book one of the "privilege" class rooms (❻), which are beautifully decorated with antique furnishings. The hotel-restaurant has an enjoyable regional menu at €25.50, but you may prefer the more relaxed atmosphere at the offshoot brasserie, *La Fontaine d'Evraud*.

△ Troglodyte house, Saumurois

Three kilometres north of Fontevraud, just off the main road to Montsoreau, is the ⚘ *Domaine de Mestre* (☎02.41.51.75.87, Ⓦwww.dauge-fontevraud .com; ❹), a handsome old farmhouse complex that has been converted into an artisanal soap factory and chambres d'hôtes; the rooms are charming in a rustic, nineteenth-century way, and there's a good table d'hôte most evenings.

Doué-la-Fontaine and around

The outwardly unremarkable town of **Doué-la-Fontaine** owes its local fame to a quirk of geology. It lies on a bed of *falun* limestone (see box on p.260) that has produced a number of fascinatingly weird troglodyte cave sites and a reputation for growing fabulous roses – some seven million are exported from here every year, amounting to over half of France's annual production. The caves may be dramatic, but the town is stranded in a flat and deeply rural corner of France that feels an awfully long way from the sophistications of Saumur, let alone Tours or Paris.

Tufa and falun

The beguiling milk-and-honey colour of the towns and villages of the Loire comes from the region's classic stone: *tuffeau*, or **tufa** in English. It's a pale, soft, creamy variety of limestone that you can sink a thumbnail into and is easily quarried. From pre history right up to modern times, local people used to burrow into the long escarpments that run parallel to the rivers, creating hobbit-like tunnel homes and at the same time quarrying stone for building houses in the valley. The **troglodyte cave-dwellings** were warm in winter, cool in summer, weatherproof and easily defensible. Many have now been abandoned or turned into garages, wine cellars or chicken coops, but they are increasingly being renovated and restored. It's even possible to stay at a few hotels and chambres d'hôtes that offer troglodyte rooms, the nicest being at Azay-le-Rideau (see p.266), Cunault (see p.253) and Turquant (see p.253). The harder varieties of tufa, as found around Bourré, on the Cher (see p.174), were used for the great châteaux and churches of the Loire, and the demand for this stone also created hundreds of kilometres of cave-like quarry tunnels. Many are now used for giant, commercial mushroom farms, especially in the Saumurois, and you can tour smaller, tourist-oriented versions throughout the region.

Doué-la-Fontaine, just south of Saumur, has a different geology. It stands on a great plateau of **falun** (soft shellstone), another type of limestone but with a deeper, more golden colour. It is packed with tiny shell fossils and you can scrape it away with a fingernail almost as if it were compacted sand. Unlike tufa, *falun* lies flat, and the people of Doué were forced to quarry straight down into the bedrock. Over generations, cave-villages were created, the houses ringing the edge of shallow, arena-like depressions. It's estimated that as much as two-thirds of the population around Doué once lived underground, which sounds barbaric until you see how neat and effective these cave-houses actually are. Excess stone could be broken up and used to lime the fields, reducing the soil's natural acidity. Where *falun* was quarried commercially, the premium on grazing and farmland round Doué meant that the quarrymen tried to keep the roof intact. They first created a narrow trench and then gradually cut the stone away underneath, leaving the region pockmarked with giant, gourd-shaped quarries whose size you'd never guess from the narrow opening above.

Doué and the region around it, including the excellent **zoo**, are best visited on a day-trip, but there's no train and only a thin **bus** service between Saumur and Doué (2–4 daily). In any case you'll need wheels to get around between the various sights, so if you don't have a car think about renting a bicycle in Saumur and making a long day of it.

Doué-la-Fontaine

If you were just passing through **DOUÉ-LA-FONTAINE**, 13km southwest of Saumur, you might not give it a second glance. There's no château, only a ruined Carolingian house and the shell of a Romanesque collegiate church, and the three central squares – place du Champ de Foire, place Vénard and place des Fontaines – fail to make much of an impression. But two lovely rose gardens, a pair of peculiar quarries, a museum of old shops and a quite wonderful zoo make Doué an enjoyable place to visit. Unusually, all the sights lie on the outskirts of town. Doué's thriving rose industry really flourishes during the **Journées de la Rose** (daily 9.30am–8pm; €7; Ⓦwww .journeesdelarose.com), a festival of rose-growing held for five days around the national holiday on 14 July. Some 100,000 prize specimens are presented in the town's amphitheatre and the giant cave-galleries underneath it – an extraordinary spectacle.

The **tourist office** is at 30 place des Fontaines (July & Aug Mon–Sat 9.30am–12.30pm & 2–7pm, Sun 10am–1pm; Sept–June Mon–Fri 9.30am–12.30pm & 2–5.30pm, Sat 9am–12.30pm; ☎02.41.59.20.49, ✉tourisme.doue .la.fontaine@orange.fr). You can **rent bikes** at Cycles Mouillien, 3 rue des Fontaines (☎02.41.59.13.58). There are two simple **hotels**, both on place du Champ de Foire; the welcoming *Dagobert* (☎02.41.83.25.25; ❸) has the edge for its recently refurbished rooms, but it's hard to think why you'd choose to stay in Doué. Both hotels have **restaurants**; this time, it's the *Hôtel de France* (☎02.41.59.12.27; restaurant closed Mon) that is the more enticing – the decor in the dining room may be rather startling, but the food is decent and prices moderate, with menus from €17.

La Cave aux Sarcophages

Hidden away just inside the ring road, near the exit roundabout for Montreuil-Bellay, is the eeriest of Doué's strange troglodyte attractions, **La Cave aux Sarcophages**, at 1 rue Croix Mordret (June–Sept daily 2–7pm; €4.50). Between the sixth and ninth centuries, stone coffins were quarried here on an almost industrial scale. The attraction of a stone sarcophagus was a powerful one for a Merovingian aristocrat, as the composition of the *falun* rock (see box, opposite) made it ideally suited for preserving flesh as long as possible – an important factor if you're expecting bodily resurrection at an imminent Last Judgement. It's estimated that over 30,000 such coffins were extracted from an area of some 11,000 square metres, though you're only shown a few areas where broken sarcophagi were left in situ. There's not, therefore, a lot to see, though there's something spooky about the whole idea, and the **guided tour** (in English if there are no French groups waiting, otherwise you're just given a written translation) is extremely informative, describing how the caves were transformed into hiding places in later, more troubled times.

Les Perrières

The most dramatic of Doué's troglodyte sites is the "*caves cathédrales*" at **Les Perrières**, 545 rue des Perrières (May to mid-Oct Tues–Sun 10am–12.30pm & 2–7pm; €4.50), signposted off the ring road on the way into town from Saumur. This is a classic scooped-out quarry site on the traditional pattern (see box, opposite), so there's nothing to see in particular apart from the flowers and plants that grow profusely all around, but as you walk through the long under-ground chambers, 20m high in places, you'll feel suitably ant-like and insig-nificant. Occasional lamp-lit tours take place on Tuesday evenings (contact the tourist office for information). Doué actually has a second, similar complex, but as it's cleverly used as the town dump it's not exactly on the tourist circuit.

Zoo de Doué

Even if you wouldn't normally visit a zoo, you might think about calling in at the **Zoo de Doué** (mid-Feb to April & Oct to mid-Nov 10am–6.30pm; May–Sept 9am–7.30pm; €14, children aged 3–10 €8; ⓦwww.zoodoue.fr). It makes brilliant use of a warm, sheltered situation in one of the region's complexes of *falun* quarries, and endless streams and bamboo thickets conspire to create a powerful Lost Eden feel. If you have reservations about animal captivity, console yourself with the thought that the zoo is committed to a major conservation scheme for endangered species, and the animals are at least constrained by natural rock instead of bars. Bears occupy a rocky hollow, leopards cruise about in a kind of stone gulch, giraffes poke their heads above the top of their quarry pit and pythons and anacondas slumber in dark, steamy tunnels. Various animal feeding times are advertised throughout the day. To get there, follow the signs west out of town towards Cholet, along the D960; the zoo is at the very edge of town, almost 3km from the centre. If you don't have wheels, you could hop on a Cholet-bound bus but they're not frequent enough to be useful.

Nearby, just off the road to Cholet, **Les Chemins de la Rose** (mid-May to mid-Sept daily 9.30am–7pm; €6) is a very English-style garden, filled with some ten thousand rose bushes featuring over eight hundred varieties.

Troglodyte sites north of Doué-la-Fontaine

A particularly fascinating trio of troglodyte sites lies just north of Doué-la-Fontaine – though you'll need French to get the most out of them. At **ROCHEMENIER**, 6km north, you can tour the **Village Troglodytique** (Feb, March & Nov Sat & Sun 2–6pm; April–Oct daily 9.30am–7pm; €4; ⓦ www.troglodyte.info). This was a complete troglodyte village, used by a group of ordinary farming families until a hundred years ago. You can see their barns, cowsheds and cellars, with old farm implements on display, and the living quarters, complete with windows, beds, ovens and all the accoutrements of farm life. The most fascinating chambers are the communal ones, particularly the large village hall, whose walls are scored with pick marks to prevent echoes, and the extraordinary subterranean chapel with its mock Gothic arches. The optional guided tour is in French only, so buy the excellent, inexpensive booklet in English, which fills in all the details of daily life. One hundred metres along the main road, you can sample a €21 menu of "heritage" fare – mushrooms followed by traditional *fouaces* breads stuffed with *rillettes* and goat's cheese – in troglodyte surroundings at *Les Caves de la Genevraie* (☏ 02.41.59.34.22; July & Aug closed Mon, Sept–June closed Mon–Fri).

Just 2km north of Rochemenier, on the D69 between Doué and Gennes, **DÉNEZÉ-SOUS-DOUÉ** is the site of the bizarre **Cave aux Sculptures** (April–Oct Tues–Sun 10.30am–1pm & 2–6.30pm; €4). Housed under a protective concrete roof, the walls of the cavern are lined with a host of naïve and cartoon-like statuettes which mock religion, morality, the state and the ruling class. The cave was only rediscovered in 1950, so the exact origin and meanings of the sculptures are obscure, but current thinking attributes them to a sixteenth-century quasi-Masonic sect. The figures may represent celebrities of the day, including François I and Catherine de Médicis.

There's another troglodyte farming hamlet at **La Fosse des Forges** (Feb & Nov Sat & Sun 2–6pm; March–May & Oct daily 10.30am–12.30pm & 2–6.30pm; June–Sept daily 9.30am–7pm; €€). The site isn't as substantial as Rochemenier's, but it's run with dedication by the owner, who plans to retire to his own troglodyte house here. The tour is largely in French but even if you don't grasp the finer details, everything is pointed out with delightful enthusiasm, from eel traps to chimneys and traditional feather dusters. To get there, take the tiny D214 out of Doué-la-Fontaine to the tiny village of **FORGES**, 4km north, and follow the signs for 1km.

Montreuil-Bellay

Approached from the north, **MONTREUIL-BELLAY**, 18km south of Saumur, presents one of the most idyllic views in the region. On the far side of the old stone bridge across the Thouet, the château rises up like the very model of a medieval castle, its giant chapel, sturdy fortifications and whimsical turrets looming high above feathery ranks of poplars that sway and stir in constant motion on the banks of the river.

As is clear from its imposingly elevated situation, the **château** (April–Oct Mon & Wed–Sun 10am–noon & 2–5.30pm; guided tour €7, grounds only €3.50) began life as a defensive fortress, one of many built by the aggressive Foulques Nerra, an eleventh-century count of Anjou. Most of the present structure, however, dates from the fifteenth century, under the d'Harcourt family. The guided tour (usually in French only) of the main body of the d'Harcourts' château, the **Château Neuf**, takes you through a succession of late-medieval rooms sumptuously decorated and redecorated at various points between the fifteenth and twentieth centuries and preserving traces of every epoch. If you're lucky you may also be shown the two superimposed d'Harcourt **family chapels** – the lower of which was gorgeously frescoed in the 1480s, with angels making music in the sky-blue vaulting and a large Crucifixion filling one wall; they are often only shown to visitors on group tours but you could just try asking. You're sure, however, to be shown the seventeenth-century bedroom of the beautiful but rebellious **duchesse de Longueville**, who was exiled here between 1652 and 1654, and the furnishings and religious objets d'art collected by the late Mme Augustine de Grandmaison. But the château's proudest treasure is the elaborately studded **marriage coffer** of Marguerite de Valois, "la reine Margot", which dates from her later-annulled marriage to Henri IV. At the end of the tour you are shown the grand kitchens and vaulted **cellars**, where you can taste (and buy) the wines made by the current owners. The "grounds only" ticket allows you to explore the **canons' lodgings**, a curious quartet of diminutive towers with roofs like witches' hats. Each had a private wine cellar and steam bath inside – surprising amenities for monk's cells.

The barn-like Gothic **collégiale** is visited separately from the château (daily 8.30am–7/8pm) – on Sunday mornings you can even see the parishioners trooping across the drawbridge to Mass. Note the black funereal band halfway up the wall, which displays the coats of arms of the château's various deceased owners. The **town** preserves substantial vestiges of its medieval walls, notably a powerful gatehouse, but the most appealing place to wander is down beside the **River Thouet**, where paths and a pontoon bridge lead to some idyllic picnic spots. In summer, you can rent **canoes and kayaks** from a spot close to the bridge (May, June & Sept Sat & Sun 2–6pm; July & Aug daily 2–6pm; at other times call ☎06.82.30.44.52).

Practicalities

Bus #4 runs to and from Saumur nine times daily (30min). Line #9 provides a skeletal service to Doué-la-Fontaine and on to Angers, but there are just three buses daily. The **tourist office**, place du Concorde (March & Oct Tues–Fri 9.30am–1pm & 2.30–6pm; April to mid-June & Sept Tues–Sat 9.30am–1pm & 2.30–6pm, Sun 10.30am–12.30pm & 2.30–5.30pm; mid-June to end Aug Mon–Sat 9.30am–1pm & 2.30–7pm, Sun 10am–1pm & 2–5pm; ☎02.41.52.32.39, ⓦwww.ville-montreuil-bellay.fr) can provide lots of information on the town's historic buildings.

There are just two good **hotels**, sharing the same management. The *Relais du Berry*, 96 rue Nationale (☎02.41.53.10.10; ❸) has a relaxing, spacious feel, with a refurbished older wing and a modern annexe offering smart rooms, some (❺) with château views; the *Splendid' Hôtel*, 139 rue du Docteur-Gaudrez (☎02.41.53.10.00, ⓦwww.splendid-hotel.fr; ❸), is slightly less expensive, and a little old-fashioned in feel. Guests at both can use the heated pool and sauna facilities at the *Relais*. The 🍴 *Demeure des Petits Augustins*, place des Augustins (☎02.41.52.33.88, ⓔlespetitsaugustins@yahoo.fr; ❹) is run by a local history enthusiast and offers three antique-furnished **chambres d'hôtes** in a gorgeous, vine-covered seventeenth-century townhouse.

The *Splendid' Hôtel* has a decent – if sometimes hit-and-miss – **restaurant**. You could also try the *Auberge des Isles* (☎02.41.50.37.37), which does simple grills and salads at an attractive location down on the riverbank; or the rather more formal *Hostellerie St-Jean*, 432 rue Nationale (☎02.41.52.30.41; closed Sun evening and Mon), where you'll find elegant and traditional cooking. The lavishly appointed, four-star **campsite**, *Camping Les Nobis* (☎02.41.52.33.66, ⓦwww.campinglesnobis.com; closed Oct–Easter) has a swimming pool and a good location beside the Thouet.

Le Coudray-Macouard

Eight kilometres north of Montreuil-Bellay, on the road to Saumur, the village of **LE COUDRAY-MACOUARD** is another contender for the title of the region's prettiest village. An attractive, twelfth-century chapel and the sixteenth-century **Seigneurie du Bois** are the chief monuments, but just wandering about the medieval streets is enjoyable enough, especially in summer, when there's usually a serious attempt at the local "village in bloom" prize under way. There's also a silk workshop, **La Magnanerie** (daily except Sat: April to mid-June & mid-Sept to mid-Oct 2–6pm; mid-June to mid-Sept 11am–6pm; €5), which is attempting to revive the long-moribund traditions of French silk-making. Silkworms are bred here, fed on mulberry leaves, and the precious thread from their cocoons collected and woven to produce small quantities of Anjou silk.

Château de Brézé

As you approach the **château de Brézé** (daily: Feb to mid-April & Oct–Dec Tues–Fri 2–6pm, Sat & Sun 10am–6pm; mid-April to Sept daily 10am–6.30pm; tunnels €8.15, château and tunnels €14; ⓦwww.chateaudebreze.com), 7km west of Le-Coudray-Macouard, it looks like a typically noble but unexceptional sixteenth-century château. The creamy-white tufa walls are handsome, and the situation on top of a minor local hill rather fine. It's only when you pass through the outer walls and walk across the courtyard and onto the entrance bridge, however, that Brézé's astounding feature reveals itself. The château perches on what can only be described as a rocky island, surrounded on all sides by Europe's deepest dry moat. Certainly, its sides are more like cliffs than walls, and it echoes with the high croaks of jackdaws.

The inner wall of the moat is riddled with tunnels and chambers, forming a maze of passageways that lie beneath the château proper. This originally formed a defensive **roche** – a kind of mirror-image underground castle – that dates back, in parts, to the eleventh century, though the deepest levels are fifteenth- and sixteenth-century. You can explore the tunnels at leisure on the less-expensive entry ticket, taking in grain silos, silkworm chambers and even stables. Some children will love the "firing hole", which comes ready-equipped with a toy gun, and the "Cathédrale d'Images", an exceptionally large cave-chamber where spooky music plays over projected images of troglodyte sites.

The main **château** is still occupied by the present Count, one Bernard de Colbert, who married the last Dreux-Brézé heiress in 1959. Her family had owned the château in unbroken line since 1682, when they swapped their home in Brittany with Louis II de Bourbon-Condé – known in France as "Le Grand Condé" for his superb management of Louis XIV's military campaigns. Condé himself had acquired Brézé in 1650 by marrying the last heiress of the

Maillé-Brézé family – and it was the Maillé-Brézés who were responsible for digging the deeper levels of the moat. They put the quarried stone to good use by enlarging and improving their château with a Renaissance *logis*, which is still the most handsome of the château's three wings.

Unfortunately, you don't currently get to see the Renaissance wing on the guided tour of the château **interior** – though there are plans to open up its long gallery for visitors. Instead, you're shown a handful of rooms decorated in sumptuous nineteenth-century style by a scion of the house who was also a bishop. You also get to see a room decorated in the sixteenth century for the arrival of Cardinal Richelieu, and the seventeenth-century kitchens, which were in use until 1991. Altogether, it's distinctly less thrilling than the tunnels beneath.

Le Puy-Notre-Dame and around

The tiny village of **LE PUY-NOTRE-DAME**, 6km west of Montreuil-Bellay, is dwarfed by the **collégiale Notre-Dame** (daily 9am–6pm), a church whose bizarre size is explained by its position on the pilgrim route to Santiago de Compostela and its possession of a great medieval relic: the **Girdle of the Virgin**. Pregnant women in particular may want to pay their respects to the jewelled reliquary – the *ceinture* is supposed to help childbirth, and was borrowed at various times by Anne de Bretagne (see box on p.97) and Anne of Austria, the mother of Louis XIV. The church itself is an airy, pale-walled space under a lofty Angevin vault. Look out for the choir stalls, riotously carved in the sixteenth century.

A signpost beside the collégiale signals the beginning of a gentle, two-hour **circular walk** through the woods and vineyards south of the village, one of a number set up in the region by the Parc Naturel Régional Loire-Anjou-Touraine (see box on p.253). At the edge of the village is a small museum of silk-making, **La Soie Vivante** (April, Sept & Oct daily 2–5pm; May–Aug Mon & Sun 2–6pm, Tues–Sat 10am–noon & 2–6pm; €4.50), based around two working Jacquard looms and various silk-related paraphernalia. It's modest enough, but an interesting reminder of this almost-vanished local industry.

At **SANZIERS**, 3km southeast of Le Puy, you can visit the **Cave Champignonnière de St-Maur** (April–Sept daily 10am–noon & 2–6pm; Oct Sat & Sun 2–6pm; €4.50), another underground mushroom farm-cum-troglodyte attraction. The sixteenth-century quarry site is moderately impressive, and there's a rather good demonstration (though in French only) of how various rustic quarry tools were once used, as well as tastings of the proprietor's wines and – of course – his mushrooms.

If you want **to stay**, the enterprising owner of the silk museum runs a friendly and efficient **chambres d'hôtes** operation, *Le Chai de la Paleine* (☏02.41.38.28.25, ⊛www.relais-du-bien-etre.com; ❸), with a dozen simple but tasteful rooms, some sleeping three or four. The ⚑ *Château Tour Grise*, rue des Ducs d'Aquitaine (☏02.41.38.82.42, ✉contact@latourgrise.com; ❹), is a very attractive option, its two stone-walled and heavily-beamed rooms set in the converted outbuildings of an organic winemaker's manor house, overlooking a courtyard garden.

West of Saumur

Once you're free of the suburbs of Saumur, the riverside **D751** becomes one of the loveliest roads in the whole Loire region, squeezed between the escarpment and the south bank of the river. Drivers and cyclists with time on their hands can potter along this delightful backroad, passing miniature meadows and diminutive vegetable plots shaded by poplars and willows, while the heavier, Angers-bound traffic rushes along the trunk road on the opposite bank.

If you don't have transport, you could catch **bus** #5 from Saumur towards Angers, but the service is very infrequent (2–4 daily), especially outside school terms, so check the timetables carefully before committing yourself. You'd do better to rent a bicycle in Saumur.

Chenehutte and Trèves

Just beyond the suburban villages of St-Hilaire-St-Florent, on the D751, a warren of tufa caves has been made over into the **Musée de Champignon** and **Parc Miniature Pierre et Lumière** (Feb to mid-Nov daily 10am–7pm; €11.50 for both tours, €6.50 for one only; W www.musee-du-champignon .com). You can visit either attraction separately, or both together. If you're keen to see mushrooms growing underground, the former is worth trying, but the *parc miniature* is more impressive, an underground collection of scale models of Loire châteaux and cities, all of them cunningly sculpted out of the soft rock. There's a good Fontevraud, measuring about two metres square.

Eight kilometres out of Saumur on the D751, a sixteenth-century priory atop the cliff at **CHÊNEHUTTE-LES-TUFFEAUX** has been turned into the luxury *Le Prieuré* **hotel** (T 02.41.67.90.14, W www.prieure.com; ❽). If you want to stay here, make sure to book one of the actual priory rooms – Hilton meets King Arthur in style – rather than the modern pavilions in the grounds.

A couple of kilometres further down the road, the higgledy-piggledy **église St-Aubin** in the pretty hamlet of **TRÊVES** hides a wonderfully carved porphyry font and the effigy of one Robert le Maczon, who was a companion of Joan of Arc and built the adjacent **keep**, now ruined.

Cunault

The pot of gold at the end of the D751 is the giant **église Notre-Dame** at **CUNAULT**, 12km west of Saumur, a Romanesque pilgrimage church overlooking a beguiling bend in the Loire. The powerful, eleventh-century **belfry** is the earliest such tower in Anjou. From the western portal, with its sculpted Virgin and Flamboyant Gothic window, you can gaze in one magnificently untrammelled line down the nave to the high altar. Romanesque imagination is given free rein in the sculpture of the hundreds of capitals, with demons vomiting forth the column beneath them or supporting the vault above, Atlas-like, on their arched backs. Other capitals are more restrained, mostly simple but elegant representations of the traditional acanthus leaf. The curving **ambulatory**, where hundreds of pilgrims would once have filed around the sanctuary, is filled with light. Tucked away on its south side is the extraordinary thirteenth-century **chasse de St-Maxenceul**, a reliquary chest carved from a single block of walnut with scenes of Christ, the Virgin and the apostles. On the north side, look out for an awkward but strangely moving early sixteenth-century **pietà** in polychrome stone. If you can time your visit for **Gregorian Mass** (chanted by a visiting choir every Sunday at 11.15am) or one of the summer **concerts** (July & Aug: Sun at 5pm) or **organ recitals** (May: Sun at 5pm), so much the better.

The ancient, stony **village** is tiny but still manages to show off a handsome Renaissance priory and a private **château** (closed to visitors), built in a mongrel mixture of architectural styles, mostly in the nineteenth century. The **chambres d'hôtes** ⚜ *Les Bateliers*, 28 rue de Beauregard (T 06.67.18.66.73, W bateliers .chez-alice.fr; ❸) offers a rare chance to stay in a cave room; the two ordinary

△ Cyclists crossing the bridge at Les Rosiers-sur-Loire

rooms are attractive enough, but try to book the "troglodyte" suite (⑤), a beautiful vaulted chamber with a sunny terrace outside and a kitchen within. The 🏠 *Manoir de Beauregard* (☎02.41.67.92.93; ⑤) offers two gorgeously furnished chambres d'hôtes – one with a lovely river view – in an aristocratic manor house on the edge of the village; you may have to share the bathroom between the two rooms, otherwise both rooms can be booked together for a bargain €115. The charming hosts will make a picnic lunch for cyclists.

Gennes

Just over a kilometre beyond Cunault, **GENNES** is best known for its **Roman amphitheatre**, signposted off the D70 on the way southwest out of town (April–June Sun 3–6.30pm, July & Aug Mon–Fri & Sun 10am–6.30pm; €3); if you speak French the optional, free guided tour is interesting, but there's little to see apart from a sunken, sandy circle surrounded by broken-down stone seats. More rewarding – as long as they've pruned the trees recently – is the view from the **monument to the cadets of Saumur** (see box on p.250), perched high on the hilltop beside the ruined church of **St-Eusèbe**. The back lanes immediately inland are worth exploring for the concentration of Megalithic **dolmens and menhirs**, but you'll need a good map to track down more than a handful; tourist offices can help – try the branches in Saumur or Angers.

Gennes is a fairly unattractive village strung out along and above the main road, but it has an excellent and surprisingly stylish **restaurant**, 🏠 *L'Aubergade*, 7 ave des Cadets (☎02.41.51.81.07; closed Tues lunch & Mon), just short of the bridge across the Loire. It uses regional produce but gives it a serious twist with judicious use of spices, tropical fruits and more than a touch of Latin flair.

A distinctive suspension bridge, built immediately after World War II, leads across to the north bank, where the village of **LES ROSIERS-SUR-LOIRE** is distinguished by a curious Renaissance bell tower rising high above the main square. The village's charm is, however, spoilt by the trunk road.

Travel details

Trains

Saumur to: Angers (14 daily; 20–30min); Tours (12 daily; 45min).

Buses

Doué-la-Fontaine to: Angers (4–6 daily; 1hr); Montreuil-Bellay (3 daily; 40min); Saumur (2–4 daily; 30min).

Saumur to: Angers via the south bank (2–4 daily; 1hr 30min); Angers via the north bank (4 daily; 1hr–1hr 30min); Fontevraud (4–6 daily; 35min); Le Mans (1–2 daily; 2hr); Montreuil-Bellay (9 daily; 30min).

6

Central Anjou

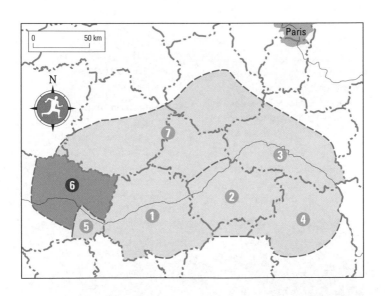

CHAPTER 6 # Highlights

✳ The Tapestry of the Apocalypse Housed in the château d'Angers, this medieval masterpiece depicts the unfolding of the Apocalypse in one hundred metres of vivid woven colour. See p.278

✳ Les Tonnelles, Béhuard One of Anjou's finest gastronomic restaurants, *Les Tonnelles* is also its best located, on the holy island of Béhuard. See p.285

✳ The Layon valley The sunny microclimate of the Côteaux du Layon, just south of Angers, allows the local wine-growers to produce some of France's finest sweet white wines. See p.286

✳ Château de Brissac The tour of this extravagant seventeenth-century château offers a taste of aristocratic opulence; you can even stay in some of the originally furnished rooms. See p.288

✳ Au Cabernet d'Anjou, Le Thoureil This ancient mariners' bar has a lovely terrace overlooking the Loire – a great place for drinks at sunset. See p.291

✳ Château du Plessis-Bourré Inside this belligerent-looking moated castle is a fascinating ceiling dating back to the fifteenth century, painted with alchemical symbols and riddles. See p.292

✳ Château de Montgeoffroy There's a *Marie Celeste* feel to this eighteenth-century château, built and decorated just before the Revolution and scarcely touched since. See p.296

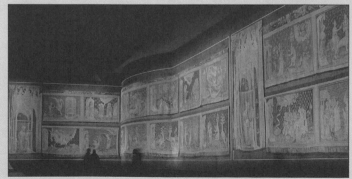

△ Tapestry of the Apocalypse, Angers

6

Central Anjou

Anjou is the most diverse of the Loire's regions, unsure whether to face west towards the sea or inland up the "royal Loire". Historically, it is linked with its eastern neighbours far more than with Brittany to the west – the counts of Anjou ruled Touraine in the eleventh century, and the two regions formed the heart of the Plantagenet empire some two hundred years later. Yet Anjou has a remarkably different feel from other Loire Valley regions. Dark, rugged schist replaces pale, creamy stone as the favoured building material, the horizons seem to widen and there's the faintest tang of sea salt in the air – a sensation that grows stronger as you travel west. This chapter covers only central Anjou, the heartland of the region. The southeastern pocket, known historically as the Saumurois, is covered separately in chapter 5.

Anjou's capital, **Angers**, is a spruce cathedral town with a single unmissable highlight, the Tapestry of the Apocalypse, housed in the city's ruined château. You could happily spend a few days visiting the city's other churches and museums, and enjoying its modest but upbeat nightlife. Otherwise, Anjou's superb vineyards are likely to lure you out into the countryside. Lazing around the Loire and its tributaries between visits to wine-makers and châteaux can fill a good summer week around Angers, as long as you have your own transport – otherwise it's a two-buses-a-day problem, or no buses at all. Worthy exceptions are the vineyards at **Savennières**, which you can reach by train, and **St-Aubin-de-Luigné**, which is served by fairly regular buses and where you can rent rowing boats during the summer. If you want to explore the beguiling villages and gentle wine valleys of the **Layon** and **Aubance**, you'll definitely need a car or bicycle.

Anjou has more **châteaux** than any other Loire region, but most are in private hands and can't be visited. Among the few which can, **Le Plessis-Bourré** looks like a true castle, complete with moat and drawbridge, while **Le Plessis-Macé** retains only its outbuildings, though even these are very grand. Both are isolated in the watery countryside north of Angers. **Serrant**, southwest of Angers, and **Brissac**, in the Aubance valley, are seventeenth-century giants, their architecture as extravagant as their furnishings. East of Angers, the perfectly preserved interiors of **Montgeoffroy** offer a window on a more charming, eighteenth-century vision of aristocratic life. By contrast, René d'Anjou's château at **Baugé**, to the northeast, is an empty shell, albeit recently filled with a hi-tech historical museum, but the fascinating and little-visited town around it makes a worthy destination, and you could spend a day or two exploring the forested countryside.

From mid-June to mid-July, the **Festival d'Anjou** (Ⓦ www.festivaldanjou .com) brings a programme of theatre and musical events to churches, châteaux and concert halls.

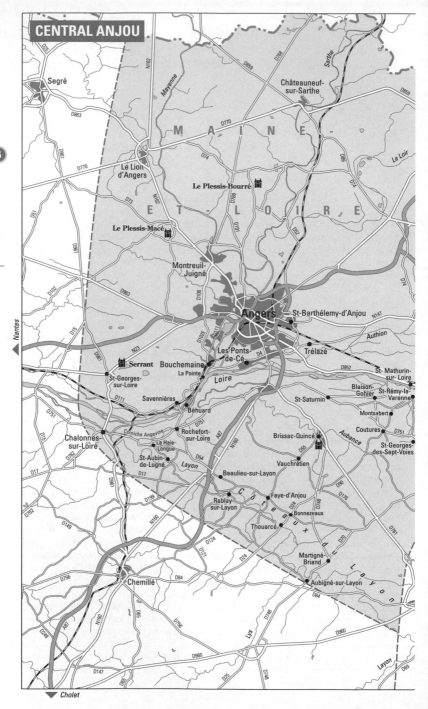

◀ Nantes

Segré

Châteauneuf-
sur-Sarthe

M A I N E -

Le Lion
d'Angers

Le Plessis-Bourré

E T   L O I R E

Le Plessis-Macé

Le Loir

Montreuil-
Juigné

Angers — St-Barthélemy-d'Anjou

Les Ponts-
de-Cé

Trélazé

Authion

Serrant   Bouchemaine

St-Mathurin-
sur-Loire

St-Georges-
sur-Loire

La Pointe

Loire

Savennières

Blaison-
Gohier

St-Rémy-la-
Varenne

St-Saturnin

Béhuard

Montsabert

Corniche Angevine

Rochefort-
sur-Loire

Coutures

Chalonnés-
sur-Lôire

La Haie-
Longue

Brissac-Quincé

St-Georges-
des-Sept-Voies

St-Aubin-
de-Lugné

Layon

Vauchrétien

Aubance

Beaulieu-sur-Layon

Rablay-
sur-Layon

Faye-d'Anjou

Bonnezeaux

Thouarcé

Martigné-
Briand

Chemillé

Aubigné-sur-Layon

Lys

Layon

▼ Cholet

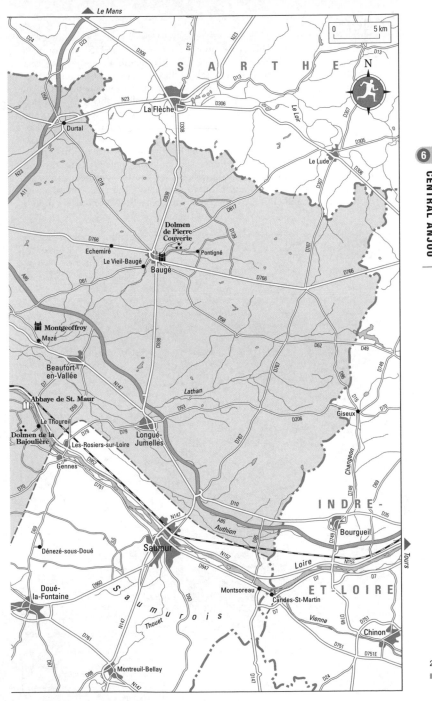

Angers

As capital of the historic region of Anjou, the city of **ANGERS** (pronounced *on-jay*) maintains a certain proud distance from its neighbours – the city isn't quite on the Loire river and does not fall within the classic Loire region. Yet Angers looks very much like a Loire town, its ruined château gazing down on the broad River Maine and its abandoned quays recalling the long-vanished river trade. Although larger than Tours and Orléans in terms of population, the city feels homely and provincial, overshadowed by the great Breton capital of Nantes, 75km west.

On the surface, Angers is a handsome, largely nineteenth-century place – Henry James, offended by the newness of its buildings, called it "stupidly and vulgarly modernized". Even if the old quarter has mostly vanished, the town centre and medieval suburb of **La Doutre**, just across the river, retain some fine old townhouses and churches, and the **cathédrale St-Maurice** is a superb

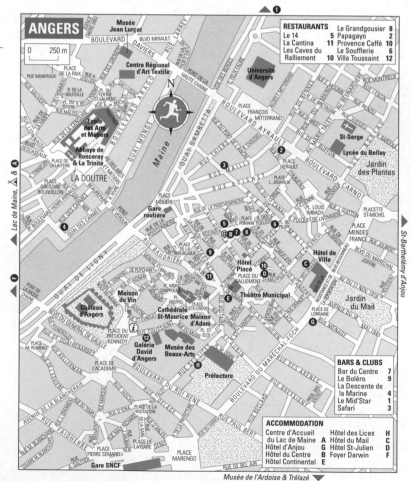

example of the twelfth-century Angevin style. Unusually, two of the city's most compelling attractions are tapestries. One is ancient – the breathtaking **Tapestry of the Apocalypse**, kept in the ruined château; the other modern – the similarly apocalyptic **Chant du Monde**, housed in a twelfth-century hospital. In the evenings, a youthful population and the presence of two major universities help drive a relaxed **bar** and **restaurant** scene.

Some history

Angers gets its name from a Celtic tribe, the **Andecavi**, but only really took shape under the Romans, as Juliomagus. "Barbarian" invasions threatened the city for much of its early life, culminating in destructive Viking raids in the mid-ninth century. Only under the warlike **counts of Anjou**, who took control from the tenth century, was the city made truly secure – in fact, their efforts ensured that it became the power-base of a miniature empire. Under the prolific castle builder **Foulque Nerra**, the "Black Falcon" (987–1040), the Angevins managed to subdue both the Saumurois and Touraine, and were only prevented from making further conquests by the obduracy of the counts of Blois. Later generations enlarged their territories by marriage rather than warfare – Count Foulques V brought the Maine region, to the north, within the family fief, while his son, **Geoffroi "Plantagenêt"** – so-called because he habitually planted a sprig of broom (*genêt*) in his headgear – wed Matilda of England, daughter of Henry I, in 1128, gaining control of Normandy. Geoffroi's son, Henri, pulled off an even bigger coup by marrying Eleanor of Aquitaine in 1152, thereby effectively taking over her vast dominions in southwestern France (see box on p.256). Just two years later he became Henry II of England. Angers grew rapidly in the brief Plantagenet heyday, even if its overlords actually preferred to live elsewhere.

After the Plantagenet collapse, the city passed into the hands of the French royal family. As regent, Louis IX's mother, Blanche de Castille, had the city encircled by giant **fortifications** from 1230; the walls were completed in just ten years in the face of the waxing power of an independent Brittany. Monasteries grew in the shelter of the walls, and Angers' life as a major **university town** began with the founding of a school of law in 1244. In the mid-fourteenth century, the French king Jean le Bon gifted Anjou to his son Louis who, as the first semi-autonomous **duc d'Anjou**, set about raising the status of his new capital with commissions for new château buildings and a great tapestry series depicting the apocalypse. Louis' grandson, René d'Anjou (see box on p.277), made further improvements, establishing Angers as a thriving artistic and mercantile centre. It continued to flourish into the sixteenth century and beyond, the city's now greatly expanded **university** attracting two of Renaissance France's greatest writers: the satirist Rabelais, from Chinon, and the poet Joachim du Bellay, from western Anjou.

In the 1790s, the entire region, including Angers itself, was thrown into turmoil when the conservative and ultra-Catholic Vendée region immediately south and west of Anjou rose up against the Revolution. But like so many Loire towns, it was the arrival of the railways in the mid-nineteenth century that most affected Angers, as the port trade slowly dwindled and died. In 1875 a private, **Catholic university** was established immediately west of the city centre. Today, the 10,000 students at "*la Catho*" still make up a powerful presence in the city, along with their 16,000 rivals at the modern, public Université d'Angers, founded in 1971 on the opposite bank of the River Maine. Meanwhile, the Institut National d'Horticulture, or INH, turns out hundreds of plant experts each year, many of them bound for highly technical jobs in Anjou's thriving horticulture industry.

Arrival and information

The **gare SNCF** is south of the centre, about a ten-minute walk from the château. Bus #2 towards "Trélazé" (bus #22 on Sun) makes the journey to the tourist office and château via the central place du Ralliement; you can also take bus #3 (towards Dezière) to place du Ralliement; a flat-rate **bus** ticket, which you can buy on board, costs €1.10. The **gare routière** is down by the river, just past the Pont de Verdun on place Molière.

The main **tourist office** is on place du Président Kennedy, facing the château (May–Sept Mon–Sat 9am–7pm, Sun 10am–6pm; Oct–April Mon 2–6pm, Tues–Sat 9am–6pm, Sun 10am–1pm; ☎02.41.23.50.00, Ⓦwww.angers loiretourisme.com). You can buy a **city pass** (€14 for 24 hours; €21 for 48), which allows unlimited access to the tapestries as well as the city's museums and galleries. Useful **online** information can be found at the city's official website, Ⓦwww.ville-angers.fr. There's an **Internet café**, Cyber-éspace, at 25 rue de la Roe, on the corner of rue Bodinier (Mon–Thurs 9am–10pm, Fri & Sat 9am–midnight, Sun 2–8pm; €1 per 15min).

Accommodation

The city's thriving commercial life pulls in a steady business clientele, so there's rarely a problem finding somewhere to stay. Charming city-centre **hotels**, especially those at the budget end of the scale, are in shorter supply, however, so it's worth booking ahead.

Hotels

Hôtel d'Anjou 1 bd du Maréchal Foch ☎02.41.21.12.11, Ⓦwww.hoteldanjou.fr. Part of the Best Western chain, but not overwhelmingly large or commercial, with just over fifty rooms. The prices guarantee a largely business clientele, but its central location makes it a useful option for tourists too. ❼

Hôtel du Centre 12 rue St-Laud ☎02.41.87.45.07. Occupies a lively, city-centre spot above one of the most popular bars on a pedestrianized street – double-glazing keeps out the worst of the noise. The rooms have been recently renovated throughout, with laminate flooring and pastel paintwork. ❸

Hôtel Continental 12–14 rue Louis de Romain ☎02.41.86.94.94, Ⓔle.continental@orange.fr. This well-equipped and efficiently run hotel offers good service and a bright pastel decor. The location on a quiet street just off place Ralliement is good, but note that it can get busy with businesspeople during the week. ❹

Hôtel des Lices 25 rue des Lices ☎02.41.87.44.10. The setting is very genteel, in a balustraded townhouse on an elegant town-centre street, but the large, bright and comfortable rooms are a bargain, and the welcome genuine. Closed first half of Aug. ❷

Hôtel du Mail 8 rue des Ursules ☎02.41.25.05.25, Ⓔhoteldumailangers @yahoo.fr. Old-fashioned and extremely attractive two-star set in a seventeenth-century building with a courtyard. The two dozen rooms are tastefully done in fresh, bright colours and the location in a quiet corner of the centre is excellent. Parking is available for a small extra charge. ❹

Hôtel St-Julien 9 place du Ralliement ☎02.41.88.41.62, Ⓦwww.hotelsaintjulien.com. Large hotel right in the centre of the city, offering a good spread of cheaply modernized but perfectly acceptable rooms. Some of the prettier little rooms under the roof have views over town, while a slightly higher price secures a minibar and armchair. ❹

Hostels and campsite

Centre d'Accueil du Lac de Maine 49 ave du Lac de Maine ☎02.41.22.32.10, Ⓦwww .lacdemaine.fr. Rather swish hostel-style accommodation beside a lake, complete with extensive sports facilities. It's a twenty-minute bus ride into town: take bus #6 (bus #11 7.30pm–midnight, bus #26 on Sun) either from the train station or bd Générale-de-Gaulle. Private rooms €35.10 for one person, €39.20 for two; dorms €17. You can rent canoes at the Base

Nautique in the complex. There's also a campsite here (see below).

Camping du Lac de Maine ave du Lac de Maine ☏02.41.73.05.03, ✉camping@lademaine.fr. Sandy campsite next to a lake with lots of facilities, including a pool. Located off the D111 south of the city centre, close to the hostel (see above). Closed Oct–March.

Foyer Darwin 3 rue Darwin ☏02.41.22.61.20, ⓦwww.foyerdarwin.com. Inexpensive young workers' hostel twenty minutes' walk west of La Doutre, near the Belle-Beille campus; take bus #6 or #8. Single rooms cost €13.35, doubles €21.80.

The city centre

Angers' city centre slopes gently down to the bank of the Maine, circumscribed to the south and east by a series of wide, busy boulevards which follow the line of the old city walls, demolished on Napoleon's orders in 1807. The heart of Angers is the nineteenth-century, Neoclassical **place du Ralliement**, with the two stucco-fronted, pedestrianized avenues of **rue Lenepveu** and **rue St-Laud**, just to the north, forming the city's main axes. Medieval Angers lies immediately west, where the **château** guards the main bridge across the Maine, the **Pont de la Basse-Chaine**, and the **cathédrale St-Maurice** towers above the wide river quays.

The château

The **château** (daily: May–Aug 9.30am–6.30pm; Sept–April 10am–5.30pm; €7.50) is a formidable early medieval fortress, its air of impregnability accentuated by the darkness of the western Anjou schist from which it's built, offset by pale bands of tufa. The kilometre-long curtain wall is buttressed by seventeen circular towers – once crowned by pepper-pot roofs – that grip the rock below. You can stroll round the length of these ramparts, looking down on the town, the château gardens first created under René d'Anjou (see box, below) and the waters of the Maine. In the centre of the château enclosure are a few

Anjou's last king

As claimant to the thrones of Naples, Sicily and Jerusalem, as well as ruler of the duchy of Anjou in the mid-fifteenth century, **Le Bon Roi René** (Good King René) styled himself a king rather than a duke, though he never succeeded in actually controlling any part of his royal patrimony. René twice failed to conquer Naples, but at least his claim was convincing, as it had been directly bequeathed to Louis I of Anjou, his grandfather. The nominal title of King of Jerusalem, by contrast, had simply been bought by an ancestor, Charles I of Anjou, in 1277. The only coronation René attended was that of his friend Charles VII, in 1429.

But René's court, which moved between Angers, Baugé and Saumur – as well as up the Loire and down the Rhône to Provence – was certainly regal. Chivalric ideals were celebrated in elaborate festivals and pageants in which René himself cut a splendid figure, dressed in black armour and riding a black-coated horse emblazoned with the insignia of his Order of the Crescent Moon. His motto was "burning desire", and he wrote a classic of romance literature, *Le Livre du Cœur d'amour épris*.

It was the swansong of the Middle Ages, and didn't last. René had no sons and was too poor to supply his daughter with an adequate dowry. Princesse Marguerite was eventually married off to Henry VI of England, but after years of interminable English warfare she fled back to France, where Louis XI offered her protection in exchange for Anjou and Touraine. She agreed, effectively bringing Anjou's autonomy to an end.

heavily restored remnants of the **great palace** of the counts of Anjou: the chapel was built in about 1410 by Louis II and Yolande d'Aragon, as were the adjacent royal apartments, to which René d'Anjou added a vaulted gallery in 1450. Both were bombed in World War II, but have since been reconstructed. They are now used for occasional tapestry exhibitions. Guided tours of the château (free) are in French, but you can pick up an English-language audio guide which covers some of the castle's history.

The Tapestry of the Apocalypse

Woven between 1373 and 1382 for Louis I of Anjou, the **Tapestry of the Apocalypse** was originally 140m long, of which 100m now survives. From the start, it was treated as a masterpiece, and only brought out to decorate the cathedral of Angers on major festival days. It takes as its text John's vision of the Apocalypse, as described in the Book of Revelation, re-creating the saint's vision in seventy stunningly rendered, nightmarish scenes. Be warned that air conditioning keeps the temperature inside low.

The sheer grandeur of the conception is overwhelming, but the tapestry's horrifying brilliance lies in its details: the skeletal face of the horseman Death, the minutely observed clothing of the servants of God fighting the Dragon, and the flowers, mountains and trees that form a disturbingly naturalistic backdrop. The colours – rich golds, greens and blues woven on alternating deep red and dark blue ground – are even more impressive.

Amazing as they are, the original colours were still more vivid – as you can see if you buy the handy English-language booklet (€5.50), which contains photographs of the tapestry's unfaded reverse side. Astonishingly, this is no chaotic tangle of wool ends, as would be normal for a tapestry, but a perfectly finished mirror image of the front which remained hidden and pristinely preserved behind the tapestry's back lining until it was removed for repair in 1981.

The booklet comes in handy if you plan to follow the story right through, though a Bible would be even better. In brief: the Day of Judgement is signalled by the breaking of the seven seals – note the four horsemen – and the seven angels blowing their trumpets. As the battle of Armageddon rages, Satan – first depicted as a seven-headed red dragon, then as the seven-headed **lion-like Beast** – marks his earthly followers. The holy forces retaliate by breaking the seven vials of plagues, whereupon the Whore of Babylon appears mounted on the Beast. She is challenged by the Word of God, seen riding a galloping horse, who chases the hordes of Satan into the lake of fire, allowing the establishment of the heavenly Jerusalem.

You'll need a drink after all that, and handily enough you can head straight out of the château and into the **Maison du Vin**, 5bis place du Président Kennedy (March, April & Oct–Dec Tues–Sat 9am–1pm & 3–6.30pm, May–Sept Tues–Sat 9am–1pm & 3–6.30pm, Sun 9am–1pm), where the very professional and helpful staff will offer you wine to taste before you buy, and provide lists of winegrowers to visit.

Cathédrale St-Maurice

The most dramatic approach to the **cathédrale St-Maurice** is via the quayside, from where a long flight of steps leads straight up to the mid-twelfth-century portal, which shows another version of the Apocalypse. Built in the 1150s and 1160s, the cathedral exemplifies the Plantagenet style – in fact, it's probably the earliest example in France of this influential architectural development, in which the keystones of the vault are raised above the level of the ordinary wall arches, creating a dome-like effect. The three aisle-less bays of the nave span a distance of over 16m. The lofty Plantagenet vaulting, known locally as the Angevin style, creates structural strength as well as a faintly Byzantine feel.

The earliest stained glass, in the north wall of the nave, is late twelfth or early thirteenth-century; the window depicting the Virgin and Child is especially famous for its design and rich colours. In the choir, one window is dedicated to Thomas Becket, murdered on the orders of Henry Plantagenet. The fifteenth-century rose windows in the transepts are impressive, with Christ's earthly suffering, in the north transept, facing Christ in Glory to the south – note the red and blue of his robe, inspired by the Tapestry of the Apocalypse. The stone carving on the capitals and the supports for the gallery are beautiful, but the cathedral is over zealously furnished with a grandiose high altar and pulpit and a set of tapestries that can't compete with Angers' other woven treasures.

If the river damp is getting into your bones, you could always light a candle to **St Maurice**, who is traditionally invoked against gout and cramps. His sainthood dates from his captaincy of the largely Christian Theban Legion, which was massacred in the late third century for refusing to sacrifice to the old Roman gods.

Galerie David d'Angers and Musée des Beaux-Arts

Angers' most famous son took the name of his home city as a *nom de plume*. **David d'Angers** (1788–1856) was the premier sculptor of the post-Napoleonic era, and his works seem to grace every major public building in the country, most notably the frieze of Paris's Panthéon. In Angers, his statue of St Cecilia adorns the cathedral chancel, but his best works are exhibited in the **Galerie David d'Angers** (June–Sept daily 10am–7pm; Oct–May Tues–Sun 10am–noon & 2–6pm; €4), a space dramatically created by glassing over the ruins of a thirteenth-century church, the **église Toussaint**. The sculptor was a prime activist in mid-nineteenth-century republican struggles and a close friend of many great Romantic artists and thinkers of the time, many of whom are celebrated here in busts or bronze medallions. You can also visit the adjacent **cloister,** a smoothly arcaded space.

The **Musée des Beaux-Arts**, at 10 rue du Musée (June–Sept daily 10am–7pm; Oct–May Tues–Sun 1–6pm; €4), is housed in the **Logis Barrault**, a proudly decorated mansion built by a wealthy late fifteenth-century mayor. Years of extensive restoration have cleaned up – and in some places entirely remade – the Flamboyant Gothic stone carving. Eighteenth- and nineteenth-century paintings dominate the collection, with works by Watteau, Chardin and Fragonard, as well as Ingres' operatic *Paolo et Francesca* – the same subject depicted by Rodin in *The Kiss* – and a small collection devoted to Boucher's *Génie des Arts*. You'll also find Lorenzo Lippi's beautiful *La Femme au Masque*, and a room devoted to the history of Angers.

The rest of town

The medieval **Maison d'Adam**, on place Ste-Croix, in front of the cathedral, sports some wonderful carved characters, including one bearing an alarming set of genitals. A block northeast, **rue de l'Oisellerie** is lined with carved, half-timbered houses that were once bird-shops (*oiselleries*). The hub of modern Angers, **place du Ralliement**, lies a few steps further west. Its main landmark is the nineteenth-century **Théâtre Municipal**, which still thrives today.

Angers' best shopping is to be found on **rue Lenepveu**, where the chief sight is the **Hôtel Pincé**, at no. 32. The facade of this Renaissance mansion positively crawls with Italianate decoration. It usually houses the **Musée Pincé,** whose prize exhibits are some Oriental and Greek ceramics, but the museum is closed for works – probably until 2009. Some of the exhibits are occasionally displayed on a temporary basis elsewhere; check at the tourist office if you're interested.

If the cathedral hasn't sated your appetite for Angevin vaulting, make for the **église St-Serge**, on ave Mairie-Talet, north of the centre (Mon–Sat 9am–7pm, Sun 2–6pm; free). Formerly part of an abbey – you can visit the chapter room, cloister and refectory – it is now enclosed within the university grounds. Inside the church, a superb early Gothic choir rises from the slenderest of columns. Close by is the verdant and relaxing **Jardin des Plantes** (8am–dusk; free).

La Doutre

The district facing the château from across the river is known as **La Doutre**, from the French *d'outre Maine*, which simply means "the other side of the Maine". Like Paris's Left Bank, it's the focus of the city's student life and has a relatively relaxed, downbeat feel; similarly, it preserves a few mansions and houses dating from the medieval period. The riverfront is dominated by the elite **ENSAM**, the École Nationale des Arts et Métiers, which hot-houses the cream of the region's students.

Abbaye de Ronceray and la Trinité

Facing onto La Doutre's central square, place de la Laiterie, the **Abbaye de Ronceray** was founded by Foulques Nerra in the early eleventh century, but its ancient buildings are now occupied by one of France's elite *grandes écoles*, training the leading students of aerospace technology. The abbey church hosts art exhibitions, and it's worth visiting just to see the Romanesque galleries of the old abbey.

Inside the twelfth-century **église de la Trinité**, an exquisite Renaissance wooden spiral staircase fails to mask a great piece of medieval bodging – the corner wall is bent around the adjacent abbey. The high vaulting of the nave is unusual, the ribs of the middle section meeting inside a stone ring offset by a tiny dome behind, which gives a delightful effect like a suspended spider's web. Perhaps the design was too ambitious, as a significant twist in the line of the roof has developed over the course of the centuries.

Musée Jean Lurçat et de la Tapisserie Contemporaine

In the north of the area, a short way from the Pont de la Haute-Chaine (about fifteen minutes' walk from the château), the **Hôpital St-Jean**, at 4 boulevard Arago, was built by Henry Plantagenet in 1174 as a hospital for the poor, a function it continued to fulfil until 1854. With its airy Angevin vault springing energetically from two perfect rows of columns, it makes a dramatic setting for the **Musée Jean Lurçat et de la Tapisserie Contemporaine** (June–Sept daily 10am–7pm; Oct–May Tues–Sun 10am–noon & 2–6pm; €4), which contains the city's astonishing twentieth-century tapestry, **Le Chant du Monde**. The tapestry sequence was designed by Jean Lurçat in 1957 in response to Angers' Tapestry of the Apocalypse; his own commentary is available in English. It hangs in a vast vaulted space, the original ward for the sick, or Salle des Malades. The first four tapestries deal with "La Grande Menace", the threat of nuclear war: first the bomb itself; then "Hiroshima Man", flayed and burnt, with the broken symbols of various world religions seemingly falling away from him; then the collective massacre of the "Great Charnel House"; and finally the last dying rose falling with the post-Holocaust ash through black space – the "End of Everything". From then on, the tapestries celebrate the joys of life: "Man in Glory in

Peace", "Water and Fire", "Champagne" ("that blissful ejaculation", according to Lurçat); "Conquest of Space", "Poetry" and "Sacred Ornaments". Modern tapestry is an unfamiliar art, and at first Lurçat's use of stark, bright colours on a heavy black ground can be overwhelming – or, to some, uncomfortably reminiscent of a heavy metal T-shirt. The Romanesque **cloisters** at the back are worth a peek.

There are more modern tapestries in the adjoining building, where a significant collection has been built up around the donation by Lurçat's widow of several of his paintings, ceramics and tapestries. Among the most interesting works are the abstract, almost three-dimensional tapestries of Thomas Gleb, who died in Angers in 1991. Gleb's experimentation with depth is developed by Josep Grau Garriga, whose huge, rough collages, bulging all over with rope-ends, matted straw and old sacks, are exhibited in the next room.

If you want to explore Angers' contemporary tapestry micro-industry further, call in at the neighbouring **tapestry workshops** at 3 boulevard Daviers (Mon–Fri 10am–noon & 2–4pm), which groups together a number of artists. Even if there isn't someone on hand who's willing to show you around, you should be able to at least track down information on private exhibitions.

The suburbs

The château de Pignerolle, in the satellite village of **ST-BARTHELÉMY D'ANJOU**, 4km east of Angers (signposted off the N147), is home to the **Espace Européen de la Communication** (Feb, March, Nov & Dec Sat 2.30–6pm, Sun 10am–12.30pm & 2.30–6pm; April–Oct daily 10am–12.30pm & 2.30–6pm; €5.50, children aged 12–18 €2.50; ⓦwww.musee-communication .com), a typically histrionic French science and technology museum. It's quite good fun, with everything from Leonardo's helicopter drawings to German submarines brought into play, and fantastical scenes of the future, but don't expect to come out much the wiser.

For something completely different, you could go on a guided tour around the **Distillerie Cointreau**, just off the ring road between Angers and St-Barthelemy d'Anjou, where the famous orange liqueur has been distilled since the mid-nineteenth century (tours May, June, Sept & Oct daily 10.30am & 3pm, Sun also 4.30pm; July & Aug daily 10.30am, 2.30pm, 3pm & 4.30pm; Nov–April Mon–Sat 3pm, Sun 3pm & 4.30pm; call ⓣ02.41.31.50.50 for times of tours in English; €5.50; take bus #7 from boulevard Maréchal Foch to the stop "Cointreau"). You'll learn a lot about the Cointreau brothers and how marvellous the drink is, a little bit about distilling techniques and very little about the recipe – which isn't quite as secret as Cointreau likes to make out, if the number of rival brands of *triple sec* is anything to go by. You also get to see rows of gleaming copper stills – and to taste a sip of a cocktail at the end of the tour.

The **Musée de l'Ardoise** (July to mid-Sept Tues–Sun 2–6pm; mid-Sept to Nov & mid-Feb to June Sun 2–6pm; demonstrations at 3pm; €5.50) is rather lost in the industrial satellite village of **TRÉLAZÉ**, 2km southeast of the centre. It's not a museum as such, rather a demonstration of traditional slate-mining techniques by former miners, on the site of an open-cast mine which still produces some of the finest-quality slate in the world. It helps if you understand a little French, but just watching a sexagenarian split a giant block of stone into millimetre-perfect, size-graded slates using a big wooden hammer and a pair of outsize clogs is fairly astounding, even if you don't get the commentary. If your French is up to it, you could even arrange to visit the mine proper: call ⓣ02.41.96.70.70.

Eating

Angers' lively atmosphere spills over into its **restaurant** scene, which is varied and forward-looking. You can find traditional dishes cooked in Anjou wines and using local Angevin produce, of course, but you're by no means restricted to them.

Le 14 14 rue Bodinier ☏02.41.20.15.20. The bright red shop front of this hugely popular restaurant is striking enough, but it's no preparation for the eccentricity of the inside, capped off by a rusty bicycle hanging from the ceiling. Beneath the bike, the stone-walled dining room is crammed with chattering diners tucking into the speciality bruschetta (€9–13). Closed Sun, Mon & first two weeks of July.

La Cantina 9 rue de l'Oisellerie ☏02.41.87.36.34. Relaxed café-bistro serving rich dishes from south-western France such as *magret de canard* (duck steak). It's good for a hearty meal, with straightforward fish and meat *plats* and salads from around €10. Closed Mon.

Les Caves du Ralliement 9 place du Ralliement ☏02.41.88.47.77. Busy brasserie beneath the Provence Caffè (see opposite). Good for inexpensive *moules* or *steak frites* with a beer – the *plats du jour* are under €10 – or perhaps a seafood platter with a glass of Muscadet. Best on sunny days, when you can sit at an outside table enjoying the view of the imposing theatre across the square. Closed Sun.

Le Grandgousier 7 rue St-Laud ☏02.41.87.81.47. Specializes in meat grilled on a wood fire. A good-value €15 menu is served before 9.30pm (Mon–Fri only), and there's also an enticing €24 menu in the evening. Both include selected Anjou wines to accompany each dish. Closed Sun.

Papagayo 44 bd Ayrault ☏02.41.87.03.35. Friendly bar-bistro near the university campus, with a great atmosphere in term-time and a kitsch little conservatory room for summer. Serves decent brasserie food, with a good lunchtime menu at €10 and *plats* for around €13 in the evening. Closed Mon lunch, Sat lunch & Sun.

Provence Caffè 9 place du Ralliement ☏02.41.87.44.15. Classic French food with an emphasis on fish and rich, Mediterranean flavours. The rather solemn service is offset by a cheerily Provençal colour scheme. Evening menus from €26. Closed Mon, Sun & three weeks in Aug.

Le Soufflerie 8 place du Pilori ☏02.41.87.45.32. Popular café specializing in soufflés, both large and savoury (at around €11) and small and sweet (around €8). The location on the corner of a bustling crossroads is prime for people-watching. Closed Sun, Mon & four weeks in July/Aug.

Villa Toussaint 43 rue Toussaint ☏02.41.88.15.64. Fashionable, ultra-contemporary bar-restaurant serving high quality seafood (platters from €14), with sushi featuring on certain menus. The leafy terrace is a lovely spot in summer. Closed Sun.

Drinking and nightlife

In the daytime, you can sample Anjou wines in the Maison du Vin de l'Anjou (see p.278). For evening drinking, make for the lively, late night **bars** around rue St-Laud: *Bar du Centre*, below *Hôtel du Centre*, is usually full of young Angevins, and there's a cluster of popular Irish-type places at the bottom end of the road, around place Romain. Just beyond the square, at 23 rue du Mail, *Safari* (closed Mon) is a trendy bar with a twenty-something clientele and DJs playing anything from salsa to hip-hop most nights of the week from around 9pm. Over in **La Doutre**, *La Descente de la Marine*, at 28 quai des Carmes, a popular old-time bar with a strong nautical flavour, that attracts students and locals of all ages for an outdoor early evening *apéro* on the quay.

Among the full-on **clubs**, *Le Boléro*, 38 rue St-Laud, is popular and central, with an unpretentious, sometimes cheesy music policy, while *Le Mid'Star*, 25 quai Félix Faure, is the biggest and best-known venue. *Chabada*, 56 bd du Doyenné, in the Monplaisir quarter just north of St-Serge (take a taxi) puts on live music; to find out about concerts, go to the FNAC music store on rue Lenepveu or check online at ⓦ www.lechabada.com.

Festivals

At the end of May, the **Tour de Scènes** festival (Ⓦ www.tourdescenes.com) brings rock and world music acts to the squares and quais of the city centre for four days of free concerts. On Tuesday and Thursday evenings throughout July and August, the **Festival Angers l'Eté** features excellent jazz and world music gigs in the atmospheric Cloître Toussaint, the cloisters behind the Galerie David d'Angers; you can book tickets in advance at the tourist office of the FNAC store on rue Lenapveu; most cost €9 but a handful are free. In early September, the festival **Les Accroche Cœurs** brings a host of theatrical companies, musicians and street-performers for three days of surreal entertainment. More theatre is laid on from mid-June to early July in the **Festival d'Anjou,** when open-air productions are staged in châteaux and other dramatic locations throughout the region; details can be found at Ⓦ www.festivaldanjou.com.

Listings

Bike rental A desk in the tourist office rents bikes and mountain bikes for €14 a day. Otherwise, Anjou Bike Center, in the nearby riverside hamlet of Blaison-Gohier (☎ 02.41.57.10.52, Ⓦ www .anjou-bike-center.com), offers self-guided cycling holidays, as well as ordinary bike rental; the village itself is a fair distance from Angers, but the company can deliver bikes to any hotel.

Boats Numerous companies rent out canoes and run guided kayak trips on the five rivers in the vicinity of Angers. Try: Canoe Kayak Club d'Angers, 75 av du lac de Maine (on the Maine and Lac de Maine; ☎ 02.41.72.07.04, Ⓦ ckcac .free.fr); Club Nautique d'Écouflant, rue de l'île St-Aubin, Écouflant (Sarthe, Mayenne, Loir, Maine; ☎ 02.41.34.56.38, Ⓦ www.kayakecouflant.com); and Club de Canoe Kayak les Ponts de Cé, 30 rue Maximin Gelineau, Les Ponts de Cé (on the Loire; ☎ 02.41.44.65.15, Ⓦ www.canoelespontsdece .new.fr). The tourist office has details of more sedate trips on sightseeing boats.

Car rental Budget 14 rue Denis Papin ☎ 02.41.24.96.18; Anjou Auto Location, 100 av Victor Chatenay ☎ 02.41.18.59.18; Europcar, 10 rue Fulton ☎ 02.41.24.05.89; Hertz, place de la Gare ☎ 02.41.88.15.16.

Cinemas Les 400 Coups, 12 rue Claveau ☎ 02.41.42.87.39, usually shows foreign films

in their original language (version originale, or "v.o."). For the latest blockbusters try the Gaumont Multiplexe, 1 av des Droits de l'Homme ☎ 08.92.69.66.96, though films are generally dubbed into French.

Email and Internet You can get online at 48 rue Plantagenet, near Les Halles (Mon–Sat 9am–7pm; €4 per hour); 37 rue Bressigny, near bd Foch (same times and prices); 25 rue de la Roë, just east of place de la République (Mon–Sat 9am–10pm, Sun 2–8pm).

Emergencies Ambulance ☎ 15; Centre Hospitalier, 4 rue Larrey ☎ 02.41.35.36.37.

Laundries 9 place Hérault; 1 rue Bodinier; 10 place des Justices; 118 rue de Létanduère.

Market A number of markets are held throughout the city from Tuesday to Saturday, including a flower market on place Leclerc on Saturday – Anjou is a major flower-growing region – and an organic produce market on rue St-Laud on Saturday.

Pharmacies For details of late-night pharmacies, phone the police on ☎ 02.41.57.52.00.

Police Commissariat, 15 rue Dupetit-Thouars ☎ 02.41.57.52.00.

Taxis Accueil Taxi Angevin ☎ 02.41.34.96.52; Allo Anjou Taxi ☎ 02.41.87.65.00.

South of Angers

There's no particular historical or geographical integrity to the area immediately south of Angers. Most of the sights included in this section lie within the parallel valleys of the **Layon** and **Aubance**, modest rivers that flow northwest towards Angers on the left bank of the Loire, watering sunny, gently undulating country thick with vines. There are a number of gentle attractions, plus the massive **château de Brissac**, but the real draw is wine. You can tour the vineyards of the sweet white wine *appellations* of Côteaux du Layon, Quarts de Chaume and Bonnezeaux; by contrast, **Savennières**, on the north bank of the Loire, is an outpost of excellence for dry white wine. Just north of here, you can take in a second sixteenth-century giant, the **château de Serrant**, and the pilgrim island of **Béhuard**, which has a sanctuary devoted to Mary.

The whole swathe of Anjou to the south of Angers is really car- or cycle-touring territory, though you can get to Brissac-Quincé in the Aubance valley by **bus** #9 from Angers, and the château at Serrant can be reached by a combination of bus and honest foot-work.

Château de Serrant

The **château de Serrant** lies 15km southwest of Angers, 2km short of **ST-GEORGES-SUR-LOIRE** (guided tour only: mid-March to June & Sept daily except Tues 9.45am–noon & 2–5.15pm; July & Aug daily 9.45am–5.15pm; Oct to mid-Nov Wed–Sun 9.45am–noon & 2–5.15pm; €9.50; Ⓦwww.chateau-serrant.net). From the outside, it's a domineering rather than a graceful structure, its walls built with a striking and typically Angevin combination of purply-brown schist edged with creamy tufa, while heavy, bell-shaped slate cupolas press down on the massive corner towers. If you don't have your own transport, you could take one of the **buses** (lines #7 and #18) from Angers to St-Georges-sur-Loire, and double back on foot to the château.

Construction was begun in 1539 but the château was added to, discreetly for the most part, up until the eighteenth century. In 1759 it was sold to an Irishman, Francis Walsh, to whom Louis XV had given the title Count of Serrant as a reward for Walsh's help against the old enemy, the English – Walsh had provided the ship for Bonnie Prince Charlie to return to Scotland for the 1745 uprising. The Walsh family married into the ancient La Trémoïlle clan, whose descendants – via a Belgian offshoot – still own the château.

The massive rooms are packed with the trappings of old wealth, but the guide's endless cataloguing of the tapestries, paintings and furniture shouldn't put you off appreciating some real gems, including a complete first edition of Diderot's *Encyclopédie*. Much of the decor dates from the late nineteenth and early twentieth centuries, but it has all been blended in tastefully. You are also shown the Renaissance staircase, the sombre private chapel designed by Hardouin Mansard, a bedroom prepared for Napoleon (who only stopped here for a couple of hours) and the vaulted kitchens.

The north bank of the Loire west of Angers

If you leave Angers via La Doutre and the north bank of the River Maine, you'll quickly pick up signs to the D111 and **BOUCHEMAINE**, an old river port just short of the mouth (*bouche*) of the Maine, some 10km from Angers. Suburban **bus** line #6 provides a regular service from Angers. There are a couple of good **restaurants**, nicely positioned down on the quayside, the most atmospheric being *Le Noë Inondable* (closed Sun), an old-fashioned Loire mariners' bar with a bright conservatory dining room added on; the food – inexpensive steaks and fish dishes – is simple but good.

Roughly a kilometre downstream, **LA POINTE** lies at the actual confluence with the Loire – from here on west, the Loire attains majestic proportions in all but the driest months. It's a good place to picnic, beside the broad quays with their stone groins projecting into the wide waterway. Alternatively, try the lovingly prepared fish dishes at *La Terrasse* restaurant, place Ruzebouc (☎02.41.77.11.96; closed Sun), which has a good weekday lunch menu (€16.50; evenings from €23) and a big view. Plain but decent **rooms** are available at the adjacent *Hôtel Ancre de Marine* (☎02.41.77.14.46; ❸). **Canoes** and **kayaks** can be hired inexpensively from the very professional Club Nautique de Bouchemaine (☎02.41.77.22.35; kayaks €5 per hour), just off the road between Bouchemaine and La Pointe; you can also book long, guided descents of the Loire.

Savennières

Seven kilometres downstream of Bouchemaine, on the north bank of the Loire, the comfortable village of **SAVENNIÈRES** is best known as an *appellation* with a huge reputation for dry whites – in fact it's regarded as one of the very few truly first-class Loire wines (see p.357). Typically, the actual area of production is tiny, with vines spread across just three hills on the fringes of the village, but the quality is exceptional. An excellent place to taste and buy is at the **Domaine du Closel**, Château des Vaults, 1 place du Mail (Mon–Sat 9am–6pm; free; ⓦwww.savennieres-closel.com), where *madame* is a true enthusiast who speaks English and runs her estate on organic principles. Other *vignerons* can easily be found both in and around the village – just follow the signs. It's also worth a look at the extremely ancient **église St–Pierre**, right in the centre. The oldest parts – best seen in the fishbone patterning of the brick on the west front – date from as far back as the tenth century. The south portal probably received its geometric patterns some hundred years later, while the Romanesque apse is a relative latecomer, dating from the twelfth century.

If money is no object, head roughly 2km east of town towards Epiré and turn off at signs to the elite vineyard of **Coulée de Serrant** (Mon–Sat 9am–noon & 2–6pm; free; ⓦwww.coulee-de-serrant.com), where the Chenin Blanc vines flourish in an unusually steep, well-protected and sunny micro-valley. Sadly, the tiny size of the *appellation*, and the fact that it's all under one proprietor, means that you can't taste unless you promise to buy. If you do, expect to pay a minimum of around €40 per bottle for the most recent vintage, and many times that for older wines.

Béhuard

The D106 south of Savennières takes you underneath the TGV line, across the first of a pair of Loire bridges and straight onto **BÉHUARD**, a peaceful, verdant, mid-stream island with a tiny village hidden away among its poplar trees. The secretive feel is emphasized by the ban on motor traffic in the village – you have to park your car and walk a few metres. At the centre of things is the pilgrim church of **Notre–Dame** (daily 9am–6.30pm), perched on a rock to avoid the frequent floods. It's a lovably eccentric structure, built in the 1470s on the orders of Louis XI, the nephew of René d'Anjou (see box on p.277). Loire mariners have come here for centuries to pray to the Virgin for protection, and her principal statue now occupies a niche halfway up the north wall of the sanctuary, covered by an embroidered mantle. The beautifully carved misericords inside date back to Louis XI's time.

Nearby, an open-air pilgrim church occupies a large field – signalled by a giant figure of Christ on the cross, neatly framed by two Lombardy poplars. There are plentiful opportunities for **walking** by the river (bathing is dangerous and illegal) and on paths between gardens and orchards. For a real treat, book in at the superb – and Michelin-starred – **restaurant**, *Les Tonnelles* (☎02.41.72.21.50;

closed Sun evening & Mon), which has a beautifully restrained, contemporary dining room and a lovely outside terrace under vines. The menu is highly seasonal, but expect a lot of perfectly sauced fish and shellfish dishes; the €24 lunch menu is fantastic value, or you can spend anything up to around €80 for an evening meal with wine.

The Layon valley

Heading south from the bridge over the Loire at Béhuard, after 3km you come to a small town called **ROCHEFORT-SUR-LOIRE** – it actually lies on a parallel branch of the river known as the **Louet**. There's little to see other than the very ruined **château de St-Offrange**, though a lively market takes place on Wednesday mornings, and you can **swim** and hire **canoes** and **pedalos** from a pleasant sandy "beach" on the north bank of the Louet, right next to the bridge. West of Rochefort, the D751 climbs steeply to the top of the **Corniche Angevine**, a surprisingly steep bluff that rears up alongside the banks of the Louet for some 9km. There's a fine view from the road: the southern slopes are lined with vines, while to the north green meadows stretch to the Loire's main channel.

At **LA HAIE LONGUE**, 3km west, you can turn down off the Corniche into the vine-covered **Layon valley**, one of the region's warmest and most enticing corners, dotted with curious *moulins à cavier* – hut-like windmills built on conical-shaped stone platforms. The valley has an unusually sunny microclimate, a factor that the local *vignerons* rely on to create their famous **Côteaux du Layon** wines (see Contexts, p.358), which need hefty doses of summer sunshine as well as autumnal "noble rot" to produce their honeyed flavour. You can stop off at lots of small, attractive villages, and wine-growers advertise tastings on roadside hoardings everywhere.

St-Aubin-de-Luigné and Chaume

The handsome, schist-built manor houses of **ST-AUBIN-DE-LUIGNÉ**, 3km southeast of La Haie Longue, are gathered in a relatively steep fold of the hills, making for a very picturesque scene. The best view is from the **Moulin Guérin**, a former windmill turned viewing tower rising up from the vine-covered hills overlooking the village. In summer, old-fashioned wooden **rowboats** can be rented inexpensively for dabbling in the waters of the Layon (May to mid-June Sun 2–7pm; mid-June to mid-Sept daily 2–7pm; ☎02.41.78.52.98). For a **restaurant** meal, try *Le Clézio*, 9 place de l'Eglise (☎02.41.78.33.15; closed Sun evening, Mon, & Tues evening), which serves good, simple Angevin cuisine. Wine-growers can be found all over the village, but committed wine buyers should also make for the elite **Quarts de Chaume** *appellation*, which covers a minuscule area between St-Aubin and Beaulieu-sur-Layon, with just half a dozen wine-growers. Even in a less well-regarded year, a bottle of this stuff will cost upwards of €20, about double the price of an "ordinary" Côteaux du Layon.

Beaulieu-sur-Layon to Thouarcé

At **BEAULIEU-SUR-LAYON**, 25km due south of Angers, the **église Notre-Dame de l'Assomption** is in fact just the choir section of a once larger twelfth-century church. It stands on rue de la Mairie, a few steps away from the newer church in the main square. It's a curious, beautiful structure; inside, the half-dome of its apse preserves a naïve but moving Christ in Majesty surrounded by the symbols of the evangelists.

Pretty **RABLAY-SUR-LAYON**, 2km southeast of Beaulieu, has reinvented itself as an art and craft village, with a sizeable population of local artisans. They exhibit at the **Village des Artistes**, place du Mail (March–June & Sept–Nov Fri–Sun 2.30–6.30pm; July & Aug Tues–Sun 10am–noon & 2.30–6.30pm; Dec daily 2–6pm; free), alongside works by French and international artists. There's a pleasant picnic spot in the centre of the village, beside the Layon.

THOUARCÉ, 9km upstream of Rablay-sur-Layon, is the largest village within the *appellation* of **Bonnezeaux**, which produces some of the best sweet wines in the world. It's only slightly larger than its *grand cru* rival, Quarts de Chaume, but there are a dozen or so producers, so you can sample freely before you buy. Thouarcé has a dedicated wine festival at the beginning of August, and two good **restaurants** make it an excellent stopping place at any time: ✹ *Le Relais de Bonnezeaux*, just off the road between Thouarcé and the village of Bonnezeaux (☎02.41.54.08.33; closed Mon, Tues evening & Sun evening), is the place to go for gastronomic food, with a lovely situation in a modernized country train station overlooking the steep, vine-combed slopes and an excellent range of menus from around €30 to €55 – the more expensive menus come with carefully selected wines. An excellent place to have a well-cooked, inexpensive lunch is the friendly, vine-covered *Auberge du Cheval Blanc*, on place du Prieuré, Thouarcé (☎02.41.54.04.40; open lunchtimes and Sat evening only).

Martigné-Briand and Aubigné-sur-Layon

The cruelly dilapidated state of the **château** (guided tours only: July & Aug Tues–Sun 10am–6pm; €2; Ⓦwww.chez.com/chateaumartigne) at **MARTIGNÉ-BRIAND**, 7km southeast of Thouarcé, is the result of its location on the borders of the Vendée, a conservative region which rose up in favour of the monarchy in the wake of the Revolution. The château was the first true Renaissance château in Anjou, but was burnt and partially dismantled by Revolutionary troops in 1793 and today presents a stark, though rather lovely face to the world. An enthusiastic local association runs guided tours. Martigné-Briand was not only a political boundary: a natural, geological frontier signals the beginning of the **Saumurois** (covered in chapter 5), as the more steeply undulating, schist-formed hills of the western Massif Armoricain, centred around Brittany, change into the gentler limestone slopes of the Paris basin. It's very easy to see the divide, as slate-roofed Angevin houses constructed in drab-coloured schist give way to the paler, limestone-built, tiled-roof homes typical of the central Loire Valley.

Just 3km from Martigné-Briand, on the southern bank of the river, honey-coloured **AUBIGNÉ-SUR-LAYON** usually makes a strenuous effort in the national "village in bloom" competition, with appealing results in the warmer months. Short, signposted walking circuits show off the priory, the old lime kiln, the washhouse and other modest local sights, but the main attraction is the **église St-Denis**, with its eleventh-century nave, twelfth-century choir and eighteenth-century trompe l'oeil wall-paintings in the transepts. You can sample the local Côteaux du Layon wines at the **château d'Aubigné**, which lies at the end of a short driveway that leads under the fortified gatehouse beside the church's west end; the actual château is ruined, but the wines – sweet and sparkling – are excellent.

Layon valley practicalities

The most enjoyable way to explore the Layon valley is by **bicycle**, and it's close enough to be feasible as a long day-trip from Angers; the only alternative is to drive, as public transport is sparse. There's a maximum of three **buses** a day up the Layon from Angers (lines #12, #17 and #24), though on some days there are no services at all; there are slightly more frequent buses on line #6, which connects Angers with Rochefort-sur-Loire and St-Aubin-de-Luigné.

For information on the valley, the largest and most helpful **tourist office** is in Beaulieu-sur-Layon, on the main rue St-Vincent (June–Aug Mon–Sat 10am–noon & 2–6pm, Sat & Sun 10am–1pm; Sept–May Mon–Fri 1.30–5.30pm; ☏02.41.78.65.07). They can give advice on walks in the area – ask for the free map *Promenades et Randonnées à Beaulieu-sur-Layon*. Otherwise, look online at ⓦwww.loire-layon-tourisme.com.

The best of the half-dozen **hotels** in the area is the welcoming *Grand Hôtel*, 30 rue René Gasnier, Rochefort-sur-Loire (☏02.41.78.80.46, ⓦwww.le-grand -hotel.net; ❷), a pleasantly old-fashioned place with a decent restaurant. Failing that, try *Le Castel* in Brissac-Quincé (see opposite) or the simple, family-friendly **hostel** (☏02.41.78.65.07; Mon–Fri only; €12 per person per night) run by the tourist office in Beaulieu-sur-Layon, which offers private two- to four-bed rooms during the week. Among the most attractive **chambres d'hôtes** in the region are the very peaceful *Domaine de l'Etang*, 3km from Martigné-Briand on the road to Thouarcé (☏02.41.59.92.31, ⓦwww.domaine-etang .com; ❹); the guest rooms have been converted from an old stable block at the end of the large garden, and there's a swimming pool. Another good option is *Au Logis de la Brunetière*, Faye d'Anjou (☏02.41.54.16.24; ❹), which has three welcoming rooms set in a picturesque Angevin farmhouse. Rochefort has an excellent, well-equipped **campsite**, *Saint Offrange*, route de Saven-nières (☏02.41.78.82.11; closed mid-Sept to mid-June), St-Aubin-de-Luigné a slightly more modest municipal site (☏02.41.78.33.28; closed Nov–April) and Thouarcé the pleasant *Camping de l'Ecluse*, rue des 3 Ponts (☏02.41.54.14.36; closed mid-Sept to mid-April).

The Aubance valley

The **Aubance valley** begins just northwest of Doué-la-Fontaine, in the Saumurois (see p.259), and the river flows for some 30km through delightful, bucolic countryside before joining the Loire close to Angers. The **château de Brissac** is the main draw, but if you do want to explore the area in depth, call in at the tourist offices in Angers or Brissac-Quincé and pick up a copy of the excellent map, *Carte de Randonnées Brissac–Loire–Aubance* (€4), which details twenty-odd walking tours lasting from ninety minutes to six hours. Every minor château, windmill, *cabane de vigne* (old-fashioned vine-growers' hut), church and viewpoint in the area is clearly marked.

If you've got young children in tow, the **Parc de Loisirs de l'Étang** (April, May & Oct Sat & Sun 11am–6pm; Easter fortnight & June–Aug Tues–Sun 10.30–7pm; €6.50, children under 1m tall free; ⓦwww.parc-etang.com) near St-Saturnin, 3km from Brissac-Quincé, makes an obvious destination. It's basically a giant adventure playground and farm-zoo, with a big but gentle waterslide, a rope bridge, kayaking on the lake, horse-drawn carriages and donkey rides.

Brissac-Quincé

Twenty kilometres southeast of Angers, **BRISSAC-QUINCÉ** is dominated by its tall, weighty and altogether rather exaggerated château, known as the **château de Brissac** (guided tours only: April–June, Sept & Oct daily except Tues 10.15am–12.15pm & 2–6pm; July & Aug daily 10am–6.30pm; €8.50, ⓦwww.brissac.net) after the line of dukes who have owned it since 1502. The village itself is rather sleepy, except during the Thursday morning market, but it's pleasant enough, and does very nicely out of two local wine *appellations*. Apart from the château, the chief sight in the village is the Renaissance **église St-Vincent**, named after the patron saint of wine-growers, which has a fine set of stained-glass windows.

The **château** lies just down the hill from the centre, an ugly duckling frozen halfway through its transformation into a swan. On the main west front, two round towers survive from an earlier, fifteenth-century fortress, the château's ill-proportioned seventeenth-century facade awkwardly wedged between them. Under the original rebuilding plan, the old fortified towers were to be pulled down, but the death of duc Charles II in 1621 brought the project to a standstill. In the latter half of the nineteenth century, the astute marriage of the eleventh duke to Jeanne Say, from the giant sugar company now known as Beguin-Say, provided the funds for numerous improvements, notably laying out the grounds as an English park. The twelfth duke did just as well with May Schneider, the heiress of the great French steel dynasty. The marquis de Brissac, son of the thirteenth duke, married a ballerina, and now lives on site, managing the château's thriving tourist business and its **vineyard**, which has been since 1515. You can buy a separate wine-tasting ticket (€3.50), which also allows you to stroll around the large park, along the forest path, round the *étang* and down beside the banks of the Aubance.

The guided tour is the only way to see the **interior**. Thankfully, rather than visit all 303 rooms you are only shown the most impressive, many of which have sumptuous ceilings. You're taken round the dining room, with its painted "marble" musician's gallery, up the superb Louis XIII staircase to the seventeenth-century bedchambers, then along the Grand Gallery and "hunting chambers", with their sixteenth-century tapestries, and into the Gothic chapel and the enormous private opera house up on the second floor – one of Jeanne Say's little modifications. On the way round, the guide points out the most fabulously expensive of the endless cabinets, wardrobes and bits of china, as well as portraits ranging from seventeenth-century oils to present-day photos.

Practicalities

The **tourist office**, 8 place de la République (May–Sept Mon–Sat 10am–12.30pm & 2–6pm, Sun 10am–1pm; Oct–April Mon–Fri 2–5pm, Thurs also 2–5pm, Sat 9.30am–12.30pm; ☎02.41.91.21.50, ⓦwww.ot-brissac-loire-aubance.fr), can provide detailed information on touring the Aubance valley.

If you want to **stay**, the only hotel in Brissac-Quincé is *Le Castel*, 1 rue Louis-Moron (☎02.41.91.24.74, ⓦwww.hotel-lecastel.com; ❸), beside the bridge over the Aubance. It's modern in style, but spick and span, with comfortable beds. The most luxurious option is to stay at the ⚜ château itself, which offers some of the most amazing – and expensive – **chambres d'hôtes** (☎02.41.91.22.21, ⓦwww.brissac.net; ❾) you'll find anywhere: for around €400 you can stay in a real seventeenth-century room, as shown to visitors, with genuine period furnishings – the Louis XIII room even has a bathroom on the far side of a secret door. Just down the road in St-Melaine-sur-Aubance, 4km northwest, the ⚜ *Logis de l'Appartenance* (☎02.41.45.27.44, ⓦappartenance.canalblog.com; ❹) offers some very attractive chambres d'hôtes, set in a modernized sixteenth-century farmhouse with a small tower and a swimming pool. Three kilometres southwest of Brissac in Vauchrétien, meanwhile, the *Moulin de Clabeau* (☎02.41.91.22.09, ⓦwww.gite-brissac.com; ❹) has three pretty, spacious bedrooms in an old watermill on the Aubance, with a wonderful beamed living room.

If you're looking for a **restaurant** meal, try *Le Haut Tertre*, 1 place du Tertre (☎02.41.91.79.95; closed Sun evening), a contemporary bistro-style place in an old setting, with a reasonably priced menu of grilled meats, salads and fish dishes. Alternatively, the *Pizzeria du Château*, 8 place du Tertre (☎02.41.54.27.28) does excellent pasta dishes and salads as well as pizza, and has a terrace with a great view of the château.

Between the Aubance and the Loire

North of the Aubance lies a delightful swathe of undulating farmland speckled with orchards and patches of woodland. Much of this is limestone territory, and very similar in ambience to the neighbouring Saumurois (covered in chapter 5). **Dolmens**, ruined windmills and private châteaux – some sporadically open to visitors in the summer months – dot the landscape, but oddly enough the two most captivating sights are both underground – literally, under the ground – **contemporary art** sites. The south bank of the Loire is particularly attractive hereabouts, and you can cycle this stretch on the **Loire à Vélo** route (see p.42); the route crosses over to the north bank at **St-Rémy-la-Varenne**, where there's a medieval priory. West of here, and downstream of Blaison-Gohier – a village heavily colonized by wealthy citizens of Angers – the landscape changes to the harder-edged profile of Anjou schist and slate.

Around St-Georges-des-Sept-Voies

Just outside **ST-GEORGES-DES-SEPT-VOIES**, 11km east of Brissac-Quincé, is the bizarre **Hélice Terrestre de l'Orbière** (daily: May–Sept 11am–7pm; Oct–April 2–6pm; €4). It's not all that easy to find, but the roadsigns will get you there eventually. Until his death in 1996, artist Jacques Wasminski gouged out a series of curling, interweaving tunnels in the soft tufa, sculpting their inner surfaces with elaborate, swirling geometric patterns that recall Mayan stonework and the creepy biomorphic passageways of the film *Alien*. Children, in particular, love exploring this mind-expanding, whole-body artwork, especially the spherical chamber which echoes any sound you make with bell-like resonance.

Lost in the countryside just 2km north of St-Georges is one of the best-preserved ancient burial sites in France, the **Dolmen de la Bajoulière**. It's even harder to find than L'Orbière: a sign on the D128 roughly 1km east of St-Georges takes you to the farms of La Lussière and La Roche; continue north from the latter for a hundred metres or so to the hamlet of La Fontaine, where a signposted lane leads through to a track, at the end of which is the dolmen and a cluster of picnic benches. You can't miss it when you get close: it measures all of seven by seven metres, and has a perfect stone cap. It's thought to date from around 2500 BC.

Around Coutures

There's another, more modest dolmen 3km west of St-Georges, on the edge of the village of **COUTURES**. The main draw here, however, is the **Manoir de la Caillère** (May–Oct Tues–Sun 10am–7pm; Nov–April Sat & Sun 10am–7pm), where artist Richard Rak exhibits and sells his work in a set of tufa caves located just outside Coutures proper, close to the privately owned château de Montsabert. There's a philosophical bent and more than a touch of Surrealism in Rak's mostly collage-style works, which use found objects, terracotta pieces, bits of paper and feathers, as well as traditional paint. Many make fascinating use of the cave space – don't miss *La Promenade des Anglais*, a curious penguin-like sculpture. M Rak lives right next door in a troglodyte house, so if the gate is open – as it usually is when he's at home – then the gallery is too. There's no entry fee, but a donation of €3 would be welcomed; if you want to buy, the cost can run into thousands.

Right beside the château is one of the best-equipped **campsites** in the region, the *Camping Parc de Monsabert* (☎02.41.57.91.63, ⓦwww.parcdemontsabert .com; closed mid-Sept to April). It has plentiful sports facilities, including indoor and outdoor pools, and you can **rent bikes**.

The south bank of the Loire

Six kilometres north of Coutures, just short of the bridge across the Loire leading to St-Mathurin, the small, sleepy village of **ST-RÉMY-LA-VARENNE** conceals the half-ruined and half-restored **Prieuré de St-Rémy** (June & Sept Sat & Sun 10am–noon & 3–6pm; July & Aug Mon–Fri 3–7pm, Sat & Sun 10am–noon & 3–6pm; €2.50). The modest priory complex is hidden away behind high walls, and what you actually see on the visit rather depends on how the works are progressing – at the time of writing they looked set to continue at least into 2008. The chief points of interest are the *logis*, with its painted Renaissance chimney, the twelfth-century chapterhouse, with its Romanesque frescoes, and the largely fourteenth-century church.

A three-kilometre signposted **nature trail** takes you through the "Grande Ile" – the wildlife-rich meadows between the village and the river. You could also try to find your way up to the Dolmen de la Bajoulière (see opposite). It's a pleasant five-kilometre **walk** but you'll have to find your own way: take the road heading south from the east end of the village, past the Lavoir de Rochereau; continue up to the crossroads at Marigné and walk through the village along the slightly larger road leading to the hamlet of La Fontaine; a lane leads from here to the dolmen. A third way to get out into the countryside may help enthuse reluctant children: at Gog'âne, a farm at Boissay, 1km east of St-Rémy (☎02.41.45.21.25 or 06.82.15.02.26, ⓔgog-ane@terre-net.fr), you can hire **donkeys** to carry a picnic or a small child aged under ten years or so. Mme Brilhaut will provide you with as many donkeys as you need, plus a route map and a suggested picnic spot; hire of one donkey costs €25 for half a day.

The impressive seventeenth- and eighteenth-century **Abbaye de St-Maur**, on the riverbank 3km east of St-Rémy, has recently been taken over as a holiday centre for groups, and isn't open to visitors. It can't even be seen easily from the south side of the river – but if you get the chance to look across from the north bank, it's well worth doing so.

For a special lunch stop or sunset drink, head 6km east to **LE THOUREIL**, where 🍴 *Au Cabernet d'Anjou*, on place de l'Eglise (Sept–June open Thurs–Sun noon–2.30pm only), is an authentic 300-year-old mariners' bar complete with in-house *tabac* and a wonderful sunny terrace overlooking the river. The restaurant isn't terribly attractive – it's a modern extension – but the hearty, inexpensive steaks, omelettes and salads are just the thing for a simple meal at an outside table. Better still, come at sunset, sit back with an inexpensive glass of sparkling Saumur and watch the terns darting about over one of the loveliest stretches of the Loire.

North of Angers

Immediately **north of Angers**, the rivers Sarthe, Mayenne and Loir converge in a boggy mess of water and pastureland. It's not a particularly enticing area

– unless you head further upstream into the peaceful, green valleys of the Loir and Sarthe (see chapter 7) – but the châteaux of **Le Plessis-Bourré** and **Le Plessis-Macé** make for interesting excursions from Angers, or a good diversion if you're approaching from the north. You'll need your own transport to get to both. The wooded plateau of northeastern Anjou is even shorter on highlights, though the ancient market town of **Baugé** is a good stopping place for its château and relic of the True Cross, and **bus** connections to Le Mans, Saumur and Angers make it a feasible destination if you're using public transport. West of the Mayenne, in the agricultural northwest of Anjou, you'll find little of note except the peaceful, green countryside, though you can walk or take a cruise along the river itself.

Château du Plessis-Macé

The graceful, low-slung buildings of **Le Plessis-Macé**, just off the main north-bound N162, 14km out of Angers (guided tours only: April–June & Sept to mid-Nov daily except Tues 1.30–5.30pm; July & Aug daily 10.30am–6.30pm; €5.50, ⓦ www.chateau-plessis-mace.fr), are scarcely grand enough to be called a château. In fact they were originally only the *communs*, or outbuildings, of the larger fortress which now lies next to them in flinty ruins. This early fortress was built in the twelfth century by one du Plessis to protect the Angevin capital from the belligerent Bretons, to the west, and the acquisitive counts of Blois, to the east. The elaborate, pale-coloured tufa stonework that still projects above the dark schist walls is mid-fifteenth-century work, dating from the same era as the similarly elaborate windows, doors and gables of the habitable part of the château. It's this later part of the château – built by Louis de Beaumont, a chamberlain of Charles VII and a cousin of the original Plessis family – that is visited today.

The obligatory **guided tour** is in French, but there's an English-language leaflet that helps with translation, and if the guides aren't too busy you may get your own tour in English. The main doorway leads under a heavily corniced **balcony** – from an architectural point of view, the highlight of the château. It was originally a kind of bridge between kitchen and *logis*, and the carved tufa has been exceptionally well preserved by the overhanging roof. Much of the **interior** was remodelled in the mid-nineteenth century by the Walsh family of Serrant (see p.284), who bought the château from an uncle of the great Angevin poet Joachim du Bellay (see p.342) in the 1680s. The decor may not be original, therefore, but there's lots of fine furniture, ranging from Louis XIII chairs to Charles X cabinets and eighteenth-century tapestries. The **chapel**, at the end of the tour, is dominated by an elaborately carved fifteenth-century tribune.

Château du Plessis-Bourré

Confusingly, the château at **Le Plessis-Bourré**, 17km north of Angers between the Sarthe and Mayenne rivers (guided tours in French and English only: mid-Feb to end March, Oct & Nov daily except Wed 2–6pm; April–June & Sept Mon, Tues & Fri–Sun 10am–noon & 2–6pm, Thurs 2–6pm; July & Aug daily 10am–6pm; closed Jan & Dec; €9, ⓦ www.plessis-bourre.com), has nothing to do with the du Plessis who built the nearby château du Plessis-Macé. The name derives instead from the old French word for a palisade, or fortress, allied with the surname of Jean Bourré, the powerful fifteenth-century treasurer of France who built it. It took just five years to built, and was completed in 1473, but Bourré's haste is explainable less by defensive urgency than by his own mania for building – he was also responsible for the great château at Langeais, among

△ Château du Plessis-Bourré

many others. The château may look as if it still expects an attack across its vast moat, spanned by an arched bridge with a still-functioning drawbridge, but the large, decorated windows herald a new, more luxurious era. This château was built to receive important visitors, among them Louis XI and Charles VIII, and it is suitably flamboyant.

The first three rooms on the ground floor are a surprise, beautifully decorated and furnished in the Louis XVI, XV and Régence styles respectively, but things revert to type in the huge Gothic Salle du Parlement, with its earthenware-tiled floor and massive sculpted fireplace. The highlight of the tour comes in the Salle des Gardes, just above, where the original, deeply coffered ceiling stems from Bourré's fashionable interest in alchemy. Every inch is painted with **allegorical scenes**: sixteen panels depict alchemical symbols such as the phoenix, the pregnant siren and the donkey singing Mass, while eight cartoon-like paintings come with morals attached – look out for "Chicheface", the hungry wolf that only eats faithful woman; its victim is supposed to be Jean Bourré's wife. You leave via the 36-metre-long library, with its collection of fans, and the serene chapelle Ste-Anne.

Baugé and around

The largely flat and heavily wooded northeastern corner of Anjou has its modest capital in **BAUGÉ**, 36km east of Angers. Unless you arrive on a market day (Monday afternoon and Saturday morning), the town may not look all that inviting at first glance, with its Neoclassical court building, contemporary town hall and fifteenth-century château glaring at each other across the gravel expanse of the place de l'Europe as if engaged in a Mexican standoff. But explore a little further and you'll discover the remnants of a rather lovely fifteenth-century town, especially along rue de la Girouardière and rue Basse, and around the ancient **place du Marché**, where you'll find a number of venerable houses.

Every summer, in late July and early August, the Manoir des Capucins, 500m outside Baugé on the road to Le Lude, hosts an **opera festival** in a specially constructed theatre in the grounds. With its post-performance dinners, it's rather like a relaxed version of England's genteel Glyndebourne opera – and turns out to be run by English enthusiasts. Tickets and information can be had at ⓦ www.operadebauge.org.

The château and Hôtel Dieu

The opportunities for hunting in the local forests weren't lost on the dukes of Anjou, who took one of the eleventh-century keeps of Foulque Nerra, the warlike count of Anjou, and turned it into a relatively luxurious château. The single wing on place de l'Europe is all that remains of the **château de Baugé** (daily: mid-March to mid-April & mid-Sept to end Oct 1.30–5.30pm; mid-April to mid-Sept 10am–12.30pm & 1.30–5.30pm; ⓦ www.chateau-bauge .com; €7, or €9 with entry to the *apothicairerie*), the dreamy chivalric castle built by René d'Anjou (see box on p.277) as a kind of country pleasure-palace in the 1450s. The exterior preserves a glimmer of former grandeur, its biscuit-coloured stone offset by the pale tufa of the cross-shaped windows, and its main staircase tower ennobled by a carved Gothic portal. Sadly, there's little left of the interior other than the palm-tree vault at the top of the newel of the great staircase, and the original beamed ceilings.

As if to compensate, the insides have been transformed into an audio-visual experience dedicated to the life of "Good King René" – the walls are lit up with chivalric projections and video reconstructions of the battle of Vieil-Baugé (see opposite), while dramatic music plays. The film is available in English; unfortunately, if you're outnumbered by French visitors it's unlikely you'll get to see this version. Your ticket also gives access to a fairly dry museum of local art and history.

The more expensive entrance ticket books you a place on one of the hourly tours (usually in French, but you are given an English-language leaflet) of the **Hôtel Dieu**, which stands 100m north of the château. Established in 1639, this huge charitable hospital was mostly complete by the end of the seventeenth century, and remained in active use until 1998. Progressive modernizations mean there's little left of the interior of the **grande salle des malades**, but the sheer size of this seventeenth-century open ward is remarkable, and you can progress through to the double-height hospital chapel – which also served another, larger ward originally on the floor above. Most impressive is the **apothicairerie**, which has been preserved completely intact since 1675, along with all 600 of its beautiful jars of unguents, spices and medicinal potions. Many are still full, including those containing such wonderful medicines as sheep's blood and worm oil – there's even a mummified human finger.

Hospice de la Girouardière

If you follow rue du Mail down from the château, crossing the nineteenth-century axis of rue Victor Hugo then bearing right along rue de la Girouardière, you'll come to the **Hospice de la Girouardière**. A religious institution founded in 1783 to look after incurables, they now look after the mentally handicapped. Ring on the doorbell (Mon & Wed–Sun 2.30–4.15pm; free) and a nun will take you through to a room off the hospice's modern chapel, where the **Vraie Croix d'Anjou** is displayed in a heavily fortified safe-cabinet. The faithful still come here in large numbers to seek spiritual inspiration from this unusually large fragment of the True Cross – one of the pieces unearthed in Jerusalem in the fourth century and brought back to France by a Crusader in the thirteenth century – but more secular-minded visitors may be more astonished by its fourteenth-century decoration, encrusted with rubies and sapphires and adorned with two heartbreaking miniature figures of Jesus on the Cross, made from solid gold. The relic has had a curious afterlife: adopted by René d'Anjou as the symbol of the region, it later became known as the Cross of Lorraine after his marriage to Isabelle of Lorraine and its two-armed shape was adopted as the symbol of the French Resistance in World War II.

Le Vieil-Baugé and Pontigné

Five villages in the **Baugeois**, the countryside around Baugé, are locally famous for their churches' tall, octagonal steeples, added in the eighteenth century to sturdy Romanesque towers and given an extraordinary quarter-turn twist – an effect that adds a certain *je ne sais quoi*. Two of the most distinctive are within walking distance of Baugé. **LE VIEIL-BAUGÉ**, 2km southwest of Baugé, was the site of an important battle that pitted the French and their Scots allies against the English in 1421; the result was the first setback for England in the wake of their great victory at Agincourt, just six years earlier. The dramatic (and accidental) lean of the church's steeple makes it look quite extraordinary, and the interior is no less interesting, with its airy early twelfth-century choir and sixteenth-century transept.

The twist on the steeple of the **église St-Denis** at **PONTIGNÉ**, 5km east up the River Couasnon, is particularly extreme, while the chapels of the transept are home to some captivating early thirteenth-century **wall-paintings**. It's easy to see why art historians have dubbed the unknown artist "the Master of the Big Feet". If you're heading out from Baugé, stop off just over halfway by the sign for the **Dolmen de la Pierre Couverte**, an ancient megalith reached by a pretty path through the woods. Two kilometres south of Pontigné lies the **Forêt Domaniale de Chandelais**, an ancient forest traced by motorable and eminently cyclable avenues.

If you've got bored kids in tow, you could take them off to **Holly Park**, 5km west of Baugé on the edge of **ÉCHEMIRÉ**. It's a miniature theme park with a kind of canoeing aqua-rollercoaster, as well as a normal rollercoaster and other funfair attractions. Opening hours outside the central summer months are complex and highly variable (July & Aug usually 10.30am–6.30pm; €9, children aged under 12 €7, children under 1m tall free), so check at the tourist office in advance or call ☎02.41.89.70.25.

Practicalities

The **tourist office** is inside the château (mid-June to mid-Sept daily 10am–12.30pm & 1.30–6.30pm; mid-Sept to mid-June Mon–Sat 11.30am–12.30pm & 1.30–6pm; ☎02.41.89.18.07, ⓦwww.tourisme-bauge.fr.st). Baugé makes a peaceful place to overnight: the best **hotel** is the *Boule d'Or*, in the centre of town at 4 rue du Cygne (☎02.41.89.82.12, ⓕ02.41.89.06.07; restaurant closed Sun evening & Mon; ❹), a comfortable, old-fashioned two-star in the Logis de France stable. Failing that you could try the *Grand Turc*, 9 ave Jeanne d'Arc (☎02.41.89.10.36; ❷), a no-frills no-star mostly used by itinerant workers, but clean and friendly enough. Both have **restaurants** catering perfectly to their clientele.

If you've got transport, you could head out to *Le Logis de Poëllier*, in Poëllier, off the D211 south of Echemiré, 7km west of Baugé (☎02.41.89.20.56, ⓦwww .logis-de-poellier.fr; ❹), an attractive *gîte* and **chambres d'hôtes** complex created in the genteel tufa buildings of a sixteenth-century farmhouse; a hearty table d'hôte is available on request. The municipal **campsite** (☎02.41.89.14.79; closed mid-Sept to mid-May) is on chemin du Pont des Fées, beside the River

Couasnon, 300m from the centre; there's a heated **swimming pool** next to it, and you can rent bikes.

Château de Montgeoffroy and around

Perfectly preserved down to its last exquisitely aristocratic decorative detail, the **château de Montgeoffroy** – just outside the village of **MAZÉ**, 22km west of Angers – is the swansong of the ancien régime (guided tour only: mid-March to mid-June & mid-Sept to mid-Nov 10am–noon & 2.30–6pm; mid-June to mid-Sept 10am–6pm; €9). The approach road sets the tone: at once imposing and tasteful, it moves through finely wrought-iron gates and up a long drive that seems to lead straight into the large, handsome windows at the centre of the main facade.

The property has been in the possession of the Contades family since 1676, but the present château was built between 1772 and 1776, on the eve of the Revolution, drawing heavily on local peasant labour and craftsmanship – a factor that may have helped save it. It was the brainchild of **Louis-Georges-Erasme de Contades**, a field marshal of France who had carried the crown for Louis XVI's coronation and was looking to spend a luxurious retirement in the country. The Revolution may have spoiled his plans, but he refused to emigrate, finally succumbing to an apoplexy in 1795 at the age of 92. The marshal's architects decided to preserve two sixteenth-century towers at the edges of the outbuildings, bearing witness to the Contades' feudal origins, but the central wing is a perfect, elegant and utterly coherent specimen of the Louis XVI style. The interior is painted entirely in subtly different shades of cool greys and blues, with warm parquet flooring throughout and light streaming through the French windows. The furniture, too, almost all dates from the early 1770s, as testified by the detailed record books kept during the building work.

The **guided tour** (usually in French, but English tours may be available on request) begins with the two main suites on the ground floor, each admirably designed for gracious living. The **salon d'hiver** (winter room) faces north and is relatively small and easily heated, while the **salon d'été** (summer room) looks south onto the sunny courtyard. The oval **dining room** is superb, draped with warm fabrics, lined with muted grey *boiseries* (wood panelling) and heated by a florid porcelain stove. The tour continues outside with the Ste-Catherine **chapel** – another sixteenth-century survival, with carved, painted bosses on the Angevin vaults and a fine stained-glass window – and the copper-pot-lined **kitchen**. The latter is particularly interesting as it had the only original tap in the château, all the rest of the water being brought by servants. Finally there are the spacious stables, notably the polygonal **tack room**, pungent with the smell of horses and leather, its walls lined with saddles, bridles and whips.

Beaufort-en-Vallée

At **BEAUFORT-EN-VALLÉE**, 6km east of Mazé, the outrageously oversized and over-sculpted **église Notre-Dame** was commissioned by Jeanne de Laval after the death of her husband, René d'Anjou, in 1480. The nave and northern transept date from this era, as well as the bell tower, which was completed in 1542; the rest is pure nineteenth-century Gothic fantasy. The stained glass from this later epoch is particularly extravagant, created by Parisian glassmaker Edouard Didron.

South of Beaufort lies the rich horticultural land of the Authion valley; at **Les Rosiers–sur–Loire** (see p.268), 11km south of Beaufort, you can cross the Loire into the heartland of the **Saumurois** (covered in chapter 5).

Travel details

Trains

Angers to: Le Mans (17 daily; 40min–1hr 20min); Saumur (14 daily; 20–30min); Savennières (3–5 daily; 10min); Tours (12 daily; 1hr–1hr 30min).

Buses

Angers to: Baugé via Beaufort-en-Vallée (3 daily; 1hr 15min–1hr 30min); Baugé via Jarzé (2–3 daily; 1hr); Bouchemaine/La Pointe (every 40min; 25min); Brissac-Quincé (5–7 daily; 30min); Doué-la-Fontaine (4–6 daily; 1hr); Rochefort-sur-Loire (4–5 daily; 40min); Saumur via Gennes (1–4 daily; 1hr 30min); St-Aubin-de-Luigné (4–5 daily; 45min); St-Georges-sur-Loire (for Serrant; 5–7 daily; 40min); Thouarcé via the Layon valley (up to 3 daily; 50min).
Baugé to: Le Mans (2 daily; 1hr 15min); Saumur (2 daily; 45min).

7

The northern approaches

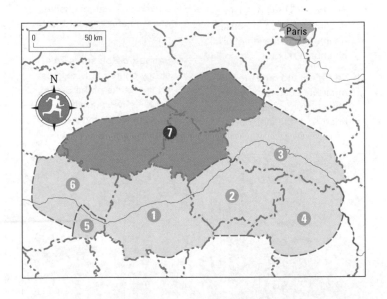

CHAPTER 7

Highlights

✳ **Chartres cathedral** The jewel of France's Gothic cathedrals is set in the plain of the Beauce, halfway to Paris but within easy striking distance of the Loire. See p.303

✳ **Châteaudun** A proud late-medieval château towers above the Loir in this sleepy provincial town. See p.307

✳ **Trôo** The tufa escarpment overlooking the Loir at Trôo is riddled with cave-houses – three of them even offer chambres d'hôtes. See p.312

✳ **Le Mans' old quarter** The medieval quarter of Vieux Mans spreads along a low ridge, with the fabulous

cathédrale St-Julien at its highest point. See p.318

✳ **Mulsanne straight** Heading south from Le Mans towards Tours, the main road follows the 24-hour racetrack for an exhilarating stretch. See p.320

✳ **Picnicking by the river** The sleepy River Sarthe is perfect for settling down on a riverbank with baguettes, cheeses and charcuterie. See p.321

✳ **Saints de Solesmes** The abbey church at Solesmes, on the banks of the Sarthe, contains two superb sixteenth-century sculpture groups. See p.323

△ Châteaudun

The northern approaches

Heading south from Normandy or the Paris region, most visitors hurtle through the quiet, deeply rural country north of the Loire on their way to the Loire Valley proper. This is, after all, a great swathe of undistinguished agricultural land, stretching from the grain-growing plains of the **Beauce**, on the eastern side, watered by the **River Loir**, to the pastures and orchards of the **Maine** to the west, drained by the **Sarthe**. Those who linger, however, will discover a quietly rewarding back-country that is best explored by imitating one of the sleepy rivers and meandering slowly south towards the Loire. As for the region's two magnificent cathedrals, in the cities of **Chartres** and **Le Mans**, they are well worth going out of your way to see.

Famously, Chartres is visible for miles around, rising up above the flat fields of the Beauce like an image from a Flemish landscape painting. South of the city, the Loir – a tributary of the Loire – passes through two attractive provincial towns: **Châteaudun**, famous for its château, and **Vendôme**, chiefly known for its canals and its Gothic church. Downstream from Vendôme, the Loir is lined with picturesque villages. Many, such as **Lavardin** and **Montoire-sur-le-Loir**, are graced by ancient churches preserving Romanesque wall-paintings. The riverbank village of **Trôo** is fascinating for its troglodyte cave-houses, while further downriver lie the poet Ronsard's manor house at **La Possonnière** and the giant Renaissance château at **Le Lude**.

Over to the west, if the famous race track of the "24 Heures" can't persuade you to stop in **Le Mans**, the city's historic quarter and magnificent cathedral might. Heading south down the River Sarthe towards Anjou, you can have your pick of pretty villages – **Asnières-sur-Vègre**, **Juigné-sur-Sarthe** and **St-Denis-d'Anjou** – or stop off at the pottery museum at **Malicorne-sur-Sarthe**. Most beguiling of all is the thriving monastery at **Solesmes**, where you can hear Gregorian chant and see the sixteenth-century sculptures known as the "saints de Solesmes".

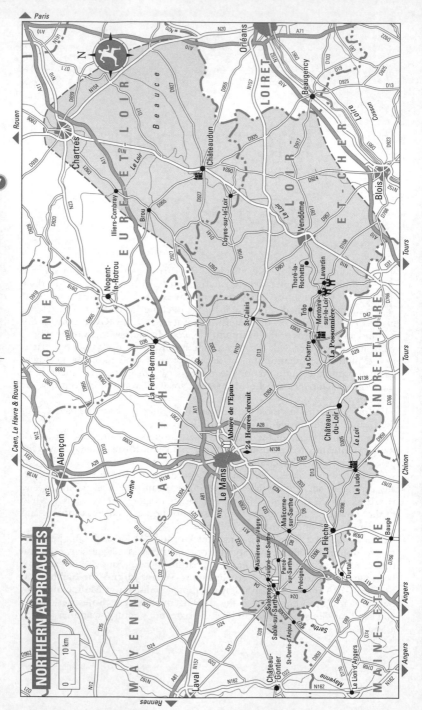

Chartres

When King Philippe-Auguste visited **Chartres** to mediate between Church and townsfolk after the riots of October 1210, the cathedral chapter noted that "he did not wish to stay any longer in the city but, so as to avoid the blasphemous citizens, stayed here only for one hour and hastened to return". Chartres' modern visitors – bussed in to see the famous cathedral and bussed straight out again – often stay little longer, which is a great pity, as the little town at the cathedral's feet has its own charm. The cathedral itself is one of the world's most astounding buildings. It is best experienced early or late in the day, when the quiet scattering of people leaves the acoustics unconfused, and – if it's sunny – the colours of the stained glass are projected into the interior.

Arrival and information

If you're travelling down to the Loire by **train**, services run from Paris's Gare du Montparnasse at least every hour on weekdays, but note that there are slightly fewer trains at weekends, especially on Sundays; the journey takes roughly one hour. From the **gare SNCF**, it's less than ten minutes' walk to the cathedral and **tourist office** (April–Sept Mon–Sat 9am–7pm, Sun 9.30am–5.30pm; Oct–March Mon–Sat 10am–6pm, Sun 10am–1pm & 2.30–4.30pm; ℡02.37.18.26.26). The latter can supply free maps and help with accommodation.

Among Chartres' handful of **hotels**, *Le Grand Monarque*, 22 place des Epars (℡02.37.18.15.15, ⓦwww.bw-grand-monarque.com; ⓻), is something of an institution, and by far the swishest in town, with well-appointed rooms decked out in luxurious fabrics. Otherwise, the tiny, old-fashioned ⚘ *Chêne Fleuri*, 14 rue de la Porte Morard (℡02.37.35.25.70; ❷), is hidden away in the nicest part of town, down by the old ramshackle houses and streets along the river Eure. The rooms are small and cheaply furnished, but full of character; it has a good restaurant, and you can eat out in the garden on sunny days. The rest of the hotels are uninspiring, but the modern two-star *Bœuf Couronné*, 15 place Châtelet (℡02.37.21.72.13, ℻02.37.21.72.13; ❸), is decent enough, and has some inexpensive rooms without bathrooms (❶). The clean, modern **youth hostel**, *Auberge de Jeunesse de Chartres*, 23 ave Neigre (℡02.37.34.27.64, ⓦwww .auberge-jeunesse-chartres.com; €11.30) sits on the opposite bank of the river, fifteen minutes' walk from the cathedral, while the **campsite**, *Camping des Bords de l'Eure*, is down beside the river at 9 rue de Launay (℡02.37.28.79.43, ⓦwww.auxbordsdeleure.com; closed mid-Nov to mid-April).

The cathedral

The **Cathédrale Notre-Dame** (daily: 8.30am–7.30pm; free) was built with prodigious speed between 1194 and 1260. As a result, it preserves a uniquely harmonious design. An earlier, Romanesque structure burnt down in 1194, but the church's holiest relic – the **Sancta Camisia**, supposed to have been the robe Mary wore when she gave birth to Jesus – was discovered three days later, miraculously unharmed. It was a sign that the Virgin wanted her church lavishly rebuilt – at least, so said the canny medieval fundraisers.

The astounding size of the cathedral is entirely due to the presence of the Sancta Camisia. In the medieval heyday of the **pilgrimage to Santiago de Compostela**, hordes of pilgrims on their way south to Spain would stop here to venerate the relic. The church accommodated them with a sizeable crypt which they could shuffle round, taking their turn to view and honour the relic, and a nave large enough to sleep in – the sloping floor evident today allowed

CHARTRES

Paris

RESTAURANTS
Café Serpente 2
L'Estocade 3
Le Pichet 1
Le St-Hilaire 4

ACCOMMODATION
Auberge de Jeunesse
de Chartres **A**
Le Bœûf Couronné **B**
Le Chêne Fleuri **D**
Le Grand Monarque **C**

PLACE
DROUAISE

BOULEVARD JEAN-JAURÈS

AVENUE BETHOUART

BOULEVARD CHARLES PEGUY

RUE MURET

RUE DE LA BRÈCHE

RUE CHANTAULT

PONT DU
MASSACRE

Eure

RUE DU MASSACRE

St-André

FONTAINE

RUE DU MOULIN A TAN

Musée des
Beaux-Arts

ST-NICHOLAS

RUE DES LISSES

Gare
SNCF

Centre
International
du Vitrail

RUE CARDINAL PIE

Jardins de
l'Evêché

RUE DE LA CORROIERIE

BOULEVARD FOCH

RUE DE LA COURONNE

NICOLE R. FELIBIEN

Cathédrale
Notre-Dame

Gare
routière

AVENUE J. DE BEAUCE

PLACE
CHATELET

ⓘ

CLOITRE NOTRE-DAME

ACACIAS S'-EMAN

RUE DE LA TANNERIE

RUE DU BOURG

PORTE GUILLAUME

BOULEVARD CLEMENCEAU

Maison Picassiette

PERCHERONNE

RUE DE
BETHLEEM

SERPENTE RUE

PLACE DE LA
POISSONERIE

RUE DES ECUYERS

Eure

BOULEVARD
DE LA RESISTANCE

RUE HARLEVILLE

RUE ST-MEME

PLACE
BILLARD

RUE SOLEIL D'OR

RUE DE LA PIE

RUE DES GRENETS

RUE DE LA FOULERIE

Jean Moulin
Memorial

PLACE
MARCEAU

St-Aignan

RUE ST-PIERRE

RUE PORTE
MORARD

PLACE
MORARD

Orléans &

PLACE
DES EPARS

POÊLE PERCÉE

R. ST-FRANÇOIS

PLACE DES
HALLES

RUE ST-MICHEL

St-Pierre

GRAND FAUBOURG

RUE
MAUNOURY

BOULEVARD=CHASLES

PLACE
PASTEUR

BOULEVARD DE LA COURTILLE

N

0   100 m

Tours

Le Mans

---

for it to be washed down more easily. The Sancta Camisia still exists, though after many years on open display it was recently rolled up and put into storage. It may yet be restored to the cathedral.

The geometry of Chartres is unique in being almost unaltered since its consecration, and virtually all of the **stained glass** is original thirteenth-century work. Many of the windows in the nave were donated by craft guilds and merchants, whose symbols can often be seen in the bottommost pane. Some of the stories fit the donors' work, such as the carpenters' window showing Noah's ark. The largely twelfth-century "**Blue Virgin**" window, in the first bay beyond the south transept, is venerated by art-lovers and worshippers alike.

Chartres may be the best-preserved Gothic cathedral in Europe, but if a group of medieval pilgrims suddenly found themselves here they would be deeply dismayed. The paint and gilt work that once brought the portal sculptures to life has vanished, while the walls have lost the whitewash that reflected the vivid colours of the stained-glass windows so well. Worse still, the high altar has been brought down into the body of the church, among the hoi polloi, and chairs cover up the thirteenth-century **labyrinth** on the floor of the nave (except on Fridays between April and October, when you can trace its two-hundred-metre-long route all the way to the centre).

The cathedral's **stonework** is captivating, particularly the **choir screen**, which curves around the ambulatory, depicting scenes from the lives of Christ and the Virgin. Its sculptor, Jehan de Beauce, was also responsible for the design of the Flamboyant Gothic north spire. Outside, hosts of sculpted figures stand like guardians at each **entrance portal**. Like the south tower and spire which abuts it, the mid-twelfth century **Royal Portal** actually survives from the earlier Romanesque church, and it's interesting to compare its highly stylized figures with the more naturalistic sculptures on the north and south porches, completed half a century later.

△ An imp, Chartres cathedral

You have to pay to visit the crypt and treasury, though these are relatively unimpressive. Crowds permitting, it's worth climbing the **north tower** (May–Aug 9.30am–noon & 2–5.30pm, Sun 2–5.30pm; Sept–April Mon–Sat 9.30am–noon & 2–4.30pm, Sun 2–4.30pm; €6.10) for its bird's-eye view of the sculptures and structure of the cathedral. There are **gardens** at the back from where you can contemplate the innovative flying buttresses.

The rest of town

Though the cathedral is the main attraction, a wander round the town of Chartres has its rewards. Occasional exhibitions of modern and ancient stained glass are displayed in a medieval wine and grain store, now the **Centre International du Vitrail**, at 5 rue du Cardinal-Pie on the north side of the cathedral (Mon–Fri 9.30am–12.30pm & 1.30–6pm, Sat & Sun 10am–12.30pm & 2.30–6pm; €4; ⓦwww.centre-vitrail.org). The **Musée des Beaux-Arts** (May–Oct Mon & Wed–Sat 10am–noon & 2–6pm, Sun 2–6pm; Nov–April Mon & Wed–Sat 10am–noon & 2–5pm, Sun 2–6pm; €2.70), in the former episcopal palace just north of the cathedral, has some beautiful tapestries, a room full of works by the French Fauvist Maurice de **Vlaminck** and an excellent *Sainte Lucie* by the Spanish Baroque painter **Zurbarán**. There are good temporary exhibitions, too.

Behind the museum, rue Chantault leads past old townhouses to the **River Eure** and Pont du Massacre. You can follow this reedy stream, lined with ancient wash-houses, upstream via rue du Massacre on the right bank; the cathedral appears from time to time through the trees. Closer at hand, on the left bank, is the Romanesque church of **St-André**, now used for art exhibitions, jazz concerts and so on.

A left turn at the south end of rue de la Tannerie, then third right, will bring you to one of Chartres' more eccentric tourist attractions. The otherwise ordinary **Maison Picassiette**, at 22 rue du Repos (April–Oct Mon & Wed–Sat 10am–noon & 2–6pm, Sun 2–6pm; €2.40), is entirely decorated with mosaics. The strange adornments were the work of the owner, Raymond Isidore, a local road-mender and later cemetery-caretaker. Between 1938 and 1962, two years before his death, Isidore used bits of broken pottery and glass to create a strange yet moving example of Christian Naïve art –"I took the things that other people threw away", as he put it.

Back at the end of rue de la Tannerie, the bridge over the river brings you back to the **medieval town**, where can you wander about spotting little details such as the sixteenth-century carved salmon that decorates a restaurant at the eastern end of place de la Poissonnerie. A large **food market** takes place on place Billard and rue des Changes on Wednesday and Saturday mornings, and there's a morning **flower market** on place du Cygne (Tues, Thurs & Sat).

At the edge of the old town, on the junction of boulevard de la Résistance and rue Collin-d'Harleville, stands a memorial to **Jean Moulin**, Prefect of Chartres until he was sacked by the Vichy government in 1942. When the Germans occupied the town in 1940, Moulin refused to sign a document claiming that Senegalese soldiers in the French army were responsible for Nazi atrocities. He later became de Gaulle's number-one man on the ground, co-ordinating the Resistance, but died at the hands of Klaus Barbie in 1943, on his way to a concentration camp in Germany.

Eating and drinking

For a snack, there are lots of places with outside tables opposite the south side of the cathedral, on rue Cloître-Notre-Dame: try the *Café Serpente*. For a proper **restaurant** meal, *Le Pichet*, 19 rue du Cheval Blanc, almost under the northwest spire (℡02.37.21.08.35; closed Wed, Tues eve & Sun eve), has a cosy interior full of gingham and bric-a-brac, and serves simple dishes like steak or Greek salad for around €10–14. The slightly more upmarket *L'Estocade*, 1 rue de la Porte Guillaume (℡02.37.34.27.17; closed Mon, Sun evening & Nov–April), has a lovely situation down by the River Eure, and serves good, traditional *cuisine bourgeoise*. The genteel 🍴 *St-Hilaire*, 11 rue du Pont St-Hilaire (℡02.37.30.97.57; closed Mon & Sun), offers refined regional dishes (menus €25–40) in a sweet little upstairs dining room.

The Loir

Source d'argent toute pleine,
Dont le beau cours eternal
Fuit pour enrichir la plaine
De mon païs paternel.

A la source du Loir, from Le quatriesme livre des odes (1550), Pierre de Ronsard

The poet Ronsard, who was born and buried beside the **Loir**, described it as "a full, silver stream whose beautiful course forever flows, enriching the plains of my native land". It is indeed one of the loveliest of the Loire's tributaries, like a junior version of its big sister – typically placid but prone to moody floods, its largely untamed banks lined with willow, alder and poplar trees, and dotted here and there with fishermen and punt-like wooden boats.

The river starts its course a few kilometres west of Chartres and flows roughly south, passing below the walls of the great castle at **Châteaudun** on its way into the Loir-et-Cher *département*. At **Vendôme**, which has a superb Gothic church and is one of the few decent-sized towns in the northern Loire, the river turns west. This, the **Vendômois** region, is one of the Loir's loveliest stretches, flowing past scattered vineyards, ruined castles and frescoed Romanesque churches around **Lavardin** and **Montoire-sur-le-Loir**, then on past the troglodyte village of **Trôo**, towards Ronsard's birthplace at **La Possonnière**. Continuing west, it forms a dividing line between the forests of northern Touraine and the rich, hedgerow-lined fields of Normandy as it enters the *département* of the Sarthe. In this downstream stretch, the chief sight is the giant Renaissance château at **Le Lude**. Finally, the river pours into the Sarthe and then the Maine, immediately north of Angers and just a few kilometres upstream of the Loire.

Châteaudun

The name of **CHÂTEAUDUN**, 44km south of Chartres, comes from two words that both mean fortress (Latin *castellum* and Celtic *dunum*), which rather underlines the fact that the town's château is the main thing to see – a beacon of interest in the middle of the endless, flat arable fields of the Beauce. It's also easy to visit by train, as it's on the main SNCF line (not the high-speed TGV line) between Tours and Paris-Austerlitz.

The château

The large, late medieval **château** (daily: April–June, Sept & Oct 10am– 12.30pm & 2–6pm; July & Aug 10am–7pm; Nov–March 10am–12.30pm & 2–5pm; €6.50, or €7.50 with Musée Municipal) lies at the western end of town. Its rough keep and two wings jammed together at right-angles give it a half-finished and forbiddingly Gothic air. Its most famous resident, Jean Dunois, the **"Bastard of Orléans"**, built the shorter of the two wings and its attached chapel. Dunois was Charles VII's ablest military captain, the companion of Joan of Arc and the chief instrument in the "liberation" of France from the English between the 1420s and 1450s. As the son of Louis d'Orléans and nephew of Charles VI, he was always destined to be powerful, but his illegitimacy meant that his titles and possessions had to be won as much by merit as breeding: Châteaudun was a gift from his admiring older brother, the poet Charles d'Orléans (see p.144). Dunois' other property, however, Beaugency (see p.201), came as part of his wife's dowry.

The longer of the two wings was built by Dunois' grandson, François II, **duc de Longueville**, in the 1510s. Scarcely fifty years separate it from the earlier work, but its architecture betrays a subtle but seismic shift in French taste. Dunois' elegant staircase, in the angle between the two wings, uses an ecclesiastical, Flamboyant Gothic vocabulary, while Longueville's larger staircase, although outwardly similar, is carved inside with delicate Classical motifs culled from the Italian Renaissance – the first time these had been applied anywhere in the Loire Valley. A stark counterpoint is provided by the massive, brooding presence of the **Great Tower**, built by Thibaud V, comte de Blois, in 1170.

The **interior** retains plenty of original giant roof beams and fireplaces, but the fifty-odd sixteenth- and seventeenth-century **tapestries** have only been hung here in recent years. The best of them follow wonderfully bold designs by the early seventeenth-century French painter Simon Vouet. But the most interesting part of the visit is to the **Ste-Chapelle**, built by Dunois in the 1450s and 1460s to house a piece of the True Cross. Skeins of stone seem to hang between the painted ribs of the vault, light floods in from the generous Gothic windows, and statues line the walls. The Madonna and Child immediately left of the altar is late fourteenth century, while the others were mostly commissioned at the time the chapel was built. The armoured, laurel-crowned figure positioned a little lower than the others, third in on the right-hand side, is thought to be Dunois himself – don't miss the grille beside the entrance to the crypt, which once guarded the remains of his heart. The chapel is lovely, but you'll have to make an effort to conjure up the original effect, when it was entirely painted in bright colours, with stained glass throughout. A splendidly colourful wall-painting of the Last Judgement still fills the wall of the southern chapel.

The **Great Tower**, with its massive, bell-shaped chambers, can only be visited on the optional guided tour (French only; tours at 11am & 3pm; June–Sept also at 4.30pm; free). It's worth joining even if you don't speak French. The topmost chamber contains a staggering wooden roof made up of five tiers of star-shaped beams extending up into the tower. The largest and lowest tier is a full 14m across, and almost all the timber is original, dating from the fifteenth century. On the tour, you also get to see the rooms above the Ste-Chapelle: the servant's chapel and the upper chapel, with its wooden barrel vaulting.

The rest of town

The new town, rebuilt after a disastrous fire in 1723, occupies a small grid of streets on top of a promontory on the left bank of the Loir. At its centre lies **place du 18 Octobre**, an old-fashioned market square lined with trees and little shops and overlooked by the eighteenth-century Hôtel de Ville. The fountain at the centre celebrates the first clean water to be pumped up from the Loir, in 1860. Immediately north of the square is the **Musée Municipal**, at 3 rue Toufaire (April–June & Sept Mon & Wed–Sun 9.30am–noon & 1.30–6pm; July & Aug daily 9.30am–6.30pm; Oct–March Mon & Wed–Sun 9.30am–noon & 1.30–5pm; €3.50, or €7.50 with château), a charmingly random collection of local curiosities, minor paintings, porcelain and archeological titbits. The highlights are a mock-up of a typical "Beauceron" peasant interior, and a fabulous collection of bright and exotic birds hand-stuffed by a local marquis in the nineteenth century.

The western end of town, between the château and the sixteenth-century abbey church of **La Madeleine**, survived the great fire, so there are plenty of handsome fifteenth- to seventeenth-century houses to admire, especially on the cobbled **rue St-Lubin**, which descends steeply towards the river. The two hundred steps of the **passage St-Pierre** provide a picturesque route to the Loir, leading from the château car park down to **rue des Fouleries**, which runs right along the riverbank below the town walls. A picnic spot in the middle of the Loir offers a fine view of the château's cliff-like northern facade. Halfway along rue des Fouleries lies the entrance to the **Grottes du Foulon** (April & May daily 2–6pm; June–Sept daily 10am–noon & 2–6pm; Oct–March Sat & Sun 2–6pm; €6; www.grottes-du-foulon.net), a large, naturally formed cave chamber. You'll need to speak French to get much out of the obligatory guided tour, on which the guide shows how the millions of flint geodes that stud the roof can be cracked open to reveal chalcedony, opal and quartz. The tour concludes with a sound-and-light show on a "fire and water" theme. In July and August, you can rent **canoes and kayaks** immediately opposite, from the Club Canoë Kayak Dunois (℡02.37.45.53.36).

Practicalities

Trains to Tours, Paris and Chartres run from the **gare SNCF**, a good ten minutes' walk northeast of the centre, on boulevard Grindelle. The central **tourist office** (mid-June to mid-Sept Mon–Sat 9am–1pm & 2–6pm, Sun 10am–1pm; mid-Sept to mid-June Tues–Sat 9am–noon & 2–6pm; ℡02.37.45.22.46, www.ville-chateaudun.com) is opposite the museum, at 1 rue de Luynes. If you want to **stay**, the best bet is the newly restored *Hôtel St-Michel*, 28 place du 18 Octobre (℡02.37.45.15.70, www.hotelstmichel .net; ❸), a handsome old post-house hotel with reasonably cheery rooms. Alternatively, the clean and welcoming *St-Louis*, 41 rue de la République (℡02.37.45.00.01, www.lesaintlouishotel.fr; ❸), has a good situation roughly 200m east of the main square. For a **restaurant** meal, the *Arnaudière*, 4 rue St-Lubin (℡02.37.45.98.98; closed Sun eve & Mon), has an atmospheric decor of old beams and stone walls, and serves considered traditional cuisine – expect to pay at least €30 a head. For something simpler, try *Le Commerce* (closed Mon), a friendly brasserie on place du 18 Octobre.

Vendôme

VENDÔME, 33km northwest of Blois, is an ancient, watery place, surrounded by two branches of the Loir and criss-crossed by miniature canals. The south bank is overlooked by a ruined castle atop a high rocky cliff, while a sizeable modern town spreads to the north. The old centre islanded between the two is the main draw, however, a likeably old-fashioned town that preserves some fine old buildings, notably the **église de la Trinité**, a Flamboyant Gothic church that's cathedral-like in its ambition.

Originally part of the county of Anjou, both town and château were bought by the Bourbon family in 1371. Vendôme became a hotbed of ultra-Catholicism during the sixteenth-century Wars of Religion, a crime for which it was pillaged by the forces of none other than **Henri IV**, the town's erstwhile duke. Other than being the birthplace of **Rochambeau**, the hero of American independence at the battle of Yorktown, Vendôme failed to distinguish itself in succeeding centuries. In the postwar era, the town has transformed itself into a thriving industrial centre for electronics and white goods.

The Town

The old town is centred on **place St-Martin**, a piazza-like space which echoes every hour to the musical chimes of its fifteenth-century bell tower (see box on p.204). Immediately to the east, you can't miss the exuberant Flamboyant Gothic facade of the **église de la Trinité** (daily 9am–dusk), which was probably conceived by Jehan de Beauce, the master of Chartres cathedral, in the early sixteenth century. The church originally belonged to a major Benedictine abbey founded in 1032 by the count of Anjou, Geoffroy Martel. As legend has it, he saw three burning spears fall from the sky into a spring at the spot, and brought two precious relics to his new church: the arm of St George and the *Sainte Larme*, a crystal-encased tear supposed to have been shed by Christ on the tomb of Lazarus. Their presence attracted thousands of pilgrims, and the resulting wealth allowed the church to be continually added to and rebuilt. As a result, practically every medieval architectural style is represented, ranging from the Romanesque transepts and belfry to the tall, narrow Rayonnant choir and Flamboyant facade. The most beautiful stained-glass window is the mid-twelfth-century **Majesté Notre Dame**, in the chapel behind the high altar.

The abbey buildings were converted into a military barracks under Napoleon, but in recent years have become the home of the **Musée de Vendôme** (April–Oct Mon & Wed–Sun 10am–noon & 2–6pm; Nov–March Mon & Wed–Sat 10am–noon & 2–6pm €3), a large but basically modest museum of folk crafts and local art works – chief among which are the animated metal sculptures by local twentieth-century artist Louis Leygue. Adjacent to the museum entrance is the **chapterhouse** (open access), in which you can still see a huge eleventh-century wall-painting depicting the Supper at Emmaus and Jesus's miraculous fishing episode, among other less visible scenes.

Rue du Change, the ancient and now pedestrianized high street, runs north past the gate of the watery **Parc Ronsard**, which is surrounded by canalized offshoots of the Loir. The park is overlooked to the north by the largely seventeenth-century **Hôtel de Ville**, once the austere **Collège des Oratoriens**, as attended – and profoundly loathed – by the novelist Honoré de Balzac. "A fat little boy with chubby cheeks and a red face", he was visited just twice in six years by his mother, and frequently punished for naughtiness by being locked up under the stairs. "Without books," he wrote, "this system of punishment would have totally brutalized me." You can peek inside the handsome courtyard during office hours. The park also looks onto a fifteenth-century manor, the **Hôtel du Saillant**, a medieval washhouse from the same era and now the tourist office (see opposite), as well as some massive plane trees planted in the mid-eighteenth century. On the east side of rue du Change, opposite the park entrance, the sedate **boat tour** round town (July & Aug daily 2–7pm; €5), takes in the elaborate floral displays set up each year by the town hall.

Remnants of the medieval town walls still stand on the banks of the Loir. The **Porte St-Georges**, a fifteenth-century fortified gateway, lies at the southernmost end of rue Poterie, which runs 200m west of the parallel rue du Change. The thirteenth-century **Tour de l'Islette** can best be seen by turning off rue du Change at its northern end, opposite the Romanesque **chapelle St-Jacques**, and following rue du Puits to a footbridge across the northern branch of the Loir. From here, you can turn south at place de la Liberté down rue Antoine de Bourbon – passing the thirteenth-century **Porte d'Eau**, which supplied Vendôme's mills and tanneries with water – and finally turning right to cross the Loir again and approach the Trinité church from behind its apse.

It's a steep climb up to the broken remnants of the **château** (daily 9am–dusk; free); continue south along rue du Change past place St-Martin, then cross the Loir on rue St-Bié and follow the rampe du Château up and round. The castle was originally run by the quasi-monastic Knights Templar as a wayfaring sanctuary for pilgrims but fell steadily into ruin from the sixteenth century onwards. Today, there's nothing much to see other than ruined towers and a fine view across town.

Practicalities

The **tourist office** is housed in the Hôtel du Saillant, 47 rue Poterie (Mon–Sat 9.30am–12.30pm & 2–6pm; ☎02.54.77.05.07, ⓦwww.vendome.eu), and in summer there's also an information point on the rue du Change (July & Aug daily 2–7pm). The **gare SNCF** lies ten minutes' walk north of the centre on rue Darreau, off the busy Faubourg Chartrain; you're more likely to arrive at the high-speed **gare TGV** 5km northwest of town, however, and this is conveniently connected by shuttle buses to the central place de la Liberté. If you want to rent **bikes** to explore the Loir valley, make for Cyclo'tech, 71 ave Ronsard (☎02.54.72.23.28), a fifteen-minute walk west of the centre towards the gare TGV.

There's one attractive, central **place to stay**, the *Auberge de la Madeleine*, 6 place de la Madeleine (☎02.54.77.20.79; ❷), an old-fashioned hotel on a pretty square at the north end of rue Poterie. Otherwise, there's a reliable three-star, *Le Vendôme*, 15 Faubourg Chartrain (☎02.54.77.02.88, ⓦwww.hotel vendomefrance.com; ❹), just outside the centre on the main road to Chartres; the rooms aren't anything special but they're clean and well kept. The *Auberge de la Madeleine* has a good traditional **restaurant** (closed Wed), with menus from €16. For simpler, more modern cuisine, try *Le Moulin du Loir*, 21 rue du Change (closed Mon), a restaurant and bar with great outdoor seating overlooking a weir (summer only). Local speciality **chocolates** in meringue cases, called Saintes Larmes, are sold at the Confiserie Bouard, 9 place St-Martin.

The Vendômois

The stretch of the Loir downstream of Vendôme, as far as La Chartre, all falls within the northern part of the *département* of the Loir-et-Cher, an area known traditionally as the **Vendômois**. This is the heart of the Loir valley: green, sedate and relaxing, the river lined with cave-houses and cave-cellars cut into the tufa escarpment (see box on p.260). You'll need your own wheels to get about, and cycling is particularly rewarding as the distances and gradients are both small. For comprehensive local information on the area, including addresses of local chambres d'hôtes, contact the tourist office in Vendôme (see above), or check online at www.loir-valley.com.

The pretty, peaceful village of **THORÉ-LA-ROCHETTE**, 9km west of Vendôme, is typical of this stretch of the Loir valley, its rock-cut *caves* used to store the wines of the surrounding Côteaux du Vendômois, a minor local *appellation*. In summer, a single-carriage 1950s **tourist train** (June & Sept 1–15 Sat & Sun 2.25pm; July & Aug Sat 2.25pm, Sun 9.30am, 2.25pm & 5.30pm; €10, children under 16 €7.50) runs three-hour round trips down to Trôo and back via Montoire-sur-le-Loir, along a leafy stretch of line. You should book in advance at the tourist office in Vendôme.

Lavardin and Montoire-sur-le-Loir

Crammed into a verdant side-valley 19km west of Vendôme, the tiny village of **LAVARDIN** is absurdly pretty. The ruined walls of its medieval castle, which once guarded the border between the Plantagenet lands and the northern holdings of the Capetian kings of France, cascade down from a hilltop promontory towards the old stone houses of the village. At the heart of the village lies a beautiful and surprisingly large Romanesque church, the **église St-Genest**, which preserves some wonderful, rust-coloured twelfth- to fourteenth-century wall-paintings in its choir. There's an excellent and very atmospheric **restaurant** down beside the river, the ✠ *Relais d'Antan* (☎02.54.86.61.33; closed Mon & Tues; menus from €27). It's surprisingly high-class for such a small village, showcasing the excellent and imaginative cuisine of its chef-owner.

On the opposite, north bank of the Loir, just under 2km away, **MONTOIRE-SUR-LE-LOIR** is a modest market town with another ruined castle – and two unusual claims to fame. It was at the train station here that Pétain met Hitler in October 1940 to agree the Vichy's government's official policy of collaboration, an event remembered by a modest exhibition on the spot. Nowadays, the town is celebrated for its summer festival of folk and world music, the **Festival International de Montoire** (⟳festival.montoire.free.fr), which attracts hundreds of artists and thousands of spectators, with a giant parade bringing the week-long festivities to a close on August 15.

During the rest of the year, the museum **Musikenfete**, just off place Clemenceau (Tues–Sat: March–Sept 10am–noon & 2–6pm; Oct–Dec 2–6pm; €5.60), shows off scores of unusual instruments from around the world accompanied by videos of musicians playing them. You can even have a go on some instruments yourself.

Close by, on the broad, horse-chestnut-lined market square, is the **tourist office**, at 16 place Clemenceau (April–Sept Mon–Sat 10am–noon & 3–7pm, Sun 11am–1pm; Oct–March Tues–Sat 10am–noon & 3–5pm; ☎02.54.85.23.30, ℮otsi@montoire-sur-le-loir.net), which can provide you with a key to the **chapelle St-Gilles** (same hours as tourist office; €3), a Romanesque chapel with three bold eleventh-century paintings of Christ covering its half-dome vaults. To get to the chapel, take rue Ronsard south off place Clemenceau, and turn right immediately after the bridge. For accommodation and food, make for the *Hôtel du Cheval Rouge*, 1 place Foch (☎02.54.85.07.05; ❸), a genteel, old-fashioned **hotel-restaurant** with an emphasis on the latter role. It offers inexpensive rooms (❷) with shared bathrooms.

Trôo

Seven kilometres downstream of Montoire, the troglodyte village of **TRÔO** (pronounced to rhyme with "no") rises gently in a series of rocky tiers from the north bank of the river. The hilltop is capped by the **collégiale St-Martin**, an imposing Gothic structure, but the real interest lies in the relatively lowly houses of the village itself, spread out along two main transverse lanes, the rue

Basse and the rue Haute, which are connected by steep stone stairways. Most of the houses are, in fact, caves – even the ones with conventional facades connect with the elaborate, seven-tiered network of some 4km of tunnels that riddles the hillside from top to bottom. During the Middle Ages, when it's thought that most of the caves were cut, for defensive reasons, the rich would have lived on the upper levels, and the poor down at the bottom. In all, the village had over four thousand inhabitants. Today, just thirty or so troglodyte houses are occupied on a permanent basis, most by incomers.

Beside a stairway joining rues Basse and Haute, in the very centre of the village, is the **Cave des Amis de Trôo** (hours vary, but generally April–Nov Mon–Fri 1.30–7pm, Sat & Sun 11am–7pm; €3, or €5 with Cave Yuccas, Ⓦwww.troglosites.asso.fr). This is a good place to start exploring, as it houses an exhibition on the geology of the area, the orchids and subtropical plants that thrive on the microclimate, the local folk traditions and the bat population – seventeen of France's thirty species can be found in and around Trôo. Even if you don't speak French, there's plenty to be gleaned. You can also enquire here about taking a tour of the **caforts des Montaigus** (free), a section of squared-off quarry tunnels with a reconstruction of how the caves might have been used in prehistoric times.

Just above the Cave des Amis, the delightful **Cave Yuccas** (April–June, Sept & Oct Mon–Fri 2–6pm, Sat & Sun 10.30am–7pm; July & Aug daily 10.30am–7pm; €3, or €5 with Cave des Amis), so called because yucca plants grow abundantly against the sunny, south-facing rock, has been done up as a traditional troglodyte house, complete with chimneys and a bread oven, and furnished with old-fashioned tables, chairs and beds. There are various curiosities elsewhere in the village, including the **Grotte Pétrifiante** – a cave-spring that slowly coats any objects left there in limestone – the old bakery and a much-venerated statue of St Gabriel, but the most enjoyable thing to do is test the dramatic echo inside

△ Troglodyte house, Trôo

the **puits qui parle**, or "talking well", which is found at the top of the village, 100m beyond the collégiale. On the opposite side of the river, the **église St-Jacques-des-Guérets** shelters twelfth-century wall-paintings.

The most characterful **accommodation** options are, of course, troglodyte dwellings, and two particularly attractive chambres d'hôtes sit side by side in the very centre of the village. ⚜ *L'Escalier Saint Gabriel* (☎02.54.72.50.34, ⓦbandbcave.com; ❸) has two large rooms with antique furnishings and cooking facilities, and a sunny terrace. The neighbouring *L'Éperon* (☎02.54.72.55.68, ⓔsolange.guilloux@orange.fr; ❹) is also beautifully appointed but not quite so cave-like, as there is less naked, exposed stone and more conventional walling. A third option, run by Sabine and Paul Lallemand (☎02.54.72.57.87, ⓔsabine .lallemand@orange.fr; ❸) is more of a gîte for hire by the week, but often has space for a night or two; the larger of the two gîtes here is the more attractive. All three dwellings can be found at ⓦwww.troo.com.

For something more elegant, there are sumptuously appointed bedrooms at the ⚜ *Château de la Voute* (☎02.54.72.52.52, ⓦwww.chateaudelavoute .com; ❻), a large eighteenth-century house overlooked by two medieval towers, situated towards the foot of the village. At Trôo's east end, on the road out towards Montoire, is the *Auberge Ste-Catherine*, carrefour Ste-Catherine (☎02.54.72.51.23; ❸; closed Jan), a friendly, family-run hotel in a venerable tufa-built house. It offers half a dozen simple rooms, and well-cooked French classics in a stone-vaulted dining room (menus from €20; closed Sun eve & Mon). *Le Petit Relais*, next to the collégiale, is an attractive if touristy **restaurant** offering a *menu du jour* for under €20.

La Possonière

In 1524, the poet **Pierre de Ronsard** (see p.343) was born at the manor house of **La Possonière**, 11km west of Trôo (late March to May & Oct to mid-Nov Thurs–Sun 2–6pm; June & Sept Tues–Sun 2–6pm; July & Aug daily 10am–7pm; €6). The main building is a refined, early-fifteenth-century gentleman's residence commissioned by Ronsard's father. The other side of the L-shaped courtyard is formed by a miniature tufa cliff into which troglodyte rooms have been dug out, with elaborate doorways adorned with inscriptions in French or Latin describing their use. The main house also wears its literary credentials on its sleeves, its doors and windows captioned with quirky epigrams and the family emblem of a flaming rose bush – a typically Renaissance visual pun on *roses ardentes* (burning roses) – "Rons-ard" for short. There's not much to see inside, other than an exhibition dedicated to the poet – for which you'll need good French – but there are regular classical **concerts** in summer, and the garden is beautiful.

Ronsard asked to be buried on the **Île Verte**, the midstream "green island" at Couture-sur-Loir, 1km north. His wish was only honoured for a few years: his body was later exhumed and transferred to the Prieuré de St-Cosme, near Tours (see p.76). The island remains a peaceful place to sit or stroll.

The village offers one charming **hotel-restaurant**, the *Auberge du Poète*, 6 rue Pasteur, right behind the church (☎02.54.72.55.96, ⓦwww.aubergedupoete .fr; ❸). It's a quintessential French country hotel, with modest but clean and comfortable rooms, and a bar-restaurant serving inexpensive country cuisine to guests and locals.

Le Lude

Strategically situated at the ancient border between Touraine, Anjou and the Maine – Le Mans, Tours and Saumur are all less than 50km distant – is the mighty château of **Le Lude** (April–Sept daily 10am–12.30pm & 2–6pm; guided tours afternoons only; closed Wed in April, May & Sept; gardens €4.60, château €6; Ⓦwww.lelude.com). The shape is basically medieval, a central keep defended by four belligerent, machicolated corner towers whose rough-hewn thirteenth-century foundations are still exposed in the deep, dry moat. The decoration, however, is pure early Renaissance, dating from the 1520s. The windows are outlined in finely carved tufa, the walls studded with Classical medallions, and the towers joined by arcaded terraces topped by balustrades. All this was the work of **Jean Gendrot**, architect to Jacques de Daillon, who presumably developed his tastes while serving in François I's Italian wars. The last of the Daillon family died in 1685, and the château fell slowly into disuse until 1751, when it was bought by Joseph Duvelaër, a merchant who had made his fortune in the East Indies. He bequeathed it to his niece, Françoise Butler, who squeezed the supremely Classical **Louis XVI façade** between the towers of the east front in 1787, just before the Revolution.

Françoise Butler's aristocratic descendants still occupy the château, which gives the guided tour of the **interior** (often available in English on request; afternoons only; free) a voyeuristic frisson – there are family photos everywhere. The stony **vestibule** is the only complete Renaissance room, though many original painted wall panels and beams were uncovered in the nineteenth century. Similarly, the exceptional **Oratory** – actually an Italian-inspired *studiolo*, or room intended for private study, meditation and storage of fine art – was only discovered in 1853, its walls entirely painted with representations of Old Testament stories and its vaulted ceiling covered in birds, flowers and nymph-like figures. Both are early sixteenth century, the ceiling probably from the school of Primaticcio, the great decorative artist behind François I's palace at Fontainebleau. Many of the other rooms visited on the tour preserve elegant Louis XVI decorative schemes, or are nineteenth-century reconstructions packed with old Flemish tapestries and antique furnishings.

Even if you don't join a tour of the interior, you can explore the passageways that link both sides of the moat underneath the château, and the extensive terraced **gardens**, which fall away towards the Loir. On the first weekend in June, a large **garden festival** takes over château and grounds. Thousands of plants are on sale or display, and there are various workshops – for which you'll need excellent French.

The adjacent village of **LE LUDE** is rather dull, but there are plenty of shops for stocking up on picnic supplies. Alternatively, the hotel-**restaurant** *La Renaissance*, 2 ave de la Libération, on the road out towards La Flèche (☎02.43.94.63.10; ❹; restaurant closed Sun eve & Mon), offers fairly pricey, classic French cuisine, as well as a good, inexpensive *menu du jour*.

Le Mans and around

LE MANS, the historic capital of the Maine region, is taken over by car fanatics in the middle of June for the famous 24-hour race. During the rest of the year, however, it is unfairly under-visited. As a large, industrial and traditionally left-wing city, its atmosphere could hardly be more different from bourgeois Tours, 80km to the south, but the two cities share a passion for *rillettes*, a kind of potted pork meat, as well as a good deal of history: Le Mans was the favourite home of the Plantagenet family, the counts of Anjou, Touraine and Maine. The tiny

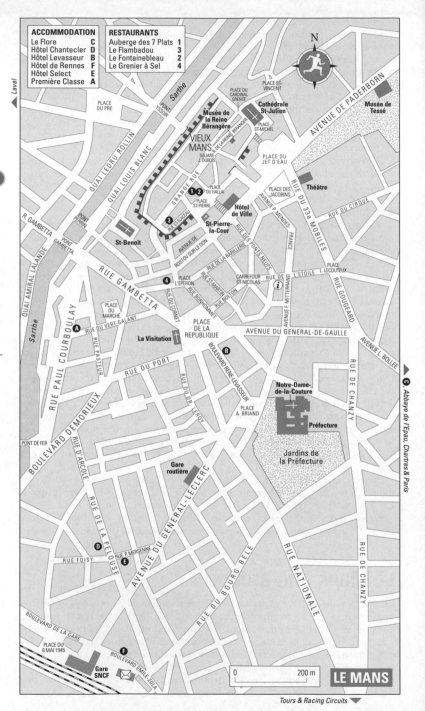

ACCOMMODATION
Le Flore   C
Hôtel Chantecler   D
Hôtel Levasseur   B
Hôtel de Rennes   F
Hôtel Select   E
Première Classe   A

RESTAURANTS
Auberge des 7 Plats   1
Le Flambadou   3
Le Fontainebleau   2
Le Grenier à Sel   4

N

◄ Laval

► G, Abbaye de l'Épau, Chartres & Paris

PLACE DU PRE

PONT YSSOIR

Sarthe

PLACE DU CARDINAL GRENTE

PLACE ST-VINCENT

PLACE ST-MICHEL

Cathédrale St-Julien

Musée de Tessé

AVENUE DE PADERBORN

Musée de la Reine Bérangère

R. DE LA REINE BÉRANGER

VIEUX MANS

SQUARE J. DUBOIS

PLACE DU JET D'EAU

RUE DU 33e MOBILES

Théâtre

QUAI LEDRU ROLLIN

QUAI LOUIS BLANC

GRANDE RUE

PLACE DU HALLAI

PLACE ST-PIERRE

PLACE DES JACOBINS

AVENUE P. MENDES-FRANCE

RUE DU CIRQUE

R. GAMBETTA

PONT PERRIN

PONT GAMBETTA

Hôtel de Ville

St-Pierre-la-Cour

RUE DES PONTS NEUFS

St-Benoît

RUE SÉJEZEAU

AVENUE DE ROSTOV-SUR-LE-DON

RUE DE LA BARILLERIE

RUE DE L'ÉTOILE

PLACE L. LECOUTEUX

QUAI AMIRAL LALANDE

Sarthe

RUE GAMBETTA

PLACE DE L'ÉPERON

RUE ST-MARTIN

CARREFOUR ST-NICOLAS

RUE DE

AVENUE F. MITTERRAND

i

RUE GOUGEARD

RUE DU CORNET

RUE BONHOMMET

RUE BOLTON

PLACE DU MARCHÉ

RUE PAUL COURBOULAY

RUE DU VERT-GALANT

PLACE DE LA RÉPUBLIQUE

AVENUE DU GENERAL-DE-GAULLE

AVENUE L. BOLLÉE

A

La Visitation

RUE PASTEUR

RUE DU PORT

BOULEVARD RENÉ-LEVASSEUR

B

RUE DU DR. LEROY

PLACE A. BRIAND

Notre-Dame-de-la-Couture

Préfecture

RUE DE CHANZY

PONT DE FER

BOULEVARD DEMORIEUX

RUE D'ARCOLE

Gare routière

Jardins de la Préfecture

RUE DE LA PELOUSE

RUE P. MERSENNE

D

E

RUE FOISY

AVENUE DU GENERAL-LECLERC

RUE DU BOURG BÉLÉ

RUE NATIONALE

RUE DE CHANZY

BOULEVARD DE LA GARE

PLACE DU 8 MAI 1945

Gare SNCF

BOULEVARD EMILE-ZOLA

F

0   200 m

LE MANS

Tours & Racing Circuits ▼

old quarter, in the shadow of the magnificent cathedral, is splendidly preserved, while outside town you can visit the serene Cistercian abbey of Epau and, of course, the racetrack.

Arrival and information

The hub of modern Le Mans is the **place de la République**, with its assortment of Belle Epoque facades and fountains and more modern office blocks. A brand new tram line is being installed in 2007 and 2008, running from the square north to the university and south to the racetrack; for now, bus #16 runs between place de la République and the **gare SNCF** via ave Général-Leclerc, where the **gare routière** is located. The **tourist office**, on rue de l'Étoile (April–June & Sept Mon–Fri 9am–6pm, Sat 9am–noon & 2–6pm, Sun 10am–noon; July & Aug Mon–Sat 9am–6pm, Sun 10am–12.30pm & 2.30–5pm; Oct–March Mon–Fri 9am–6pm, Sat 9am–noon & 2–6pm; ☏02.43.28.17.22, ⓦwww.lemanstourisme.com), lies a couple of minutes' walk east of place de la République. What with its miniscule historic centre and profound motor-racing traditions, Le Mans really isn't cycling territory, and to rent one you'll need to make your way to the northern suburb of La-Chapelle-St-Aubin, where you'll find Veloland at 1 rue du Moulin-aux-Moines (☏02.43.51.16.00); take bus #8 to its terminus, "Moulin aux Moines".

Accommodation

Unless your visit coincides with one of the big racing events during April, June or September (see p.320), you should be able to find **accommodation** easily without having to book, though disappointingly, there's nothing in the old town. At race times, prices can quadruple, and most places are booked up months in advance.

Hotels

Hôtel Chantecler 50 rue de la Pelouse ☏02.43.14.40.00, ⓦwww.hotelchantecler.fr. This quiet, independent three-star has a pleasing mix of efficiency and friendliness. The standard rooms are rather dull in terms of decor, but well fitted-out. There are also two large, airy suites available (❻), which are rather good value, sleeping up to four people. ❺
Hôtel Levasseur 5–7 bd René Levasseur ☏02.43.39.61.61, ☏02.43.39.61.65. This two-star hotel has a good location just off place de la République, but it's rather rambling inside, and the rooms feel a bit functional. ❹
Hôtel de Rennes 43 bd de la Gare ☏02.43.24.86.40, ☏02.43.87.02.95. This simple, inexpensive hotel right next to the station is well maintained and pleasantly decorated in bright colours. Inexpensive rooms with shared bathrooms are available, and all rooms are double-glazed. ❷
Hôtel Select 13 rue du Père-Mersenne, off ave du Général-Leclerc ☏02.43.24.17.74. Under the new ownership, the rooms here are being slowly refurbished with en-suite bathrooms. It looks set to be a smart budget option, and especially good value for families, who can have a room with a double bed and two bunks for €48. ❷
Première Classe 40 rue du Vert-Galant ☏02.43.24.19.41, ⓔpremiereclasse.lemans @lsfhotels.com. This businesslike, anonymous chain hotel is a no-frills place, with hard beds and lino flooring. It's clean and perfectly adequate, with a handily central location, so makes a good fallback option. ❷

Hostel

Le Flore 23 rue Maupertuis ☏02.43.81.27. 55, ⓔflorefjt@noos.fr. This is mainly a workers' hostel, but it has some beds reserved for HI members (€12). It's close to the centre, with a 24-hour reception and a cheap canteen offering three meals per day. Take ave du Général-de-Gaulle from place de la République, continue along ave Bollée, and rue Maupertuis is the third on the left; or catch the Citadine bus from the station or République to stop "Flore".

The City

The modern centre of Le Mans is **place de la République**, bordered by a mixture of Belle Epoque buildings and more modern office blocks, and the Baroque bulk of the **église de la Visitation**. Almost all the sights lie inside the beautiful **old quarter**, on the raised ground immediately west of the cathedral.

Cathédrale St-Julien

At the crown of the old town is the immense **cathédrale St-Julien**, on cobbled place du Cardinal Grente (daily: late June to late Sept 8am–7pm; late Sept to late June 8am–noon & 2–6pm; free). The approach from the east, up the steps from **place du Jet d'Eau** and past the forest of flying buttresses that props up the incredibly tall Gothic choir, is undeniably dramatic. The older half of the cathedral, the nave, was only just completed when Geoffroi le Bel – the count of Maine and Anjou who wore a sprig of *genêt* (broom) in his hat, hence Planta-genet – married Matilda, daughter of Henry I of England, in 1129, founding the Plantagenet line. The cathedral is one of the greatest Romanesque structures in France, in both scale and decorative ingenuity. According to Rodin, the sculpted figures of the south porch were rivalled only by those at Chartres cathedral and the Parthenon in Athens; sadly, they are now blurrred by weathering. The archaic lozenge patterns of the **west front** date right back to the 1050s, when the nave was begun, but the most ancient stone of all is propped up against the southwest corner, a strangely anthropomorphic, pink-tinted **menhir** that may be a last remnant of a prehistoric sacred site at this spot. Local tradition would have you put your fingers in the holes for good luck.

Inside, for all the power and measured beauty of the Romanesque structure, it's impossible not to be drawn towards the High Gothic choir. At the transept, there's a vertiginous leap up to the 34-metre-high thirteenth-century vault. The whole choir is filled with coloured light, filtered through the stained-glass windows, but the brightest colours are found in the **chapelle de la Vierge**, at the easternmost end of the choir, where the stunning vault is painted with angels singing, dancing and playing medieval musical instruments, set against a lustrous red background. The **sacristy**, on the south side of the ambulatory, is worth seeing for its single central column, which seems to fountain out into the vault above.

The city centre

The old quarter, known as **Vieux Mans**, lies on a hill above the River Sarthe to the north of the central place de la République. Its medieval streets, a hotch-potch of intricate Renaissance stonework, medieval half-timbering, sculpted pillars and beams and grand classical facades are still encircled by the original third- and fourth-century **Gallo-Roman walls**, which are among the best-preserved in Europe and run for several hundred metres. Their shape, and the elaborate geometric details set into their pink brick, are best viewed from the river, which can be accessed by steep steps from the south side of place du Cardinal Grente.

Local crafts and history are showcased at the **Musée de la Reine Bérengère**, rue de la Reine-Bérengère (daily except Mon: May–Sept 10.30am–12.30pm & 2–6.30pm; Oct–April 2–6pm; €2.80, or €6 with Musée de Tessé), which is named after Queen Bérengère of Navarre, the wife of Richard the Lionheart. The museum is dull, but the house is a beautiful fifteenth-century construction, one of many on the street. The **Maison des Deux-Amis**, opposite, gets its name from the carving of two men (the "two friends") supporting a coat of arms between the doors of numbers 18 and 20.

Heading away from the cathedral, you enter the equally ancient **Grande Rue**. Further down on the left, just off place St-Pierre, a sixteenth-century apothecary's shop known as the **Maison d'Adam et Eve** is superbly carved, the pair of original sinners apparently contemplating a gigantic toffee apple.

In the 1850s, a road was tunnelled under the quarter – a slum at the time – helping to preserve its self-contained unity. The road tunnel comes out on the south side, by an impressive **monument to Wilbur Wright** – who tested an early flying machine in Le Mans – and into place des Jacobins, the vantage point for the St-Julien apse. From here, you can walk east through the park to the **Musée de Tessé** (July & Aug Tues–Sun 10am–12.30pm & 2–6.30pm; Sept–June Tues–Sat 9am–noon & 2–6pm, Sun 10–noon & 2–6pm; €4, or €6 with Musée de la Reine Bérengère), where the highlight is an exquisite enamel portrait of Geoffroi le Bel, which was originally part of his tomb in the cathedral. Otherwise, it's a very mixed bag of paintings, furnishings and sculptures, while in the basement there's a full-scale reconstruction of the ancient Egyptian tomb of Queen Nefertari, the principal wife of Ramesses the Great.

On summer nights, the cathedral and various other buildings in the old quarter are illuminated in a **son et lumière** show, called *la Nuit des Chimères* (daily: July 11pm; Aug 10.30pm; free), the highlight of which is a parade of mythical monsters projected along the length of the Gallo-Roman walls.

It's worth making a brief foray out of the old quarter to see the **church of Notre-Dame-de-la-Couture**, on place Aristide-Briand. The Gothic choir and nave mostly date from the twelfth and thirteenth centuries, but you can still

The 24 Heures du Mans

Le Mans' associations with automobiles began early, when local bell-founder Amadée Bollée built the world's first car in 1873 – though it was steam-powered, as Gottlieb Daimler's internal combustion engine only appeared in 1887. Over a century later, Le Mans has a huge Renault factory operating in its southwest suburbs, and the **24 Heures** race is a giant of the racing calendar, attended by a quarter of a million petrolheads – 80,000 of them British.

The first big race at Le Mans was the Grand Prix de l'Automobile Club de l'Ouest in 1906. Two years later, **Wilbur Wright** took off in his prototype aeroplane, alongside what is now the fastest stretch of the racetrack, remaining in the air for over ninety minutes and setting a new record in the process. 1923 saw the first 24-hour car race, run on the present 13.6-kilometre circuit, with average speeds of 92kph (57mph). It established the classic rule – that all drivers must make repairs on the circuit. The original suicidal start, which saw drivers running to their cars from a standing line-up, was only abolished in 1970, the year Porsche began their legendary winning streak. In 1979, the actor Paul Newman finished second; the following year a Frenchman, Jean Rondeau, won in a car he had built himself.

These days, expensively backed professional teams dominate. In 2003, the race was won by a British team, Bentley, the first time they had taken the chequered flag since 1930. The three drivers had covered some 5000km (3000 miles) in the 24 hours, averaging around 210kph (130mph). For one member of the team, **Tom Kristensen** this was his fourth victory in as many years and his fifth overall. Reverting to his usual Audi R8 the following year, Kristensen went on to win again – and in 2005 he finally passed Jacky Ickx's 23-year-old record of six wins at Le Mans. In 2006, however, he was beaten into third place by a different and somewhat unusual Audi, the R10 – the first diesel-powered car ever to win the 24 Heures.

see some of the stonework and round arches belonging to the earlier Roman-esque church, especially down in the crypt, which once housed the remains of St Bertrand.

The racetrack and Musée de l'Automobile

The **Sarthe circuit**, on which the world-renowned **24 Heures du Mans** car race takes place each year, stretches south from the outskirts of the city, along ordinary roads. The simplest way to get a taste of the track is just to take the main road south of the city towards Tours, a stretch of ordinary highway which follows the infamous **Mulsanne straight** for 5.7km – a distance that saw race cars reach speeds of up to 375kph (230mph), until two chicanes were introduced in 1989, bringing the revs down a few notches. You can follow the straight down to the Mulsanne corner, turn along the D140 towards Indi-anapolis and the Arnage corner, then follow the D139 to the Ford corner, at the entrance to the Bugatti circuit – the dedicated race track section of the 24-hour route.

Races

During the three-day **race weekend**, held from Friday to Sunday in mid-June, you'll need a ticket to get anywhere near the circuit, as the roads all around are barred off and access is tightly controlled. Tickets can be bought direct from the organizers at ⓦ www.lemans.org, or via the tourist office, and cost €61 for all three days, €25 for trial days (Fri & Sat), and €39 for race day, which is always on a Sunday. You'll need a separate ticket (€61–102) to get access to the grand-stands of the Bugatti circuit: be sure to book well in advance. Many enthusi-asts' clubs and ticket agencies offer tour packages including accommodation – otherwise impossible to find at race times – and the crucial parking passes; try ⓦ www.clubarnage.com or ⓦ www.pageandmoy.com, or look through the adverts in a motor-sports magazine. True petrol heads book themselves a place at one of the circuit-side campsites. At other times of the year you can attend the **Le Mans Classic**, in September, and the bikers' **24 Heures Moto**, in early April, among other races.

Musée de l'Automobile

The **Musée de l'Automobile** (daily: Feb–May & Oct–Dec 10am–6pm; June–Sept 10am–7pm; €7) is on the edge of the Bugatti circuit, the dedicated track section of the main Sarthe circuit. As a stunning parade of some 150 vehi-cles, ranging from the humble 2CV to classic Lotus and Porsche race cars, the museum speaks for itself, but there's also a good attempt to document the early history of car racing, including automobile anatomy and automated assembly. The visit ends with audio-visual displays examining the world of car racing, including a simulated high-speed track.

The Abbaye de l'Epau

If car racing holds no romance, there's another outing from Le Mans of a much more contemplative nature, to the Cistercian **Abbaye de l'Epau** (daily 9.30am–11.30am & 2–5.30pm; opening hours may vary in summer to accom-modate exhibitions; ☎02.43.84.22.29; €3), 4km out of town off the Chartres–Paris road. If you haven't got your own transport, take bus #14 from place de la République in Le Mans to the "Pologne" stop, from where it's a five-minute walk. The abbey was founded in 1229 by **Bérengère**, or Berengaria of Navarre, the wife of Richard the Lionheart – though they rarely saw each other, and never had children, perhaps because of Richard's probable homosexuality. In fact, Richard repeatedly spurned her, and formally repudiated her in 1196, after which she retired to Anjou and then, after fighting his brother John for a share of the rapidly diminishing Plantagenet territories in France, to Le Mans.

The abbey stands in the Cistercian's favoured rural setting, and has remained more or less unaltered since its early fifteenth-century restoration after a fire. You can visit the huge dormitory under its wooden barrel vault, and the typically plain abbey church, but the **chapterhouse**, whose four columns support a web of ribbed vaulting protecting Bérengère's original **tomb**, is more interesting. Her slightly outsized effigy clutches a book, representing her "life story".

Eating and drinking

In the centre of town, the **cafés** and **brasseries** on place de la République stay open till late, while on nearby place l'Eperon there's a very good, if pricey, traditional French **restaurant**, ☆ *Le Grenier à Sel* (☎02.43.23.26.30; closed Sun & Mon; menus from €18). The interior has a restrained, contemporary feel, with cool, pale colours, but the food has warmer and more classic tendencies: on the €60 tasting menu, mains might include beef with truffled potatoes, and scallops with pork belly in a cream of morel mushrooms. The most atmospheric restaurants are located in the labyrinthine streets of Vieux Mans, the old quarter. The *Auberge des 7 Plats*, 79 Grande-Rue (☎02.43.24.57.77; closed Sun & Mon), does a good range of inexpensive *plats* and a good-value menu at €15. For a special occasion, make for the rustic *Le Flambadou*, 14bis rue St-Flaceau (☎02.43.24.88.38; closed Sat lunch & Sun), which offers very meaty dishes from Périgord and the Landes (main courses around €15). Nearby on place St-Pierre, *Le Fontainebleau* (☎02.43.14.25.74; closed Mon & Tues) has pleasant outside seating facing the Hôtel de Ville and serves classic French cuisine, with menus from €17.50.

There's a daily **market** in the covered halls on place du Marché, plus a bric-a-brac market on Wednesday, Friday and Sunday mornings on place du Jet-d'Eau, below the cathedral on the new town side.

The Sarthe valley

The **River Sarthe** begins its course some 30km north of Le Mans, from where it winds southwest through the heart of the historic Maine region before joining the Mayenne just north of Angers. The most beautiful stretch of river lies between Le Mans and the border with Anjou, a picturesque backwater corner of France made up principally of *bocage* – an English-style landscape of small fields, orchards and patches of woodland criss-crossed by hedgerows and streams. You can picnic at picturesque villages such as **Asnières-sur-Vègre** and **St-Denis-d'Anjou**, and visit the ceramics centre of **Malicorne-sur-Sarthe**, but most fascinating of all is the Benedictine monastery at **Solesmes**, whose abbey church houses two extraordinary sculptural groups.

Malicorne-sur-Sarthe

Follow signs off the Le Mans ring road towards Allones and you'll quickly find yourself on the D23, one of the more attractive roads leading southwest towards Anjou. After 35km you'll arrive at **MALICORNE-SUR-SARTHE**, a centre of pottery production since Roman times, and of fine faïence (glazed earthenware, or majolica) since 1747. Two faïence workshops are still in business, while the entire history of local ceramics is displayed at the **Espace Faïence**, 24 rue Victor-Hugo (Easter–Oct daily 10am–7pm; Nov–Easter Mon & Wed–Sun 10am–12.30pm & 2.30–6.30pm; €6), a large, modern gallery and museum stacked with ceramics ranging from beautifully glazed eighteenth-century pieces to contemporary art works. If you want to explore further, Malicorne's **tourist office**, 3 place du Guesclin, beside the bridge (℡02.43.94.74.45, ⓦwww.ville-malicorne.fr) can help arrange visits to the two active faïence workshops. It also rents out **boats**, kayaks and pedalos for paddling about on the river – the centre of the village overlooks a broad, attractive stretch with weirs, watermills and a small island. There's little else to do apart from visit the plain but very old **église St-Sylvestre**, an eleventh-century structure housing the fifteenth-century tomb-effigy of local lord Guy de Chaource.

⅄ *La Petite Auberge*, 5 place du Guesclin (℡02.43.94.80.52; menus from €16; closed Mon; Oct–March closed Mon–Fri & Sun eve), is an excellent place for a **restaurant** meal, serving up gourmet dishes, with an emphasis on fish, on a sunny terrace overlooking the river. The riverbank **campsite** *Le Port Ste-Marie* (℡02.43.94.80.14; closed Nov–March), which has an open-air swimming pool, is close at hand.

Asnières-sur-Vègre

From Malicorne-sur-Sarthe, the D8 leads to **Parcé-sur-Sarthe**, 10km west, a picturesque riverside village with a number of rustic eighteenth-century houses. Prettier still is **ASNIÈRES-SUR-VEGRE**, 7km north of Parcé – to get there you'll have to cross back over the Sarthe, as if heading east, then turn immediately left on the D57 through Avoise. Asnières is entirely constructed in the golden local stone and is centred on a twelfth-century humpback bridge over the River Vègre, a tributary of the Sarthe. Signposts point out various ancient houses and other local landmarks such as the **manoir de la Cour**, a large shell of a thirteenth-century manor house, and the **église St-Hilaire**, a simple parish church with a Gothic choir and Romanesque nave, the latter decorated with beautiful wall-paintings that were only discovered underneath the whitewash in 1950. It's a pleasant stroll across the bridge and up the hill to the elegant, eighteenth-century **château de Moulin Vieux**, though the château is private and the grounds only sporadically open for visits.

The **restaurant** *Le Pavillon*, in the centre of the village, is usually open for snacks and simple meals, but this is perfect picnic territory. If you want to stay locally, there are two excellent if pricey **chambres d'hôtes** in the nearby countryside, both set in fifteenth-century buildings on the Vègre and well-signposted from the centre. The atmospheric ⅄ *Manoir des Claies*, 2km northwest of the village (℡02.43.92.40.50, ⓕ02.43.92.65.72; ❺; closed Nov–Easter), offers three welcoming and sympathetically decorated rooms, and a swimming pool in the summer months, while the *Château de Dobert*, on the minor road towards Avoise, the C4 (℡02.43.92.01.52, ⓕ02.43.92.16.16; ❼; closed July & Nov–April), is a grander place extended in the eighteenth century, with three elegant, antique-furnished bedrooms.

Solesmes and around

The D22, a sleepy back road heading southwest from Asnières towards Sablé-sur-Sarthe, reaches the river just below **JUIGNE-SUR-SARTHE**, 6km away, a medieval hilltop village with a thirteenth-century church and a fine view downriver. Below in **Port-de-Juigné**, a local enthusiast has opened **l'Amusant Musée** (open on reservation only: daily except Mon & Fri;

☎02.43.92.44.62; €6, children under 16 €4), a private toy museum crammed into two tiny rooms. If you can arrange a mutually convenient time – 3pm is preferred – the English-speaking owner will engagingly demonstrate many of his two thousand or so old-fashioned and contemporary toys for you, and let you discover others for yourself. Most visitors seem to find some forgotten treasure from their own era.

Just over 1km west of Juigné, the **abbaye de St-Pierre** (Ⓦwww.solesmes .com) at **SOLESMES** dominates the valley bottom. The bulk of the castle-like monastic buildings are the work of the reforming Dom Guéranger, who refounded the Benedictine monastery in 1833, some forty years after it had been broken up in the Revolution. There are now over sixty brothers, following St Benedict's original rule of poverty, chastity and obedience, and doing research – theoretical and practical – into Gregorian chant. The monks welcome visitors to their sung services at 10am (High Mass), 1pm (Sext), 1.50pm (None), 5pm (Vespers) and 8.30pm (Compline), and young men are received freely as guests on retreat.

Most visitors, however, come to see not the monks but the extraordinary **saints de Solesmes**, two monumental groups of statues in the transepts of the abbey church – the nave of which dates back to the first priory, founded here in 1010. The extraordinarily naturalistic *Entombment* group in the **south transept** dates from around 1500. It is framed by an arch that drops down at the centre into a stone case inscribed with the words *factus in pace loc eius* ("his place having been made in peace"). Once a year, on Easter Monday, this reliquary displays the **Holy Thorn**, a relic from Jesus' crown brought back from the Crusades in the twelfth century by the local lord of Sablé.

In the 1530s, the monks decided to outdo the work in the south transept by filling the **northern side** with some hundred figures of saints and biblical scenes. The statues themselves are similar in style to the earlier group, apparently caught in motion, but the architectural framing is in the full grip of the Renaissance, crawling with columns, medallions and floral and scallop-shell motifs. The main scene shows the burial of Mary, while above is her Assumption into heaven.

Three kilometres downstream of Solesmes, the small, semi-industrialized town of **SABLÉ-SUR-SARTHE** doesn't have much to recommend it – a poultry slaughterhouse is one of its biggest employers. Still, it does have all the usual facilities of a fair-sized town, as well as good TGV and train connections to Le Mans and Angers, and you could linger in the little river port at its heart, or browse the local pâtisseries for the speciality shortbread-like biscuits, known as *sablés* ("sandies").

Practicalities

Sablé-sur-Sarthe has a useful **tourist office** on the central place Raphël-Elizé (Mon–Sat 10am–noon & 2–5.30pm; ☎02.43.95.00.60, Ⓦwww.sable -sur-sarthe.com). If you want to **stay** in the area, the *Grand Hôtel de Solesmes*, 16 place Dom-Guéranger (☎02.43.95.45.10, Ⓦwww.grandhotelsolesmes.com; ❻), has a superb location immediately opposite the abbey, and a three-star rating for its room sizes, sauna and modern facilities. The actual rooms, however, are in an ugly modern block and not half as swish as you'd think from the building's facade and reception. The restaurant is overly fussy and somewhat overpriced, with menus starting at €25. Sablé-sur-Sarthe's handful of hotels are uninspiring, but the **restaurant** *Le Saint Martin*, 3 rue Haute St-Martin, just off the main square (☎02.43.95.00.03; closed Sun evening & Mon), serves excellent traditional French cuisine, with lots of reasonably priced à la carte options.

St-Denis-d'Anjou

Eleven kilometres beyond Sablé-sur-Sarthe along the D309, **ST-DENIS-D'ANJOU** is one of the most beguiling of the region's little villages. At its heart is the **église St-Denis**, a chaotically constructed mongrel building whose most interesting feature is the set of rustically sketched sixteenth-century wall-paintings that brighten the nave. The rest of the village repays a wander. Rue des Halles leads behind the church, across the stream, past some lovely old houses and a slate *pissoir*, and onto **place des Halles**, where the large, timber-roofed market hall dates from 1509. You can turn left to return via the smithy and fifteenth-century **manoir**, or continue round via **rue du Puits Morin**, one of the best-preserved medieval streets.

Despite its modest size, the village has a number of excellent places to eat and stay. The part-fifteenth-century ✻ *Auberge du Roi René* (☎02.43.70.52.30, Ⓦ www.roi-rene.fr; ❹), managed exuberantly and with a definite personal touch by a husband-and-wife team, has four characterful and homely **chambres d'hôtes**, decorated with antique furniture and a real eye for nineteenth-century style. The **restaurant** is deeply atmospheric, too, with its massive stone fireplace and beamed ceiling; the menus feature inventive and sometimes hearty dishes, with prices ranging from €20 to €40. Set in an old post-house, the *Hostellerie La Calèche*, rte d'Angers (☎02.43.70.61.00, Ⓔhostellerie.lacaleche@orange.fr; ❸), is more of a conventional provincial **hotel** – welcoming, family-run and with just seven modern, bright and unfussy rooms and a traditional, inexpensive restaurant (closed Sun eve & Mon). *Le Logis du Ray* (☎02.43.70.64.10, Ⓔecoleattelageduray@laposte.net; ❹) runs some attractive chambres d'hôtes as a sideline from its horse-and-carriage business, while deep in the countryside near Varennes, a pretty hamlet on the Sarthe, 5km southeast of St-Denis, the **organic farm** ✻ *La Morlière* (☎ & Ⓕ02.43.70.91.65; ❸) offers a welcoming "ecologîte" – everything is built and run in a sustainable way – and two simple but cosy chambres d'hôtes in a restored farm outbuilding.

Travel details

Trains

Chartres to: Châteaudun (5 daily; 1hr); Le Mans (11 daily; 1hr 15min–1hr 45min); Paris Montparnasse (at least hourly; 1hr); Tours (usually requires change; 4–6 daily; 2hr 10min–3hr 20min).
Le Mans to: Angers (17 daily; 35min–1hr 10min); Paris (hourly; 1hr); Tours (7 daily; 1hr).
Sablé-sur-Sarthe to: Angers (6–11 daily; 20–35min); Le Mans (6–11 daily; 20–30min).

Vendôme to: Châteaudun (2–3 daily; 40min); Tours (10 daily; 30min–1hr).

Buses

Chartres to: Châteaudun (4–8 daily; 1hr); Orléans (9 daily; 1hr 10min–1hr 45min); Tours (2 daily; 1hr 40min).
Le Mans to: Baugé (2 daily; 1hr 15min); Saumur (1–2 daily; 2hr).
Vendôme to: Blois (5–6 daily; 1hr–1hr 35min); Châteaudun (4 daily; 45min–1hr).

Contexts

Contexts

History

T he role of the Loire region in French history has been rather like the
river itself: generally sleepy and placid, though its easy flow has at times
been disrupted by violent floods. Chief among these disruptive episodes
were the Plantagenet era in the twelfth century; the last years of the
Hundred Years War, when Joan of Arc roused the French to victory in 1429;
and the late fifteenth and early sixteenth centuries, when the Loire was in
the vanguard of the French Renaissance. Since then, the region's political and
commercial influence has steadily dwindled, the river has silted up, and the
Loire Valley has now settled into a comfortable provincial existence.

Prehistory

The Atlantic Ocean has come and gone many times over the terrain that now
makes up the Loire, like a vast tide in geological time. The deposits it repeatedly
left behind now form the **Bassin Parisien**, which extends across much of
northern France towards Paris. Most of the region's typically soft, chalky rock,
known as *tuffeau blanc*, or **tufa**, was laid down towards the end of the Upper
Cretaceous period, roughly ninety million years ago, during the era geologists
call the Turonian, after Touraine. In the Miocene era, between 15 million and 9
million years ago, the sea invaded up the Loire as far the site of modern-day
Blois, creating the Mer des Faluns, named after the **faluns**, or fossilized shells,
that characterize the rock. From around this time, the Alps began to be pushed
upwards, causing the River Loire to change its course from the north – it once
flowed into the Seine – to the west.

The earliest peoples may have arrived in the Loire Valley as much as 100,000
years ago, but little evidence predates the flint and bone fragments found at La-
Roche-Cotard, near Cinq-Mars-la-Pile. Dated to around 32,000 BC, these are
thought to belong to the Neanderthal Mousterian culture, and include an
enigmatic flint supposedly shaped in the form of a face. The most significant
Stone Age finds in the Loire, however, belong to the age of **megaliths**. In the
centuries around 3000 BC, hundreds of dolmens (burial chambers) and menhirs
(single standing stones) were erected all over the Loire – roughly 150 have been
found in the region, with a particularly high concentration in the Saumurois. It
is impossible to reconstruct more than a fragmentary picture of life at this time,
but it seems that a thriving trade followed the rivers, flints from Anjou being
transported up the Loire across to the Rhône and down to the Mediterranean
– archeologists have turned up goods here from as far away as Greece. The land
between the rivers was heavily forested, as is recalled by the many place names
ending in *-euil*, such as Bourgueil and Montreuil, which comes from the Gallic
word "*ialos*", meaning "clearing".

Celts and Romans

When Julius Caesar began his conquest of what he called Gaul in 58 BC, he
found a sophisticated Iron Age people living in fortified villages across the

region we know as France. The Romans referred to their enemies as either Gauls or Celts, but didn't trouble to enquire too deeply into their origins. They probably arrived in the region from the east in around 500 BC, perhaps bringing with them the culture we know as "Celtic", and settling alongside – or even among – earlier peoples. By the time Caesar encountered them, they were loosely gathered into tribes: the Turones from what is now Touraine; the Carnutes from between Chartres and the Orléanais; the Andecavi from Anjou; and the Bituriges from Bourges – whose name means "kings of the world". These tribes were by no means as "barbarian" as the Romans generally imagined them to be: they minted their own coins, traded across long distances and seem to have had centralized religious practices. Caesar's account of his campaign, the *Conquest of Gaul*, refers to a great druidic meeting in the Forest of the Carnutes, probably held in the vicinity of modern St-Benoît-sur-Loire, in what was called the *omphalos*, or navel, of the country. Valuable material evidence of this druidic culture was found near Orléans in 1861, when the Treasure of Neuvy-en-Sullias was discovered, its sophisticated cast-bronze animals and figurines indicating some kind of veneration of forest creatures.

Caesar found the Carnutes particularly hard to subdue. In 53 BC, the people of Cenabum, the capital of the Carnutes on the site of modern-day Orléans, rose up against the Romans. Caesar responded by razing the city, an action that helped spark a pan-Gaulish uprising. In the ensuing war, the Carnutes sent some 12,000 troops to the aid of the Gaulish leader Vercingetorix; most were massacred at the siege of Alésia, in 52 BC.

Roman rule over a pacified Gaul brought the well-known benefits: order, straight roads, aqueducts, trade with the empire, country villas, wine and towns. The chief cities of the Loire – or the Liger, as the Romans called the river – were all founded in this era. Most were built on Celtic sites, including Juliomagus (Angers), Caesarodunum (Tours), Vindinium (Le Mans), Vindocinum (Vendôme), Avaricum (Bourges) and Aurelianum (Orléans). Le Mans and, to a lesser extent, Tours, still preserve their Gallo-Roman walls, and near Luynes, you can see a stretch of the aqueduct that once supplied Tours with water.

The Franks

From the third century, Gaul began to be invaded by fresh waves of incomers from the east. At much the same time, Christianity was spreading fast throughout the empire. The bishop St Gatien is known to have preached in Tours in around 250 AD, but Christianity only became established at the end of the fourth century, with the arrival of **St Martin** (see box on p.75). In the early fifth century, two groups of probable Germanic origin, the **Franks** and the Visigoths, fought it out over Touraine, while Attila's Huns attacked Orléans – only to be repulsed by troops rallied by another early bishop, St Aignan. By 485, the Franks, under Clovis, had finally crossed the Loire and won control of Gaul, establishing the **Merovingian** dynasty. As described by the chronicler Gregory of Tours, Clovis converted to Christianity and summoned a council of bishops to Orléans, where they drew up the **Lex Salica**, the legal code of the Franks, which established the rule that daughters could not inherit land – this "salic law" was to become very significant in the dynastic struggles that ensued.

Years of vicious and fratricidal power struggles followed, until the palace mayor Charles Pepin, known as Charles Martel, "the Hammer", usurped his

Merovingian overlords. He defeated the invading Arab armies in 732, the battle taking place somewhere on the plateau between southern Touraine and northern Poitou. Local legend claims that the prisoners were settled in the **Pays du Véron**, the spit of land between the Loire and Vienne, and that the local population is still darker skinned than in neighbouring *communes*.

Martel's grandson, **Charlemagne** (747–814) presided over a massive expansion of the Frankish territories well beyond the boundaries of modern-day France. Sadly, little remains of this miniature **Carolingian** renaissance, other than a few scraps of decorative fragments on the church at Azay-le-Rideau and the oratory chapel near St-Benoît, built by Theodulf, Charlemagne's counsellor and bishop of Orléans. Of the great centre of learning established by **Alcuin of York** at Tours, nothing remains except Carolingian minuscule, the superbly readable script – it invented spaces between words, for one thing – on which the exact shapes of all modern European letters are based.

Capets and Plantagenets

From the end of the eighth century, **Viking** raiders began to make incursions up the Loire, besieging Tours in 843, sacking Angers in 854 and taking control of Normandy, to the north of the Loire region, in the early tenth century. The ensuing chaos hastened the final collapse of the Carolingian empire, ushering in an era of highly militarized local lords. The area between Orléans and Paris belonged to the Robertians, who under Hugues le Grand became the most powerful family in France. Le Grand's son, **Hugues Capet** – named after the famous cape of the local patron St Martin (see box on p.75) – was eventually elected king of the Franks in Ste-Croix cathedral, in Orléans, in 987, thus beginning the **Capetian** dynasty. The coronation only gave him notional overlordship over his feudal vassals, however, and he had little power outside his own territories in the Orléanais and Ile de France.

Over to the west, the counts of Anjou and Blois fought it out over Touraine. Under **Foulque Nerra** (972–1040), the "Black Falcon" of Anjou, the Angevins (the people from Anjou) won decisively, and protected their enlarged territories with a string of fortified keeps, a number of which – Loches and Langeais, in particular – still survive. Nerra went on to conquer Maine and the Vendômois, establishing Anjou as one of the most powerful counties in France.

The Plantagenet empire

In the early twelfth century, the Angevin count Geoffroi le Bel – called "**Plantagenêt**" for his habit of wearing a sprig of broom (*genêt* in French) in his hat – made two moves that significantly extended the territories belonging to Anjou. In 1110, he married Matilda, the daughter and heir of Henry I of England, and he later conquered Normandy in 1144. His son, Henri Plantagenêt (Plantagenet in English) did even better, marrying **Eleanor of Aquitaine** (see box on p.256) and inheriting the English throne as **Henry II**, which made him master of a miniature empire stretching from the Scottish border to the Pyrenees, and incorporating roughly a third of France – a far larger territory than that controlled by the Capetian king, Louis VII.

War between the Capets and Plantagenets was almost inevitable, especially as Eleanor had previously been Louis' wife; the sporadic clashes that ensued were named the "**First Hundred Years War**". By 1189, the rebellion of Henry's

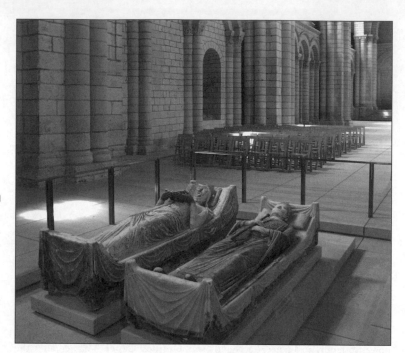

△ The tombs of Henry Plantagenet and Eleanor of Aquitaine, Fontevraud

elder sons forced him to sue for peace, and he died in Chinon a broken man (see box on p.102). In the first years of the thirteenth century, his youngest son, John "Lackland", lost most of the empire to Philippe-Auguste, the martial son of Louis.

The Loire now lay wholly in Capetian hands, and under Louis VIII it was parcelled up and given to the royal children in appanage, meaning it could be held as a semi-autonomous territory under the Crown. The main purpose of the system was to provide the royal children with an independent source of income. Louis' youngest son was given Anjou and Maine, becoming **Charles I d'Anjou** (numerals being used for scions of powerful families as well as kings). His eldest son, **Louis IX**, signed the Treaty of Paris in 1259, officially ending the First Hundred Years War. Under its terms, all that remained of the Plantagenets' continental territories was Gascony, in Aquitaine. It soon proved to be a contentious bit of land.

Charles I used his Angevin power-base to launch the conquest of Naples and Sicily between 1265 and 1268 – the twin kingdoms whose titles he had been granted by the pope. He didn't hold onto the territories for long, but the claim to their titles passed down to his descendants – along with the title to king of Jerusalem, which Charles bought in 1277.

The origins of the Valois kings

The last Capetian monarch, Charles IV, died in 1328 without a male heir. Two nobles came forward to claim the throne. One was **Philippe de Valois**, a descendant of Charles I d'Anjou and nephew of Philippe IV. The other was

Edward III of England, who based his title on being the grandson of Philippe IV through his mother – Philippe's daughter – Isabelle. The salic law clearly ruled out Edward's claim, and in 1328 **Philippe VI** was duly crowned at Reims. He was the first of the Valois line, the dynasty that so favoured the Loire over the next two hundred years.

In 1341, Philippe applied the **gabelle** – the salt tax on which royal revenue was based – to the whole of France. Much of France's salt came up the Loire from Brittany, and the tax began to be applied rigorously along its length. Soon afterwards, the boatmen who worked on the Loire formed a **guild** to protect themselves against rapacious tolls levied by the land-owning aristocrats on either bank. It was one of the first signs of the rising confidence of local tradesmen, an early hint of the Loire-based rise of the bourgeoisie.

The Hundred Years War

Edward III had initially done homage to Philippe VI as feudal overlord of the remaining English territory in Aquitaine, but in 1337 he repudiated his oath and launched what became known as the **Hundred Years War**. The English landed in France in 1346 with the dual aims of making Edward III's claim to the French throne a reality and recapturing the lost Plantagenet territories of Anjou, Normandy and the wider duchy of Aquitaine. At **Crécy**, in northern France, the English won a decisive battle, decimating the French cavalry. They almost immediately signed a truce. Thus began a succession of brief conflicts followed by periods of peace, forming a pattern that lasted for 116 years. English armies and mercenary bands roamed throughout northern and western France, alternately gaining, losing and simply terrorizing the lands they passed through, which often included the Loire. The wars were a tragedy for the peasantry, in particular, as their lives became steadily more brutish and insecure. The arrival of the **Black Death** in 1348 devastated the Loire region along with the rest of France, killing as much as a third of the population.

A second major French defeat, at **Poitiers** in 1356, led to the imprisonment in England of Philippe's son, Jean le Bon. Jean's elder son succeeded him as Charles V, pursuing a more successful policy of gradually chipping away at the territories held by the English in northern and southwestern France until, in 1369, he seized all of Aquitaine. Meanwhile, Charles V's brothers – the dukes of Anjou, Berry (see box on p.226) and Burgundy – ruled their allotted provinces in appanage, growing rich and powerful, especially after they became regents for the child king Charles VI, from 1380. Over in England, the dethronement of Richard II in 1399 and his subsequent death brought an end to the Plantagenet line there.

Joan and the Dauphin

The wars between France and England received new impetus when the Burgundian duke **Jean sans Peur** ("the Fearless"), son of Philippe le Hardi, threw in his lot with the English in 1414. In 1415, the English armies arrived under the warlike Henry V, defeating the French at **Agincourt** on October 25 and taking control of most of northern France over the next four years. In 1418, the Burgundians occupied Paris, and in 1420 Charles VI was forced to sign the **Treaty of Troyes**, which disinherited his son and heir, the **Dauphin Charles**, in favour of Henry V of England. The Dauphin fled to the Loire and the territories he had inherited from his uncle, Jean de Berry, moving frequently between his châteaux in Bourges, Mehun-sur-Yèvre, Chinon and Loches.

In 1421, the battle of **Baugé**, in northern Anjou, stemmed the English advance. The following year, Charles had himself proclaimed king of France at Mehun-sur-Yèvre, although he controlled no more than a fraction of the country – his enemies mockingly calling him the "little king of Bourges". Advisers such as **Georges de la Trémoïlle**, from Sully-sur-Loire, counselled him to follow a pacifying, diplomatic solution, while others such as **Dunois**, of Châteaudun and Beaugency, wanted confrontation. The Loire became the front line. In 1426, Charles won a minor battle at Montargis, north of Orléans, but two years later the English were able to lay siege to Orléans, threatening Charles's heartlands. The situation was parlous, and might well have ended in complete defeat had it not been for the arrival at court, in 1429, of **Joan of Arc** (see box on p.191), a peasant girl who galvanized Charles into action with promises of divine support. The English were driven back, the Dauphin crowned as Charles VII at Reims in July 1429, and Joan burnt at the stake in 1431.

The royal Loire

Over the next twenty years, **Charles VII** drove the English out of all France except for a pocket around Calais; Paris was retaken in 1436, Le Mans in 1448. The Loire was now no longer an island of vulnerable French territory, but the heartland of a kingdom rapidly growing in wealth, population and confidence. From the 1450s, the court embarked on an era of luxury centred on the Loire Valley. Aside from Charles's personal knowledge of the region, earned during the hard times of the war, the valley's attractions were obvious. Its climate was excellent, the forests provided good hunting, the vines produced excellent **wine** and there was a pre-existing network of fine châteaux between which the court – still itinerant at this time – could move. The Loire also had the advantage of being politically reliable, having backed the Crown during the wars – unlike Paris. Charles installed his mistress, **Agnès Sorel** (see p.129), in Loches and indulged in hunting, jousting and other chivalric pursuits with his sophisticated relative, **René d'Anjou** (see box on p.277), who had his own miniature court to the west. In Blois, the poet-duke **Charles d'Orléans** set up a third, relatively modest court, which later grew famous as the site of the **Concours de Blois**, a poetry contest held in the late 1550s (see p.144).

For the court, it was a time of prosperity and ease, and even for the local **peasantry** life grew less hard. The threats of war and plague steadily receded, and from 1450 the harvests did not fail for an unbroken period of seventy years. Populations began to grow again, especially in the towns of the Loire where there was new employment on the fringes of the court circle. In the country-side, a kind of peasant aristocracy took shape in the form of the smallholder *fermiers*, or *coqs de village*, who acted as intermediaries between journeymen peasants, and merchants and the local *seigneur*, or lord. In the towns, the *aisés*, or well-to-do merchants and artisans, began to form the basis of what would

The Loire kings

Charles VI	1380–1422	Louis XII	1498–1515
Charles VII	1422–1461	François I	1515–1547
Louis XI	1461–1483	Henri II	1547–1559
Charles VIII	1483–1498	François II	1559–1560

become the bourgeoisie. The Loire, as ever, formed a crucial trade artery, its shallow-drafted sailing vessels carrying goods from the Atlantic ports deep into the centre of France, from where they were shipped across to Paris or over into the Rhône valley, for access to the Mediterranean.

In 1461, **Louis XI** came to the throne, making Tours the home of the court in preference to Paris. He established a major silk industry in the city, and set about uniting the various territories of France, inheriting Anjou, Maine and Provence after the death of René in 1481, and winning control of Burgundy and Picardy a year later. During his reign, the merchant classes grew steadily more powerful. The most powerful families were all intermarried and financially intertwined, and in 1465 the Beaunes, Briçonnets and Berthelots formed a powerful syndicate, protected by Jean Bourré, who built Langeais and Le Plessis-Bourré.

In the last years of his life, Louis succumbed to paranoia, barricading himself into his château at **Plessis**, just outside Tours. In 1483, he was succeeded by his 13-year-old son **Charles VIII**, though the kingdom was effectively run for the next seven years by **Ann de Beaujeu** from her seat in Gien. She had to fight both Brittany and domestic rebels. The malcontents – **Louis d'Orléans**, son of the poet Charles, and François I d'Orléans-Longueville, son of Dunois – were defeated at Beaugency in 1485, and later banished, while the skirmishes with Brittany were resolved by the forced marriage of Charles to Anne Bretogne at Langeais in 1491 (see box on p.97).

Charles VIII

By the close of the fifteenth century, the Loire had become the centre of a rich, large and well-ordered kingdom. After scarcely fifty years of peace, the French now turned their attention beyond their borders, to **Italy**, where Ferdinand of Naples had just died. Re-invoking the Angevin claim to the throne, Charles VIII invaded in August 1494 and conquered Naples by February 1495, his swift victory partly due to the new invention of iron cannon balls and partly to the age-old technique of treating the opponent with extreme cruelty – such that the murder, rape and firestorm left in the army's wake was known as the *furia francese*. By July 1495, however, Charles was forced to retreat across the Alps, and he had lost all his gains by December.

The French brought back two things that changed the shape of French history. The first was **syphilis**, which the French called the "Neapolitan sickness" (the Neapolitans, by contrast, called it the "French disease"). The second was a taste for Italianate architecture, which soon mushroomed into a full-blooded passion for all things Italian, ushering in the rediscovery of Classical learning and taste in the **French Renaissance**. Charles began elaborate works on his château at Amboise, but in 1498 hit his head on a doorway while on his way to watch a game of tennis (see p.84) and died, suddenly, without heirs.

Louis XII

Under the salic law, the heir to the throne had to be traced through the male line. Louis d'Orléans, the son of the poet Charles and great nephew of Charles VI, duly ascended the throne as **Louis XII** in 1498, and quickly set about getting rid of his infertile wife, **Jeanne de France**, whom he had married in 1476 under the orders of her father Louis XI – ironically, in an attempt to ensure the termination of the rival Orléans line. An infamous annulment was quickly granted in Tours. Jeanne founded an order of nuns in Bourges and later took the veil herself. Louis was now free to secure Brittany by marrying Charles's widow, Anne de Bretagne, which he did in 1499.

Louis made **Blois** his capital, bringing the merchant classes fully within the circle of power for the first time in French history and relying increasingly on their financial acumen and resources. He continued the **Italian wars**, his Loire-based captain Charles II d'Amboise (see p.166) helping conquer Milan. The French brought back the Milanese duke Ludovico Sforza as a prisoner and held him captive in Loches (see p.131). More significant in the long term was the arrival of Italian artists and craftsmen, who were set to work decorating proto-Renaissance châteaux such as **Chaumont** and the Louis XII wing at **Blois**.

François I and the Renaissance

François I, a cousin of Louis XII, became king through yet another failure in the male line. According to an English chronicler, he was "a goodly prince, stately of countenance, merry of chere, brown coloured, great eyes, high nosed, big lipped, fair breasted". He was also six-foot tall, courageous, charming and well educated: a true Renaissance prince. During his reign, the fortunes of the Loire Valley reached their zenith. The importation of Italian artists and Renaissance ideas continued to gather pace, and the king built fabulous new lodgings at **Amboise** – where he had been brought up and to which he later invited **Leonardo da Vinci** (see box on p.87) – and **Blois**, as well as a vast new château at **Chambord**.

The turning point came in 1525, when François I was defeated at **Pavia** while prosecuting yet another futile and aggrandizing military campaign in Italy. The king was made prisoner by Charles V of Spain: "all is lost," he said, "except my honour and my life." When he returned to France, in 1526, he found his **finances** in dire need of attention. Huge loans had been required for châteaux construction, the Italian wars and the king's ransom of two million gold écus, and the daily expenditure on a court of some 10,000 people was vast. Initially, the necessary income had been supplied by the same group of *haut bourgeois* families that had begun to grow wealthy under Louis XI, but the whole financial system collapsed in the great accounting scandals of the late 1520s. In 1527, the arch-financier **Jacques de Beaune-Semblançay** was hanged at the age of eighty – more because the king owed him millions than because of any wrongdoing – and many of his cronies and relations were brought down with him. As the royal investigations progressed, the hitherto suspiciously hasty construction of two of the newest and most sumptuous country residences – Gilles Berthelot's **Azay-le-Rideau**, and **Chenonceau**, built by Thomas de Bohier and Catherine Briçonnet – was brought to an abrupt halt. Berthelot fled the country in 1527, while the Bohiers were forced to give Chenonceau to the Crown in 1533.

It was the end of the Loire's golden age. François steadily abandoned the region for Paris and his new palaces at the Louvre and Fontainebleau, and turned his attention to fighting the new menace to the kingdom's unity: Protestantism.

The Wars of Religion

On October 18, 1534, placards appeared in Paris and Amboise, entitled: *True articles on the horrible, great and insufferable abuses of the papal mass*. One was even found on the door of the king's bedchamber. It was the first murmuring of an impending civil war of bewildering complexity, known as the **Wars of Religion**. For a while, however, civil war seemed a distant prospect. During the reign of Henri II, who succeeded François I in 1547, and his wife **Catherine de Médicis**, from the powerful Medici clan of Florence, the court continued its life of peripatetic luxury. Thousands of people would move lock, stock and barrel from one Loire château to another, living a life dedicated to pleasure, and giving balls of legendary decadence – most famously in the **château de Chenonceau** (see p.89). On the back of this elaborate court culture, literature reached a new peak with the creation of the **Pléiade**, a group of seven writers who aimed to reinvent French poetry following Classical and Italian models; chief among them were locally born **Pierre de Ronsard** (see p.343) and **Joachim du Bellay** (see p.342). Meanwhile, **François Rabelais** from Chinon wrote his landmark tales *Gargantua* and *Pantagruel* (see p.343).

It was only after Henri died in a jousting accident in 1559 – a splinter from a broken lance lodged in his eye – that the simmering religious tensions boiled over. In 1560, came the **Tumult of Amboise** (see p.85), swiftly followed by François de Guise's massacre of Huguenot worshippers in 1562. From this time, the name of **Guise**, belonging to the powerful dukes of Lorraine, became inextricably associated with an ultra-Catholic faction pitted against the Protestant **Huguenots**. The Guises were determined to make the Crown enforce religious unity, while the Huguenot leaders sought guarantees of religious toleration. Catherine de Médicis – who became sometime regent and influential powerbroker for the next thirty years during the reigns of her three sons François II, Charles IX and Henri III – attempted to hold the balance of power. At first she pursued a policy of moderate (by sixteenth-century standards) toleration, but neither Guises nor Huguenots could ever be satisfied. Immediately after the massacre of 1562, the Huguenot leader, the prince de Condé, seized **Orléans**, followed by other cities along the Loire. Protestantism was particularly strong in the Loire, where it had found favour among the burgeoning middle classes; **Saumur**, in particular, became a Huguenot stronghold, as was **Sancerre**, at the opposite end of the region. Huguenots rampaged through the region's cathedrals and churches in an iconoclastic fury, and for much of the next twenty years civil war raged across France. For once, ordinary people were willing participants.

In Paris, the **St Bartholomew's Day Massacre** of August 24, 1572 saw Protestants murdered in the streets by mobs or agents of the Guises, and the violence spread rapidly; hundreds, perhaps thousands were murdered in the towns of the Loire; the attacks in Bourges, Saumur and Angers were particularly vicious. In 1574, Henri III came to the throne, and in 1576 Henri de Guise formed the radical **Catholic League**, after which the conflict deepened. The next stage of the wars acquired the name of the **War of the Three Henrys**, after Henri III, Henri, duc de Guise, and Henri de Navarre, the leader of the Protestant cause and the heir to the throne. In May 1588, the king was forced to abandon Paris by rampaging supporters of the Catholic League. He fled to Tours, where he made peace with Henri de Navarre; their joint armies defeated the troops of the League just outside the city. In December, in an attempt to resolve the crisis definitively, the king summoned the French parliament, the Etats Généraux, to Blois, where he had Henri de Guise murdered (see box on p.147). Catherine died a few days later, and Henri III himself was assassinated by a fanatical Catholic the following year.

The Bourbons

From 1589, Henri de Navarre ruled as **Henri IV**, taking the name of his father, Antoine de Bourbon, as the name of his dynasty. It was to be the last. Henri's coronation had to take place at **Chartres**, as Reims was still in the hostile hands of the Catholic League, but after renouncing Protestantism, he swiftly pacified his kingdom. The 1598 Edict of Nantes allowed a degree of religious freedom. Not all French Catholics were reconciled, however, and the king was assassinated by a radical Catholic in 1610. He was succeeded by his 8-year-old son, Louis XIII, whose mother, **Marie de Médicis**, acted as regent.

Under Henri IV, a Protestant academy had been set up in Saumur, but the Bourbon court was now firmly established in Paris, and the Loire was forgotten by the main stream of national affairs. The populations of the main towns fell throughout the seventeenth century and the region steadily became little more than another provincial backwater. As early as 1617 **Blois** was considered far enough from court to be a suitable place of exile for Marie de Médicis, sent there by the newly assertive Louis XIII to keep her out of state affairs. She escaped in 1619, but was soon replaced at Blois by Louis' rebellious brother, **Gaston d'Orléans**, who devoted himself to building the fourth and last of the château's wings. In the 1630s, **Cardinal Richelieu**, Louis XIII's chief minister, attempted to promote a revival by planning a new town in southern Touraine, modestly called Richelieu, but few investors were interested. The main economic activity took place along the rivers, which carried ever-increasing amounts of trade to Paris, a route facilitated by the building of a **canal** linking the Seine and the Loire in the mid-seventeenth century.

Louis XIV may have briefly sheltered in Gien during the tax revolts of the **Fronde** in 1652, and he later enjoyed summer sojourns in **Chambord** – where **Molière** performed the première of the *Bourgeois Gentilhomme* – but he did nothing to promote the region. In fact, his **revocation of the Edict of Nantes** in 1685 seriously undermined the Loire's prospects. Thousands of Protestants, many of them from the prosperous middle classes, fled renewed religious persecution. Tours and Saumur were particularly hard hit, while Orléans rode out the crisis on the strength of its thriving river trade and burgeoning vinegar industry, and Angers and Blois maintained brisk business in wine and spirits. During the eighteenth century, Angers also laid down the foundations of its fruit and market-gardening industries, and opened up large-scale slate mines. In the countryside, however, peasant life remained a matter of bleak subsistence.

The Revolution and the nineteenth century

The **Revolution** of 1789 and the proclamation of the Republic in 1792 affected the Loire less than other French regions. The church lost all its extensive landholdings, which were redistributed among the peasantry, but the nobility mainly kept their châteaux and attached lands. Both governing classes and peasantry largely accepted the decrees from Paris, and only in the southwest of the region was there serious trouble, when the "Whites", or Royalist, Catholic conservatives of the Vendée and western Anjou, mobilized against revolutionary troops in 1793. Saumur and Angers suffered under the revolutionary backlash, but the murderous "Terror" of 1793–4 left the Loire largely untouched. The fluctuating price of grain seemed to be the peasantry's chief concern, and later, under Napoleon, the threat of conscription.

During the **nineteenth century**, technology slowly revolutionized society. Agriculture became more productive and potentially profitable, and for the first time the countryside started to boom in comparison with the towns. Steam-boats, introduced in the 1830s, briefly invigorated the river trade by cutting journey times by more than half – it used to take the **mariners** just under a week to sail from Orléans to Angers, and up to three times that in the opposite direction. But the **train line** between Orléans and Tours was completed in 1845, and the Paris–Orléans route just one year later. Trade quickly shifted from the capricious, weather- and season-dependent Loire to the reliable trains instead. With the end of channel dredging, the river's navigable channels quickly silted up. Steadily, cities and towns turned their backs on the river, building new civic squares and landmark buildings inland, beside the train stations. In just a few years, the once-vibrant quays were abandoned.

Napoleon III's disastrous **Franco–Prussian war** of 1870 was quickly followed by the siege of Paris and the fall of the Second Empire. On October 7, the Minister of the Interior, **Léon Gambetta**, fled in a hot air balloon, landing at Tours where he briefly formed a government – the first time the region had tasted anything approaching national significance since the parliaments held in Blois during the Wars of Religion. The only French victory in the entire sorry affair occurred at Coulmiers, just west of Orléans, in November 1870, though the victorious Armée de la Loire lost three times as many troops as the Prussians and, in any case, the battle had almost no effect on the progress of the war. As the politicians jockeyed for power in the new Third Republic, the **comte de Chambord** (see box on p.159) was approached with a view to establishing a constitutional monarchy, but his uncompromising **White Flag Manifesto** of 1871 effectively scotched Bourbon chances. The region's wine industries were devastated by the depredations of the **phylloxera beetle** between 1876 and 1883. In the later nineteenth and the early twentieth century, the Loire again lapsed into provincial obscurity, though the foundations of later growth were laid with the establishment of Orléans' pharmaceutical industry.

The World Wars

The fighting of **World War I** killed tens of thousands of the region's young men, one of them being the author **Alain Fournier**, who died defending Paris in September 1914 during the desperate battle of the Marne. The trenches lay hundreds of kilometres to the north, but the Loire was close enough and safe enough to receive train- after train-load of the injured and mutilated. In the winter of 1918–19, the **Spanish influenza** killed yet more people, including the elderly and women and children weakened by four years of malnourishment.

In the aftermath of the war, rural areas all over France suffered, and the Loire was no exception. Grain prices – still a major concern – collapsed, unemployment was rife, and the economic benefits of the peace were slow to filter through. Socialism grew in popularity, though the Loire region remained relatively conservative, cut off from affairs in Paris, let alone elsewhere in Europe. Germany, certainly, seemed very far away.

World War II

The German invasion at the beginning of **World War II** was sudden, fast and devastatingly effective. On June 10, 1940, the government fled south from Paris towards **Tours**, quartering itself in various nearby châteaux – most of them not connected by telephone. When **Winston Churchill** arrived at the Préfecture, the offices of the regional government, on June 13, he found the place deserted. He eventually tracked down the errant national government later that day, but could do nothing to persuade it to fight. The same night the Germans bombed Tours, and then occupied Paris the next day, even as the French government fled south again, to Bordeaux. Meanwhile, millions of **refugees** and leaderless soldiers streamed south across the bridges of the Loire. The Germans savagely strafed and bombed the riverside quarters of the Loire towns, causing the partial destruction of many of the loveliest among them – notably Orléans, Tours, Blois and Gien. The French destroyed their own bridges. On June 17, **Marshal Pétain** broadcast his call for an armistice; the next day, **Général de Gaulle** delivered his radio-call for resistance from London. Most mayors responded to this murder and destruction by declaring their towns "open", stating that they would not resist the Occupation. Only in Saumur was the Loire successfully held against the advancing Germans – astonishingly, by mere cadets (see box on p.250). But their resistance lasted just three days. On June 22, the **armistice** was signed, dividing France into occupied and unoccupied sectors.

The peace deal split Touraine in two. The new border ran along the Cher east of Tours – right through **Chenonceau** – then turned southwest. Chinon and everywhere west lay under German control, while Loches, southeastern Touraine and most of the Berry formed part of the new **Vichy France**. On October 24, at the railway station of **Montoire-sur-Loir**, Hitler and Pétain met to agree the official policy of collaboration.

Other than a few sporadic episodes of genuine heroism – such as the stance taken by **Jean Moulin**, the prefect of Chartres (see p.306) – the experience of the Loire was typically mixed. Collaboration, both reluctant and enthusiastic, could be found alongside passive or active resistance, and profiteering went hand in hand with severe deprivation. Rivalries and hatreds established at this time are still a matter of passionate debate, a situation fomented by a recent spate of books naming names in the wake of the release of official records. At the time, most of the peasantry just put up with the Germans as best as they could. Thousands of young agricultural workers were sent away to work the fields in Germany, while the deportation of Jews, Roma people, homosexuals and dissidents began in 1942. On November 11 the same year, the Germans completed the occupation of France. The regime grew harsher and resistance stiffer.

British and American troops stormed the **Normandy beaches** on June 6, 1944, but it wasn't until mid-August that the Allied armies reached the Loire. The Liberation was tinged with sadness. Allied bombing in the prior weeks had completed the destructive work begun by the Germans in 1940, and many towns lay partially in ruins, especially along the riverbanks.

The Loire since 1945

At the end of World War II, the Loire was still a deeply traditional region. Peasants – not an insulting term in France – still wore clogs and worked the soil, often by hand, while aristocrats still occupied their châteaux and the middle classes confined themselves to the towns. Many rural people lived largely on what they grew themselves, and market day was the highlight of the week. Much of that is still true today, though a good deal has changed.

Cars and tractors replaced horses in the 1950s, at the same time as the economic growth of the cities sucked thousands in from the countryside.

Bombed-out quarters were rebuilt, at first rapidly and carelessly, later with more concern for aesthetics. From the 1960s, state spending increased dramatically. In 1964, the first of four **nuclear power stations** was built on the Loire, at Avoine, near Chinon, and market gardens were established using the warm – and supposedly radiation-free – water from the cooling towers. River pollution grew steadily – mostly due to over-use of fertilizers rather than heavy industry – and hydroelectricity dams upstream led to **salmon** numbers plummeting from hundreds of thousands to mere hundreds; fishing for salmon, once the symbol of the Loire, is still banned today. Public **universities** were set up in Orléans, Tours and Angers in the late 1960s and early 1970s, and at around the same time the **wine industry** regenerated itself: *appellations* were re-established, vineyards replanted and quality more tightly controlled. Tourism, too, grew exponentially with the help of government backing and a new entrepreneurial spirit among the region's private-château owners – faced with giant tax bills, there was little else they could do. In 1990, the high-speed **TGV**, or *train à grande vitesse*, arrived in Vendôme from Paris. As it has steadily spread its electrified tentacles south and west into the heart of the region, it has brought with it thousands of buyers of **second homes**, at first from the Paris region – many people even commute – and later from the UK. Certain pockets of the Loire are particularly popular with *les Anglais*, notably the Maine *département*, north of Angers, and the region around Chinon. Comparisons are often made locally with the Plantagenet days.

The rediscovery of tradition

Despite the many social and technological changes, the Loire remains a quietly conservative region. The **old customs** are maintained in subtle ways: small vegetable plots can be seen everywhere, for example, tiny scraps of country vineyard provide wine for many town tables, and hunting is practised with passion by rich and poor alike – rich and poor men, that is. Church-going is no more prevalent than elsewhere in republican France, but Sundays are respected as days for visiting the family or eating out in a restaurant. Family-owned businesses from *charcuteries* to shoe shops still hold out against the multinationals, and even supermarkets source much of their food products locally. Most obviously, the cooking in homes and restaurants alike is resolutely regional, with few concessions to even Parisian fads, let alone foreign styles of cooking.

If anything, the Loire has become *more* traditional in recent years. The **heritage industry** has helped ignite a powerful kind of local patriotism that encompasses anything from rebuilding the old wooden boats used by the Loire mariners to rediscovering ingredients and dishes enjoyed in the Middle Ages. Many château owners are enthusiastically restoring their homes, helped by government grants and, since 2005, by a change in the law which allows them to direct works themselves. Previously, they had been obliged to employ artisans and architects officially certified to work on historic monuments – an expensive business.

In such an atmosphere, tourism is not so much voyeurism as a matter of taking part in the region's rediscovery of itself. Every village and town has plans to redevelop the quays, to put boats back on the river and to outdo the river festivities of neighbouring *communes*. There are even signs that the various administrative territories that parcel up the valley are starting to be able to work together: since 2006, the new Loire à Vélo cycle route (see p.42) has traced the course of the river from Orléans to downstream of Angers. Everywhere there is evidence of a desire to somehow turn back to where it all began: the Loire itself.

Writers of the Loire

L iterature and the Loire have been intertwined since the medieval era, when **Guillaume de Lorris** and **Jean de Meun**, both from the Orléanais, wrote the *Romance of the Rose*. The fifteenth-century poet **François Villon** spent time in the region – much of it in prison – but it was in the Renaissance that the Loire truly came to the fore. Three of the greatest writers of the epoch were born in the region: **François Rabelais**, near Chinon, **Pierre de Ronsard**, in the Vendômois, and **Joachim du Bellay**, in Anjou. *La Belle au bois dormant*, the most famous of Charles Perrault's seventeenth-century fairy tales, was supposedly inspired by the château d'Ussé, but the Loire only became prominent again in the nineteenth century, notably through the work of **Honoré de Balzac**, who was born in Tours and based a number of his novels in Touraine. Alexandre Dumas successfully exploited the region's rich past in his historical thrillers *La Dame de Montsoreau* and *Le Vicomte de Bragelonne* (*The Man in the Iron Mask*), and Alfred de Vigny did the same in his *Cinq Mars*. The regions surrounding the Loire Valley proper have also been fertile ground for fiction: the Beauce region, just north of the Loire, is the setting for Emile Zola's powerful evocation of peasant life, *La Terre*; Joris-Karl Huysmans' *La Cathédrale* celebrates Chartres; while Marcel Proust's *A la récherche du temps perdu* opens in the author's childhood home in Combray (Illiers), just southwest of Chartres. South of the Loire, the rustic life of the Berry is portrayed in fine, naturalistic detail in Georges Sand's *Le Meunier d'Angibault, Jeanne* and *La Mare au diable*, while the atmosphere of the Sologne is superbly conjured in Maurice Genevoix's *Raboliot* and **Alain-Fournier**'s *Le Grand Meaulnes*. For reviews of books available in translation, see p.348.

Very little is known about the two authors of the *Romance of the Rose*, but their names indicate that they both came from the Loire region: Guillaume de Lorris, from the village of the same name in the Forêt d'Orléans, and Jean de Meun from Meung-sur-Loire. Guillaume probably wrote the original 4000-line poem in the 1230s, Jean de Meun adding his 18,000 lines some forty years later. In its final form, the *Romance* was a medieval bestseller, reproduced in hundreds of beautifully illuminated manuscripts, and influencing generations of poets, including Geoffrey Chaucer. It takes the form of a dream vision and allegorical tale about a Lover's journey towards his Rose, variously helped and thwarted on the way by such figures as Pleasure, Courtesy, Rebuff and Jealousy. Guillaume de Lorris's part is a relatively straightforward coded account of the progression of a love affair, containing, as he put it "the whole art of love ... anyone who aspires to love should pay attention".

The dream begins, from the *Romance of the Rose*

In this delightful month, when Love excites
All things, one night I, sleeping, had this dream.
Methought that it was full daylight. I rose
In haste, put on my shoes and washed my hands,
Then took a silver needle from its case,
Dainty and neat, and threaded it with silk.
I yearned to wander far outside the town
To hear what songs the birds were singing there
In every bush, to welcome the New Year.
Basting my sleeves in zigzags as I went

I pleased myself, in spite of solitude,
Listening to the birds that took such pains
To chant among the new-bloom-laden boughs.
Jolly and gay and full of happiness
I neared a rippling river which I loved;
For I no nicer thing than that stream knew.
From out a hillside close thereby it flowed,
Descending full and free and clear and cold
As water from a fountain or well.
Though it was somewhat lesser than the Seine,
More broad it spread; a fairer ne'er I saw.
Upon the bank I sat, the scene to scan,
And with the view delight myself, and lave
My face in the refreshing water there;
And, as I bent, I saw the river floor
All paved and covered with bright gravel stones.
The wide fair mead reached to the water's edge.
Calm and serene and temperate and clear
The morning was. I rose; and through the grass
Coasting along the bank I followed the stream.

Translated by Harry W. Robbins

(Syracuse University Press, 2002)

François Villon

More is known about the life of **François Villon** than most medieval poets, mostly because he was continually in trouble with the law. Born in 1431, he studied at Paris in the 1450s, where he burgled the Collège de Navarre and managed to kill a priest during a riot. He seems to have fled Paris, and attended Charles d'Orléans' poetry contest at Blois (see p.144), which required all the poets attending to compose a ballad beginning with a first line written by Charles himself; all the subsequent lines had to contain antitheses. Villon was later imprisoned by the Bishop of Orléans at Meung-sur-Loire (see box on p.200) – a sentence railed against with superb spleen in his most famous poem, a brilliant and rebelliously spirited mock will entitled *Le Testament* ("The Will"). Back in Paris, he was arrested again in 1462 and seems to have been sentenced to death or banishment – whereupon he disappears from the record.

From the *Ballad*, written for the contest at Blois

I die of thirst beside the fountainhead;
I chatter, tooth on tooth, as hot as fire.
A foreigner in my own land I tread;
Ardently shivering, by the brazier perspire.
Bare as a worm, in presidential attire,
I laugh in tears and hope without a hope;
I take more comfort in despair to mope;
Enjoy myself with no pleasure under the sun;
Forceful with no strength or power to cope,
So well received, thrown out by everyone.

I'm certain of uncertainty ahead;
Since everything's so clear, confused as mire;
Doubt nothing but what's certain, taken as read;
An accident all knowledge I acquire.
I always win yet stay a loser, sure-fire;
Bid folk good night as daybreak spreads its scope.
And, lying down, fear falling off the rope.
Legacy await, though neither heir nor son,
And, rolling in it, without a bean I lope,
So well received, thrown out by everyone.

Taken from *Poems of François Villon*, translated by Peter Dale (Anvil Press Poetry, 2001)

Joachim du Bellay

Joachim du Bellay was born in around 1522 into a noble family from Liré, a village beside the Loire in the far west of Anjou. He is counted among the coterie of seven lyric poets – five of whom were from the Loire region – grouped around Pierre de Ronsard (see opposite). Known as the Pléiade, after the stars of that constellation, the group aimed to revive French literature by emulating the works of Greece, Rome and Renaissance Italy, while writing in their native language. In 1553, du Bellay went to Rome, where he seems to have fallen in love and been bitterly disappointed – at least, if the emotions described in his two greatest collections, *Les Antiquitez de Rome* and *Les Regrets*, both published in 1558, are to be trusted. As he put it, "I did not find Rome in Rome". The two sequences, however, are among the finest written in French, at once deeply personal and highly accomplished, pushing forward the possibilities both for poetry and the French language. He died in 1560, and is buried in Paris's Notre-Dame cathedral.

Sonnet from *Les Regrets*

Happy the man who, like Ulysses, went
Sailing afar; or him who won the fleece,
Then, wise and worldly grown, returned to Greece,
Amongst his own, to live and die content.
Alas! When shall I end my banishment,
To see my village rooftops smoke, to cease
My wandering, see my humble home, in peace,
More grand to me than realm magnificent?
More do I love the home my fathers made
Than Rome's bold palaces, in pride arrayed:
More do I love fine slate than marble rare;
More than their Tiber do I love my Loire;
Their Palatine, more my Liré by far;
And more than sea's salt breeze, Anjou's soft air.

Taken from *Lyrics of the French Renaissance: Marot, du Bellay, Ronsard*, with English versions by Norman R. Shapiro (Yale University Press, 2002)

Pierre de Ronsard

Pierre de Ronsard was born at La Possonnière (see p.314) in 1524. Educated at the Collège de Navarre – as burgled by François Villon – he became the foremost of the Pléiade poets. In 1552, Ronsard published his greatest collections, the *Second Livre d'Amours* and the *Amours de Cassandre*. His poems were immediately recognized as masterpieces, and still reach a wide audience – partly because of their obsession with roses, used as symbols of beauty and mortality. In later life, Ronsard lived between Paris and Vendôme; he died in 1585 at St-Cosme, where he had been nominated prior.

Sonnet from *Le Second Livre d'Amours*

Just as, upon the branch, one sees the rose's
Bud bloom in May, young blossom newly spread
Before the sky, jealous of its bright red,
As Dawn, sprinkling her tears, the morn discloses;
Beauty lies in its leaf, and love reposes,
Wafting its scent on tree, bush, flowerbed:
But, lashed by rain or torrid heat, soon dead,
Leaf after leaf its fragile grace exposes.
So too, blooming with youth, as earth and heaven
Honoured your beauty, to Fate was it given
To slay your flesh, which now in ash reposes.
Take thus these tears that I, in tribute, shed,
This jug of milk, these blossoms heaped, outspread,
So that in death, as life, that flesh be roses.

Taken from *Lyrics of the French Renaissance: Marot, du Bellay, Ronsard*, with English versions by

Norman R. Shapiro (Yale University Press, 2002)

François Rabelais

François Rabelais was born near Chinon in around 1494, an episode "described" in typically Rabelaisian manner in the extract below. He trained first as a monk and later studied medicine. In 1532, he published *Pantagruel*, a heady mix of serious humanistic learning, satire and earthily exuberant comedy. The book was almost immediately condemned as obscene by the Sorbonne. In 1533, came the prequel, *Gargantua*, and in 1537 he became attached to the court of François I, later visiting Italy as part of the retinue of Cardinal Jean du Bellay, the cousin of the poet Joachim. The Third Book was drier and safer, but the scurrilously antipapal content of the Fourth Book lost him his position and may even have landed him in prison. Rabelais died in Paris soon after, in 1553.

Gargantua's birth, from *Gargantua*

Whilst they were pleasantly tattling on the subject of drinking, Gargamelle began to feel disturbed in her lower parts. Whereupon Grandgousier got up from the grass, and comforted her kindly, thinking that these were birth-pangs and telling her that since she had been resting under the willows she would soon be in a good state. She ought to take new heart, he said, at the coming of her new baby. For although the pains would be somewhat severe, they would nevertheless be quickly over, and the joy which would follow after would banish all her pain, so that only the memory of it would be left. [...]

A little while later she began to groan and wail and shout. Then suddenly swarms of midwives came up from every side, and feeling her underneath found some rather ill-smelling excrescences, which they thought were the child; but it was her fundament slipping out, because of the softening of her right intestine – which you call the bum-gut – owing to her having eaten too much tripe, as has been stated above.

At this point a dirty old hag of the company, who had the reputation of being a good she-doctor and had come from Brizepaille, near Saint Genou, sixty years before, made her an astringent, so horrible that all her sphincter muscles were stopped and constricted. Indeed you could hardly have relaxed them with your teeth – which is a most horrible thought – even if you had copied the method of the devil at the Mass of St Martin, when he wrote down the chatter of two local girls and stretched his parchment by tugging with his teeth.

By this misfortune the cotyledons of the matrix were loosened at the top, and the child leapt up through them to enter the hollow vein. Then, climbing through the diaphragm to a point above the shoulders where this vein divides in two, he took the left fork and came out by the left ear.

As soon as he was born he cried out, not like other children: "Mies! Mies!" but "Drink! Drink! Drink!", as if inviting the whole world to drink, and so loud that he was heard through all the lands of Booze and Bibulous.

I doubt whether you will truly believe in this strange nativity. I don't care if you don't. But an honest man, a man of good sense, always believes what he is told and what he finds written down. Is this a violation of our law or our faith? Is it against reason or against Holy Scripture? For my part I find nothing written in the Holy Bible which contradicts it. If this had been the will of God, would you say that he could not have performed it? For goodness' sake do not obfuscate your brains with such an idle thought. For I say to you that to God nothing is impossible. If it had been His will women would have produced their children in that way, by the ear, for ever afterwards.

Was not Bacchus begotten by Jupiter's thigh? Was not Rocquetaillade born from his mother's heel, and Crocquemouche from his nurse's slipper? Was not Minerva born from Jupiter's brain by way of his ear, and Adonis from the bark of a myrrh-tree, and Castor and Pollux from the shell of an egg laid and hatched by Leda? But you would be even more flabbergasted if I were now to expound to you the whole chapter of Pliny in which he speaks of strange and unnatural births; and anyhow, I am not such a barefaced liar as he was. Read Chapter three of the seventh book of his *Natural History*, and don't tease my brain any more on the subject.

Taken from *The Histories of Gargantua and Pantagruel*, translated by J.M. Cohen (Penguin)

Honoré de Balzac

Honoré de Balzac, the giant of nineteenth-century "realism", was born in Tours in 1799. Despite being sent away to school in Vendôme, and then moving to Paris, Touraine remained the novelist's spiritual home, the only place where he could rest and recover his creative powers – he described the sensation of returning to the region as like being "buried up to the neck in foie gras". Balzac wrote a number of his novels in Saché, at the house of Jean de Margonne, the father of his illegitimate brother, and later in life considered buying the château de Moncontour, near Vouvray. Most of the ninety novels of his great sequence, *La Comédie humaine*, are Paris-based, but a few are set in the Loire: most evocatively, *Le Lys dans la vallée*, a tale of troubled young love, with the countryside around Azay-le-Rideau as a spectacular backdrop; *Eugénie Grandet*, an unflinching story about frustrated love set in provincial Saumur; *Louis Lambert*, which draws heavily on Balzac's own experiences in Vendôme; and *Le Curé de Tours*, a novella about petty ambition and rivalry in the shadow of Tours' cathedral.

M Grandet's house, from *Eugénie Grandet*

Two pillars supported the arch above the doorway, and for these, as also for the building of the house itself, a porous crumbling stone peculiar to the district along the banks of the Loire had been employed, a kind of tufa so soft that at most it scarcely lasts for two hundred years. Rain and frost had gnawed numerous irregular holes in the surface, with a curious effect; the piers and the voussoirs looked as though they were composed of the vermicular stones often met with in French architecture. The doorway might have been the portal of a jail. Above the arch there was a long sculptured bas-relief of harder stone, representing the four seasons, four forlorn figures, aged, blackened and weatherworn. Above the bas-relief there was a projecting ledge of masonry where some chance-sown plants had taken root; yellow pellitory, bindweed, a plantain or two, and a little cherry tree, that even now had reached a fair height.

The massive door itself was of dark oak, shrunk and warped and full of cracks; but, feeble as it looked, it was firmly held together by a series of iron nails, with huge heads, driven into the wood in a symmetrical design. In the middle there was a small square grating covered with rusty iron bars, which served as an excuse for a door knocker which hung there from a ring, and struck upon the menacing head of a great iron bolt. The knocker itself, oblong in shape, was of the kind that our ancestors used to call a "jaquemart", and not unlike a huge note of exclamation. If an antiquary had examined it carefully, he might have found some traces of the grotesque human head that it once represented, but the features of the typical clown had long since been effaced by constant wear. The little grating had been made in past times of civil war, so that the household might recognize their friends without before admitting them, but now it afforded to inquisitive eyes a view of a dank and gloomy archway, and a flight of broken steps leading to a not unpicturesque garden shut in by thick walls through which the damp was oozing, and a hedge of sickly-looking shrubs. The walls were part of the old fortifications, and up above upon the ramparts there were yet other gardens belonging to some of the neighbouring houses.

Taken from *Eugénie Grandet*, translated by Ellen Marriage (Everyman's Library)

The Indre valley, from *Le Lys dans la vallée*

With no other sustenance than a dimly seen object that filled my soul, I found infinite love written in the long ribbon of water streaming in the sun between two green banks, in the rows of poplars adorning this vale of love with their flickering lace-work, in the oak trees rising between the vineyards on the ever-changing slopes that the river rounds off, and in the shadowy horizons shifting athwart each other. If you want to see nature in the beauty and purity of a betrothed, go there on a spring day; if you want to soothe the bleeding wounds of your heart, return there during the last days of autumn. There, in springtime, Love flutters his wings in mid air; there, in autumn, one thinks of those who are no more. There the sick lungs inhale a kindly freshness, and the eye reposes upon golden copses that impart their peaceful sweetness to the soul.

At this moment, the mills situated on the falls of the Indre were giving voice to this quivering valley, the poplars were swaying in their glee, there was not a cloud in the sky, birds were singing, grasshoppers chirping, everything there was melody. Do not ask me again why I love Touraine; I do not love it as one does one's birthplace, or as one loves an oasis in the desert; I love it as an artist loves art; I love it less than I do you; but, without Touraine, maybe I might not now be living.

Alain Fournier

Alain Fournier was born Henri Alban at La Chapelle-d'Angillon, in the Sologne, in 1886. Much like the watchful and forlorn narrator of *Le Grand Meaulnes*, he was the son of a country schoolteacher – the atmosphere of the provincial schoolroom, and of the Sologne in general, suffuses the novel. *Le Grand Meaulnes* was published in 1912, drawing heavily on the author's unrequited love for a woman he had met by chance in Paris. In 1914, he began his second novel, but was forced to join the army in August that year. He was killed within a month, during fighting on the Meuse.

Meaulnes' journey, from *Le Grand Meaulnes*

At daybreak he set out again. But his knee had swollen and was hurting him. So sharp indeed was the pain that he was forced to stop and rest every few minutes. In the whole of the Sologne it would have been hard to find a more desolate spot than the region in which he now found himself. Throughout the morning he saw no one but a shepherdess guiding her flock some distance away. He called out, and attempted to run, but she disappeared without having heard him.

He limped on in the direction she had taken but his progress was dishearteningly slow . . . Not a roof, not a living soul, not even the cry of a curlew from the reeds of the marshes. And over all this desolation streamed the thin and frigid light of a December sun.

It must have been getting on for three in the afternoon when he at last saw the spire of a turret above a large grove of fir trees.

"Some forsaken old manor," he surmised. "Some deserted pigeon-house . . ."

But he kept wearily to his course. At a corner of the wood he came upon two white posts marking the entrance to an avenue. He turned into it and had not gone far when he was brought to a halt in surprise and stood there, stirred by an emotion he could not have defined. Then he pushed on with the same dragging steps. His lips were cracked by the wind which at moments almost took his breath away. And yet he was now sustained by an extraordinary sense of well-being, an almost intoxicating serenity, by the certitude that the goal was in sight, that he had nothing but happiness to look forward to. It reminded him of days gone by when he would nearly faint with delight on the eve of the midsummer fête, when out in the village street they would be setting up fir trees and his bedroom window was obstructed by branches.

Then he scoffed at himself for rejoicing at the prospect of "a tumble-down pigeon-house full of owls and draughts . . ."

Disgruntled, he paused, half inclined to turn back and walk on till he came to a village. As he stood trying to make up his mind, his eyes fixed on the ground, he noticed that the avenue had been swept in wide symmetrical circles, as on very special occasions at home. It was like the high street at La Ferté on the morning of Assumption . . . He could not have been more surprised had he come upon a group of holiday-makers stirring up a cloud of dust as if it were June . . .

"And yet," he mused, "of all places for a fête – this wilderness!"

Taken from *Le Grand Meaulnes*, translated by Frank Davison (Oxford University Press)

Books

There's a big discrepancy between the large number of novels set in the Loire and the small number of non-fiction books about the region – in English, at least. In history, the Loire tends to feature only as background to its historical celebrities, of which the three most notable are women: Eleanor of Aquitaine, Joan of Arc and Catherine de Médicis. For more on local literature, see "Writers of the Loire" (p.340).

History and biography

Robert Gildea *Marianne in Chains: In Search of the German Occupation 1940–45*. This controversial work of war history is really an intimate biography of Chinon, a town chosen largely for its ordinariness. Rejecting the heroic view of the Occupation as Resistance versus collaborators, Gildea depicts the compromises and everyday hardships of life under the Nazis.

Mary Gordon *Joan of Arc*. Gordon's simple and moving retelling of Joan's story places the woman herself at the forefront.

Gregory of Tours *History of the Franks*. This sixth-century chronicle by a bishop of Tours won't be everyone's favourite bedtime reading, though some fascinating and occasionally scurrilous tales lurk among the drier passages.

J.H. Huizinga *The Waning of the Middle Ages*. A superb read, this book creates a detailed and fascinating portrait of life in the fourteenth and fifteenth centuries. Focuses on Burgundy, but also has plenty of material on the French court in general.

R.J. Knecht *The Rise and Fall of Renaissance France, 1483–1610*. Unimpeachably accurate and detailed, though, as you might expect from an academic historian, there's little attempt to create atmosphere. Still, the subject matter of this

500-page tome – focusing mostly on François I and the Wars of Religion – is exciting enough to help keep the pace up.

R.J. Knecht *Catherine de' Medici*. Knecht puts the final nail in the coffin of the "Black Legend" of the *Reine Margot* in this serious, historical portrait of a powerful Renaissance queen fighting for her family interests in the face of religious warfare and national chaos.

Marion Meade *Eleanor of Aquitaine*. This chatty, journalistic biography tries to focus directly on Eleanor in order to conjure up a picture of her as a woman. As a result, it sometimes strays into embarrassing emotional speculation and lacks the necessary breadth of historical context. Readable, nonetheless.

Marina Warner *Joan of Arc*. The most illuminating and erudite of all the books on Joan, placing her within the spiritual and intellectual traditions of her time. Beautifully written, too.

Alison Weir *Eleanor of Aquitaine: By the Wrath of God, Queen of England*. Despite the title, Weir's scholarly biography focuses just as much on Eleanor as a French ruler as an English queen, while a wealth of contextual detail makes this as much a history of the life and times of the Plantagenet empire as of Eleanor herself.

CONTEXTS | Books

Fiction

Honoré de Balzac *Eugénie Grandet*. This taut novella is one of Balzac's masterpieces. Set entirely in bourgeois, nineteenth-century Saumur, it exists in a claustrophobic world of half-strangled emotion, bitter irony and defiant hope. The detail is intensely naturalistic, while the plot and the characters – the miser Grandet, his daughter Eugénie and her flashy cousin Charles – could almost come from a fairy tale. See p.345.

Honoré de Balzac *The Lily of the Valley*. Not one of Balzac's best efforts, with an irritatingly sentimental, semi-autobiographical hero and a meandering plot revolving around his idealized mistress's marriage to a monster. The descriptions of the landscape around Azay-le-Rideau, however, are beautiful. See p.345.

Alain-Fournier *Le Grand Meaulnes*. Widely available in English, and sometimes translated as *The Wanderer* or *The Lost Domain*, this early twentieth-century classic is at once a coming-of-age novel, a wistful love story and a gentle hymn to youthful idealism. It draws heavily on the author's own childhood in the Sologne. See p.348.

Joanne Harris *Five Quarters of the Orange*. The bestselling author spins a disturbing yarn about a troubled, food-obsessed family growing up in a Loire village under German occupation. When "Framboise" returns as a middle-aged woman, the traumas of the past soon resurface. Much darker and more ambitious than the average summer read, though some find the quirky foodie themes profoundly irritating.

Joris-Karl Huysmans *The Cathedral*. This rich, experimental novel was published towards the end of Huysmans' life, in 1898. It ostensibly continues the spiritual journey of the ex-Satanist hero, Durtal, but the chief protagonist is really Chartres cathedral, whose symbolism is described in learned and mesmerizing detail.

François Rabelais *Gargantua and Pantagruel*. This outrageous parody of a sixteenth-century epic is extravagantly inventive, savagely satirical, filthy, erudite and, after nearly five hundred years, still very funny. The first book tells the life story of the giant Gargantua and his mock-heroic exploits in the Chinonais. See p.343.

George Bernard Shaw *Saint Joan*. Shaw may be out of fashion, but this was one of his most successful dramas. The Joan he creates is sassy, provocative and lovable, and he depicts the corrupt political world encircling her with a very modern kind of satirical absurdity.

Emile Zola *The Earth*. This dark, elemental tale of brutish peasant life was Zola's favourite among his own novels. It is set in the 1860s on the plain of the Beauce, between Vendôme and Châteaudun. As the title suggests, the real hero is *la terre* itself.

Poetry

Joachim du Bellay You'll have to look hard to find translations of du Bellay on his own, so go for *Lyrics of the French Renaissance*, a beautiful edition of Marot, du Bellay and Ronsard from Yale University Press, with skilful verse translations by American academic Norman R. Shapiro. See p.342.

Guillaume de Lorris and **Jean de Meun** *The Romance of the Rose*.

This long, thirteenth-century poem is really two works: Lorris's poem is a highly allegorical dream vision of desire, while Meun adds on an extended commentary on medieval life. Two good prose translations of the *Romaunt de la Rose* are available in paperback, from OUP and Princeton University Press. See p.340.

See p.340.

🏃 **Pierre de Ronsard** Various translations and collections of Ronsard's work are available, but Penguin's *Selected Poems* is particularly good as it supplies the original French along with a straightforward prose translation. Otherwise, you could opt for Yale's edition of Renaissance lyric poets (see under Joachim du Bellay, above). See p.343.

François Villon *The Legacy and the Testament*. Villon isn't widely translated into English, though Anvil Press Poetry recently published an excellent and affordable bilingual edition, including all of *The Testament*, with bold verse translations by poet Peter Dale. See p.341.

Art and architecture

🏃 **André Chastel** *French Art: the Renaissance 1430–1620*. The great French art historian defines what is distinctively French about French art in this, the second book of his three-volume work. Insightful and superbly illustrated.

Ivan Cloulas and **Michèle Bimbenet-Privat** *Treasures of the French Renaissance: Architecture, Sculpture, Paintings and Drawings*. Excellent commentaries by two French scholars make this beautifully produced, glossy art book a good guide to the wider artistic context of the Loire châteaux.

🏃 **Mark Girouard** *Life in the French Country House*. Girouard meticulously re-creates the social and domestic life of the French châteaux, starting with the great halls of early castles and ending with the commercial marriage venues of the twentieth century. Fascinating.

Robert Polidori and **Jean-Marie Pérouse de Montclos** *Châteaux of the Loire Valley*. Relatively original photography makes this one of the better coffee-table books. The text is reasonably accurate and salted with interesting quotations.

Miscellaneous

John Ardagh *France in the New Century: Portrait of a Changing Society*. This overview of contemporary France concentrates on the last twenty years in Paris and the regions, with an emphasis on politics. Nothing in particular on the Loire, but good background nonetheless.

Jacqueline Friedrich *A Wine and Food Guide to the Loire*. The authoritative English-language (American) survey. Out of print, though, so you'll have to shop around online.

John Higginson *Cycling the River Loire*. Some useful tips, but the routes have been made largely redundant by the post-2006 construction of the *Loire à Vélo* cyclepaths.

Henry James *A Little Tour in France*. James spends a healthy proportion of his "little tour" poking his nose around the great Loire towns and châteaux, and commenting on them with a characteristic mix of snootiness and penetrating observation.

Hugh Palmer *The Most Beautiful Villages of the Loire.* This solid coffee-table book has thin text but wonderful photographs that, for once, don't focus exclusively on the châteaux.

Judy Smith *Holiday Walks in the Loire Valley.* Details 32 walks in the Loire Valley, most ranging from 5km to 15km and most within the classic "Val de Loire". Useful maps included.

Roger Voss *The Wines of the Loire.* An odd combination of technical facts and statistics with engagingly personal accounts of visits to winemakers. Out of print and out of date, but there's still plenty of useful guidance on the classic vineyards.

Wine

The Loire is the kid sister of French wine regions: lively, charming, full of promise and often not taken seriously by friends of her rich older brothers, Bordeaux and Burgundy. As a wine region, the geographical area covered by the Loire is unusually large, extending almost 400km from Sancerre, in the very centre of France, to Nantes, on the Atlantic coast. The soil and climate are particularly varied, as are the wines. There are two-dozen different *appellations* to discover, ranging from crisp, white Sancerre to honeyed Bonnezeaux, and from a zesty, youthful Touraine *primeur* to a heady old Chinon red. The Loire is subdivided into four main wine regions: **Centre**, which means Sancerre and the wines of the Haut Berry; **Touraine**, which also includes the region around Blois; **Anjou–Saumur**; and, over the border in Brittany, **Nantes**. Because of their Breton origins, the wines of the Nantais, notably Muscadet, are not discussed here. The following is only an introduction to the main wine styles of the Loire. Incredibly detailed information is available free at tourist offices in all wine areas, including maps of the well-signposted **wine roads**, or *routes des vignobles*, lists of addresses of wine *caves* and advice on finding growers who speak English, if need be. For serious research, try to get hold of a copy of Jacqueline Friedrich's opinionated *Wine and Food Guide to the Loire* or Roger Voss's charming *Wines of the Loire* (unfortunately, both are out of print). Alternatively, Chris Kissack's excellent website, ⓦwww.thewinedoctor.com, specializes in the Loire, and contains plentiful background information and detailed tasting notes. Some recommendations on partnering **food and wine** are given below, but for more on the cuisine of the Loire, see "Basics" (p.35).

Due to the northerly climate, **vintages** are particularly important in the Loire, especially for red wines, as the grapes only ripen properly in sunnier, drier years. The heatwave of 2003, for instance, was very good for most reds, but Sancerre whites tended to suffer. In general, 2000 to 2006 are all regarded as good years for Loire wines; 2002 and 2005 were particularly special – up there with the great year, 1997. It's impossible to generalize any further, however, as different regions and even different wine-makers can produce wines of higher or lower quality in any given year.

Touraine wines

Most of the Touraine wine you can buy outside the region is the standard, white Apellation d'Origine Contrôlée (AOC) **Touraine**, much of it pretty ordinary stuff with an unfortunate astringency resulting from not-quite-ripe Sauvignon Blanc grapes. The better-quality wines can be appealing, however, with a good balance of acidity and sweetness and a heady floral nose. **Vouvray** has its own separate and very well-known *appellation*, while the tiny **Touraine Azay-le-Rideau** AOC is starting to produce some good Chenin Blanc whites. Red AOC **Touraine** wine is less commonly seen, and not much missed, though some interesting reds are being produced under the more tightly controlled **Touraine Amboise** and **Touraine Mesland** *appellations*, which allow a blend of Gamay with smaller amounts of Cabernet Franc and Côt. The former is sold everywhere in and around Amboise, east of Tours, while the latter is centred around the Blésois villages of Monteaux and Mesland, on the right bank of the Loire opposite Chaumont.

Vouvray and Montlouis

Some of the best wines in the Loire are born in the chalky uplands of **Vouvray**, which slope back from the Loire just east of Tours, but there's still a fair amount of sulphurous rubbish, too. The trick is to follow a local recommendation and avoid buying blind, as all too often you can't tell from the label what's inside. Vouvray is always white but it can be *sec* (dry), *tendre* (half-dry) or *demi-sec* (slightly sweet), and in good years it can be *moelleux* (sweet) and even *doux* or *liquoreux* (very sweet). Unusually, the best sweet wines are not limited to those produced by the fabled "noble rot", but also grapes dried on the vine, or *passerillé*. Sparkling wines are covered on p.361. Vouvray's character varies enormously, but basically it's the classic expression of the Chenin Blanc grape (see box below) on its classic Loire soils – either *aubuis*, which is chalky Loire tufa, or *perruches*, which is a flinty *silex*. The latter is found more abundantly near the southern edge of the plateau, and creates a more severe, complex and mineral-flavoured wine. *Aubuis*, by contrast, produces a true Loire Chenin, with a smoky dampness in the nose, an apricot or apple fruitiness on the palate and a firm acidity to hold all the flavours together. It goes perfectly with fish and white meats – the *sec* perhaps best with shellfish, *demi-sec* with white sauces.

Most Vouvray vignerons make different wines from individual parcels of land, which complicates buying, but among the famous names to look out for are Domaine Huet (especially their Le Haut Lieu, Clos de Bourg and Le Mont wines), Marc Brédif, Domaine des Aubuisières, Château Gaudrelle, Domaine Champalou, Clos Baudoin and Clos Naudin. Of the two cooperatives, the Cave des Producteurs du Vouvray, in Vouvray's Vallée Coquette, is the higher rated.

Montlouis, across the river, makes very similar wines that tend to age a little faster and cost a little less. There's an excellent Cave Cooperative in Montlouis itself, but if you want to follow the wine roads, make for the villages of Husseau, on the Loire, and St-Martin-le-Beau, at the far side of the *appellation*, on the Cher. At the former, look for the *caves* of Dominique Moyer, Claude Levasseur and Yves et François Chidaine; at the latter, make for G&G Deletang.

White wine grapes

The great grape of the white wines of Touraine and Anjou is **Chenin Blanc**, known locally as **Pineau de la Loire**. It is increasingly planted in California and South Africa, but only achieves its potential in the Loire Valley. Wines made with the Pineau are typically redolent of honey, quince, grilled almonds and lime leaves, often with a distinctive smell of wet wool or musty stone – not unlike the limestone caves in which it often matures. It is capable of producing a bewildering range of wine styles ranging from sweet to dry, as well as sparkling, and notorious for having a "closed" period – wines made with the Chenin Blanc tend to be drinkable young but then lose the best of their flavour for a period of anything from five to ten years. You'll need to find an all-too-rare older wine to discover the best of the grape. **Sauvignon Blanc** is the staple of Sancerre, Pouilly-Fumé and ordinary Touraine. It thrives in a cool climate, producing superbly crisp, grassy, smoky-perfumed wines at its best. At its worst, it can make an astringently acidic wine whose smell is commonly described as "cat's pee on a gooseberry bush".

Chinon and Bourgueil

Facing each other across the Loire are the two great red wine *appellations* of Touraine: **Bourgueil**, on the north bank, and **Chinon**, on the south. Both rely almost solely on the Cabernet Franc grape, as grown in Bordeaux – which means they risk comparison with their more famous southern cousin. A good bottle can silence claret-loving detractors, maturing for up to thirty or forty years and offering up rich spicy, truffle-like flavours in age. An indifferent bottle, however, can be a little thin and unrewarding, and is best enjoyed young, lightly chilled and without fuss. Some drink most Bourgeuil and Chinon wines in this way, but a typical Chinon or Bourgeuil should be aged for at least five years. If you're expecting a classic wine like a Burgundy or an old Bordeaux, or a loud, super-fruity New World offering, you'll be disappointed. These wines are typically light on the palate, gently laced with warm earthiness and the lingering taste of summer fruits, and sometimes perfumed with violets.

It's hard to pick out differences between the two. Chinon, which catches a little more sunshine, is perhaps bigger and more rounded, while Bourgueil is sometimes rougher-edged, with more tannin – qualities particularly pronounced in **St-Nicolas-de-Bourgueil**, a separate *appellation* just west of Bourgueil itself. If you know the origin of the wine, it's more helpful to talk about the different types of soil, as all three *appellations* share the same basic types. The gravelly, sandy soil of the valley bottoms produces a fast-maturing, rustic wine best suited to drinking young, while the chalky limestone-clay of the plateaux lends itself to smoother, more serious, longer-maturing wines. The wines are often used locally in rich meat sauces, and tend to go well with meat and game in general. Their fruitiness also makes them an excellent partner for cheese, especially goat's cheese. Even if you're not serving them chilled, they shouldn't be too warm, perhaps three or four degrees below room temperature.

Top Chinon names include the legendary Charles Joguet, in Sazilly, and Couly-Dutheil and Château de la Grille, on the edges of Chinon itself – Couly-Dutheil's famous **Clos de l'Echo** site is right behind the château. There are also rich pickings around the village of Cravant-les-Côteaux, where Bernard Baudry is one of the best-known producers. For excellent Bourgueil wines, look for **Domaine de la Lande** and Domaine de la Coudraye, in Bourgueil, and Pierre-Jacques Druet, in the Hameau de la Croix-Rouge, just outside Benais. In the St-Nicolas *appellation*, the Domaine Joël Taluau, on the road to Chevrette, is a well-established producer, while Frédéric Mabileau is a relative newcomer.

Cheverny, Cour-Cheverny and Valençay

Thanks to their celebrated châteaux, three of the most minor Touraine appellations bear the most famous names. All three are in the east of the wine-growing area, and acquired their AOC status relatively recently. The most unusual and interesting of the trio is **Cour-Cheverny**. Uniquely, this white wine is made using the Romorantin grape, which was supposedly introduced to the region by François I. Romorantin doesn't exactly make a royal wine, however: Cour-Cheverny wines are typically even more acid than their Sauvignon Blanc neighbours. That said, their lemony acidity goes perfectly with a fatty white fish, and they age unusually well. Domaine des Huards and Philippe Tessier are names to look out for.

Cheverny has only been an appellation contrôlée since 1993, and it's still finding its way in the world. The area centres on the château but extends up the left bank of the Loire towards Orléans. You can find whites made using

Sauvignon Blanc with, unusually, a small amount of Chardonnay added to lend a little roundness. Reds run the gamut from Gamay and Pinot Noir to Cabernet Franc and Cabernet Sauvignon, while rosés rely on the Pineau d'Aunis and Grolleau grapes. **Valençay** has only just made AOC status – in 2004 – and remains something of a curiosity. Two thirds of the production is spicy, fruity red, with the lively flavours of the Gamay grape dominating, helped out by Pinot Noir, Côt and the Cabernets. Try it young, on the cool side, and served with rabbit or chicken. Whites tend to be flinty Sauvignons – again, with some Chardonnay blended in.

Jasnières and the Côteaux

Fashionable Parisian restaurants and wine-sellers started a trend for this previously obscure wine a few years back, pushing **Jasnières** into the national wine consciousness. The main drawback for this *appellation* is its northern latitude – Jasnières is closer to Le Mans than Tours, situated in the Loire Valley near Vendôme. Yields are kept very low to ensure only the ripest grapes get through, but in colder, wetter years the acidity can be intolerably high, producing a poor, tight-lipped wine. A good vintage can be exceptional, however, especially if you can wait six or seven years for the Chenin Blanc flavour to really open up. The leading wine-makers are Joël and Ludovic Gigou of the Domaine de la Charriere, based in La Chartre-sur-le-Loir.

The names of the neighbouring appellations of **Côteaux du Loir** and **Côteaux du Vendomois** barely register outside the region – but then the latter has only been AOC since 2001. Both areas produce predominantly Chenin Blanc whites, but with some fascinating, peppery *vin gris* (ultra-pale rosé) made with the Pineau d'Aunis – try it with a fish *friture*. You can sometimes find a few red wines, too. The heart of the Côteaux du Vendomois appellation

△ Wine *cave*, Saumur

is around Thoré-la-Rochette, where you'll find the producers Emile Hérédia –
who makes organic wines – and Patrice Colin.

Anjou and Saumur wines

Even by Loire standards, Anjou makes an extraordinary variety of white wines,
especially if you include those of the Saumurois, with which they are normally
grouped. By volume, rosé is the leading wine, but there are significant amounts
of usually unexceptional **AOC Anjou** and **AOC Saumur** – names which can
refer to both white wines made with the Chenin Blanc grape and red wines
made with a mixture of Cabernet Franc and Cabernet Sauvignon. The more
interesting red wines come under the **Anjou-Villages, Anjou-Villages-**
Brissac and **Saumur-Champigny** *appellations*, while **Savennières** is the elite
appellation for dry whites. There's also a fair amount of **Anjou Gamay**, which
has seen passing trends as an alternative *primeur* to the ubiquitous Beaujolais.
But the most extraordinary wines produced in this region are the exquisite
sweet wines of the **Côteaux du Layon** and, to a lesser extent, the **Côteaux**
de l'Aubance.

Rosés

Anjou's reputation suffers from the glut of bargain-priced rosé wines that
dominate the market, with supermarket own-brand wines flooding Britain
every year in early summer. **Rosé d'Anjou** can make pleasant summer

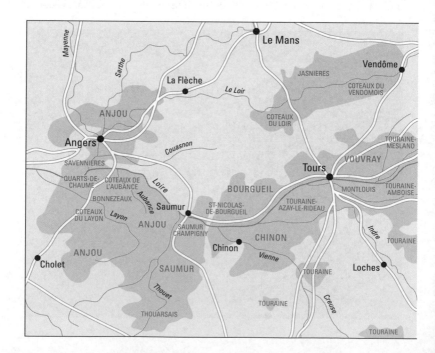

drinking, but more typically it's over-sweet and dull. The drier, more aromatic **Rosé de Loire** *appellation* tends to be superior. Both are made with varying mixtures of the Cabernet Franc, Cabernet Sauvignon, Côt, Gamay, Grolleau and local Pineau d'Aunis grapes, but Rosé d'Anjou relies primarily on the Grolleau. The **Cabernet d'Anjou** and much rarer **Cabernet de Saumur** rosé *appellations* both restrict themselves to just the two Cabernet grapes, but they're very different in style. The former is fruity and semi-sweet, making a good dessert wine, while the latter is dry, lively and highly floral, and perfect with grilled and spiced meats.

Savennières

The white wines of **Savennières** are in a class of their own. The unusually steep, south-facing slopes around this small western Anjou village are made of volcanic schist, which soaks up every available ray of sunshine. Yields are kept tiny, and the local techniques are highly rarified. Many producers follow complex variations on organic growing methods that are designed to express the character of the local *terroir* to the greatest possible degree. The wine itself is equally unusual – deep golden in colour, ageing superbly up to thirty years, but almost exclusively dry. One wine writer has described Savennières as having "the distant beauty of an ice maiden". The grape variety is Chenin Blanc, which offers up some surprising flavours in this context: white peaches, minerals, jasmine, camomile, quinine and, later in life, dried fruit, beeswax and honey. It's a classic served alongside fish in a *beurre blanc*, especially the Loire favourites, *sandre* and salmon. A Savennières should only be very lightly chilled, certainly not lower than 10°C. The top-rated vineyards are Roche-aux-Moines and Coulée de Serrant – the latter so small as to be exclusively owned by one

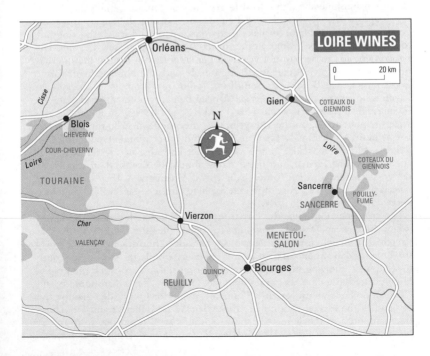

The classic red wine grape of the Loire is the **Cabernet Franc**, locally called the **Breton**, probably because it arrived here from Brittany. The grape is best known for its use in Bordeaux, mostly as a junior partner in the blend, though it plays a bigger role in Pomerol and St-Emilion, with their limestone soils and damper climate. Its finest expression, however, is in the Loire, where its popularity partly stems from its ability to ripen early and resist cold winters. It produces wonderfully silky, summery reds, smooth, pungent and with a distinctive taste of raspberries. It is often drunk young, but the better wines should be laid down. The traditional local grape is the **Grolleau**, or Groslot, a robust grape now best served by its use in rosé. As in Beaujolais, **Gamay** is popular as a *primeur* – made for drinking very young. Less common are Cabernet Sauvignon, the classic grape of Bordeaux, Burgundy's **Pinot Noir** – used for red Sancerre – and the plummy **Malbec**, known locally as the Côt.

wine-maker, the philosophical Nicolas Joly, who follows the "biodynamic" theory of wine-making. Other great Savennières wines include the Domaine du Closel; Château d'Epiré, in the adjacent hamlet of Epiré; Domaine du Baumard, based in Rochefort-sur-Loire; and Château Pierre Bise's Clos de Colaine, based in Beaulieu-sur-Layon.

Côteaux du Layon

The Layon valley and the slopes, or *côteaux*, that surround it, is one of the few areas in France where climate and topography come together to allow the autumnal growth of a fungus called *botrytis cinerea*. Morning mist and hot afternoon sunshine allow this **"noble rot"** to develop, weakening the skin of the grape so that it shrivels and dehydrates, causing the sugars inside to concentrate. Growers have to make many *tries*, or passes through the vineyard, to handpick the grapes where noble rot has set in to the required extent. The result is one of the finest sweet wines in France, a serious rival to the internationally better-known Sauternes, though made with the Loire's Chenin Blanc grape rather than Bordeaux's Sémillon. The main flavour of a Côteaux du Layon is honey, but the sweetness is balanced by herby notes and fruity acidity – you might detect apricot, citrus zest and figs, and it's easy to imagine oversweet grapes bursting in the late-year, late-afternoon sun. The top wines can last a lifetime, and slowly become more and more pungent with spices – delicate and yet muscular at the same time. The idea of "dessert wine" is anathema to the French, and these wines should be drunk as an apéritif or paired with foie gras and other liver pâtés. Alternatively, they can partner sauced fish, and make a superb match for blue cheese – especially Roquefort. Serve cool, at around 8 to 10°C.

The *appellation* **Côteaux du Layon** extends along the length of the Layon valley, from near Doué-la-Fontaine to Chalonnes-sur-Loire. Within that stretch are two elite mini-*appellations*: **Quarts de Chaume**, near Rochefort-sur-Loire, and **Bonnezeaux**, around Thouarcé. At both, the slopes face south to southwest, allowing the maximum afternoon sunshine to reach the grapes. Highly rated Bonnezeaux wines include Domaine de la Sansonnière and Château de Fesles, both based in Thouarcé, while for Quarts de Chaume the top end of the market is dominated by Château de Bellerive and Domaines Baumard, both in Rochefort-sur-Loire. Other Layon producers to look out for include Château Pierre-Bise, in Beaulieu-sur-Layon; Philippe Delesvaux, at La Haie Longue, near St-Aubin-de-Luigné; and Domain Jo Pithon, just outside St-Lambert-du-Lattay.

Saumur-Champigny

The name "Champigny" supposedly comes from the Latin *campus ignis*, meaning "field of fire", and refers to the sunny microclimate that favours this sheltered corner of the Saumurois. It is this warm weather that allows the region to produce top-quality red wines, all of which are dubbed **Saumur-Champigny** to distinguish them from the local white wines. Like its great rival, Chinon, the grape variety is Cabernet Franc, and the flavours are similar: raspberry, strawberry, cherry, sometimes vanilla, with distinctive violet notes.

The area is well defined, stretching back from the south bank of the Loire between Saumur and the border with Touraine. The principal wine town is St-Cyr-en-Bourg, in the southwestern corner of the *appellation*, but you'll find growers in all the villages along the Loire, too: Montsoreau, Turquant, Parnay and Dampierre. The biggest and, some say, the most innovative wine producer is Domaine Filliatreau, based at La Grande Vignolle, in Turquant. The well-regarded Domaine de Nerleux, Château du Hureau and Château de Chaintres are all based in handsome châteaux – the first in St-Cyr-en-Bourg, the last two in Dampierre-sur-Loire.

Centre wines

Unlike the rest of the Loire region, the **Sauvignon Blanc** – a relative of the Cabernet Sauvignon, which originally came from Bordeaux – is the chief grape variety for white wines from the Centre region. One name dominates: **Sancerre**. Its dry whites are exported all over the world, and sold at high prices relative to other Loire wines. Explore a little further afield, however, and you'll find subtly different offerings at **Menetou-Salon**, a few kilometres west of Sancerre, where the whites are more forgiving and floral, and can be better value, and at **Pouilly-Fumé**, on the east bank of the river, where the wines lean in the opposite direction, towards flinty austerity. **Pouilly-sur-Loire** comes from the same area as the Fumé, but is made with the frankly inferior Chasselas grape. Less well known than any of these are the tiny *appellations* of **Reuilly** and **Quincy**, isolated on the left bank of the Cher, west of Bourges. In the **Côteaux du Giennois**, north of Sancerre down the Loire, they make a straightforward, lightweight red from a mix of the Gamay and Pinot Noir grapes, and a white that often tastes like a rather slight Pouilly-Fumé.

Sancerre

Sancerre is one of the few Loire regions with a serious international reputation. Made with the **Sauvignon Blanc** grape, the white wines are traditionally dry, crisp and acid – you could almost describe the flavour as green. Increasingly, however, wine-growers are using New World techniques to get as much fruity, floral flavour as possible out of the grape. It's unusually difficult to get to know the wines of Sancerre, as most growers' holdings are very small, and often split up into tiny parcels on a number of different vineyards. What's more, the growers aren't allowed to name the vineyard or origin on the label, even if there is only one; instead, they have to put their own name to it, or resort to *cuvée* names that hint slyly at the vineyard of origin. And there are three very different types of **soil**. On the western hilltops are the *terres blanches*, or Kimmeridgean chalk soils, which produce the classic Sancerre, especially when combined with wines from the drier *caillottes*, or pebbly limestones (on their own, wines grown on the *caillottes* are more suitable for younger, easier drinking). Just a fifth of the territory is *silex*, the flint-clay soil that many believe makes the finest Sancerre whites of all – complex, steely, powerful and best drunk aged a few years. All can be drunk as apéritifs, but they also go well with white meats and creamy dishes, the acidity cutting through the fat. The big names are Alphonse Mellot and Vacheron in Sancerre itself; Lucien Crochet, in Bué; and Henri Bourgeois, in Chavignol, but it's well worth trying out smaller wine-makers. Pascal and Nicolas Reverdy, in the hamlet of Maimbray, are known for their reds.

Red Sancerre is much harder to find outside the region, but it can be exceptional in a good year. Like red Burgundy, which is geographically quite close, it is made with the **Pinot Noir** grape, which can produce a surprisingly pale, thin-looking wine that browns quite quickly. Some drinkers find it offputting, and the nose is even more extraordinary, a composty smell that some describe as like raw meat or rotting fruit. The flavour is less heavy and full-bodied than Burgundy, but can be just as complex, rich with spicy, earthy tones; it goes well with game, duck and meaty fish dishes. It can be very enjoyable when drunk young and lightly chilled. Sancerre's soft, fruity **rosé** enjoyed a brief fashion in the 1970s, but is relatively uninteresting.

Pouilly-Fumé

Not to be confused with Burgundy's Pouilly-Fuissé, the wines of Pouilly-Fumé are twinned with Sancerre and, as such, fall definitively within the Loire wine region. In terms of geography, however, Pouilly lies on the east bank, in Burgundy, and you won't, therefore, find it in this guidebook. This needn't deter wine buyers, who need only drive across the bridge from St-Satur, and turn right onto the D553 for **Tracy-sur-Loire**, one of the main wine *communes*, situated on a delightful stretch of the Loire. You can then continue to the main village of **Pouilly-sur-Loire**, as well as Les Berthiers, just off the N7, and nearby St-Andelain.

Pouilly-Fumé is, if anything, even more serious than Sancerre: gun-metal flinty, mineral-flavoured and sometimes severe. Roger Voss, writing in *Wines of the Loire*, claims that the wines "express the character of the Sauvignon Blanc in complete simplicity". Top wine-makers include Château de Nozet, just north of Pouilly; the impressive Château de Tracy, close to the river; and the Dagueneau brothers: Jean-Claude, in Les Berthiers, and Didier, in St-Andelain.

Reuilly and Quincy

The twin vineyards of **Reuilly** and **Quincy** are minuscule, together covering barely a tenth of the area of Sancerre, and for years they were scarcely known outside the region. The popularity of Sauvignon Blanc has galvanized the local producers in the last decade or so, however, and the wines are now gaining a reputation as a quirky, insider's alternative to Sancerre – as promoted in the restaurants of Paris. A good bottle of either can be wonderfully aromatic, slightly tart with the flavour of gooseberries. Reuilly also comes in rosé, made with Pinot Noir and Pinot Gris, and in good years it can be very interesting: soft, fresh and perfumed with red fruits. The red Reuilly wines, made with Pinot Noir, are not highly regarded.

Sparkling wines

The sparkling wines of the Loire are made in exactly the same way as champagne, and, indeed, they called themselves that before the wine-growers of the actual Champagne region started to object. **Méthode traditionelle** is now added to the label to denote a serious sparkling wine made in the traditional way. The Loire's sparklers are, on the whole, excellent value – a good sparkling Vouvray or Saumur typically costs roughly half the price of an inferior bottle of champagne, where you're paying for the brand. If you're in Saumur or Vouvray, a visit to the rock-cut *caves*, where thousands of racked-up bottles take advantage of the ideal cool conditions to mature, is a must. If you're not, a glass or two as an apéritif is just as obligatory – in France, sparkling wines are not restricted to celebrations.

Saumur

The longest-established Loire sparkling wine is **Saumur** *mousseux*, often marketed as Saumur Brut. Saumur was the first town in the Loire to use the champagne technique, and some of the great houses are still owned by champagne-makers: Gratien & Meyer is part of Alfred Gratien Champagne, while Langlois-Château is owned by Bollinger. Bouvet-Ladubay, which is part of the Taittinger stable, produces some of the best sparkling Saumur wines. The local giants – whose budget-priced wines may be relatively disappointing – are Ackerman-Laurance and Veuve Amiot. Saumur mostly relies on the local Chenin Blanc, but with various admixtures of Cabernet Franc and Champagne's Chardonnay grape to moderate any acid hardness in the Brut. *Demi-secs* can be packed with honeyed flavour, especially when aged, and Gratien & Meyer even make a sparkling red.

Vouvray

Connoisseurs are particularly keen on **Vouvray**, an *appellation* just east of Tours that makes around half of its wines into sparklers, depending on the year. Most common is the full-pressure *mousseux*, usually known as Vouvray Brut, which is crisper and less heady than champagne, the acidity and quince or apple-like fruitiness of the Chenin Blanc grape balancing any creamy sweetness. Some people prefer it to champagne, but it has to be said that an inferior Vouvray can be rather thin. Don't ignore the honeyed *demi-secs* and the gently fizzing *pétillant* wines, which can be superb. **Montlouis**, just across the Loire from Vouvray, makes similar, often slightly lighter sparkling wines.

Crémant de la Loire

One sparkling wine to watch out for is **Crémant de la Loire**, which is growing in popularity – and with good reason. Unusually, these are blended wines from across Touraine and Anjou, but the quality is assured by regulations insisting on very low grape yields, hand harvesting and bottle ageing for at least a year. The wine is usually made with sixty percent Chenin Blanc and 25 percent Cabernet Franc, with the champagne grape Chardonnay (15 percent) adding a familiar creamy richness.

Language

Language

French

rench can be a deceptively familiar language because of the number of words and structures it shares with English. Despite this, it's far from easy, though the bare essentials are not difficult to master and can make all the difference. Even just saying "Bonjour madame/monsieur" and then gesticulating will usually get you a smile and helpful service. People working in tourist offices, hotels and so on, almost always speak English and tend to use it when you're struggling to speak French – be grateful, not insulted.

Pronunciation

One easy rule to remember is that **consonants** at the ends of words are usually silent: Tours is thus pronounced "toor", Orléans is "or-lay-on" and Angers "on-jay". Otherwise they are much as in English, except that: *ch* is always "sh", *c* is "s", *h* is silent, *th* is the same as "t", *ll* is like the "y" in yes, *w* is "v", and *r* is growled (or rolled). **Vowels** are the hardest sounds to get exactly right, but they rarely differ enough from English to make comprehension a problem – though note that *au* sounds like the "o" in "over", as in *aujourd'hui* ("oh-jor-dwi") *oi* becomes "wa", as in Blois ("Blwa") and adding "m" or "n" to a vowel, as in *en* or *un*, adds a nasal sound, as if you said just the vowel with a cold.

Basic words and phrases

French nouns are divided into masculine and feminine. This causes difficulties with adjectives, whose endings have to change to suit the nouns they qualify – you can talk about *un château blanc* (a white castle), for example, but *une tour blanche* (a white tower). If you're not sure, stick to the simpler masculine form – as used in this glossary.

oui	yes	demain	tomorrow
non	no	le matin	in the morning
s'il vous plaît	please	l'après-midi	in the afternoon
merci	thank you	le soir	in the evening
pardon/Je m'excuse	sorry	maintenant	now
pardon	excuse me	plus tard	later
d'accord	OK/agreed	à une heure	at one o'clock
bonjour	hello	à trois heures	at three o'clock
au revoir	goodbye	à dix heures	at ten-thirty
bonjour	good morning/ afternoon	et demie	
		à midi	at midday
bonsoir	good evening	un homme	man
bonne nuit	good night	une femme	woman
au secours!	help!	(pronounced "fam")	
aujourd'hui	today	ici	here
hier	yesterday	là	there

ceci	this one
celà	that one
ouvert	open
fermé	closed
entrée	entrance
sortie	exit
grand	big
petit	small
plus	more
moins	less
un peu	a little
beaucoup	a lot
bon marché/ pas cher	cheap
cher	expensive
bon	good
mauvais	bad
chaud	hot
froid	cold
avec	with
sans	without

Numbers

un	1
deux	2
trois	3
quatre	4
cinq	5
six	6
sept	7
huit	8
neuf	9
dix	10
onze	11
douze	12
treize	13
quatorze	14
quinze	15
seize	16
dix-sept	17
dix-huit	18
dix-neuf	19
vingt	20
vingt-et-un	21
vingt-deux	22
trente	30
quarante	40

cinquante	50
soixante	60
soixante-dix	70
soixante-quinze	75
quatre-vingts	80
quatre-vingt-dix	90
quatre-vingt-quinze	95
cent	100
cent-et-un	101
deux cents	200
trois cents	300
cinq cents	500
mille	1000
deux milles	2000
un million	1,000,000

Days and dates

janvier	January
février	February
mars	March
avril	April
mai	May
juin	June
juillet	July
août (pronounced "oot")	August
septembre	September
octobre	October
novembre	November
décembre	December

lundi	Monday
mardi	Tuesday
mercredi	Wednesday
jeudi	Thursday
vendredi	Friday
samedi	Saturday
dimanche	Sunday

le premier août	August 1
le deux mars	March 2
le quatorze juillet	July 14
deux mille cinq	2005

Talking to people

Bonjour monsieur/ madame	Hello (daytime)

Bonsoir monsieur/ madame	Hello (evening)		

Similarly with requests:

Bonsoir monsieur/ madame	Hello (evening)	S'il vous plaît, une chambre pour deux?	We'd like a room for two?
Parlez-vous anglais?	Do you speak English?	S'il vous plaît, un kilo d'oranges?	Can I have a kilo of oranges?
Comment ça se dit en français?	How do you say it in French?	où?	where?
Comment vous appelez-vous?	What's your name?	comment?	how?
Je m'appelle...	My name is...	combien?	how many/how much?
Je suis...	I'm...	c'est combien?	how much is it?
...anglais[e]	...English	quand?	when?
...irlandais[e]	...Irish	pourquoi?	why?
...écossais[e]	...Scottish	à quelle heure?	at what time?
...gallois[e]	...Welsh	quel est?	what is/which is?
...américain[e]	...American		
...australien[ne]	...Australian		
...canadien[ne]	...Canadian		
...néo-zélandais[e]	...a New Zealander		
... néerlandais[e]	...Dutch		

Getting around

autobus/bus/car	bus
gare routière	bus station
arrêt	bus stop
voiture	car
train/taxi/ferry	train/taxi/ferry
bâteau	boat
avion	plane
navette	shuttle
gare (SNCF)	train station
quai	platform
Il part à quelle heure?	What time does it leave?
Il arrive à quelle heure?	What time does it arrive?
un billet pour...	a ticket to...
aller simple	single ticket
aller retour	return ticket
compostez votre billet	validate your ticket
vente de billets	ticket office
combien de kilomètres?	how many kilometres?
combien d'heures?	how many hours?
autostop	hitchhiking
à pied	on foot
Vous allez où?	Where are you going?
Je vais à ...	I'm going to...
Je voudrais descendre à ...	I want to get off at...

Je comprends	I understand
Je ne comprends pas	I don't understand
S'il vous plaît, parlez moins vite	Can you speak slower?
Comment allez-vous?/Ça va?	How are you?
Très bien, merci	Fine, thanks
Je ne sais pas	I don't know
Allons-y	Let's go
A demain	See you tomorrow
A bientôt	See you soon
Fichez-moi la paix! (aggressive)	Leave me alone
Aidez-moi, s'il vous plaît	Please help me

Questions and requests

The simplest way of asking a question is to start with **s'il vous plaît** (please), then name the thing you want in an interrogative tone of voice. For example:

S'il vous plaît, la boulangerie?	Where is there a bakery?
S'il vous plaît, la route pour le château?	Which way is it to the château?

LANGUAGE | Basic words and phrases

la route pour…	the road to…	pompe	pump
près/pas loin	near	crevaison	puncture
loin	far	réparer	repair
à gauche	left	clef	spanner
à droite	right	rayon	spoke
tout droit	straight on	pneu	tyre
à l'autre côté de	on the other side of	roue	wheel
à côté de	next to		

derrière	behind
devant	in front of
avant	before
après	after
sous	under
traverser	to cross
pont	bridge
centre ville	town centre
vieille ville	old town

Cars

garer la voiture	to park the car
le parking	car park
défense de stationner/ stationnement interdit	no parking
essence	fuel
super	4-star petrol/gas
sans plomb	unleaded
gas-oil	diesel
faites le plein!	fill it up!
huile	oil
station-service	petrol station
garage	service station
gonfler les pneus	put air in the tyres
tomber en panne	to break down
assurance	insurance

Cycling

je voudrais louer un…	I'd like to hire
vélo	bicycle
VTT ("vay-tay-tay")	mountain bike
freins	brakes
broken	cassé
chaîne	chain
les vitesses	gears
gonfler	inflate
chambre à l'air	inner tube

Accommodation

je voudrais réserver	I'd like to reserve/book
une chambre pour une/deux personne(s)	a room for one/two persons
avec un grand lit	with a double bed
avec deux lits	with two singles
avec douche	with a shower
avec salle de bain	with a bath
avec lavabo	with a sink
avec WC dans le palier	with a shared bathroom
pour une/deux/ trois nuits	for one/two/three nights
Je peux la voir?	Can I see it?
une chambre sur la cour	a room on the courtyard
une chambre sur la rue	a room over the street
premier étage	first floor
deuxième étage	second floor
avec vue	with a view
clef	key
repasser	to iron
faire la lessive	do laundry
draps	sheets
couvertures	blankets
eau chaude	hot water
eau froide	cold water
Est-ce que le petit déjeuner est compris?	Is breakfast included?
Je voudrais prendre le petit déjeuner	I would like breakfast
Je ne veux pas de petit déjeuner	I don't want breakfast
chambres d'hôtes	bed and breakfast
table d'hôte	evening meal at a B&B
On peut camper ici?	Can we camp here?
camping	campsite
tente	tent

un emplacement	tent space
foyer	hostel
auberge de jeunesse	youth hostel

Health

médecin	doctor
pharmacie	chemist
hôpital	hospital
Je ne me sens pas bien	I don't feel well
médicaments	medicines
ordonnance	prescription
Je suis malade	I feel sick

J'ai mal à la tête	I have a headache
mal à l'estomac	stomach ache
douleur	pain
ça fait mal	it hurts
préservatif	condom
pilule du lendemain	morning-after pill

Other needs

timbres	stamps
banque	bank
argent	money
toilettes	toilets
police	police
téléphone	telephone

Food and drink terms

Basic words and phrases

déjeuner	lunch
dîner	dinner
menu	set menu
à la carte	individually priced dishes
entrées	starters
les plats	main courses
une carafe d'eau	a carafe of water
eau minérale	mineral water
eau gazeuse	fizzy water
eau plate	still water
carte des vins	wine list
un (verre de) rouge/ blanc	a glass of white/red wine
Je voudrais réserver une table	I'd like to reserve a table
pour deux personnes, à vingt heures et demie	for two people, at eight thirty
Je prendrai le menu à quinze euros	I'm having the €15 set menu
monsieur/madame!	Waiter!
l'addition, s'il vous plaît	the bill/check please
une pression	a glass of beer
un café	coffee (espresso)
un crème	white coffee
un café au lait	big bowl of milky breakfast coffee

Cooking terms

bio or biologique	organic
cru	raw
cuit	cooked
fumé	smoked
pimenté	spicy
salé	salted/savoury
sucré	sweet

Essentials

beurre	butter
bouteille	bottle
couteau	knife
cuillère	spoon
à emporter	takeaway
formule	lunchtime set menu
fourchette	fork
huile	oil
lait	milk
moutarde	mustard
œuf	egg
pain	bread
plat	main course
poivre	pepper
sel	salt
sucre	sugar
table	table
verre	glass
vinaigre	vinegar

Snacks

un sandwich/une baguette	a sandwich
croque-monsieur	grilled cheese and ham sandwich
panini	toasted Italian sandwich
tartine	buttered bread or open sandwich
crêpe	pancake
galette	buckwheat pancake
omelette	omelette
...nature	plain
...aux fines herbes	with herbs
...au fromage	with cheese
salade de tomates	tomato salad
salade vert	green salad

Wine terms

un verre de...	a glass of...
une bouteille de...	a bottle of...
un quart/demi de rouge/blanc	a quarter/half-litre of red/white house wine
rouge/rosé/blanc	red/rosé/white wine
sec	dry
demi-sec	fairly sweet
doux	very sweet
brut	dry sparkling wine
pétillant/mousseux/ méthode traditionelle	sparkling
biologique/bio	organic
biodynamique	organic plus New Age ideas
appellation d'origine controlée (AOC)	the top level of quality controlled wine – wine from one estate
VDQS	the second level
vin de pays	the third level – wine from one region
vin de table/vin ordinaire	the lowest level – who cares where it's from?

Soups (soupes) and starters (hors d'œuvres)

assiette anglaise	plate of cold meats
assiette composée	mixed salad plate, usually cold meat and vegetables
bisque	shellfish soup
bourride	thick fish soup
consommé	clear soup
crudités	raw vegetables with dressings
hors d'œuvres	combination of the above plus cold meats
potage	thick vegetable soup
soupe à l'oignon	onion soup with rich cheese topping
velouté	thick soup, usually fish or poultry

Fish (poisson), seafood (fruits de mer) and shellfish (crustaces/coquillages)

alose	shad
anchois	anchovies
anguilles	eels
barbue	brill
bigourneau	periwinkle
brème	bream
brochet	pike
cabillaud	cod
calmar	squid
carrelet	plaice
colin	hake
congre	conger eel
coques	cockles
coquilles St-Jacques	scallops
crabe	crab
crevettes grises	shrimps
crevettes roses	prawns
daurade	sea bream
éperlan	smelt or whitebait
escargots	snails
flétan	halibut
friture	deep-fried small fish
gardons	roach
goujons	gudgeon
hareng	herring
homard	lobster
huîtres	oysters

lamproie	river lamprey
langouste	spiny lobster
langoustines	saltwater crayfish (scampi)
limande	lemon sole
lotte de mer	monkfish
loup de mer	sea bass
maquereau	mackerel
merlan	whiting
moules (marinière)	mussels (with shallots in white wine sauce)
palourdes	clams
raie	skate
rouget	red mullet
sandre	pike-perch or zander
saumon	salmon
sole	sole
thon	tuna
truite	trout
turbot	turbot

Fish dishes and terms

arête	fish bone
assiette de pêcheur	assorted fish
beignet	fritter
darne	fillet or steak
en beurre blanc	in a butter, shallot and white-wine sauce
en matelote	in a red-wine stew
friture	method of deep-frying small fish
fumé	smoked
fumet	fish stock
gigot de mer	large fish baked whole
grillé	grilled
hollandaise	butter and vinegar sauce
à la meunière	in a butter, lemon and parsley sauce
mousse/mousseline	mousse
pané	breaded
quenelles	light dumplings

Meat (viande) and poultry (volaille)

agneau	lamb
andouille	pork sausage
andouillette	tripe sausage

bavette	French cut of beef equivalent to flank
bifteck	steak
bœuf	beef
boudin blanc	sausage of white meats
boudin noir	black pudding
caille	quail
canard	duck
caneton	duckling
contrefilet	sirloin roast
dinde/dindon	turkey
entrecôte	rib steak
faisan	pheasant
faux filet	sirloin steak
foie	liver
foie gras	pâté of force-fed duck/ goose liver
gibier	game
gigot (d'agneau)	leg (of lamb)
grenouilles (cuisses de)	frogs (legs)
grillade	grilled meats
hâchis	chopped meat or mince hamburger
langue	tongue
lapin/lapereau	rabbit/young rabbit
lard/lardons	bacon/diced bacon
llèvre	hare
mouton	mutton
museau de veau	calf's muzzle
oie	goose
onglet	French cut of steak
os	bone
pâté au biquion	pâté of pork, veal and goat
pintade	guinea fowl
porc	pork
poulet	chicken
poussin	baby chicken
rillettes	pork mashed with lard and liver
rillons	cubes of fatty pork
ris	sweetbreads
rognons	kidneys
rognons blancs	testicles
sanglier	wild boar

tête de veau	calf's head (in jelly)
tournedos	thick slices of fillet
tripes	tripe
tripoux	mutton tripe
veau	veal
venaison	venison

Meat and poultry dishes and terms

aile	wing
blanquette, daube, estouffade, hochepôt, navarin, ragoût	types of stew
blanquette de veau	veal in cream and mushroom sauce
bœuf bourguignon	beef stew with Burgundy, onions and mushrooms
carré	best end of neck, chop or cutlet
cassoulet	casserole of beans, sausages and duck/goose
choucroute	pickled cabbage with peppercorns, sausages, bacon and salami
civet	game stew
confit	meat preserve
coq au vin	chicken slow-cooked with wine, onions and mushrooms
côte	chop, cutlet or rib
cou	neck
cuisse	thigh or leg
en croûte	in pastry
épaule	shoulder
farci	stuffed
au feu de bois	cooked over wood fire
au four	baked
garni	with vegetables
gésier	gizzard
grillade	grilled meat
grillé	grilled
magret de canard	duck breast
marmite	casserole
médaillon	round piece
mijoté	stewed

pavé	thick slice
poêlé	pan-fried
râble	saddle
rôti	roast
sauté	lightly fried in butter
viennoise	fried in egg and breadcrumbs

Terms for steaks

bleu	almost raw
saignant	rare
à point	medium rare
bien cuit	well done
très bien cuit	very well done
brochette	kebab

Garnishes and sauces

auvergnat	with cabbage, sausage and bacon
béarnaise	sauce of egg yolks, white wine, shallots and vinegar
bonne femme	with mushroom, bacon, potato and onions
bordelaise	in a red wine, shallot and bone-marrow sauce
boulangère	baked with potatoes and onions
bourgeoise	with carrots, onions, bacon, celery and braised lettuce
chasseur	white wine, mushrooms and shallots
châtelaine	with artichoke hearts and chestnut purée
diable	strong mustard seasoning
forestière	with bacon and mushroom
fricassée	rich, creamy sauce
mornay	cheese sauce
pays d'auge	cream and cider
périgourdine	with foie gras and possibly truffles
piquante	gherkins or capers, vinegar and shallots

| provençale | tomatoes, garlic, olive oil and herbs |
| savoyarde | with gruyère cheese |

Vegetables (légumes), herbs (herbes) and spices (épices)

ail	garlic
anis	aniseed
artichaut	artichoke
asperge	asparagus
avocat	avocado
basilic	basil
betterave	beetroot
blette/bette	Swiss chard
cannelle	cinnamon
capre	caper
cardon	cardoon, a beet related to artichoke
carotte	carrot
céleri	celery
cèpes	ceps/edible boletus
champignons (de Paris)	mushrooms
chou (rouge)	cabbage (red)
choufleur	cauliflower
concombre	cucumber
cornichon	gherkin
echalotes	shallots
endive	chicory
épinard	spinach
estragon	tarragon
fenouil	fennel
fèves	broad beans
flageolets	flageolet beans
gingembre	ginger
girolles	chanterelles
haricots	haricot beans (French/string)
verts	string beans
rouges	kidney beans
beurres	yellow snap beans
laurier	bay leaf
lentilles (vertes)	(green) lentils
maïs	maize (corn)
menthe	mint
moutarde	mustard
oignon	onion

panais	parsnip
pâte	pasta or pastry
pélandron	type of string bean
persil	parsley
petits pois	peas
pieds bleu/jaune	blue/yellow-foot mushrooms
pignons	pine nuts
piment (rouge/vert)	(red/green) chilli pepper
pleurotes	oyster mushrooms
pois chiche	chick peas
pois mange-tout	snow peas
poireau	leek
poivron (vert/rouge)	(green/red) sweet pepper
pommes de terre	potatoes
primeurs	spring vegetables
radis	radish
riz	rice
safran	saffron
salade verte	green salad
sarrasin	buckwheat
tomate	tomato
trompettes de la mort	horns of plenty
truffes	truffles

Vegetable dishes and terms

beignet	fritter
duxelles	fried mushrooms and shallots with cream
farci	stuffed
feuille	leaf
fines herbes	mixture of tarragon, parsley and chives
gratiné	browned with cheese or butter
à la grecque	cooked in oil and lemon
jardinière	with mixed diced vegetables
mousseline	mashed potato with cream and eggs
parmentier	with potatoes
petits farcis	stuffed tomatoes, aubergines, courgettes and peppers

râpée	grated or shredded
à la vapeur	steamed
en verdure	garnished with green vegetables

Fruit (fruit) and nuts (noix)

abricot	apricot
acajou	cashew nut
amande	almond
ananas	pineapple
banane	banana
brugnon, nectarine	nectarine
cacahouète	peanut
cassis	blackcurrant
cérise	cherry
citron	lemon
citron vert	lime
datte	date
figue	fig
fraise (de bois)	strawberry (wild)
framboise	raspberry
fruit de la passion	passion fruit
grenade	pomegranate
groseille	redcurrant
marron	chestnut
melon	melon
mirabelle	small yellow plum
myrtille	bilberry
noisette	hazelnut
noix	walnuts or nuts in general
orange	orange
pamplemousse	grapefruit
pêche	peach
pistache	pistachio
poire	pear
pomme	apple
prune	plum
pruneau	prune
raisin	grape
reine-claude	greengage

Fruit dishes and terms

agrumes	citrus fruits
beignet	fritter
compôte	stewed fruit
coulis	sauce of puréed fruit
crème de marrons	chestnut purée
flambé	set aflame in alcohol
frappé	iced
tapée	dried (local apples and pears)

Desserts (desserts or entremets) and pastries (pâtisserie)

brioche	sweet, high-yeast breakfast roll
clafoutis	heavy custard and fruit tart
crème Chantilly	vanilla-flavoured and sweetened whipped cream
crème fraîche	sour cream
crème pâtissière	thick, eggy pastry-filling
crêpe suzette	thin pancake with orange juice and liqueur
fromage blanc	cream cheese
gaufre	waffle
glace	ice cream
macaron	macaroon
madeleine	small sponge cake
mousse au chocolat	chocolate mousse
parfait	frozen mousse, sometimes ice cream
petit-suisse	a smooth mixture of cream and curds
petits fours	bite-sized cakes/ pastries
poires belle hélène	pears and ice cream in chocolate sauce
tarte Tatin	upside-down apple tart
yaourt/yogourt	yoghurt

Cheese

assiette de fromage	plate of selected cheeses
cendré	dusted with ash
chèvre	goat's cheese
fermier	farm-produced
frais	fresh/unmatured
sec	dry (strong)

Glossary

alimentation food

Angevin/Angevine from Anjou; a man/woman from Anjou

appellation (d'origine) contrôlée government certification guaranteeing the quality of a French wine; often written AOC

autoroute motorway/freeway

Berrichon/Berrichonne from the Berry region; a man/woman from the Berry

boulangerie baker's

centre ville town centre

chambres d'hôtes B&B accommodation in a private house

charcuterie sells cold meats and other pre-pared foods

département administrative division of France, roughly equivalent to a English county

dégustation tasting, as in wine tasting

église church

étang a marshy pond or small lake

fief land held under the feudal system

foyer residential hostel for young workers and students

fromagerie cheese shop

gare routière bus station

gare SNCF train station

gîte (d'étape) privately rented, government-regulated accommodation

halles market

hôtel particulier mansion or townhouse

Hôtel de Ville town hall (in a city)

Mairie town hall

marché market

patisserie cakeshop

Pietà statue or image of Jesus's body in Mary's arms

plats du jour daily specials

pont bridge

quartier district in a town or city

rue street

seigneur the lord of a château

Solognot/Solognote from the Sologne; a man/woman from the Sologne

tabac tobacconist's, also selling bus/metro tickets and phone cards

table d'hôte a communal dining table in a home or restaurant

Tourangeau/Tourangelle from Touraine; a man/woman from Touraine

traiteur delicatessen

Architectural terms

These are either terms you'll come across in the *Guide*, or come up against while travelling around.

abbaye abbey

ambulatory passage round the outer edge of the choir of a church, behind the high altar

apse semicircular termination at the east end of a church

arcade series of arches; in a church, the bot-tommost of usually two or three well-defined horizontal sections, below the triforium

Baroque largely seventeenth-century style of art and architecture distinguished by dyna-mism and extreme ornateness

beaux-arts fine arts

capital top of a column, often carved

Carolingian dynasty (and art, sculpture, etc) named after Charlemagne; mid-eighth to early tenth centuries

chancel part of a church containing the altar and sanctuary

château mansion, country house, castle

château fort castle

choir the part of a church between the altar

and nave, used by the choir and clergy

chevet east end of a church

Classical architectural style incorporating Greek and Roman elements: pillars, domes, colonnades, etc; dominant in France from the seventeenth century

clerestory upper storey of a church, incorporating the windows

collégiale collegiate church (run by canons)

communs the outbuildings of a château, often with stables

cornice decorative line dividing the facade from the roof

crypt area of a church usually under the choir, sometimes used for burial

cul-de-lampe decorated base of a corbel or projecting bit of masonry

donjon castle keep

dormer upright window projecting from a sloping roof

échauguette bartizan, or overhanging corner turret

église church

First Renaissance from the early sixteenth-century

Flamboyant late style of Gothic architecture (c.1450–1540) characterized by elaborate, "flame-like" stone-carving

Gallo-Roman from the Roman era in France

hôtel (particulier) mansion or town house

loggia open gallery or arcade

logis noble wing of a château, often a dedicated building

machicolation openings pierced in a parapet for dropping stones etc on attackers

Merovingian dynasty (and art, etc), ruling France and parts of Germany from sixth to mid-eighth centuries

misericord shelf under a choir seat for leaning against, often carved

narthex entrance hall or porch of a church

nave main body of a church, usually at the west end and flanked by aisles

newel the main upright post of a staircase

œil-de-bœuf small, circular "bull's-eye" window, often set into the roof

porte gateway

Rayonnant mid-period style of Gothic architecture (c.1340–1450) characterized by chapels radiating from the apse

Régence architecture/design style from 1715–23

Renaissance in architecture, a Classically influenced, rationally planned style developed in fifteenth-century Italy and imported to France in the early sixteenth century

retable altarpiece

Roman Romanesque (easily confused with Romain – Roman)

Romanesque early medieval architecture (eleventh to thirteenth centuries) distinguished by rounded arches and naive sculpture; called Norman in Britain

stringcourse horizontal band of stone dividing a facade

stucco heavy limestone plaster used for decoration

tour tower

transept transverse arms of a church

triforium wall-passage at middle-level of a church, between the arcade at the lowest level and the clerestory above

trompe-l'oeil artistic effect that deceives the eye, usually with the illusion of depth

tufa creamy, crumbly limestone typical of the Loire region

tympanum sculpted panel above a church door

voussoir wedge of stone around an arch

Travel
store

UK & Ireland
Britain
Devon & Cornwall
Dublin **D**
Edinburgh **D**
England
Ireland
The Lake District
London
London **D**
London Mini Guide
Scotland
Scottish Highlands
& Islands
Wales

Europe
Algarve **D**
Amsterdam
Amsterdam **D**
Andalucía
Athens **D**
Austria
Baltic States
Barcelona
Barcelona **D**
Belgium &
Luxembourg
Berlin
Brittany & Normandy
Bruges **D**
Brussels
Budapest
Bulgaria
Copenhagen
Corfu
Corsica
Costa Brava **D**
Crete
Croatia
Cyprus
Czech & Slovak
Republics
Denmark
Dodecanese & East
Aegean Islands
Dordogne & The Lot
Europe
Florence & Siena
Florence **D**
France
Germany
Gran Canaria **D**
Greece
Greek Islands

Hungary
Ibiza & Formentera **D**
Iceland
Ionian Islands
Italy
The Italian Lakes
Languedoc &
Roussillon
Lanzarote &
Fuerteventura **D**
Lisbon **D**
The Loire Valley
Madeira **D**
Madrid **D**
Mallorca **D**
Mallorca & Menorca
Malta & Gozo **D**
Menorca
Moscow
The Netherlands
Norway
Paris
Paris **D**
Paris Mini Guide
Poland
Portugal
Prague
Prague **D**
Provence
& the Côte D'Azur
Pyrenees
Romania
Rome
Rome **D**
Sardinia
Scandinavia
Sicily
Slovenia
Spain
St Petersburg
Sweden
Switzerland
Tenerife &
La Gomera **D**
Turkey
Tuscany & Umbria
Venice & The Veneto
Venice **D**
Vienna

Asia
Bali & Lombok
Bangkok
Beijing

Cambodia
China
Goa
Hong Kong & Macau
Hong Kong
& Macau **D**
India
Indonesia
Japan
Kerala
Laos
Malaysia, Singapore
& Brunei
Nepal
The Philippines
Rajasthan, Dehli
& Agra
Singapore
Singapore **D**
South India
Southeast Asia
Sri Lanka
Taiwan
Thailand
Thailand's Beaches
& Islands
Tokyo
Vietnam

Australasia
Australia
Melbourne
New Zealand
Sydney

North America
Alaska
Baja California
Boston
California
Canada
Chicago
Colorado
Florida
The Grand Canyon
Hawaii
Honolulu **D**
Las Vegas **D**
Los Angeles
Maui **D**
Miami & South Florida
Montréal
New England
New Orleans **D**
New York City

New York City **D**
New York City Mini
Guide
Orlando & Walt
Disney World® **D**
Pacific Northwest
San Francisco
San Francisco **D**
Seattle
Southwest USA
Toronto
USA
Vancouver
Washington DC
Washington DC **D**
Yellowstone & The
Grand Tetons
Yosemite

Caribbean
& Latin America
Antigua & Barbuda **D**
Argentina
Bahamas
Barbados **D**
Belize
Bolivia
Brazil
Cancùn & Cozumel **D**
Caribbean
Central America
Chile
Costa Rica
Cuba
Dominican Republic
Dominican Republic **D**
Ecuador
Guatemala
Jamaica
Mexico
Peru
St Lucia **D**
South America
Trinidad & Tobago
Yúcatan

Africa & Middle East
Cape Town & the
Garden Route
Dubai **D**
Egypt
Gambia
Jordan

D: Rough Guide
DIRECTIONS for
short breaks

ROUGH GUIDES

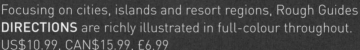

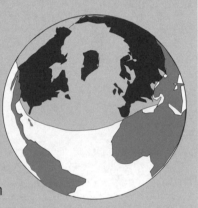

Avoid Guilt Trips

Buy fair trade coffee + bananas ✓

Save energy - use low energy bulbs ✓
- don't leave tv on standby ✓

Offset carbon emissions from flight to Madrid ✓

Send goat to Africa ✓

Join Tourism Concern today ✓

Slowly, the world is changing.
Together we can, and will, make a difference.

Tourism Concern is the only UK registered charity fighting exploitation in one of the largest industries on earth: people forced from their homes in order that holiday resorts can be built, sweatshop labour conditions in hotels and destruction of the environment are just some of the issues that we tackle.

Sending people on a guilt trip is not something we do. We know as well as anyone that holidays are precious. But you can help us to ensure that tourism always benefits the local communities involved.

Call 020 7133 3330
or visit **tourismconcern.org.uk** to find out how.

A year's membership of Tourism Concern costs just £20 (£12 unwaged)
– that's 38 pence a week, less than the cost of a pint of milk, organic of course.

Fighting Exploitation in Tourism

TourismConcern

Small print and
Index

A Rough Guide to Rough Guides

Published in 1982, the first Rough Guide – to Greece – was a student scheme that became a publishing phenomenon. Mark Ellingham, a recent graduate in English from Bristol University, had been travelling in Greece the previous summer and couldn't find the right guidebook. With a small group of friends he wrote his own guide, combining a highly contemporary, journalistic style with a thoroughly practical approach to travellers' needs.

The immediate success of the book spawned a series that rapidly covered dozens of destinations. And, in addition to impecunious backpackers, Rough Guides soon acquired a much broader and older readership that relished the guides' wit and inquisitiveness as much as their enthusiastic, critical approach and value-for-money ethos.

These days, Rough Guides include recommendations from shoestring to luxury and cover more than 200 destinations around the globe, including almost every country in the Americas and Europe, more than half of Africa and most of Asia and Australasia. Our ever-growing team of authors and photographers is spread all over the world, particularly in Europe, the USA and Australia.

In the early 1990s, Rough Guides branched out of travel, with the publication of Rough Guides to World Music, Classical Music and the Internet. All three have become benchmark titles in their fields, spearheading the publication of a wide range of books under the Rough Guide name.

Including the travel series, Rough Guides now number more than 350 titles, covering: phrasebooks, waterproof maps, music guides from Opera to Heavy Metal, reference works as diverse as Conspiracy Theories and Shakespeare, and popular culture books from iPods to Poker. Rough Guides also produce a series of more than 120 World Music CDs in partnership with World Music Network.

Visit www.roughguides.com to see our latest publications.

Rough Guide travel images are available for commercial licensing at www.roughguidespictures.com

SMALL PRINT

Rough Guide credits

Text editor: James Smart, Keith Drew
Layout: Umesh Aggarwal
Cartography: Jasbir Sandhu
Picture editor: Sarah Cummins
Production: Aimee Hampson
Proofreader: Amanda Jones
Cover design: Chloë Roberts
Photographer: James McConnachie
Editorial: **London** Kate Berens, Claire Saunders, Ruth Blackmore, Polly Thomas, Richard Lim, Alison Murchie, Karoline Densley, Andy Turner, Edward Aves, Nikki Birrell, Alice Park, Sarah Eno, Lucy White, Jo Kirby, Samantha Cook, Natasha Foges, Roisin Cameron, Joe Staines, Duncan Clark, Peter Buckley, Matthew Milton, Tracy Hopkins, Ruth Tidball; **New York** Andrew Rosenberg, Steven Horak, AnneLise Sorensen, Amy Hegarty, April Isaacs, Ella Steim, Anna Owens, Joseph Petta, Sean Mahoney
Design & Pictures: **London** Scott Stickland, Dan May, Diana Jarvis, Mark Thomas, Jj Luck, Harriet Mills, Chloë Roberts, Nicole Newman; **Delhi** Ajay Verma, Jessica Subramanian, Ankur Guha, Pradeep Thapliyal, Sachin Tanwar, Anita Singh, Madhavi Singh, Karen D'Souza

Production: Katherine Owers
Cartography: **London** Maxine Repath, Ed Wright, Katie Lloyd-Jones; **Delhi** Jai Prakash Mishra, Rajesh Chhibber, Ashutosh Bharti, Rajesh Mishra, Animesh Pathak, Karobi Gogoi, Amod Singh, Alakananda Bhattacharya, Athokpam Jotinkumar
Online: **New York** Jennifer Gold, Kristin Mingrone; **Delhi** Manik Chauhan, Narender Kumar, Rakesh Kumar, Amit Kumar, Amit Verma, Rahul Kumar, Ganesh Sharma, Debojit Borah
Marketing & Publicity: **London** Liz Statham, Niki Hanmer, Louise Maher, Jess Carter, Vanessa Godden, Vivienne Watton, Anna Paynton, Rachel Sprackett; **New York** Geoff Colquitt, Megan Kennedy, Katy Ball; **Delhi** Reem Khokhar
Special Projects Editor: Philippa Hopkins
Manager India: Punita Singh
Series Editor: Mark Ellingham
Reference Director: Andrew Lockett
Publishing Coordinator: Megan McIntyre
Publishing Director: Martin Dunford
Commercial Manager: Gino Magnotta
Managing Director: John Duhigg

Publishing information

This second edition published June 2007 by
Rough Guides Ltd,
80 Strand, London WC2R 0RL
345 Hudson St, 4th Floor,
New York, NY 10014, USA
14 Local Shopping Centre, Panchsheel Park,
New Delhi 110017, India
Distributed by the Penguin Group
Penguin Books Ltd,
80 Strand, London WC2R 0RL
Penguin Group (USA)
375 Hudson Street, NY 10014, USA
Penguin Group (Australia)
250 Camberwell Road, Camberwell,
Victoria 3124, Australia
Penguin Books Canada Ltd,
10 Alcorn Avenue, Toronto, Ontario,
Canada M4V 1E4
Penguin Group (NZ)
67 Apollo Drive, Mairangi Bay, Auckland 1310,
New Zealand

Cover concept by Peter Dyer.
Typeset in Bembo and Helvetica to an original design by Henry Iles.
Printed and bound in Singapore by SNP Security Printing Pte Ltd
© James McConnachie 2007
No part of this book may be reproduced in any form without permission from the publisher except for the quotation of brief passages in reviews.
400pp includes index
A catalogue record for this book is available from the British Library
ISBN: 978-1-84353-791-5
The publishers and authors have done their best to ensure the accuracy and currency of all the information in **The Rough Guide to The Loire**, however, they can accept no responsibility for any loss, injury, or inconvenience sustained by any traveller as a result of information or advice contained in the guide.

3   5   7   9   8   6   4   2

Help us update

We've gone to a lot of effort to ensure that the second edition of **The Rough Guide to The Loire** is accurate and up to date. However, things change – places get "discovered", opening hours are notoriously fickle, restaurants and rooms raise prices or lower standards. If you feel we've got it wrong or left something out, we'd like to know, and if you can remember the address, the price, the time, the phone number, so much the better.

We'll credit all contributions, and send a copy of the next edition (or any other Rough Guide if you prefer) for the best letters. Everyone who writes to us and isn't already a subscriber will receive a copy of our full-colour thrice-yearly newsletter. Please mark letters: "**Rough Guide The Loire Update**" and send to: Rough Guides, 80 Strand, London WC2R 0RL, or Rough Guides, 345 Hudson St, 4th Floor, New York, NY 10014. Or send an email to **mail@roughguides.com**
Have your questions answered and tell others about your trip at
www.roughguides.atinfopop.com

SMALL PRINT

Acknowledgements

James McConnachie would like to thank his editors, James Smart and Keith Drew, and everyone at Rough Guides. Especial thanks go also to Hugh Cleary, for his meticulous and judicious updating, and to Pierre Sabouraud and Samuel Buchwalder, at the CDT de Touraine.

Readers' letters

Thanks to all the readers who have taken the time to write in with comments and suggestions (and apologies if we've inadvertently omitted or misspelt anyone's name):

Christopher Hamilton, Leo Lacey, Stuart Connell, Dr Val Harris, S R McCombie.

SMALL PRINT

Photo credits

All photos © James McConnachie except the following:

Full page
Hot air balloon above Blois region © Robert Harding Picture Library Ltd/Alamy

Introduction
p.5 Place Plumereau © Vittorio Sciosia/Alamy
p.8 Tubs of harvested Chenin Blanc grapes, Indre © Cephas Picture Library/Alamy
p.8 Château de Chambord © Jon Arnold Images/Alamy
p.9 Bourges cathedral © Images-of-France/Alamy

Colour section: The château
Chateau d'Usse © David Norton Photography/Alamy

Walls of Château de Angers © AM Corporation/Alamy
Villandry Gardens © Harriet Mills
Cheverny © Robert Harding Picture Library Ltd/Alamy

Colour section: The River Loire
Kingfisher © Robert Harding 748-348
Nuclear power station Saint-Laurent-des-Eaux Pays © Robert Harding Picture Library Ltd/Alamy

Black and whites
p.90 Chenonceau © Alamy

ROUGH GUIDES

SMALL PRINT

Index

Map entries are in colour.

D

E

F

INDEX

INDEX

Map symbols

maps are listed in the full index using coloured text

― ― ― -	Chapter division boundary	🏰	Château
― ― ・・・	Departmental boundary	♜	Castle
▬▬▬	Motorway	⋒	Abbey
▪ ▪ ▪ ▪	Motorway under construction	⊙	Statue/memorial
═══	Main road	⊠―⊠	Gate
───	Minor road	⋏	Campsite
⊞⊞⊞⊞⊞	Steps	ⓘ	Tourist office
▬▬▬	Pedestrianized street (town maps)	⊠	Post office
▪ ▪ ▪ ▪	City wall/fortifications	⊞	Hospital
──▪──	Railway	🏊	Swimming pool
───	River	▬	Building
✈	Airport	⊞	Church (town maps)
♦	Point of interest	▦	Park
∴	Ruin/prehistoric site	🌲	Forest